THE AFFECTIVE ASSISTANCE
OF COUNSEL

- Atypical
  lawyer.

P. 96.

types
OF
law for
A.typ.
lawyers

P. 446

meditation
C-CULP.

you fitty boomba !!

I ♡ You
IMARA
teehee

THE AFFECTIVE ASSISTANCE
OF COUNSEL

PRACTICING LAW
AS A HEALING PROFESSION

Marjorie A. Silver

CAROLINA ACADEMIC PRESS

Durham, North Carolina

Library of Congress Cataloging-in-Publication Data

The affective assistance of counsel / edited by Marjorie A. Silver.
    p.   cm.
Includes bibliographical references and index.
10-digit ISBN 1-59460-111-9 (alk. paper)
13-digit ISBN 978-1-59460-111-8 (alk. paper)
1. Practice of law--United States. 2. Practice of law--Psychological aspects.
3. Practice of law--Social aspects. 4. Attorney and client--United States. 5.
Attorney and client-- Psychological aspects. 6. Attorney and client--Social
aspects. I. Silver, Marjorie Ann. II. Title.

KF300.S54 2007
347.73'504--dc22

                                    2006038315

Cover art design by Kimberly Newman

CAROLINA ACADEMIC PRESS
700 Kent Street
Durham, North Carolina 27701
Telephone (919) 489-7486
Fax (919) 493-5668
www.cap-press.com

Printed in the United States of America.

To David with Love & Joy

CONTENTS

Foreword   xi
Preface   xv
Acknowledgments   xvii
Introduction   xix

PART I
LAWYERING WITH INTRA- AND INTER-PERSONAL COMPETENCE

Chapter 1   Emotional Competence and the Lawyer's Journey   5
            Marjorie A. Silver

Chapter 2   Using Social Work Constructs in the Practice of Law   53
            Susan L. Brooks

Chapter 3   Lawyer Personality Traits and their
            Relationship to Various Approaches to Lawyering   79
            Susan Daicoff

Chapter 4   Making out the Ghost Behind the Words: Approaching
            Legal Text with Psychological Intelligence   109
            Aderson Bellegarde François

PART II
LAWYERING WITH CROSS-CULTURAL COMPETENCE

Chapter 5   Multicultural Lawyering: Heuristics and Biases   143
            Paul R. Tremblay
            Carwina Weng

Chapter 6   Six Practices for Connecting with Clients Across Culture:
            Habit Four, Working with Interpreters
            and Other Mindful Approaches   183
            Susan J. Bryant
            Jean Koh Peters

PART III
LAWYERING AND CIVIL DISPUTES

Chapter 7   Problem-Solving Advocacy in Mediations:
A Model of Client Representation   231
Harold Abramson

Chapter 8   Collaborative Law: Practicing Without Armor,
Practicing With Heart   259
Pauline H. Tesler

Chapter 9   The Culture of Legal Denial   279
Jonathan R. Cohen

Chapter 10 Hurting Clients   317
Edward A. Dauer

Chapter 11 Overcoming Psychological Barriers to Settlement:
Challenges for the TJ Lawyer   341
Bruce J. Winick

PART IV
LAWYERING AND THE CRIMINAL JUSTICE SYSTEM

Chapter 12 The TJ Criminal Lawyer:
Therapeutic Jurisprudence and Criminal Law Practice   367
David B. Wexler

Chapter 13 A Public Defender in a Problem-Solving Court   401
Lisa Schreibersdorf

Chapter 14 Defining the Lawyer-Self: Using Therapeutic Jurisprudence
to Define the Lawyer's Role and Build Alliances that
Aid the Child Client   411
Kristin Henning

PART V
LAWYERING WITH MINDFULNESS, SPIRITUALITY & RELIGION

Chapter 15 Awareness in Lawyering: A Primer on Paying Attention   447
Leonard L. Riskin

Chapter 16 Spirituality and Practicing Law as a Healing Profession: The Importance of Listening   473
Timothy W. Floyd

Chapter 17 Sojourner to Sojourner   493
Calvin G.C. Pang

Chapter 18 The Good Lawyer: Choosing to Believe In the Promise of Our Craft   513
Paula A. Franzese

Index   525

FOREWORD

"It was the best of times; it was the worst of times." So Charles Dickens famously began his *Tale of Two Cities*, succinctly capturing his appraisal of the London and Paris, the England and France, of 1775. As I look at a much narrower canvas, the American legal profession midway through the first decade of this new century, in the light of the important collection that Marjorie Silver has evoked and edited, the Dickensian epigram seems newly apt.

The "worst" is an old tale, happily not to be recounted here. There is a now familiar litany of exhibits: The relevant citations usually begin with Anthony Kronman[1] and Mary Ann Glendon,[2] at the head of a lengthening catalogue of indictments attesting to serious failings in the professed norms as well as the actual practices of lawyers, with deleterious impacts on them, on their clients, and on the citizenry at large.

In the decade that began about 30 years ago, several powerful critiques appeared, which drew into serious question core premises of the traditional concept of advocacy. Richard Wasserstrom (1975) doubted the justification for the prevalent emphasis on attorney role-differentiation and professional domination of clients;[3] Warren Lehman (1979) described the unspoken presuppositions that lawyers and clients each bring to their conversations, which distort their understandings of one another's intentions or priorities;[4] Leonard Riskin (1982), looking beyond the lawyer's "standard philosophical map," developed a justification for taking seriously the place of mediation in the practice and teaching of law;[5] Carrie Menkel-Meadow (1984) presented a "prob-

---

1. ANTHONY T. KRONMAN, THE LOST LAWYER: FAILING IDEAS OF THE LEGAL PROFESSION (1995).

2. MARY ANN GLENDON, A NATION UNDER LAWYERS (1996).

3. Richard Wasserstrom, *Lawyers as Professionals: Some Moral Issues*, 5 HUM. RTS. 1 (1975).

4. Warren Lehman, *The Pursuit of a Client's Interest*, 77 MICH. L. REV. 1078 (1979).

5. Leonard L. Riskin, *Mediation and Lawyers*, 43 OHIO ST. L.J. 29 (1982).

lem-solving" alternative to prevalent conceptions of the negotiation process;[6] earlier, Bill Simon (1978) had offered a comprehensive critique of the major versions of the "ideology of advocacy."[7] The critique burgeoned, and, as if foreshadowing professional "buy-in" to at least some of it, the American Bar Association's Kutak Commission (1977-1983) seemed for a time to be leading the organized Bar to rein in at least the more visibly problematic aspects of dominant approaches to the practice of law.[8]

It was not to be. The profession, evidencing some real suppleness, soberly incorporated some of the critique in casebooks and conference formats, while rejecting even modest attempts to change the rules. At the same time, it adapted quickly and powerfully year-by-year to changes in the economics and technology of what was coming to be thought of as the "production of legal services." Emergent versions of practice only strengthened the disaffection of those who had seen merit in the earlier critique. Among many examples of these are ever-increasing sub-specialization, globalization of the law firm, multi-disciplinary practice (*de facto* if not *de jure*), transformation of the meaning of partnership, enhanced opportunities, and pressures for enormous profits: The result has been a deepening of the "commodification" of both practice and teaching, and of the lives of those engaged in them.

What, then, is the "best" news? To me, the essays that follow demonstrate that it is not necessary to change professional norms to make it possible for those who find them seriously deficient to mark out a different road. That 90s exhortation, "Just do it!," is actually feasible, and does not always entail stepping off alone into an uncharted wilderness. I will refer in general terms to only an illustrative sample of exciting developments that one or more of the essays that follow present:

- A "collaborative law" movement is not only a challenging idea, it is indeed a movement already in existence. It has undertaken, for example, to practice family law in a manner thought by its practitioners to be responsive to what clients really care about, as well as to the factors that led its members to want to practice family law in the first place. Instead of debating fruitlessly with their teachers, classmates, or colleagues who

---

6. Carrie Menkel-Meadow, *Toward Another View of Legal Negotiation*, 31 UCLA L. Rev. 754 (1984).

7. William H. Simon, *The Ideology of Advocacy*, 1978 Wis. L. Rev. 30.

8. ABA Special Comm. on Prof'l Standards, Robert J. Kutak, Chairman (1977-1983).

do not share their vision, they are meeting, talking, and forming practices with those who do.

- Similarly, lawyers and students who find the concept of "therapeutic jurisprudence" valid and relevant now have the resources, in the literature and among professional colleagues, to begin to learn the skills necessary to practice it. Responsive to its opportunities as well as its dangers, they can leave off debating whether the latter should choke off serious pursuit of the former.

- By seeking to develop attributes like attentiveness and awareness as a lawyering skill and not simply a way to "unwind" after a stressful day, lawyers are transcending the polarization of thinking and doing that is so powerful both in society at large and among the profession. Beginning to think that way brings specific guides and supportive communities into view, and one does not need to persuade multitudes in order to find and follow them.

- Another polarization that has been cracked open is that between benefiting the client (one's only "proper" business) and benefiting oneself in a non-material (and therefore "self-indulgent") way. Learning to listen becomes a major lawyering priority as a spiritual practice: It serves the client, for listening to clients *is* representing them, but it is a worthy activity in the life of the lawyer as well, for it legitimates and focuses the impulse to live a life of service to others.

These are only a few manifestations of the wide-ranging challenges described and developed below, which are being acted upon and implemented day-by-day, beneath the radar screen of most academic and professional disputation. You—student, practitioner, teacher—needn't lead a parade to live your work life in ways that make sense to you. Others have come before, are coming along now, and are here as teachers/fellow-learners.

That, to me, is the message of this book. Is it "subversive," as Marjorie Silver daringly proclaims in its opening line? Well, to me that depends on how you understand the word. I don't expect the priorities and premises that animate these essays to become dominant in the profession, and the expectation that they might can be a route to burn-out and disillusionment. The deeper point, and perhaps the more relevant subversion, is that the "deviant" views needn't take over, needn't become normative. There is room for each of us to follow the path that makes sense to him or her. You are not alone. Others are walking along with you; indeed, many have been treading along already; there is much to learn, much to teach, many to support, and find support from. Like Emily Dickinson, the authors of this collection "dwell in possibility."[9] Join them, or some of them, if you decide you are or become of a mind to.

Howard Lesnick
Jefferson B. Fordham Professor of Law
University of Pennsylvania Law School
August 2006

---

9. Emily Dickinson, "I dwell in possibility" (Poem No. 657).

PREFACE

Beware. This book is subversive. It is a counter-culture book. It aims to subvert the legal profession's prevailing gladiatorial paradigm. It is, to use Professor Leonard Riskin's phrase, something off "the lawyer's standard philosophical map."[1] It promises a vision of practicing law that is likely very different than what you learned in law school, or, for those of you who are currently law students, what you have been learning in most of your law school classes.

When I first conceived the idea for this book, my intent was to produce a comprehensive compendium of the knowledge, skills, and values necessary to practice law as a healing profession. I quickly realized, however, the absurdity of that ambition. That would require a whole library, not a single volume.[2]

Instead, I set out to solicit a diverse range of contributions from authors who had something meaningful to contribute to the body of literature aimed at lawyers who desire to practice law as a calling, who are interested in developing the competencies to practice law as a healthy, healing profession, one that the lawyer finds fulfilling and rewarding and that is beneficial and therapeutic for the client. When lawyers find ways to practice law that optimize their own and their clients' wellbeing, they can recapture the moral vision that originally attracted them to the law, and, in so doing, find joy and meaning in their practices.[3]

---

1. *See infra* ch. 15: Leonard L. Riskin, *Awareness in Lawyering: A Primer on Paying Attention,* at p. 447.

2. At last count, the bibliography of the website of the International Network on Therapeutic Jurisprudence listed twenty-nine books & monographs, twenty-two symposia, and 800 articles, all published over the past fifteen years. *See* International Network on Therapeutic Jurisprudence, *TJ Bibliography, at* http://www.law.arizona.edu/depts/upr-intj/ (last visited June 29, 2006).

3. *See generally* Symposium, *Lawyering and its Discontents: Reclaiming Meaning in the Practice of Law,* 19 Touro L. Rev. 773 (2004) [hereinafter Touro Symposium]; Steven Keeva, Transforming Practices: Finding Joy and Satisfaction in the Legal Life (1999).

There exists tremendous discontent among the practicing bar. Many lawyers have found themselves unhappy or unfulfilled in their practices. Compared to other professionals, lawyers suffer disproportionately from excessive stress, substance abuse, and other emotional difficulties. Many find themselves demoralized or disillusioned about the practice of law.

Here's the good news. Recent years have witnessed a spate of both new and renewed approaches to the practice of law. Disaffected by the adversarial model, many practitioners have engaged in a quiet revolution, a marriage of theory and practice designed to maximize the healing potential of the law. The intention for this book is to inspire law students and lawyers to pursue paths and practices that will be more beneficial for more clients, and more meaningful and rewarding for more lawyers. Hopefully each reader will find something in this book that enhances his or her wellbeing in practice, so that all lawyers may realize the possibilities of careers well spent.

Marjorie A. Silver
August 2006

Acknowledgments

I have received tremendous support and sustenance from friends and family over the course of this project. First and foremost, I want to thank the nineteen extraordinary people who contributed chapters to this book, and Howard Lesnick, who wrote the Preface. Thank you all for saying "yes" when I invited you to be part of this book. Many editors complain about the difficulties they experience in trying to coordinate the efforts of multiple authors. I, instead, had minimal glitches and abundant joy working with all of you. Your commitment to this book's mission was teamed with tremendous enthusiasm, energy, and responsiveness.

In particular, I want to single out David Wexler and Bruce Winick who, over the past eight or so years that I have known them, have been friends and mentors *extraordinaires*, and have opened numerous windows and doors for me. Jean Koh Peters has been my clinical muse and dear friend. Thanks, too, to Jonathan Cohen for his wise and helpful editorial suggestions on the Introduction.

My research assistant, Stephanie Adduci, has been almost inhumanly indefatigable in doing research, footnotes, and proofreading. This book would never have been done on time without her diligence, conscientiousness, commitment, and long hours into the night. Thanks, too, to the support of Marie Litwin and the other members of Touro Law Center's faculty services team. Touro's outstanding research librarians were there whenever I needed them. And thanks to our dean, Lawrence Raful, who has supported me with his enthusiasm, a sabbatical, and multiple summer research grants.

Finally, I thank my wonderful family: my husband, Doug Block, for his almost uncanny ability to make everything read better; my daughter, Lucy Block, whose feel for metaphor enhanced my prose; my daughter-in-law Margaret Silver; and my son, Josh Silver, who gave Margaret the time and space to cast her excellent editorial eye and mind on my chapter in the weeks following the birth of their first child and my first grandchild, David Morgan Michael Silver, to whom this book is dedicated. Thank you all for your love and understanding.

INTRODUCTION

I came to realize that the best lawyers I have ever known, all had three main qualities.... They were highly competent, had unshakable integrity, and truly cared—about their families, their colleagues, their clients, and their community.... I've learned the hard way that caring about things is at least as important as being competent and ethical in life.[1]

When we represent a client, we receive into our care a human being with an array of problems and possibilities, only some of which are likely to be legal. The traditional law school curriculum, however, does not prepare its graduates well for the day-to-day practice of law. It is even more deficient in preparing students for alternative visions of what it means to be a lawyer. The first year curriculum consists largely of analyzing appellate court decisions. When we law professors speak of teaching students to "think like lawyers," what we generally mean is we want to cultivate the skills of advocacy and argument. We want them to master the ability to argue both sides of a "case," so that they may develop the necessary competence to serve as hired guns for contentious clients. In large measure, we prepare students to be players in the adversary system game.[2]

---

1. SUCCESS BRIEFS FOR LAWYERS: INSPIRATIONAL INSIGHTS ON HOW TO SUCCEED AT LAW AND LIFE 49 (Amiram Elwork & Mark R. Siwik eds., 2001) (quoting a law firm founding partner).

2. That it is viewed as a game by at least one judge is illustrated by an order out of the United States District Court in the Middle District of Florida in June of 2006. Judge Gregory Presnell issued a discovery order that read, as follows:

ORDER
This matter comes before the Court on Plaintiff's Motion to designate location of a Rule 30(b)(6) deposition.... Upon consideration of the Motion—the latest in a series of Gordian knots that the parties have been unable to untangle without enlisting the assistance of the federal courts—it is
ORDERED that said motion is DENIED. Instead, the Court will fashion a new form of alternative dispute resolution, to wit: at 4:00 P.M. on Friday, June 30, 2006, counsel shall convene at a neutral site agreeable to both parties. If counsel

Increasingly, though, law teachers—both clinical and classroom—inspired by approaches such as Therapeutic Jurisprudence, Creative Problem-Solving, and Humanizing Legal Education, are integrating into our teaching individual and systemic approaches that challenge the gladiator model of lawyering. New pedagogy is informing old courses, and new courses are evolving and taking their places in the curriculums of increasing numbers of law schools. This book bears the fruit of many of these efforts.

The contributors to this book come from widely diverse backgrounds. What they share are visions for more therapeutic, more beneficial, more helping, healing ways to practice law. This book is a resource for law professors, law students, and lawyers who share those visions.

Some History[3]

Although the emerging interest in law as a healing profession is of relatively recent vintage, the seeds can be found decades ago. As early as 1955, Erwin Griswold, former dean of the Harvard Law School, called upon the bar and the legal academy to recognize the need for human relations training in law school. Dean Griswold urged lawyers to study social science literature on human relations, noting that the average lawyer spent far more time interacting with people than reading and arguing appellate cases.[4]

Dean Griswold's call inspired Professor Howard Sacks to offer an experimental human relations course at Northwestern Law School during the 1957-58 school year.[5] The course, entitled Professional Relations, was apparently the first course at any law school to apply human relations training to lawyers.[6]

> cannot agree on a neutral site, they shall meet on the front steps of the Sam M. Gibbons U.S. Courthouse.... Each lawyer shall be entitled to be accompanied by one paralegal who shall act as an attendant and witness. At that time and location, counsel shall engage in one (1) game of "rock, paper, scissors." The winner of this engagement shall be entitled to select the location for the 30(b)(6) deposition to be held somewhere in Hillsborough County during the period July 11–12, 2006. If either party disputes the outcome of this engagement, an appeal may be filed and a hearing will be held at 8:30 A.M. on Friday, July 7, 2006 before the undersigned in Courtroom 3, George C. Young United States Courthouse ...

Case No. 6:05-cv-1430-Orl-31JGG (U.S. D. Ct. Middle D. Fla., June 6, 2006).

3. This history is drawn largely from Marjorie A. Silver, *Love, Hate and Other Emotional Interference in the Lawyer/Client Relationship*, 6 CLIN. L. REV. 259, 284-88 (1999).

4. *Id.* at 284.

5. Howard R. Sacks, *Human Relations Training for Students and Lawyers*, 11 J. LEGAL EDUC. 316, 317 (1959).

6. *Id.* at 321 n.13.

Professor Andrew Watson, a psychiatrist who later held a joint appointment at the University of Michigan law and medical schools, taught similar experimental courses.[7] In his endeavors to bridge the gap between psychiatry and the practice of law, over a twenty-year period Professor Watson published numerous articles and books for a legal audience.[8] His work explored the clinical application of psychotherapeutic insights to legal education and the practice of law. Watson urged legal educators to incorporate basic psychiatric principles into mainstream legal education.

In 1964, Harrop Freeman, a Cornell law professor, published the first coursebook devoted to the techniques and psychology of interviewing and counseling clients.[9] In a preface to the book, Dean Griswold praised the work for recognizing the importance of cultivating interpersonal skills for the effective practice of law. Dean Griswold wrote that by seeking to fill a void in legal education—a field devoted until then almost entirely to the Langdellian case method—Freeman's contribution was "almost as much a pioneering book as was Dean Langdell's *Cases on Contracts*."[10]

Another important contributor to the field was Alan Stone, Professor of Law and Psychiatry at Harvard University.[11] In a 1971 law review article, Professor Stone lamented that sixteen years had passed since Dean Griswold had made his oft-cited declaration that legal education neglected human relations training. "In spite of Dean Griswold's enthusiasm," Professor Stone wrote, "law schools … have largely ignored the responsibility of teaching interviewing, counseling, negotiating, and other human relations skills, and Harrop Freeman's work has not generated a new Langdellian dynasty."[12]

---

7. Andrew S. Watson, *The Law and Behavioral Science Project at the University of Pennsylvania: A Psychiatrist on the Law Faculty*, 11 J. Legal Educ. 73 (1958).

8. *See id.*; Andrew S. Watson, *Some Psychological Aspects of Teaching Professional Responsibility*, 16 J. Legal Educ. 1 (1963); Andrew S. Watson, *The Lawyer as Counselor*, 5 J. Fam. L. 7 (1965); Andrew S. Watson, *The Quest for Professional Competence: Psychological Aspects of Legal Education*, 37 U. Cin. L. Rev. 91 (1968); Andrew S. Watson, *Lawyers and Professionalism: A Further Psychiatric Perspective on Legal Education*, 8 U. Mich. J.L. Reform 248, 265–78 (1975); Andrew S. Watson, The Lawyer in the Interviewing and Counseling Process (1976); Andrew S. Watson, Psychiatry for Lawyers (rev. ed. 1978).

9. Harrop A. Freeman, Legal Interviewing and Counseling (1964).

10. *Id.* at ix–x.

11. Alan Stone, *Legal Education on the Couch*, 85 Harv. L. Rev. 392 (1971); Alan Stone, Law, Psychiatry, and Morality: Essays and Analysis 199 (1984).

12. Stone, *Legal Education on the Couch*, *supra*, at 428. Professor Stone notes the limitation of the Freeman book's case studies:

Cases like those collected by Professor Freeman do have some utility, but often

In the late seventies and early eighties, Professor James Elkins of the West Virginia University College of Law made several contributions to the literature advocating training in human relations.[13] In a 1983 law review article, Professor Elkins argued for the revitalization of a humanistic perspective in legal education.[14] He observed that the psychoanalytic approach, popular in the jurisprudence of the 1960s and early 1970s, had fallen into disfavor by the 1980s.[15]

Law and Humanism

Interest in the development of human relations skills in law schools was closely aligned with the law and humanism movement that gained a core of proponents in the 1970s and early 1980s. While articles advocating for an approach that paid attention to the humanistic side of lawyering began appearing in the mid- to late- sixties,[16] it was in the late seventies and early eighties

they neither have the psychological depth nor the complexity that allows for rigorous analysis; nor do they involve the student personally in a way which permits the psychological elements to come to life and be comprehended at the level of emotionally significant learning.

Id. at 429.

13. James A Elkins, *A Counseling Model for Lawyering in Divorce Cases*, 53 NOTRE DAME LAW. 229 (1977); James A Elkins, *The Legal Persona: An Essay on the Professional Mask*, 64 VA. L. REV. 756 (1978); James A. Elkins, *A Humanistic Perspective in Legal Education*, 62 NEB. L. REV. 494 (1983).

14. Elkins, *A Humanistic Perspective in Legal Education, supra.*

15. Professor Elkins speculated that the loss of interest might have been due to a growing realization among academics that the psychoanalytic or humanistic perspectives were unlikely to engender substantial change in legal education. "[L]egal educators," he wrote, moved to take up other concerns as they realized "conscious[ly] or unconscious[ly], that counseling was not going be the catalytic agent for change...." *Id.* at 508 n.56.

16. Walter Gellhorn, *"Humanistic Perspective": A Critique*, 32 J. LEGAL EDUC. 99, 99 (1982) (citing Charles A. Reich, *Toward the Humanistic Study of Law*, 74 YALE L.J. 1402 (1965); Robert S. Redmount, *Humanistic Law Through Legal Education*, 1 CONN. L. REV. 207 (1968)). The Gellhorn article is interesting in and of itself. It is a rather venomous appraisal of the humanistic movement and the book, *Becoming a Lawyer, see infra* note 17. There is some history here. Somewhere in the bowels of my files, I discovered a photocopy of fascinating correspondence between Walter Gellhorn and Jack Himmelstein from the summer of 1978. Gellhorn politely but dismissively responds to a draft Himmelstein had apparently shared with him of Jack Himmelstein, *Reassessing Law Schooling: An Inquiry into the Application of Humanistic Educational Psychology to the Teaching of Law*, 53 N.Y.U. L. REV. 514 (1978).

that the movement gained momentum. Perhaps it reached its apex in 1981, with the publication of *Becoming a Lawyer: A Humanistic Perspective on Legal Education and Professionalism.*[17]

For some, introducing humanism into the curriculum meant focusing on developing interpersonal skills;[18] for others, like the authors of *Becoming a Lawyer*, it was a call for a more value-focused legal education. This focus on values however, was coupled with renewed attention to the human element in the law: the *humanbeingness* of teachers, students and, most importantly, clients.[19] The book was an outgrowth of a federally-funded project based at Columbia Law School, the Project for the Study and Application of Humanistic Education in Law. The Project's mission was to address the perception that in the process of training law students to become lawyers, for the most part legal educators at best ignored and at worst dismissed attention to the core values that attracted many students to the study of law.[20] These values included the desire to "help people," to "make a difference," to seek justice, to have a positive impact on the world.[21] The intellectual indoctrination of law students distanced many from the ideals that provided a meaning for the work they wished to do,[22] thus threatening to separate lawyers from their own moral core.[23]

---

17. ELIZABETH DVORKIN, JACK HIMMELSTEIN & HOWARD LESNICK, BECOMING A LAWYER: A HUMANISTIC PERSPECTIVE ON LEGAL EDUCATION AND PROFESSIONALISM 2 (1981) [hereinafter DVORKIN ET AL.]. By 1983, Professor Elkins was already lamenting its decline. *See supra* note 14.

18. *See, e.g.*, David M. Hunsaker, *Law, Humanism and Communication: Suggestions for Limited Curricular Reform*, 30 J. LEGAL EDUC. 417 (1979–80). Although this article, written by a professor of speech communication at the University of Virginia, acknowledged the "values" question, its primary focus was on the need for introducing interpersonal skill development into the law school curriculum.

19. DVORKIN ET AL., *supra* note 17, at 3.

20. *Id.* at 1–2.

21. For the past twenty years or more, towards the end of each semester in Professional Responsibility, I survey students' hopes and concerns about practicing law. The most common response to the question of "What excites you most about the law?" has consistently remained responses about the possibility of "helping others."

22. *See infra* note 51 (discussing Viktor Frankl's school of logotherapy and man's search for meaning).

23. DVORKIN ET AL., *supra* note 17, at 2. When I entered the University of Pennsylvania Law School in 1970, it was at the height of the Civil Rights movement and the opposition to the Vietnam War. Many if not most of my classmates shared the vision that, armed with law degrees, we could be champions fighting for social justice and equality. Three years later, something had happened. Most of my classmates sought and found jobs at prestigious law firms. Only a few of us maintained the ideals that drew us to the law in the first

Therapeutic Jurisprudence and the Comprehensive Law Movement

Some have speculated that the disillusionment fueled by the Vietnam War and Watergate may have dampened the efforts of reformers to approach law and its problems informed by a humanistic perspective, thus precipitating the individualism and materialism that thrived in the 1980s.[24] Interest in a more humanistic approach to legal education and the practice of law may have waned, but it did not disappear. Professor Susan Daicoff has suggested that the increasing societal disillusionment with the materialistic, egocentrism of the 1980s may have paved the way for the burgeoning of developments in the last decade of the twentieth century and the beginning of the twenty-first, for what Professor Daicoff has named The Comprehensive Law Movement.[25]

Therapeutic Jurisprudence

Probably the most influential of these developments has been Therapeutic Jurisprudence (TJ). Grounded in the notion that law and legal actors cause outcomes that may be either therapeutic or anti-therapeutic, TJ calls for attention to those effects and a conscious effort, consistent with legal rights and other important values, to promote legal consequences that enhance wellbeing, and minimize those that diminish it.[26] The subsequent "marriage" of TJ with the Preventive Law model[27] calls for, in Professor Bruce Winick's words,

---

place.

For studies demonstrating that wellbeing is nurtured far more by *intrinsic* rather than *extrinsic* rewards, see *infra* ch. 3: Susan Daicoff, *Lawyer Personality Traits and their Relationship to Various Approaches to Lawyering*, at pp. 92–93.

24. *See* Susan Daicoff, *Law as a Healing Profession: The "Comprehensive Law Movement,"* 6 Pepp. Disp. Resol. L.J. 1, 47(2006).

25. *See infra* notes 36–41 and accompanying text.

26. *See, e.g.,* Dennis P. Stolle et al., *Integrating Preventive Law and Therapeutic Jurisprudence: A Law and Psychology Based Approach to Lawyering, in* Practicing Therapeutic Jurisprudence: Law as a Helping Profession 5, 7–8 (Dennis P. Stolle, David B. Wexler & Bruce J. Winick eds., 2000); International Network on Therapeutic Jurisprudence, *at* http://www.law.arizona.edu/depts/upr-intj/ (official website of the International Network on Therapeutic Jurisprudence) (last visited July 28, 2006) [hereinafter TJ Website].

27. Preventive law, which focused on proactive counseling to avoid future legal problems, dates back to the 1950s. The father of the movement was Professor Louis Brown.

"lawyers who practice their profession with an ethic of care, enhanced interpersonal skills, a sensitivity to their clients' emotional wellbeing as well as their legal rights and interests, and a preventive law orientation that seeks to avoid legal problems."[28]

TJ has had a profound impact over the past decade or so, not only on legal systems in the United States,[29] but on legal institutions around the world.[30] As the reader will learn, many of the contributors to this book are writing from, or are informed by, a TJ perspective.[31] The body of TJ-related scholarship con-

---

Along with Professor Edward Dauer and others, Professor Brown founded the National Center for Preventive Law at the University of Denver. *See* California Western School of Law Nat'l Center for Preventive Law, *Louis M. Brown Program in Preventive Law*, at http://www.preventivelawyer.org/main/default.asp?pid=brown_program.htm (last visited July 25, 2006). In 1969, Professor Brown began the first ever interscholastic *counseling* competition. Hunsaker, *supra* note 21, at 422–23.

28. *See infra* ch. 11: Bruce J. Winick, *Overcoming Psychological Barriers to Settlement: Challenges for the TJ Lawyer*, at p. 342.

29. The growth of problem-solving courts is perhaps the most dramatic example here in the United States. *See infra* text accompanying note 52 (describing problem-solving courts). *See generally* JUDGING IN A THERAPEUTIC KEY: THERAPEUTIC JURISPRUDENCE AND THE COURTS (Bruce J. Winick & David B. Wexler eds., 2003). Perhaps related to the successes of the interdisciplinary approach used in problem-solving courts, increasingly legal services offices are seeking to meet the "extra" legal needs of clients. One such example is a program of the New York-based Office of the Appellate Defender. *OAD Expands Social Work/Re-entry Program*, VII NEWS FROM THE OFFICE OF THE APPELLATE DEFENDER 1 (2006), *available at* http://www.appellatedefender.org/May%202006.pdf (last visited July 26, 2006). Another example is the Georgia Justice Project, www.gjp.org. (last visited July 26, 2006). *See infra* ch. 16: Timothy Floyd, *Spirituality and Practicing Law as a Healing Profession: The Importance of Listening*, at pp. 482–83.

30. Judges from many different countries around the world are embracing TJ principles. The National Judicial Institute in Canada is drafting a handbook on how to incorporate TJ principles into generalist courts. In July 2004, Professor Wexler participated in a workshop for New Zealand judges to help them identify and use therapeutic interventions in general court work. *See* David B. Wexler, *Therapeutic Jurisprudence: It's Not Just for Problem-Solving Courts and Calendars Anymore: International Developments*, at http://www.ncsconline.org/WC/Publications/Trends/SpeProTherapTrends2004.html (last visited Aug. 3, 2006). Last November, at their annual conference in Perth, the Western Australian Country Magistrates unanimously passed a resolution supporting the use of TJ in their courts and programs. *See* TJ Website, *supra* note 26, *Announcements*, June 3, 2005. *See also* Michael S. King, *Therapeutic Jurisprudence in the Commonwealth*, 16 COMMONWEALTH JUD. J. 19 (2006) (surveying use of TJ in the 53 independent states around the world that comprise the Commonwealth).

31. *See, e.g.*, ch. 2: Susan Brooks, *Using Social Work Constructs in the Practice of Law*; ch. 11: Bruce J. Winick, *Overcoming Psychological Barriers to Settlement: Challenges for the TJ Lawyer*; Ch. 12: David B. Wexler, *The TJ Criminal Lawyer: Therapeutic Jurisprudence*

tinues to grow at an impressive rate,[32] and numerous international interdisciplinary conferences focused on TJ theory and practices are held every year around the globe.[33]

Other forces of wellbeing have been at work. Steven Keeva's 1999 book, *Transforming Practices: Finding Joy and Satisfaction in the Legal Life*, shared the stories of numerous attorneys who—often without the benefit of a theoretical framework like TJ—have forged a variety of pathways that allow them to practice law consistent with their values and belief systems, allowing them, in Keeva's words, to find joy and satisfaction in the legal life.[34] Around the same time, a group of law professors forged an on-line Humanizing Legal Education (HLE) community. Propelled by the energy and commitment of Professor Lawrence Krieger from Florida State University, HLE attracted increasing numbers of participants, around the country and beyond, determined to find ways to re-humanize the law school experience.[35]

---

and Criminal Law Practice; Ch. 14: Kristin Henning, *Defining the Lawyer-Self: Using Therapeutic Jurisprudence to Define the Lawyer's Role and Build Alliances that Aid the Child Client.*

32. *See* Preface, *supra* note 3.

33. To date there have been three International Conferences on Therapeutic Jurisprudence: in Winchester, England in 1998, in Cincinnati, Ohio in 2001, and in Perth, Australia in 2006. Numerous TJ-related conferences have been held around the globe over the past several years. For example, the 20th annual meeting of the Australia and New Zealand Association of Law, Psychiatry and Psychology held in Auckland, New Zealand focused on Therapeutic Jurisprudence. Professor Winick chaired a panel on Therapeutic Jurisprudence at the European Association of Psychology and Law held in Lisbon Portugal in 2001, and a TJ session held at the International Association of Law and Mental Health in Amsterdam in 2002. *See* Bruce J. Winick, *Therapeutic Jurisprudence Defined, at* http://www.brucewinick.com/TherapeuticJurisprudence.htm (last visited Aug. 3, 2006). Therapeutic Jurisprudence played a significant role at the 2004 AALS Clinical Legal Education Conference, *see* The Association of American Law Schools Presents: A Conference on Clinical Legal Education, *Back to Basics, Back to the Future, at* http://www.aals.org/clinical2004/program.html (last visited Aug. 3, 2006); and was featured at The Greek Conference on Professional Responsibility in Crete in 2004. *See* The Greek Conference, *at* www.greekconference.com.au. *See also* Symposium: *Therapeutic Jurisprudence in Clinical Legal Education and Legal Skills Training*, 17 St. Thomas L. Rev. 403 (2005).

34. Preface, Keeva, *supra* note 3.

35. *See* Daicoff, *supra* note 24, at 49–50. In January 2006, this group organized an all day workshop at the annual meeting of the Association of American Law Schools, in Washington, D.C. entitled *A Search for Balance in the Whirlwind of Law School*.

The Comprehensive Law Movement

Around 2000, Professor Susan Daicoff coined the term *The Comprehensive Law Movement* (CLM) to describe the confluence of related developments, or as she has called them, *vectors*[36]—of which Therapeutic Jurisprudence is one—that comprise this "movement."[37] Professor Bruce Winick characterized these as

> [M]embers of an extended family.... [S]ome have red hair, some have brown hair and brown eyes, some have blue eyes[. B]ut when you put them all together for a group photo, a striking family resemblance is evident in each member. Yet, each member has his or her own distinctive features that are peculiar to that member only. The beauty of the movement is evident not only in the features that unify the[m] but also in their distinct and individual differences.[38]

These vectors, as described by Professor Daicoff, include the *lenses* of TJ, Preventive Law, Procedural Justice, Creative Problem-Solving, and Holistic Justice, as well as the *processes* of Collaborative Law, Transformative Mediation, Restorative Justice, and Problem-Solving Courts.[39] In her exploration of the similarities and the differences among these vectors, Professor Daicoff notes that all of them aim to "maximize the emotional, psychological, and relational wellbeing of the individuals and communities" involved,[40] and require attention to extra-legal factors.[41]

The Contents

The eighteen chapters of this book will introduce the reader to a variety of skills, techniques, values, attitudes, and information, some essential and all

---

36. "This term 'vectors' reflects the forward movement of the disciplines in the future and their convergence toward common goals." *Id.* at 3.

37. For additional summaries of the vectors that comprise the Comprehensive Law Movement, see Susan Daicoff, *The Role of Therapeutic Jurisprudence within the Comprehensive Law Movement, in* PRACTICING THERAPEUTIC JURISPRUDENCE: LAW AS A HELPING PROFESSION 465, 470–83 (Dennis P. Stolle, David B. Wexler & Bruce J. Winick eds., 2000); Susan Daicoff, *The Comprehensive Law Movement*, 19 TOURO L. REV. 825, 832–45 (2004).

38. Daicoff, *supra* note 24, at 5.

39. *Id.* at 16–38.

40. *Id.* at 5.

41. *Id.* at 9.

useful, to the *affective* practice of law.[42] In addition, you will find in these pages numerous resources to assist you further in this endeavor.

This book is divided into five parts. Part I, ***Lawyering with Intra- and Interpersonal Competence*** introduces the reader to important psychological and other social science principles that inform the human dimensions of the practice of law. The first chapter, *Emotional Competence and the Lawyer's Journey*, by this volume's editor, Professor Marjorie Silver, explains the concept of emotional competence and how it is relevant to lawyers' work. Professor Silver advocates for developing psychological-mindedness, and offers illustrations of psychological manifestations that create both obstacles and opportunities in the lawyer/client relationship. Chapter 1 also alerts the reader to the sorts of psychological and emotional dysfunction—stress, burnout, and vicarious trauma—to which the empathic lawyer has heightened vulnerability.

Chapter 2, *Using Social Work Constructs in the Practice of Law*, by clinical law professor and former social worker Susan Brooks, discusses several elements, techniques, and constructs familiar to social work and illustrates their utility for the therapeutically-inclined lawyer. These include helpful approaches to use with especially challenging clients, including those who fail to keep appointments, those who constantly call the attorney, and those whose lives are in turmoil. Professor Brooks also explores the centrality of family and community—however defined—in cultivating deep understanding of a client's needs and interests.

In chapter 3, *Lawyer Personality Traits and their Relationship to Various Approaches to Lawyering*, law professor Susan Daicoff, who holds a master's degree in clinical psychology, surveys the findings of empirical studies on lawyer

---

42. "Affective" means "of or pertaining to emotions, mood, mental state, feeling, sensibility." Biology-Online.org, *Affective, at* http://www.biology-online.org/dictionary/affective (last visited Jan. 2, 2006). The earliest reference to *affective lawyering* of which I am aware appears in Carrie Menkel-Meadow, *Narrowing the Gap by Narrowing the Field: What's Missing from the MacCrate Report—Of Skills, Legal Science and Being a Human Being*, 69 Wash. L. Rev. 593, 606 (1994), in which Professor Menkel-Meadow critiques the MacCrate Report for ignoring the affective aspects of lawyering. Subsequently, others, most prominently, Professors Peter Margulies and Linda Mills have written about *affective lawyering* in the domestic violence context. *See, e.g.*, Peter Margulies, *Representation of Domestic Violence Survivors as a New Paradigm of Poverty Law: In Search of Access, Connection, and Voice*, 63 Geo. Wash. L. Rev. 1071, 1072–73 (1995); Linda G. Mills, *On the Other Side of Silence: Affective Lawyering for Intimate Abuse*, 81 Cornell L. Rev. 1225 (1996). *See also* Linda G. Mills, *Affective Lawyering: The Emotional Dimensions of the Lawyer-Client Relation, in* Practicing Therapeutic Jurisprudence: Law as a Helping Profession 419 (Dennis P. Stolle, David B. Wexler, Bruce J. Winick eds., 2000).

personality types and traits, and discusses how these findings relate to lawyers' preferences and strengths. Professor Daicoff explores the *fit* between personality types and approaches to practicing law generally, and law as a healing profession in particular. With the caveat that the conclusions of such studies are generalizations to which there are always exceptions, this chapter may guide the reader in determining which type of law practice would fit best with her own interests and inclinations.

In the final chapter of Part I, chapter 4, *Making out the Ghost Behind the Words: Approaching Legal Text with Psychological Intelligence*, Professor Aderson François explores the significance and implications of reading legal text with psychological engagement. After discussing Howard Gardner's theories of multiple intelligences in general and as applied to lawyering in particular, Professor Francois illustrates how to use *psychological lawyering intelligence* to understand three very different written texts. All these texts, however, have one commonality: an automobile accident. The texts examined include portions of an important products liability case, *Henningsen v. Bloomfield Motors, Inc.*, F. Scott Fitzgerald's *The Great Gatsby*, and Bruce Springsteen's song, *Wreck on the Highway*.

In Part II, **Lawyering with Multicultural Competence**, four clinical law teachers and scholars focus on the unique challenges that arise in counseling clients from different cultures. Professors Paul Tremblay and Carwina Weng, in chapter 5, *Multicultural Lawyering: Heuristics and Biases*, draw from the rich social science literature on multicultural counseling. Their guidance will assist lawyers in recognizing cultural dissimilarities, developing sensitivity to how they may affect the counseling relationship, and making appropriate adjustments to accommodate differences in cultural orientations. The chapter cautions practitioners to approach cross-cultural interactions with *informed not-knowing* and *disciplined naiveté*, so as to be sensitive to both cultural variations as well as individual variations from cultural norms.

Chapter 6, *Six Practices for Connecting with Clients Across Culture: Habit Four, Working with Interpreters, and other Mindful Approaches*, by Professors Susan Bryant and Jean Koh Peters, builds on the authors' earlier work on the Five Habits of Cross-cultural Lawyering.[43] Their chapter here zooms in on a particular and critical aspect of cross-cultural lawyering: communication. The authors illustrate how communication between lawyer and client with different cultural orientations can go awry, and offer specific opportunities and corrections available to the lawyer to get communication back on course. This

---

43. *See* ch. 6 *infra* note 3.

chapter also explores in depth the special challenges of working with inter-preters when lawyer and client speak different languages, and suggests six spe-cific practices for avoiding miscommunication.

In Part III, *Lawyering and Civil Disputes*, five authors share their visions of less adversarial approaches to solving civil problems. Over the past thirty-five years or so, the alternative dispute resolution movement has increasingly gained momentum. Although it got the early attention of the courts due to the savings of time and money it afforded as compared to court litigation, re-cent years have witnessed increasing numbers of advocates who have pro-moted it for its potential in fostering harmony and healing, and receiving bet-ter results for clients.[44] These five authors are among those supporters.

Chapter 7, by Professor Harold Abramson, *Problem-Solving Advocacy in Mediations: A Model of Client Representation*, provides a framework as well as concrete advice to attorneys who represent clients in civil mediation, urg-ing a problem-solving, rather than adversarial approach. The chapter reflects the methodology developed in Professor Abramson's award-winning book, *Mediation Representation-Advocating in a Problem-Solving Process*,[45] which filled a void of available guidance on problem-solving, geared not for the me-diator, but rather for the lawyer representing a client in mediation. Ap-proaching mediation as an extension of negotiation, Professor Abramson suggests strategies for realizing the enhanced value possible when disputants focus on *interests* rather than *positions*, as well as intelligently enlist the as-sistance of the mediator.

Chapter 8, *Collaborative Law: Practicing Without Armor, Practicing With Heart*, by renowned collaborative law practitioner and author Pauline Tesler, explains collaborative dispute resolution, an increasingly preferred alternative

---

44. *See, e.g.*, Daicoff, *in* Practicing TJ, *supra* note 37, at 467–68. "These other shifts include a decreased emphasis on individualism and individual rights and liberties and an increased emphasis on preserving relationships, connectedness, identity within a commu-nity or culture, and familial ties." *Id.* at 468. Other examples include: Robert A. Baruch Bush & Joseph P. Folger, The Promise of Mediation: Responding to Conflict Through Empowerment and Recognition (1994); Robert A. Baruch Bush & Joseph P. Folger, The Promise of Mediation: The Transformative Approach to Conflict (1994); Carrie J. Menkel-Meadow, *The Many Ways of Mediation: The Transformation of Tra-ditions, Ideologies, Paradigms and Practices, in* Mediation: Theory, Policy and Practice 111 (Carrie Menkel-Meadow ed., 2001) (*reprinted in* 11 Negotiation J. 217 (1995)).

45. Harold Abramson, Mediation Representation—Advocating in a problem-Solving Process (2004). This book was the recipient of the International Institute for Conflict Prevention and Resolution for Dispute Resolution (CPR) 2004 Book Award. *See* http://www.cpradr.org. (last visited July 28, 2006).

to contentious divorce litigation, taking hold not only throughout the United States, but in many other countries as well. Collaborative law involves a contractual arrangement among the lawyers and their clients that provides a structure designed to forge agreement between the parties, one that is constructive and healing, and that focuses on the best interests of the clients and their children. Collaborative practice has had transformative effects not only on the parties, but on the lawyers who engage in it as well; it is a "poster child" for the law as a healing profession movement.[46] Ms. Tesler describes the devastating emotional toll that traditional divorce litigation exacts on parties and counsel alike, the limitations of judicially-available relief, and explains how collaborative law offers the possibility of a far superior therapeutic resolution for divorcing couples.

In Chapter 9, *The Culture of Legal Denial*, Professor Jonathan Cohen, who has written wisely and well about the role of apology in legal disputes,[47] here explores the paradox that although we are taught as children that the right thing to do is to take responsibility for our wrongdoing, and to own up to our role in causing harm, lawyers are trained to advise their clients—in particular their clients who are defendants—just the opposite. Attorneys regularly caution clients *not* to take responsibility and to deny liability. Professor Cohen writes that not only does this generally escalate conflict, it likely also has a negative impact on the defendant client's—and perhaps the lawyer's—wellbeing. The chapter examines the moral, psychological, relational, and economic risks of denial and, while recognizing the potential difficulty of having such discussions, suggests that ethical and zealous representation often requires attorneys to discuss such factors with their clients. Professor Cohen explains why attorneys should not only advise clients about their legal rights, but should also consider engaging clients with respect to their moral responsibilities.

In chapter 10, *Hurting Clients*, the inimitable Dean Emeritus and Professor Edward Dauer, one of the earliest proponents of Preventive Law,[48] explains how, although lawsuits are almost always about money, money is frequently *not* what many clients are seeking. This has been demonstrated empirically in the medical malpractice arena in studies from several countries, including the

---

46. Collaborative problem-solving is being used in other fields as well. *See, e.g.,* Barry E. Hill & Nicholas Targ, *Collaborative Problem-Solving: An Option for Preventing and Resolving Environmental Conflicts.* 36 Envtl. L. Rep. News & Analysis 10440–10455 (2006).

47. *See, e.g.,* Jonathan R. Cohen, *Apology and Organizations: Exploring an Example from Medical Practice,* 27 Fordham Urb. L.J. 1447 (2000); Jonathan R. Cohen, *Advising Clients to Apologize,* 72 S. Cal. L. Rev. 1009 (1999).

48. *See supra* note 30 and accompanying text.

United States, that Professor Dauer discusses. However, trained to reduce all hurts to money, lawyers rarely consider that alternatives—perhaps an apology, or an explanation—may really be what the client needs or wants. Money is often a poor substitute for accountability, which, as explained by Professor Dauer, may encompass any or all of *sanction, restoration, correction,* or *communication.* Professor Dauer offers sound reasons for suggesting lawyers may better counsel their civil clients by exploring with them a range of alternatives, including, but certainly not limited to, litigation. Further, to do this effectively and well, lawyers must retrain themselves to listen to—and for—their clients' authentic needs and desires.

In chapter 11, *Overcoming Psychological Barriers to Settlement: Challenges for the TJ Lawyer,* Therapeutic Jurisprudence co-founder, Professor Bruce Winick, explores the lawyer's opportunities for counseling clients on pursuing alternatives to litigation. Professor Winick starts from the premise that although litigation is rarely in the client's best interest, the hurt and anger clients often experience complicate the client's ability to appreciate why alternatives to litigation are likely to better meet her goals and interests, including her ability to achieve psychological healing and wellness. Through understanding a range of emotional and psychological responses, the TJ attorney who has enhanced interpersonal, interviewing, and counseling skills, coupled with some basic techniques from psychology, can assist the client in overcoming resistance to settlement and in successfully navigating some of life's most difficult moments.

In Part IV, *Lawyering and the Criminal Justice System,* three writers explore what therapeutic lawyering has to offer those who represent clients accused of committing crimes. In chapter 12, *The TJ Criminal Lawyer: Therapeutic Jurisprudence and Criminal Law Practice,* Professor David Wexler, who partnered with Professor Winick in founding TJ, describes how defense lawyers might use therapeutic practices and approaches to promote better outcomes for their clients. By focusing on opportunities for treatment and services early on in the process and at various points thereafter, lawyers may be able to forge agreements with prosecutors and judges for interdisciplinary, rehabilitative alternatives to incarceration. Even when incarceration is ordered, the lawyer can work with the client to increase readiness for rehabilitation and toward eventual release and reentry.

In chapter 13, *A Public Defender in a Problem-Solving Court,* Executive Director of Brooklyn Defender Services, Lisa Schreibersdorf, a criminal defense lawyer with more than twenty years experience, shares her personal story. Early in her career, Ms. Schreibersdorf developed appreciation for the multiplicity of needs that her clients presented, as well as for the profound ways in which the criminal justice system failed to meet those needs. The advent of specialized *problem-solving courts* in Brooklyn in the mid-nineties—interdisciplinary systems designed to address multiple needs and provide rehabilitation for defendants accused of crimes related to drug addiction or mental health problems[49]—offered Ms. Schreibersdorf and her clients authentic opportunities for healing and redemption. Ms. Schreibersdorf describes both the victories and the challenges of insuring vigorous client representation in a system that, while offering a pathway to health and rehabilitation, nonetheless requires defendants to waive their constitutional rights to trial.

Clinical Law Professor Kristin Henning, in chapter 14, *Defining the Lawyer-Self: Using Therapeutic Jurisprudence to Define the Lawyer's Role and Build Alliances that Aid the Child Client,* extends the application of therapeutic jurisprudence principles to representing clients in the juvenile justice system. Professor Henning focuses on forging a lawyer/client relationship that empowers the young client, gives her voice and validation, enhances positive outcomes, and promotes possibilities for lasting rehabilitation, all the while mindful of preserving the juvenile's legal rights. She explores as well the significance of family, community, and interdisciplinary partnerships in achieving rehabilitative goals, as well as the challenge of insuring client autonomy consistent with these alliances.

Part V focuses on *Lawyering with Mindfulness, Spirituality, and Religion.* While many lawyers pursue the practice of law as a healing profession for purely secular reasons, others are motivated to do so by virtue of their religious faith.[50] My experience in discussions with many caring, committed col-

---

49. These are only two examples of the kinds of problem-solving courts that have evolved in recent years. *See* Center for Court Intervention, *at* http://www.courtinnovation .org/index (last visited July 28, 2006) (website for The Center for Court Innovation that has been instrumental in creating many of these courts).

50. *See generally, e.g.,* Symposium, *Reconciling Lawyers' Professional Lives with their Faith,* 27 Tex. Tech L. Rev. 911–1427 (1996). *See also* Healing Emotions: Conversations with the Dalai Lama on Mindfulness, Emotions, and Health (Daniel Goleman ed., 1997). This interdisciplinary gathering of ten Western scholars—among them experts in the fields of psychology, physiology, behavioral medicine, and philosophy—met with the Dalai Lama in Dharamsala, India in 1991 to explore the relationship between health and emotions, including whether an ethical system of moral values could be grounded on something other than a religious belief system. *Id.* at 1, 4, 18. According to the Dalai Lama, this was necessitated by the reality that the majority of the world's peoples held no religious belief system. Was there an effective way to appeal to such persons that they had a moral obligation to address the systemic problems of poverty, illness and devastation throughout the world? *Id.* at 18. Daniel Goleman, whose work on emotional competence is discussed *infra* ch. 1: Marjorie A. Silver, *Emotional Competence and the Lawyer's*

leagues has convinced me that the subject of religion and spirituality is one that causes many lawyers discomfort. While I do not claim to understand all of the reasons for this, I believe it bears relationship to the deep ambivalence many lawyers share about the appropriate boundary between the personal and the public. Nothing is more personal than our religion, our belief system, or the fact that we subscribe to neither. For many of us, what churches we attend and what practices we employ to help us make sense out of the world and our place in it, are matters private and separate from what we do when we engage in our professional work.

For others, however, for those who experience their work as a *calling*, a *vocation*, they are integrally related. Integration of one's personal values with one's professional pursuits is arguably essential for practicing law as a healing profession. The absence of such integration contributes to a kind of moral disconnect that threatens lawyers' psychological and emotional wellbeing.[51] One may or may not participate in an organized religion or hold any spiritual belief system.[52] But unless one finds meaning in one's work other than as a source of income, it will likely be difficult to sustain one's interest, enthusiasm, and commitment over the decades of one's career.[53]

Journey, at pp. 9–12, suggests that further research on the already documented connection between negative emotions and ill health may offer such a possibility. *Id.* at 5, 33–44.

51. *See* ch. 1, *supra* note 50, at pp. 42–44. The European psychiatrist and concentration camp survivor, Viktor Frankl, developed the school of psychotherapy known as logotherapy (also known as "The Third Viennese School of Therapy"). Its premise is that man's search for meaning is intrinsic to being human, and vitally important in the pursuit of happiness. VIKTOR E. FRANKL, MAN'S SEARCH FOR MEANING 120–21 (1984). One of several studies supporting his conclusion was a survey undertaken by Johns Hopkins of about 8,000 students from forty-eight colleges. When asked what they considered "very important" to them, 16 percent chose "making a lot of money" compared to 78 percent who selected "finding a purpose and meaning to my life." *Id.* at 122.

52. One of my colleagues who falls into this category, a civil libertarian and human rights activist, has shared with me that he admires, sometimes even envies, those for whom doing good works is grounded in their religious belief system. He has tried meditation, see *infra* text at note 56, but has found it doesn't work for him.

53. Although my "google" search revealed a variety of definitions of spirituality, David Hall, former dean and professor of law at Northeastern Law School has a definition that resonates for me in his new book, THE SPIRITUAL REVITALIZATION OF THE LEGAL PROFESSION: A SEARCH FOR SACRED RIVERS (2005): "'the intentional decision to search for a deeper meaning in life and to actualize in one's life the highest values that can be humanly obtained.'" Rich Barlow, *Balancing Life and Practice: Getting Lawyers to Reset Moral Compass*, THE BOSTON GLOBE, April 2006, *available at* http://www.lexisone.com/balancing/articles/b040006h.html (last visited April 18, 2006).

In the chapters that follow, four authors share what they have discovered as sources for inspiration in their professional journeys. These chapters contain insights that many readers will likely find inspiring,[54] and practical advice that many will find useful in your journey to better serve your clients' needs and derive more satisfaction from your work. I invite any skeptical readers to approach these chapters with nonjudgmental curiosity to see what they might offer.

The first of these, chapter 15, *Awareness in Lawyering: A Primer on Paying Attention*, by Professor Leonard Riskin, describes contemplative practices that were developed and refined by Buddhists but are widely used in secular Western society.[55] He offers practical advice on how to better tune in to what your client needs to communicate, and on how to develop the capacity to be a better listener to your client, through being mentally and emotionally present. Professor Riskin, a renowned expert on both *mediation* and mindfulness *meditation*, describes the benefits of mindfulness and offers step-by-step guidance on how to cultivate this state of mind through meditation that enables the practitioner to develop nonjudgmental awareness and loving-kindness.[56]

In chapter 16, *Spirituality and Practicing Law as a Healing Profession: The Importance of Listening*, Professor Timothy Floyd explores different kinds of listening: listening to our lives, listening for opportunities for healing and reconciliation, and listening to clients and others in legal conflict. For Professor Floyd, practicing law as a healing profession requires the employment of spiritual practices. He suggests that Christianity, Judaism, and Islam are concerned with healing our brokenness, and suggests listening as a framework for both exploring our spirituality and for practicing law as a healing profession. This listening includes paying attention, seeing clearly, understanding deeply, and reaching out with empathy. Professor Floyd shares his own experiences of deep listening and spirituality in his death penalty representation work.

---

54. The words "inspiring" and "spiritual" share common roots. Both come from the Latin word *spirare*, "to breathe." WEBSTER'S THIRD NEW INTERNATIONAL DICTIONARY OF THE ENGLISH LANGUAGE UNABRIDGED 1170, 2198–99 (1993).

55. Goleman, *supra* note 50, at 5. Professor Riskin has received inspiration from Jon Kabat-Zinn, whose Stress Reduction Clinic at the University of Massachusetts Medical Center in Worcester, Massachusetts, uses Mindfulness Meditation practice to enhance the well-being and improve the medical healthfulness of, among others, chronically ill patients and medical students. *Id.* at 113–43.

56. These concepts, too, have roots in Buddhist philosophy. *See, e.g., id.* at 19, 185, 191 (on loving-kindness, towards oneself as well as others) and 120-21, 184–85 (on nonjudgmental awareness). The Dalai Lama was taken aback to learn that low self-esteem was a pervasive problem in the West. "There is no such concept as self-loathing or self-deprecation … in Tibetan culture." *Id.* at 184.

In chapter 17, *Sojourner to Sojourner*, Professor Calvin Pang invites us to accompany him on a journey to understand how spirituality informs his—and our—professional quest. For him, the spiritual is always a part of us, whether we acknowledge it, value it, or not. It is an inherent part of our being human. Professor Pang explores the challenge of maintaining awareness and being present to our spirituality, as we juggle the demands of law school and practice, and seek the extrinsic, material rewards that so often define success. He shares stories from Father Dan Edwards, a lawyer turned priest, whose faith enabled him to find redemption even in clients who had committed heinous crimes.

Chapter 18, *The Good Lawyer: Choosing to Believe in the Promise of Our Craft*, the last chapter of both this part and the book, is an inspirational essay from Professor Paula Franzese that encourages the reader to search for meaning in the face of the negativity and cynicism that pervade the legal profession. Sharing poignant stories—her own and those of others—Professor Franzese entreats us to use our knowledge and skills to bridge the gap between the world that is and the one that ought to be. She counsels us not to let the fact that we can not cure all of the world's problems stop us from taking on those that we can—and we should not underestimate our abilities to effect small miracles in the world. "[T]here are countless clients and causes out there," she writes, "some of them as yet nameless and unknown, waiting for us to make the difference that only we can make."[57]

Whatever calls to us, let it be something that sustains us throughout our lives. For some of us, that will mean fighting for social, economic, or political justice. For others it will be championing the environment. For still others, it will be providing competent legal services at reasonable prices to the members of our communities. Whatever it is, let it be something that challenges us every day to be not only the best lawyers we can be; let it be something that allows us to be the best people we can be.

I invite the reader, in a spirit of generosity and optimism, to open up to the opportunities for wellbeing that this book offers you and your clients.

Marjorie A. Silver
August 2006

---

57. Ch. 18, *infra*, at p. 521.

THE AFFECTIVE ASSISTANCE OF COUNSEL

I

Lawyering with Intra- and Inter-personal Competence

CHAPTER 1

Emotional Competence and the Lawyer's Journey

Marjorie A. Silver[*]

Introduction: The Journey Ahead

Unlike training for other helping professions, training for lawyers rarely includes exposure to principles of psychology or an exploration of the emotional aspects of practice. Yet understanding what makes human beings act and think the way they do would greatly benefit any lawyer/client relationship. It is especially critical in practicing law as a healing profession.

Lawyers need not *become* psychologists or social workers in order to practice law *affectively* and *effectively*,[1] any more than a medical malpractice lawyer

---

[*] Professor of Law, Touro Law Center.

1. In fact, there exists a real danger that lawyers who educate themselves along the lines I am suggesting in this chapter might then assume that they have acquired such qualifications. I cannot emphasize strongly enough that this is both ill-advised and dangerous. *See infra* ch. 3: Susan Daicoff, *Lawyer Personality Traits and Their Relationship to Various Approaches to Lawyering* at pp. 100–01; *infra* ch. 14: Kristen Henning, *Defining the Lawyer-Self: Using Therapeutic Jurisprudence to Define the Lawyer's Role and Build Alliances that Aid the Child Client* at p. 430. Lawyers need to recognize when they ought to collaborate with social workers and other mental health providers. *See* Paula Galowitz, *Collaboration Between Lawyers and Social Workers: Re-Examining the Nature and Potential of the Relationship*, 67 Fordham L. Rev. 2123 (1999); Sanford M. Portnoy, The Family Lawyers' Guide to Building Successful Client Relationships 4, 58–59, 118–19 (Section of Family Law, American Bar Association 2000) (stressing distinction between roles of therapists and family lawyers practicing with awareness of emotional and psychological concerns). I thus have concerns about the misleading title and its implications of an article by two clinicians whom I admire greatly. *See* Jane Aiken & Stephen Wizner, *Law as Social Work*, 11 Wash. U. J.L. & Pol'y 63 (2003). "We have come to realize that our defensive response to the accusation that what we do is social work is the wrong response. What we should be saying is: "You're right.

5

must go to medical school. But just as that lawyer needs to acquire sufficient knowledge about the human body, disease, and medicine in order to effectively represent his clients, all lawyers need to know enough about the operation of emotions and the psyche in order to appreciate the ways in which these forces may enhance or impede their work. It is insufficient, however, to only gain the ability to observe their manifestations in our clients, our adversaries, and others with whom we interact. First and foremost, we must gain sufficient self-awareness to recognize how we ourselves are affected by our psyche and emotions. Because so much of this happens at a level below consciousness, this is no simple task. Yet, as with so many skills that the lawyer must develop, time and experience will be great teachers. Our entire career is a journey in which we have repeated opportunities to hone these skills, to our benefit, as well as to the benefit of our clients, and the legal system in which we practice.

Whether or not we admit it, whether we are aware of them or not, whether or not we like it, emotions are always influencing our cognitive functioning and moral judgments.[2] Yet, as Susan Bandes has noted, "There may be no other profession whose practitioners are required to deal with so much pain with so little support and guidance."[3]

This chapter is an introduction to the realms of emotional competence and psychology, and offers several examples of how they may affect the lawyer endeavoring to practice law therapeutically. You will find other examples throughout this book. If you have already represented clients, you will likely find that some or many of the examples below have cropped up in your own experience. The field, however, is vast. This chapter reflects my work and that of others who have begun to explore the terrain of how the emotions and the psyche may impact the lawyer/client relationship. It will enable you to add to your body of knowledge, as well as your repertoire of strategies and skills for lawyering with psychological-mindedness[4] and an attention to emotions. I also hope it will inspire you to think about how the affective domain shapes your

---

What *we* do is social work, and that is why it so challenging and important." *Id.* at 63–64. Professors Aiken and Wizner, however, do acknowledge the existence of significant differences in the training and qualifications for practicing the two professions. *Id.* at 64.

2. *See infra* note 32.

3. Susan Bandes, *Repression and Denial in Criminal Lawyering*, 9 BUFF. CRIM. L. REV. 339, 342 (2006).

4. One finds numerous definitions of *psychological-mindedness*. *See, e.g.*, PubMed, *Psychological-Mindedness: A Conceptual Model, at* http://www.ncbi.nlm.nih.gov/entrez/ query.fcgi?cmd=Retrieve&db=PubMed&list_uids=1543250&dopt=Abstract (last visited July 27, 2006) (abstract of paper exploring various definitions and suggesting new conceptual model). I use it here to "denote[ ] a person's capacity to reflect on themselves, on

relationships with your clients. Through improving your relationships with your clients, you will both enhance what makes you a competent lawyer and increase your pleasure with the practice of law.[5]

Like most lawyers, I received no formal training in clinical psychology or counseling.[6] My interest grew from my experiences in the classroom and led me to explore, initially, manifestations of *countertransference* in the lawyer/client relationship.[7] That project made me curious about the impact of other emotional and psychological phenomena that arise in the lawyer's relationship with her client. On this journey I met many fellow travelers who shared my emerging interests in finding ways to practice law that enhance the client's—and the lawyer's—wellbeing.[8] Many of those fellow travelers have contributed chapters to this book.

This chapter is divided into three parts. The first explores the meaning of emotional competence and its relationship to lawyering as a healing profession. Part two describes several examples of psychological phenomena that may arise in the lawyer/client relationship. The final part looks at several manifestations of dysfunction—stress, burnout, and vicarious trauma—of which the emotionally competent lawyer must be wary; for, left unchecked, they threaten to impair our wellbeing and thus sabotage our effectiveness as helping, healing, competent counselors to our clients.

I. Setting Out:
Cultivating Emotional Competence

[An] instructor told [his] class about a time when a client had called
him and asked him, "Will, if I've just taken out a life insurance policy

---

others and the relationship between the two." Real World Solutions, *The Psychological Aspect to Executive Coaching, at* http://www.1to1coachingschool.com/Psychology_Based_ Executive_Coaching.htm (last visited July 27, 2006).

5. Enhancing your emotional competence in fact offers possibilities for improving your relationships with persons other than your clients, both within and beyond your professional life.

6. My interest has been most certainly augmented, however, as a *consumer* and *beneficiary* of quite productive psychotherapy at critical junctures in my life. For that, I wish to especially acknowledge and thank Robert E. Fischel, M.D.

7. *See infra* text accompanying notes 46–47.

8. *See supra* Introduction, at pp. xxiv, xxvii (discussing the Comprehensive Law Movement); Susan Daicoff, *The Role of Therapeutic Jurisprudence within the Comprehensive Law Movement, in* PRACTICING THERAPEUTIC JURISPRUDENCE: LAW AS A HELPING PROFESSION 465 (Dennis P. Stolle, David B. Wexler & Bruce J. Winick eds., 2000) [hereinafter PRACTICING TJ].

Can before I kill myself? [handwritten margin note]

on myself, how long must that policy be in effect before I can kill myself and my beneficiaries will still be able to collect the money?" A student shouted out, "Two years!" The instructor, who had been telling this story as a preamble to announcing that a psychologist would be coming to speak at the next class, told the man in no uncertain terms that "two years" is NOT the correct answer to that question. The most appropriate response to that question would be something such as, "Why do you ask?" or, "Is there something that has been bothering you lately?" or even, "Let's get together and talk about this."

While the student was technically correct, he was missing the point by a very wide margin. Any client who brings up suicide, however "hypothetically," is communicating a very important message that must be taken seriously.[9]

What's wrong with this picture? Did the law student overlook the possibility that this client might be contemplating suicide? Would the student have responded differently, more empathically, *before* he entered law school? If so, what has legal education wrought, and what can we do about it? How do we cultivate empathy and other interpersonal skills so necessary to serving the whole client?

Not surprisingly, most of us are resistant to acknowledging the power of our emotional lives.[10] The qualities most valued by legal educators and the bar are the abilities to analyze, to reason, and to make logical, persuasive arguments. Applicants who show most promise to excel in these areas—those that score high on the LSAT,[11] for example—are generally those most likely to be accepted into law school. Thus the personality profile of the typical law stu-

---

9. Stephanie Sogg & Wilton S. Sogg, *Coping with Adversity: Your Clients' and Your Own*, 46 Prac. Law. 25, 31 (2000).

10. The reader should be mindful that these are generalizations, to which there are many exceptions—likely among those are the law students and lawyers attracted to practicing law *affectively*. *See* Introduction, *supra* note 8 and accompanying text. As Professor Daicoff notes, the minority of law students and lawyers who are "Feelers" in the Myers-Briggs nomenclature—are likely to thrive as practitioners within the Comprehensive Law Movement. Susan Daicoff, *Law as a Healing Profession: The "Comprehensive Law Movement"*, 6 Pepp. Disp. Resol. L.J. 1, 55–59 (2006); ch. 3: Susan Daicoff, *Lawyer Personality Traits and their Relationship to Various Approaches to Lawyering* at p. 90 [hereinafter *Lawyer Personality*].

11. Law School Admissions Test. *See* Law School Admission Council, *About the LSAT*, *at* http://www.lsac.org/LSAC.asp?url=lsac/about-the-lsat.asp (last visited July 13, 2006).

dent;[12] the emphasis on rational, analytical discourse and the Socratic method in law school; the talents that are ratified and rewarded in practice: All these contribute to the devaluation and denial of emotional processes and influences.[13] *denial of emotional processes.*

Lack of self-awareness takes its toll on lawyers, leading to disproportionately high levels of stress, substance abuse, and depression.[14] Deficits in interpersonal relationship skills adversely affect our capacity to empathize with our clients, to counsel them, and to gain their trust.[15] An inability to understand the emotional undercurrents among our adversaries is also likely to limit our skill at negotiating and resolving controversies.

Lawyers also need to understand how we are perceived by others.[16] If things we say or do produce unintended, unwanted reactions in others, then we will, consequently, be less effective in our work. If we are aware of how we can act or speak in ways that produce desired results, to achieve desired goals, then we will be both more successful and, likely, more fulfilled.[17]

In his 1995 bestseller,[18] Daniel Goleman claimed that emotional intelligence, which includes a range of intra- and inter-personal skills, was more significant than several other factors, including "I.Q.,"[19] in predicting success in life.[20] In a subsequent work, Goleman cited empirical evidence demonstrat-

learning how to speak w/ others.

---

12. *See, e.g.,* Susan Daicoff, *Lawyer Know Thyself: A Review of the Empirical Research on Attorney Attributes Bearing on Professionalism,* 46 Am. U. L. Rev. 1337, 1365–66 (1997) (describing studies showing that law students and lawyers differ from general population by "marked preference for Thinking over Feeling" and that this has remained a constant over time, independent of gender influences."); Daicoff, *Lawyer Personality, supra* note 10, at pp. 87–88.

13. Marjorie A. Silver, *Emotional Intelligence and Legal Education,* 5 J. Psychol. Pub. Pol'y & L. 1173, 1181–82 (1999) [hereinafter *EI & LE*]; Marjorie A. Silver, *Love, Hate and Other Emotional Interference in the Lawyer/Client Relationship,* 6 Clin. L. Rev. 259, 278–81 (1999) [hereinafter *Love & Hate*].

14. Silver, *Love & Hate, supra,* at notes 105–111 and accompanying text.

15. Silver, *EI & LE, supra* note 13, at 1182.

16. Marjorie A. Silver, *Commitment and Responsibility: Modeling and Teaching Professionalism Pervasively,* 14 Widener L. Rev. 329, 346 (2005).

17. *Id.* (citing Joshua D. Rosenberg, *Teaching Values in Law School: Teaching Empathy in Law School,* 36 U.S.F. L. Rev. 621, 637–41 (2002) (discussing student development of awareness of how others perceive them to enable more effective lawyering).

18. Daniel Goleman, Emotional Intelligence (paperback ed. 1997).

19. "IQ" stands for intelligence quotient. *See* Howard Gardner, Multiple Intelligences: The Theory in Practice 5 (1993) (describing the development of the test by Alfred Binet).

20. Daniel Goleman, Working with Emotional Intelligence 5, 19 (1998).

ing how critical emotional intelligence is to success at work.[21] Since then, numerous legal scholars, myself included, have written about the relationship between emotional intelligence and good lawyering.[22]

Goleman's work built on that of psychologist and educator Howard Gardner, who had identified multiple kinds of intelligence not measured by stan-

---

21. *Id.* at 5–6.

Given how much emphasis schools and admissions tests put on it, IQ alone explains surprisingly little of achievement at work or in life. When IQ test scores are correlated with how well people perform in their careers, the highest estimate of how much difference IQ accounts for is about 25 percent. A careful analysis, though, suggests a more accurate figure may be no higher than 10 percent, and perhaps as low as 4 percent.

This means that IQ alone at best leaves 75 percent of job success unexplained, and at worst 96 percent—in other words, it does not determine who succeeds and who fails. For example, a study of Harvard graduates in the fields of law, medicine, teaching, and business found that scores on entrance exams—a surrogate for IQ—had zero or negative correlation with their eventual career success.

Paradoxically, IQ has the least power in predicting success among that pool of people smart enough to handle the most cognitively demanding fields, and the value of emotional intelligence for success grows more powerful the higher the intelligence barriers for entry into a field. In MBA programs or in careers like engineering, law, or medicine where professional selection focuses almost exclusively on intellectual abilities, emotional intelligence carries much more weight than IQ in determining who emerges as a leader.

Id. at 19 (references omitted).

Since EI is generally not a factor in admission to professional schools, one finds a greater range of EI than of IQ among their students and graduates.

Id. at 20.

22. *See generally* Mark Neal Aaronson, *Problem Solving in Clinical Education: Thinking Like a Fox: Four Overlapping Domains of Good Lawyering*, 9 Clin. L. Rev. 1, 7 (2002); Angela Burton, *Cultivating Ethical, Socially Responsible Lawyer Judgment: Introducing the Multiple Intelligences Paradigm into the Clinical Setting*, 11 Clin. L. Rev. 15 (2004); Kirsten A. Dauphinais, *Valuing and nurturing multiple Intelligences in Legal Education: A Paradigm Shift*, 11 Wash. & Lee Race & Ethnic Anc. L.J. 1 (2005); *infra* ch. 4: Aderson Bellegarde Francois, *Making Out the Ghost Behind the Words: Approaching Legal Text with Psychological Intelligence*; Leonard L. Riskin, *Mindfulness in the law and ADR: The Contemplative Lawyer: On the Potential Contributions of Mindfulness Meditation to Law Students, Lawyers, and their Clients*, 7 Harv. Negot. L. Rev. 1, 46–48 (2002); Erin Ryan, *The Discourse Beneath: Emotional Epistemology in Legal Deliberation and Negotiation*, 10 Harv. Negot. L. Rev. 231, 280–281 (2005) (discussing the competitive advantage of emotionally intelligent negotiators); Silver, *EI & LE, supra* note 13; Ian Weinstein, *Testing Multiple Intelligences: Comparing Evaluation by Simulation and Written Exam*, 8 Clin. L. Rev. 247 (2001). *See also Working Paper on Multiple Intelligences, at* http://www.law.nyu.edu/workways/theoretical/multintell/multintel.html (last visited July 30, 2006) (describing NYU Law Professor Peggy Davis' Workways project and its emphasis on multiple intelligences).

dardized intelligence quotient (I.Q.) examinations.[23] Goleman relied as well on the work of psychologists Peter Salovey and John Mayer, who coined the term *emotional intelligence* to further refine what Gardner intended in his identification of intra- and inter-personal intelligences.[24]

In my own work, I began (admittedly unscientifically) to use the term *emotional competence*[25] in lieu of *emotional intelligence*, in order to stress the ability lawyers have to develop this quality and set of skills, which are not "fixed" as we normally assume I.Q. to be.[26] In *Working with Emotional Intelligence*, though, Goleman described emotional intelligence as a quality that is not genetically fixed; it is a set of attributes that one usually develops as one matures, thus distinguishing it from I.Q..[27] While some may have greater native abilities than others in this domain, all human beings have the capacity to improve our emotional intelligence, and Goleman offers guidelines for doing so.[28] In addition, emotional intelligence is relatively useless unless one learns how to put it into practice. Goleman has identified an *Emotional Competence Framework* that places emotional intelligence into operation. His framework encompasses a list of twenty-five *emotional competencies* relevant to performance on the job.[29] These competencies will likely come more naturally for some of

---

23. GARDNER, *supra* note 19, at 24–25. For a discussion of all of Gardner's multiple intelligences, see *infra* ch. 4: Aderson Bellegard Francois, *Making out the Ghost behind the Words: Approaching Legal Text with Psychological Intelligence*, at pp. 113–17.

24. *See* Peter Salovey & John D. Mayer, *Emotional Intelligence*, 9(3) IMAGINATION, COGNITION AND PERSONALITY 191 (1989–90); *See also* John D. Mayer, David R. Caruso, & Peter Salovey, *Emotional Intelligence Meets Traditional Standards for Intelligence*, 27 INTELLIGENCE 267 (2000).

25. *See, e.g.*, Marjorie A. Silver, *The Professional Responsibility of Lawyers*, 13 J.L.M. 431, 432 (2006) (using *emotional competence* as surrogate for *emotional intelligence* to emphasize its ability to be learned).

26. The standard IQ score is a number that takes into account the subject's chronological and mental age. ROBERT S. FELDMAN, UNDERSTANDING PSYCHOLOGY 293 (4th ed. 1996). *But see* DAVID G. MYERS, PSYCHOLOGY 422 (7th ed. 2004) (asserting that "IQ" is only a measure of how one performs on a given test, at a given time).

27. According to Goleman, I.Q. remains relatively stable after adolescence. GOLEMAN, *supra* note 20, at 7.

28. *Id.* at 14.

29. *Id.* at 26–27.

An emotional *competence* is a learned capability based on emotional intelligence.... Our emotional *intelligence* determines our potential for learning the practical skills that are based on its five elements: self-awareness, motivation, self-regulation, empathy, and adeptness in relationships. Our emotional *competence* shows how much of that potential we have translated into on-the-job capabilities.

Id. at 24–25.

us than for others, but virtually all lawyers have the capacity to develop the emotional competencies that will enable us to practice law empathically and therapeutically.[30]

We need to recognize that emotional responses are triggered in virtually every human encounter. The goal need not be—indeed could not be—to eradicate these responses,[31] but to recognize them, analyze how, if at all, they

---

Goleman credits his PhD advisor, David McClelland, with the term "competence," representing "a personal trait or set of habits that leads to more effective or superior job performance—in other words, an ability that adds clear economic value to the efforts of a person on the job." *Id.* at 15–16 (citing David C. McClelland, 28 AMER. PSYCHOL. 1 (1973)). This use of the term *competence* (with a small *c*) appears to be synonymous with *competency. See* WEBSTER'S THIRD NEW INTERNATIONAL DICTIONARY OF THE ENGLISH LANGUAGE UNABRIDGED 463 (1993).

Goleman divides his list into Personal Competencies and Social Competencies. The Personal Competencies include (1) self-awareness ("[k]nowing one's internal states, preferences, resources, and intuitions" including emotional awareness, accurate self-assessment and self-confidence); (2) self-regulation ("[m]anaging one's internal states, impulses, and resources" including self-control, trustworthiness, conscientiousness, adaptability and innovation); and (3) motivation ("[e]motional tendencies that guide or facilitate reaching goals" including achievement drive, commitment, initiative, and optimism). The Social Competencies include (1) empathy ("[a]wareness of others' feelings, needs, and concerns" including understanding others, developing others, service orientation, leveraging diversity, and political awareness); and (2) social skills ("[a]deptness at inducing desirable responses in others" including influence, communication, conflict management, leadership, change catalyst, building bonds, collaboration and cooperation, and team capabilities).

See also infra ch. 15: Leonard L. Riskin, *Awareness in Lawyering: A Primer on Paying Attention* at p. 450 n. 9 (distinguishing EI and emotional competencies).

30. EI has components that are both cognitive and emotional. *See* GOLEMAN, *supra* note 20, at 23. Furthermore, the work of Antonio Damasio provides scientific evidence that, not only are thinking and feeling not mutually exclusive, in fact, rational decision-making is dependent on emotional input. ANTONIO R. DAMASIO, DESCARTES' ERROR: EMOTION, REASON, AND THE HUMAN BRAIN (1994). *See also* Silver, *Love & Hate, supra* note 13, at 274–75 ("One cannot know whether a decision is rational or otherwise appropriate unless one looks within to examine the irrational forces bearing on that decision.").

31. Andrew S. Watson, *The Quest for Professional Competence: Psychological Aspects of Legal Education,* 37 U. CIN. L. REV. 91 (1968):

> While I agree completely that emotions can thoroughly disrupt a lawyer's skill, I cannot overstate the folly of attempting to eliminate them. Emotions are part and parcel of the biological reactivity of the human animal and are therefore irremovable. While they may be modified and grotesquely distorted, they are always present to influence all human behavior, even that of lawyers.

Id. at 124. *See also* Samuel H. Pillsbury, *Emotional Justice: Moralizing the Passions of Criminal Punishment,* 74 CORNELL L. REV. 655, 684 (1989) (arguing that because emotion is always present, when we deny its relevance to legal decision-making, we merely push it un-

may affect the lawyer/client relationship, and respond appropriately.[32] Whether or not we are aware of it, our unconscious exerts powerful force on our thoughts and actions.[33] Not all manifestations of the unconscious, or all emotional reactions, are problematic. But we must first accept that they might be problematic in order to recognize the situations where they may impair our representation of clients, in order to avoid these consequences.

While undeniably important, it is not sufficient for lawyers to understand the disruptive, or maladaptive, expressions of emotions. Affective lawyering requires that lawyers learn to harness the power of the emotions constructively. Emotional competence includes appreciation of one's own emotional life and sensitivity to and acceptance of the emotional lives of others. It includes an attitude that acknowledges the legitimacy of emotions and their relevance to our actions, interactions, and decisions. Its actualization requires the intra- and inter-personal skills necessary to live a reflective, joyful, and connected life, rich in human relationships.[34]

---

dergound where it can do the most damage); Bandes, *supra* note 3, at 343–44 (emotion informs rational decision-making); Ryan, *supra* note 22, at 249 ("By excluding consideration of epistemological emotionality, we remain subject to its influence but powerless to refine or even resist its contribution.").

32. *See* Andrew S. Watson, *Lawyers and Professionalism: A Further Psychiatric Perspective on Legal Education*, 8 U. MICH. J.L. REFORM 248, 268 (1975) ("While the conflicts will arise regardless of how they are handled, the way they are normally resolved when not understood is to banish them from awareness through one of the psychological defense mechanisms."). Peterson notes the relevance of this insight to all of the helping professions:

> We also relate to professionals out of our childhood experiences with authority figures. If we were abused in our family, we may be careful not to question the professional. If we were neglected, we may hunger after a warm and sympathetic ear. If we fought our parents for control, we may respond combatively and battle the professional for the power. If the professional does not understand the origin of our presumptive response, has no limits, or is frightened of our anger, he or she may inadvertently feed our paranoia or encourage the negative ways we express our entitlement.

MARILYN R. PETERSON, AT PERSONAL RISK 39 (1992).

33. *See* HARROP A. FREEMAN, LEGAL INTERVIEWING AND COUNSELING 50 (1964); David B. Saxe & Seymour F. Kuvin, *Notes on the Attorney-Client Relationship*, 2 J. PSYCHIATRY & L. 209, 209–10 (1974); Andrew S. Watson, *The Lawyer as Counselor*, 5 J. FAM. L. 7, 11 (1965); ANDREW S. WATSON, THE LAWYER IN THE INTERVIEWING AND COUNSELING PROCESS 93 (1976) [hereinafter INTERVIEWING & COUNSELING].

34. Silver, *EI & LE*, *supra* note 13, at 1178. In that article, I wrote that Goleman's concept of emotional intelligence appeared to be narrower than my own. *Id.* As fleshed out by his schema of competencies in WORKING WITH EMOTIONAL INTELLIGENCE, *supra* note 20, however, the inventory of qualities he describes appears to be far more comprehensive than

What does this actually look like in practice? Imagine you are a personal injury lawyer, meeting for the first time with a client whose ten-year old daughter was killed three weeks ago by a drunken driver who ran a red light. How might emotional competence show up in this meeting? You would probably start with an appropriate expression of sympathy. Perhaps you would say something like "I am so sorry for your loss. It's hard to imagine anything more devastating than losing a child." You might acknowledge that the client may find it very difficult to talk about what happened, and tell the client that, if at any time he needs a break, to let you know. Even if the client doesn't request one, you might be aware that at certain junctures in the conversation, a break might be a good idea. You would likely have a pitcher of water and glass available for the client. You might offer coffee or tea. There would be a box of tissues on the coffee table.[35]

You would be familiar with the stages of the grieving process[36] and realize that whatever emotions the client might be experiencing while speaking with you are understandable and to be expected. If the client breaks down in tears, and seems embarrassed, you might reassure him that tears are nothing to be ashamed of. Nor is anger. Nor is feeling that it was somehow his fault that his child died.[37] You might inquire whether the client had met with a grief counselor or other professional to help him through this tragedy. You might say, "Many of my clients who have lost someone close to them have found it very useful to speak with a professional at times like this. I would be happy to give you the names of some people you could call. If you like, I could place the call while you are here."

You would give the client the time and space he needed. If the client is finding it extremely difficult to talk about what happened, you might suggest that

---

his original description of emotional intelligence had suggested, and would seem to encompass the qualities I described as well. *See also* MYERS, *supra* note 26, at 426–27 (describing Multifactor Emotional Intelligence Scale (MEIS) developed by Mayer, Salovey and Caruso to assess a person's ability to *perceive, understand* and *regulate* emotions). *See generally* Mayer et al., *supra* note 24.

35. Even how you arrange the furniture, so that you and the client can sit comfortably, without the barrier of your desk between you, bespeaks emotional competence. For such an example, see Silver, *EI & LE, supra* note 13, at 1202 (hypothesizing a "rewrite" of a client meeting based on a mélange of three works of fiction discussed in the article).

36. *See* ELISABETH KÜBLER-ROSS, DEATH: THE FINAL STAGES OF GRIEF 97 (1975) (discussing mother's working through loss of adult son to cancer); *Beware the 5 Stages of "Grief,"* http://www.counselingforloss.com/article8.htm (last visited July 27, 2006) (discussing five stages of grief).

37. KÜBLER-ROSS, *supra*, at 101.

you adjourn and schedule another meeting. You might ask if the client would find it easier to write out what he wants to tell you before your next meeting. For the reader who has previously represented clients in distress, some of these suggestions might seem obvious. And you may well have even better ideas about how to interact with such a client in an empathetic, helping way.[38]

Here's what you would *not* do. You would not say, "I know how you must feel," not even if you yourself had lost a child.[39] You would not say, "let's get right down to the legal matter that brings you here."[40] You would not speak

---

38. For other examples in the civil litigation context, see *infra* ch. 11: Bruce J. Winick, *Overcoming Psychological Barriers to Settlement,* at pp. 346–59.

39. Although it would be natural to *think* you know how the client must feel in such circumstances, what you experienced may or may not be similar to what this client is experiencing. *Cf. infra* ch. 5: Paul R. Tremblay & Carwina Weng, *Multicultural Lawyering: Heuristics and Biases,* at pp. 150–54 (discussing how individuals may or may not share any given cultural heuristic).

40. Many lawyers might disagree, as suggested by a recent column in the ABA Journal. Margaret Graham Tebo, *What Do You Expect?,* 91 A.B.A. J. 25 (2006):

> Kathy A. Biehl surprised even herself when she told a startled client that she wasn't qualified to be his therapist and his money would be better spent telling his rambling tale of woe to a mental health professional.... When [the client] started speaking again, he stuck to the legal issues of his case, never again mentioning the strictly emotional aspect. He later referred several friends to her practice.
>
> Biehl says she believes the client appreciated her honesty in reminding him that she would be billing for all of the time she spent with him and that it would be in his best interest to stick to the legal issues.

Setting appropriate boundaries for the relationship is, of course, critically important, and probably one of the biggest challenges that the therapeutically-inclined lawyer may face. I experienced this first hand in my *pro bono* work, after successfully representing a young Romanian woman in obtaining her lawful permanent resident status. Over the course of our fifteen month association I had formed a very friendly, close relationship with this woman, who had been the victim of domestic abuse. I frequently chatted with her about her custody battles and her relationship with her estranged nine year old daughter. I had made phone calls on her behalf on a variety of matters outside of our "retainer agreement." After she obtained her lawful status, I expected to move on. She, however, incredibly grateful for my assistance, continued to call me and call upon me frequently. I found myself annoyed by the demands she made on my time, and was, regrettably, sometimes rather rude to her. In her mind, I believe, I had become her friend, someone important in her life. I had a difficult time figuring out how to communicate that while I did want to keep in touch, and hear from her from time to time, I could no longer give her the kind of time and attention that I had during our professional relationship. From this experience, I learned the importance of preparing a client for the "end" of the lawyer/client relationship. *See infra* ch. 2: Susan Brooks, *Using Social Work Constructs in the Practice of Law,* at 66–67 (discussing the termination of relationship process). *See also* PORTNOY, *supra* note 1, at 110–14 (discussing boundaries and limit setting in the lawyer/divorce client relation-

or act as if the legal issues are the only issues of importance. Nor, on the other hand, would you try to act as the client's therapist.[41] And you would not push this case to the bottom of your priority pile because of the difficulty in dealing with an emotionally overwrought client.[42] Again, you could likely add to this list from your own experience.

Emotional competence is put into action when you pay attention to the human dimensions of your relationships with your clients.

II. Learning the Language: Developing Psychological-Mindedness

How does one *develop* emotional competence? What are the knowledge, skills, and attitudes (or values) that one needs to acquire? A familiarity with psychology, the body of knowledge that helps explain why human beings think, feel, and behave as they do,[43] is an important navigational tool. By learning some basic concepts, a person can develop an alertness to, an awareness of, the psyche's manifestations; that is, one can become psychologically-minded.[44] Below are some examples of ways in which psychological phenomena permeate lawyering work.[45]

---

ship). Recognizing the need to set appropriate boundaries, however, is not inconsistent with being emotionally available to the client during the professional relationship.

41. *See supra* note 1 and accompanying text.

42. For an example of such neglect, see Videotape: What Went Wrong: Conversations with Disciplined Attorneys: A Documentary (Lawrence Dubin, Weil Productions 1985) (attorney who missed statute of limitations because he thought his client was too emotionally fragile to face litigation).

43. MYERS, *supra* note 26, at 1. This book is a comprehensive widely used college text for a basic psychology course. Another is FELDMAN, *supra* note 26. The reader who lacks the time or the inclination to read such weighty tomes, might enjoy—and benefit from— ADAM CASH, PSYCHOLOGY FOR DUMMIES (2002); or, JONI E. JOHNSTON, THE COMPLETE IDIOT'S GUIDE TO PSYCHOLOGY (2d ed. 2003).

44. *See supra* note 4 (defining psychological-mindedness).

45. The reader should note that the examples I discuss below are certainly not the only ways that psychology has something to add to lawyering, and may not even be the most important ways. Rather, they are aspects of psychology that have claimed my attention and the attention of others whose work is discussed in this chapter. Jean Koh Peters, who read and commented on a draft of this chapter, invoked the metaphor of mapping: There is much that remains to be explored in this largely uncharted territory. Hopefully, the interested reader will participate in further exploration and mapping. Keep in mind that what is explored in this part is not necessarily "to scale." My lengthy discussion of countertrans-

A. Transference & Countertransference

My interest in the *psychological* aspects of lawyering actually began with an "Aha!" moment many years ago in my Professional Responsibility class. We had been discussing regulation of sexual relations between lawyers and clients, and I asked the class whether an attorney's amorous feelings towards a client might not impair the competency of the representation, even if the attorney never communicated those feelings to the client. The class's reaction—that clearly there is nothing that could be done about that!—starkly illustrated the resistance lawyers generally have to recognizing the power of emotions. Not only are lawyers not taught about psychology and the unconscious, mainstream legal education actually devalues the relevance of anything beyond rational processes in teaching students what it means to be a lawyer.[46] I decided to explore the psychoanalytic literature on transference and countertransference, and its applicability to the lawyer/client relationship.[47]

The concept of *transference* was first introduced by Sigmund Freud in 1910 in his lectures on psychoanalysis:

> In every psycho-analytical treatment of a neurotic patient the strange phenomena that is known as "transference" makes its appearance. The patient, that is to say, directs towards the physician a degree of affectionate feeling (mingled, often enough, with hostility) which is based on no real relation between them and which—as is shown by every detail of its emergence—can only be traced back to old wishful phantasies of the patient which have become unconscious.[48]

Although Freud focused on the manifestation of transference in psychoanalytic treatment, he observed that the phenomenon was not limited to psy-

---

ference, for example, is a product of my having spent several years researching the psychoanalytic literature on this subject. *See generally* Silver, *Love & Hate, supra* note 13. I have also written about emotional intelligence (part I), *see generally* Silver, *EI & LE, supra* note 13; and vicarious trauma (part III C), *see generally* Marjorie A. *Silver, September 11th, Pro Bono, and Trauma,* 7 Contemp. Issues L. 64 (2004) [hereinafter *September 11th*].

46. *See supra* text accompanying notes 12–13.

47. This discussion of transference and countertransference is excerpted (with some modification) from Silver, *Love & Hate, supra* note 13.

48. Sigmund Freud, *Five Lectures on Psycho-Analysis, Leonardo da Vinci, and Other Works,* Fifth Lecture, *in* XI The Standard Edition of the Complete Psychological Works of Sigmund Freud 51 (James Strachey ed., 1957) (1910) [hereinafter *Fifth Lecture*]. *See* Silver, *Love & Hate, supra* note 13, at 262–63.

choanalysis, and, indeed, was manifest in all human relationships.[49] Human beings carry emotional baggage from early relationships and unload that baggage in the relationships they form later in life. Transference may involve strong positive (love-transference)[50] or negative (hate-transference)[51] emotions, and these emotions will affect how clients relate to their attorneys.[52] Freud cautioned analysts to resist urges to act on the transference, and encouraged them to learn to deal with it appropriately.[53]

Freud soon named the related phenomenon of the analyst's response to the patient's transference: countertransference.[54] As with transference, countertransference exists in all human relationships,[55] but is most notable and potentially problematic in those relationships involving an imbalance of power.[56]

---

49. Freud, *Fifth Lecture* (1910), at 51–52; *See also* Lewis R. Wolberg, M.D., The Technique of Psychotherapy 309 (1954).

50. Sigmund Freud, *Observations On Transference-Love, in* XII The Standard Edition of the Complete Psychological Works of Sigmund Freud 159–171 (James Stachey ed., 1957) (1911–13); Leon J. Saul, *The Erotic Transference*, 31 Psychoanalytic Q. 54 (1962).

51. Sigmund Freud, *Introductory Lectures on Psycho-Analysis* (Part III), *in* XVI The Standard Edition of the Complete Psychological Works of Sigmund Freud 444 (James Stachey ed., 1957) (1916–17) [hereinafter *Introductory Lectures, Part III*]; D.W. Winnicott, *Hate in the Countertransference*, 3 J. Psychotherapy Prac. & Res. 350, 350 (1994).

52. For more on transference and the lawyer/client relationship, see, *e.g.*, Portnoy, *supra* note 1, at 58, 114–17; Andrew Watson, Psychiatry for Lawyers 3–8 (1978); Robert M. Bastress & Joseph D. Harbaugh, Interviewing, Counseling, and Negotiating 190–93 (1990). *See also infra* note 110 and accompanying text (on humiliated rage as manifestation of transference).

53. Freud, *Observations on Transference-Love, supra* note 50, at 170; Freud and others later came to see transference, when properly managed, as a useful tool in psychoanalysis. Freud, *Introductory Lectures, Part III, supra* note 51, at 444; Heinrich Racker, Transference and Countertransference 18 (1968); Joseph Sandler, *Countertransference and Role-responsiveness*, 3 Int. Rev. Psychoanalysis 43 (1976).

54. Sigmund Freud, *Nuremberg Congress Paper: The Future Prospects of Psycho-analytic Theory, in* XI The Standard Edition of the Complete Psychological Works of Sigmund Freud 144–45 (James Stachey ed., 1957) (1910). Psychoanalytic literature yields a wide range of definitions for both transference and countertransference. *See* Silver, *Love & Hate, supra* note 13, at 264–65 nn.24–28.

55. *See* Howard F. Stein, The Psycho-Dynamics of Medical Practice: Unconscious Factors in Patient Care 47 (1985); Lucia E. Tower, *Countertransference*, J. Amer. Psychoanalytic Ass'n 224, 232–34 (1956).

56. *See* Linda M. Jorgenson & Pamela K. Sutherland, *Lawyers' Sex with Clients: Proposal for a Uniform Standard*, 12 Fair$hare 11 n.38 (1992) (citing Thomas L. Shaffer, *Undue Influence, Confidential Relationship, and the Psychology of Transference*, 45 Notre

And, needless to say, the attorney/client relationship is one of those that generally involves such an imbalance.

Countertransference acquired notoriety in large measure due to its manifestation in scandalous and not infrequent sexual relationships between numerous therapists and their patients, often with dire consequences for emotionally vulnerable patients.[57] Such relationships understandably were condemned by the profession. Both the American Psychiatric Association in 1973 and the American Psychological Association in 1977 adopted ethical rules forbidding sexual relationships between therapists and their patients.[58]

The problem became a grave one for lawyers as well, who faced disciplinary charges[59] and civil liability[60] for sexual liaisons with their clients. The most egregious cases tended to arise in family law practice.[61] In 1992 the ABA issued formal opinion 92-364, which, while not prohibiting sexual liaisons between lawyers and clients outright, strongly discouraged them and identified various problems that could result in a violation of ethics rules. The opinion concluded that in disciplinary or other proceedings, an attorney who has engaged in sexual relations with a client would have the burden to prove

---

DAME LAW. 197, 214–15 (quoting 16 COLLECTED WORKS OF CARL G. JUNG 218 (H. Read et al. eds., 2d ed. 1966))).

57. *See generally* SEXUAL EXPLOITATION IN PROFESSIONAL RELATIONSHIPS (Glen O. Gabbard ed., 1989). For additional sources, see Silver, *Love & Hate, supra* note 13, at 266 n.31.

58. American Psychiatric Association, *The Principles of Medical Ethics With Annotations Especially Applicable to Psychiatry*, 130 AM. J. PSYCHIATRY 1058, 1061 (1973); APA Ethical Standards for Psychologists, Principles 6 ("sexual intimacies with clients are unethical") (APA 1977); *id* at 7 ("psychologists do not exploit their professional relationships with clients, supervisees, students, employees, or research participants sexually or otherwise") (APA 1981).

59. *See* Linda Mabus Jorgenson & Pamela K. Sutherland, *Fiduciary Theory Applied To Personal Dealings: Attorney Client Sexual Contact*, 45 ARK. L. REV. 459, 499 n.11 (1992) (informal survey of state bar associations' disciplinary proceedings dealing with sexual harassment and contact by attorneys); For a partial compilation of the numerous disciplinary actions involving sexual relations between attorneys and clients, see Silver, *Love & Hate, supra* note 13, at 268 n.39.

60. *See, e.g.,* Catherine Holand Petersen & Candace Mathers, *Developing Personal Relationship, Impairing Attorney-Client Relationship*, 14 FAIR$HARE 26 (1994) (discussing specific malpractice case finding liability).

61. *See, e.g.,* Thomas Lyon, *Sexual Exploitation of Divorce Clients: The Lawyer's Prerogative?*, 10 HARV. WOMEN'S L.J. 159 (1987) (exploring causes and effects of sexual relations between divorce lawyers and their clients and comparing them to therapist-client relationship).

such relations *did not* violate any ethical responsibilities.[62] Ten years later, the ABA revised the *Model Rules of Professional Responsibility* to include an explicit prohibition:

> A lawyer shall not have sexual relations with a client unless a consensual sexual relationship existed between them when the client-lawyer relationship commenced.[63]

Whether by virtue of personal ethics, regulation, self-control, or a combination of factors, most attorneys will refrain from acting on erotic feelings they may have for their clients. But that does not solve the countertransference problem. Attorneys need to recognize that strong feelings towards their clients—whether positive or negative—need to be addressed to assure a functional, healthy, healing attorney/client relationship.

For effective psychotherapy, an understanding of countertransference must be both doctrinal and personal. Analysts-in-training, for example, both study the theory, and then explore their own countertransference responses in their personal analyses and re-analyses.[64] Neither law students nor attorneys generally receive any such training, however, and thus they generally have no access to a structured protocol for addressing problematic countertransference when it arises.

Countertransference, insufficiently understood, creates the danger of boundary violations, which both therapists and lawyers alike must avoid. Boundary violations are the crossing of the line between professional and client that defines the helping relationship within which they interact.[65] Sex-

---

62. ABA Comm. on Ethics and Prof'l Responsibility, Formal Op. 92-364 (1992).

63. AMERICAN BAR ASSOCIATION, MODEL RULES OF PROF'L CONDUCT R. 1.8(j) (2002). The comments to the rule are virtually identical to the reasoning in ABA Formal Op. 92-364. Many state codes contain prohibitions of one form or another on sexual relationships between lawyers and clients. *See* Silver, *Love & Hate*, *supra* note 13, at 269 nn.44–45 (describing then extant and pending state rules on such relationships).

64. *See* FRIEDA FROMM-REICHMAN, PRINCIPLES OF INTENSIVE PSYCHOTHERAPY 42 (1950); Kenneth S. Pope & Glen O. Gabbard, *Individual Psychotherapy for Victims of Therapist-Patient Sexual Intimacy*, *in* SEXUAL EXPLOITATION IN PROFESSIONAL RELATIONSHIPS 100 (Glen O. Gabbard ed., 1989). *But see* Stuart W. Twemlow & Glen O. Gabbard, *The Lovesick Therapist*, *in* SEXUAL EXPLOITATION IN PROFESSIONAL RELATIONSHIPS 85 (Glen O. Gabbard ed., 1989) ("offenders were more likely than non-offenders to have undergone therapy or analysis").

65. *See* PETERSON, *supra* note 32, at 74–75:
> Boundaries are the limits that allow for a safe connection based on the client's needs. When these limits are altered, what is allowed in the relationship becomes ambiguous. Such ambiguity is often experienced as an intrusion into the sphere

ual intercourse with a distraught and emotionally vulnerable patient or client is a relatively obvious example of such a boundary violation. Yet boundary violations may occur even without sexual transgressions.[66] It is not sufficient to merely resist sexual impulses towards one's client.[67] Harm to the relationship and consequently harm to the client may happen without any physical or sexual component. Lawyers need to be sensitive to the possible crossing of boundaries *before* the fiduciary relationship is abridged.

1. Love Countertransference

It seems likely, for example, that for every lawyer who succumbs to a sexual liaison with a client, a hundred are tempted but resist. Imagine such a lawyer, and observe how countertransference might cause problems:

Adam is a 50 year-old lawyer with a criminal law practice and a solid reputation as an ethical, competent, and thorough attorney. Belle seeks representation for a felony drug charge. She is young, lovely, and treats Adam with awe. Adam finds himself strongly attracted to her. He looks forward to their meetings. It comes to pass that the prosecutor offers Belle a plea deal. Adam discusses the deal with her, but does not push it very hard (as he might with other clients). Belle denies her guilt to him and Adam believes her. He tells her that if she is innocent, then they should go to trial. Placing her trust in his advice, she agrees. They go to trial. Belle is convicted and sentenced to twice the time she would have served had she accepted the deal that the prosecutor offered.

2. Hate Countertransference

Now imagine Adam with a different client, Carl. Carl shares two characteristics with Belle. He is the same age, and has also been arrested on a felony drug charge (no relationship to Belle's alleged offense). Carl has a strong effeminate affect. Adam finds him annoying and obsequious, and dreads their

---

of safety. The pain from a violation is frequently delayed, and the violation itself may not be recognized or felt until harmful consequences emerge.

See also supra note 40 (discussing boundary issues).

66. *See* STEVEN B. BISBING, LINDA MABUS JORGENSON, & PAMELA K. SUTHERLAND, SEXUAL ABUSE BY PROFESSIONALS: A LEGAL GUIDE 461, 463–64 (1995); Carter Heyward, *Book Review: When Boundaries Betray Us: Beyond Illusions of What is Ethical in Therapy and Life,* by Marie Fortune, THE CHRISTIAN CENTURY, May 18, 1994, at 524; Twemlow & Gabbard, *supra* note 64, at 86.

67. *See* PETER RUTTER, SEX IN THE FORBIDDEN ZONE 195 (1989); WATSON, INTERVIEWING AND COUNSELING, *supra* note 33, at 85.

encounters. Despite Carl's claim of innocence—he says he was framed by a neighborhood miscreant who threatened "I'm gonna get you, faggot"—Adam pushes the deal offered by the prosecution. Carl begins to cry, which greatly annoys Adam. He chastises the young man and advises him to "grow up and act like a man." Carl, cowered, agrees to the plea.

3. Countertransference and Self-Awareness

Now both of these scenarios might profitably be analyzed in terms of lawyer ethics and professional responsibility,[68] but our focus here is elsewhere. *Why* did Adam respond so differently in the two situations? If Adam did breach his professional responsibilities in these cases, what is the explanation? And how might he have avoided doing so?

It might be useful to know more about Adam. He has been married to the same woman for twenty years. His marriage has reached the comfort and complacency of its middle years. Also, Adam has a twelve year-old son who cries easily when his feelings are hurt. Knowing something about counter-transference, we might be able to proffer a good guess as to why Adam behaved in these situations as he did.[69] And if Adam acquired a degree of self-awareness, he might know as well, and perhaps avoid such aberrant behaviors.

Whatever the reasons for emotional interference in the lawyer/client relationship, it is important that the lawyer strive to ensure that the competency of the representation is not compromised. There is no magic bullet for eviscerat-

---

68. For example, did Adam provide competent representation? *See* AMERICAN BAR ASSOCIATION, MODEL RULES OF PROF'L CONDUCT R. 1.1 (2003). Did Adam adequately investigate the charges against Belle and Carl before rejecting or pushing the plea deals offered by the prosecution in their respective cases? *See id. See also* AMERICAN BAR ASSOCIATION, STANDARDS RELATING TO THE ADMINISTRATION OF CRIMINAL JUSTICE § 4-4.1 (*The Defense Function:* Duty to Investigate) (1992). Should he be accountable for not doing so? What if Carl were in fact innocent?

69. *Cf.* T.P. Hackett, *Which Patients Turn You Off? It's Worth Analyzing,* 46 MED. ECON. 94, 96 (1969):

A doctor who remains oblivious of his bias may not only be less able to help a patient, but may literally hurt him. For instance, I recall the surgery instructor who taught us how to use a sigmoidoscope. He was a burly guy who still looked like the football player he'd been in college. I observed—as did other interns—that when he performed sigmoidoscopies on effeminate men, he would never use enough lubricant, thus causing them considerable and unnecessary pain. I give him the benefit of the doubt and say he was unaware of what he was doing. He made no derisive comments about such men, but what he did to them spoke the true feelings he couldn't acknowledge: He needlessly hurt them. It wasn't malpractice, but it was not good medicine.

ing emotional responses that interfere with our abilities to function as we would like. In an ideal world, perhaps we would all have the time and money to undergo personal analysis, to explore our hopes, dreams, and fantasies with a well-trained guide.[70] However, as this is neither feasible nor essential for most of us, it is fortunate that less costly and time-consuming alternatives are available.[71]

When countertransference troubles an attorney, a range of responses may be appropriate. The efficacy of any response may well depend on the severity of the problem.[72] The first step, of course, is recognition that a problem or potential problem exists. The goal is to make the Unconscious conscious.[73] The mere acknowledgment of uncomfortable feelings may suffice to render such feelings more manageable.[74] In their clinical education text, Professors

---

70. *See* WATSON, INTERVIEWING AND COUNSELING, *supra* note 33, at 82:

> I have often been queried about whether or not lawyers, judges, and other professionals should be "psychoanalyzed." My response has been that under ideal circumstances, because lawyers are constantly serving as counselors, and since the subjects of their work are always people, they and their profession would profit much by that form of learning and experience.

See also James A Elkins, *The Legal Persona: An Essay on the Professional Mask*, 64 VA. L. REV. 756, 758–59 (1978) ("The essential unresolved question is whether insight for effective self-scrutiny is possible without the encouragement and guidance of an experienced psychoanalyst or psychotherapist."); Saxe & Kuvin, *supra* note 33, at 216 ("[I]t is respectfully submitted that optimally the prototypical attorney should himself have undergone some formal psychoanalysis or psychotherapy.").

71. *See* WATSON, INTERVIEWING AND COUNSELING, *supra* note 33, at 82 ("Needless to say, to require such a learning experience would be totally infeasible.").

72. *See* WATSON, PSYCHIATRY FOR LAWYERS, *supra* note 52, at 21; Martin A. Silverman, *Countertransference and the Myth of the Perfectly Analyzed Analyst*, 54 PSYCHOANALYTIC Q. 175, 177 (1985).

73. *See* Freud, *Introductory Lectures, Part III, supra* note 51, at 435; Joseph Allegretti, *Shooting Elephants, Serving Clients: An Essay on George Orwell and the Lawyer-Client Relationship*, 27 CREIGHTON L. REV. 1, 13 (1993) (quoting WATSON, PSYCHIATRY FOR LAWYERS, *supra* note 52, at 7).

74. *See* WATSON, PSYCHIATRY FOR LAWYERS, *supra* note 52, at 8:

> Since transference is unconscious, the question arises whether one can do anything about it. The answer is something of a paradox. The mere acknowledgment of the possibility of such unconscious reactions permits the participants to look more objectively at relationships and to question causes. The capacity to accept the possibility that one's feelings about another may be due to unconscious and unrealistic coloring rather than to the other's reality traits, is a major step toward understanding. Without awareness of transference phenomena, people are over- or under-convinced by their own emotional response and have no opportunity to work out any understanding of them.

Bastress & Harbaugh suggest the lawyer start by asking the following series of questions, designed by psychotherapist Lewis Wolberg, to elicit evidence of countertransference:[75]

1. How do I feel about the client?

2. Do I anticipate the client?

3. Do I over-identify with, or feel sorry for, the client?

4. Do I feel any resentment or jealousy toward the client?

5. Do I get extreme pleasure out of seeing the client?

6. Do I feel bored with the client?

7. Am I fearful of the client?

8. Do I want to protect, reject, or punish the client?

9. Am I impressed by the client?

If any of questions two through nine elicit an affirmative response, we should then ask "Why?"[76] We might recognize that the client reminds us of a

---

75. BASTRESS & HARBAUGH, *supra* note 52, at 491. *See also* Saxe & Kuvin, *supra* note 33, at 212–215 (canvassing variety of reactions that should alert attorney to possible existence of neurotic conflicts affecting representation):
> 1. Feelings of depression or discomfort (anxiety) during or after time spent with certain clients ....
> 2. Carelessness with regard to keeping appointments with the client or allowing trivial maters that could easily be postponed to interfere with time apportioned to the client.
> 3. Repeatedly experiencing affectionate feelings toward the client ... this affectivity may cause the attorney to prolong the case as a rationalization to maintain the interpersonal relationship and further may eventually lead to seduction....
> 5. Repeated neglect by the attorney of certain files....
> 7. A conscious awareness, that the attorney is deriving satisfaction from the client's praise, appreciation and other evidences of affection.
> 8. Becoming disturbed, consciously, by the client's persistent reproaches and evident dissatisfaction with the merits of the case.
> 9. Perhaps the most important of all responses to which the attorney should be alert, is a feeling of boredom or drowsiness when either he talks or listens to the client.

In my opinion, the precise list of questions is of far less import than the attorney's realization that good practice requires attention with thoughtful curiosity to one's emotional reactions provoked by the representation.

76. Wolberg follows his list of questions with the following advice to the therapist, advice that is beneficial to the attorney as well:
> Should answers to any of the above point to problems, then ask why such feelings and attitudes exist. Is the patient doing anything to stir up such feelings? Does the patient resemble anybody the therapist knows or has known, and, if so, are any

close family member and that we are revisiting an emotional pattern played out with a parent or sibling.[77] However, it is altogether possible that we will not have a clue as to why we are experiencing such an intense, troubling reaction. Nonetheless, recognizing that a problem exists in our emotional response to the client may be sufficient to obtain control over the problem.[78] It may be unnecessary to identify the source; the very act of raising the reaction to a conscious level may make it possible to control the feeling or diffuse its force sufficiently to avoid any problems in the representation.

What if that is not enough? A psychotherapist would likely seek advice from a trusted friend or colleague to help gain perspective.[79] We lawyers, though, are far more likely to seek legal advice than personal advice on such matters. Given that personal skills are as important to effective legal representation as is knowledge of legal strategies and doctrine, lawyers need to overcome that resistance. The very process of telling a friend or colleague about one's emotional reactions to a client may enable a lawyer to gain perspective on and control over interfering countertransference reactions.[80]

* Countertransference *

---

attitudes being transferred to the patient that are related to another person? What other impulses are being mobilized in the therapist that account for the feelings? What role does the therapist want to play with the patient? Mere verbalization to himself of answers to these queries, permits of better control of unreasonable feelings. Cognizance of the fact that he feels angry, displeased, disgusted, irritated, provoked, uninterested, unduly attentive, upset or overly attracted, may suffice to bring these emotions under control. In the event untoward attitudes continue, more self-searching is indicated. Of course it may be difficult to act accepting, non-critical and non-judgmental toward a patient who is provocatively hostile and destructive in his attitudes towards people, and who possesses disagreeable traits which the therapist in his everyday life would criticize.

WOLBERG, *supra* note 49, at 491. *See also* PORTNOY, *supra* note 1, at 117–18 (discussing managing transference).

77. WOLBERG, *supra* note 49, at 491.

78. *See id. See also* Otto Kernberg, *Notes on Countertransference*, 13 J. AMER. PSYCHO-ANALYTIC ASS'N 38, 42 (1965).

79. *See id.*; Joan S. Meier, *Notes from the Underground: Integrating Psychological and legal Perspectives on Domestic Violence in Theory and Practice*, 21 HOFSTRA L. REV. 1295, 1354 (1993).

80. *See* WATSON, INTERVIEWING AND COUNSELING, *supra* note 33, at 25, 81; WATSON, PSYCHIATRY FOR LAWYERS, *supra* note 52, at 10–11; James R. Elkins, *A Counseling Model for Lawyering in Divorce Cases*, 53 NOTRE DAME LAW. 229, 244 (1977). Of course, any such disclosure must guard against revealing any privileged communications. MODEL RULES OF PROF'L CONDUCT R. 1.6(a) (2002); MODEL CODE OF PROF'L RESPONSIBILITY DR 4-101(B) (2002).

A therapist who finds that strong emotional reactions are interfering with the therapy may seek guidance through consultation[81] or reanalysis.[82] If still unable to overcome such difficulties, the therapist may find it necessary to refer the patient to someone else for treatment.[83] Likewise, if a lawyer is unable to gain control over emotional responses to the client, it may be necessary to refer the client elsewhere for representation.[84] Nonetheless, in certain kinds of representation referral may not be a viable option. Clients represented by legal aid lawyers or public defenders may have nowhere else to go. The socioeconomic disparities between lawyers and clients in such cases may further exacerbate countertransference problems.[85] For these attorneys, training in handling countertransference may be of critical importance.

Although therapy or analysis may not be necessary for all lawyers, those who repeatedly experience problematic emotional reactions to their clients may require professional treatment.[86]

4. Countertransference Understood

Adam, had he understood something about countertransference, might have been conscious that he was erotically attracted to Belle.[87] Adam might

---

81. *See* Hans W. Loewald, *Transference-countertransference*, 34 J. Am. Psychoanalytic Ass'n 275, 275 (1986).

82. *See* Leslie R. Schover, *Sexual Exploitation by Sex Therapists*, *in* Sexual Exploitation in Professional Relationships 147 (Glen O. Gabbard ed., 1989); Silverman, *supra* note 72, at 177.

83. *See, e.g.* Lewis R. Wolberg, 2 The Technique of Psychotherapy 488 (4th ed. 1988); Schover, *supra* note 82, at 147.

84. *See* Watson, Psychiatry for Lawyers, *supra* note 52, at 21; David A. Binder Paul Bergman & Susan C. Price, Lawyers as Counselors: A Client-Centered Approach 64 (1991) (recommending, where possible, referral to another attorney if lawyer lacks all empathy for client).

85. *See infra* notes 92–96 and accompanying text.

86. *See* Mark K. Schoenfield & Barbara Pearlman Schoenfield, Interviewing and Counseling Clients In a Legal Setting 331 (1977); Watson, Psychiatry for Lawyers, *supra* note 52, at 11.

87. *See* Tower, *supra* note 55, at 230 (Psychoanalyst Lucie Tower reported that "in [her] experience virtually all physicians, when they gain enough confidence in their analysts, report erotic feelings and impulses toward their patients, but usually do so with a good deal of fear and conflict."). *See also* Theodore Jacobs, *Posture, Gesture, and Movement in the Analyst: Cues to Interpretation and Transference*, 21 J. Am. Psychoanalytic Ass'n 77, 88–90 (1973) (discussing his erotic countertransference reaction to female patient).

Reflection

have noticed that he contemplated their meetings with heightened anticipation. He then might have seen these deviations from his usual responses to clients as warning signs. If so, he likely would have responded differently than he did. He would probably have caught himself abandoning his usual—and usually appropriate—skepticism about his client's protestations of innocence. Hopefully, he would have investigated the charges against Belle more thoroughly. Were he then to conclude that strong evidence existed of Belle's culpability, he would probably have utilized his excellent powers of persuasion to convince Belle to accept the favorable plea deal.[88]

Awareness of his attraction to Belle probably would have been less of a stretch for Adam than confronting and understanding his more complicated feelings towards Carl—and their genesis. An appreciation of the effects of unresolved conflicts or presumptions about differences in gender, race, culture, or sexual orientation might have enabled Adam to examine his own conflicted feelings about homosexuality.[89] Individual analysis or therapy might have enabled Adam to understand his impatience with his twelve-year-old son who so easily dissolved in tears. Possibly, Adam might have come to realize that his anger at his son derived from insecurity about his own masculinity. Understanding countertransference, Adam might have realized that his disgust with Carl was triggered by his perception (conscious or not[90]) that Carl was gay (accurate or not), and derived from similar anxiety. If Adam came to understand these fears, they might have lost their powerful grip on him. Were he able to dissipate his annoyance with Carl, he might have been able to hear and process Carl's claim of innocence, and, if warranted upon further investigation, he might have agreed with Carl's decision to proceed to trial.

Our individual psyches affect the intensity of countertransference in our professional lives. Each of us brings to the representation some unresolved—often unconscious—biases in favor of or against persons based on their individual or group characteristics.[91] We may have emotional reactions to a client

---

88. *See* Randy Bellows, *Notes of a Public Defender, in* THE SOCIAL RESPONSIBILITIES OF LAWYERS 69, 89–90 (Philip B. Heymann & Lance Liebman eds., 1988) (on critical importance of persuading client to accept favorable plea deal).

89. *Cf.* Gertrude R. Ticho, *Cultural Aspects of Transference and Countertransference*, 35 BULL. MENNINGER CLINIC 313, 318–21 (1971) (discussing negative effects of her own cultural biases on analytical relationships).

90. *Cf.* Charles Lawrence, *The Id, the Ego, and Equal Protection: Reckoning with Unconscious Racism*, 39 STAN. L. REV. 317, 330–44 (1987) (discussing largely unconscious nature of contemporary white racism).

91. *See id.* at 330.

based on any number of variables, including race, ethnicity, language, religion, gender, sexual orientation, age, physical appearance, physical or mental disability, substance abuse problems, or economic status.[92] These reactions—again, often unknowingly—may affect the quality of our representation.

Another variable affecting countertransference is the kind of representation involved. The greater the degree of power imbalance and emotional intensity of the situation, the greater is the likelihood that transference and countertransference may interfere with competent representation.[93] Thus countertransference is likely to pose the greatest problems in the contexts of child abuse, criminal defense, domestic violence,[94] immigration, matrimonial practice,[95] and representation of mentally ill persons.[96]

---

92. *See generally* ch. 5: Tremblay & Weng, *supra* note 39; *see also* ch. 6: Susan Bryant & Jean Koh Peters, *Six Practices for Connecting with Clients across Culture: Habit Four, Working With Interpreters and Other Mindful Approaches* at p. 186 (discussing Habit Five, biases, and stereotypes).

93. *See supra* note 56 and accompanying text; Silver, *Love & Hate, supra* note 13, at 260–61(discussing effect of power imbalance in lawyer/client relationship). *See also* Paul N. Gerber, *Commentary on Counter-Transference in Working with Sex Offenders: The Issue of Sexual Attraction*, 4 J. CHILD SEXUAL ABUSE 117, 120 (1995) (describing intensity of countertransference in work with sex offenders).

94. *See* Meier, *supra* note 79.

95. *See, e.g.,* Allwyn J. Levine, *Transference and Countertransference: How it Affects You and Your Client*, 15 FAM. ADVOC. 14 (1992):

> In no other field of jurisprudence is one dealing with the most private aspects of people's lives and their most precious possessions—their children. Divorce, in and of itself, is a psychologically draining experience. For all clients, it stirs up feelings of abandonment, separation, dependency, and anxiety— unmatched in intensity by any other situation. A matrimonial lawyer is thus thrust into a veritable minefield of psychological traps and pitfalls.

For a comprehensive guide to the special challenges faced by family law attorneys, written by a clinical psychologist who specializes in marital therapy, see PORTNOY, *supra* note 1.

96. *See* Michael Perlin, *Ethical Issues in the Representation of Individuals in the Commitment Process*, 45 L. & CONTEMP. PROBS. 161, 163 (1982) ("[I]ssues raised by investigating ethical standards in civil commitment representation may dredge up unconscious feelings which lead to avoidance—by clients, by lawyers, and by judges—of the underlying problems.") *See also* Winnicott, *supra* note 51 (discussing negative (hate) countertransference in treatment of psychotic patients):

> However much he loves his patients he cannot avoid hating them, and fearing them, and the better he knows this the less hate and fear will be the motive determining what he does to his patients.

Id. at 350.

most clients feel

B. Shame & Humiliation

The previous discussion explores how countertransference may affect attorneys' representations of their clients. Yet it is only one of many psychological manifestations that, if not sufficiently understood, may negatively impact the legal services provided. Another is shame and humiliation. Psychiatrist Aaron Lazare and attorney Wilton Sogg[97] have collaborated to provide us with some excellent guideposts on how shame and humiliation may operate in the attorney/client relationship—and what the attorney can do about it.[98]

Lazare and Sogg suggest something that is, for most of us, far from intuitive: Most clients likely experience some degree of shame or humiliation by virtue of having a legal problem that brings them to the attorney's door in the first place. Clients may view their legal problems as evidencing personal defects or inadequacies.[99] We ask clients to divulge uncomfortable personal information to us, in order to help address their legal problems. And few of us—lawyers or clients—are comfortable discussing our own shame or humiliation.[100]

Yet, according to Lazare and Sogg, shame may well be a healthy emotion. Shame is something one experiences when one fails to live up to her own expectations. It can occur alone or in relationship to another. It is often a healthy emotion, because it means we have certain ideals and standards, and care about what others think of us.[101]

Lazare and Sogg identify three components to shame: the shame-inducing event, the individual's vulnerability to experiencing shame, and the social context, including the other persons involved in the event.[102] They offer exam-

---

97. I am indebted to Wilton Sogg for his review and comments on an earlier draft of this section of the chapter.

98. Aaron Lazare & Wilton S. Sogg, *Shame, Humiliation, and Stigma in the Attorney-Client Relationship*, 47 Prac. Law 11 (2001).

99. *Id.* at 12.

100. "It is shameful in itself to admit that one feels ashamed." *Id.*

101. *Id.* Humiliation, which is generally maladaptive, however, is almost always the result of how someone else treats us, and is manifested by a belief that the treatment was undeserved. *Id.* In most of the article, Lazare & Sogg discuss shame and humiliation interchangeably. *Id.* I do as well.

102. *Id.*

ples, in a variety of practice settings, of the kind of *shame-inducing events* that the client may present to the attorney:[103]

PRACTICE SETTING	SHAME-INDUCING PROBLEMS
Employment Relations	Employers: Unfair labor practices; strikes. Supervisors: Sexual harassment.
Family Businesses	Unsuitability or unwillingness of child to take over leadership of family business.
Estate Planning	Disclosure of financial circumstances.
Tax Practice	Audits; deficiencies; liens; penalties; asset seizures.
Medical Malpractice	Indignities of litigation; harm and injury to patients.
Litigation, generally	Depositions; cross-examinations about personal matters; financial circumstances; alleged wrong-doing.
Family Law	Abandonment; divorce; loss of custody; loss of home; net worth; earnings; exposure of secrets.
Law Enforcement	Registration of sex offenders.
Business Organizations	Accusations of failure to meet fiduciary obligations.

Lazare and Sogg explore how the experience of shame may be exacerbated by a person's *vulnerability* to a range of needs, desires, and expectations:

- The need to be loved and taken care of, not rejected;
- To be strong and powerful, not weak;
- To succeed or win, not fail or lose;
- To be clean and tidy, not messy and disgusting;
- To be good, not bad;
- To be whole and complete in physical and mental makeup, not defective.[104]

---

103. Adapted from Lazare & Sogg, *supra* note 98, at 13.

104. *Id.* at 14. "A multitude of day-to-day issues involving self-esteem may be subsumed under these categories." *Id.* "In the legal setting ... self-esteem may be associated with

We all differ in the degree to which we are vulnerable to these desires, and whether and to what extent a person may experience shame will, of course, vary from client to client. A client's cultural background, too, may affect how and when he experiences shame.[105]

An additional factor is the *social context* in which the client finds himself. Many of the logistics involved in the legal system are stressful, and stress may worsen the degree to which one experiences shame:

> Clients who visit large lawyers' offices or court complexes for the first time often brave unfamiliar traffic, search frantically for a parking space in high-priced lots, and make their way through a labyrinth of buildings, passing busy and seemingly indifferent court or law firm employees as they search for the right courtroom or lawyer's office. In the elevator, they hear lawyers or police officers openly discussing how trials are unfolding. Even if they are in court for something as simple as a traffic ticket, they hope they do not meet any acquaintances that may ask, "What are you doing here?" These clients may understand-ably feel bewildered, harassed, exposed, insignificant, and incompe-tent. They are not quite sure at that moment what preoccupies them most—their legal problem, their insignificance, or arriving late.[106]

All of this occurs before the client enters the lawyer's office and is required to reveal personal information that in and of itself may elicit shame. The shame that a client experiences in exposing her legal problems is often increased by the legal processes that follow. Clients must engage first with their own lawyer, and later with others who have different loyalties and agendas. The process and procedures of litigation in particular, in which clients are forced to tell their

---

wealth, social status, public office or reputation, strength, dexterity, intellectual acuity ... etc." *Id.*

105. *See, e.g.,* Marc Lacey, *Leading Player in Darfur's Drama: The Hapless Camel,* N.Y. TIMES, Dec. 5, 2005, at A4 ("If a man sees one of his camels being stolen and does not risk his life to recover it, he is an embarrassment to the tribe, nomads say. The man's wife would have reason to leave him, they say."). I have learned in working with undocumented im-migrant women who have been physically and psychologically abused by their spouses that, for some, speaking about the abuse, even to another woman, can be incredibly uncom-fortable. *See infra* ch. 6: Bryant & Peters, at p. 214 (discussing culture & shame). However, the lawyer must be cautious about making any assumptions based solely on a client's cul-ture; any individual may—or may not—respond in a culturally stereotypical manner. *See infra* ch. 5: Tremblay & Weng at pp. 150–54 (cautioning about use of heuristics in indi-vidual cases).

106. Lazare & Sogg, *supra* note 98, at 14.

stories subject to often hostile cross-examination in both depositions and at trial, likely will intensify the experience of shame and humiliation.[107]

How an individual responds to shame, of course, also varies from one client to another. An *adaptive* response may well be to take steps to solve the problem that brought the client to the lawyer's office in the first place, or to take steps to make sure that the problematic behavior does not occur again.[108] The client charged with a DWI offense may cease getting behind the wheel when she has had more than one drink. The client facing a tax audit might develop bookkeeping procedures to guard against future problems with the IRS. The lawyer has a constructive role to play in suggesting and supporting the client's adaptive responses to shameful occurrences.[109]

The lawyer needs to be on alert to maladaptive responses as well. These often include depression, avoidance, and anger. Lawyers should realize that a client who fails to reveal all the relevant information about a situation, who breaks appointments, or fails to follow the attorney's advice, may be engaging in avoidant behavior as a result of the humiliation they experience. So, too, the client who angers easily, and directs that anger at the attorney or the attorney's office colleagues may be manifesting what Lazare and Sogg call *humiliated rage*. A client with a history of firing attorneys, filing complaints with the bar association, or bringing lawsuits against attorneys or others, may well be reacting out of humiliated rage.[110]

Clients have no monopoly on shame and humiliation. Lawyers, because of their tendency towards perfectionist personality traits, are also particularly prone to these emotions.[111] These tendencies may be exacerbated by the often

---

107. *See id.* at 14–15. The greater likelihood of shame and humiliation through litigation processes is yet another argument for seeking non-litigious alternatives, as discussed in several of this book's chapters. *See infra* Part III: Lawyering and Civil Disputes, chs. 7–11.

108. Lazare & Sogg, *supra* note 98, at 15.

109. Lazare and Sogg suggest that in appropriate circumstances, the lawyer can use shame constructively:

> John, I've known you and your family for 20 years. You just have to keep better records and pay your taxes on time. You can't expect me to keep on cleaning up your messes.

Id. at 17.

110. *Id.* at 15. Such outbursts and acting out may well be manifestations of transference. *See, e.g.,* WATSON, PSYCHIATRY FOR LAWYERS, *supra* note 52, at 193 (discussing transference as explanation of clients whose actions and words provoke attorneys to anger). *See also* BINDER ET AL., *supra* note 84, at 248–50 (discussing "[c]lients who are hostile, angry and explosive" *Id.* at 248).

111. *See generally* Daicoff, *supra* note 1.

indeterminate amounts of information and research that lawyers are expected to master in order to render competent and competitive legal advice.[112]

Lawyers who are aware of the origins and manifestations of shame are much better equipped to respond in constructive, adaptive ways. Lazare and Sogg suggest that by starting with the assumption that shame is a natural byproduct of a client's legal problem, and factoring in any particular client's degree of susceptibility, the lawyer can devise strategies and responses to manage the social context so as to (1) diminish the client's shame; (2) avoid making it worse; and (3) recognize and manage her own shame.[113]

The lawyer who practices law as a healing profession is halfway there. The lawyer should approach the client with Rogerian "unconditional positive regard,"[114] respectfully, and nonjudgmentally.[115] Attention to the effect of unfamiliar, often intimidating physical space, may help diminish its impact. The lawyer should avoid having the client wait beyond the appointment time, and should minimize interruptions during their meeting. When delays and interruptions are unavoidable, the lawyer should apologize. The lawyer should treat the client as an equal, addressing her by appropriate title and surname in the absence of permission to be less formal. Respecting the client's preferred boundaries as to communication and privacy, asking the client where she prefers to be telephoned or to receive mail, all help to bolster the client's positive self regard.[116]

Lazare and Sogg suggest that revealing personal information may be a useful tool in minimizing the client's shame. A comment such as "I have been through a divorce myself and I know what an emotional challenge it can be," may decrease the client's feelings that a divorce is something of which to be ashamed. It is, however, a tactic fraught with risk. The lawyer must guard against burdening the client with her own problems, appearing superior for having already solved them, or having the client experience the lawyer's strategy of sharing as offering insincere support.[117] What the lawyer intends may differ from what the client hears. The lawyer thus needs to be sensitive to how her communications to the client are received.

---

112. *See* Lazare & Sogg, *supra* note 98, at 15–16.

113. *Id.* at 16.

114. *See* CARL R. ROGERS, ON BECOMING A PERSON: A THERAPIST'S VIEW OF PSYCHOTHERAPY 283–84 (1961) (attributing phrase to unpublished work by Ph.D. candidate Stanley Standal).

115. *See* ch. 2: Brooks, *supra* note 40, at p. 72 (discussing nonjudgmentalism as critical social work attribute).

116. Lazare & Sogg, *supra* note 98, at 16.

117. *Id.* at 17.

(handwritten margin note: What to say to a client humiliated client)

If the lawyer perceives that the client is feeling humiliated, she might acknowledge the feelings without labeling them. Statements such as "I know coming to see a lawyer may feel uncomfortable," or "a divorce is often a very stressful process," may help validate, and thus diminish the negative impact of what the client is experiencing.[118] Genuine, sincere acknowledgement of the client's strengths in coping with the problem can also be quite supportive.[119] Helping the client to have reasonable expectations, to realistically understand the dimensions of the problem, the factors that contributed, and the possible outcomes—both legal and practical—may help diminish the client's shameful feelings. Frequently, clients blame themselves—even if they don't verbalize such blame to the lawyer—for matters that were beyond their control. Helping them to understand the limits of their responsibility can be extremely therapeutic.[120]

More challenging is the client who fails to follow the lawyer's advice, or who continues to engage in behavior that aggravates the client's legal problems. What the lawyer wants to avoid is lecturing the client, or having each meeting be a replay of what has gone before. If the lawyer can nonjudgmentally explore the reasons why the client has failed to follow her advice, she may help her client see the ways in which he undermines his own expressed objectives.[121]

Recognizing one's own shame is challenging, for the lawyer as well as the client. Expressing anger at the client, finding oneself humiliating the client, avoiding the client, or dreading meetings with the client may be signals that the lawyer experiences shame or humiliation in the relationship. Once acknowledged, the lawyer has the opportunity to pursue therapeutic responses. As with experiences of countertransference discussed above, acknowledging the existence of the emotion may be sufficient to resolve the problem. In extreme cases, the lawyer may need to refer the client elsewhere. If the lawyer finds this to be a sufficiently frequent problem that is negatively affecting her ability to practice law competently, she should consider professional counseling.[122]

---

118. *See id.* at 17. ("Ultimately, helping the client identify these emotions helps dissipate some of the suffering.").

119. *See id.* ("The lawyer may be the only one who can see courage and heroism in the client's coping behavior").

120. *See id.* at 17–18.

121. *See id.* at 18. *See also* ch. 2: Brooks, *supra* note 40, at pp. 72–76 (discussing constructive approach to difficult clients).

122. *See supra* note 86 and accompanying text.

Appended to Lazare and Sogg's article is a useful "Practice Checklist for Shame, Humiliation, and Stigma in the Attorney-Client Relationship." Lazare & Sogg, *supra* note 98, at 19–21. An online version of their article and checklist is available for purchase at www.ali-aba.org.

C. Denial and Other Defense Mechanisms

Professors Bruce Winick and Susan Bandes have identified some of the challenges lawyers face in dealing with psychological defense mechanisms such as denial, minimization, and repression. Professor Winick has focused on the effect of these mechanisms on client behavior,[123] while Professor Bandes has concentrated on their effect on lawyers, particularly in the representation of criminal defendants.[124]

Denial is one of a range of defense mechanisms, which are (largely) unconscious psychological strategies we use to control anxiety.[125] These defense mechanisms enable us to suppress painful, anxiety-producing information, thus, according to Freud, making it possible for us to keep functioning day to day.[126]

Denial is in many situations a useful defense mechanism. By allowing us to push upsetting thoughts or reality out of consciousness, we are able to keep functioning. Thus, it is most useful when there is nothing to be done to change a disturbing reality.[127] However, in many situations, denial may keep

---

123. Bruce J. Winick, *Client Denial and Resistance in the Advance Directive Context: Reflections on How Attorneys Can Identify and Deal With a Psycholegal Soft Spot*, 4 PSYCHOL. PUB. POL'Y & L. 901 (1998), *reprinted in* PRACTICING THERAPEUTIC JURISPRUDENCE, Ch. 12, at 327–55 [hereinafter *Denial & Resistance*]; *see* Winick, *supra* note 38, at pp. 353–57.

124. Bandes, *supra* note 3.

125. FELDMAN, *supra* note 26, at 469–70; *see also* Winick, *Denial & Resistance, supra* note 123, at 330–32.

126. Winick, *Denial & Resistance, supra* note 123, at 331; Winick, *supra* note 38, at p. 354. *See also* Bandes, *supra* note 3, at 351–52 (describing varying definitions of denial in psychological literature).

127. *See* Bandes, *supra* note 3, at 353–54. Let me share a personal example to illustrate the adaptive use of denial. Not so long ago, my annual mammogram showed some thickening in my left breast, and I was notified that a follow-up procedure was necessary. When I called to make an appointment for the follow-up, I was given a date four weeks in the future. Concerned that, were there a malignancy, this should be determined sooner rather than later, I called my doctor, who assured me that there was nothing to worry about, that the follow-up procedure was a product of the radiologist's extreme caution. She said there was no reason to worry about waiting four weeks.

On the one hand, this news was reassuring. On the other, what if my doctor were wrong? Surely, there was a *chance* that there might, in fact, be a problem, a possible malignancy? But if I continued to ruminate about the "what ifs?" for the next four weeks, it would have been extremely difficult to function day to day. Instead, whenever the thought entered my consciousness, I just pushed it away. And, as it turned out, what had appeared to be a thickening was merely a cloudy picture of normal breast tissue. The follow-up picture revealed that there was, in fact, nothing to worry about. I would suggest this was a constructive use of denial.

us from taking constructive action. A refusal to "face the facts" may, in the long run, be harmful to us and those for whom we care.[128]

How is this relevant to the work of the lawyer? Oftentimes, as Professor Winick has described, clients may be avoiding dealing with important issues to avoid the anxiety that such issues produce. Professor Winick's 1998 article, for example, explores client denial in the advance directive context.[129] For most of us, discussions about our own aging, incapacity, and death produce a great deal of anxiety. Clients are often resistant to engaging in discussions and planning about end of life matters, and may well engage in denial in order to avoid them. Such situations are what Professor Winick and others have described as *psycholegal softspots*, legal procedures, processes, or interventions that are likely to exacerbate or diminish the client's psychological distress.[130] As such planning is generally in the client's long term interest, this kind of denial will usually be maladaptive. A lawyer who understands denial is likely to be more effective in engaging the client in constructive advance decisionmaking.

In his chapter in this book on overcoming psychological barriers to settlement, Professor Winick offers several other practice settings where clients might engage in maladaptive denial. The matrimonial client might refuse to accept that his marriage is beyond repair. Similarly, the businessman may be unable to accept and plan for the dissolution of a partnership. A defendant in a personal injury lawsuit may be unable to accept responsibility for the injury she caused.[131] In each instance, understanding that denial is a common, human reaction to the situation may enable the lawyer to help the client face up to reality and facilitate the lawyer's ability to counsel the client effectively and appropriately. Professor Winick discusses strategies and interventions that the lawyer may employ.[132]

In her article, Professor Bandes explores how defense mechanisms such as denial and repression may affect the criminal defense lawyer.[133] How, emo-

---

128. Contrast the example above with one that Professor Winick uses, of the woman who discovers a lump in her breast, and, unable to deal with the thought that it might be a malignant tumor, ignores it. Winick, *Denial & Resistance, supra* note 123, at 331. Given the high cure rate when breast cancer is caught early, the failure to follow-up could, literally, be the difference between life and death. Certainly this is a maladaptive use of denial.

129. Winick, *Denial & Resistance, supra* note 123.

130. David B. Wexler, *Practicing Therapeutic Jurisprudence: Psycholegal Soft Spots and Strategies, in* PRACTICING TJ, *supra* note 8, at 45, 48.

131. Winick, *supra* note 38, at p. 353.

132. Winick, *Denial & Resistance, supra* note 123, at 333–47; Winick, *supra* note 38, at pp. 355–57 (discussing motivational interviewing).

133. Bandes, *supra* note 3.

tionally, does one defend clients accused of horrific crimes? How is one able to do that, year after year? What emotional toll does it take to be a good criminal lawyer? And at what cost? What happens to that lawyer when she leaves the office and goes home? "What emotions do criminal lawyers need to deny or repress, or in some way place at a safe remove? On what level of awareness does the denial occur, and how permanent is it?"[134]

Professor Bandes' interest in this subject is rooted in her four years as a state appellate defender in Illinois after law school.[135] Even when she was able to rationally respond to the constant question of "How can you represent those people?," she wondered about the *emotional* processes that allowed her to do so, and what might be the connection to the burnout she felt that contributed to her decision to leave that work.[136] Bandes describes some of the strategies she and her colleagues employed:

> There were certain obvious strategies for avoiding thinking about the emotions surrounding the defense of those accused (or convicted) of gruesome crimes. One was the use of euphemisms, or code.... We referred to murders, rapes, as "the incident in question" or "the alleged incident." A truly horrifying case had "bad facts." A fun case was often one with interesting or gory facts. We felt we could not afford to focus on the victim or to imagine the experience of the crime.... [W]e felt loyalty to our clients. We knew them and their families as human beings, we cared about them, we drew much of our strength and motivation from their desperate need for our help. Our clients' needs were serious, immediate and palpable. Our job was to help our clients, which meant to get their convictions reversed or their sentences reduced. And like all good lawyers, we took pride in a job well done....
>
> [A]t some point it became clear that all this "not thinking about" was taking its toll. There were emotions I couldn't afford to explore, and I was no longer sure that they were all easily confined to my professional life.[137]

Bandes' article is her attempt to understand what happened to her, and what happens generally to lawyers who take on the work of representing those accused or convicted of terrible crimes. She concludes that some amount of

---

134. *See id.* at 349.
135. *Id.* at 348.
136. *Id.* at 348–49.
137. *Id.* at 349–51.

denial—in fact, often a great deal—is necessary for a lawyer to undertake representation of clients who may have committed horrendous acts.[138] For those who represent such clients on an ongoing basis, denial is both necessary for psychological survival, and, simultaneously, an occupational hazard. The hazard is a disengagement from emotions that may undermine the lawyer's empathy with the client, as well as leak into the lawyer's personal life.[139] The result is often burnout,[140] psychic numbing,[141] or worse.[142]

These hazards are not limited, of course, to those lawyers engaged in criminal defense work. As Bandes notes, prosecutors, judges, law enforcement personnel, and others are also vulnerable.[143] Also at risk are those who represent victims of torture, trauma, and others who have endured horrific experiences.[144] It is critically important for lawyers who do this work to develop a repertoire of healthy coping mechanisms.

Some strategies for coping are discussed in greater detail in the next Part, which focuses on lawyers' stress, burnout, and vicarious trauma.

III. Maintaining the Course: Avoiding and Surviving Stress, Burnout, and Vicarious Trauma

Developing one's emotional competence includes gaining knowledge and acquiring strategies that enable one to avoid debilitating stress,[145] as well as to

---

138. *Id.* at 374.

139. *Id.* at 375–78.

140. *Id.* at 378–79. For a discussion of Burnout, see *infra* notes 165–80 and accompanying text.

141. *Id.* at 378.

142. "In their extreme form, the mechanisms the lawyers employ are characteristic of a moral disengagement that is at the root of a host of antisocial or destructive behaviors." *Id.* at 376. *See also* David Barnhizer, *Princes of Darkness and Angels of Light: The Soul of the American Lawyer*, 14 NOTRE DAME J.L. ETHICS & PUB. POL'Y 371, 429–30 (2000) (discussing the necessary moral compartmentalization of criminal defense work). *Cf.* Benedict Carey, *In the Execution Chamber, the Moral Compass Wavers*, N.Y. TIMES, Feb. 7, 2006, at F1 (on how prison personnel charged with executing capital offenders cope with the moral burden through moral disengagement).

143. Bandes, *supra* note 3, at 344–46.

144. *See infra* notes 180–207 and accompanying text (discussing vicarious trauma).

145. *See* GOLEMAN, *supra* note 18, at 231–60 (ch. 15: *The Cost of Emotional Illiteracy* (discussing how to avoid depression and other psychic disorders)).

survive major distress and trauma should it happen.[146] Stress is certainly no stranger to lawyers' lives. Over the past two decades, empirical evidence has painfully documented the toll that repeated stress may exact in the form of depression, alcoholism, and other substance abuse.[147] Burnout is another debilitating-manifestation of repeated stress.[148] Vicarious trauma, too, is an occupational risk for lawyers whose clients have faced horrific circumstances. This part explores these risks and offers some emotionally intelligent strategies for avoiding or remedying the harm they may cause.

A. Stress

lawyers have trauma a because clients head such torrible experiences.

In his excellent book written especially for lawyers, Amiram Elwork explains why lawyers suffer from *distress* disproportionately to the general population, and offers strategies for managing stress.[149]

The stress reaction, as Elwork explains, is composed of a sequence of triggers:

$$\text{Stimulus} \rightarrow \text{Thought} \rightarrow \text{Emotion} \rightarrow \text{Behavior.}^{150}$$

For example, suppose you are taking a walk in the city with a young child. All of a sudden, the child darts out into the street, into the path of an oncoming car. That would be the stimulus. The thought produced by the stimulus would be that the child is in great danger of serious injury. The emotion triggered by the thought would likely be fear.[151] The behavior triggered by the emotion might be to dart out after the child and pull her to safety.[152]

Now to place this in the lawyer's context. Stimulus: Your supervisor assigns you to draft a complaint in a personal injury case. The statute of limitations is one week away. Thoughts: "I need to get on this right away, because if I

---

146. *Id.* at 200–14 (ch. 13: *Trauma and Emotional Relearning*).

147. *See, e.g.,* G. Andrew H. Benjamin et al., *The Role of Legal Education in Producing Psychological Distress Among Law Students and Lawyers,* AM. B. FOUND. RES. J. 225 (1986); G. Andrew H. Benjamin et al., *The Prevalence of Depression, Alcohol Abuse, and Cocaine Abuse Among United States Lawyers,* 13 INT'L J.L. & PSYCHIATRY 233, 233–34 (1990).

148. *See* Bandes, *supra* note 3, at 379–83 (discussing relationship of denial and burnout among criminal defense attorneys).

149. AMIRAM ELWORK, STRESS MANAGEMENT FOR LAWYERS (3d ed. 2007).

150. *Id.* at 45, 101.

151. There would of course be a series of physical reaction as well which, combined with your thoughts, creates the emotion of fear. *Id.* at 45–46.

152. However, if the fear is overwhelming, the result might be panic and an inability to react in time to save the child. *See id.* at 46.

don't, our client will lose his right to recover, my firm will face a malpractice suit, and I might lose my job." Emotions: Fear, anxiety. Behavior: You put less pressing matters aside, and work on the complaint.

As the above examples demonstrate, a certain amount of stress is essential as a motivator. Too much stress, though, results in *distress.* This distress often manifests itself as substance abuse, depression, and other forms of anxiety disorders—problems that are disproportionately high among attorneys.[153]

Elwork identifies factors endemic to the legal profession, as well as individual traits and circumstances that contribute to the high levels of stress among attorneys. Most obvious are the time pressures, long hours, lack of time to spend with family, and, certainly, the economic bottom line. For some that means worrying about generating sufficient business to meet payroll; for others, especially for those in most law firms, it is the competition and pressure to increase billable hours and the firm's profit margin.[154]

Lawyers tend to share certain personality characteristics as well that increase their distress.[155] Lawyers tend to be perfectionists,[156] and this drive to produce a perfect brief, a perfect complaint, a perfect oral argument, takes its emotional toll. As discussed previously, lawyers' preferences for rationalism and logical thinking often make them less able to process strong emotions—both theirs and their clients—in a healthy way.[157] This, too, contributes to high stress levels,[158] as does the ethic of workaholism that pervades the profes-

---

153. *See id.* at 13–18 (discussing studies demonstrating disproportionately high incidence of these problems among attorneys). *See also generally* MARJORIE A. SILVER, SUBSTANCE ABUSE, STRESS, MENTAL HEALTH AND THE LEGAL PROFESSION: COURSE CURRICULUM AND TEACHERS GUIDE (2004), *available at* http://www.nylat.org/lawschoolrelated/documents/courseinabox.pdf (last visited May 15, 2006).

154. ELWORK, *supra* note 149, at 19–24. Other stressors Elwork discusses include the competition caused by increasingly large numbers of lawyers entering the profession, the slowdown of the economy, and corporate streamlining, all of which contribute to lower morale and higher anxiety. *Id.* at 20–21. Another contributing factor is related to the moral confusion discussed *infra* notes 167–72 and accompanying text. Many lawyers have ambivalent feelings about the work they do, especially when it causes harm to third parties. And certain areas of practice, such as criminal and family law, tend to be particularly stressful. ELWORK, *supra* note 149, at 22. *See also generally* Bandes, *supra* note 3; Barnhizer, *supra* note 142.

155. *See generally* Daicoff, *supra* note 1.

156. ELWORK, *supra* note 149, at 22–23, 30–31.

157. *See* discussion *supra* notes 10–13 and accompanying text.

158. ELWORK, *supra* note 149, at 23. Elwork cites as a fact of life, the "feelings of hostility, cynicism, aggression, fear and low self-esteem" that the adversary system generates.

sion.[159] Finally, Elwork notes the insatiable drive for success as a contributing factor for many lawyers:

> These lawyers seldom enjoy their success. They live in the future, not in the present. No level of achievement is savored for very long before it is interrupted by the pressures of newly set ambitions. Success is elusive in that it is perpetually anticipated rather than experienced. Happiness is always foreseen, but seldom felt.[160]

Elwork's book introduces the reader to a range of stress management techniques, with a primary focus on methods for interrupting habitual thought processes that trigger distressful reactions.[161] Section V of his book presents simple exercises designed to interrupt automatic patterns of thoughts/emotions, allowing the reader to replace any automatic, dysfunctional patterns with more constructive alternatives.[162] The goal is to shift one's focus from the problem to the solution.[163] Elwork suggests that this form of cognitive or rational-emotive therapy holds special appeal for many lawyers, given our cognitive, rational preferences.[164]

What is key, however, is for the lawyer to find one or more strategies that work to keep stress levels under control and to keep the lawyer on course emotionally.

B. Burnout

The social psychologist Professor Christina Maslach defines burnout as follows: BURNOUT

> Burnout is a syndrome of emotional exhaustion, depersonalization and reduced personal accomplishment that can occur among in-

---

Id. at 24, 28–29. He also notes the special challenges that women and minorities face in the profession. *Id.* at 33–39.

159. *Id.* at 26–28. Elwork's advice for those forced to work in antagonistic, stressful environments is to work less and spend more time with family and friends, advice he realizes is far more easily delivered than followed. *Id.* at 29.

160. *Id.* at 31.

161. *Id.* at 49–123.

162. The book contains a sample of a "daily log" that the reader can use to deconstruct the automatic process of Stimulus → Thought → Emotion → Behavior, allowing one to develop adaptive alternatives. *Id.* at 110.

163. *Id.* at 107.

164. *Id.* at 109.

dividuals who do 'people work' of some kind. It is a response to the chronic emotional strain of dealing extensively with other human beings, particularly when they are troubled or having problems. Although it has some of the same deleterious effects as other stress responses, what is unique about burnout is that the stress arises from the *social* interaction between helper and recipient.[165]

Susan Bandes described the burnout she and other criminal defense attorneys experienced as a product of the denial in which they engaged to survive the emotional toll of doing criminal defense work.[166] Similarly, Professor David Barnhizer described the emotional and moral burnout experienced by many attorneys as a function of navigating the disconnect between positions we take on behalf of our clients, and our own personal sense of morality.[167] While Barnhizer notes that this problem may be heightened among criminal defense attorneys,[168] he recognizes it as a phenomenon that a lawyer in virtually any field might experience when the role of advocating for one's client clashes with one's personal sense of right and wrong.[169] The risk of burnout and other distress responses is exacerbated by the state of moral and legal ambiguity that is the lawyer's lot.[170] The irony is that those who enter the law for the most altruistic of purposes—including lawyers who want to be helpers and healers—might be exactly those individuals most susceptible to burnout and other stress reactions.[171] The more one cares, the more intensely one may experience the frustrations of being unable to achieve desired goals, whether because of lack of resources, government bureaucracy, or any number of other obstacles. Or, the attorney may find herself in conflict with the client over what the goals of the representation are or should be.[172] And, when this later problem arises, it is the lawyers who represent poor people and other clients who have no realistic choice of attorneys that are most likely to find themselves forced to take positions inconsistent with their own moral compasses.

---

165. Christina Maslach, Burnout: The Cost of Caring 3 (1982).

166. Bandes, *supra* note 3, at 348–51, 379–83.

167. Barnhizer, *supra* note 142, at 429–30.

168. *Id.* at 450–51.

169. *Id.* at 451–52.

170. *Id.* at 453–55.

171. *See id.* at 452 (citing Anne Ferguson, *Career Burnout: Causes and Cures*, Mgmt. Today, July 1989, at 122).

172. An attorney who fails in persuading an admittedly guilty drug addict to accept a treatment plan in lieu of incarceration might well be an example. *See generally infra* ch. 13: Lisa Schreibersdorf, *A Public Defender in a Problem-Solving Court.*

*The more committed you are, the more
you care, the more likely you are to burn out*

Thus there is a basic paradox at the heart of burnout. The more committed one is to social justice, the more involved one is in giving voice to the mar-
ginalized members of our society, the more likely one may be to experience
burnout. This is true not only of criminal defense work—although it may be
particularly acute in those circumstances—but in any work where one is constantly confronting seemingly insurmountable challenges of limited resources
and opportunities. In such circumstances, the lawyer risks experiencing moral
disengagement from the values of justice and fairness that drew him to become a lawyer engaged in public interest work.

In her research, Professor Maslach interviewed lawyers who described
symptoms of burnout:

> "It's painful to say it, but maybe I'm just not cut out for this kind of
> work," said one attorney in legal services. "I thought of myself as a
> sensitive and caring person, but often I'm *not* sensitive and caring
> when I'm with my clients—so maybe I'm really deluding myself
> about the real me." With the crumbling of self-esteem, depression
> may set in, and some will seek counseling or therapy for what they
> believe are their personal problems. Others will change their jobs,
> often to abandon any kind of work that brings them into stressful
> contact with people.[173]

Burnout, then, is a defensive response to excessive stress, an affective flat-
tening or shutting down that renders one emotionally empty and comparatively ineffective professionally. Its repercussions generally spill over into one's
personal relationships as well, and may lead to any number of other dysfunctional conditions.[174] Maslach emphasizes the importance of self-care to prevent or ameliorate burnout, including self-awareness,[175] rest, and relaxation.[176]
Having realistic expectations is also important,[177] as is balance:

> If all the knowledge and advice about how to beat burnout could
> be summed up in one word, that word would be *balance*. Balance be-

---

173. MASLACH, *supra* note 165, at 5.

174. *See, e.g.,* Barnhizer, *supra* note 142, at 450–52.

175. MASLACH, *supra* note 165, at 98–99 ("Research has found that therapists … who
have been trained to recognize and deal with countertransference, are better able than other
therapists to handle the emotional exhaustion of burnout." *Id.* at 99.).

176. *Id.* at 100–01.

177. *Id.* at 133–34 ("When people do not know ahead of time about the emotional demands of the job, their expectations as they enter that job will be decidedly out of line with
reality." *Id.* at 134.).

*• realistic expectations
+
• balance*

giving + getting • stress + calm • work + home.

tween giving and getting, balance between stress and calm, balance between work and home.[178]

And balance is at the core of what Maslach describes as *detached concern*, in which the lawyer or therapist genuinely cares about the client, but is able to maintain sufficient psychological distance from the client's problems to avoid becoming overwhelmed by them.[179]

To stay on course, the emotionally competent lawyer, while maintaining an empathic connection, needs to take measures to keep her balance and to distance herself from her clients' problems.

C. Vicarious Trauma

Burnout generally results from sustained, chronic, stressful work.[180] Vicarious trauma, though, may occur through a counselor's intensive work with a single client.[181]

Only recently has there been explicit acknowledgment of the emotional, physiological, cognitive, and behavioral effects frequently suffered by care-

---

178. *Id.* at 147.

179. *Id.* at 147–48. Maslach acknowledges that achieving this balance is no simple task: Although this balanced state of detached concern may sound good in theory, it is not always clear how to achieve it in practice. The skills that are necessary to maintain professional detachment may be quite different from those used to maintain interested concern—in fact, they may even be in conflict. Indeed, some practitioners talk about moving back and forth between these two states, rather than trying to combine them.

Id. at 148.

180. *Id.* at 11. "[T]he burnout syndrome appears to be a response to chronic, everyday stress (rather than to occasional crises)." *See also* Andrew P. Levin & Scott Greisberg, *Vicarious Trauma in Attorneys*, 24 Pace L. Rev. 245, 248 (2003) (describing burnout as a progressive response to the prolonged stress of therapeutic relationships that results in fatigue, demoralization, and withdrawal personally and professionally); Barnhizer, *supra* note 142, at 450 ("True burnout ... is a chronic condition, what one researcher has called 'a general erosion of the spirit,' that can have severe consequences: loss of enthusiasm for work or family, trouble concentrating, reduced creativity, depression, alienation, even paranoia or psychosis. Burned-out workers may lose all sense of meaning in their lives and begin drinking or using drugs. Marriages suffer and careers erode.").

181. Levin & Greisberg, *supra* note 180, at 246 (citing I. Lisa McCann & Laurie Anne Pearlman, *Vicarious Traumatization: A Framework for Understanding the Psychological Effects of Working with Victims*, 3 J. Traumatic Stress 131 (1990)).

givers who work with traumatized populations.[182] Happily, though, there is now a substantial body of work that explores what is alternatively labeled vicarious traumatization, secondary traumatic stress (STS), or compassion fatigue.[183] While the literature has primarily addressed the impact on trauma therapists, many of those writing have recognized that similar problems exist for other professionals, first responders, and caregivers whose work brings them into contact with trauma survivors.[184] Those who bear witness to patients' and clients' stories of pain and anguish are in jeopardy of suffering symptoms that mirror the symptoms of those who experienced the trauma directly—thus the terminology *secondary* or *vicarious* trauma.[185] The effect is often cumulative; the more one is immersed in trauma work, the more likely one is to experience the negative effects of vicarious trauma.[186]

Several years ago, in the wake of September 11th, 2001, I interviewed lawyers who had volunteered their services to individuals and families who lost loved ones and livelihoods in the terrorist attacks. I was interested in learning about the nature of the emotional toll exacted from those who undertook this work.[187] Not surprisingly, hardly any of these lawyers were prepared for the special challenges of representing survivors of trauma.[188]

---

182. COMPASSION FATIGUE: COPING WITH SECONDARY TRAUMATIC STRESS DISORDER IN THOSE WHO TREAT THE TRAUMATIZED xiv (Charles R. Figley ed., 1995) [hereinafter COMPASSION FATIGUE].

183. *Introduction to the Second Edition, in* SECONDARY TRAUMATIC STRESS xix (B. Hudnall Stamm ed., 2d ed. 1999) [hereinafter SECONDARY TRAUMATIC STRESS].

184. *See, e.g.,* Laurie Anne Pearlman, *Self-Care for Trauma Therapists: Ameliorating Vicarious Traumatization, in* SECONDARY TRAUMATIC STRESS, *supra* note 183, at 51, 52; Mary Ann Dutton & Francine L. Rubinstein, *Working with People with PTSD: Research Implications, in* COMPASSION FATIGUE, *supra* note 182, at 83.

185. Debra A. Neumann & Sarah J. Gamble, *Issues in the Professional Development of Psychotherapists: Countertransference and Vicarious Traumatization in the New Trauma Therapist,* 32 PSYCHOTHERAPY 341, 343–44 (1995).

186. Laurie Anne Pearlman & Karen W. Saakvitne, *Treating Therapists with Vicarious Traumatization and Secondary Traumatic Stress Disorders, in* COMPASSION FATIGUE, *supra* note 182, at 51.

187. *See generally* Silver, *supra* note 45.

188. In actuality, most of the caregivers who worked with the September 11th survivors and their families—social workers, therapists and lawyers—are both direct *and* secondary victims of that trauma. Through both direct witness, live television coverage, and the repeated televised replays of the terrorist attacks over the hours and days that followed, most of us in New York—perhaps the entire nation and much of the world—experienced the traumatic events of September 11th directly. The attorneys I interviewed occupied a spectrum of how directly the trauma of September 11th and its aftermath touched their

In the United States, whether an attorney through prior experience or training has had the opportunity to learn about trauma, or grieving, or to develop the necessary intra- and inter-personal skills, or psychological-mindedness to represent clients who are trauma victims — is virtually serendipitous.[189] Only a few of the lawyers with whom I spoke had any background in psychology, and then only from studies or work outside of law school.[190] Most of the attorneys had neither had any relevant experience, nor had ever received any training that would prepare them for working with trauma survivors, or enable them to recognize and discuss a client's needs for therapeutic interventions. Nor had they learned to appreciate how they might be affected, emotionally and psychologically, by the work they were doing.[191]

Many of these lawyers were puzzled by their emotional and psychological responses to their clients. In the representation of trauma survivors, such confusion can be hazardous to the attorney's health, and may well compromise the quality of the representation. Whether clients are traumatized because of individual experiences, or because of mass disasters, lawyers need to know about what to expect, both for their clients' wellbeing and for their own.[192]

I will share the story of one of the attorneys whom I interviewed, Susan Cartwright.[193] This was the first *pro bono* work she had ever done. Susan, who graduated law school in 1998, was an associate at a large midtown intellectual property law firm. Susan volunteered with the New York City Bar's Septem-

---

lives. The question was not whether they had experienced trauma, but rather to what degree.

189. Silver, *September 11th, supra* note 45, at 71.

190. Some were better prepared than others because of their prior work experiences. One lawyer had been an emergency medical worker for six years. Another had done a 400-hour externship on the psychiatric unit of a hospital, as a requirement for earning her masters in forensic psychology.

191. One exception was Saralyn Cohen, *pro bono* coordinator at a major New York law firm. Through representation of asylum seekers, Saralyn had developed an understanding of the importance of working with a team when representing survivors of trauma. Thus she made sure to have a social services person, a mental health professional and a physician to augment and support what she was able to do for her clients with her legal skills. Author's interview with Saralyn Cohen (April 22, 2003).

192. Vicarious trauma doesn't just affect caregivers and lawyers. Judges, too, report experiencing symptoms of secondary trauma arising out of their work. *See* Peter G. Jaffe et al., *Vicarious Trauma in Judges: The Personal Challenge of Dispensing Justice*, 54 Juv. Fam. Ct. J. 1 (Fall 2003).

193. This is a pseudonym.

ber 11th project[194] out of her frustration of wanting, needing to do something. For her, the experience was an emotional roller coaster, yet it was clear from our discussion that it had also been a transformative one:

> [T]he emotional issues aside and the pain and the tragedy and all that aside, this has been a very good experience for me, on many levels. Knowing that I am able to really counsel. The firm has been supportive, but they sort of let me do this on my own. I would go around the office and seek advice from senior members of the firm on certain issues, but for the most part I've had to find my way, and that's a good experience for me too. And also, getting the feedback from other attorneys who are more senior than me when I talk to them and they would say, wow, I can't believe you even got this, or were able to accomplish that, that's amazing. Also, the six attorneys on this [case] are all much older than I am, have been practicing longer than I have, but would consistently defer to me when there's a situation specifically dealing with the client because I have the closest relationship with the client. I also think that the client will be a part of my life, for the rest of my life. That we've become friends throughout this process and I regard him highly, and he regards me highly and this is a man who is 52 and I'm 32, so it's very interesting how that works out. It's been a positive experience, just as frustrating as hell, but a really positive experience.[195]

But for Susan, as for so many of the lawyers I interviewed, the work took its toll. Susan described to me the intense and emotionally demanding relationship she had developed with her client who had lost his same-sex domestic partner in the collapse of the Twin Towers. The partner had been the cou-

---

194. *See* Silver, *September 11th, supra* note 45, at 64:

After the events of September 11th 2001, the Association of the Bar of the City of New York mobilized a *pro bono* response unlike any other in history. Thousands of lawyers sought and received training as facilitators. These facilitators operated as legal problem-solvers, lawyers who would serve as legal liaisons to individuals and families who lost loved ones and livelihoods in the terrorist attacks. The services provided ran the gamut of the clients' legal needs. In addition to assisting in obtaining expedited death certificates, arranging for estate administration, and filing claims for death benefits, lawyer/facilitators, backed by expert mentors, helped clients with landlord/tenant, insurance, and family law issues.

195. Author's interview with "Susan Cartwright" (August 29, 2002).

ple's primary breadwinner, and the survivor was in tremendous distress—emotionally and financially. Susan reported that for some time she got so wrapped up in her client's life that she felt she could not separate herself from her work. She would get very frustrated when she hit roadblocks in obtaining benefits and services for her client. She would berate herself, question her own competence, have to constantly remind herself that she was dealing with a bureaucracy, and that there was only so much over which she had any control. Frequently she would go home and cry. Her health suffered—physically and emotionally.[196]

Susan's story demonstrated how, in addition to the emotional toll this work takes on the attorneys who do it, it was often difficult to separate themselves, and their own lives, from those of their clients. September 11th representation, especially as designed by the architects of the facilitator/problem-solver model,[197] encouraged if not commanded a broader view of the lawyer's role than that to which most attorneys traditionally subscribe. While on one hand, this fostered a more therapeutically oriented approach, it also potentially exacerbated the boundary confusion that many attorneys experience in their relationships with clients.[198]

In order to better understand vicarious trauma, I met with two professionals who worked with trauma survivors. I first met with social worker Nancy Arnow, who ran the Project Liberty component of Safe Horizons. As an organization employing specialists in trauma and its effects, Project Liberty provided free mental health services to organizations coping with the aftermath of September 11th. Among these organizations were some of the law firms who had, as institutions, undertaken September 11th representation. A significant part of what Project Liberty provided was basic information about what those who had experienced trauma either directly or secondarily might expect. According to Ms. Arnow, just knowing the normal reactions that trauma survivors experience was tremendously helpful in supporting the caregivers' coping mechanisms.[199]

---

196. *Id.*

197. *See* Silver, *September 11th, supra* note 45, at 64.

198. *See* Lynda L. Murdoch, *Psychological Consequences of Adopting a Therapeutic Lawyering Approach: Pitfalls and Protective Strategies*, 24 SEATTLE U. L. REV. 483, 489 (2000):

> In order to decrease overidentification with a client, a professional must delicately balance neutrality and objectivity with involvement and concern. The professional must develop a detached style of interaction in order to prevent blurring of identity boundaries and maintain nonjudgmental objectivity.

See also generally ch. 2: Brooks, *supra* note 40.

199. Author's interview with Nancy Arnow (May 16, 2003).

Andrew Levin, a psychiatrist who has studied vicarious trauma among attorneys working with survivors of domestic violence and criminal defendants,[200] agreed. If an attorney can recognize symptoms about which she has previously learned—whether they are her client's symptoms or her own—she will be far less likely to experience debilitating vicarious trauma. If one knows what to expect, one's reaction can be "Aha! I recognize that!" Rather than "Oh my god, what do I do now?" or "What did I do to cause the client to act that way?" And if the lawyer has difficulty coping with those experiences, she will know where she can turn for help.[201] Thus knowledge is the first line of defense against vicarious trauma.

In her book, *Representing Children in Child Protective Proceedings: Ethical and Practical Dimensions*, Professor Jean Koh Peters discusses the relevance of the social science literature on vicarious trauma to the work of lawyers who represent traumatized children.[202] What she writes has significant implications for all attorneys who represent trauma survivors, whether they be survivors of terrorist attacks, other acts of mass violence or oppression, or individual crises. After describing vicarious trauma, Professor Peters examines how *self-care* is essential to counteracting the effects of working with trauma survivors. Informed by the work of psychotherapists Neumann and Gamble[203] she writes—and I agree[204]—that it is the lawyer's *ethical responsibility* to care for herself—be it through diet, exercise, music, meditation, spending time with loved ones and friends, psychotherapy, or all of the above. If the caregiver does not meet her own emotional, psychological, and physical needs, she will be in no position to competently care for her client. As Neumann and Gamble write, "[I]f therapists [substitute attorneys] do not care for themselves, they are at much greater risk of hurting their clients."[205]

---

200. *See generally* Levin & Greisberg, *supra* note 180. In comparing the experiences of these attorneys to those of other caregivers, the authors found that the attorneys demonstrated significantly higher levels of secondary traumatic stress, as well as burnout. *Id.* at 250.

201. Author's interview with Andrew Levin, June 10, 2003.

202. *See* JEAN KOH PETERS, Chapter 9: *The Lawyer-as-Context II: Fulfilling the Ethical Duty to Address Occupational Hazards that Imperil Client Service: Stress, Burnout, Vicarious Traumatization, in* REPRESENTING CHILDREN IN CHILD PROTECTIVE: PROCEEDINGS: ETHICAL AND PRACTICAL DIMENSIONS 421–87 (2d ed. 2001).

203. *See* Neumann & Gamble, *supra* note 185, at 345.

204. Silver, *supra* note 25, at 435.

205. Neumann & Gamble, *supra* note 185, at 345. *See also* Arin Greenwood, *Ripple Effects: Education and Self-Care Can Help Lawyers Avoid Internalizing Client Trauma*, 92 A.B.A. J. 20 (2006).

In his book, *Opening Up*, James Pennebaker discusses numerous studies demonstrating that oral and written expressions of thoughts and feelings about traumatic experiences have both preventive and therapeutic benefits for physical as well as mental wellbeing.[206] By expressing their own feelings about the traumatic events described by their clients, lawyers may be able to prevent or ameliorate symptoms of secondary trauma. Lawyers might consider keeping journals and developing support groups with other lawyers undergoing similar experiences.[207]

But there may well be times when these strategies are insufficient. At such times, lawyers should seek counseling from trained trauma specialists to help them maintain or recover their emotional balance and get them back on course.

Conclusion: Continuing On

Professor Lynda Murdoch has noted that lawyers who practice with a therapeutic orientation are likely at a higher risk to suffer burnout,[208] vicarious trauma,[209] as well as other hazards of caregiving.[210] These hazards include over-identification with clients, challenges in finding an appropriate balance between neutrality and involvement, and difficulties in identifying and managing transference and countertransference.[211] As increasing numbers of lawyers move towards practicing law as a healing profession, the greater is the need for training in the knowledge, skills, and values necessary to enhance emotional competence, to cultivate psychological-mindedness, to anticipate psychological hazards, and to develop strategies to prevent or control their interference in lawyers' professional relationships.

---

206. JAMES. W. PENNEBAKER, OPENING UP 34, 86–88, 103 (1997).

207. Some of the attorneys I interviewed told me that they were able to cope and keep on doing this work because they had someone with whom they could share and receive empathy. Debra Steinberg and Saralyn Cohen, both married to Israeli men, shared with me that their husbands did not want to hear the details of their September 11th work. Debra and Saralyn were grateful that they had each other to talk to, and they talked long and often. Author's interviews with Debra Browning Steinberg (October 31, 2002) and interview with Saralyn Cohen, *supra* note 191.

208. Murdoch, *supra* note 198, at 489–90.

209. *Id.* at 483, 493–94.

210. *Id.* at 483.

211. *Id.* at 489–93.

The lawyer's navigational tool kit should include basic knowledge about psychology and emotions. Just as important, though, are self-awareness and self-care, without which we might lose our way. Although few of us received any training about such matters in law school, there is reason for optimism that this is changing.[212] Hopefully, this chapter has enlarged the reader's knowledge of many of the psychological and emotional concepts that can impede or enhance the lawyer's effectiveness. What we have here explored, however, is merely the tip of the proverbial iceberg. The vast majority of us will never have the opportunity to develop the knowledge and expertise of those who have been trained in the psychodynamic professions, those who practice clinical social work or psychotherapy. Borrowing a concept from Professors Tremblay, Weng, and others, therefore, I urge you to approach this undertaking with humility, with *informed not-knowing* and *disciplined naiveté*.[213] Consider where your client—or you—may be coming from emotionally or psychologically, but be humble about your conclusions. There will likely be occasions when you should refer your client to another professional.[214] When I interviewed attorneys who had volunteered for September 11th representation,[215] I spoke with a lawyer who stated he would never presume to refer paying clients to a mental health professional, believing it to be outside of his role as an attorney.[216] Yet paying attention to a client's emotional struggles is an integral part of being a problem-solver. A lawyer can ease a grieving client's burden in finding needed support services, whether they be tax planning, investment strategies, or therapy. Yet most lawyers are far more likely to feel comfortable in offering advice with respect to financial matters than with per-

---

212. The numbers of law students who will be introduced to these subjects is increasing. This is evidenced by the growing interest among clinical law professors in Therapeutic Jurisprudence and the healing possibilities of law, *see, e.g.*, Symposium, *Therapeutic Jurisprudence in Clinical Legal Education and Skills Training*, 17 St. Thomas L. Rev. 403 (2004–05), as well as by the increasing number of stand-alone courses devoted to a helping, healing, more therapeutic approach to the practice of law. Eighteen law schools that offer such courses are listed on the website of the International Network on Therapeutic Jurisprudence, *at* http://www.law.arizona.edu/depts/upr-intj/ (last visited July 12, 2006). However such courses are certainly not yet considered part of any school's core curriculum. Perhaps this, too, may change over time.

213. *See* ch. 5: Tremblay & Weng, *supra* note 39, at nn.15, 17 and sources cited therein.

214. *See* Winick, *Denial & Resistance, supra* note 124, at 336 (discussing sensitivity with which such referrals should be discussed with client); Portnoy, *supra* note 1, at 118–20 (offering suggestions for making successful referrals).

215. *See supra* text accompanying note 187.

216. Silver, *September 11th, supra* note 45, at 70.

sonal matters such as counseling or psychotherapy. The attorney who possesses the knowledge and resources to facilitate both legal and non-legal services for the client will greatly enhance possibilities for a therapeutic outcome.

Consider developing a relationship with a knowledgeable mental health professional with whom you might consult, not only in times of need, but also for preventive check-ups; someone with whom, within the constraints of the attorney-client privilege, you could explore what comes up in your relationships with your clients: transference, countertransference, shame, humiliation, denial, trauma, and any other psychological processes or problems that may arise.

The resources cited in this chapter and others will further your journey to enhance your knowledge and understanding. Developing self-awareness and insuring self-care, however, are ultimately up to you, the reader. I welcome you on a wonderful journey towards emotional wisdom.

CHAPTER 2

USING SOCIAL WORK CONSTRUCTS IN THE PRACTICE OF LAW

*Susan L. Brooks**

Introduction

Ms. T, a 59-year-old woman with chronic back pain and complications from diabetes, contacts a law school's legal clinic to see if the clinic can assist her in appealing the denial of her application for disability benefits. The clinic students meet with her once, and they believe they have had a successful interview. Nevertheless, Ms. T misses her second appointment, and does not call immediately to reschedule.

Mr. H, a 30-year-old father who is in the midst of a divorce involving a custody battle, calls his lawyer several times a day, wanting to fill the lawyer in on every move of his soon-to-be ex-spouse. Twice in the past two weeks, he has shown up at the lawyer's office without an appointment.

Ms. S, a 46-year-old widow with no children, contacts a lawyer seeking legal assistance to file for bankruptcy. The first time she meets with her lawyer, he smells alcohol on her breath, and she proceeds to tell him how she feels depressed and has difficulty getting out of bed in the morning. She has recently experienced the deaths of her husband and both of her parents.[1]

* Clinical Professor of Law, Vanderbilt University Law School. J.D. New York University, 1990; M.A. in Social Work. University of Chicago, School of Social Service Administration, 1984; B.A. University of Chicago, College, 1983. I would like to express heartfelt appreciation to Marjorie Silver for her support and her tremendous editorial skills. Special thanks also goes to David Wexler and Bruce Winick for inspiring as well as encouraging my work over the years.

1. For more examples of such dilemmas taken from actual practice experiences, see *infra* ch. 6: Susan J. Bryant & Jean Koh Peters, *Six Practices for Connecting with Clients across*

Law students in clinical programs as well as practicing lawyers may face these types of clients and/or situations, regardless of the legal setting in which they work or the type of law they practice. Most experienced lawyers have developed their own strategies for dealing with such circumstances when they arise. But if they are honest, it may well be that, for the most part, they simply follow their gut feelings. Such responses may or may not be "therapeutic" for clients; in other words, they may or may not enhance clients' wellbeing. If acting therapeutically toward clients is an important value, our work must not simply be based on gut feelings, but rather must be grounded in well-established and evidence-based theoretical principles and approaches. In other words, if we care about maximizing the law's potential to be a healing profession, we need to be able to rely upon a sound, comprehensive framework in responding to dilemmas presented by clients.

This chapter proposes that constructs taken from the field of social work, often referred to as "generalist" social work constructs, offer such a comprehensive and well proven approach. I will describe a number of these core constructs in this chapter, and then demonstrate their usefulness in approaching the types of client dilemmas articulated above.[2]

The underpinning for this approach is a critical perspective known as therapeutic jurisprudence (TJ).[3] TJ is part of an international movement pro-

---

Culture: Habit Four, Working with Interpreters, and Other Mindful Approaches, at pp. 184–85, 188–89; 201–03, and *infra* ch. 5: Paul R. Tremblay & Carwina Weng, *Multicultural Lawyering: Heuristics and Biases*, at pp. 171–73; 175–77; 178–81.

2. This chapter represents a synthesis of the ideas presented in several recent articles addressing the use of social work constructs in the law. *See* Susan L. Brooks, *Practicing (and Teaching) Therapeutic Jurisprudence: Importing Social Work Principles and Techniques into Clinical Legal Education*, 17 St. Thomas L. Rev. 513 (2005) [hereinafter *Importing Social Work Principles*]; Susan L. Brooks, *Building Effective Relationships with Students, Clients, and Communities*, 13 Clin. L. Rev. __ (forthcoming 2006) [hereinafter, *Building Relationships*]; Susan L. Brooks, *Representing Children in Families*, 6 Nevada L. J. 836 (2006) [hereinafter *Representing Children in Families*]. A significant portion has been reprinted from the forthcoming article in the Clinical Law Review.

3. In a recent essay, I introduced some of these ideas from the standpoint of importing core social work elements into clinical legal education. Much of that article was devoted to elucidating the reasons why social work offers both a useful and an appropriate normative framework for therapeutic jurisprudence in the clinical teaching setting. *See* Brooks, *Importing Social Work Principles*, *supra* note 2. I have also summarized therapeutic jurisprudence and core social work elements in earlier works. *See generally* Susan L. Brooks, *A Family Systems Paradigm for Legal Decision Making Affecting Child Custody*, 6 Cornell J.L. & Pub. Pol'y 1 (1996) [hereinafter *Family Systems Paradigm*]; Susan L. Brooks, *Therapeutic Jurisprudence and Preventive Law in Child Welfare Proceedings: A Fam-*

moting the exploration of the law's impact on client wellbeing. When the core social work constructs described in this chapter are combined with TJ, they comprise a theory and a structure that can translate into our work with clients, and thus can assist us in building effective relationships with clients.

The first part of the chapter discusses the relationship between social work and therapeutic jurisprudence. Part II then explores a number of micro-level constructs that is, constructs pertaining to the dynamics of the one-on-one relationship between the helping professional and the client, taken from the social work field. By presenting these constructs, I hope to offer lawyers[4] a handful of useful tools and techniques that can be applied in their day-to-day work with clients. Many of these ideas will be readily identifiable, although lawyers may not have previously been exposed to them as such, because these processes are generally not discussed in the legal literature. Nevertheless, as will become apparent, naming these familiar processes and dynamics is useful to the extent that it makes them less intimidating and thus more manageable for us and our clients. Part III focuses on macro-level constructs, which are broader theoretical constructs that can inform our work with individual clients as well as groups, including families and communities. After describing some of the more useful constructs, in Part IV, I will illustrate their applicability by revisiting the three scenarios mentioned at the outset of this chapter.

I. Therapeutic Jurisprudence and Social Work

Therapeutic Jurisprudence, or TJ, is an interdisciplinary movement that studies the role of law as a therapeutic agent.[5] This movement, co-founded

---

ily Systems Approach, 5 PSYCHOL. PUB. POL'Y & L. 951 (1999) [hereinafter Therapeutic Jurisprudence]; Susan L. Brooks, The Case for Adoption Alternatives, 39 FAM. CT. REV. 43 (2001) [hereinafter Adoption Alternatives].

4. Here and throughout the rest of this paper, references to "lawyers" or "practitioners" are equally applicable to law students. Some of my examples are drawn from my experience teaching students at the Vanderbilt Legal Clinic, a program of Vanderbilt Law School, in which I and several of my colleagues supervise students on actual legal matters. My clinic, which is called the Child and Family Law Policy Clinic, involves supervision of students on matters related to the representation of children, youth, parents, and extended family members who are in some way involved in the child welfare system.

5. See, e.g., DAVID B. WEXLER, THERAPEUTIC JURISPRUDENCE: THE LAW AS A THERAPEUTIC AGENT (1990); Bruce J. Winick, The Jurisprudence of Therapeutic Jurisprudence, 3 PSYCHOL. PUB. POL'Y & L. 184, 185 (1997). For more information about TJ, including a comprehensive bibliography of TJ scholarship, see the International Network on Thera-

well over a decade ago by two legal scholars, David Wexler and Bruce Winick,[6] now has an international following among judges, lawyers, and mental health professionals.[7] TJ examines the extent to which our laws, policies, and practices have therapeutic or anti-therapeutic consequences for those who are affected by them.[8] TJ promotes exploration of the effects of laws and the legal system on the wellbeing of the persons they are supposed to serve. A TJ inquiry asks: is this particular law or aspect of the legal system 'therapeutic' or 'anti-therapeutic' for the persons affected by it?[9] Identifying and understanding what is anti-therapeutic ideally will lead to positive law reform.[10]

Given that the law is designed to uphold many values, such as due process and fairness, it nevertheless appears that many lawyers, particularly those who wish to practice law as a healing profession, are seeking to promote "higher values" in their practice. They want to see their clients' lives, and perhaps society itself, improve in some measurable way.[11] Occasionally, tensions may

---

peutic Jurisprudence, *at* http://www.therapeuticjurisprudence.org (last visited Mar. 26, 2006). Professors Wexler and Winick have contributed chapters to this book. *See infra* ch. 12: David B. Wexler, *The TJ Criminal Lawyer: Therapeutic Jurisprudence and Criminal Law Practice*; ch. 11: Bruce J. Winick, *Overcoming Psychological Barriers to Settlement: Challenges for the TJ Lawyer.*

6. *See generally* David B. Wexler, *An Introduction to Therapeutic Jurisprudence, in* DAVID B. WEXLER, THERAPEUTIC JURISPRUDENCE: THE LAW AS A THERAPEUTIC AGENT (1990); DAVID B. WEXLER & BRUCE J. WINICK, LAW IN A THERAPEUTIC KEY: DEVELOPMENTS IN THERAPEUTIC JURISPRUDENCE (1996).

7. This international following is evidenced by the TJ web site (http://www.therapeuticjurisprudence.org) and listserve (tjsp@topica.com), which reflect a high level of participation by scholars and practitioners of many disciplines from around the globe.

8. *See generally* DAVID B. WEXLER & BRUCE J WINICK, ESSAYS IN THERAPEUTIC JURISPRUDENCE (1991); DAVID B. WEXLER & BRUCE J. WINICK, LAW IN A THERAPEUTIC KEY: DEVELOPMENTS IN THERAPEUTIC JURISPRUDENCE (1996); PRACTICING THERAPEUTIC JURISPRUDENCE: LAW AS A HELPING PROFESSION (Dennis P. Stolle et al. eds., 2000).

9. Robert G. Madden & Raymie H. Wayne, *Social Work and the Law: A Therapeutic Jurisprudence Perspective*, 48 SOCIAL WORK 338, 339 (2003) [hereinafter Madden & Wayne I] (citing Dennis P. Stolle & David B. Wexler, *Therapeutic Jurisprudence and Preventive Law: A Combined Concentration to Invigorate the Everyday Practice of Law*, 39 ARIZ. L. REV. 25, 25–33 (1997)). It is also important to point out that TJ does not take the position that therapeutic goals should replace other goals of the law, such as fairness and due process. It simply posits that, all else being equal, the law should aim toward therapeutic goals. *Id.* at 340.

10. David B. Wexler, *Reflections on the Scope of Therapeutic Jurisprudence*, 1 PSYCHOL. PUB. POL'Y & L. 220, 224 (1995) [hereinafter *Reflections*] (quoting Christopher Slobogin, *Therapeutic Jurisprudence: Five Dilemmas to Ponder*, 1 PSYCHOL. PUB. POL'Y & L. 193, 196 (1995)).

11. I have stated this same position in a recent article discussing what TJ can offer to clinical legal education in terms of guidance for building effective relationships with students, clients, and communities. *See* Brooks, *Building Relationships, supra* note 2.

arise among these goals, but there is no reason to assume that they are necessarily contradictory.

Assuming agreement that, all else being equal, the law should work in ways that are therapeutic for our clients, how do we assess its therapeutic value? This is a tough question, but one with which we must grapple if TJ is to be worth pursuing at all. In other words, a TJ inquiry must be grounded in a particular normative framework,[12] if we are truly be able to determine whether a given practice, or rule, or law, is indeed therapeutic for the clients we represent.[13]

For many years, I have posited that the core elements of the social work provide a comprehensive, useful, evidence-based[14] framework that should inform the understanding of what is therapeutic.[15] Other scholars likewise have proposed that social work principles and values offer a normative framework

---

12. "A normative framework states how things ought to be. It serves as a baseline from which to evaluate the current state of affairs. A normative framework shapes the way people conceptualize problems and the solutions they seek." Robert G. Madden & Raymie H. Wayne, *Constructing a Normative Framework for Therapeutic Jurisprudence Using Social Work Principles as a Model*, 18 Touro L. Rev. 487 (2002) [hereinafter Madden & Wayne II].

13. Interestingly, TJ itself does not dictate a particular normative framework; rather, it sets up a line of inquiry, and is not prescriptive as to outcomes, processes, or roles. The TJ movement simply promotes the use of social science research to inform the understanding of what is therapeutic or anti-therapeutic, as the case may be. I have stated elsewhere that the lack of a particular normative framework for assessing the therapeutic value of our work in representing clients is problematic. For a more thorough discussion of this concern, see Brooks, *Representing Children in Families, supra* note 2.

14. The effectiveness of social work-based approaches has been demonstrated time and time again to address a wide range of issues related to vulnerable children and families. Professional practice journals such as Social Work and Child Welfare are devoted almost entirely to presenting this research. Specifically, family systems theory has been proven effective through research on Multi-Systemic Therapy (MST) and Functional Family Therapy (FFT), both of which have been evaluated primarily in the field of juvenile delinquency. For a detailed discussion of these approaches, see Kristin Henning, *It Takes a Lawyer to Raise a Child?: Allocating Responsibilities Among Parents, Children and Lawyers in Delinquency Cases.* 6 Nevada L. J. 836, 843–44 (2006) (citations omitted).

15. Much of this writing has focused on my work in the field of child advocacy/family law, but the ideas are equally applicable to other areas of legal representation. Perhaps the natural fit I have always perceived between my social work background and my current role as a clinical law teacher explains why the notion of a *therapeutic* jurisprudence has resonated with my sense of my work as a teacher, advocate and scholar.

for TJ.[16] This body of knowledge represents a relatively cohesive set of ideas, some of which are familiar to and have already been embraced by legal scholars and practitioners, such as client self-determination, cultural competence, and social justice.[17] On the other hand, social work principles also include important theoretical approaches that are generally unfamiliar to most lawyers, including family systems theory.[18]

Within the legal field, many practitioners may sincerely believe they are already incorporating at least some of these approaches into their work. Nevertheless, lawyers stand to gain a tremendous amount from looking beyond our own discipline and drawing upon the rich body of literature that has been developed in the social work field. This literature contains much that is relevant to lawyers' work, including how individuals function within families and the larger community. A useful way to understand this range of perspectives is the distinction that is also drawn in the TJ literature between micro-level analysis and macro-level analysis.[19] Micro-analytic TJ focuses on particular rules, procedures, and roles, as compared with macro-analytic, which looks at broader considerations, such as entire areas of law.[20]

As I have noted elsewhere,[21] the social work profession represents a synthesis of theories and practice approaches that has developed over time by incorporating elements from other mental health fields as well as the social sciences.[22] Its overarching goal is to help people to become increasingly

---

16. Madden & Wayne II, *supra* note 12; *See also* Barbara A. Babb, *An Interdisciplinary Approach to Family Law Jurisprudence: Application of an Ecological and Therapeutic Perspective,* 72 IND. L.J. 775, 788–806 (1997) (discussing the "ecology of human development theory" articulated by prominent social work scholar, Professor Uri Bronfenbrenner, and its relationship to TJ and family law).

17. *See, e.g.,* DAVID A. BINDER ET AL., LAWYERS AS COUNSELORS: A CLIENT-CENTERED APPROACH 1 (2d ed. 2004); Lori Klein, *Doing What's Right: Providing Culturally Competent Reunification Services,* 12 BERKELEY WOMEN'S L.J. 21 (1997); MARTHA R. MAHONEY ET AL., SOCIAL JUSTICE: PROFESSIONALS, COMMUNITIES, AND LAW: CASES AND MATERIALS (2003).

18. Madden & Wayne II, *supra* note 12; *See generally* Brooks, *Adoption Alternatives, supra* note 3, at 43.

19. *See* Wexler, *Reflections, supra* note 10, at 220, 226, 229–36.

20. *Id.* at 226, 229–36.

21. *See* Brooks, *Importing Social Work Principles, supra* note 2.

22. "The theories that ground social work practice are derived from the fields of sociology, psychology, economics, human biology and political science. These disciplines provide social workers with the ability to understand human behavior, development, mental health, family and group dynamics, cultures, and political processes to allow for intervention at whatever system level is warranted by an ecological assessment." Madden & Wayne II, *supra* note 12, at 496.

self-sufficient by enhancing their adaptive skills and abilities, while simultaneously decreasing existing environmental barriers.[23] The balancing of individual, community, and societal interests, as well as the systems orientation creates a solid model from which to build a normative framework for TJ.[24]

One clear source of identification of many of the core elements of social work is the *Code of Ethics of the National Organization of Social Workers (NASW)*.[25] The core values identified in the *Code* are: (a) service; (b) social justice; (c) dignity and worth of the person; (d) importance of human relationships; (e) integrity; and (f) competence.[26] Other guiding ethical principles described in the *Code* include commitment to clients' self-determination, informed consent, cultural competence, social diversity, awareness of conflicts of interest, and privacy and confidentiality.[27]

The *Code* also defines the social worker's responsibilities to the broader society, by stating that social workers should promote the general welfare of society at the local and more global levels. It goes on to state that social workers should advocate for improved living conditions and should promote social, economic, political, and cultural values and institutions that are compatible with the realization of social justice.[28]

These core social work elements are reflected in the social work literature describing the "generalist" approach to practice.[29] The literature includes many concepts pertaining to the professional relationship with the client, which is expressly viewed as offering a model for the client's other relationships.[30] The literature also defines important relationship-enhancing characteristics including warmth, empathy, and genuineness.[31]

---

23. *See id.* at 494–95.

24. *See id.* at 495. This approach is referred to the in social work literature as the "generalist" approach to social work. *See* JOHN POULIN ET AL., STRENGTHS BASED GENERALIST PRACTICE 2 (2d ed. 2005).

25. *See* the NATIONAL ASSOCIATION OF SOCIAL WORKERS (NASW), CODE OF ETHICS (1999), *available at* http://www.socialworkers.org/pubs/code/code.asp (last visited Mar. 26, 2006).

26. *Id.*

27. *Id.*

28. *Id.*

29. *See, e.g.,* KAREN K. KIRST-ASHMAN & GRAFTON H. HULL, JR., UNDERSTANDING GENERALIST PRACTICE 1 (4th ed. 2004); POULIN ET AL., *supra* note 24, at 2.

30. *See* BEULAH COMPTON ET AL., SOCIAL WORK PROCESSES 247–48 (7th ed. 2005); *see also* KIRST-ASHMAN & HULL, *supra* note 29, at 100–01. "Modeling" offers an overarching micro-level construct for thinking about client representation. *See infra* text accompanying note 40.

31. KIRST-ASHMAN & HULL, *supra* note 29, at 49–53.

Further, the generalist approach emphasizes the importance of a strengths orientation, which incorporates client[32] self-determination and empowerment. The strengths orientation, also known as a strengths-based approach, is a feature of family systems theory,[33] but has also developed into a specific orientation in its own right. The strengths-based approach emphasizes the client's inherent resources and coping abilities, rather than focusing on deficits or problems.[34] Clients are seen as being capable of change, and are partners and active participants in the change process.

The social worker's role is to help clients recognize, marshal, and enhance their inherent abilities.[35] Strengths-based generalist social work practice involves the formation of a helping relationship between a professional and an individual, family, group, organization, or community for the purpose of empowerment and promotion of social and economic justice.[36] The professional collaborates with the client and/or with the systems that may assist the client, while focusing on the client's strengths and resources.[37]

II. Micro-Level Constructs

The micro-level constructs that are compatible with practicing TJ reflect fundamental elements of "planned change" relationships that have been embraced by the profession of social work.[38] I have found many of these concepts

---

32. It must be kept in mind, however, that the term "client", when used in a social work context, does not necessarily mean the same thing as it does in a legal context. For lawyers, clients are often thought of as individuals. Of course, many lawyers represent entities, such as corporations or partnerships, but these types of representation tend to be discussed in the legal literature as aberrations to the general rules that apply to clients as individuals, rather than a fully accepted aspect of legal practice. For social workers, the 'client' may be an individual, a couple, a group, or an entire family. For this reason, the literature often refers to "client systems." *See, e.g.*, POULIN ET AL., *supra* note 24, at 8–9 (2d ed. 2005).

33. *See infra* text accompanying notes 54–69.

34. *See* KIRST-ASHMAN & HULL, *supra* note 29, at 27; POULIN ET AL., *supra* note 24, at 2.

35. *Id.*

36. *See* POULIN ET AL., *supra* note 24, at 3.

37. *Id.*

38. Planned change is "the development and implementation of a strategy for improving or altering 'some specific condition, pattern of behavior, or set of circumstances that affects social functioning,'" KIRST-ASHMAN & HULL, *supra* note 29, at 27 (citation omitted). Planned change is a process whereby a social worker engages a client; assesses issues, strengths, and problems; establishes a plan of action; implements the plan, eval-

to be useful in processing information with students that arises out of their clinical work, but these concepts are equally useful for practicing lawyers. They reflect ways of understanding and naming interpersonal phenomena. By naming them, the field of social work has created a language for considering important therapeutic aspects of our professional relationships that might otherwise go unnoticed. Naming these phenomena also normalizes them. Once lawyers recognize these as elements that commonly occur in helping relationships, they will often feel more at ease discussing them.[39]

A. Modeling

The first set of concepts relate to modeling, which offers an overarching construct for thinking about our work with clients. Social workers are taught to be cognizant of the fact that, over time, if one is doing one's job successfully with clients, the clients will begin to observe the ways one interacts with them, and will begin to mirror those interactions with others.[40] For example, a client who has a difficult time dealing with angry feelings in general has outbursts during interactions with the social worker. The social worker talks calmly and quietly to the client during these outbursts and, in doing so, demonstrates that angry feelings can be expressed and worked through in a calm, controlled manner. Over time, the client has fewer outbursts, and begins to express anger in a calmer manner as well. Perhaps even more importantly, the client also begins to deal with angry feelings differently in her interactions with others in her family and community.

Similarly, lawyers need to be cognizant of the role and positive potential of modeling. They must be aware that clients will mirror what they observe in our interactions with them in their own interactions with others. The more practitioners are aware that modeling is taking place, the more they can challenge themselves to be intentional in the ways they model.

------

uates its effects; terminates the process; and follows up to monitor the client's ongoing status. *Id.* Another term to describe this type of professional relationship is "problem-solving," which relates to the same set of processes. The term "problem" has become disfavored as part of the social work field's increased emphasis on client strengths. In this paper, I will also refer to such relationships interchangeably as problem-solving relationships and helping relationships.

39. The chosen examples are concepts that have stood out as useful in my experience as a clinical teacher, and are by no means an exhaustive list.

40. *See* COMPTON ET AL., *supra* note 30, at 247–48; *see also* KIRST-ASHMAN & HULL, *supra* note 29, at 100–01.

B. Boundaries/Limit Setting

Another useful set of interrelated concepts are boundaries and limit-setting.[41] A planned change relationship must be understood as having boundaries, both in terms of the definition of the issues to be addressed and the goals of the relationship. Early in the relationship, the definition of the issues and the goals of the relationship are established through a negotiation or "contracting" process between the helping professional and the client.[42] In that process, the professional may have to set limits with the client to clarify exactly what issues can and cannot be addressed in the course of the representation.

For instance, it is not uncommon that a client wants to know personal information about a social worker, or wants the social worker to assist the client with matters that are unrelated to their original understanding of the work they were going to do together. In these instances, the social worker must decide how and to what extent to set limits with the client and to assert professional boundaries. This is not necessarily an 'all or nothing' proposition, and it often requires processing with the client the concerns underlying the request, such as the specific reasons the client wants to know personal information, or, what has changed in the client's life such that he or she wants the social worker to take on a new role.

Awareness of boundaries and limit setting is an ongoing process in helping relationships. Clients may introduce additional issues, or issues that are outside of the expertise of the professional. Clients may also, often unconsciously, try to place the professional in a different role, such as that of a family member.

Attentiveness to boundaries and limit setting can be particularly useful for legal practitioners. Lawyers often struggle with establishing clear boundaries and with setting limits, partly because they are so eager to be helpful and to succeed, and partly because the legal culture tends to promote the notion that a lawyer should be available to his or her client at all times and under all circumstances.[43] Encouraging lawyers to be self-reflective about these issues will serve them well throughout their professional careers.

---

41. *See* COMPTON ET AL., *supra* note 30, at 244.

42. *See* KIRST-ASHMAN & HULL, *supra* note 29, at 292–97; COMPTON ET AL., *supra* note 30, at 222–23.

43. The notions of boundaries and limit-setting are an area where further attention is definitely warranted, not just in terms of how we teach students in the legal clinic, but in terms of the future of the profession. It is a well-known fact that our profession is plagued by a high incidence of substance abuse and depression among practicing lawyers. This may be an area where we can benefit a great deal from what the field of social work offers. Social workers are educated and closely supervised on the issues of limit setting and boundaries, while there generally seems to be little or no discussion of these issues in law schools.

C. Transference/Countertransference

A third useful set of interrelated concepts are transference and counter-transference. These concepts, drawn from the psychoanalytic literature, have been discussed by other clinicians writing from a TJ perspective, such as Marjorie Silver, the editor of this volume.[44] Transference has been described as the irrational attribution of characteristics to another person and response to that person in terms of these attributes.[45] It involves a client 'transferring' feelings from one relationship (usually a primary relationship such as with the client's mother or father) to another (the planned change relationship). Countertransference is the reaction of the professional to the client along similar lines as transference.[46]

In the social work context, transference often is identified in terms of a client becoming enamored with the social worker in a way that does not fit the nature of the professional relationship. Transference can also be observed in situations in which the client's response to a simple statement or question by the social worker seems intensely emotional or 'out of whack' in some manner. Similarly, countertransference would be typified by a social worker who feels a strong affinity or a strong dislike for a particular client.[47]

D. Constructs Related to the Phases of a Planned Change Relationship

Social work also offers a set of concepts that pertain to the phases or stages of a planned change relationship, and the dynamics that arise in each phase.

Instead, law students are taught about the duty of zealous advocacy. While recognizing that the lawyer's ethical duties may place somewhat different obligations on lawyers with respect to when, where, and how they can set limits and establish boundaries, the point is that regardless of the outcome, these are concerns that deserve reflection and conscious decision making.

44. *See, e.g.,* Marjorie A. Silver, *Love, Hate, and Other Emotional Interference in the Lawyer/Client Relationship,* 6 Clin. L. Rev. 259, 262–65 (1999); *supra* ch.1: Marjorie A. Silver, *Emotional Competence and the Lawyer's Journey* at pp. 17–28.

45. *See* Silver, *Love & Hate, supra* note 44.

46. *Id.* at 265–74.

47. These constructs were taught as part of the 'core' social work curriculum two decades ago when I studied for my master's degree. In scouring several well-accepted social work texts today, I could not find any reference to this terminology. Apparently, these issues are identified differently and/or are taught using different language in today's social work programs. *See* Compton et al., *supra* note 30, at 154–57 (focusing on "The Helping Person").

The four main phases within every planned change relationship are: (1) engagement; (2) assessment; (3) intervention; and (4) evaluation. Each of the phases reflects discrete tasks, although there are also tasks that are common to more than one phase.

Considering helping relationships in terms of phases offers a structure within which to understand the important tasks that need to be accomplished, and to ensure that the helping professional gives each task its due.[48] The following discussion highlights four important tasks and relational dynamics that arise during the four phases within the lawyer-client relationships. These four constructs are engagement; readiness for change; partialization; and termination.

1. Engagement

Central to the initial phase is the concept of engagement. Legal scholars often talk about this phase in terms of "developing rapport" with clients, but rapport is only one aspect of engagement. Engagement of clients involves a broader set of skills, including reflective listening, empathy, and assessment.

Lawyers can benefit by thinking about their initial goal as engagement, because it indicates that there is more to entering into the attorney-client relationship than merely developing a rapport. Legal practitioners tend to want to compartmentalize these aspects of the beginning of the relationship, rather than appreciating that all of these skills must be integrated and put into practice throughout the work with the client. They are, however, especially critical at the beginning.

For instance, a lawyer might think, "Well, I'll start the interview by chatting with the client about the weather and trying to make him comfortable. Then I'll try to move to the 'real purpose,' which is to gather the important legal facts so that we can begin to build our case." Instead, the lawyer needs to understand that the entire first interview and beyond must be devoted to engaging the client; meanwhile, the lawyer generally will still be able to gather pertinent information. If the lawyer fails to understand this principle, there is a risk that the client will not engage and will not return for the second appointment. Even if the client does return, the lawyer-client relationship may be fundamentally impaired.

2. Readiness for Change

Another key aspect of the engagement as well as the assessment and intervention phases is the client's "readiness for change," or, as it used to be re-

---

48. In this part of the paper, the focus is on individual clients, but the same is true if the client is an entity, such as a community group.

ferred to "resistance."[49] Social workers are taught to expect that, even very early in the planned change relationship, the client may seem to waver or express reticence to continue working on the issues that spurred the client to seek help. Social workers are trained to understand that it is human nature to resist change, or at least to resist the work that it takes to make significant changes.[50]

Readiness for change is an especially useful concept for newer practitioners. New lawyers often experience frustration and a personal sense of failure when a client who seemingly was desperate to obtain legal help then cancels several appointments, or is hard to reach. Of course, many things might account for a client's disappearance,[51] but helping beginning practitioners to appreciate the idea of readiness for change assists them in maintaining a professional approach to their work, rather than personalizing what has occurred.

3. Partialization

Another concept that is useful throughout the planned change relationship is what social workers call "partialization."[52] This concept can be as useful for ourselves as practitioners as it is for our clients. The idea of partializing is to try to break down a complex set of issues into simpler parts. Partialization is suggested for social workers as a tool for helping a client who feels overwhelmed to figure out where to begin. The social worker will guide the client to try to focus on just one small thing at a time, and to try to accomplish something with respect to that small thing, rather than trying to tackle the whole bundle of issues. It should be readily apparent how this concept can be equally useful to law students, who at times, may also feel overwhelmed not only by their clients' issues, but also in general by the demands of their roles as students and as student attorneys. We lawyers, too, often have

---

49. The shift in terminology seems to reflect an effort within the social work field to make the terminology more consistent with a strengths orientation. Another example would be, as previously mentioned, referring to the helping relationship as a "planned change" relationship rather than a "problem-solving" relationship. *See supra* note 38.

50. "Readiness for change" is a concept that is useful not only in the beginning phase, but also in the assessment and intervention phases of the relationship, when much of the work actually takes place. *See* KIRST-ASHMAN & HULL, *supra* note 29, at 152. For a detailed discussion of the assessment and intervention phases, see COMPTON ET AL., *supra* note 30, at 194–301.

51. *See infra* pp. 71–72.

52. *See* COMPTON ET AL., *supra* note 30, at 176–77, 218–19.

to juggle many clients, cases, and demands on our time; partialization thus may be useful in coping with the stresses of our own professional and personal lives.

These constructs complement one another and work in concert—for example, partialization and modeling. A lawyer finds himself panicking. He has just received an urgent call from a client suggesting that there is a crisis in the client's life. Now, the lawyer and the client both feel immobilized by the situation. The lawyer needs to begin by partializing the situation, first in terms of his own feelings of panic. This means breaking down what confronts him into simpler parts and thinking through what might be a first step, rather than trying to resolve the entire crisis at once. If the lawyer can internalize this technique in order to deal with his own feelings, then he can hopefully assist the client to do exactly the same thing— to begin to figure out a first step rather than a solution for the entire crisis. In this way, both the lawyer and client learn important problem-solving tools.

4. Termination

Finally, the field of social work emphasizes the importance of how one ends a planned change relationship. Likewise, it is important for lawyers to pay attention to the evaluation phase, which focuses in part on ending the lawyer-client relationship.[53] Law students in the setting of the legal clinic or externship must move through these phases with clients in a relatively short time, given that many clinics and externships operate on a fourteen or fifteen-week basis. It is often the case that the client will not have completed the work by the time the student leaves, and therefore will have to work through terminating with one student and then engaging with someone new. Moreover, many clients have experienced very traumatic endings of previous important relationships as a result of abandonment or rejection of another sort. Ending the relationship will always be difficult for such clients. On the other hand, it is also a typical part of life that people come and go and move on. By paying attention to the termination phase, practitioners can transform the ending into a constructive process for themselves and for their clients.

Lawyers often need to be made aware that ending with a client is not merely a matter of saying good-bye at their final hearing. Many fail to appreciate the

---

53. *See* COMPTON ET AL., *supra* note 30, at 303–35. This process is sometimes referred to as "termination." *See* KIRST-ASHMAN & HULL, *supra* note 29, at 277–87.

impact their relationship and their work may have had on the client even within a short span of time. Paying attention to the termination phase therefore not only assists the client, it also provides a basis for lawyers to become more aware of their accomplishments.

For instance, a student in my legal clinic was representing a fourteen-year-old young man over the course of the semester. In the student's mind, the relationship was not terribly strong. The client was reluctant to open up and discuss his feelings, and the student felt like there really had not been that much contact between them. When I first mentioned that it was important for the student to prepare the client for their ending, as well as to mark the ending with the client in an important way, the student seemed reluctant. Nevertheless, the student went along with my suggestion, and created a special ending, in which the student brought food as well as a Polaroid camera to the last client meeting, so that she and the client could 'celebrate their ending,' and the client could have a photo of them to keep. Afterward, the student acknowledged that the client was very emotional at the last meeting, and thanked the student for working with him. The relationship obviously had been more important to the client than the student initially recognized.

Appreciating the importance of termination also returns this discussion to one of the unique challenges of practicing law in a therapeutic manner. Lawyers tend to not want to pay attention to "touchy-feely" things such as saying good-bye or marking endings with clients. However, if we care about law as a healing profession, we must pay attention to the phases of a relationship, including the often awkward termination phase. This is not merely an issue for child or adolescent clients. Many adult clients also find transitions to be very difficult, and struggle with feelings of loss and abandonment based on earlier childhood experiences. These issues certainly arise in family law practices, but they arise in many other types of legal settings as well. In poverty law practices, for example, in which clients have often experienced repeated instances of abandonment and other types of trauma in their lives, endings are often fraught with significance. Indeed, even with more affluent, corporate clients, endings are important, if for no other reason than to preserve positive relationships for unforeseen legal needs that may arise in the future.

Having outlined a number of important micro-level constructs drawn from the social work field, I now turn to several key macro-level constructs that also reflect core social work elements.

III. Macro-Level Constructs

A. Family Systems Theory

Family systems theory is a holistic approach to human development, and is a fundamental theme in social work theory and practice.[54] It is sometimes referred to broadly as ecological theory or the ecology of human development.[55] As mentioned earlier, this approach incorporates a strengths-based, non-judgmental orientation, as well as an understanding of family dynamics and human development. Family systems theory advocates studying the entire family in order to understand the individual within that family, whether an adult or child.[56] The family is a system that functions in many ways similar to the natural ecosystem. Whatever one member of a family does in some way affects the larger family dynamic. Thus the whole is greater than the sum of the parts, and the individual cannot truly be understood outside the context of the family system.[57] It must also be kept in mind that the term family does not simply refer to the nuclear biological family. It needs to be defined broadly in terms of bonds of intimacy, and therefore can easily include extended family, as well as neighbors and friends in some instances.[58]

This theory provides a specific orientation toward understanding a child's best interests.[59] Since the child is part of the family system, the child's best interests are coextensive with the family's best interests when those interests are properly understood.[60] The key point here is that those interests are co-ex-

---

54. "The theories that ground social work practice are derived from the fields of sociology, psychology, economics, human biology and political science. These disciplines provide social workers with the ability to understand human behavior, development, mental health, family and group dynamics, cultures, and political processes to allow for intervention at whatever system level is warranted by an ecological assessment." Madden & Wayne II, *supra* note 12, at 496. *See supra* text accompanying notes 25–29.

55. *See, e.g.,* Babb, *supra* note 16, at 788–90. The 'au-courant' terminology for essentially this same set of ideas is "ecological theory," to make it apparent that we are concerned about the broader systems in which an individual exists, as well as that individual's family.

56. For a more detailed description of family systems theory, see Brooks, *Family Systems Paradigm, supra* note 3, at 4–8.

57. *See id.* at 5.

58. *See id.* at 4.

59. Although it is a specific orientation, family systems theory is not monolithic. There are many schools and a vast literature in this area. Nevertheless, there are some general principles and common themes.

60. *See* Brooks, *Family Systems Paradigm, supra* note 3, at 12–14.

tensive *when properly understood*; it may be the case that the family members themselves do not fully understand their mutual interests.[61]

Two important and unique concepts in family systems theory are mutual interaction and shared responsibility. Since the family is an interactive and dynamic system, everything that occurs within the family, including an individual's behavior, is attributable in some way to the family as a whole. These concepts also mean that every family member is important to what happens to any family member and to improving each family member's functioning.[62]

Mutual interaction and shared responsibility, in the family systems context, are simply descriptive of the family dynamic. They by no means imply shared "blame" or liability in the legal sense—they simply are ways to characterize how a family functions in psychological terms. Although these concepts may be difficult to appreciate in the legal context,[63] they are essential components of understanding families and how they actually operate.[64]

---

61. For instance, in an earlier paper, I discussed the well-known U.S. Supreme Court case of Parham v. J.R. *See* Brooks, *Therapeutic Jurisprudence, supra* note 3, at 960–61 (citing Parham v. J. R., 442 U.S. 584 (1979)). *Parham* concerned in part a situation in which parents "voluntarily" admitted their child to a state mental institution. Although a majority of the Court decided that no additional legal protections were needed based on the notion that parents generally act in the best interests of their children, the dissenters and many advocates agreed that this is precisely the type of scenario in which the interests of children are likely to be in direct conflict with those of their parents. *See id.* at 961. A family systems approach would suggest that the apparent conflict in such a case reflects a failure of the family members to appreciate their mutual interests. It certainly may be the case, for instance, that parents are blaming their child rather than addressing problems that exist in their marital relationship. In such a case, family therapy would be the most effective intervention, rather than a more legalistic approach that would create a further gap between parents and child, such as offering a contested hearing in which the parents and child would each have separate lawyers.

62. *See* Brooks, *Family Systems Paradigm, supra* note 3, at 5.

63. As suggested above, mutual interaction and shared responsibility are inconsistent with the general approach of our legal system. This dissonance is apparent in the area of family law, which tends to attach responsibility for acts that occur within the family to a single individual. For instance, divorce law has traditionally been fault-based, meaning that to secure a divorce, one party has to be deemed to be liable for the break-up of the marriage. Family systems theory would suggest that both parties, as well as anyone else who is part of a family system, must necessarily contribute to the dynamics within a marriage, and ultimately, whether it "succeeds" or "fails."

64. The failure to appreciate this phenomenon, I have argued, often undermines the effectiveness of legal responses to concerns such as child abuse and neglect, including legal advocacy on behalf of children. *See* Susan L. Brooks & Ya'ir Ronen, *On the Notion of Interdependence and its Implications for Child and Family Policy*, 17 J. FEMINIST FAM. THERAPY 23 (2006).

It is critical to understand these two important principles in the context of two other aspects of family systems theory. First, family systems approaches are descriptive and not evaluative, and focus more on present situations than on past conduct. Second, family systems approaches focus on family strengths[65] rather than on pathology. These last two characteristics mean that family systems theory approaches families from a non-judgmental posture.[66] Accordingly, this approach emphasizes the importance of understanding "what is,"—describing current functioning, as opposed to "why"—past history, and the need for insight.[67]

The idea of focusing on current functioning fits with notions of mutual interaction and shared responsibility because the helping professional can observe these qualities through the interactions that take place in her presence. This concept is also consistent with a non-judgmental approach insofar as the need to understand why a particular behavior exists is often accompanied by attaching blame to a particular individual. Family systems theory generally operates with the philosophy that people have unused or under-used competencies and resources that may be brought forth when constraints are removed. Together with the emphasis on current functioning and the non-judgmental approach, the competency-based emphasis of the family systems model allows professionals to empower the family and to build a positive treatment atmosphere.[68]

Family systems theory offers a framework and a thought process. It does not preference a particular outcome. There is no doubt that family members do not always act in ways that are consistent with the family's best interests. Once a family systems analysis is applied to a particular set of facts, for instance in the context of an abuse or neglect situation, it may lead to a conclusion that a family should remain intact, or that it should not, depending on the circumstances.

Further, the recognition that an understanding of the family system is essential to an understanding of a child does not mean that the child is a nonentity or should have his or her viewpoint or 'voice' disregarded. There is

---

65. Rocco A. Cimmarusti, *Family Preservation Practice Based Upon a Multisystems Approach*, LXXI CHILD WELFARE 241, 246 (1992).

66. *See* Brooks, *Family Systems Paradigm, supra* note 3, at 8. A family systems approach is completely foreign to the way our legal system operates, particularly in the area of child and family law. Our legal system is not set up to take account of family systems, but rather to focus on individuals' rights and responsibilities. *Id.* at 9–11.

67. *See* Brooks, *Family Systems Paradigm, supra* note 3, at 8.

68. *Id.*

nothing inconsistent with an approach that supports the importance of respecting what children think and feel and believe, and a family systems approach. Indeed, recognizing the importance of the family system in and of itself gives voice to what children are often unable to articulate for themselves.[69]

B. Appreciating Difference: The Role of Culture

Elsewhere, I have emphasized the importance of the integration between family systems thinking and cultural competence, which is also fundamental to social work principles and values.[70] Two other chapters in this book address the role of culture so well, however, that I will only briefly highlight a few of the many helpful ideas they offer.

Both chapters offer a great deal of practical guidance for approaching cross-cultural attorney-client relationships and interactions. Tremblay and Weng suggest a posture of "informed not-knowing" which is an orientation that respects differences, but guards against making assumptions about how such differences will matter.[71] They also offer several very useful heuristics[72] to assist lawyers in understanding, respecting, and working with clients' preferences and values, particularly those from cultural backgrounds different than that of the lawyer.

---

69. *See* Susan L. Brooks, *Re-Envisioning "Child Welfare" as a New Agenda for the Child*, *in* THE CASE FOR THE CHILD—TOWARDS THE CONSTRUCTION OF A NEW AGENDA (Ronen et al. eds., forthcoming 2006) [hereinafter *New Agenda*]. In that chapter I describe a typical example of this phenomenon, which I have witnessed in both my careers practicing social work and law. A child or young person exhibits challenging or anti-social behaviors, and the institutional response is to treat the child as the one who has the "problem". In reality, the child is simply acting out as a result of dysfunction that exists elsewhere in the family system, such as a situation in which the parents are experiencing marital difficulties. If a professional person can help the family first to acknowledge, and second, to address that other dysfunction, the young person will experience a great sense of relief, and probably their problematic behavior will subside. *Id.*

70. *See, e.g.*, Brooks, *Building Relationships, supra* note 2; Brooks, *Representing Children in Families, supra* note 2; Brooks, *Adoption Alternatives, supra* note 3. Carwina Weng and Paul Tremblay, in their chapter in this volume, acknowledge that social work researchers have been studying the interplay of culture and technique for decades. *See* Tremblay & Weng, *supra* note 1, at p. 146.

71. Tremblay & Weng, *supra* note 1, at pp. 149–50.

72. "Heuristics represent a method of inquiry which employs generalizations and maxims to guide education or a learning process." Tremblay & Weng, *supra* note 1, at p. 150. Tremblay and Weng offer several heuristics in an effort to offer an orientation to cross-cultural practice which respects differences, but also avoids making false assumptions about how differences will matter from the client's standpoint. *See id.*

Tremblay and Weng further discuss the importance of the lawyer's understanding of her own cultural background. This critical concern about the lawyer's own potential biases is also explored in the chapter by Sue Bryant and Jean Koh-Peters. Their chapter discusses six practices[73] for promoting cross-cultural communication, including Habit Four, which focuses on moments of faltering communication.

Bryant and Peters also describe three dynamics that drive cross-cultural competence. These dynamics are: (1) nonjudgment; (2) isomorphic attribution; and (3) daily practice and learnable skill.[74] These dynamics fit well with the family systems approach described above, and also dovetail nicely with the approach presented by Tremblay and Weng. Of course, nonjudgment speaks for itself, and has also been emphasized as an important feature of family systems thinking. Isomorphic attribution asks the lawyer to try to attribute the same meaning to the client's conduct that was intended by the client, rather than solely as understood from the lawyer's perspective. This dynamic requires an understanding of countertransference, as well as an appreciation of one's own cultural biases. Isomorphic attribution may also be an area in which the heuristics described by Tremblay and Weng can assist the lawyer in being mindful and avoiding the interference of her own biases.

Finally, it is significant that Bryant and Peters emphasize the importance of daily application of the skills and dynamics they discuss. Their notion helps lawyers to realize that cultural competence is neither innate nor can it be magically acquired only by a select few—instead, similar to the other micro- and macro-level constructs described in this chapter, it can be learned through thoughtful and reflective practice and constant reinforcement.

IV. Applications

We can now revisit the three scenarios presented at the beginning of the chapter, which can be addressed using a number of the constructs presented above: (a) Ms. T represents a client who misses appointments, or fails to fol-

---

73. The six practices are essentially: (1) employ narrative as a way of seeing the client in context; (2) listen mindfully; (3) use parallel universe thinking (which I refer to as reframing, *see infra* text at note 76); (4) speak mindfully, taking into account the client's culture; (5) work effectively with interpreters; and (6) apply the Habit Four analytical process continuously to identify miscommunication and appropriate corrective measures. *See* Bryant & Peters, *supra* note 1, at p. 188.

74. *Id.* at pp. 186–87.

low through in some other way after initially seeking legal representation; (b) Mr. H represents a client who frequently calls or shows up unannounced at the law office; and (c) Ms. S. represents a client who seems overwhelmed by 'extra-legal' stressors, such as financial struggles, marital difficulties, or other social or personal issues.

A. The "No-Show" Client

Ms. T's failure to keep her second appointment or to call immediately to reschedule may be attributable to a number of factors. In attempting to process this conduct, the lawyer needs to slow down and try to consider a range of possibilities, before deciding how to respond. Bryant and Peters suggest this as Habit Three, which they refer to as "Parallel Universe Thinking," in which the lawyer seeks "other possible explanations or meanings for clients' words and actions."[75] Social work parlance might describe this same technique as "reframing."[76]

One possibility, as articulated above, is that the lawyer has failed to engage Ms. T.[77] Another possibility, though, is that she is demonstrating a lack of readiness for change.[78] Typically, clients contact a lawyer when they are in a crisis or feeling some immediate legal pressure. Once they come in and are able to discuss their issues, several things may happen. They may feel some immediate relief simply by telling someone else their story. They may also realize rather quickly, although perhaps not consciously, that resolving their legal dilemma is going to involve more change on their part than they previously considered or are ready to make at this particular time. The amount of the work that will be required on their part may thus make it difficult for them to follow through at that point in time. These feelings, which are all perfectly

---

75. *Id.* at 4. They identify this habit as playing a "vital role in cross-cultural communication." *Id.* at p. 186 n.4.

76. *See* KIRST-ASHMAN & HULL, *supra* note 29, at 333, 336–37; COMPTON ET AL., *supra* note 30, at 412. Reframing is defined as viewing a problem or an issue with a new outlook or understanding it in a new way. It is sometimes also referred to as "relabeling" or "redefining". KIRST-ASHMAN & HULL, *supra* note 29, at 337. Social workers often use reframing to try to offer a more positive perspective on something that is seemingly negative. In this way, reframing can potentially help one person—the lawyer— to empathize more effectively with another person—the client—or to understand content more clearly from the client's perspective. *Id.*

77. *See supra* p. 64.

78. *See supra* pp. 64–65.

normal and natural, typify the concerns that often underlie the client's apparent failure to respond.[79]

So, how should a lawyer respond to a client such as Ms. T, who does not show up or follow through with the next appointment or phone call? By recognizing that readiness for change is an expected part of the helping process, the lawyer can be mindful not to react to the client's failure to follow through, and can take a more patient and thoughtful approach. At the same time, the lawyer may eventually need to take steps to set appropriate limits with Ms. T. Setting limits in this context would involve communicating by letter or otherwise that the lawyer is available to assist her, but if the lawyer does not hear from her by some reasonable date, the lawyer will have to assume that Ms. T no longer wishes the lawyer's assistance at this time. Nevertheless, the same communication should make it clear that the lawyer may be available to assist Ms. T at some point in the future.

Once these limits are set, Ms. T can then choose whether or not to go forward, but she also knows that the lawyer's time is valuable, and that the lawyer does not intend simply to sit and wait indefinitely for her to decide whether or not to pursue the lawyer's services. Indeed, setting appropriate limits may actually help to bring about greater readiness for change on the client's part. If, for example, part of Ms. T's resistance is stemming from some kind of transference in which she expects the lawyer to react angrily to a missed appointment, the lawyer's calm, supportive limit-setting may reassure the client and make it easier for the client to return for the next session. The lawyer's response also models for her a constructive way of establishing professional boundaries.

B. The Client Who Won't Stop Calling

Just as practicing lawyers experience clients who seem to disappear, we also have clients who seem to want to come home with us, or at least seem to need to check in with us numerous times a day, such as Mr. H. Such clients may stir up a great deal of counter-transference on the lawyers' part, because these clients tend to test the lawyer's professional boundaries dramatically. Again, the habit of mindfulness is most useful in this context as well.[80] Before re-

---

79. In the true spirit of Parallel Universe Thinking or reframing, it is also worth mentioning that a client's failure to keep an appointment may also be completely unrelated, such as a flat tire, illness, etc.

80. See Bryant & Peters, *supra* note 1, at pp. 196–200.

sponding to the client, the lawyer needs to be aware of her own emotional re-action to the client, and to be careful not to let those feelings interfere with her response to the client.

The lawyer's next step (after checking her own emotional reaction) should be to try to understand what is causing Mr. H to call frequently. It may be that Mr. H simply does not have a functioning support system, such as his own family and friends. It may also be the case that he has some other non-legal issues, such as mental health needs, that are not being addressed elsewhere. The lawyer in this situation again needs to employ the technique of reframing,[81] and also needs to continue to assess Mr. H's situation to determine if there are appropriate referrals that can be made to address his other unmet needs. At the same time, invariably the lawyer will have to set limits so that Mr. H recognizes that he cannot call as frequently as he might wish. The lawyer may also need to make it clear that she has limited time, even within a particular meeting or phone call.

Lawyers generally may not believe that they can or should set these types of limits with clients, especially if a client is paying them. However, there are at least two important reasons for the lawyer to set such limits. First, if Mr. H lacks respect for the lawyer's boundaries, it is likely that Mr. H is treating other people in a similar manner. Thus, by failing to address the issue with Mr. H, the lawyer is essentially doing him a disservice, and increasing the likelihood that Mr. H will transgress other people's boundaries and jeopardize his situation. Further, by modeling appropriate limits and boundaries with Mr. H, the lawyer may teach Mr. H an important set of skills that can assist him in other aspects of the lawyer's life.

Second, the lawyer/client relationship may suffer if the lawyer does not set limits effectively. The lawyer may build up such resentment toward Mr. H that it compromises his representation. The stress of Mr. H's demands on the lawyer's time may cause the lawyer to lash out, either at Mr. H or at others in the lawyer's life.

C. The Client Whose Life is in Turmoil

Ms. S's scenario raises some of the same issues as does that of Mr. H. Clients whose lives are in turmoil are often dealing with 'extra-legal' problems, such as social and emotional issues. Such clients, too, may not have an effective natural support system in place, which most of us rely upon to help reg-

---

81. *See supra* text accompanying note 76.

ulate our lives. Again, the lawyer needs to be assessing the client's situation on an ongoing basis to gain a genuine understanding of her situation, and to make appropriate referrals where necessary.

As described above, the construct of partialization may be helpful in situations in which a client appears to be in crisis.[82] By helping the client to try to break down the situation into smaller parts, both the lawyer and the client can experience some immediate relief, and also identify concrete steps to begin to address the crisis. In the case of Ms. S, being mindful of boundaries is also very important. The lawyer may have a genuine interest in trying to help Ms. S. with her apparent depression, but that type of professional help properly lies outside of the lawyer's expertise. Partialization combined with an awareness of boundaries on the lawyer's part may assist the lawyer and Ms. S to focus on identifying appropriate resources in the community to address her possible depression and other non-legal issues.

D. Family Systems Theory and the Role of Culture

In each of the scenarios described above, the lawyer should bear in mind the overarching constructs of family systems theory and the role of culture. For instance, if a client expresses feeling overwhelmed, in order to be effective in assisting that client, the lawyer needs to know something about the client's family system as well as the client's culture. The lawyer needs to know something about the family system both so that the lawyer can fully appreciate the potential sources of the client's stress, and also can identify possible resources the client may draw upon for support in the midst of the crisis. The lawyer also needs to know something about the client's culture to be able to determine whether and to what extent the client's expression of feeling has a particular cultural meaning, which will assist the lawyer in responding appropriately.

Conclusion:
Social Work Constructs and Best Practices

The social work constructs described in this chapter, particularly the macro-level constructs of family systems theory and cultural competence, offer guidance for lawyers who aspire to practice therapeutic jurisprudence. One

---

82. *See supra* pp. 65–66.

way to approach this guidance is to think in terms of best practices. By focusing on "best practices" we return to the question of how we pursue a therapeutic approach to representation—that is, how the social work constructs described in this chapter translate into our day-to-day representation of clients. In my early work, I identified five guidelines for child custody decision making that are consistent with a family systems approach, including making sure we identify the members of the family system, consider their mutual interests, and maintain family ties and continuity wherever possible.[83] More recently, I have defined five basic principles that I believe more fully take into account considerations of culture combined with family systems thinking.[84] Although I have identified these principles in the context of representing children, they potentially have much broader applicability to lawyer-client relationships. They are as follows: (1) respect the dignity of all individuals and families; (2) approach every individual as a member of a family system; (3) respect individual, family, and cultural differences; (4) adopt a non-judgmental posture that focuses on identifying strengths and empowering families; and (5) appreciate that families are not replaceable.[85]

First, we must start from a place of respecting the dignity of all individuals and families, and believing that, with support, most if not all families can draw upon their own strengths to provide what is needed for their children. Second, we must also approach every client not as an isolated individual, but as an essential member of a family system that is not solely defined by blood, but by bonds of intimacy.

Third, we must respect differences, including cultural differences, and not allow cultural biases or any other biases to obstruct our ability to think about clients in a therapeutic manner. Culture is inclusive of race and ethnicity, but it goes beyond those perhaps more easily identifiable attributes to encompass more subtle and nuanced aspects of family life. This aspect of best practices will generally require us to slow down in making assessments of our clients' situations. We must not simply react to things we hear about a client's expe-

---

83. *See* Brooks, *Family Systems Paradigm, supra* note 3, at 14–20. The five guidelines are:

(1) identify the members of the family system; (2) consider the mutual interests of all members; (3) maintain family ties and continuity wherever possible; (4) emphasize current status; and (5) focus on family strengths.

84. *See* Brooks, *Representing Children in Families, supra* note 2; Brooks, *New Agenda, supra* note 69.

85. This discussion is largely reprinted from a forthcoming chapter in a book focusing on presenting new models for child advocacy. *See* Brooks, *New Agenda, supra* note 69.

riences that are different from our own; rather we should approach those observations or revelations as the beginning of a learning process in which we partner with clients to understand their cultures and to try to work within their cultural norms and expectations to find mutually agreeable solutions.

Fourth, we must adopt a non-judgmental posture. This idea reinforces all of the other recommendations discussed above. But what I am positing here goes beyond simple neutrality. It requires an affirmative stance that focuses on strengths and on empowerment of clients. We must not approach clients as "them" versus "us." We must join with them and collaborate with them in their struggles and in their successes.

Fifth, we must appreciate that families cannot ever truly be replaced in the lives of our clients. This recommendation pertains especially to the situation of children who we may encounter in the legal system. Children are adaptive, and they often will be able to form new attachments, but that is not the same as replacing a parent or other loved one. Again, this should cause us to slow down, and think before we act.[86]

The point of this chapter has been to demonstrate how an understanding of social work constructs can assist lawyers who wish to practice law as a healing profession. By translating these constructs into practice guidelines, I hope it is apparent that social work constructs can guide and enrich our practice in ways that are grounded in the realities of our clients' lives, and, at the same time, are consistent with the highest values and aspirations of our own profession.

---

86. This principle may also be interpreted to state: "do no harm." Nevertheless, as noted earlier, incorporating this basic principle into decision making around children will not always lead to keeping families together. The point here is that we must recognize that there is always a cost to separating children from their families, whether temporarily or permanently, and we must fully and carefully weigh that cost in our decision making. There may well be times when we decide that the risk of keeping a particular family together is too great, and therefore the cost of separation is necessary. If we make that decision, however, we must acknowledge that the cost is there to ensure that the child receives all of the services that are needed to address the accompanying issues of grief and loss that the child is sure to experience. For a detailed discussion of the impact of separation and loss on children, see VERA I. FAHLBERG, A CHILD'S JOURNEY THROUGH PLACEMENT 1 (1991).

CHAPTER 3

Lawyer Personality Traits and their Relationship to Various Approaches to Lawyering

Susan Daicoff*

Introduction

This chapter will explore some of the empirical research on the personality traits of lawyers and then relate those traits, typical and atypical, to the

---

* Professor, Florida Coastal School of Law. The excellent research assistance of Elizabeth Roach, the able support of Holly Bolinger, and the encouragement of Professor Marjorie Silver are gratefully acknowledged. The author acknowledges that a significant portion of this chapter represents a synthesis of ideas previously published in an expanded, condensed, or different form in the following publications: Susan Daicoff, Lawyer, Know Thyself: A Psychological Analysis of Personality Strengths and Weaknesses (2004) [hereinafter Lawyer, Know Thyself; Susan Daicoff, *Lawyer, Know Thyself: A Review of Empirical Research on Attorney Attributes Bearing on Professionalism*, 46 Am. U. L. Rev. 1337 (1997) [hereinafter *Lawyer, Know Thyself*]; Susan Daicoff, *Asking Leopards to Change Their Spots: Can Lawyers Change? A Critique of Solutions to Professionalism by Reference to Empirically-Derived Attributes*, 11 Geo. J. Legal Ethics 547 (1998) [hereinafter *Asking Leopards*]; Susan Daicoff, *Making Law Therapeutic For Lawyers: Therapeutic Jurisprudence, Preventive Law, and the Psychology of Lawyers*, 5 Psych., Pub. Pol'y. & Law 811 (1999) [hereinafter *Making Law Therapeutic*]; Susan Daicoff, *Law as a Healing Profession: The "Comprehensive Law Movement,"* 6 Pepperdine Disp. Resol. J. 1 (2006); and Susan Daicoff, *Afterword: The Role of Therapeutic Jurisprudence Within the Comprehensive Law Movement* [hereinafter *Afterword*], in Practicing Therapeutic Jurisprudence: Law as a Helping Profession 465-9 (Dennis P. Stolle, David B. Wexler & Bruce J. Winick, eds. 2000) [hereinafter Stolle et al].

practice of law as a healing profession. Specifically, it will suggest ways in which these traits might impede or enhance your ability to practice law as a healing profession and is designed to help you identify your personal strengths and weaknesses, in this area. Identifying your strengths and weaknesses can lead to making better career choices within the law, both in terms of substantive practice area and approaches to lawyering.

I. Lawyer Personality Traits

The first reported studies investigating personality traits of lawyers, as compared to nonlawyers, appear in the late 1950s and 1960s.[1] The following forty or fifty years of empirical research on lawyer personality are scattered, haphazard, and incohesive.[2] However, a review of this research does suggest that there are a number of traits making up the typical lawyer personality. These fall loosely into eight broad traits, grouped into three categories: our drive for achievement or success, our decision-making preferences, and our interpersonal relating style.[3] As a note of caution, all of these conclusions may be overgeneralizations and thus inaccurate, in the sense that not all lawyers are "typical" and not all of the traits suggested by the research may be typical of lawyers. However, the general statements in this chapter are offered as guides to assist you in identifying your individual preferences and characteristics, as you develop your own approach to lawyering and the law.

---

1. *See, e.g.,* Michael J. Patton, *The Student, the Situation, and Performance During the First Year of Law School,* 21 J. Legal Educ. 10, 39–44 (1968) (discussing law students and social support); Paul Van R. Miller, *Personality Differences and Student Survival in Law School,* 19 J. Legal Educ. 460 (1967), Paul Van R. Miller, The Contribution of Non-Cognitive Variables to the Prediction of Student Performance in Law School (1965) (unpublished Ph.D. dissertation, University of Pennsylvania) (on file with University Microfilms, No. 66-4630); Barbara Nachmann, *Childhood Experience and Vocational Choice in Law, Dentistry, and Social Work,* 7 J. Couns. Psychol. 243 (1960), Wagner P. Thielans, Jr., *Some Comparisons of Entrants to Medical and Law School, in* The Student Physician 140–141 (Robert K. Merton et al. eds., 1957); James J. White, *Women in the Law,* 65 Mich. L. Rev. 1051, 1069 (1967); Seymour Warkov & Joseph Zelan, Lawyers in the Making (National Opinion Center, 1965); L.D. Eron, *The Effect of Legal Education on Attitudes,* 9 J. Legal Educ. 431 (1957).

2. *See, e.g.,* A.B.A. Commission on Women in the Profession, Basic Facts From Women in the Law: A Look at the Numbers (Dec. 1995). *See also* Daicoff, Lawyer, Know Thyself, *supra* note *, at 26–42, 46 n.55.

3. Daicoff, *Lawyer, Know Thyself, supra* note *, at 1337, 1403–1410 (1997) (identifying multiple traits in addition to those discussed here).

A. Drive to Achieve

1. Achievement Orientation

A 1984 study examined lawyers in the context of three main motivators: a need to achieve, a need for affiliation with other people, and a need for power over others. If you grouped people's basic needs into these three types, lawyers tended to need achievement much more than affiliation or power. Law library directors and judges, in contrast, tended to score higher on needs for power, perhaps not surprisingly.[5] This emphasis on achievement, as measured against an external standard of excellence, echoes the emphasis on scholastic achievement and reading found in the childhood memories and early family lives of lawyers.[6] Therefore, our primary psychological need or motivation may be to achieve.

In law school, this is likely channeled into achieving grades and honors; in practice, it may be focused on win/loss records, financial gains, damage awards, partnership in the firm, professional prestige and honors, and Martindale-Hubbell ratings. While an achievement orientation may not be troublesome per se, if it is channeled into achieving things that are scarce, it can cause a lot of frustration. For example, Lawrence Krieger has noted that if the goal of every law student is to be in the top 10% of the class, grade-wise, then 90% of students will inevitably be frustrated and disappointed.[7] Lawyers are not likely to stop being achievement-oriented, but we can redefine our achievement goals in ways that are likely to create more satisfaction and less frustration.

2. Competitiveness, Dominance, Ambition, Aggression, Masculinity

Other traits seem to echo or support this drive for achievement. Some studies suggest that we are competitive, dominant, ambitious, and aggressive.[8] For example, one study confirmed that lawyers are competitive and

---

4. *See* Leonard H. Chusmir, *Law and Jurisprudence Occupations: A Look at Motivational Need Patterns*, Com. L.J., May 1984, at 231–235.

5. *Id.* at 233–234.

6. *See* Nachmann, *supra* note 1, at 243, 244, 248.

7. He wrote: "I recently asked our entire first year class how many wanted to be in the top 10% of the class. The affirmative response from 90% of the class indicates the potential problem: if this want is perceived as a need, most of the class must eventually see themselves as failures." Lawrence S. Krieger, *What We're Not Telling Law Students—and Lawyers—That They Really Need to Know: Some Thoughts-In-Action Toward Revitalizing the Profession From Its Roots,* 13 J.L. & Health 1, 11 (1998–99).

8. *See generally* Chusmir, *supra* note 4. The term "dominance" is used here in the sense of socially ascendant or striving to the top, but does not necessarily mean controlling or domineering.

hard driving.[9] As children, we had an active approach to life and focused on self-discipline instead of submission to authority.[10] As prelaw students, we tended to score higher on measures of dominance and lower on measures of deference to others and self-abasement on standard psychological personality tests.[11] As law students, we reported that we became more aggressive and more ambitious as we experienced more stress in law school.[12] Female lawyers have described themselves as "masculine," meaning argumentative, competitive, aggressive, and dominant, and then indicated that they viewed this as desirable.[13]

These traits can be quite useful when an active, aggressive approach is needed, such as when a client needs vigorous advocacy against an intractable opponent. However, when they are overused, or deployed in the wrong settings, such as in collaborative dispute resolution, they can become obstacles to successful client representation.

3. Characteristics of High-Grade Achieving Law Students

Pessimism, distant peer relationships, and a strong work ethic may be indirectly rewarded in law school.[14] One study found that higher grade achiev-

---

9. Janet S. St. Lawrence et al., *Stress Management Training for Law Students: Cognitive Behavioral Intervention*, 1 BEHAV. SCI. & L. 101 (1983).

10. Nachmann, *supra* note 1, at 243, 244.

11. Martin J. Bohn, *Psychological Needs of Engineering, Pre-Law, Pre-Medical, and Undecided College Freshmen*, 12 J.C. STUDENT PERSONNEL 359, 360 (1971). The test used was the Adjective Check List (*Id.* at 361, citing H.G. GOUGH & A.B. HEILBRUN, JR., MANUAL FOR THE ADJECTIVE CHECKLIST (1965)). It was scored for 15 psychological needs according to a standardized system. The engineering and premedical students' scores were close to the mean on all the scales. Also, the prelaw students' scores were the mirror image of the undecided students' scores (e.g., high on abasement and deference and low on self-confidence, dominance, and exhibition), indicating that college freshmen who are undecided about their career choices have the opposite needs of those who expect to enter law school.

12. Robert Stevens, *Law Schools and Law Students*, 59 VA. L. REV. 551, 678–679 (1973). Students who felt tense throughout law school were more likely to say they became more ambitious as law school progressed. Students who saw the law school atmosphere as very competitive were more likely to say they became more ambitious as a result of law school. Students who perceived faculty-student relations as warmer and more frequent were also more likely to become more ambitious during law school. *Id.*

13. Sue Winkle Williams & John C. McCullers, *Personal Factors Related to Typicalness of Career and Succession in Active Professional Women*, 7 PSYCHOL. WOMEN Q. 343, 350 (1983); Jane W. Coplin & John E. Williams, *Women Law Students' Descriptions of Self and the Ideal Lawyer*, 2 PSYCHOL. WOMEN Q. 323, 327–332 (1978).

14. Patton, *supra* note 1, at 43–45; Jason M. Satterfield et al., *Law School Performance Predicted by Explanatory Style*, 15 BEHAV. SCI. & L. 95, 100–104 (1997).

ing law students reported a pessimistic outlook on life (good things happen to me by chance; it's all my fault if bad things happen to me), while lower grade achieving law students endorsed a more optimistic attitude (good things happen to me because I deserve them and work for them; bad things happen to me by sheer bad luck).[15] Another found that higher grade achieving law students reported that their relationships with their peers were more professional and distant in tone, while the lower grade achieving students reported more warm and collaborative relationships with their fellow students.[16]

This "work-hard, it's-all-up-to-me" attitude can be useful when it produces a strong work ethic, determination, and persistence. However, it may also produce a "loner" style and a tendency to avoid delegating tasks or relying on or trusting others. In settings where a collaborative approach with others is called for, this attitude can become a hindrance.

4. Economic Bottom Line Orientation

Most lawyers went to law school for three main reasons: an interest in the subject matter, a desire for intellectual stimulation, and a desire for advancement.[17] However, a strong fourth reason was a desire for prestige, success, and material rewards.[18] As we progressed through law school, many of us who espoused altruistic motives for entering law and a desire for public interest work found that we became more interested in private law firm practice by the end of our legal education.[19] After law school, we tended to focus on the "economic bottom line," often ignoring non-economic factors that non-lawyer individuals would find relevant or persuasive in various situations.[20] For example, non-lawyers found it important, when evaluating the desirability of an offer of settlement of a lawsuit arising from a car accident, whether the defendant drove a Toyota or a BMW, whether or not the defendant apologized, and the size of

---

15. David G. Meyers, Social Psychology 104–105 (2d ed. 1987); Satterfield et al., *supra* note 14, at 100–104.

16. Patton, *supra* note 1, at 42–43.

17. Stevens, *supra* note 12, at 575–577, 614; James M. Hedegard, *The Impact of Legal Education: An In-Depth Examination of Career-Relevant Interests, Attitudes, and Personality Traits Among First-Year Law Students*, 4 Am. B. Found. Res. J. 791, 814 (1979).

18. Stevens, *supra* note 12, at 577, 578.

19. Hedegard, *supra* note 17, at 805 n.34, 825 (finding this shift in interest occurring in Brigham Young University law students from their orientation week of law school to the end of their first year); Robert Granfield, *Learning Collective Eminence: Harvard Law School*, 33 Soc. Q. 503, 518 (1992).

20. Russell Korobkin & Chris Guthrie, *Psychology, Economics, and Settlement: A New Look at the Role of the Lawyer*, 76 Tex. L. Rev. 77, 121–122, 137 (1997).

the defendant's opening offer.[21] Lawyers ignored these factors and focused instead solely on how much money was being offered in the settlement proffer.[22] This is a "show me the money" approach we often learn in the first few years of practice, if not in law school.

However, experience shows that litigants often want more than simply money; they may want (1) an apology from the defendant,[23] (2) the defendant to make a change in the circumstances that led to the cause of action,[24] (3) a chance to tell their story and be heard,[25] or (4) a chance to participate in the decision-making process.[26] If we as lawyers focus solely on the economic bottom line in resolving legal matters for clients, we can miss the whole picture for some clients. Thus, it is critical to be able to listen carefully to the client to determine the particular client's wants and goals in the legal matter, being careful to listen for emotional, psychological, and non-economic needs and desires[27] and being aware that we may, as lawyers, be quick to dismiss these concerns as irrelevant, useless, undesirable, or unattainable.

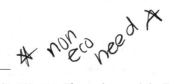

---

21. *Id.* at 101–103, 111. The apology and the "lowball" or reasonable opening offer relate to the defendant's attitude, interpersonal skills, and overall approach to others, which are clearly non-economic factors. One could argue that the car make and model are, however, economic factors, as they might relate to how much the defendant can afford to pay you. However, I would argue that the car make and model might be used to assess the effect of the payment on the defendant's wellbeing and financial position, and in that way it would be important to someone who cared about the effect of the settlement on the other. Used in this way, it can become a non-economic, interpersonal, other-oriented factor.

22. Korobkin & Guthrie, *supra* note 20, at 137.

23. *See generally* Jonathan R. Cohen, *Advising Clients to Apologize*, 72 S. Cal. L. Rev. 1009 (1999). *See also* Stephen B. Goldberg et al., *Saying You're Sorry*, 3 Negotiation J. 221 (1987) (discussing the benefits of an apology in a mediated settlement).

24. This was one of the goals of the plaintiffs portrayed in A Civil Action (Touchstone Pictures 1998).

25. Tom R. Tyler, *The Psychological Consequences of Judicial Procedures: Implications for Civil Commitment Hearings*, in Law in a Therapeutic Key: Developments in Therapeutic Jurisprudence 9–11 (David B. Wexler & Bruce J. Winick eds., 1996).

26. *Id.* at 6–7 (citing E. Allan Lind et al., *In the Eye of the Beholder: Tort Litigants' Evaluations of Their Experiences in the Civil Justice System*, 24 Law & Soc'y Rev. 953, 968–971 (1990)).

27. Steven Keeva, *What Clients Want: People who come to Arnie Herz seeking legal help leave with some unexpected solutions*, 87 A.B.A. J. 48, 50 (2001).

B. Decision-Making Preferences

Most lawyers are likely to be rational, logical, and analytical.[28] Lawyers have described themselves as "cold and quarrelsome."[29] Most lawyers tend to prefer to make decisions on the basis of rights, duties, logic, reason, analysis, and obligations, rather than on the basis of interpersonal harmony, personal relationships, or mercy.[30] As children, our families were not likely to have emphasized interpersonal relations, emotions, or others' feelings as much as other pre-professionals' families did (such as graduate social work students).[31] This de-emphasis may be evidenced in law school by an increased interest in a "rights orientation" and a decreased interest in an "ethic of care," as a decision-making style (described below).[32]

There are three traits relating to moral development and decision-making that may distinguish lawyers from the general population. These are: a "Stage 4 (Rules and Regulations)" morality,[33] a "rights orientation,"[34] and a "Thinking" preference.[35] These three traits were defined by social scientists Kohlberg, Gilligan, and Myers and Briggs, respectively.

1. Moral Development

Lawrence Kohlberg, a Harvard professor, postulated that our moral development progresses somewhat linearly through a set of six stages as we mature and develop.[36] These stages range from a Stage 1 morality of: "I'll do whatever

---

28. Lawrence R. Richard, Psychological Type and Job Satisfaction Among Practicing Lawyers in the United States 233–234 (1990) (unpublished Ph.D. dissertation, Temple University) (on file with author).

29. Heather M. McLean & Rudolf Kalin, *Congruence Between Self-image and Occupational Stereotypes in Students Entering Gender-Dominated Occupations*, 26 J. BEHAV. SCI. 142, 153–154 (1994).

30. Larry Richard, *How Your Personality Affects Your Practice The Lawyer Types*, 79 A.B.A. J. 74, 77–78 (1993).

31. Nachmann, *supra* note 1.

32. Sandra Janoff, *The Influence of Legal Education on Moral Reasoning*, 76 MINN. L. REV. 193, 226, 227 (1991).

33. Lawrence J. Landwehr, *Lawyers as Social Progressives or Reactionaries: The Law and Order Cognitive Orientation of Lawyers*, 7 Law & Psychol. Rev. 39, 44 (1982).

34. Erica Weissman, Gender-Role Issues in Attorney Career Satisfaction (1994) (unpublished Ph.D. dissertation, Yeshiva University) (on file with author).

35. *See generally* Richard, *supra* note 28.

36. *See* Landwehr, *supra* note 33, at 39–41; *see also* 2 LAWRENCE KOHLBERG, THE PSYCHOLOGY OF MORAL DEVELOPMENT: ESSAYS IN MORAL DEVELOPMENT 344 (1984) [hereinafter KOHLBERG].

I please as long as I don't get caught," to a Stage 4: "I follow the rules," to a Stage 6: "I follow universal ethical principles that transcend laws and creeds."[37] Most individuals' morality stops developing somewhere around Stages 3, 4, or 5; most never reach Stage 6.[38]

A 1992 study found that an overwhelming proportion of lawyers functioned at Stage 4, a rules and regulations-type morality, in contrast to the general American population, whose morality was scattered across Stages 3, 4, and 5 more uniformly.[39] This result is not surprising, given the law's emphasis on rules, black-letter law, rights, and duties, but it does point out how different we may be from the society and clients we serve.

Kohlberg's six-stage theory and methodology were questioned by Carol Gilligan, another Harvard professor, who argued that Kohlberg's scheme did not adequately measure human moral development and mis-measured the moral development of women, often characterizing it as a "lower stage" than men's.[40] She theorized that moral development could be assessed on a continuum from a "rights orientation," which was focused on rights, duties, and obligations, to an "ethic of care," which focused instead on interpersonal harmony, mercy, context, and avoiding harm to people and relationships.[41] While data on the care/rights dimension is limited on lawyers, there is evidence that law school strongly inculcates a rights orientation in law students. Those who come to law school with an ethic of care tend to shift to a rights orientation as early as the first year of law school.[42] Other limited research found that female lawyers with a rights orientation were more satisfied with their careers than were those with an ethic of care.[43]

Care → rights

---

37. KOHLBERG, *supra* note 36, at 175; Landwehr, *supra* note 33, at 40 n.2 (citing Lawrence Kohlberg, *The Cognitive-Developmental Approach to Moral Education, in* READINGS IN MORAL EDUCATION 44, 50–51 (Peter Scharf ed., 1978)).

38. *See generally* KOHLBERG, *supra* note 36. For example, we might think of Gandhi's behavior as exemplifying Stage 6 morality.

39. Landwehr, *supra* note 33, at 44–46.

40. John M. Murphy & Carol Gilligan, *Moral Development in Late Adolescence and Adulthood,* 23 HUM. DEV. 77, 94–96, 101–102 (1980).

41. *See generally* Carol Gilligan et al., *Contributions of Women's Elimination of Sex Bias in Moral Development Theory and Research, Final Report to National Institute of Education* (1982), *cited in* KOHLBERG, *supra* note 36, at 344.

42. Janoff, *supra* note 32, at 219–222, 226.

43. Weissman, *supra* note 34, at 107. This was not true for male lawyers in this study, but this study admits that its sample size was limited to a small number of New York lawyers, so it may not be representative of lawyers as a whole. *Id.* at 107–108.

2. Personality Preferences

Finally, a test developed by Isabel Myers and Katharine Briggs to assess one's personality preferences also distinguishes lawyers from the general population; this is the "Myers-Briggs Type Indicator," which assesses individuals' preferences along four continua: Introversion/Extraversion; Sensing/Intuiting; Thinking/Feeling; and Judging/Perceiving.[44] Thinkers prefer "logical analysis, principles, cool and impersonal reasoning and cost/benefit analyses" and are "more tolerant of conflict and criticism."[45] Feelers prefer "harmonizing, building relationships, pleasing people, making decisions on the basis of [their own] ... personal likes and dislikes, and being attentive to the personal needs of others." Feelers prefer avoiding conflict and criticism.[46]

There is more data on the Myers-Briggs preferences of lawyers than on almost any other trait.[47] Lawrence Richard's massive study in 1994 concluded that not only did Thinking predominate in the legal profession, but Think-

---

44. Richard, *supra* note 28, at 28–29. Each continuum describes an individual personality trait. For example, Extraversion and Introversion are an attitude. "Extraverts focus on the outer world and feel energized by contacts with other people; introverts focus on their inner world and often feel drained if they spend too much time with other people. Introverts are likely to enjoy quiet concentration, thinking things through, and reflecting. Extraverts like to talk things out with others .... Sensing and intuition are two different ways of perceiving and processing incoming information. Sensors attend to concrete, real world things and enjoy working with real facts and details. Intuitors would rather think about the big picture, abstract ideas, and global themes, learn new things, and solve complex problems .... Thinking and feeling are two different ways of making decisions .... Judging and perceiving are general approaches to life. Judgers prefer structure, schedules, closure on decisions, planning, follow through, and a cut-to-the-chase approach. They tend to work on one task at a time and like to complete projects. Perceivers prefer a 'go with the flow and see what develops' approach. They are the kind of people who have several projects spread all over their desks, all of which are in process, in flux, and being worked on." *See also* Daicoff, Lawyer, Know Thyself, *supra* note *, at 32–33 (citing Susan J. Bell & Lawrence R. Richard, Full Disclosure: Do You Really Want to Be a Lawyer? (2d ed. 1992)). A useful website is http://www.keirsey.com (last visited Oct 20, 2006), which provides an online test that gives the taker a rough estimate of their Myers-Briggs "type." The actual Myers-Briggs Type Indicator is available only through administration by qualified, credentialed professionals.

45. Richard, *supra* note 28, at 233.

46. *Id. See also* Bell & Richard, *supra* note 44, at 152.

47. Richard, *supra* note 28, at 238 (noting at least eleven other studies of the Myers-Briggs "type" of lawyers and law students and reporting that his study involved data on the type of about 1,200 lawyers).

Sensus: real facts

ing-type individuals were more likely to be satisfied with the law as a career.[48] In fact, he concluded that the traits of Extraversion, Thinking, and Judging were associated with job satisfaction among lawyers.[49] A majority of the lawyers in Richard's 1994 study preferred Introversion, Intuiting, Thinking, and Judging; in contrast, a slight majority of the general population preferred Extraversion, Sensing, and Feeling.[50] Other studies have found that Thinkers and Introverts were less likely to drop out of law school and made higher grades than Feelers or Extraverts.[51]

These traits—the rights orientation, Thinking preference, and a Stage 4 morality—are quite adaptive to the traditional practice of law. They tend to focus our analyses on rules, black letter law, relative rights, obligations, duties, logic, and rationality, rather than on more subjective concerns such as emotions, relationships, mercy, harmony, or nebulous "universal values." In decision-making, these traits probably produce in the decision-maker the ability to make consistent decisions, which is quite important in a legal system that relies on precedent and stare decisis.

However, these traits may be less conducive to collaborative, cooperative, or therapeutic forms of law practice, as they may discourage lawyers from considering or valuing extralegal factors such as relationships, emotional wellbeing, feelings, desires, wants, or psychological needs. Randall in 1995 stated that Thinking law students might be "likely to undervalue factors such as the im-

---

48. *Id.* at 250. *See also* BELL & RICHARD, *supra* note 44, at 153.

49. Richard, *supra* note 28, at 250. These studies taken together do suggest that Introverts were more satisfied in law school and Extraverts were more satisfied in law practice, but this may have to do with the fact that law school requires a great deal of solitary, reading, researching, and writing, whereas law practice, particularly litigation, can afford Extraverts the interpersonal contact they enjoy.

50. Richard, *supra* note 28, at 229 tbl. 91. According to Richard: (a) about 65% of the adults in the United States prefer Extraversion, whereas 56% of lawyers prefer Introversion; (b) about 68% of the United States population prefer Sensing, whereas 56% of lawyers prefer Intuiting; (c) about 60% of all men and 35% of all women in the United States prefer Thinking, whereas 81% of male lawyers and 66% of female lawyers prefer Thinking; and (d) about 55% of the U.S. population prefer Judging, whereas 63% of lawyers prefer Judging. *Id.* "Introversion and intuiting preferences are relatively stable across one's lifetime, suggesting that these characteristics are preexisting, meaning present before law school." Personal communication with Larry Richard (Aug. 24, 1995); *see also* DAICOFF, LAWYER, KNOW THYSELF, *supra* note *, at 34 tbl. 2.1. Note 44, *supra* provides a description of these traits.

51. *See, e.g.,* Vernellia R. Randall, *The Myers-Briggs Type Indicator, First Year Law Students and Performance,* 26 CUMB. L. REV. 63, 81, 92 (1995–1996).

portance of human relationships in legal problems, the human side of legal issues, the role of values in legal decision-making, and the art of communication."[52] These are often the very factors integrated into legal analysis by the practice of law as a healing profession; thus Thinkers may want to first, explicitly
recognize the importance of these factors and second, make an effort to consider them when deciding how to approach a particular client or legal problem.

For example, an employment lawyer who assists an employee in implementing an accommodation in the workplace under the Americans with Disabilities Act may or may not integrate factors such as the employee's relationship with his or her superiors, co-workers, and subordinates into the analysis
of how to accomplish the goal of putting the accommodation in place. Rose
Daly-Rooney has argued that co-worker envy and workplace dissension can
be minimized by considering workplace relations and including co-workers in
an open discussion of the need for the accommodation, rather than by maintaining confidentiality of the accommodated employee.[53] One might imagine
a recovering alcohol-dependent employee who, after treatment for chemical
dependency, is allowed to come to work late every day in order to attend daily
meetings of Alcoholics Anonymous. Co-workers who are unaware of the disability and the accommodation might simply see the situation as one of fa-
voritism towards the accommodated employee and harbor resentment against
him or her, thus reducing morale and cooperation in the workplace overall.
The relationship between the employee and his or her co-workers could deteriorate, if his or her confidentiality is maintained and the resentment of others grows. Including co-workers in the design and implementation of this accommodation can prevent these concerns. Daly-Rooney argues that this
approach can provide a better overall result for the client than simply implementing the accommodation, with confidentiality, and without co-workers'
input. It is important to acknowledge, however, that the competing concerns
must be carefully balanced. Although the lawyer should consider all these factors, and discuss them with the client, concerns about confidentiality are not
irrelevant, and ultimately it must be the client's decision whether or not to
breach confidentiality and disclose his or her status to co-workers.

---

52. *Id.* at 93 (citing Mary H. McCaulley & Frank L. Natter, Psychological
(Myers-Briggs) Type Differences in Education 158 (1974)).

53. Rose A. Daly-Rooney, *Designing Reasonable Accommodations through Co-Worker
Participation: Therapeutic Jurisprudence and the Confidentiality Provision of the Americans
With Disabilities Act, in* Law in a Therapeutic Key 371–78 (David B. Wexler & Bruce J.
Winick eds., 1996).

Lawyers who have a preference for an ethic of care or a Feeling orientation may well gravitate to practicing law as a healing profession, as these atypical traits may be assets to the lawyer engaged in this form of law practice. Feelers or care-oriented lawyers may naturally consider extralegal factors in their analysis of a client's problem and be able to weave a sensitivity to or reliance on those factors into the resolution of the legal matter. For example, they may understand the psychological need of a civil plaintiff for an apology from the defendant/tort-feasor[54] and readily combine an opportunity for a face-to-face "apology and for-giveness" meeting between the litigants into the settlement of the lawsuit.

The Myers-Briggs trait of Judging deserves a note, here. Judgers tend to prefer work involving "structure, schedules, closure on decisions, planning, follow through, and a 'cut-to-the-chase' approach."[55] Judgers may experience discomfort with silence and impasse and, due to a desire for closure, suggest an outcome or seek to impose a solution on the parties. While this trait could be very useful to the traditional litigator or judge, the ability to tolerate am-biguity, silence, impasse, and flexibility can be more important in healing forms of practice, particularly in cooperative dispute resolution. The founder of collaborative law, Stuart Webb, sometimes describes the moment of silence where everyone realizes, in a conference, that there is no agreement as a "magic moment."[56] He explains that the impact of this realization, if allowed to continue and "sink in," can motivate the participants to find new and cre-ative solutions to the dispute. They may realize that they do, indeed, want to resolve it and they also may realize that they cannot resolve it without some shift occurring. This silence, if allowed to continue, can be followed by great creativity by the parties, ultimately leading to a fully mutual, consensual, party-driven solution.[57]

C. Interpersonal Relating Style

Despite our socially ascendant, competitive, confident exterior, there is evidence that internally lawyers may often feel insecure, awkward, and de-

---

54. Jonathan R. Cohen, *Legislating Apology: The Pros and Cons*, 70 U. Cin. L. Rev. 819, 853–854 (2002).

55. Richard, *supra* note 28, at 233–234. Sixty-three percent of lawyers surveyed by Richard preferred Judging. *Id.*

56. Videotape: The Melrose Seminar (Pauline H. Tesler and Stuart Webb 2000) (on file with author) (discussing the "magic moment" at a collaborative law seminar in Dallas, TX on January 1, 2000).

57. *Id.*

fensive, particularly under stress.[58] We desire to be seen as socially ascendant and confident, but internally may be feeling awkward, resulting in an outward display of defensiveness. There is evidence that we may respond to stress by becoming more ambitious and more aggressive, which may add to our difficulties in relating to others.[59] There is also evidence that we may tend not to rely on the support of others when we are stressed, preferring instead perhaps to handle our tension alone[60] or to resort to substance abuse, which is rampant in the legal profession.[61] Thus, lawyers may not typically view interpersonal relationships as comfortable, easy, or a primary source of support and comfort.

The modern practice of law is a stressful environment; certainly, dealing constantly with people and clients in conflict with one another can be stressful as well. If legal practice and conflict resolution are often stressful, and if we tend to rely on the above coping strategies when under stress, then we may indeed often be ineffective interpersonally in legal matters and conflict situations. As lawyers, some of our coping mechanisms may result in a dominant and yet defensive posture at worst, and avoidance of people at best.[62]

Interpersonal relationships are frequently, if not always, involved in legal work. Interpersonal dynamics are integral to family law, employment law, corporate law, estate planning, mediation, and many forms of dispute resolution. Lawyers require excellent interpersonal and collaborative skills in order to successfully build lawyer-client relationships, work with other lawyers, and resolve disputes between parties. Because of this, and because of lawyers' potential to deemphasize interpersonal relations, training in interpersonal relations should be an essential part of training to be a lawyer, particularly in a healing approach.

---

58. Stephen Reich, *California Psychological Inventory: Profile of a Sample of First-Year Law Students*, 39 PSYCHOL. REP. 871, 873 (1976).

59. Stevens reported that as law students felt more tension, they reported that they became more ambitious and aggressive. Stevens, *supra* note 12, at 678.

60. *Id.*

61. Alcoholism is well-documented in the legal profession; studies consistently report that about 18–19% of lawyers has an alcohol problem, which is about twice the rate found in the general population. *See, e.g.,* G. Andrew H. Benjamin et al., *The Prevalence of Depression Alcohol Abuse, and Cocaine Abuse Among United States Lawyers*, 13 INT'L. J.L. & PSYCHIATRY 233, 244 (1990).

62. In addition, lawyers' substance abuse can lead to client neglect and malpractice. D. Muchogrosso, *Profile of Legal Malpractice—A Statistical Study of Determinative Characteristics on Lawyers' Professional Liability Fund*, OR. S.B.A. (May 1986) (internal program memorandum).

Laws: eco bottom line.

The more we value they

D. Lawyers' Values, Satisfaction, and Wellbeing

Lawyers' values are also relevant. As previously noted, lawyers tend to be focused on the "economic bottom line." Recent research, however, reveals that, when lawyers (as early as law school) begin to focus on and value external rewards, such as grades, money, prestige, fame, the approval of others, and awards, we are more likely to develop a decreased sense of wellbeing—in other words, distress and dissatisfaction. This recent research underscores the importance of lawyers discovering, maintaining, or rediscovering our "intrinsic" values—those things that are intrinsically satisfying to us.

The loss of our intrinsic values begins in law school. Law school witnesses many changes in law students, including important changes in values,[63] such as: (1) becoming more cynical about the legal profession, but also more protective of it;[64] (2) becoming less intellectual, less philosophical and introspective, and less interested in abstractions, ideas, and the scientific method;[65] (3) shifting from an ethic of care to a rights orientation;[66] and (4) shifting from a focus on intrinsic satisfactions to a focus on extrinsic rewards, as early as the first year.[67] Specifically, we become less interested in community, intimacy, and personal growth and more interested in appearance and attractiveness; as this shift from intrinsic values to extrinsic values occurs, we also become more psychologically distressed and experience an overall decline in our wellbeing.[68]

Therefore, a renewed focus on intrinsic values is critical for all lawyers. However, it may be particularly important for lawyers seeking to practice law

---

63. *See generally* Daicoff, Lawyer, Know Thyself, *supra* note *, at 69–77.

64. *See* Don S. Anderson et al., *Conservatism in Recruits to the Professions*, 9 Austl. & N.Z. J. Soc. 42, 44 (1973); Kurt M. Saunders & Linda Levine, *Learning to Think Like a Lawyer*, 29 U.S.F. L. Rev. 121, 146 (1994).

65. Hedegard, *supra* note 17, at 836–837. He suggested that perhaps some of this was attributable to law students simply becoming more interested in realistic, pragmatic concerns, rather than in abstract ideas, as a natural process of moving towards graduation and the practice of law. *Id.*

66. Janoff, *supra* note 32, at 226, 211.

67. Kennon M. Sheldon & Lawrence S. Krieger, *Does Legal Education Have Undermining Effects on Law Students? Evaluating Changes in Motivation, Values, and Well-Being*, 22 Behav. Sci. & L. 261, 281 (2004) (studying the emotional well-being of Florida State University law students and comparing it to that of advanced undergraduate students at the University of Missouri).

68. *Id.*

as a healing profession. For example, if the lawyer intrinsically values helping others or making a difference in others' lives, then there is a good fit between this form of practice and those intrinsic values. Such intrinsic values may actually be assets in the practice of law as a healing profession.

For example, as a high school and college student, I naively stated that I wanted to "help people."[69] Despite the beauty pageant simplicity of this stated goal, it held weight and importance for me then (and still does). During law school, it became clear that helping people was not highly valued by my peers; instead, the external rewards of high grades, law review, Order of the Coif, and a plum job with a silk stocking private law firm were. So, being naturally competitive, ambitious, and aggressive, and having other, achievement-oriented traits of the typical lawyer, I set about to achieve the goals that others thought were valuable. Years later, after much self-assessment, I was able to recall that "helping others" was an intrinsic value of mine, and discovered that unless my job or career contained some element of helping others, I would not be satisfied. I also discovered that "making a difference" was important to me and was able to incorporate this feature into my career as a law professor. I suspect that every lawyer needs to find fulfillment of some element of his or her intrinsic values in his or her job in order to be satisfied and effective as a lawyer.[70]

Intrinsic values can be as varied as: bringing people together, resolving disputes efficiently and cheaply, upholding individual constitutional rights, being an effective and thorough trial lawyer, helping businesses succeed, or bringing resources (rights, power) to the underdog. For lawyers whose intrinsic values are to enhance individuals' emotional and mental wellbeing or to preserve and enhance harmonious personal relationships, the practice of law as a healing profession has enormous appeal. Not only are they likely to be quite satisfied with this form of practice, they are likely to excel at it. For some lawyers who have submerged or lost their intrinsic values, training to engage in this form of practice may assist them in rediscovering those intrinsic values and incorporating them into their work in a way that promises greater satisfaction and wellbeing for them.

E. Self Assessment Tools

Therefore, it is important for each of you to identify your intrinsic values, those things that you would do even without compensation, those

---

69. 7 Oak Hall School Aerie 28 (1976–77) (Susan Daicoff's personal statement).
70. *See* Sheldon & Krieger, *supra* note 67, at 263–264.

things that are intrinsically satisfying to you. It is also helpful to identify your strengths and weaknesses, career aptitudes, and interests. The most useful tools I have found are the Keirsey Temperament Sorter, which is reproduced in David Keirsey's book, *Please Understand Me II* and is online,[71] and a series of career and vocational aptitude and interest tests administered by a psychologist.[72] Any exercise or test that requires you to assess your values, interests, and preferences can be helpful as you begin to identify your strengths and weaknesses and how they might best be melded into a professional career.

One exercise that is useful in identifying your intrinsic values is to ask yourself questions such as: What would you do, work-wise, even if you weren't being paid for it? In what part of your work or studies do you find yourself "losing yourself" and losing track of time, because the activity is so absorbing? What part of your work or study do you enjoy the most? What motivates you to get up in the morning and greet your day? On what activities or endeavors do you spend the most time?

Another exercise is to write your own eulogy; write what you would like your family to say about you, your best friend to say about you, and your professional peers to say about you.[73] A third exercise is to identify the clients and causes you would most enjoy representing and the clients and causes you would most detest representing.[74]

Identifying and understanding your intrinsic values and satisfactions can guide you toward a particular area of the law and practice setting. However, even beyond particular areas of the law and practice settings, there are choices to make about how one approaches lawyering. The next section explores different approaches to lawyering and their relationship to lawyer personality traits.

---

71. DAVID KEIRSEY, PLEASE UNDERSTAND ME II: TEMPERAMENT CHARACTER INTELLIGENCE (1998). The on-line instrument can be accessed (for a relatively small fee) online, *available at* http://www.keirsey.com/ (last visited Oct. 20, 2006).

72. G. F. Kuder, *Kuder Occupational Interest Survey* (Science Research Associates, Inc. 1991). This test is available through Science Research Associates, Inc., 155 N. Wacker Dr., Chicago, IL 60606; E. R. Strong et al., *Strong-Campbell Interest Inventory* (Consulting Psychologists Press, Inc. 1985). This test is available through Consulting Psychologists Press, Inc., 577 College Ave., Palo Alto, CA 94306.

73. *See* Lawrence S. Krieger, *The Inseparability of Professionalism and Personal Satisfaction: Perspectives on Values, Integrity and Happiness*, 11 CLIN. L. REV. 425, 435–437 (2005) (describing this exercise).

74. See App. 1 for an example of the questions one might use to explore these preferences.

II. Relationship of Traits to Lawyering Styles

A. Typical and Atypical Traits

From my study of the lawyer personality research, I concluded that approximately eight traits described the typical lawyer. These traits are: competitiveness,[75] a preference for social dominance,[76] a tendency to become aggressive and ambitious under stress,[77] an economic bottom-line orientation,[78] an achievement orientation,[79] a Thinking preference,[80] a rights orientation,[81] and a de-emphasis on emotional or interpersonal matters.[82] I also argued that these traits were likely to be assets in litigation, hardball negotiation, and vigorous advocacy before a tribunal.[83]

The atypical lawyer is likely to have one or more atypical traits. The atypical lawyer, therefore, might be altruistic, cooperative, affiliation-oriented, Feeling-oriented, care-oriented, or highly attuned to emotional or interpersonal dynamics. However, the atypical lawyer is likely to have a mix of typical and atypical traits, since it is probably necessary to have some typical traits in order to complete the rigor of law school.

For example, a lawyer with a strong Feeling preference who is also highly competitive and achievement-oriented may complete law school and pass the bar, but feel as if he or she is "swimming against the tide"[84] in law school and

---

75. Stevens, *supra* note 12, at 674–675; Patton, *supra* note 1, at 43, 44; John M. Houston et al., *Assessing Competitiveness: A Validation Study of the Competitiveness Index*, 13 PERSONALITY & INDIVIDUAL DIFFERENCES 1153, 1155 (1992); Williams & McCullers, *supra* note 13 at 350.

76. Coplin & Williams, *supra* note 13, at 327–332; Bohn, *supra* note 11, at 360.

77. Stevens, *supra* note 12, at 677–678.

78. Korobkin & Guthrie, *supra* note 20, at 77.

79. Chusmir, *supra* note 4, at 231–235.

80. Miller, *supra* note 1, at 464–466; Frank L. Natter, *The Human Factor: Psychological Type in Legal Education*, 3 RES. PSYCHOL. TYPE 55, 56–58, 63 (1981); Richard, *supra* note 28, at 233–234; Randall, *supra* note 51, at 80–81, 86–87, 91–92, 96–97.

81. Janet Taber et al., *Project, Gender, and Legal Education & the Legal Profession: An Empirical Study of Stanford Law Students and Graduates*, 40 STAN. L. REV. 1209, 1248–1251 (1988); Janoff, *supra* note 32, at 226, 227; RAND JACK & DANA C. JACK, MORAL VISIONS AND PROFESSIONAL DECISIONS: THE CHANGING VALUES OF WOMEN AND MEN LAWYERS 130–55 (1989).

82. Janoff, *supra* note 32, at 226, 227.

83. Daicoff, *Asking Leopards*, *supra* note *, at 574–590.

84. BELL & RICHARD, *supra* note 44, at 153.

in traditional private law practice. In fact, in the traditional practice of law, a Feeling orientation may operate as a liability, rather than an asset.

Most of the atypical traits lend themselves well to practicing law as a healing profession. For example, lawyers with an ethic of care or a Feeling preference might be attracted to relational modes of law practice, such as mediation, collaborative law,[85] transformative mediation,[86] restorative justice,[87] and peacemaking circles,[88] because these modes emphasize relationships and collaboration between individuals. In fact, atypical traits that are a liability for lawyers in traditional forms of practice may actually be assets in more cooperative, healing forms of law. For example, interpersonal sensitivity and psychological sophistication may cause great angst for lawyers in traditional practice, who see not only the legal aspects of the client's problem, but also the emotional, relational, and psychological aspects. These sensitivities, however, are quite helpful in practicing therapeutic jurisprudence,[89] collaborative law, and other forms of healing law practice. These lawyers may also be comfortable collaborating with non-lawyer experts, such as mental health experts, in resolving the client's problem. Finally, an inclination towards affiliation with others (contrasted to achievement or power over others)[90] might give a lawyer the interpersonal sensitivity necessary to collaborate well, cooperate with others, and assist the client in preserving the client's interpersonal relationships.

B. Lawyering Styles and Professionalism

Most lawyers have heard of zealous advocacy—this was a concept originally espoused in Canon 7 of the *Model Code of Professional Responsibility*,[91] which is now found only in one comment to one rule, Rule 1.3, of the *Model Rules of Professional Responsibility*.[92] For at least the last 20 years, the dominant method

---

85. Daicoff, Lawyer, Know Thyself, *supra* note *, at 183–184.

86. *Id.* at 178–179.

87. *Id.* at 182–183.

88. Mary Ellen Reimund, *The Law and Restorative Justice: Friend or Foe? A Systematic Look at the Legal Issues in Restorative Justice*, 53 Drake L. Rev. 667, 677 (2005) (discussing peacemaking circles).

89. Daicoff, Lawyer, Know Thyself, *supra* note *, at 180–181.

90. Chusmir, *supra* note 4, at 231.

91. Model Code of Prof'l Responsibility Canon 7 (1981).

92. Model Rules of Prof'l Conduct R. 1.3 cmt. 1 (2003).

of lawyering has been zealous advocacy.[93] However, besides the "zealous advocate," there are other orientations to lawyering that may be a better fit for lawyers with atypical preferences and values. Rob Atkinson has a very useful taxonomy of lawyers; he splits the profession into three types: Types I, II, and III.[94] Type I is the neutral partisan or zealous advocate who finds value in representing the client to the fullest extent of the law, who presses for every advantage for the client allowable, and who does not question the morality or wisdom of his or her client's chosen goal or end.[95] The Type I lawyer is criticized sometimes for being a hired gun, but this is the type of lawyer who can represent repugnant or socially unpopular clients and causes with zeal and enthusiasm. Without the Type I lawyer, the social and civil reforms of the 1960s might not have occurred. Thus the Type I lawyer is quite valuable.[96]

Lawyers who identify themselves as Type I often explain that they find value in ensuring that their clients receive their full legal, sometimes constitutional, rights. For example, a Type I lawyer might be fulfilled by zealously representing a criminal defendant who is guilty but whose confession was coerced, because of the importance of enforcing the Fifth Amendment. This type of lawyer may find upholding the integrity of the adversarial system and of the United States Constitution intrinsically satisfying.

On perhaps the other end of the spectrum is Atkinson's Type III: the "true believer." This type of lawyer cannot, in good conscience, represent clients or causes which are morally or personally repugnant to the lawyer or conflict with the lawyer's own morals, values, and beliefs. This type of lawyer by definition brings his or her own morals and values into the lawyer-client relationship and feels comfortable discussing and evaluating the morality or desirability of the client's stated goals with the client.[97] The *Model Rules of Professional Responsibility* endorse this approach, in Rule 2.1,[98] but remind us in Rule 1.2 that the client determines the ultimate goals of the legal representation and the

---

93. Carrie Menkel-Meadow, *The Trouble with the Adversarial System in a Postmodern, Multicultural World*, 38 WM. & MARY L. REV. 5, 12–14, 40 (1996) (discussing the history of the adversarial system and comparing the different rules of professional responsibility).

94. Rob Atkinson, *A Dissenter's Commentary on the Professionalism Crusade*, 74 TEX. L. REV. 259, 305, 308, 309 (1995).

95. *Id.* at 305–306.

96. *See* Monroe H. Freedman, *The Trouble with Postmodern Zeal*, 38 WM. & MARY L. REV. 63, 68–69 (1996) (arguing that, while collaborative approaches are sometimes desirable, his experience has led him to conclude that zealous advocacy can be useful in certain cases, such as civil rights cases).

97. Atkinson, *supra* note 94, at 310.

98. MODEL RULES OF PROF'L CONDUCT R. 2.1 (2003).

lawyer determines the means to those ends.[99] Thus the Type III lawyer would not undertake representation if he or she could not agree with the client on the goals of the representation.[100]

Atkinson's Type II is the "wise counselor." This type of lawyer falls somewhere in between the other two types, in that he or she considers extralegal concerns, such as his or her own morals, values, and beliefs, in representing clients, but uses them only to advise and counsel clients.[101] The Type II lawyer sees his or her role as broader than simply an advocate for the client's position; the lawyer is also a counselor, advisor, and what Thomas Shaffer calls a "friend."[102] The lawyer counsels the client as to the advisability, cost, efficiency, and moral and social consequences of the client's goals, bringing his or her experience into the discussion to provide the client with the maximum information so that the client can make the best informed decision as to the ultimate ends of the legal representation.[103]

Most lawyers, despite the ascendancy of Type I zealous advocacy in recent years, would agree that all three types are acceptable approaches to lawyering.[104] Individual differences will dictate your preference. The extent to which you are comfortable discussing your values and morals with your clients, the extent to which you use your experience, both personal and professional, to advise and counsel your clients, and your ability to divorce your work from your own personal values, all determine which of these lawyer types is likely to appeal to you.

For example, Feeling-preference lawyers are not likely to be comfortable divorcing their personal values from their work, as opposed to Thinking-preference lawyers, who are more comfortable with making decisions that do not always reflect their personal values.[105] Feeling-type lawyers, therefore, might be drawn to Types II and III as lawyering styles, rather than Type I, which might attract more Thinking types.

Typical and atypical lawyers may have different lawyer-client relationships, as well. For example, atypical lawyers might have more personal, warm relationships with their clients, while typical lawyers are more likely to maintain

---

99. MODEL RULES OF PROF'L CONDUCT R. 1.2, 1.4 (2003).

100. Or, if the representation had already begun, might withdraw from representation, if permissible under the rules, see MODEL RULES OF PROF'L CONDUCT R. 1.16(b)(4) (2003) (on withdrawing).

101. Atkinson, *supra* note 94, at 308–309.

102. Robert F. Cochran, Jr. et al., *Symposium: Client Counseling and Moral Responsibility*, 30 PEPP. L. REV. 591, 598–599 (2003).

103. *See id.* at 615–625.

104. Atkinson, *supra* note 94, at 303.

105. BELL & RICHARD, *supra* note 44, at 152.

a professional distance and firm boundaries between lawyer and client. There are advantages and disadvantages to both; the atypical lawyer might have to guard against becoming inappropriately enmired and enmeshed with the client, while the typical lawyer might be too distant and be experienced as cold and uncaring.[106]

C. Proficiency with Lawyering Skills

Atypical lawyers may find training in the skills needed to practice law as a healing profession quite easy and comfortable; more typical lawyers may struggle, fail to see the importance of some of the skills, or feel as if they are being asked to become a psychologist. For example, the ability to convey basic empathy[107] to a client may come fairly easy to a lawyer with a Feeling preference, a care orientation, or affiliative needs, due to his or her natural emphasis on people and emotions; the Thinker, rights-oriented, or achieve-ment-oriented lawyer may fail to see the point of empathy, have trouble mak-ing an empathetic statement, or feel unsure when to do so. The highly com-petitive lawyer might feel that an apology by his or her client, or any empathetic statement made by either the lawyer or the client to the other side, would be a damaging admission against interest and might avoid making them or even discussing such options with the client, even though they are precisely the sorts of communications that can foster cooperation and reso-lution of a dispute.[108]

All of the foregoing are, of course, overgeneralizations. They are offered only for the purpose of helping you identify your proclivities and inclina-tions, as you train to practice law as a healing profession. All lawyers have areas of ability in their work, or assets, and areas in which their natural ten-dencies are liabilities. All lawyers have to assess these areas and work to over-come certain tendencies. Even typical traits in traditional practice can be un-

---

106. *See* Patton, *supra* note 1, at 43–45 (finding that successful law students preferred re-lationships that were professional in tone); *see also* Janoff, *supra* note 32, at 224 (explaining that a rights-oriented person tends to value objectivity and adopt an impartial standpoint).

107. Daicoff, *Making Law Therapeutic, supra* note *, at 834 (describing empathy and how lawyers with a Feeling preference can use it).

108. Cohen, *supra* note 23, at 1019–1023, 1042–1046. Anecdotally, this seems true; I had a law student relay to me a story in which a plaintiff dismissed his lawsuit against the defendant, once the defendant expressed to the plaintiff his sympathy for the plaintiff's loss. As a lawyer, I participated in the settlement of a lawsuit that followed a similar state-ment made by the defendant to the plaintiff.

wisely extreme; for example, a highly competitive nature must be tempered, even in traditional law practice, as simple negotiations with other lawyers do not progress smoothly, and deals do not close, if the lawyer insists on every advantage.

D. Reliance on Non-Legal Experts

To the extent that a lawyer feels that he or she has all the answers, is expected to have all the answers,[109] and is expected to solve the client's problem alone (attitudes that could be fostered by the interpersonally distant peer relationships found among high grade-achieving law students,[110] by a preference for Judging,[111] a desire for dominance,[112] and an achievement orientation[113]), the lawyer may struggle with relying on non-lawyer experts. He or she may be accustomed to solving client's problems alone or may distrust the expert. However, in the practice of therapeutic jurisprudence or cooperative dispute resolution, non-lawyer experts are often needed to accurately define and deal with the extralegal considerations involved in the client's case,[114] such as: interpersonal (relational) dynamics (e.g., How well are the parents going to co-parent the children after the divorce?[115]); economic needs and resources (e.g., How will this personal injury plaintiff survive years of litigation without a paycheck?); vocational abilities and choices (e.g., What earning ability does the divorcing, stay-home spouse really have?); and intrapersonal emotions of the client (e.g., How are Elisabeth Kubler-Ross' five stages of grief[116] affecting the legal planning of a terminally ill estate planning client? Is the drug-dependent criminal defendant sincerely ready for rehabilitation or in denial and simply

---

109. Janeen Kerper, *Creative Problem Solving vs. The Case Method: A Marvelous Adventure in Which Winnie-the-Pooh Meets Mrs. Palsgraf*, 34 CAL. W. L. REV. 351, 367 (1998).

110. *See* Patton, *supra* note 1, at 43–45.

111. Richard, *supra* note 28.

112. *See generally* Bohn, *supra* note 11.

113. Chusmir, *supra* note 4, at 233.

114. *See generally* Dennis P. Stolle et al., *Integrating Preventive Law and Therapeutic Jurisprudence: A Law and Psychology Based Approach to Lawyering*, 34 CAL. W. L. REV. 15 (1997) and James M. Cooper, *Towards a New Architecture: Creative Problem Solving and the Evolution of Law*, 34 CAL. W. L. REV. 297, 312–313 (1998), *cited in* Daicoff, *Afterword*, *supra* note *, at 481–483 *in* Stolle et al. *supra* note *. (giving an overview of Creative Problem Solving).

115. Kathyrn E. Maxwell, *Preventive Lawyering Strategies to Mitigate the Detrimental Effects of Clients' Divorces on their Children*, *in* Stolle et al., *supra* note *, at 161, 165–66.

116. ELISABETH KUBLER-ROSS, ON DEATH AND DYING 2–9 (1997).

paying lip service to escape a harsher sentence? Does this client need psychological counseling or simply some coaching, to be adequately prepared for civil mediation?). The lawyer practicing law as a healing profession cannot be expected to do it all, particularly when nonlegal aspects are being integrated into law practice. Reliance on and collaboration with others (such as non-lawyer experts or even the client) to identify these issues and then deal with them properly and delicately, are necessary parts of this form of law practice.[117]

Conclusion

In summary, the available empirical research on lawyer personality to date suggests that there are a handful of traits that describe the typical lawyer, at least as compared to the general public. While these traits are not descriptive of all lawyers, by any means, they can be clues to strengths and weaknesses of the individuals making up the legal profession and may explain why, when called upon to be cooperative problem solvers, resolvers of conflict, and helping professionals, we have sometimes failed. Hopefully, this chapter has helped you identify those characteristics and preferences that may stand in the way of or foster your ability to have excellent interpersonal skills, collaborative professional and lawyer-client relationships, and a sensitivity to extralegal factors such as: individuals' needs, wants, desires, goals, resources, values, relationships, and emotional wellbeing. It may have also helped you identify your values in terms of how you want to approach the lawyer-client relationship, how you will approach your role as a lawyer, how you will approach non-lawyer experts, and to what extent you will incorporate a healing approach into your law practice.

Appendix 1

Comprehensive Law Practice Course
Daicoff
Lab 1: Self-Inventory and Self-Awareness In-Class Exercises

I. Self-Inventory

This is designed to assist you in identifying your personality traits, your decision-making preferences, and your values, via the following exercises.

---

117. PAULINE H. TESLER, COLLABORATIVE LAW: ACHIEVING EFFECTIVE RESOLUTION IN DIVORCE WITHOUT LITIGATION 43–53 (2001).

A. Decision-making Styles: *Identify which you prefer, on scale of 1 to 10:*

1. Thinking vs. Feeling as a decision-making preference (see keirsey.com for an informal test); and

> THINKERS: value justice, rationality, truth, & objectivity; decisions don't reflect own personal values; can be cold & calculating; good problem-solvers.
> FEELERS: value harmony, interpersonal relationships, praise & mercy; apply their own personal values to make decisions; seek to do what's right for self & others; are sensitive to the effect of decisions on others.

> 1   2   3   4   5   6   7 • 8   9   10
> Thinking ....Feeling

2. Rights orientation vs. ethic of care as a moral decision-making preference (can be assessed with the Moral Orientation Scale).

> RIGHTS: weighs conflicting rights & duties; seeks fairness, justice, & equality; maintains & applies rules, standards, & role obligations; arrives at clear, absolute answers.
> CARE: contextual; focuses on harm to people; seeks to avoid harm, maintain & restore relationships & protect others from hurt; decides by assessing relative harm to & vulnerabilities of parties.

> 1   2   3   4   (5)• 6   7   8   9   10
> Rights ....Ethic of Care

B. Values Sort: *Read the following values, activities, and pursuits. Rank the top 15 in order of their importance to you. Feel free to add some that are not on this list.*

___Competitive—I like to win
___Spending time with family
___Spending time with friends
___Inner peace
___Greater connection to my community
___Spending time with my children; being a good parent
___Being respected and admired in my profession
___Being good at what I do
___Excelling, achieving scholastically
___Healthy body, physical fitness
___Creativity
___Being visionary
___Art
___Music

___Sports
___Current events; following politics
___Hobbies (describe:_____)
___Marriage
___Parenting
___Children
___Family
___Extended family
___Personal growth and awareness
___Spirituality
___Relationship with God
___Harmony between people
___Environmental concerns
___Championing a cause
___Leading others
___Friends
___Knowledge, education, formal learning
___Greater professional ability, experience, and acumen
___Making money
___Being financially secure
___Nature, being in nature
___Animals
___Charitable activities, giving to others, helping others
___Others (describe: _____

_____

_____

_____

_____)

C. Values Clarification: *Write your own eulogy in three sentences, based on the following three questions:*

1. What do you want your closest person (spouse, partner, best friend) to say about you?

2. What do you want your professional colleagues to say about you?

She really knew her stuff. Was able to sell salt to a slug but in a way that wasn't forced or manipulative. She was actually an honest caring lawyer who kicked butt

3. What do you want your dependents (clients, children, others whom you lead or who look up to you) to say about you?

and made social change. She always knew how to step away and come back to us - she loved work but loved us more and we always felt short. She inspired us to be better people and I am inspired to follow in her footsteps and continue her legacy. I will. I am.

II. Professional Inventory

A. Professional Roles: *On a scale of 1 (not like this) to 10 (this describes me perfectly), rate your level of agreement with the following lawyering styles:*

1. Neutral partisanship/zealous advocacy: I am comfortable detaching my own personal values from the particular client or cause that I am representing. I am able to view my legal representation as a good in itself, regardless of the ultimate goals of my client. My client is the ultimate arbiter of his or her goals; those goals are in a sense none of my business. My job is to provide the most excellent legal representation that I can, designed to help my client achieve his or her goals. Part of my job is to give my client my professional advice about the legal aspects of his or her problem.

1   2   3   4   5   6   7   8   9   10
disagree strongly ....agree strongly

2. The wise counselor: I believe that I should clearly pursue my client's aims and goals, however, I also believe that part of my role is to point out to the client extralegal concerns (such as moral, ethical, relational, emotional, psychological, etc.) that are raised by his or her wishes. The client is the final decision-maker, however, and my job is simply to provide all the options and point out the consequences.

1   2   3   4   5   6   7   8   9   10
disagree strongly ....agree strongly

3. Moral lawyering: I am unable to divorce my personal values, morals, and beliefs from my work as a lawyer. I am most comfortable and satisfied when I am representing clients and causes I truly believe in. I am interested in working with my client as equal partners to determine what his or her best interests are and what his or her goals should be. I believe part of my job as a lawyer is to give my client my honest opinion on nonlegal matters that affect the legal matter at hand.

1	2	3	4	5	6	7	8	9	10

disagree strongly ....agree strongly

4. Caring lawyering: I believe that the lawyer and client should work together as equal members of a team. They should engage in an open, honest discussion of their individual beliefs and values to define the purpose of the legal representation. I believe the lawyer should do more listening than talking. It is important to avoid harm to people, and to their relationships, when resolving legal problems.

WTF

1	2	3	4	5	6	7	8	9	10

disagree strongly ....agree strongly

5. If none of these is appealing, write your own:

I will treat my client like a human being and with respect. I must believe the client is innocent or that the crime is not horrendous but my work is most fulfilled when the client is deprived a natural right + I can act on it

B. Personal Definition of Professional Success: *Complete the following sentences:*

A good attorney is one who *can ~~successfully~~ win the case for their client and ~~create~~ possible and in positive social change while doing it.*

A successful attorney is one who *wins*

I know I will be a successful attorney when I *grow up. lol.*

for the ultimate He client is an adult with intelligence and they have final decisions are theirs owns. I will recommend counseling if the client

~~Attempts~~ but is beyond daily interaction, but otherwise, I will leave their personal lives to themselves.

I expect to be most satisfied professionally, in my work as an attorney, when
I _learn to self care,_
balance and that is not
my job to t learn I should not
be so emotionally involved in my
cases.

C. Expected Professional Strengths and Weaknesses:

As you have worked through the foregoing exercises, you have identified your personal characteristics, preferences, and values.

1. What are your best qualities? What are those characteristics that will be your greatest assets in your work as an attorney?

Examples:
Intellectual power
Verbal persuasion
Leadership skills
Written word
Insight into human dynamics and motivations
Compassion for others
Ability to detach emotionally, compartmentalize
Ability to be rational, cool-headed in conflict or in the heat of battle
Ability to be fair and impartial with two disputing parties
Others:

2. What are your weak spots? What aspects of yourself do you think will cause you the most trouble as an attorney? What is your "Achilles heel"?

Examples:
Too compassionate
Can't detach emotionally
Can't be impartial or rational about certain clients and types of cases
Have a hard time listening to others' viewpoints
Are very confident in your ability to know what's right and wrong
Stubborn
Hardheaded
Afraid of conflict

Others:

3. Do you have explicit or conscious biases that might cause you to subtly skew your advice or cause you to treat certain matters or clients differently? Optional: describe.

I value mercy over justice sometimes. — small crimes should not require jail time

4. What kind of clients or causes would you prefer to avoid?

civil rights

5. Which clients or causes would you most like to represent?

civil rights

6. What kinds of clients or situations are going to (1) push your buttons, meaning irritate you to the point of total frustration, or (2) invite your over-involvement, meaning tread on your weaknesses to the point that you become over-invested in the situation or "in over your head?"

prosecuting youths, prosecuting long crimes, depending, wallst theives / def. corps, depending murderers / rapist / molesters

7. What do you normally do when you are extremely frustrated, irritated, angry, worried, or overly stressed with a person or situation? (What are your normal reactions and coping strategies?)

stop, breath, breath again + again + then try to be alone + or listen to jam music

CHAPTER 4

Making out the Ghost Behind the Words: Approaching Legal Text with Psychological Intelligence

Aderson Bellegarde François[*]

Introduction

The law, we are often told, "is a profession of words,"[1] and "the life of the lawyer is at its heart a literary one—a life of both reading the compositions of others and of making compositions of one's own."[2] To that end, much of the education students receive in law school and quite a bit of the training young lawyers obtain in practice is designed to nurture facility with and mastery of the written and spoken word as a prerequisite skill of all good practitioners. There is, to be sure, something absolutely right about the notion of lawyer as modern Cicero, as scholarly scribe and textual critic. After all, both as metaphor and as fact, law is indeed a text. As a metaphorical story, not only is law a communal book, in which people write and rewrite the rules by which they relate to one another and the world around them, but a people's law is

---

[*] Assistant Professor of Law, Howard University School of Law.

1. David Mellinkoff, The Language Of The Law 1 (1963).

2. James Boyd White, Heracles Bow: Essays on the Rhetoric and Poetics of the Law 77 (1985).

109

also a written totem of a culture that reveals something about the people who adopt it and the ideas they profess to honor or abhor, love or fear. As a factual matter, for all of law's importance as a catalogue of public morality and registry of social consciousness, its operation comes down to nothing more substantial than the use of words—the tiny pegs of speech and lettering on which we hang meaning. So, it would not be inaccurate to say, as others have done, that the irreducible core of lawyering is that "the lawyer must read the statutes, cases, and other documents that is his or her task to understand, to interpret, and to make real in the world."[3]

Yet, the view of the profession as a life of letters, even if essentially correct, is also an awfully limited and limiting conception of law practice. The law, it might be said, is also a profession of relationships, and the life of the lawyer is at its heart a relational one—a life of both relating to the desires of others and of keeping true to one's own. Surely, if the work of, among other scholars, Peggy Davis, Marjorie Silver, Gerald Lopez, and Ian Weinstein shows anything it is that the intellectual work of good lawyering is not just literary but also deeply social, physical, and emotional.[4] But, even when, for the sake of inquiry, one concedes the importance of the idea of the lawyer as wordsmith, the danger of abiding too literally by that view is that in many precincts of legal academia and the bar that notion is defined simply and exclusively as the ability to bring strict logical reasoning and close linguistic analysis to the interpretation of written and oral texts. Becoming a lawyer may in fact mean becoming first—though not last—a close reader of text, a practiced decipherer of language, an expert interpreter of words. However, rarely is that dexterity achieved solely through the use of logical reasoning and linguistic analysis.

Speech—both content and manner, both narrative and rhetoric—displays character and reveals the self. Every text is a representation of the individual or institution that produced it; every text is an invitation to the audience to enter into a relationship with the author. That piece of the author's self may be more or less genuine and the relationship may be so fleeting as to barely register at the level of consciousness. Still, at the end of the day what the author of any text—legal or otherwise—says to the reader is always this: *By these*

---

3. *Id.* at 78.

4. Peggy C. Davis, *Law and Lawyering: Legal Studies with an Interactive Focus*, 37 N.Y.L. Sch. L. Rev. 185 (1992); Marjorie A. Silver, *Love, Hate, and Other Emotional Interference in the Lawyer/Client Relationship*, 6 Clin. L. Rev. 259, 275 (1999); Gerald Lopez, *Lay Lawyering*, 32 UCLA L. Rev. 1 (1984); Ian Weinstein, *Lawyering in the State of Nature: Instinct and Automaticity in Legal Problem Solving*, 23 Vt. L. Rev. 1 (1998).

words I want you to understand how I see myself and how I want you to see me; by these words I am telling you how I see you and how I want us to connect. So, in order to fully engage a text, it is not enough to use analytical intelligence to, say, detect the patterns of legal precedent used in a judicial opinion, nor is it enough to use linguistic intelligence to deconstruct the narrative and rhetorical structure of the opinion. Equally important is the ability to approach a legal text with a measure of *psychological intelligence* so as to attempt to gain in the author's choice of words, style, and grammar an understanding of not just the subject matter of the text, but also of the persona behind the text. Approaching a legal text with psychological lawyering intelligence is in essence the ability to reconstruct, using nothing more than the text itself, the character or image the author of the text wishes to project and the relationship the author proposes to create with the audience.

The thesis of this chapter comes then to this: The process of reading legal texts is, like the process of reading any text, a relational act between the author and the reader—one that may take place at a human remove but one that remains nonetheless relational at heart. In this relationship, the physical distance between the author and the reader is always far less than the span of time and space would suggest, for behind the words of any text, stands, like a spectral image, the lingering ghost of the author. And, however faint may be the image of the author's self, however inexact may be the reader's attempt at making it out behind the words, and however imperfect may be the clues the image holds to the interpretation of the text, such a psychological engagement with the text is not only a necessary component of good lawyering and a faithful measure of the lawyer's intellectual versatility, but also a means of giving voice to the personhood that modern legal practice would otherwise suppress.

There is something in the modern legal study and practice that leaves many students and practitioners deeply unfulfilled about the law as an institution and their place in it as professionals.[5] Perhaps it was always ever thus; perhaps

---

5. Lawrence Krieger, *The Inseparability of Professionalism and Personal Satisfaction: Perspectives on Values, Integrity and Happiness*, 11 Clin. L. Rev. 425, 426–27 (Spring 2005); Jean Stefancic & Richard Delgado, How Lawyers Lose Their Way: A Profession Fails its Creative Minds 62–72 (2005); Michael L. Rustad & Thomas H. Koenig, *Competing Visions of Angst Among Elite Lawyers*, 2006 U. Ill. L. Rev. 475, 476 ("Despite the great interest in lawyers and the unprecedented numbers of applications to law schools, lawyers are deeply conflicted about whether legal practice fits their aspirations, values, abilities and needs."); Duncan Kennedy, Legal Education and the Reproduction of Hierarchy: A Polemic Against the System 221 (2004) (denouncing the narrowness of elite legal education and contending that "there is a lot of radical legal scholarship and scholarly activity still around for the student who is willing to look for it, even if there is not the

lawyers of every era experienced an equal measure of alienation between self and profession as do modern lawyers, who time and again report a seemingly irredeemable discontent with the profession; and perhaps the only difference between modern lawyers and our forebears is that, being creatures of a more confessional culture, we are more willing to express our unhappiness with the profession and less disposed to silently accept that unhappy state of affairs as just the way of the world. But whether our sense of alienation is a symptom of an ancient professional malady or more a sign of post-modern melancholy, it is not too difficult to speak to one of its main causes: We teach, practice, think, and write about law as though it were mainly a set of commands to manage behavior, a group of institutions to achieve policies, and a collection of tools to distribute goods. And, in this awfully instrumental conception of law, the lawyer becomes something of a hired hand, whose more or less fungible knowledge and skill may be necessary for the manipulation of gears and levers, but whose distinct identity and voice hardly register above or even matter to—and might indeed be unproductive for—the proper workings of the legal machine.

No doubt, most of this will sound to non-lawyers and many lawyers as so much navel-gazing indulgence. After all, it might be said with some justification that only a profession as socially, politically, and materially successful as lawyering could afford to devote time and energy in contemplating such narcissistic questions as *Who am I? How do I fit in? What's my role?* But the fact that these questions may at first (or even second) glance appear self-absorbed does not mean that they are unimportant, or that they do not reveal a fundamental problem with a profession that, for all of its public influence, nonetheless manages to produce practitioners who believe their private selves to be separate from, if not at war with, the practice of law. Ask most lawyers who report being alienated from their profession why it is that they should feel so estranged from an occupation upon which society showers so much power, prestige, and money, and most will probably struggle to explain that which, though keenly felt, remains ironically hard to express for professionals trained in the use of words: The law, as it is conceptualized, taught, and practiced does not seem to make room for their values, their stories, their voices—in short, does not seem to make room for *them*.

---

sense of an all-inclusive, open movement to join or rebel against. It's time for something new here too"); Connie J. A. Beck et al., *Lawyer Distress: Alcohol-Related Problems and Other Psychological Concerns Among a Sample of Practicing Lawyers,* 10 J.L. & HEALTH 1 (1995–96) (highlighting significant prevalence of alcohol abuse and divorce experienced by a cross-section of lawyers).

"People," James Baldwin wrote, "evolve a language in order to describe and thus control their circumstances or in order not to be submerged by a situation that they cannot articulate."[6] If as lawyers, for all of our linguistic sophistication, we nonetheless perceive ourselves trapped in an institutional machine over which we have no meaningful control, and feel submerged by a professional sorrow we can hardly bear to express, perhaps that is because of our unnecessarily miserly relationship with the language of the law. Language "is the most vivid and crucial key to identity: It reveals the private identity, and connects one with, or divorces one from, the larger, public, or communal identity."[7] And law, in its truest sense is (or should be) a language with which we forge communities, establish cultures, and construct meaning. To think of law not only as a tool of social control but also as a constitutive language is

> to ask what place is there for me in this language, this text, this story, and to feel that you have the right to answer, is a very different way of evaluating law from thinking of it as a mechanism for distributing social goods. The central idea is not that of goods but of voices and relations: what voice does the law allow to be heard, what relations does it establish among them? With what voice, or voices, does the law itself speak?[8]

If psychological engagement with a legal text is a means by which one may begin to make out and listen to the distinct authorial voice and identity behind the text, then by definition it is also a means by which one may begin more consciously to express one's own voice and identity in the drafting of legal text. To put it simply, the old adage holds true: to read well is to write well, and to read with psychological discernment is to write with an equal measure of emotional intelligence.

I

A. The General Concept of Multiple Intelligences

In his path-breaking work, *Frames of Mind: The Theory of Multiple Intelligences*, Howard Gardner rejected the traditional definition of a uniform and

---

6. JAMES BALDWIN, *If Black English Isn't a Language, Then Tell Me What is?*, in THE PRICE OF THE TICKET: COLLECTED NON-FICTION 1948–1985, at 649 (1985).

7. *Id.* at 650.

8. WHITE, *supra* note 2, at 42.

constant notion of intelligence in favor of what he called multiple intelligences. Gardner's theory envisioned a pluralistic view of the mind, recognizing that different individuals possess, in greater or lesser degrees, potentials for different intellectual capacities that, depending on life's circumstances and social roles and contexts, they may or may not put to use in undertaking various tasks.[9] In light of that theory, Gardner defined human intelligence as "a set of skills of problem solving—enabling the individual to resolve genuine problems or difficulties that he or she encounters and, when appropriate, to create an effective product,"[10] as well as a "potential for finding or creating problems—thereby laying the groundwork for the acquisition of new knowledge."[11]

Gardner originally identified seven distinct intelligences:

1) *linguistic intelligence*, defined as "a sensitivity to the order among words—the capacity to follow the rules of grammar, and, on carefully selected occasions to violate them;"[12]

2) *musical intelligence*, defined as a sensitivity to pitch and rhythm, an ability to appreciate the relationships that obtain within a key, the properties of a musical contour, an ability to develop schemas or frames for hearing music and complete a musical segment in a way that makes musical sense;[13]

3) *logical and mathematical intelligence*, defined as an ability to "appreciate the actions that one can perform upon objects, the relation-

---

9. Howard Gardner, Frames of Mind: The Theory of Multiple Intelligences 67–69 (10th ed. 1993).

10. *Id.* at 60.

11. *Id.* at 61. In support of this definition, Gardner set up eight criteria or "signs" of an intelligence: (1) "the extent that a particular ability can be destroyed, or spared in isolation, as a result of brain damage," *id.* at 63; (2) "the discovery of an individual who exhibits a highly uneven profile of abilities and deficits" such as idiot savants, prodigies and other exceptional people, *id.*; (3) an identifiable core operation or sets of operations, *id.* at 64; (4) "a distinctive development history, along with a definable set of expert end-state performances," *id.*; (5) "the extent that one can locate its evolutionary antecedents, including capacities (like bird song or primate social organization) that are shared with other organisms," *id.* at 65; (6) the extent that experimental psychological tasks "help demonstrate the ways in which modular or domain-specific abilities may interact in the execution of complex tasks," *id.*; (7) the extent that psychometric findings from diverse arrays of intelligence tests correlate with one another, *id.* at 66; and, (8) "its natural gravitation toward embodiment in a symbolic system." *Id.*

12. *Id.* at 77.

13. *Id.* at 107–08.

ships that obtain among those actions, the statements or propositions that one can make about actual or potential actions, and the relationships among those statements;"[14]

4) *spatial intelligence*, defined as "the capacities to perceive the visual world accurately, to perform transformations and modifications upon one's initial perceptions, and to be able to re-create aspects of one's visual experience, even in the absence of relevant physical stimuli;"[15]

5) *bodily-kinesthetic intelligence*, defined as "the ability to use one's body in highly differentiated and skilled ways, for expressive as well as goal-directed purposes" and the "capacity to work skillfully with objects, both those that involve fine motor movements of one's fingers and hands and those that exploit gross motor movements of the body;"[16] and

6 & 7) *personal intelligences*, defined as "access to one's own feeling life—one's range of affects or emotions: the capacity instantly to effect discrimination among these feelings and, eventually, to label them, to enmesh them in symbolic codes, to draw upon them as a means of understanding and guiding one's behavior," as well as "the ability to notice and make distinctions among other individuals, and in particular, among their moods, temperaments, motivations, and intentions."[17]

Subsequently, in 1999, Gardner revised his list of intelligences and supplemented it with two additional intelligences: naturalistic and spiritual:[18]

8) *naturalistic intelligence*, defined as "the core capacities to recognize individuals as members of a group (specifically, a species); to distinguish among members of a species; to recognize the existence of other, neighboring species; and to chart out the relationships among the several different species;"[19] and

9) *spiritual intelligence*, defined as a "concern with cosmic or existential issues" and "a desire to know about experiences and cosmic

---

14. *Id.* at 129.

15. *Id.* at 173.

16. *Id.* at 206.

17. *Id.* at 239.

18. Howard Gardner, Intelligence Reframed: Multiple Intelligences for the 21st Century 34 (1999).

19. *Id.* at 49.

entities that are not readily apprehended in a material sense but that, nonetheless, are important to human beings."[20]

Each of the nine intelligences is composed of what Gardner called "raw components" and, arguably, each of us possesses these components in more or less equal measure.[21] However, in different individuals the raw core components of an intelligence may evolve into the more complex realization of that intelligence when these components are put to use in the service of particular social roles and functions.[22] Thus, while to some degree every normal human being possesses the phonological and grammatical processing abilities that are the core components of linguistic intelligence, in the poet these core components will manifest themselves as a lyric ability to create images with words, while in the lawyer these very same core components will manifest themselves as a rhetorical ability to convince other individuals of a course of action.

Moreover, while, according to Gardner, it is theoretically useful to think of each intelligence as distinct and separate "building blocks, out of which productive lines of thought and action are built,"[23] in the normal course of events, "the intelligences actually interact with, and build upon, one another from the beginning of life."[24] Thus, the evolution of the core components of each intelligence into more complex capacities is determined and shaped not just by the various social functions which the intelligence is made to serve, but also by the dynamic interaction among all the intelligences.[25]

In sum, Gardner's theory of multiple intelligences first proceeds from a general rejection of the notion of intelligence as being uniformly one-dimensional and unalterably innate.[26] The theory then posits that every human being

---

20. *Id.* at 54.

21. GARDNER, *supra* note 9, at 278.

22. "At the core of each intelligence, there exists a computational capacity, or information-processing device, which is unique to that intelligence, and upon which are based the more complex realizations and embodiments of that intelligence." *Id.* at 279.

23. *Id.*

24. *Id.* at 278.

25. In Gardner's words: "We can see them operating in isolated fashion, in certain unusual populations and atypical situations; and it is the opportunity to examine these special circumstances that has permitted us to identify the core operations of each domain. But in normal human intercourse, one typically encounters complexes of intelligences functioning together smoothly, and even seamlessly in order to execute intricate human activities." *Id.* at 279.

26. *Id.* at 12–30.

possesses a small set of intellectual potentials by virtue of their membership in the human species and that "every normal individual should develop each intelligence to some extent, given but a modest opportunity,"[27] but at the same time also allows that, "owing to heredity, early training, or, in all probability, a constant interaction between these factors, some individuals will develop certain intelligences far more than others."[28] Finally, the theory concludes that, while each intelligence contains core components unique to that intelligence, the complex realization of the raw potential of any single intelligence is ultimately determined by the active relationship among the intelligences, and "eventually mobilized in the service of diverse social roles and functions."[29] "The world," Gardner reminds us, "is enwrapped in meanings, and intelligences can be implemented only to the extent that they partake of these meanings, that they enable the individual to develop into a functioning, symbol-using member of his community."[30]

B. The Specific Concept of Multiple Lawyering Intelligences

A Lawyering Intelligence is a raw Gardnerian intelligence that is "eventually mobilized" in the service of the legal profession. Since Gardner defines a raw intelligence as a latent potential or developed competence, enabling the individual to resolve genuine problems and, when appropriate, to create effective products, the Gardnerian intelligence mobilized in the service of lawyering is *a latent potential or a developed ability to solve problems or create projects in the context of providing service to a client, fulfilling an institutional role, or pursuing legal scholarship.*

The two principal requisites of a Lawyering Intelligence are that it must overlap with core components of a Gardnerian intelligence and must entail a set of problem solving capacities suited to the practice of law. Determining whether a Gardnerian intelligence is indeed suited to lawyering means examining whether the particular intelligence is composed of a core set of professional operations that can be observed, critiqued, and developed through training; whether it consists of an identifiable, though not necessarily uniform, development history, through which lawyers pass in the course of pro-

---

27. *Id.* at 278.
28. *Id.*
29. *Id.*
30. *Id.* at 297.

fessional development; whether it maintains an acknowledged usefulness in areas of legal practice or scholarship; and whether it possesses a credible foundation in the array of social, scientific, and literary disciplines whose tenets, practices, and traditions provide valuable theoretical and practical insights for the legal profession.

Based upon these prerequisites, lawyering intelligences may be divided into four distinct categories, each of which is the lawyering embodiment of a Gardner intelligence: 1) *analytic intelligence*, which corresponds to Gardner's logical and mathematical intelligence; 2) *psychological intelligence*, which is equivalent to Gardner's two personal intelligences; 3) *linguistic intelligence*, which is the lawyering incarnation of Gardner's of the same name; and 4) *bodily intelligence*, which is the lawyering realization of Gardner's bodily-kinesthetic intelligence.[31]

Since my ultimate goal is to focus here on psychological intelligence, I will leave for another time and place a full discussion of the contours and contents of analytic, linguistic, and bodily intelligence. However, for now, this much bears saying: In no way do I mean for the concept of lawyering intelligence to be taken as being substantively different from Gardner's notion of multiple intelligence.[32]

---

31. Other legal scholars have examined the implications of Gardner's theory for the legal classroom. *See, e.g.,* Ian Weinstein, *Testing Multiple Intelligences: Comparing Evaluation By Simulation And Written Exams*, 8 CLIN. L. REV. 247 (2001). Some have taken a view far different than I adopt here by expanding beyond the "Gardnerian nine" the list of lawyering intelligences. For example, Professor Angela Burton has developed a catalogue of intelligences in her article titled *Cultivating Ethical, Socially Responsible Lawyer Judgment: Introducing The Multiple Intelligences Paradigm into the Clinical Setting*, 11 CLIN. L. REV. 15 (2004). That my application of the Gardnerian intelligences would differ from that of others is, it seems to me, perfectly consistent with Gardner's own view of his theory as a never-ending project. In his words:

> [I]t becomes necessary to say, once and for all, that there is not, and there can never be, a single irrefutable and universally accepted list of human intelligences. There will never be a master list of three, seven, or three hundred intelligences which can be endorsed by all investigators. We may come closer to this goal if we stick to only one level of analysis (say, neurophysiology) or one goal (say, prediction of success at a technical university); but if we are striving for a decisive theory of the range of human intelligence, we can expect never to accomplish our search.

GARDNER, *supra* note 9, at 60.

32. Since Gardner initially proposed his theory more than twenty years ago, discussions of the practical applications of multiple intelligences to various fields have at times followed a certain semantic drift, along which any skill at which individuals or professionals excel is referred to as an "intelligence," even though the particular skill may not necessarily fit Gardner's rather precise definition of the term intelligence or meet his even more exacting cri-

One of the principal virtues of Gardner's theory is that every single one of his intelligences is scrupulously grounded in and meticulously substantiated by scientific research in biology, genetics, experimental psychology, and evolutionary history. In this way, Gardner is clear that by intelligence he does not mean "talent," "common sense," or "originality," or even "wisdom," but rather a biologically-based set of "building blocks out of which productive lines of thought and action are built."[33] In proposing a concept of Lawyering Intelligences based upon Gardner's work, I do not then presume to create a new catalogue of intelligences but simply mean to do that which Gardner himself anticipated when he noted that intelligences are *unmediated* intellectual capacities that *evolve* into more complex realizations "through their implementation in cultural tasks."[34] Since a Lawyering Intelligence is a Gardnerian intelligence mediated through the culture of the legal profession, it would not do to simply isolate certain lawyering skills and call them lawyering intelligences no matter how central those skills happen to be to the culture of lawyering.[35] Rather, as I have indicated earlier, each lawyering intelligence must track core components of a Gardnerian intelligence. Thus, by necessity the Lawyering Intelligences must be limited to analytic, psychological, linguistic, and bodily intelligences, corresponding respectively to the Gardnerian logical-mathematical, personal, linguistic, and bodily-kinesthetic intelligences.[36]

---

teria for the concept. Admittedly, in certain educational or professional environments, there may well be salutary purposes for equating a skill with a Gardnerian intelligence insofar as doing so may serve to bring respect to a needed but heretofore neglected aspect of professional training. But, it seems to me, that, when one consciously uses Gardner's vocabulary to describe lawyering, one may have a concomitant obligation to also abide by the criteria of his theory even if, as a result, essential aspects of law practice end up not quite fitting the definition of a separate and distinct intelligence but must instead be folded into one or more of the four lawyering intelligences.

33. *Id.* at 279.

34. *Id.*

35. Thus, for my purposes, I will leave aside the question of whether there exists a negotiating intelligence, or an interviewing intelligence, or an ethical intelligence, though those skills are in different ways and for different reasons essential to effective and ethical practice.

36. A word of explanation is necessary regarding the difference in nomenclature between some of lawyering and Gardnerian intelligences—i.e. psychological as opposed to personal intelligences. The difference in taxonomy is not meant to signal a more substantive distinction, but only exists to highlight the fact that Gardner's multiple intelligences are being examined through the specific domain of lawyering, and to acknowledge that, while a particular lawyering intelligence may indeed consist of core components of a Gard-

C. Psychological Lawyering Intelligence:
The Lawyer as Student of Self and Others

Psychological lawyering intelligence is an intra-personal ability to access one's range of perspective, affect, emotion, and desire as a means of understanding and managing one's behavior, as well as an interpersonal ability to assess other individuals' range of perspective, affect, emotion, and desire as a means of understanding and influencing those other individuals or institutions within which they function. The core components of this intelligence, which Howard Gardner characterizes as two separate but related "personal intelligences," consist of a lawyer's capacities to recognize and monitor human motivation and behavior, whether such motivation or behavior is driven by the lawyer's own emotional makeup or that of others with whom the lawyer is expected to interact, and whether such motivation or behavior can be observed face-to-face or needs to be monitored at a distant remove.

We all have patterns of emotions that significantly impact our behavior toward others even in the context of a professional environment. Moreover, since every social institution is created by, built upon, and functions through individuals, the emotions, biases, and prejudices of those individuals will inevitably shape the goals and actions of those institutions. Psychological intelligence recognizes that, both at the individual and institutional level, the words we speak, the decisions we make, the actions we take, are not just motivated by rational individual thought processes or by fixed institutional procedures, but also driven by such frustratingly human needs and emotions as status, ego, fear, greed, regret, ambition, friendship, and love.

To be sure, in the conventional culture of legal education, or even some traditional environments of professional practice, the notion of a lawyer needing to be *a student of self and others* is usually received with skepticism, though even the least thoughtful practitioner daily relies on some measure of psychological intelligence to, among other things, negotiate with colleagues,

---

nerian intelligence, the lawyering enculturation of the intelligence necessarily means that it may not contain every one of the core components of that intelligence as Gardner defines it. For example, among the core components of linguistic intelligence is a "sensory" sensitivity to "the sounds, rhythms, inflections and meters of words—that ability which can make even poetry in a foreign tongue beautiful to hear." While the lawyering incarnation of linguistic intelligence does consist in part to a sensitivity to the sheer beauty of words insofar as that beauty may increase the rhetorical impact on a legal audience, it remains that the lawyer's sensitivity to the poetics of language need not—and in most instances does not—extend as far as that of the poet.

counsel clients, plan an appearance before a judge, or even supervise junior associates. Still, it is all too rare for many practitioners and some scholars to explicitly refer to these activities in terms of *psychological* intelligence. Perhaps this has less to do with a substantive rejection of the notion of psychological intelligence than with a cultural antipathy to the vocabulary of emotions and psychology, as well as with an understandable suspicion against lawyers using psychological techniques and tools with which they barely have a rudimentary familiarity. If so, psychological intelligence in no way asks the lawyer to assume the role of therapist or other cognitive professional for which the lawyer is not trained. Even in the case of an individual client, whose problems may require solutions that are not strictly law-based, the lawyer may not under the guise of exercising psychological intelligence counsel the client in ways and about matters that go beyond the lawyer's expertise and training; a lawyer is not a priest, therapist, or social worker and should not try to be. But any lawyer with any degree of self-awareness knows perfectly well that, for good or for ill, his or her actions are often driven by psychological desires barely within the lawyer's comprehension, and that his or her interactions with others are often shaped by emotional forces barely within the lawyer's control; what is true of the lawyer as an individual is no less so of others with, for or against whom the lawyer works.[37] In this sense, psychological intelligence merely requires the lawyer to develop and cultivate a measure of judgment about how psychological dynamics present in all human interaction shape legal actions and discourse.

II

A. Approaching Legal Text with Psychological Intelligence

By now it is a commonplace that psychological intelligence is called for whenever lawyers engage with other human beings.[38] Whether the lawyer is

---

37. *See* Linda Mills, *Affective Lawyering: The Emotional Dimensions of the Lawyer-Client Relation, in* PRACTICING THERAPEUTIC JURISPRUDENCE: LAW AS A HELPING PROFESSION 419 (Stolle et al. eds., 2000).

38. DAVID F. CHAVKIN, CLINICAL LEGAL EDUCATION: A TEXTBOOK FOR LAW SCHOOL CLINICAL LEGAL PROGRAMS 127 (2002).

interviewing a witness,[39] counseling a client,[40] picking a jury,[41] negotiating against opposing counsel, or participating in a mediation session,[42] it is usually taken for granted that the outcome of the interaction will be determined not just by the substantive legal and factual issues involved, and not just by the structural format of the interaction, but also by the psychological dynamics at play.[43]

Even human interactions that take place in the choreographed atmosphere of work are marked by complex sets of psychodynamic forces that serve to both bridge and create distance between people. When, in the course of their professional obligations, lawyers engage with others, they enter, however fleetingly, into relationships whose outer boundaries may appear generic and superficial, but whose inner dynamics are as unique and profound as those of any personal relationship. In these lawyering relationships—as in personal ones—individuals come with unique modes of communication, narratives, emotions, and values, and unique sets of professional, emotional, cultural, and political baggage such that whenever one person tries to communicate with another, something always gets lost in translation. Differences (or similarities) in personal history, belief systems, class, race, sex, and other social markers operate as filters through which each person sees and understands the other, and each person has to assume the impossible burden of cutting across these barriers and connecting with another, whose thoughts and reality they can never, in spite of all best efforts and intentions, truly and fully know or understand.

---

39. *See* Gisli H. Gudjonsson, The Psychology of Interrogations, Confessions and Testimony (1992).

40. Carolyn Copps Hartley & Carrie J. Petrucci, *Practicing Therapeutic Jurisprudence: A Collaboration Between Social Work and Law*, 14 Wash. U. J.L. & Pol'y 133 (2004).

41. *See generally* Antony Page, *Batson's Blind-Spot: Unconscious Stereotyping and the Preemptory Challenge*, 85 B.U. L. Rev. 155 (2005); Michael Owen Miller & Thomas A. Mauet, *The Psychology of Jury Persuasion*, 22 Am. J. Trial Advoc. 549 (1999).

42. *See* Clark Freshman, *The Lawyer-Negotiator as Mood Scientist: What We Know and Don't Know about How Mood Relates to Successful Negotiation*, 2002 J. Disp. Resol. 1.

43. As Marjorie Silver states, "lawyers must acknowledge that emotional responses are triggered in virtually every human encounter. The goal need not be—indeed could not be—to eradicate these responses. Rather the goal should be to recognize them, analyze how, if at all, they may affect the lawyer/client relationship, and resolve them appropriately. Therefore the lawyer must understand the dynamics of transference and counter-transference in lawyer/client relationships. Whether or not we so acknowledge, our unconscious exerts powerful force on our thoughts and actions." Silver, *supra* note 4, at 275. *See supra* ch. 1: Marjorie A. Silver, *Emotional Competence and the Lawyer's Journey*, at p. 13.

But that psychological distance is not just the result of unconscious and innate differences between people; it is also created by the quite conscious and quite practiced desire we all have to deliberately create and control the image of ourselves in the eyes of those with whom we interact. All of us approach even the most fleeting of encounters as an opportunity to shape the way the world perceives, understands, and appreciates us. Put any two people in a room together and charge them with accomplishing a specific task and the results will be that their interaction will operate on two distinct levels: At one level they may more or less successfully achieve the task at hand; at another barely hidden level they will furiously play out minor psychological dramas designed to shape the image of how each sees the other. Often that image will have little to do with who the other person "really" is or what is "really" going on in the room, but will greatly be affected by the nearly automatic processes of transference and counter-transference, pursuant to which we project unto others and others project unto us attitudes and associations from past relationships.[44] Still, whether the attempt is worthwhile or futile, there is present in every human interaction the desire to make the world see and believe in our imagined self. A witness does not take the stand just to tell the facts that he or she knows and remembers, but also to put out to the courtroom the persona that he or she has over the years crafted for himself or herself. Similarly, a lawyer does not counsel a client just to help solve the problem at hand, but also to project the image of the professional the lawyer imagines himself or herself to be. In this sense, every interaction is an opportunity to say: *Here is who I am and who I want to be, and here is how I want you to see and remember me.*

Nowhere is the need to project one's psychological persona to and establish a relationship with an audience more evident than in written texts.[45] That is, even the most formalistic of written legal document is both a projection of the psychological persona of the author and an invitation to the audience to establish a relationship with the author on the basis of that professed persona. In this, legal writing is no different than any other genre of writing. What makes an epic poem an epic poem, a mystery novel a mystery novel, or a political speech a political speech is not just that each meets the expectations of their audience by following a fairly set formula, but also that each reveals important traits the author has or desires to have and that, in the very choice of words, grammar, and style, each text is an attempt at convincing the audience

---

44. *Id.*

45. Anthony G. Amsterdam & Jerome Bruner, Minding the Law 165–193 (2000).

that the author possesses those traits. Similarly, what makes a judicial opinion a judicial opinion, or a brief a brief, is not just that each follows a prescribed format, but that each may reveal a personal or institutional portrait of the author. In other words, behind the words of any written legal text stands, like a ghostly avatar, the self the author wishes to project or sometimes cannot help but projecting, and learning to make out the psychological avatar behind the words holds an important clue for understanding the text. As professor James Boyd White explained in the context of rhetorical argument:

> Every time one speaks as a lawyer, one establishes for the moment a character—an ethical identity, or what the Greeks called an ethos—for oneself, for one's audience, and for those one talks about, and proposes a relationship with them. The lawyer's speech is thus always implicitly argumentative not only about the result—how should the case be decided?—and the language—in what terms should it be defined and talked about?—but about the rhetorical community of which one is at that moment a part. One is always establishing in performance a response to the question "What kind of community should we who are talking the language of the law establish with each other, with our clients, and with the rest of the world? What kind of conversation should the law constitute, should constitute the law?

Approaching a legal text with psychological lawyering intelligence is then an attempt to reconstruct, using nothing more than the text itself, the character or "ethos" of the author, and the relationship the author proposes to create with the audience. This attempt at recreating the author's character and understanding the relationship with the audience does not alone hold the key to unlocking the meaning of the text but, together with disciplined analytical and linguistic interpretation, this psychological reconstruction may provide a fuller understanding of the text. Thus, when interpreting, say, a written judicial text it is not enough to use analytical intelligence to detect the patterns of legal precedent used in the text, nor is it enough to use linguistic intelligence to deconstruct the narrative and rhetorical structure of the text. Equally important is the ability to use a measure of psychological intelligence to monitor and recognize the implicit values, beliefs, and accepted wisdoms, and unspoken personal motives the author attempts to illuminate or conceal in his or her choice of words, grammar, and style. That psychological reconstruction may be accurate or flat out wrong, may get to a deeper textual truth, or may result in nothing but shallow psychoanalysis, may, in a phrase, succeed or fail. But, that approaching a text with psychological intelligence may lead to faulty or empty conclusions is no reason to eschew the attempt itself since the same dangers apply to logical and linguistic approaches to legal interpretation.

Speaking of the use of rhetoric in written text, the critic Wayne C. Booth writes that "an author cannot choose to avoid rhetoric; he can choose only the kind of rhetoric he will employ."[46] Similarly, an author cannot choose to erase all traces of the ghost behind the written text; he or she can choose only its shape and features.

B. An Example of Using Psychological Intelligence in the Interpretation of Written Texts

Consider three texts, each describing an automobile accident; the first is an excerpt from *Henningsen v. Bloomfield, Inc.*,[47] a key decision in the development of the law of products liability; second is an excerpt from *The Great Gatsby*, in which F. Scott Fitzgerald describes the scene of the automobile accident, the consequences of which will ultimately lead to the death of the main character, Jay Gatsby;[48] and third are the full lyrics of a song by Bruce Springsteen, describing a motorist's reaction upon coming to a fatal automobile accident on the highway.[49]

1. Henningsen v. Bloomfield Motors, Inc.

Henningsen was decided in 1960 and tells the story of Claus H. Henningsen, who purchased a new Chrysler automobile from Bloomfield Motors, Inc., a New Jersey car dealership, as a mother's day present for his wife, Helen Henningsen. After the car apparently malfunctioned and caused Mrs. Henningsen to crash into a highway embankment, the Henningsens sued the manufacturer and dealer, claiming negligence and breach of express and implied warranties. At trial, the negligence counts were dismissed and the case submitted to the jury solely on the theory of breach of implied warranty of merchantability. The jury returned verdicts in favor of plaintiffs. Defendants appealed and plaintiffs cross-appealed from the dismissal of their negligence claim. The Supreme Court certified the case prior to consideration in the Appellate Division.

Since, Mr. Henningsen had purchased the car from Bloomfield Motors rather than Chrysler, the main issue on appeal was whether in a products li-

---

46. Wayne C. Booth, The Rhetoric of Fiction 149 (2d ed. 1983).

47. 32 N.J. 358, 161 A.2d 69 (1960).

48. F. Scott Fitzgerald, The Great Gatsby (1925).

49. Bruce Springsteen, *Wreck on the Highway, on* The River (Sony 1980).

ability claim based on the contractual doctrine of warranty breach, a manufacturer was liable to the ultimate user of a product for a manufacturing defect in the absence of a direct contractual privity relationship between the consumer and the manufacturer. In siding with the consumer, the Supreme Court essentially did away with the privity requirements in product liability cases and reasoned as follows:

> Under modern conditions the ordinary layman, on responding to the importuning of colorful advertising, has neither the opportunity nor the capacity to inspect or to determine the fitness of an automobile for use; he must rely on the manufacturer who has control of its construction, and to some degree on the dealer who, to the limited extent called for by the manufacturer's instructions, inspects and services it before delivery. In such a marketing milieu his remedies and those of persons who properly claim through him should not depend 'upon the intricacies of the law of sales. The obligation of the manufacturer should not be based alone on privity of contract. It should rest, as was once said, upon the "demands of social justice."[50]

The above summary of the decision is offered merely to help frame the discussion but for our purposes, the key passage of the opinion is the Court's description of the accident that caused Mrs. Henningsen's injuries:

> *The new Plymouth was turned over to the Henningsens on May 9, 1955. No proof was adduced by the dealer to show precisely what was done in the way of mechanical or road testing beyond testimony that the manufacturer's instructions were probably followed. Mr. Henningsen drove it from the dealer's place of business in Bloomfield to their home in Keansburg. On the trip nothing unusual appeared in the way in which it operated. Thereafter, it was used for short trips on paved streets about the town. It had no servicing and no mishaps of any kind before the event of May 19. That day, Mrs. Henningsen drove to Asbury Park. On the way down and in returning the car performed in normal fashion until the accident occurred. She was proceeding north on Route 36 in Highlands, New Jersey, at 20—22 miles per hour. The highway was paved and smooth, and contained two lanes for northbound travel. She was riding in the right-hand lane. Suddenly she heard a loud noise "from the bottom, by the hood." It "felt as if something cracked." The steering*

---

50. *See Henningsen*, 161 A.2d at 83 (1960) (citation omitted).

wheel spun in her hands; the car veered sharply to the right and crashed into a highway sign and a brick wall. No other vehicle was in any way involved. A bus operator driving in the left-hand lane testified that he observed plaintiffs' car approaching in normal fashion in the opposite direction; "all of a sudden (it) veered at 90 degrees and right into this wall." As a result of the impact, the front of the car was so badly damaged that it was impossible to determine if any of the parts of the steering wheel mechanism or workmanship or assembly were defective or improper prior to the accident. The condition was such that the collision insurance carrier, after inspection, declared the vehicle a total loss. It had 468 miles on the speedometer at the time.[51]

If speech is character, then lawyers learn early to recognize in the words of the typical judicial opinion individual and institutional authors who are, or wish to appear to be, careful, meticulous, dispassionate, fixated with precise details, tied to tradition, uncomfortable with emotion, suspicious of poetic eloquence, concerned with larger social themes, but, above all else, faithful to established authority. Certainly, these characteristics are all too evident in the brief description of the automobile accident in *Henningsen*: the careful account of the car's inspection (*No proof was adduced by the dealer to show precisely what was done in the way of mechanical or road testing ... It had no servicing and no mishaps of any kind before the event of May 19*); the meticulous retracing of the car's driving history (*Mr. Henningsen drove it from the dealer's place of business in Bloomfield to their home in Keansburg. Thereafter, it was used for short trips on paved streets about the town*); the precise establishment of factual details (*That day, Mrs. Henningsen drove to Asbury Park. She was proceeding north on Route 36 in Highlands, New Jersey, at 20—22 miles per hour; [the car] had 468 miles on the speedometer at the time*); the dispassionate and emotionally flat description of what must have terrifying moments for Mrs. Henningsen (*She was riding in the right-hand lane. Suddenly she heard a loud noise "from the bottom, by the hood." It "felt as if something cracked." The steering wheel spun in her hands; the car veered sharply to the right and crashed into a highway sign and a brick wall. No other vehicle was in any way involved*).

Of course, insofar as these characteristics reveal a deliberate and cautious author, this may be less a function of the author's psychological predilections than the traditional expectations of the form in which the author works. Law is, after all, an inherently conservative institution; it is cautious, it seeks to

---

51. *See Henningsen*, 32 N.J. at 368–69, 161 A.2d at 75.

preserve that which already exists, and it resists radical change. Among the professions of words—literature, philosophy, psychology, etc.—the law may well be unique in requiring its practitioners to hide the very instances when they are being the most creative. Novelists win Nobel prizes by convincing people that their work is unlike any other that preceded it; lawyers win cases by persuading judges that their argument—no matter how creative, no matter how new—is really very much like existing binding or persuasive doctrines. But to say that the psychological profile of the author of a legal text may be shaped by the professional milieu in which he or she operates is simply to acknowledge a truth common to all texts—legal or otherwise: They carry the indelible mark of the narrative and rhetorical traditions of the genre out of which they emerge.

But, for the legal reader and legal writer, the point of drawing out the psychological profile of the author is, as indicated previously, not just for the purpose of understanding the author's persona but more importantly to become more consciously aware of the type of relationship the author wishes to establish with the reader on the basis of that persona. The critic Wayne C. Booth says it best in the context of reading literature when he argues that the act of reading is in the end an act of moral imagination because a literary text forces us to confront who we are while we are reading, and almost always changes us by virtue of the reading experience we have had.[52] That is, Booth maintains, reading aims to establish a "literary friendship" between author and reader: The author attempts not only to bring to life the author's conception of a factual and moral world, but also to subtly train the reader to accept, respect, and ultimately function in that world; the reader in turn not only begins to internalize the moral dictates of the world described in that particular text but, little by little, to export the world of that text into other texts.[53]

Certainly, this is what it means to be trained "in the law." It is not just that one learns that law is a conservative and cautious institution—that point becomes very evident very quickly barely a few days into law school. Rather, the more the legal reader begins to learn to interpret legal texts, and the more the reader begins to understand the character of the individuals and institutions who produced the text, the more the reader also becomes the "ideal" reader for those authors: careful, precise, detail-oriented, tradition-bound, and authority-driven. In short, the legal reader becomes the idealized incarnation of the writer.

---

52. WAYNE C. BOOTH, THE COMPANY WE KEEP: AN ETHICS OF FICTION 53 (1988).
53. *Id.*

None of this, incidentally, is offered as a critique of legal writing. The point here is not that the moral cautiousness and conservative instinct of a legal writer and reader are necessarily bad things—under some circumstances, they may be; under others, they may not be. Instead, the point to bear in mind is that the psychological transformation brought about by Booth's literary friendship may be absolutely necessary for the reader to fully engage with a text, but—and this goes to the heart of this chapter's thesis—this transformation will harden into unthinking and unfeeling reading habits and interpretive behaviors unless the reader becomes self-conscious about it. For example, the least that law school teaches students is how to become deliberate and conservative readers. Undoubtedly, that interpretive skill is indispensable to good lawyering. However, unless the reader becomes and remains aware that the psychological price he or she pays for acquiring that useful skill is that he or she is in the process subtly transformed into the "ideal" reader of the individuals and institutions who produced the text, then he or she is less likely to question, doubt, and challenge the text in new and meaningful ways; and, what is perhaps worse, as a writer he or she is less likely to abandon law's moral cautiousness and conservative instinct even when it would make perfect sense to work and speak to an audience in a different mode.

"In each text," Professor White explains, "the writer establishes a relationship with his or her reader, a community of two ..."[54] But if, as the Greeks believed, craft reveals character, then that relationship and community of two is created, maintained, and nurtured by the psychological transformation the writer's craft effects on the reader's character. The interpretive friendship between legal writer and legal reader is one based on moral cautiousness and conservative instinct. In and of itself, this act of friendship is not wrong, but it can become maladaptive for the reader if he or she never questions the basis of the friendship.

One way of making the point evident is to consider the remaining two texts of an automobile accident beginning with *The Great Gatsby*.

2. The Great Gatsby by F. Scott Fitzgerald

F. Scott Fitzgerald published *The Great Gatsby* in 1925. The novel tells the story of Jay Gatsby and Daisy Buchanan, two of the most memorable characters in American fiction, but the central figure is the narrator Nick Carraway, who, as the voice of the novel, also serves as the voice of the novelist. The story

---

54. James B. White, When Words Lose Their Meaning 13 (1984).

takes place during a single summer, though earlier events of the characters' life are recounted in complex, layered flashbacks.

In the summer of 1922, Nick, the son of a "well to-do" Midwestern family, travels East to New York City to work as a bond trader. He rents a house on the Eastern Shore of Long Island, fifty yards from Long Island Sound and where, just across the water, lives his cousin Daisy with her wealthy husband Tom Buchanan. On his first night at the rental house, Nick catches the first glimpse of his neighbor Gatsby, standing on the darkened lawn of his mansion and staring at the "green light" across the sound at the end of the dock of Daisy's house. In time, Nick will come to learn from Gatsby himself that, as a poor young man, he had fallen in love with Daisy only to have her break off their engagement. Now five years later, after making his fortune under mysterious circumstances, Gatsby has settled on Long Island to be close to Daisy. He befriends Nick and uses their acquaintance in order to gain entrance to the Buchanan household and renew his romance with Daisy. When she first sees Gatsby again, Daisy, whom Fitzgerald describes as having "a sad and lovely [face] with bright things in it, bright eyes and a bright passionate mouth," takes up with him with a seeming unconsidered insouciance, as though she had not left him behind five years ago, and as though he had not spent every moment of those years waiting for her.

Meanwhile, Tom, Daisy's husband, is having the latest of one of his many affairs with Myrtle Wilson, the wife of George Wilson, Tom's local mechanic. Though Tom does not realize it, Daisy is perfectly aware that Myrtle Wilson is his mistress. One day, on their way to an outing in New York City, Gatsby, Nick, Tom, Daisy, and her friend Jordan stop at Wilson's shop. Tom suggests the stop as an excuse to see his mistress who lives in an apartment above the shop with her husband. During the visit, Myrtle Wilson notices Tom at the wheel of Gatsby's car and mistakenly believes it to be Tom's. Later that evening, Tom returns to Long Island in his own car with Nick and Jordan, while ahead of them Daisy and Gatsby drive back in Gatsby's car with Daisy at the wheel. As they speed past Wilson's shop, Myrtle Wilson, wanting to speak to Tom, runs into the street waving at Gatsby's car, not realizing that it is Daisy at the wheel. She is struck and killed instantly. Daisy speeds away without stopping but not before George Wilson catches a glimpse at the car. When Nick, Tom, and Jordan reach the accident, Tom tells George Wilson that he does not own and was not driving the car that struck his wife. Days after the accident, Daisy and Tom hurriedly leave Long Island. Gatsby, who all along had nurtured the hope of winning Daisy back, stays behind even though he knows that the car will eventually be traced back to him. Indeed, George Wilson tracks him down at home and, in mistaken revenge for the death of his wife, murders him.

Gatsby is buried in a lonely ceremony; only Nick and an old Gatsby associate attend. As Nick looks back on the summer just ended, his final thoughts serve as both the story's coda and, in a way, Gatsby's eulogy:

> As I sat here, brooding on the old unknown world, I thought of Gatsby's wonder when he first picked out the green light at the end of Daisy's dock. He had come a long way to this blue lawn and his dream must have seemed so close that he could hardly fail to grasp it. He did not know that it was already behind him, somewhere back in that vast obscurity beyond the city, where the fields of the republic rolled on under the night.
>
> Gatsby believed in the green light, the orgiastic future that year by year recedes before us. It eludes us then, but that's no matter—tomorrow we will run faster, stretch our arms farther.... And one fine morning—
>
> So we beat on, boats against the current, borne back ceaselessly into the past.[55]

As with the Henningsen's opinion, while the preceding description and passage helps to provide context to the story, for our purposes the key text of the novel is Fitzgerald's description of Daisy's running down Myrtle Wilson at the wheel of Gatsby's car:

> *The "death car," as the newspapers called it, didn't stop; it came out of the gathering darkness, wavered tragically for a moment and then disappeared around the next bend. Michaelis wasn't even sure of its color— he told the first policeman that it was light green. The other car, the one going toward New York, came to rest a hundred yards beyond, and its driver hurried back to where Myrtle Wilson, her life violently extinguished, knelt in the road and mingled her thick, dark blood with the dust*
>
> *Michaelis and this man reached her first but when they had torn open her shirtwaist still damp with perspiration they saw that her left breast was swinging loose like a flap and there was no need to listen for the heart beneath. The mouth was wide open and ripped at the corners as though she had choked a little in giving up the tremendous vitality she had stored so long.[56]*

---

55. FITZGERALD, *supra* note 49, at 152.
56. *Id.* at 119.

By now, enough has been written about the law *and* literature and law *as* literature movement to draw some evident contrasts between this excerpt from *The Great Gatsby* and the prior excerpt from *Henningsen*. As the rhetorician Gerald Wetlaufer notes:

> If the purpose of a judicial opinion is to close what has been open, the motive behind literature is likely to be the desire to open what has been closed. Thus, literature is likely to celebrate and explore the problematic, the uncertain, the ambiguous, the subjective, the irrational, the insoluble. It will, at least usually, acknowledge and examine the multiplicity of perspectives and the personal contingency of reality ... Indeed it will confront the limits of knowledge and reason, often casting the rational and logical not as the hero but as the fool.[57]

Here, even the brief description of the car accident demonstrates many traits of a psychological literary profile: the favoring of the irrational and ambiguous (*The "death car," as the newspapers called it, didn't stop; it came out of the gathering darkness and then disappeared around the bend*); uncertainty (*Michaelis was not even sure of its color*); imprecision of details (*the other car, the one going toward New York, came to rest a hundred yards beyond*); limited knowledge and reason (*they saw her left breast was swinging loose and there was no need to listen to the heart beneath*); subjective perspective (*The mouth was open and ripped at the corners as though she had choked a little in giving up the tremendous vitality she had stored so long*). In other words, by creating a sense of uncertainty and doubt, the writer invites a very different interpretive friendship with the reader than that created by the *Henningsen* author. Whereas, the judicial author projected himself as cautious, deliberative, and conservative and, thereby, encouraged the reader to adopt a similar stance as the key for the correct interpretation of the text, here the fiction writer offers himself as unsure, flawed, and eager to confess that the reality being described is not just as he found it but as he constructed it. If the ideal legal reader is one who looks for certainty and remains grounded in authority, the ideal fiction reader would seem to favor doubt and would search for meaning in the text anchored and burdened only by his or her imagination.

But, while on the surface it may seem that an interpretive friendship based on uncertainty, imagination, and doubt is ill-suited to the tasks of interpreting legal texts, in fact the two forms of friendship—one based on moral cau-

---

57. Gerald Wetlaufer, *Rhetoric and Its Denial in Legal Discourse*, 76 VA. L. REV. 1545, 1594 (1990).

tiousness and conservative instinct, the other on contingent reality and imaginative uncertainty—do share an important feature. The *Henningsen* writer created a portrait of the accident with a list of precise factual details: The exact speed of the car, the driver's destination, the weather conditions, the surface of the road, the cracking of the motor, the crash into the highway sign and wall. These details may at first seem coldly dispassionate but it is precisely because of their seemingly slow, methodical, and objective accretion that the writer is able to paint a vivid sense of the exact place and time of the accident. Similarly, Fitzgerald succeeds in creating just as stunning a sense of time and place, not with accumulated details but with impressionistic snapshots: The death car, the gathering darkness, blood in the dust, the open shirtwaist damp with perspiration, the breast loose like a flap, the mouth ripped at the corners, the stilled heart beneath.

It is not enough to say that the differences between the two descriptions of the accidents is that the *Henningsen* court is concerned with establishing the factual basis for its holding, whereas Fitzgerald wishes to use lyrical images in the service of his narrative. Perhaps there is indeed more precision in *Henningsen* and more poetry in *The Great Gatsby*, but that surface difference becomes almost irrelevant when, as mentioned previously, one considers the fact that, in its own way, the *Henningsen* scene is just as vivid as the one from *The Great Gatsby*. What is relevant for our purposes are the different types of psychological persona and interpretive relationship each writer offers the reader in order to achieve the very aim of making the accident real and immediate. In *Henningsen*, the accident becomes vivid because the writer has succeeded in creating this deliberate persona, thereby convincing the reader to pay close attention to every detail of the description. Once the reader's attention becomes focused on the details, then the sheer precision and weight of these accumulated facts bring the scene to life: The reader learns to be detail-oriented because the writer models the importance of details. By contrast, in *The Great Gatsby*, the accident comes to life because the writer has succeeded in creating this self-doubting persona, thereby forcing the reader to complete images the writer has sketched in only the broadest of strokes. Once the reader's attention is unanchored by the details of the text, then the sheer lyricism and starkness of these abbreviated images cause the reader to complete the rest of the scene.

At this point, it should be made clear that a deliberate psychological profile is not exclusive to legal writers any more than a self-doubting persona belongs solely to fiction writers. The two examples above were chosen mainly because, insofar as the most common legal stance is one grounded in established authority and the most common fiction counterpart relies on contingent reality, then it is easier to demonstrate the idea of using psychological intelligence in the interpretation of text by analyzing two excepts as starkly different as *Henningsen* and *The Great Gatsby*. So, just as the earlier statement that the typical interpretive friendship between legal writer and reader is grounded in moral cautiousness and conservative instinct was not offered as a negative critique of legal writing, so too here the notion that the typical interpretive friendship between fiction writer and reader is based on doubt and imagination is not offered as a positive endorsement of fiction writing. The point, again, is that being aware of the psychological persona behind the words of the writer and the resulting psychological transformation these words effect on the reader, does help the reader become more sophisticated in interpreting the text. In the case of the legal reader, this means not just becoming the idealized cautious reader, but also bringing to legal texts the more self-doubting and imaginative persona of the fiction reader.

This combined persona may be best demonstrated by considering the third description of an automobile accident, this time in the song *Wreck on the Highway* by Bruce Springsteen.

3. Wreck on the Highway, by Bruce Springsteen

Wreck on the Highway first appeared on Springsteen's 1980 Album "*The River*." Unlike the respective passages from *Henningsen* and *The Great Gatsby*, the Springsteen song is reproduced here in its entirety. As such, and again unlike the prior excerpts, there is not much of a back story to summarize for the song. This is not to say that Springsteen did not have a back story in mind, nor is it to say that it is not possible to place the song in the larger context of Springsteen's considerable work. Rather, the point of comparing these three texts is not to engage in a scholarly deconstruction of their meaning but to use them to demonstrate how the reader might begin to use psychological intelligence to conjure up the character of the respective authors of the texts.

Still, even though the goal is not to engage in a full review of the song or the album, two points are worth making: First, as an album "*The River*" is usually regarded as the culmination of a trilogy that began with the 1975 album "*Born to Run*" and continued in 1978 with "*Darkness at the Edge of Town*." Together, these three albums show Springsteen conjuring a cast of working class men and women, who find themselves moving from the reckless optimism of youth to the humbling limitations of life's middle years. In the course of the three albums the very same characters materialize time and time again at different stages of their lives: They fall in love, get married, start work, become unemployed, get caught up in crime, and struggle to reconcile the facts of their lives with the promises of the American dream. So, the unnamed narrator in *Wreck on the Highway*, who feels himself powerless to the cries of the young man dying amid "blood and glass" as "the rain tumbled hard and cold," could be the same man, now older and chastened, who in younger days believed in his heart that he was "born to run" and used to call out to his girlfriend to "ride through mansions of glory in suicide machines / Sprung from cages out on highway 9, / Chrome wheeled, fuel injected / and steppin' out over the line." But tonight, exhausted, melancholic, he rides alone "at the end of a working day" and sits up in darkness, watching his baby sleep and "thinking 'bout the wreck on the highway."

The second point to make about the song is this: The image of the car and the highway is one of the most iconic metaphors in American artistic life, providing endless themes for movies, novels, and song lyrics. Springsteen, perhaps more than any other modern American musician, uses the imagery of cars to explore a host of ideas, ranging from love to despair, from freedom to alienation. *Wreck on the Highway* is one of four songs on *The River* that uses the imagery of cars and the highway: In *Stolen Car*, the car is evidence of the hero's desperation; in *Drive all Night*, it is the measure of love and devotion; in *Sherry Darling*, it is the symbol of the loss of freedom; and in *Wreck on the Highway*, it is a reminder of life's fragility:

Last night I was out driving
Coming home at the end of the working day
I was riding alone through the drizzling rain
On a deserted stretch of a county two-lane
When I came upon a wreck on the highway

There was blood and glass all over
And there was nobody there but me
As the rain tumbled down hard and cold
I seen a young man lying by the side of the road
He cried Mister, won't you help me please

An ambulance finally came and took him to Riverside
I watched as they drove him away
And I thought of a girlfriend or a young wife
And a state trooper knocking in the middle of the night
To say your baby died in a wreck on the highway

Sometimes I sit up in the darkness
And I watch my baby as she sleeps
Then I climb in bed and I hold her tight
I just lay there awake in the middle of the night

Thinking 'bout the wreck on the highway[58]

Wreck on the Highway lies somewhere between the precise accretion of details of *Henningsen* and the lyrical imagery of *The Great Gatsby*. Like the *Henningsen* author, Springsteen is very precise in creating a sense of time and place: *the end of the work day, a stretch of two-lane highway, blood and glass all over, an ambulance driving away to Riverside, sitting up in darkness, thinking about the wreck on the highway*. At the same time, like Fitzgerald in *The Great Gatsby*, Springsteen paints a stark scene in just a few broad strokes: *alone through a hard and cold rain, Mister, won't you help me please, a state trooper knocking in the middle of the night, then I climb in bed and hold her tight*. Thus, the writer's persona combines a reticent precision with contingent ambiguity, and the interpretive friendship the writer offers the reader is based on that mixed psychological profile. In this way, the ideal interpreter of the song is one who possesses the deliberate persona of the legal reader as well as imaginative consciousness of the fiction reader.

At the present stage of his career, Springsteen has achieved the sort of iconic status that needs no more mythologizing. If his fans, who ironically seem to utterly lack the quiet reticence that is the artist's greatest attribute, are to be believed, Springsteen is either the greatest musician who has ever lived, or the reincarnation of Jesus, the Buddha, and Shakespeare combined. But at the risk of sounding like yet another fawning offering at the altar of "*Bruuuuuce*" the demigod, the fact remains that his writing persona of reticent precision and contingent ambiguity is one to which writers of legal texts should aspire. If the irreducible definition of legal writing is writing that seeks in one way or another to persuade its audience, then neither the *Henningsen* nor *The Great Gatsby* writing persona is likely to fit the bill: The latter is too unsure, too lyrical, and too doubting to command the authority in which persuasion needs to remain grounded, while the former is too cautious, too deliberative, and too conservative to spark the inspiration from which persuasion needs to take flight. The writing persona reflected in *Wreck on the Highway* combines the two: It demands reticence as much as lyricism, precision as much as imagination, certainty as much as doubt.

Are these not, in the final analysis, the very psychological tools a good lawyer needs for intelligent, rigorous, and creative interpretation of legal text?

---

58. "Wreck on the Highway" by Bruce Springsteen. Copyright © 1980 Bruce Springsteen (ASCAP). Reprinted by permission. International Copyright secured. All rights reserved.

Conclusion

Reading is an act of interpretive friendship. The writer uses words to model and project a psychological persona to the reader and the reader, in turn, even if only for a moment, internalizes and mirrors that persona, thereby becoming, again even if only for a moment, the ideal audience for the writer. This psychological transformation, though subtle, is inevitable. That is why law students and novice lawyers can be the most rigidly conservative readers of legal texts: They often unthinkingly and unfeelingly take up the most salient characteristics of the legal texts they are trained to read but, in the process, they also become alienated from a profession they believe requires them to cultivate the moral cautiousness and conservative instinct of their persona while suppressing all other parts of their nature that speak to self-doubt, reflection, and imagination.

This need not be so; the interpretive friendship of legal reading need not be so cramped and miserly. Even when interpreting legal texts the reader can and should remain open to the doubtful and imaginative aspects of the writer's persona as a way of cultivating a full imaginative life and rich authorial voice of his or her own. In the final analysis, this intellectual versatility is the true, universal mark of all good lawyers: an ability to bring to the study and practice of law a depth and breadth of thought and perspective mined out of the fullness and chaos of human knowledge and experience.[59] This ability, which is neither innate nor terribly mysterious, but learned and eminently teachable,[60] rests ultimately on a willingness to approach the legal profession as a device for the exercise of inquisitiveness and doubt.

---

59. By now, it is the norm in clinical education that the practice of law is seen, theorized and taught as a multidisciplinary profession:

> As the academy moves beyond a model of legal education predicated upon the case method and the assimilation of self-contained bodies of legal doctrine, legal educators should also recognize similar limitations in models of lawyering and lawyering instruction that stem from the treatment of clients as compartmentalized legal problems. Newer lawyering models, which shift the focus from vindication of legal rights and injuries to creative problem solving, stress the need to transcend doctrinal areas, legal fora, and professional disciplines to fully address client problems. In increasing numbers, lawyers in both public interest and private practice settings are working collaboratively or cooperatively with professionals in other disciplines to address client problems in a more holistic, efficient, comprehensive, and cost-effective fashion.

Margaret Martin Barry et al., *Clinical Education for this Millennium: The Third Wave*, 7 CLIN. L. REV. 1 (2000).

60. "Legal problems are like elephants: examining them from only one perspective gives a distorted image of the whole. In order to understand legal problems, lawyers often need

To paraphrase the novelist Mark Helperin, though traditional legal academia may be constructed to serve above all else logical dogmatism, linguistic certainty, and economic calculation, thoughtful lawyers learn from the day-to-day experience of dealing with people—be they clients, judges, colleagues, or students—that the measure of good practice is not just logic but also poetic storytelling; not just economics, but also psychological subtlety; not just linguistics but also physical performance.[61] Lawyers learn as well, and if they remain open-minded, they never stop learning, that the legal profession contains within it a multitude of intellectual disciplines and that, when all is said and done, what is required of legal practitioners and scholars alike is doubt, imagination, curiosity, and skepticism. To be a good lawyer one must be disciplined and obstinate in fashioning one's practice as an un-remitting pursuit of learning and an unrelenting exercise in self reflection, to become, if you will, the closest modern incarnation of and most faithful heir to a renaissance person. Without this, lawyering hardens into a repetitive and unreflective profession devoid of personal fulfillment, in which young lawyers quickly turn and remain disillusioned about both the intellectual integrity and higher ideals of their work.[62] With it, the practice of law, though de-manding, will be full, and the lawyer will keep the faith and, as the novelist Mark Helperin writes not about law but about love, "stay in the fight unto the very last."[63]

---

to examine them from the perspective of multiple disciplines. Likewise, successful legal problem-solving sometimes means that lawyers need to be able to collaborate with other professionals in order to address a client's problems." Kim Diana Connolly, *Elucidating The Elephant: Interdisciplinary Law School Classes*, 11 WASH. U. J.L. & POL'Y 11, 14 (2003); *See also* V. Pualani Enos & Lois H. Kante, *Who's Listening? Introducing Students to Client-Centered, Client-Empowering, and Multidisciplinary Problem-Solving in a Clinical Setting*, 9 CLIN. L. REV. 83 (2002) (describing multidisciplinary approach to train novice students to interview women about intimate partner violence, and to train the upper-level students who supervise them throughout their participation in the project).

61. "Embracing multidisciplinary perspectives, as an instrument, when closely examining course material cuts two ways. In one direction, the instrument is a microscope through which students will gain deeper insight into the law in general and specific issues. In the other direction, by looking through the instrument from the vantage point of the legal materials, it becomes a telescope through which the students will gain deeper insight into the nature and reach of these multidisciplinary materials." Bailey Kuklin & Jeffrey W. Stempel, *Continuing Classroom Conversation Beyond the Well-Placed "Whys?"*, 29 U. TOL. L. REV. 59, 61 (1997).

62. *See generally* Krieger, *supra* note 5.

63. MARK HALPERIN, MEMOIRS FROM ANTPROOF CASE 514 (1995).

Psychological lawyering intelligence is no more the Rosetta Stone of the interpretation of legal text than logical reasoning or linguistic analysis. It is, however, a device for the pursuit of learning and the exercise of self-refection. And it is, when all is said and done, a measure of the lawyer's intellectual versatility.

II

Lawyering with Cross-Cultural Competence

CHAPTER 5

MULTICULTURAL LAWYERING: HEURISTICS AND BIASES*

*Paul R. Tremblay***

*Carwina Weng****

If we can make the subject of cross-cultural lawyering one that our students and we can talk about, our collective capacity to practice law in non-discriminatory and culturally-sensitive ways will increase access and substantive justice to our clients.[1]

I. Introduction

A. The Multicultural Critique of Models

This chapter sets out to explore how lawyering skills, and especially legal interviewing and counseling, might begin to accommodate differences in culture between a lawyer and her client. It attempts to learn from the rich literature on multicultural counseling in non-legal disciplines to suggest discrete changes to the profession's prevailing approaches to working with clients who come from cultures different from the lawyer's.

---

* This chapter combines ideas first developed by the respective authors in articles published in the Clinical Law Review. *See* Paul R. Tremblay, *Interviewing and Counseling Across Cultures: Heuristics and Biases*, 9 CLIN. L. REV. 373 (2002); Carwina Weng, *Multicultural Lawyering: Teaching Psychology to Develop Cultural Awareness*, 11 CLIN. L. REV. 369 (2005). Some of the ideas previously expressed in those articles have evolved in this iteration. The authors wish to thank Jeremy Eggleton and Michael Yeung for their research assistance.

** Clinical Professor of Law, Boston College Law School.

*** Clinical Associate Professor of Law, Indiana University School of Law.

1. Susan Bryant, *The Five Habits: Building Cross-Cultural Competence in Lawyers*, 8 CLIN. L. REV. 33, 99 (2001).

Let's assume, as we begin, that you are a second year law student who has recently enrolled in a law school clinical program. (Everything we say here will apply equally well to experienced lawyers, but we'll use the example of a student.) Your clinical placement happens to be a civil program, where you will represent low income clients in family, housing, welfare, and Social Security disputes. This is your first opportunity to practice law, and you are at once excited and very scared about your performance in this setting.

One of the primary missions of your clinical program, you notice, is to teach you basic skills in interviewing and counseling. That makes sense, of course. You've never done that kind of thing before, and you worry that if you interview poorly you may miss critical facts and end up less prepared for the advocacy you will be performing. Similarly, if you counsel ineptly, your client may make a decision she will later regret, or end up accepting a course of action that causes her serious harm. So you are quite open to the idea of learning these skills. You have purchased a textbook that your teachers use to help you understand the underlying theories and practice of these skills.[2]

These interviewing and counseling texts are interesting creatures, when you think about them. You notice when you study books on those topics that they tend to offer "models" for you to use, at least provisionally and tentatively, while you are learning a new professional skill. This makes sense to you. If books are to be of any help, they should suggest reasonably explicit and concrete ways to perform the skills that they purport to teach you. For instance, the most prominent interviewing and counseling book, *Lawyers as Counselors*, offers a very elegant model for conducting an initial interview with a client.[3] That authority suggests four stages of an interview. You begin with a "preliminary problem identification," and transition through a "preparatory explanation" to the second "chronology" stage where you learn the time-gener-

---

2. For the sake of our discussion here, let us assume that you had been assigned one of the two leading textbooks on these topics, sources which were written about a decade ago and have not yet included in their pages a substantial component dedicated to the specific issues of cultural difference. We refer to DAVID BINDER ET AL., LAWYERS AS COUNSELORS: A CLIENT-CENTERED APPROACH (1990) [hereinafter BINDER ET AL. 1990], and ROBERT M. BASTRESS & JOSEPH D. HARBAUGH, INTERVIEWING COUNSELING AND NEGOTIATING: SKILLS FOR EFFECTIVE REPRESENTATION (1990). More recent textbooks have included at least some explicit attention to the cultural difference phenomenon. *See, e.g.,* ROBERT F. COCHRAN ET AL., THE COUNSELOR-AT-LAW: A COLLABORATIVE APPROACH TO CLIENT INTERVIEWING AND COUNSELING 203–21 (1999); DAVID BINDER, PAUL BERGMAN, SUSAN PRICE & PAUL R. TREMBLAY, LAWYERS AS COUNSELORS: A CLIENT-CENTERED APPROACH 34–40 (2d ed. 2004).

3. *See* BINDER ET AL. 1990, *supra* note 2, *passim.*

ated narrative of your client. You then follow with an important "theory verification" segment where you return to topics to flesh out facts that are critical to your legal theory. Finally, you end with a "closing" stage where you try to conclude your session in a way that makes future agendas clear, offer provisional advice if possible, but resist premature diagnosis or judgment about the client's case even if the client asks strongly for your opinion. The model endorsed by these authors not only helps you out with a very explicit agenda for your meeting, but it also suggests for each stage the kinds of questions that you ought to use (open-ended during stages one and two, more narrow and focused during the theory verification stage, etc.), and teaches you about the importance of empathy, active listening, and rapport development—critical components of an interview.

A model like that from *Lawyers as Counselors* develops from the learned experience of its authors, combined with some established theories of psychology and human interaction. It includes critical assumptions about your goals in the professional activity and about the ways that people tend to react to, and within, various interpersonal events. So, for instance, an interviewing model assumes that your goals in an initial interview are to learn all the relevant facts about the problem for which the client seeks your assistance, to establish rapport and a working relationship between the lawyer and her client, and to test for credibility in both directions (to gauge your client's and to bolster yours with him). The model further assumes important things about the ways in which people interact. Some of those assumptions seem pretty obvious (being kind and warm is more likely to establish good rapport than being unkind and brusque), while others are things which you learn from the book that you might not otherwise have known intuitively (for instance, open questions allow the client to speak more freely and tell his story more satisfactorily than closed questions; sustained eye contact is effective in showing concern and interest; open body language is more inviting and encouraging than folded-limbs, closed body language; a chronological narrative is a particularly effective vehicle for understanding a story most completely and in a less distorted way; etc.).

Now here's the puzzle for those, like you, who wish to learn a new skill from a course or a book or a model (as well as for those who create the books, courses, and models). The puzzle arises from the role of culture, background, and learning styles in our understanding of the effects of interpersonal behavior. Put simply, many, and perhaps even most, of our assumptions about how people interact, and about the meaning of their expressions, are *culturally influenced*. If all the persons in the world, or, more modestly, all the persons in your lawyering community world, shared with you the same basic, overall way of communicating, interacting, and understanding the world, then models for professional skills would be, or could be, pretty reliable. They wouldn't be *perfect*, because an occasional individual might have some idiosyncratic quirk that throws off your structured plan, but they'd be pretty effective just about all the time. If, though, the community in which you work is filled with a variety of interpersonal patterns, and a multiplicity of ways of understanding the world, then any "model" faces a distinctly more onerous challenge.

Of course, we now know that the latter is far more accurate a description of our experience than the former. Much of what we understand about interpersonal effectiveness is connected to cultural understandings, learned practices, and traditional customs. For example, your family background, race, gender, ethnicity, socioeconomic status, and sexual orientation, and those characteristics of your clients, matter a great deal in the interviewing and counseling process. In other fields, most notably social work and mental health counseling, researchers have been arguing and writing about the interplay of culture and technique for decade. In the field of lawyering practice, this topic has begun to receive serious attention only in recent years.

This chapter intends to explore, begin to understand, and offer some practice suggestions about this critical aspect of learning interviewing and counseling skills. Does our recognition of the cultural influences on skills training mean that models are useless, or that they can never work? We're not as pessimistic as that. That conclusion overlooks the many ways in which persons from varying backgrounds share ways of communicating and relating, and the many ways in which the client-centered models taught in law schools foster tolerance for difference. But of course a model cannot assume too many cross-cultural similarities. The first challenge, then, is to identify where models can serve reliably and where they risk fostering misunderstanding.

The second challenge is to articulate for lawyers how they ought to proceed when some parts of the traditional models might not apply. The task here is to appreciate and respect the differences among your clients, but without resorting to stereotypes or stubborn myths about race, sex, ethnicity, and culture. To ignore likely differences in culture is an invitation to malpractice in counseling; at the same time, to presume you know what those differences will be once you know your client's race or sex or cultural background is an invitation to dehumanize your client, and to apply generalizations that may not apply to him. Here's an apt story: In the movie *Annie Hall*, the comedian Alvy Singer, played by Woody Allen, meets at an Adlai Stevenson presidential rally Alison Porchnik, a campaign staffer for Stevenson, played by Carol Kane. After Alvy learns that Alison's graduate thesis is entitled "Political Commitment in Twentieth Century Literature," he says,

Alvy: So you're, like, New York, Jewish, left-wing, liberal intellectual, Central Park West, Brandeis University, socialist summer camp, father with the Ben Shahn drawing on the wall, ah, strike-oriented, kind of—stop me before I make a complete imbecile of myself ...

Alison: No, that was *wonderful*. I love being reduced to a cultural stereotype.

Alvy: I'm a bigot, I know—but for the left .... [4]

A primary ambition of this chapter is to confront the quandary just described, and to propose some lawyering process conceptions that might allow you to resolve the dilemma. Our suggestions focus on the two concepts of *heuristics* and *biases*, as we describe below (we steal those terms from some pioneering work in another field by two cognitive scientists, Amos Tversky and Daniel Kahnemann[5]). Our suggestions proceed from an effort to be, as one writer has put it, "'cross-eyed,' with one eye always clearly focused on the differences, and the other eye clearly focused on the similarities"[6] between dominant culture and minority culture clients.

This goal seems especially critical to your training as a professional. Your effectiveness as a lawyer, as a helping professional for clients who need your advice and skill, depends almost entirely on how well you can understand your client's story, needs, and goals. Plus, as we also develop later, your effectiveness as a lawyer also depends on how well you understand your own culture, your own biases, and the lenses through which you perceive the world. We offer some suggestions on both fronts—understanding a bit better where your clients might be coming from, and understanding a bit better why you are who you are—so that you can better manage the interaction between the two fronts.

B. Setting the Stage for Our Discussion

Before we introduce the heuristics and biases themes, we need to set the stage with a few preliminary observations that should help you as we move along.

---

4. ANNIE HALL (United Artists Films 1977).

5. Amos Tversky & Daniel Kahneman, *Judgments Under Uncertainty: Heuristics and Biases*, *in* JUDGMENT UNDER UNCERTAINTY: HEURISTICS AND BIASES (Amos Tversky et al. eds., 1982).

6. PAUL B. PEDERSEN, CULTURE-CENTERED COUNSELING INTERVENTIONS: STRIVING FOR ACCURACY 28 (1997).

First, what do we mean by the elusive word "culture"? If we want to teach you about cultural competence or awareness, you deserve to know what we mean by the term culture. While commentators describe or use the term in many different ways, the following definition seems appropriate for our purposes:

> [C]ulture [is] all the customs, values, and traditions that are learned from one's environment. [I]n a culture there is a "set of people who have common and shared values, customs, habits, and rituals; systems of labeling, explanations, and evaluations; social rules of behavior; perceptions regarding human nature, natural phenomena, interpersonal relationships, time, and activity; symbols, art, and artifacts; and historical developments.[7]

We are all part of some culture, and likely many cultures, understanding culture in this way. At the same time, though, "[c]ulture is performed, ... fluid/emergent ... [and] improvisational."[8]

The first part of this chapter focuses on the contrasts between what many see as the dominant United States culture, usually understood to mean White, Eurocentric practices and patterns, and non-dominant cultures, representing the practices and patterns of ethnic and religious minority communities as well as members of the disabled, poor, and gay, lesbian, transgender, and bisexual communities.[9] Our claim is that discrete communities tend to share certain preferences, styles, patterns, and values, and that a better lawyer will understand that the cultural background of a lawyer or a client matters—it can affect how that person will behave and respond to behaviors suggested by skill models or by theories of good lawyering. So, given that theme, one might predict that a woman raised in, or living in, a Mexican-American family will likely possess certain characteristics which the lawyer ought to understand and anticipate. Her ethnic background, reflecting the culture in which she lives or

---

7. Gargi Roysircar Sodowsky et al., *Ethnic Identity in the United States*, *in* HANDBOOK OF MULTICULTURAL COUNSELING 123, 132 (Joseph G. Ponterotto et al. eds., 1995) (quoting Gargi Roysircar Sodowsky et al., *Moderating Effects of Sociocultural Variables on Acculturation Variables of Hispanics and Asian Americans*, 70 J. COUNSELING & DEV. 194 (1991)).

8. Joan Laird, *Theorizing Culture: Narrative Ideas and Practice Principles*, *in* RE-VISIONING FAMILY THERAPY: RACE, CULTURE, AND GENDER IN CLINICAL PRACTICE 24 (Monica McGoldrick ed., 1998) [hereinafter RE-VISIONING FAMILY THERAPY]. *Compare* Laird *with* PEDERSEN, *supra* note 6, at 29 ("Culture is complex, but not chaotic. There are *patterns* that make it possible to manage complexity.").

9. We note here that while White Eurocentric patterns may not be dominant in many parts of our nation, they do tend to dominate the lawyering world.

was raised, is thus relevant to the task of good lawyering. The lesson for professionals is this: "It is not appropriate or helpful to insist that ethnic minority clients who come from a value system differing from the Eurocentric worldview be subjected to interventions that are often incompatible with their norms.... [I]t is mandatory that we know what [the cultural values] are for every client system of color with which we interact."[10]

We stress here, though, that culture is neither static nor easily knowable, and thus the risks of misapplying cultural generalizations to any individual client are obviously a source of some worry. So, not only do we acknowledge that culture is "socially constructed, evolving, emergent, and occurring in language,"[11] but that intersectionality (that is, our possessing several cultures at the same time) renders many cultural designations suspect. And the role of assimilation is similarly critical to any understanding of the influences of a traditional culture on a member of an ethnic minority community.[12]

The suggestions we make in our first part, those regarding heuristics, intend to recognize these objections and worries. As Ruth Dean and others have written, the realization that most professionals will never become culturally competent does not mean that those professionals—and we mean you here—ought not continue to explore, with curiosity and humility, the ways in which cultures tend to express their traditions, values, and beliefs.[13] In this process, the client is the expert, and you try to understand, as best you can, the life

---

10. Rowena Fong, *Culturally Competent Social Work Practice: Past and Present, in* CULTURALLY COMPETENT PRACTICE: SKILLS, INTERVENTIONS, AND EVALUATIONS 4, 6 (Rowena Fong & Sharlene Furuto eds., 2001) [hereinafter CULTURALLY COMPETENT PRACTICE].

11. Ruth G. Dean, *The Myth of Cross-Cultural Competence*, 82 FAM. SOC'Y: J. CONTEMP. HUM. SERV. 623, 625 (2001). *See also* Laird, *in* RE-VISIONING FAMILY THERAPY, *supra* note 8.

12. *See* T.K. OOMMEN, CITIZENSHIP, NATIONALITY AND ETHNICITY 63 (1997); Anthony E. Varona, Blind Justice and Invisible Walls: Exposing and Surmounting Barriers to Legal Services through Cultural-Sensitive Lawyering 46–47 (1992) (unpublished J.D. research project, Boston College Law School) (on file with the authors). Anthony Verona is Associate Professor of Law, American University.

13. *See* Dean, *supra* note 11, at 624. As Professor Dean writes:

I ... propose a model in which maintaining an awareness of one's lack of competence is the goal rather than the establishment of competence. With "lack of competence" as the focus, a different view of practicing across cultures emerges. The client is the "expert" and the clinician is in a position of seeking knowledge and trying to understand what life is like for the client. There is no thought of competence—instead one thinks of gaining understanding (always partial) of a phenomenon that is evolving and changing.

and worldview of your client.[14] As one writer vividly describes it, you ought to proceed with "*informed not-knowing.*"[15] We like that phrase a lot.

We approach the "informed not-knowing" idea by using the concept of "heuristics." *Heuristics* represent a method of inquiry which employs generalizations and maxims to guide education or a learning process. It has achieved particular significance in the past decade within the field of behavioral psychology, which attempts to explain human behavior not through classical economic rationality but instead through the operation of sometimes less-than-rational thinking patterns on which most of us rely to organize our worlds.[16] In contrast to the behavioral psychologists' understanding of heuristics as reflexive operations guiding decisionmaking without much conscious deliberation, we employ the concept as a more explicitly deliberative operation. The key point about heuristics is that they rely on generalizations which are not absolute, but are more tentative and preliminary.

The central premise of the heuristics idea is this: A lawyer working with a client can neither assume that the client's cultural preferences do not matter (as some of the dominant culture models imply), nor be certain that the specific differences of which the lawyer is aware will call for predictable variations in their interaction. The former danger we label as cultural imperialism; the latter, stereotyping. What the good-faith lawyer needs is an orientation to cross-cultural practice which respects differences but does not guess incorrectly how the differences will matter.

If *every* aspect of the interviewing and counseling process were open for reconsideration in cross-cultural contexts, a lawyer would feel powerless about how to proceed. The models suggested for dominant culture interactions would have no guiding relevance. A review of the extensive literature on the topic of cross-cultural practice, though, shows that in those settings everything is not open to reconsideration. In fact, there are several identifiable, reasonably predictable ways in which cultures will differ, and will influence their

---

14. *See id. See also* Harlene Anderson & Harold Goolishian, *The Client Is the Expert: A Not-Knowing Approach to Therapy, in* THERAPY AS SOCIAL CONSTRUCTION 25 (Sheila McNamee & Kenneth J. Gergen eds., 1992).

15. Laird, *in* RE-VISIONING FAMILY THERAPY, *supra* note 8, at 21 (*quoting* V. Shapiro, *Subjugated Knowledge and the Working Alliance: The Narratives of Russian Jewish Immigrants,* 1 IN SESSION: PSYCHOTHERAPY IN PRACTICE 9 (1995)) (emphasis added).

16. *See, e.g.,* BEHAVIORAL LAW AND ECONOMICS (Cass R. Sunstein ed., 2000); Christine Jolls et al., *A Behavioral Approach to Law and Economics,* 50 STAN. L. REV. 1471 (1998); Russell Korobkin & Chris Guthrie, *Psychological Barriers to Litigation Settlement: An Experimental Approach,* 97 MICH. L. REV. 107 (1994).

members. A culturally competent lawyer can anticipate the areas where difference is most likely to arise, and, equally importantly, the direction in which the differences are most likely to proceed. Knowing that, a lawyer can anticipate provisionally the places where her model's world view might not be the same as that of her culturally different client, remaining open to possible misunderstanding, the possibility of conversation about the differences, if appropriate, and the possibility of adjustment to accommodate the differences.

It is in this fashion that we suggest you consider the idea of heuristics. By identifying the places where cultures are most apt to differ, and by knowing a bit about how each culture differs on these scores, you can plan for a session with a culturally different client by the use of tentative generalizations accompanied by a *disciplined naïveté*[17] regarding interpersonal dynamics about which you previously may have felt some real, but possibly misplaced, confidence. Part II describes several areas in which you might expect predictable differences among cultures, and proposes heuristics to employ when working with clients from those non-mainstream cultures.

There is another orienting topic to cover before we move on. In the "heuristics" section of this chapter, we will assume that the skill models typically available to law students and lawyers will apply, at least presumptively, with dominant culture (usually understood as White American) clients, and that the pressing question for students and lawyers is how, if at all, the dominant culture models ought to be changed with clients who are not from that dominant culture. This assumption or premise narrows the focus of our inquiry, of course. As many have written, and as the above definition of culture suggests, *all* counseling is cross-cultural—even an interaction between a male, WASP lawyer from Newton Centre, Massachusetts and his male, WASP client from the same city. But the traditionally taught lawyering skills models have been developed with an eye to suggesting behaviors most apt to work generally, and if there is a cultural skew in the models it would be (and we believe it plainly has been) in favor of the dominant, Eurocentric conception of a per-

---

17. The idea of disciplined naïveté as a critical virtue of cross-cultural counseling has been suggested by David Sue & Derald Wing Sue, Counseling the Culturally Different 115 (3d ed. 1999) [hereinafter Sue & Sue 1999]; Sue Bryant, *see* Bryant, *supra* note 1, at 62; and Jean Koh Peters, Representing Children in Child Protection Proceedings: Ethical and Practical Dimensions 249–50 (2001). *See also* Dean, *supra* note 11, at 623 (proposing "a model based on acceptance of one's lack of competence in cross-cultural matters"); Laird, *in* Re-Visioning Family Therapy, *supra* note 8, at 23 (describing "informed not-knowing").

sonality. In working with a client who may not share the expected personality conceptions, you want to consider how to adjust your skill sets.

Note, though, that this premise or assumption leaves out *your* cultural background. There are important ways in which a lawyer's cultural background affects the work about which we write here. To the extent that the skills taught in law school seek to maximize your client's comfort and trust, you may rely on the traditional models when working with dominant culture clients, for those models are apt to be pretty reliable for that purpose. If you happen to share that client's dominant culture background, then, presumably, your use of the models will be uncomplicated (except to the extent that using the models themselves is a challenge, which we ought not underestimate, and except to the extent, as just noted, that all counseling is cross-cultural). If you do not share your client's dominant culture background, then you will be working with models crafted with your client in mind, but not necessarily with your culture in mind. As we see below, a critical responsibility of cross-cultural practice is to understand, respect, and work with your client's preferences and values. The models help you do so in the setting where you are working with a dominant culture client, because they assume the dominant culture perspective (for both lawyers and clients). In this respect the skills privilege your client's cultural preferences and values, but not yours.

Your cultural background and preferences are the subject of our last section of this chapter. There, we address the importance for any lawyer of understanding his or her cultural identity, including biases, stereotypes, values, and comfort patterns. Many sophisticated writers about cross-culture counseling teach us that no lawyer enters into an attorney-client relationship without a complex package of learned behaviors, assumptions, and biases. Not only do you need to know something about how different cultures might respect different values, customs, and practices, but you also must "move[] from being culturally unaware to being aware and sensitive to [your] own cultural issues and to the ways that [your] own values and biases affect culturally diverse clients."[18] Understanding your complex package and identifying its components explicitly is a critical step in becoming a better cross-cultural lawyer, as that awareness might allow greater appreciation for the culture of your client and minimize the perception of the client as the one who is "different." We try to show you ways to accomplish that goal.

---

18. Donald B. Pope-Davis & Jonathan G. Dings, *The Assessment of Multicultural Counseling Competencies, in* HANDBOOK OF MULTICULTURAL COUNSELING, *supra* note 7, at 287, 287–88.

II. Heuristics

The heuristics concept is an effort to resolve, in a pragmatic kind of way, two apparent hurdles that arise upon the discovery that the typical lawyering models are constructed upon dominant culture assumptions, which may not apply necessarily in minority-culture contexts. The two hurdles are (1) confronting your uncertainty whether *any* of the suggestions from a previously acceptable model ought to apply in cross-cultural practice (or, put another way, your not knowing which of the assumptions underlying the models ought to be rethought in any given encounter); and (2) your worry that in responding to culturally different clients you will rely on stereotypes which might not work with the particular individual with whom you happen to be working. These hurdles are no small challenge. If you use dominant culture models faithfully regardless of the cultural background of your client, you will no doubt fail in some respects as a lawyer. So you opt to adapt the models, but you wish to know which parts of the model are likely to be inappropriate for culturally different clients. And, even if you can figure out that puzzle, you encounter the further worry that you will presume in some kind of slavish way that your client must share some characteristics of her culture, and that feels like unfair stereotyping.

The idea of heuristics might help you on both of these counts. First, as we see, there are a limited range of heuristics which will likely apply. That responds to your first concern. Not everything is subject to revision in cross-cultural practice, but certain predictable items ought to command your attention. Those items (including kinesics, proxemics, paralanguage, relational qualities, scientific orientation, and perhaps a few others) will call for a set of heuristics. In all other respects the models remain in place. In addition, because we work with heuristics and not rules or models, you minimize the stereotyping risk. The idea of a heuristic is that you assume tentatively—with your "disciplined naïveté" and "informed not-knowing"—a certain presumption about the behavior you're about to encounter, and better to assume some culturally predominant qualities than some culturally unlikely ones. Because you're applying heuristics, many of your presumptions prove to have been mistaken, but with some training you'll be flexible enough to adjust when your expectations seem unfounded.

The vast literature on cross-cultural counseling in the fields of social work and psychotherapy has identified several important areas in which cultures are most apt to differ. A lawyer who fails to understand these differences, or to anticipate that some such differences might exist, risks misunderstanding, insulting, or offending her client. The following sections summarize some of the most critical areas, with a brief explanation of how certain cultures tend to differ from the dominant American culture. A culturally competent lawyer ought to have available to her resource materials which would explain the cultural traits, customs, and values that she can expect to encounter in her work with diverse clients. That kind of book-research, though, has limited usefulness. It might be supplemented with other means of understanding ethnic culture, including attending cultural events in the community where your clients live, and speaking with your clients about these topics. As one writer has cautioned, "Be tactful and discreet and quietly compare any book learning against the actual situation. Use book learning as an aid to understanding, *not* as a template into which the world will actually be fitted."[19]

In reviewing these places where cultures tend to differ in some predictable ways, we attempt to suggest a level of practical application for concepts which sometimes remain a bit theoretical in their discussions. It is quite common, in textbooks written for social work or mental health professions as well as in the few resources emerging for lawyers, to observe authors insisting that professionals anticipate and understand cultural differences in their work with clients, but without offering adequate guidance to the professionals about *how* to accomplish those tasks. The areas we describe here hardly achieve the goal of adequate guidance, but they do represent a beginning effort to turn the discussion to a more concrete level.

A. Proxemics

The concept of *proxemics* refers to "perception and use of personal and interpersonal space."[20] Cultures tend to develop relatively unambiguous norms concerning appropriate physical distance in social interactions. Most lawyering counseling texts attend to proxemics, and do so with the expected dominant culture norms in mind. For instance, one respected interviewing and counseling text reports on the research available on the effect of distance, including the respect for some "critical space," on effectiveness of communication, and reporting that "experiments indicate that ... five and one-half feet is the preferred distance between people...."[21] Another central text refers its

---

19. FRAN CRAWFORD, JALINARDI WAYS: WHITEFELLAS WORKING IN ABORIGINAL COMMUNITIES 56 (1989), *quoted in* Dean, *supra* note 11, at 629.

20. DAVID SUE & DERALD WING SUE, COUNSELING THE CULTURALLY DIFFERENT 53 (2d ed. 1990) [hereinafter SUE & SUE 1990].

21. THOMAS L. SHAFFER & JAMES R. ELKINS, LEGAL INTERVIEWING AND COUNSELING IN A NUTSHELL 225 (3d ed. 1997). While this book seems to assume some universality of

readers to the "[s]ubstantial literature … devoted to how offices should be dec-orated and arranged to put clients at ease," after suggesting that lawyers "[h]ave an area of your office which is conducive to personal conversation rather than attempting to communicate across a large and often messy desk."[22] A very common suggestion in interviewing and counseling texts is to reduce the psy-chological barriers between lawyer and client by meeting face-to-face rather than across a desk.[23]

All of these suggestions make important sense, and are necessary for be-ginning lawyers to understand. But, as Derald Wing Sue and David Sue re-mind us, "different cultures dictate different distances in personal space."[24] Many cultures, including Latin American, African, Black American, Indone-sian, Arab, South American, and French, prefer discourse at a much closer distance than White American culture finds comfortable or appropriate.[25] Other cultures, such as the British, maintain a greater distance than traditional American custom.

You now may see for the first time in this discussion how a set of heuris-tics about proxemics might assist you when you are working with a minority culture client. The academy's dominant culture training will have established for you certain relatively reflexive feelings about social distance, and you might well in a dominant culture meeting rely on those understandings in deciding how close to your client you will sit, how you might arrange your furniture, and so forth. When you meet with a client from a different culture, however, you might want to assume a bit more naïveté about these issues. You can rely on some generalizations (the heuristic) about how your client will react to so-cial distance. If you have read that "[m]any Latina/o people often prefer half

---

the effect of distance and other proxemics on communication and rapport, it is in fact quite vivid in its recognition of the importance of the particular client's needs, including a partly-in-jest suggestion that lawyers use furniture on wheels and permit clients to choose which office furniture arrangement works best for them. *See id.* at 224.

22. BINDER ET AL. 1990, *supra* note 2, at 85–86.

23. *See, e.g.,* FRED E. JANDT, EFFECTIVE INTERVIEWING 31–32 (1990); BASTRESS & HAR-BAUGH, *supra* note 2, at 135–36.

24. SUE & SUE 1990, *supra* note 20, at 53 (citing Nan M. Sussman & Howard M. Rosen-feld, *Influence of Culture, Language and Sex on Conversation Distance,* 42 J. PERSONALITY & SOC. PSYCHOL. 66 (1982) and Aaron Wolfgang, *The Function and Importance of Nonverbal Behavior in Intercultural Counseling, in* HANDBOOK OF CROSS-CULTURAL COUNSELING AND THERAPY (Paul B. Pedersen ed., 1985)).

25. *Id. See also* ALLEN E. IVEY & MARY BRADFORD IVEY, INTENTIONAL INTERVIEWING AND COUNSELING: FACILITATING DEVELOPMENT IN A MULTICULTURAL SOCIETY 35 (4th ed. 1999).

[the dominant culture] distance, and those from the Middle East may talk practically eyeball to eyeball,"[26] you might assume—with some tentativeness—that your usual social distances might inaccurately imply aloofness or disinterest in meetings with Latina/o or Middle Eastern clients, and therefore attempt a bit closer contact. Of course, your own social background and cultural influences cannot be ignored either, so you will search for a setting that accommodates the (possibly) different preferences of your client with your own comfort levels.

This first example of the use of heuristics invites us to consider the risk of being wrong. The perhaps most respected work on cross-cultural counseling in the psychotherapy literature offers the following caveat to its readers:

> It is extremely difficult to speak specifically about the application of multicultural strategies and techniques in minority families because of the great variations not only among Asian Americans, African Americans, Latino/Hispanic Americans, Native Americans, and Euro-Americans, but because large variations exist within the groups themselves.... Worse yet, we might foster overgeneralizations that would border on being stereotypes. Likewise, to attempt an extremely specific discussion would mean dealing with literally thousands of racial, ethnic, and cultural combinations, a task that is not humanly possible.[27]

These sophisticated observers of cultural patterns concede that cultural competence is anything but a precise science, and that making assumptions about an individual because of her race or cultural background may lead to mistakes. How do you work with this uncertainty?

The concept of heuristics is intended to respond to precisely this problem of uncertainty. Our advice to you is this: If you were to apply automatically the dominant culture model and ignore the cultural differences which might be in play (because of your legitimate worry about being wrong), you would face a risk of error in that direction. It seems far more prudent, given the risks of error in both directions, to assume tentatively that the known generalizations *apply*, rather than that they do not apply. The heuristics are just that—preliminary orientations from which you will deviate based upon your own pragmatic judgments arising from your interaction with the culturally different client. It is better, in short, to err by assuming provisionally that the cul-

---

26. IVEY & IVEY, *supra* note 25, at 35.
27. SUE & SUE 1999, *supra* note 17, at 115.

tural generalizations will apply, than to err by assuming provisionally that they do not.

This first heuristic example also invites another consideration which will arise in each heuristics area that we explore in this chapter—whether you ought simply to talk to your client about the matters that you suspect will be different from the model's suggestions. The concern is this: Might you, amidst conditions of uncertainty, *ask the client* about his cultural preferences and any differences that you might be expecting? The answer to this question will often be "yes," but not necessarily always. Later parts of this chapter will address some ways cultures differ in their reactions to and respect for an attorney's status, comfort level with engaging in dialogue, and valuing autonomy. The culturally different client's preferences on *those* items may affect significantly the prospect for the attorney and client to engage in a mutual exploration of the differences.

In the case of proxemics, some decisions will simply not be subject to collaborative decisionmaking. It would be hard, I imagine, for you to have a productive conversation with a new client about how close to him you ought to stand. You might, by contrast, set up your office in a way that permits you to offer him a choice that includes your provisional assessment of how his culture would arrange such a meeting room, but that interaction might be distorted by his need to defer to your authority, if that cultural value is central to him.

This discussion of heuristics about proxemics invites one final thought about the enterprise of working as a lawyer with culturally different clients. Without an appreciation of cultural preferences about proxemics, many lawyers might interpret "inappropriate" (from a dominant culture perspective) use of physical space as odd, deviant, or "difficult." Similar culturally-specific behaviors might even lead a professional inappropriately to suspect mental illness. The benefits of provisional heuristics and reinforced naïveté include a more sustained appreciation and tolerance for "difficult" behaviors, especially when combined with an examination of your own personal cultural assumptions, values, and biases.

B. Kinesics

The term *kinesics* refers to the way in which bodily movements are used and interpreted. It includes such things as facial expressions, eye contact, hand shakes, posture, gestures, and similar physical movements. "[K]inesics appears to be culturally conditioned, with the meaning for body movements strongly linked to culture."[28]

---

28. SUE & SUE 1990, *supra* note 20, at 54.

The role of kinesics in legal interviewing and counseling is sometimes quite explicit and central, and in other ways it is more subtle. It seems clear, though, that your attempts to achieve effective and meaningful communication and rapport with your clients will be influenced (and evaluated) by your reading of kinesics. A culturally inept lawyer will misread cues, to the detriment of the relationship; and a culturally competent lawyer will understand her clients' cues more accurately, to the benefit of the relationship.

As with proxemics, kinesics may be approached by the employment of heuristics. You can learn about patterns of physical behavior common to various cultures, and approach a meeting with a culturally different client with the tentative expectation that your client will act consistently with her culture. Some of the most common sources of misunderstanding, or of offending another, include the following:

Eye contact: We rely on eye contact, or its absence, to communicate a great deal about feelings, truthfulness, confidence, and comfort level. In the dominant culture, eye contact has some seemingly shared meaning. Those in the dominant culture usually understand a strong, unwavering gaze to indicate honesty, self-assurance, and comfort. By contrast, shifting eye contact or very little eye contact tends to communicate, in the dominant culture, just the opposite—lack of self-esteem, discomfort, and possibly untruthfulness.[29] The textbooks that teach effective lawyer/client relations rely on these generalizations in recommending that lawyers master eye contact as an appropriate rapport-building tool.[30]

Both the dominant culture and less mainstream cultures recognize that messages are sent by eye contact, but not all cultures agree on the positive/neg-

---

29. An inability to sustain eye contact for more than a second or two at a time can be informative. Client persistence in glancing away from you immediately after making eye contact evidences nervousness or, possibly, deceit (hence the term "shifty-eyed"). A client who never, or almost never, looks at you indicates a severe state—perhaps a total breakdown in trust, an intense dislike, extreme nervousness, psychiatric or physical illness, or some combination of these. BASTRESS & HARBAUGH, *supra* note 2, at 139.

30. *See, e.g.,* COCHRAN ET AL., *supra* note 2, at 63 ("[G]eneral factors that contribute to an effective interview include … making and keeping eye contact throughout the interview"); Binder et al. 1990, *supra* note 2, at 50 (in using silence as a facilitator, you should "keep your attention on the client and give other non-verbal cues (such as leaning forward, maintaining eye contact, or nodding your head) to indicate your expectation that the client will continue speaking"); *id.* at 254 (suggesting the use of "[d]irect eye contact," a serious expression, and a few shakes of the head to communicate to a suspected lying client that you are not fooled by his lie).

ative valences of this cue. For instance, studies of kinesics within Black communities have shown that Blacks make less frequent eye contact than Whites, especially when listening. White Americans tend to engage in more sustained eye contact when listening and less when speaking; Black Americans tend to exhibit the reverse pattern—more eye contact when speaking and less when listening.[31] This latter phenomenon can, within dominant culture circles, lead to an inference that the listener is inattentive, uncomfortable, or bored. Eye contact patterns are also different in some Asian cultures, notably Japanese and Chinese, where avoiding eye contact is considered a sign of respect,[32] and in traditional Navajo society where eye contact is also deemed inappropriate.[33]

Facial Expressiveness: Within the dominant culture individuals intuit a great deal from the facial expressions of those with whom they interact. They take pleasure in the smile, and attribute positive qualities, including intelligence and personality, to those who smile often.[34] If their clients demonstrate "inappropriate" facial expressions (not smiling when politeness or the pleasurable context would call for a smile, or not frowning at painful moments), they might assume that the clients are somehow "off." Again, as with proxemics or with eye contact, those cues and inferences are valuable and frequently reliable, but they are almost entirely culturally determined (and, even within the dominant culture, may be gender-based as well). Certain Asian cultures in particular teach that restraint of strong feelings is a virtue, and a sign of maturity and wisdom. Thus, smiling may indicate discomfort.[35] That cultural trait has led dominant culture observers to misconstrue Asians as inscrutable, unfeeling, deceptive, and sneaky. In the American Black culture the customs may also be different about expressing emotions, facially and otherwise, including less smiling and more expressions of unhappiness than the dominant culture custom finds appropriate.[36]

Hand Shaking: It is a universally expected ritual in the dominant American culture for two persons when meeting in a professional or work context to

---

31. SUE & SUE 1990, *supra* note 20, at 56; Michelle Jacobs, *People from the Footnotes: The Missing Element in Client-Centered Counseling*, 27 GOLDEN GATE U. L. REV. 345, 358–59 (1997).

32. *See* WANDA M. L. LEE, AN INTRODUCTION TO MULTICULTURAL COUNSELING 104–13 (1999).

33. IVEY & IVEY, *supra* note 25, at 87.

34. SUE & SUE 1990, *supra* note 20, at 54 (citing Sing Lau, *The Effect of Smiling on Person Perception*, 117 J. SOC. PSYCHOL. 63 (1982)).

35. IVEY & IVEY, *supra* note 25, at 87.

36. *See* LEE, *supra* note 32, at 76–87.

shake hands, and guide books on successful professional behavior will offer suggestions about how to communicate the best messages when shaking hands.[37] Obviously hand shaking is a cultural artifact, and as such it may develop variations in differing cultures. Latinos, for instance, tend to shake hands more vigorously, frequently, and for a longer period of time than in the dominant American culture, according to the literature. In some Moslem and Asian countries, touching with the left hand is considered taboo, while in some Asian cultures assertive hand shaking, especially by women, is not considered proper.[38]

C. Time and Priority Considerations

Most of us can relate stories of our frustration with clients who miss appointments, or show up late, and seem not at all apologetic about the inconsiderateness of their behavior. "I really wonder whether [name the client here] really cares about this case as much as I do. And s/he's getting these valuable legal services free!" is a comment we have heard not infrequently in our clinics. Such reactions are entirely sensible given the dominant culture world view shared by many students and teachers. Prevailing American culture, especially as it is known in the law office, respects time as a commodity and an appointment as an organizing construct for allocating that scarce commodity.

Clients who "abuse" our allocation of this resource *may well be* inconsiderate and uninterested in their legal problem. But the cross-cultural perspective suggests other explanations, which your disciplined naïveté and thinking about "parallel universes"[39] might encourage you to consider. In some cultures, time considerations simply have a different meaning than in our dominant culture. Hispanic culture, the researchers tell us, does not consider time in the same literal and specific fashion that most law offices tend to do.[40] Sue

---

37. *See, e.g.,* TERENCE BRAKE ET AL., DOING BUSINESS INTERNATIONALLY: THE GUIDE TO CROSS-CULTURAL SUCCESS 118 (1995).

38. SUE & SUE 1990, *supra* note 20, at 55; *see also* ANN CADDELL CRAWFORD, CUSTOMS AND CULTURE OF VIETNAM 108 (1966).

39. *See* Bryant, *supra* note 1, at 70–72; PETERS, *supra* note 17, at 307–312. The "parallel universe" habit asks lawyers to "brainstorm alternative explanations for client behavior that initially puzzles or annoys the lawyer," and "to challenge his or her own assumptions [about client behavior] with fact." PETERS, *supra* note 17, at 248–250.

40. *See* FREDDY A. PANIAGUA, ASSESSING AND TREATING CULTURALLY DIVERSE CLIENTS: A PRACTICE GUIDE 37 (1994); Earleen Baggett, *Cross-Cultural Legal Counseling*, 18 CREIGHTON L. REV. 1475, 1490 (1985); Harold Cheatham et al., *Multicultural Counseling and Therapy II: Integrative Practice, in* COUNSELING AND PSYCHOTHERAPY: A MULTICUL-

and Sue distinguish between the "future" time orientation of middle-class White Americans, the "past-present" time orientation of Asian Americans and Latino Americans, and the "present" orientation of American Indians and African Americans.[41] It is very easy, but culturally hegemonic, to assume that the rest of the world views time and appointments in the same way that the dominant culture does.

Another explanation for the difference in respecting appointments rests with many of our clients' lived experience in poverty. Not only do our clients have frequent bureaucratic experiences in which a 9:00 a.m. appointment means being called at 10:30 a.m., but their lives will often be filled with more stresses and crises than we can imagine in our organized law firm world.

D. Narrative Preferences

The dominant culture models for interviewing and counseling encourage you to provide the maximum space for an undistorted client narrative. The goal of most legal interviewing and counseling books is to suggest the best techniques for learning the client's story from the client's point of view. It is hard to disagree with that goal, one which seems to hold across differing cultures, since a lawyer cannot begin to do a lawyer's job without knowing the facts of the client's case and the solutions that the client has in mind. This shared goal serves as an apt example of the point made earlier in this chapter—that cross-cultural interactions will not call into question *everything* that one might learn about the lawyering process from within the dominant culture.

This unambiguous goal of the counseling process does encounter some complications in the context of culturally different clients, however, even if it is not a culturally-driven goal. The complications arise from two assumptions of the dominant culture models. First, the models wisely advise the use of open-ended, undirected questions as primary vehicles by which to learn a client's story, but individuals from some cultures will resist that narrative technique. Second, the models implicitly (and at times explicitly) assume a commitment to autonomy as a critical premise of the lawyer/client interaction. The dedication to autonomy may in fact be a culturally-manifested construct in the dominant American culture. To the extent that models assume autonomy as a "good," they may fail to achieve their aims with some culturally different clients.

TURAL PERSPECTIVE 170, 177 (Allen E. Ivey et al. eds., 4th ed. 1997) [hereinafter COUNSELING AND PSYCHOTHERAPY].

41. SUE & SUE 1990, *supra* note 20, at 125–29.

To the extent that we are looking for workable heuristics, it is fair to conclude that the narrative-based focus of the dominant culture models will work
in most settings, and hence can serve as a reliable technique most of the time.
But some cultures, and some persons within some cultures, may resist the fundamental techniques of silence and open questions used to encourage the
client to talk most of the time. As a culturally competent counselor, you might
alter your heuristics in settings where this risk appears to be a possibility. For
instance, Michelle Jacobs reminds us that Black clients may feel considerable
distrust of a White professional.[42] With such clients techniques that call for
open, free-flowing narrative by the client might not be effective until a trusting relationship has been affirmed. Other observers tell us that some cultures
might respond less well to unstructured, non-directive techniques, especially
those cultures which favor verbal restraint over verbal expressiveness.[43]

The commitment to autonomy affects the counseling process in significant,
if perhaps subtle, ways. That value, so deeply-entrenched in American culture, causes lawyers to strive for strict neutrality in their counseling processes
(a paradigmatic quality of "client-centered counseling") and to search hard for
evidence of the client's *personal* values. These important elements of the dominant culture counseling models will be appropriate most of the time, but not
always. Research has shown that some non-Western cultures find non-directiveness in counseling to be much less effective than the American models assume. Parallels to psychotherapy may be apt here. Critics of the dominant
psychotherapy schools observe that "therapists tend to prefer clients who exhibit the YAVIS syndrome: young, attractive, verbal, intelligent, and successful."[44] Therapy works best when the clients are verbally, emotionally, and be-
haviorally expressive, and, conversely, less well when the clients are not so
expressive. In cultures which discourage self-disclosure, such as Japanese or
some Latino cultures, an interviewer expecting the client to provide a narra-

---

42. Jacobs, *supra* note 31, at 384–91.

43. *See* SUE & SUE 1990, *supra* note 20, at 71 (noting the resistance of Asian cultures to
"attending" (non-directive) techniques versus "influencing" (directive) techniques).

44. *Id.* at 33 (citing WILLIAM SCHOFIELD, PSYCHOTHERAPY: THE PURCHASE OF FRIEND-
SHIP (1964)). Sue and Sue report a later commentator's label for the obvious reciprocal
less-preferred clients: "QUOID," for quiet, ugly, old, indigent, and culturally dissimilar.
BINDER ET AL. 1990, *supra* note 2, at 21 (citing N.D. Sundberg, *Cross-Cultural Counseling
and Psychotherapy: A Research Overview, in* CROSS-CULTURAL COUNSELING AND PSY-
CHOTHERAPY (A. J. Mansella & Paul B. Pedersen eds., 1981)). For further discussion of the
YAVIS preference, see PATRICIA D'ARDENNE & ARUNA MAHTANI, TRANSCULTURAL COUN-
SELING IN ACTION 41, 87 (2d ed. 1999).

tive tale may be disappointed. Once again, there is the accompanying risk that the lawyer will perceive a client who does not participate in the narrative, revealing process as difficult, dishonest, or uncooperative.

In similar fashion, the client-centered model of counseling taught in law schools assumes a "Rogerian" non-directive stance on the part of the lawyer.[45] This fundamental premise of dominant culture counseling models flows from the value of autonomy, with its insistence that a client's choices be determined by the client and not by the lawyer. That goal of the counseling process may seem to many law students quite self-evident, but it, too, is influenced by cultural assumptions and American and Eurocentric value structures. Many culturally different clients find a non-directive process frustrating and unhelpful. Cultures which value action and results more highly than process, insight, and deliberation look for more active direction from professionals. Relying on the dominant models with clients whose world orientation is different from that of the dominant culture can cause difficulty in the process and unhappiness on the part of the clients.

E. Relational Perspectives: Individualism versus Collectivism

The concern about presuming a commitment to autonomy and therefore to non-directiveness in counseling connects to another very common issue in multicultural counseling settings. The dominant culture models are largely individualistic, reflecting quite understandably the individualistic themes of the legal profession's ethics generally. Most interviewing and counseling models assume a single client describing his or her legal issue, making decisions for himself or herself, and grounding those decisions on the client's personal values. On occasion that world is expanded to include spouses,[46] but even that scenario is exceptional. The profession's ethics rules regarding confidentiality and conflicts of interests discourage lawyers from "pluralizing" the lawyer-client relationship, and the lawyering models tend to follow that lead.

The literature on cross-cultural interactions is rich with examples where the dominant cultural assumption of individual deliberation about personal

---

45. *See, e.g.,* BASTRESS & HARBAUGH, *supra* note 2, at 26–27 (citing CARL ROGERS, CLIENT-CENTERED THERAPY (1951)).

46. *See, e.g.,* Teresa Stanton Collett, *The Ethics of Intergenerational Representation*, 62 FORDHAM L. REV. 1453 (1994); Russell G. Pearce, *Family Values and Legal Ethics: Competing Approaches to Conflicts in Representing Spouses*, 62 FORDHAM L. REV. 1523 (1994).

values is quite inconsistent with minority cultural understandings and customs. In one vivid example, Charles Waldegrave quotes a Samoan individual who has been asked "what do you think?" and answers,

> It is so hard for me to answer that question. I have to think. What does my mother think? What does my grandmother think? What does my father think? What does my uncle think? What does my sister think? What is the consensus of those thoughts? Ah, that must be what I think.[47]

In her brilliant and evocative account of the American medical profession's interaction with a very dissimilar culture, the anthropologist Anne Fadiman documents how deep differences in world view can cause enormous misunderstanding in a professional relationship, even where both sides act in good faith toward a common goal.[48] Fadiman recounts the experiences of the Lees, a Hmong family living in Merced, California, after their daughter Lia suffers a mysterious and life-threatening illness. The well-meaning doctors at the Merced community hospital diagnose Lia's symptoms as a serious form of epilepsy; to the Hmong family, Lia is experiencing "when the spirit catches you and you fall down," an event caused by the evil *dab* spirit and most likely related to some important earlier ritual having been missed in Lia's life. Amidst the scores of agonizing stories Fadiman reports of intolerable frustrations felt by the Lee family toward the medical staff, and the medical staff toward the family, we learn of the implicit and deep connections among the extended Hmong family and community as they collectively care for Lia and search for her cure. The story one encounters is far from that of a nuclear family deciding in "substituted judgment" fashion what Lia would want. The Hmong traditions and world views do not distinguish between immediate family, extended family, the larger Hmong community, and the historical Hmong ancestry—all are vividly present as implicit context for the ways that the Lees live their lives and raise their daughter.

Lia's story arises in the context of medicine, and shows dramatically the dangers of misunderstanding across cultural gulfs. A recent research study of Latino families in litigation arrived at similar conclusions, in a more empirical fashion than the Fadiman account. [49] The study investigated the experi-

---

47. Charles Waldegrave, *The Challenge of Culture to Psychology and Postmodern Theory*, *in* RE-VISIONING FAMILY THERAPY, *supra* note 8, at 404, 407.

48. ANNE FADIMAN, THE SPIRIT CATCHES YOU AND YOU FALL DOWN: A HMONG CHILD, HER AMERICAN DOCTORS, AND THE COLLISION OF TWO CULTURES (1997).

49. *See* Steven Weller et al., *Fostering Culturally Responsive Courts: The Case of Family Dispute Resolution for Latinos*, 39 FAM. CT. REV. 185 (2001).

ences of recently-arrived Latino families, primarily from Mexico and Central America, in court-annexed mediation services in family law disputes. The authors found, in concluding that "[t]he justice system needs to better understand the culture of Latino family life and the ways in which Latinos interact with government authority," that the traditional mediation service offerings failed to account for the "collectivist orientation" of Latino families. The well-intended diversion methods offered by the court system misunderstood the significant influence of extended family and community leaders in Latino culture, and the "holistic" problem-solving orientation of that culture.

These three examples show us the need for a heuristic for the collectivist world view when working with culturally different clients. The Samoan, Hmong, and Latino cultures are hardly alone in their implicit acceptance of a connectedness to a larger family or community. Cross-cultural therapy researchers point out similar orientations among Haitians,[50] African Americans,[51] Asian Americans,[52] and Native Americans.[53] Paulette Moore Hines and Nancy Boyd-Franklin write, "In contrast to the European premise, 'I think, therefore, I am,' the prevailing African philosophy is 'We are, therefore, I am.'"[54] The individualism so cherished in the dominant culture may, in fact, be a less prevailing orientation overall. Your counseling practices could be affected significantly by this shift in world view, as you explore consequences to and values not only of your client, but also of his extended community. Less apparent, but equally important, are the changes that this heuristic might suggest for your interviewing practices. Not only might you invite more "strangers" into your interview meetings, but you may alter your strategy of "learning the client's story" in order to learn the story as it might look to others in the client's immediate circle.[55]

---

50. *See* Amy Bibb & Georges J. Casimir, *Haitian Families, in* ETHNICITY AND FAMILY THERAPY 97, 105 (Monica McGoldrick et al. eds., 2d ed. 1992).

51. Paulette Moore Hines & Nancy Boyd-Franklin, *African American Families, in* ETHNICITY AND FAMILY THERAPY, *supra* note 50, at 66, 70.

52. *See* SUE & SUE 1990, *supra* note 20, at 36.

53. *See* Michael Yellow Bird, *Critical Values and First Nations Peoples, in* CULTURALLY COMPETENT PRACTICE, *supra* note 10, at 61, 64–67.

54. Hines & Boyd-Franklin, *supra* note 51, at 66, 70.

55. But watch out about waiver of the attorney client privilege. According to most doctrine, the attorney-client privilege is waived if a friend, relative, or other non-essential person joins a meeting between the lawyer and the client. *See* FED. R. EVID. 503(a)(4); United States v. Evans, 113 F.2d 1457, 1464 (7th Cir. 1997) (privilege inapplicable absent showing that third party's presence was necessary to accomplish the object of the consultation).

Tolerance about difference is not necessarily without its anxieties, especially when the difference clashes with important values of our own. The Western preference for individuality and autonomy tends to include a strong commitment to egalitarianism in relationships. You may consider it your goal in "client-centered" counseling to achieve a measure of independence for your clients in their decisionmaking capacity. In working with cultures different from the dominant one, you may encounter a tension between egalitarian norms and the well-established sex roles of a minority culture. David Sue and Derald Wing Sue tell a story of an ineffective therapist who failed to appreciate the importance of a woman's expected role in a Hispanic family, and the power of *Machismo* within that culture. The counselor worked from his established world view that resisted patriarchy, and in doing so he failed to understand the needs of both members of the couple with whom he worked. "Therapists," Sue and Sue caution us, "should not judge the health of a family on the basis of the romantic egalitarian model characteristic of White culture."[56] Another pair of commentators offer the same advice in the context of Southeast Asian American clients. They write that we may need to accept "chauvinism to tolerate Confucius's teaching and centuries-old traditions."[57]

F. The Limits of Scientific Rationality

Our final heuristic is one that has frequent significance in the medical/psychotherapeutic field, and may have similar importance to your work with

---

56. SUE & SUE 1999, *supra* note 17, at 116.

57. Kazumi Nishio & Murray Bilmes, *Psychotherapy with Southeast Asian American Clients, in* COUNSELING AMERICAN MINORITIES: A CROSS-CULTURAL PERSPECTIVE (Donald R. Atkinson et al. eds., 4th ed. 1993). It is important to note, however, that the tolerance defended in the text is not a universally accepted moral or political position, at least with respect to some controversial cultural practices. As Joan Laird writes, "Others, more concerned about subjugation and injustice, take a very different stance. [One author], for example, argues that every therapeutic act is a political one, and that clients need to be helped to deconstruct not only their self-narratives but also the dominant culture narratives and discursive practices that constitute their lives." Laird, *in* RE-VISIONING FAMILY THERAPY, *supra* note 8, at 33. One particularly troubling cultural practice that offends many moral sensibilities is female genital mutilation. For a discussion of the multicultural feminist reaction to that practice, see Isabelle R. Gunning, *Global Feminism at the Local Level: Criminal and Asylum Laws regarding Female Genital Surgeries,* 3 J. GENDER RACE & JUST. 45 (1999); Isabelle R. Gunning, *Arrogant Perception, World-Traveling and Multicultural Feminism: The Case of Female Genital Surgeries,* 23 COLUM. HUM. RTS. L. REV. 189, 194–97 (1992).

clients on legal matters. The dominant culture is, not surprisingly, deeply committed to scientific rationality, and its counseling models reflect that orientation. One primary aim in legal counseling is to predict for clients the likelihood of differing outcomes, allowing a careful comparison of the available alternatives so that the client may choose the one which best serves his purposes. This structure allows for the most careful, reasoned client decisionmaking, even if recent work in the behavioral psychology field demonstrates that individuals rely on distorted reasoning in making many important decisions.

While conventional counseling models encourage you to respect the idiosyncratic wishes and values of your clients (and insist upon an anti-paternalistic stance on the part of lawyers), it is fair to say that the models do not easily accommodate mysticism, voodoo, and other "bizarre"[58] or irrational decisionmaking vehicles. Cross-cultural theorists tell us, though, that many non-Western cultures rely heavily on native rituals, beliefs, and practices which are not likely to be seen by United States-educated lawyers as "scientifically rational."

Anne Fadiman's story of the Hmong family and community in Merced, California is an apt example of how impatient dominant culture professionals can be when faced with unconventional rituals.[59] To her American doctors, Lia suffered from a complex seizure disorder treatable with sophisticated medical intervention, including significant medication regimens. To her Hmong family, Lia's spirit had been invaded by an evil *dab* spirit, and the only way to banish the *dab* was through indigenous healing arts, rituals, dermal treatments, and shamanism. The Hmong shaman was known as a *txiv neeb*,

> who was believed to have the ability to enter a trance, summon a posse of helpful familiars, ride a winged horse over the twelve mountains between the earth and the sky, cross an ocean inhabited by dragons, and (starting with bribes of food and money and, if necessary, working up to a necromantic sword) negotiate for his patients' health with the spirits who lived in the realm of the unseen.

The *txiv neeb*, his rituals, and his advice were enormously important to the Lees and their Hmong community, but his suggestions were of no use what-

---

58. *See* Bryant, *supra* note 1, at 2 (describing, as a trait of a culturally competent professional, "the capacity to make 'isomorphic attributions'… the capacity to enter the cultural imagination of another, as 'perceiving as normal things that at first seem bizarre or strange'" (quoting RAYMONDE CARROLL, CULTURAL MISUNDERSTANDINGS: THE FRENCH/AMERICAN EXPERIENCE 2 (1988))).

59. FADIMAN, *supra* note 48.

soever to the medical staff at Lia's hospital. Indeed, at one deeply painful juncture in Fadiman's story of Lia's illness the local Department of Child Protective Services obtained a court order and removed Lia from the Lee home, because the Lees were relying on indigenous Hmong remedies and refusing (or
failing) to comply with the medical directives from the hospital.

The Fadiman account does not, and cannot, conclude that the doctors were
wrong in their medical treatment of Lia or that they were negligent in fulfilling their professional medical obligations to her. Nor does her narrative imply
necessarily that the Lees were wrong in their noncompliance with the medical
treatment plans ordered by the hospital staff. It does convey acutely, though,
the depth of misunderstanding, distrust, and frustration engendered on both
sides of the cultural gulf by the narrow and limited focus of the medical personnel on their well-established traditional medical assumptions.

Fadiman's history is perhaps the most elaborate account of the centrality
of non-scientific rituals and beliefs in a different culture, but it is hardly the
only one. The literature on cross-cultural counseling shows us that many other
cultures hold strong attachments to deep-seated traditions which conventional
thinking might find less than scientific. A form of witchcraft, or "Obeah," is
common and important in Jamaican society.[60] Voodoo practice is deeply respected and common in Haitian culture.[61] American Indians have long practiced traditional healing rituals.[62] Puerto Rican children have been shown to
respond best to native folk-tale therapy when compared to more traditional
Western therapy.[63] Many other cultures no doubt respect similar traditional
practices and rituals.

You may find that this heuristic arises less often in your lawyering work
than others described above, and it may arise more infrequently in law than
in, say, medicine. But we have experienced a couple of disorienting moments
for which this heuristic might have helped. One of us worked with a client, a
woman from China, who genuinely feared that an individual important to her
case was a witch. We have also met clients who refuse to believe in the "sci-

---

60. *See* Janet Brice Baker, *Jamaican Families, in* ETHNICITY AND FAMILY THERAPY, *supra*
note 50, at 85, 92–93.

61. Bibb & Casimir, *supra* note 50, at 101.

62. Sandra K. Choney et al., *The Acculturation of American Indians: Developing Frame-*
works for Research and Practice, in HANDBOOK OF MULTICULTURAL COUNSELING, *supra*
note 7, at 73, 87.

63. Donald R. Atkinson & Susana M. Lowe, *The Role of Ethnicity, Cultural Knowledge,*
and Conventional Techniques in Counseling and Psychotherapy, in HANDBOOK OF MULTI-
CULTURAL COUNSELING, *supra* note 7, at 387, 404.

ence" of psychotherapy and counseling, and whose beliefs are disrespected in the world of lawyers and judges.

Your heuristic on this topic will encourage a nurturing of your "isomorphic attributions"[64] and your disciplined naïveté when working with culturally different clients. Your open-mindedness and tolerant acceptance of very different ways of thinking about problem-solving will reduce the likelihood of serious misunderstanding between you and your culturally different clients, and will forestall your concluding that the "bizarre" ways in which your clients respond to your carefully reasoned legal analyses of their problems means that something is seriously amiss with your clients.

III. Biases and Cultural Self-Awareness

Part II of this exploration of cross-cultural counseling has identified several heuristics which you might employ to reduce the risk of misunderstanding when you work with culturally different clients. The "heuristic" idea is intended to guide your work generally and provisionally, suggesting topics and areas where differences between cultures are most apt to exist.

The latter part of this chapter intends to complicate your life a bit more, but necessarily and importantly so. We turn here to the idea of "bias," and how it affects and interferes with your likely success even with the best heuristics and the most forthright discipline about naïveté. Unlike its use in the work of the decisional theorists, the term bias in this context refers to its more common meaning—prejudice, intolerance, distrust, belief in the inferiority of others. We explore briefly the role of one's own biases in the cross-cultural counseling endeavor. The biases that we need to consider are not as much the conscious, deliberate ones—most, if not all, readers of a work such as this are likely deeply opposed to prejudice and discrimination—as the implicit, unconscious ways in which our own cultural heritages, whatever they may be, influence our world view and our deep-seated assumptions about how the world works.

We start with a look at how these implicit, unconscious biases come to be. Each of us has subconscious cognitive categories, called schemas, that we automatically employ when we encounter other people and events. A schema is simply a means of organizing information "to identify objects, make predic-

---

64. *See* Bryant, *supra* note 1, at 56. "Isomorphic attribution" means "to attribute the same meaning to behavior and words that the person intended to convey." *Id.*

tions about the future, infer the existence of unobservable traits or properties, and attribute the causation of events."[65] A schema thus enables us to process information quickly and largely automatically. We create our schemas through the experience of our daily lives, from personal encounters, second-hand information, the media, etc. Behavior becomes associated with race, gender, age, roles, and character traits. Physical characteristics like skin color, gender, and age are readily perceived and therefore are more likely to become salient features in our cognitive categories. Each category then becomes a reference point for the people we meet, and we interact with others based on the category that is activated. If we do not question the expectations evoked by the activated category, insensitive behavior can result.

Here's one vivid example of what we mean. At a recent clinical education conference, a clinical teacher approached a fellow clinician (one of the authors) and asked her if she knew the Hong Kong—U.S. dollar exchange rate. What had struck the first teacher most about the other clinician was not that she is a clinician or an American—even though they were in Canada—but that she looks (and is) Asian (-American). For him, her ethnicity seemed to evoke a schema that said, Asian appearance = person knowledgeable about Hong Kong. And so he asked his question.

This kind of social categorization operates on an automatic level. Based on your own characteristics, you sort others into "in-groups" sharing characteristics with you and "out-groups" that do not.[66] The separation of others into in-groups and out-groups further influences the way in which you view others. So, if you have limited experience with members of different cultures, then the behavior of those few members of the out-group culture becomes more salient and might be seen as representative of that culture. In addition, you might use your in-group as a reference point for interpreting your own behavior as well as that of others. On a subconscious level, you might exaggerate differences among groups and favor members of your in-group over members of out-groups. Generally speaking, "[i]n-groups are more highly valued, more trusted, and engender greater cooperation as opposed to competi-

---

65. Linda Hamilton Krieger, *The Content of our Categories: A Cognitive Bias Approach to Discrimination and Equal Employment Opportunity*, 47 STAN. L. REV. 1161, 1188–89 (1995); Kim Taylor-Thompson, *Empty Voices in Jury Deliberations*, 113 HARV. L. REV. 1261, 1290–91 (2000).

66. *See* Bryant, *supra* note 1, at 64 ("Habit One first asks students to list and diagram similarities and differences between themselves and their clients and then to explore the significance of these similarities and differences.").

tion, and those with the strongest in-group affiliation also show the most prejudice."[67]

The challenge is to recognize when a schema about an out-group might also be a stereotype — "a generalized description of a group of people that has usually developed over time on the basis of cross-cultural interactions"[68] — so that you can learn to avoid reliance on it. Because a stereotype can become ingrained in a schema, the stereotype can create an unconscious expectation that an individual will conform to the stereotype. If the expectation is distorted or illusory, then you might unconsciously be biased in the way you interact with the person, who might be your client.

When your client comes from a culture different from yours, the risk of stereotyping is greater. If you are like most of the world, you will recall negative experiences with members of the client's culture more readily than you will recall negative experiences with members of your own culture. Thus, you run the risk of expecting negative behavior and then finding it, whether or not it actually occurred. In addition, you are more likely to attribute behaviors of the out-group client to his character traits if those behaviors fit your expectations, but to situational factors if his behaviors seem aberrant.[69] So, then, you might start to label your client who does not return phone calls as rude or uncaring instead of considering that work, personal, child-related, or other factors might account for the delay.[70]

To consider how these schemas are created and how they can affect your behavior, let us consider a real situation from our clinical practice. This is a story of a White student attorney working with a Black public housing tenant who was being evicted for nonpayment of rent. During her first meeting with the client, the student was shocked when her client informed her that she had lied to the clinic's intake worker about how much rent she owed to her landlord (the client had told the intake worker that she owed no rent). The student was equally surprised that the client had not paid rent that she seemingly could afford to pay under the rules governing public housing.

---

67. American Psychological Association, *Guidelines on Multicultural Education, Training, Research, Practice and Organizational Change for Psychologists* 19–20 (August 2002), *available at* http://www.apa.org/pi/multiculturalguidelines/formats.html (last visited Feb. 11, 2006) [hereinafter APA Guidelines] (citations omitted).

68. *Id.* at 11 (citation omitted). Familiarity with a stereotype should not imply prejudice, which is the "endorsement of negative attitudes toward and stereotypes about groups." *Id.* at 21; Taylor-Thompson, *supra* note 65, at 1291.

69. Krieger, *supra* note 65, at 1192–93 (citations omitted).

70. *See* discussion *supra* note 39.

After the client revealed and corrected the misinformation she'd given to the intake worker, the student continued the interview, asking questions about the rent that was due.[71] The client told the student that the housing authority had miscalculated some of her rent by failing to give her a mandatory rent freeze after she stopped receiving public assistance because she was working. She also informed the student that she had made efforts to pay the rent actually owed but that her money orders had been lost or stolen and, further, that she no longer had the money order receipts for the rent she did pay. On the one hand, this explanation was possible, as tenants often use money orders when they have no checking account; on the other hand, it was hard to believe that so many money orders had been lost or stolen, and that the receipts were also missing. The student did not know how to react to this part of the client's story, and, after asking whether the client still had her receipts from purchasing the money orders, did not push her farther.

After the student had left the clinic, though, the client confided, to the student's supervisor, that her explanation of lost and stolen money orders was not true. The client shared with the supervisor that she had in fact refused to pay the rent because of the racist and condescending attitude of the housing authority manager toward her. She was unwilling to negotiate with the manager but instructed the supervisor to offer a shorter, higher-level payment plan to the White housing authority lawyer who had charged the housing manager to correct the calculation of the tenant's rent. She based her more favorable offer on her willingness to work with a lawyer with whom she did not have a contentious history and on her desire to show her manager that she was a good and worthy tenant.

From this example, you can see that there are at least three ways in which the "bias" reality might affect your work with clients, and the rich literature from disciplines outside of law might help us understand each of these. First, as a professional you need to explore and confront your own cultural influences and the extent of your unconscious (or conscious) biases, including your own racism, sexism, classism, and homophobia. Second, your learned preferences might interfere with your appreciation of your clients' stories, to the detriment of your client's legal case, or with the clients' willingness to trust and confide in you. And third, it is important to your effectiveness as a lawyer

---

71. The student never asked the client why she had lied. Few students and lawyers probably would have. Had the student done so in a nonjudgmental manner, her interest in the client's motivations might have repaired any harm that may have occurred from the initial reaction of judgment and assumption.

to understand how societal and historical racism affects, and has affected, your clients' lives and the stories they bring to you as a helping professional, including how they view you.

Let us explore each of these ideas separately. For each of these topics, the discussion here is tentative and preliminary. Talking about race, class, gender, and power is complicated and often threatening to professionals, especially among lawyers. The suggestions here, borrowed from other professional worlds, might facilitate their discussion in the legal profession. As we discuss these three ideas, we will relate them back to this story.

A. Self-Awareness

In their portrayal of the "five habits of cross-cultural lawyering," Sue Bryant and Jean Koh Peters suggest a three-step process "for good cross-cultural lawyering:"

1. Identify assumptions in our daily practice.
2. Challenge assumptions with fact.
3. Lawyer based on fact.[72]

That first step—where you identify explicitly the assumptions which form the basis of your work—is essential to good lawyering generally, and especially so in cross-cultural practice. There are two components of this idea, both rather challenging, but one more easily confronted than the other.

The first, and more accessible, component touches on the relationship between your cultural identity and your lawyering performance. You possess some cultural identity (or identities) and have learned from your community (or communities) certain beliefs, habits, customs, ways of thinking, and values. These elements help define who you are, and your lawyering activities cannot but reflect them. You may not think very explicitly about those beliefs, habits, values, and so forth—they are just part of who you are and how you see the world. Now, your clients (and your colleagues, and any one else who is not you) will possess different identities, instilled from different communities, with different beliefs, customs, values, and so forth. Some will be very dissimilar from you; others, less so. But nobody will share all of your preferences with you.

---

72. PETERS, *supra* note 17, at 249; Bryant, *supra* note 1, at 64–99.

So the first part of the Peters and Bryant challenge is to recognize that you have assumptions and to understand where your assumptions come from, what they are, and how they influence your professional work. Having done so, you can better anticipate where your clients' preferences might depart from yours. You probably won't easily or necessarily change who you are, but you might appreciate better why your clients (and your colleagues) seem to see the world in ways that you do not and why they might see you and the legal system in ways you do not.

The researchers and theorists of multicultural counseling regularly include this important advice, which is at the heart of the "cultural competence" movement. Some of these sources offer exercises to unpack cultural assumptions and refine cultural identity. Certain exercises are intended for groups or for pairs, allowing a person to appreciate his or her cultural influences comparatively. Others may be performed alone. The exercises often require the participants to identify "who [they] are," as well as what values and practices are most important to them.[73] Other experts recommend developing a "family genogram," a map of your immediate and extended family which includes

---

73. For instance, one popular college course text offers a "Describing Cultural Identity" exercise which works as follows in a classroom setting:

Objective

To identify the complex culturally learned roles and perspectives that contribute to an individual's identity[.]

Instructions

In the blanks below, please write answers in a word or phrase to the simple question "Who are you?" Give as many answers as you can think of but try to identify at least 20 descriptors. Write the answers in the order that they occur to you. You will have 7 minutes to complete the list.

I AM _____

I AM _____

[Repeated 18 more times]

Debriefing

Ask volunteers to read their list out loud and count the numbers of others in the class who also used approximately the same label. Keep count of all the labels on a flipchart, blackboard, overhead, or whiteboard[, identifying which responses were] given by all, by many, by some, by few, or by only one to demonstrate the extent of similarity or difference in the group. If students would prefer to keep their identity labels confidential, their lists can be turned in anonymously and coded by the instructor for feedback to the class later. The instructor may use these data to discuss the importance of between-group and within-group differences.

PEDERSEN, *supra* note 6, at 271.

"your own perceptions of the relationships with and between family members."[74] The genogram will help you understand your intergenerational context and situate you within a wider culture. Jean Koh Peters and Sue Bryant use a similar device of Venn diagrams to chart "degrees of separation/connection" between a lawyer and her client.[75]

The story of Lia Lee, the Hmong child whose medical crises were documented in Ann Fadiman's book, offers powerful insights about a medical culture far short on reflection about its own unexamined assumptions. At the end of her book, Fadiman reports a conversation with the anthropologist and psychiatrist Arthur Kleinman, of Harvard Medical School, about the Lee saga. Kleinman's observations about the Merced doctors' interactions with the Hmong family apply with equal force to the legal community:

> [Y]ou need to understand that as powerful an influence as the culture of the Hmong patient and her family in this case, the culture of biomedicine is equally powerful. If you can't see that your own culture has its own set of interests, emotions, and biases, how can you expect to deal successfully with someone else's culture?[76]

The Kleinman quote provides an apt segue to the second component of the Peters and Bryant "identify your assumptions" (or, perhaps, "know thyself") suggestion. This second component is the more challenging one, but no less important to effective lawyering practice. Here, the task is not simply to understand your identity and its preferences and values; it is also to understand how your cultural background has influenced your own views about race, sex, class, and sexual orientation. It asks you to confront your own biases, your own stereotypes, and your own participation in oppressive societal practices.

Let's revisit the clinic student who was incredulous that her client had lied to the intake worker, to unpack the assumptions she brought to working with this client. At the time of the meeting, the student had little experience with legal clients. Indeed, her primary idea of a client was her mother—a white, small-business owner, married to a minister, and then involved in litigation. The student could not imagine her mother lying, especially to her lawyer, or being financially irresponsible. Hence her shock at the client's lie.

---

74. COUNSELING AND PSYCHOTHERAPY, *supra* note 40, at 43. *See also* IVEY & IVEY, *supra* note 25, at 236–37.

75. PETERS, *supra* note 17, at 264–273; Bryant, *supra* note 1, at 64.

76. FADIMAN, *supra* note 48, at 261.

Had the student stopped her reflection at this point, she could have done herself and her client a disservice. As Patricia D'Ardenne and Aruna Mahtani demonstrate in the therapeutic counseling context,

> When the counselor and client are from differing cultural backgrounds, countertransference invades the therapeutic relationship in a particularly insidious way. Counselors are unlikely to examine their own racism and cultural prejudice. As a consequence of this neglect, unacknowledged prejudice is reflected back unconsciously in the therapeutic relationship.... The dissonance in the relationship results in both parties having their beliefs about the other's culture reinforced.[77]

There is little reason to believe that the risks within the lawyer/client relationship are any less substantial.[78]

However, in supervision, the student explored her cultural expectations about clients. In so doing, she realized that her conception of a client was based on limited experience (her mother as client) and the expectation that a client can shop around for a lawyer, not that the client must market herself to a lawyer. She and her partner also considered different reasons why the client might have lied, including the possibility that the client might have believed the lie would make her a better candidate to receive a scarce intake appointment. This recognition, coupled with the client's clearing of the record, helped the student to move past her reaction to the client's lie and to appreciate the client's retraction.

Having probed her assumptions about this client, the student now would have a chance to adjust her lawyering for the next client. Most likely, the student would incorporate this experience into her existing client schema. Her client schema might now recognize that clients might lie or, more specifically, that poor, Black American clients might lie. The next time she were to encounter a poor, Black American client, she would automatically recollect this schema. That recollection might give rise to an expectation that this new client would lie. If, however, the student were to recognize that such an expectation might be generalized and generalized on too little information, then she might act differently toward this next client. She might, for example, consciously remind herself that this is a different individual, she might remember the dis-

---

77. D'ARDENNE & MAHTANI, *supra* note 44, at 92–93.

78. *See* Marjorie A. Silver, *Emotional Competence, Multicultural Lawyering and Race*, 3 FLA. COASTAL L. REV. 219, 221–29 (2002); Clark Cunningham, *The Lawyer as Translator, Representation as Text: Towards an Ethnography of Discourse*, 77 CORNELL L. REV. 1298 (1988).

cussion she had with her supervisor about why the earlier client might have lied, and she might prepare a more nonjudgmental response should the current client lie.

Such self-reflection is important not just because it helps us to understand what we prefer and value but also what deep assumptions our culture may have instilled in us. Indeed, we all need to remember that, in the United States, our lawyering takes place within a culture that includes racism, sexism, homophobia, and ethnic and cultural imperialism. While confronting our cultural biases will never be easy—as Marjorie Silver writes, "Few of us want to admit to being racists"[79]—a benefit of learning that we have cultural assumptions, however, is that we then might recognize that most of us do not consciously buy into the prejudices that these assumptions might be based upon. Rather, we can learn to distinguish between our good intentions and our unconscious biases, recognizing that it is our behavior, and its effects on our clients—not our conscious thoughts—that might be racist. From this base, we can then work to change behavior and to lawyer based on facts, not assumptions.

B. Understanding and Respecting Clients' Stories

The previous section described how you will bring your own bundle of preferences and values to your work with clients, and how that package will almost always be different, in greater or lesser extent, from the bundle your client comes with. This section reminds us of a particular concern within that larger context. As you work with different clients, you will filter their stories through the lens of your own cultural identity and your bundle of preferences and values. In doing so, you run a risk of misunderstanding your clients. Your misunderstanding may lead to frustration on your part ("My client just isn't making any sense!") and, of greater worry, your failing to achieve what your client really wants.

The remedy for this worry is easy to articulate but perhaps rather difficult to accomplish. First, the disciplined naïveté and informed not-knowing that we stressed in the discussion of heuristics play an equal role here. The client story that seems to make little sense, the strategy direction that you cannot understand, that tactic that you see as self-defeating—each might be perfectly reasonable with another's lens and another's bundle of preferences and values. Second, the better that you understand the ways in which your own bundle

---

79. Silver, *supra* note 78, at 233.

of preferences and values skews your thinking about stories, strategies, tactics and the like, the better you are likely to be in remaining less judgmental about your clients' different preferences and values.

All that said, it is important to remember that your judgments are not necessarily *wrong* just because they are part of your bundle of preferences and values. Correspondingly, your clients' choices indeed may be ill-advised. Your commitment to disciplined naïveté does not imply an abdication of your responsibility to talk directly and frankly with your clients about the hard lawyering topics on your agenda. What it does imply, though, is greater humility about the universality or inevitability of your perspective.

How do you practice disciplined naïveté and informed not-knowing when trying to understand your client's story? For lawyers in particular, this is a hard skill to develop because classroom teaching emphasizes causes of action and elements of a claim as the framework for facts and narratives, even though a client's story often does not fit easily into legal boxes. So, even when you ask an open-ended question of the client ("Tell me about your problem from its beginning"), you are acculturated to listen more closely to "facts" that fit a legal claim rather than to the client's plot line. A risk of heeding only the seemingly legally relevant facts is that you miss the context for the client's claims, her emotional and value-laden stake in the claims, and her motive in pursuing specific goals or strategies.

Let us offer another example here. Take the case of a Black woman, a domestic violence survivor, whose Nigerian ex-husband had sued her for equitable distribution of the marital estate and for shared legal custody of, and visitation with, their daughter. In the White student attorney's first interview with the client, she asked the client to explain why the client needed legal assistance. The client began by relating that her daughter from a different relationship had died a few years ago when that daughter was thirteen years old. What did the deceased daughter have to do with the complaint the ex-husband had filed for visitation and joint custody of his child? Legally, nothing. Indeed, if the client were in court and the judge asked her why she opposed her ex-husband's complaint for custody and child support, would she have started her response by describing her other daughter's death? Seemingly not.

The student did not ignore the client's starting place, but she did not understand it until later in the relationship with the client. By the end of the year, the student realized that the client had been giving her some context about why she became involved with her ex-husband, why she was vulnerable to a man who was charming and who gave her a reason to continue living—until he had married her for his green card and began to be abusive.

This context also provided the motivation later for the client's reaction to a settlement offer from the ex-husband to resolve the claim for an equitable distribution of the marital property. The couple really had no property; the dispute centered on the personal injury claims each had for a car accident they were involved in together. The ex-husband eventually agreed to waive his claim to the client's award, but the clinic's client rejected the agreement that his lawyer had drafted. The student was puzzled by her client's reaction—why did the writing matter so much, when the substantive content was exactly what the client wanted?

Disciplined naïveté and informed not-knowing helped to uncover the answer. By asking nonjudgmental "why" questions to understand the client's concerns and "what if" questions to determine her priorities, the student realized that the client was reacting from her deep sense of betrayal and fear that her ex-husband still was taking advantage of her. At that point, explicit expressions of empathy and respect for the client's emotions and context enabled the student to put aside her frustration and the client to conclude that the agreement was acceptable with only minor changes. The case settled.

This client's situation helps to illustrate the importance of disciplined naïveté and informed not-knowing in developing cultural competence. The student could not pinpoint any single cultural factor, like race or gender, or heuristic to explain the client's narrative. Rather, many factors, including the client's identities as a survivor of domestic violence and as a woman of color, played a role in setting the context for the client's narrative. The student therefore could not rely primarily on the heuristics described in Part II above to plan her interactions with the client. Rather, by exploring with the client her values, interests, and priorities, the student was able to lawyer based on the facts of the client's life, as Peters and Bryant remind us that we all should strive to do.

C. Understanding the Effects of Oppression on Your Clients' Lives

Multicultural competency experts advise professionals to understand more than the culturally linked preferences and values of their clients. They would urge you to understand at a deeper level how your clients have been formed and affected by the forces of racism, ethnocentrism, sexism, and homophobia.[80] If you are from the dominant culture and your client is not, that gulf between you will affect your relationship in many ways. Your client may distrust you and suspect that you will never understand him adequately. His pref-

---

80. *See id.* at 229–31; SUE & SUE 1999, *supra* note 17, at 31–39.

erences and values will likely be shaped by his experiences with bigotry and hatred. Your ability to empathize with him and to share his worldview will be limited because of your cultural differences, but you might increase your empathic connection to him by becoming more aware of his history and struggles, including your cultural group's role in that struggle.

There may not be any simple clinical method to accomplish this goal, but the multicultural theorists offer some suggestions, including a greater appreciation for narrative and stories. Let's take another look at the housing authority nonpayment case, to consider how we can better appreciate the client's narrative, specifically considering how racism affected her world view and interactions with the lawyer and the legal system. As we noted above, the client instructed the supervisor to offer a payment plan to the housing authority lawyer. That plan was more favorable than the one the student attorney previously had devised with the client. The client explained that she was willing to negotiate more readily with the lawyer because she had no negative experience with him, as she had with the housing authority manager.

The client and the supervisor did not discuss the fact that the client had changed her negotiation tactics. Speculation on her motivation, however, raises questions about whether unintended discrimination (race? class?) affected the client's interactions with the student. It is possible that the client had picked up on the student's judgmental reaction to the client's lie, felt in that judgment a replication of the dynamic she experienced with the housing manager, and then explained her rent arrears as the product of external mischance (lost/stolen money orders) to maintain a portrayal of herself as a client worthy of assistance. It is possible, too, that the client was less interested in engaging the student about the conduct of the case for similar reasons. With the supervisor, possibly because she was the supervisor[81] or because she is a person of color or otherwise (perceived to be) more accepting of the client's circumstances and motivations, the client shared a different aspect of herself—a person with dignity and awareness of the racism she faced—and instructed the supervisor accordingly. At the same time, regardless of who her lawyer was, the client maintained control of her chief interest—demonstrat-

---

81. This note is from Carwina Weng, whose story we are telling here: "I consider my position as a clinical supervisor to be part of my cultural makeup because my experience as a supervisor in a legal services practice in New York City and Boston has given me a cultural perspective and a set of values that I hope is more open to issues of poverty, race, and other differences. In addition, it is possible that the client reacted to me differently because of culturally-based expectations of a person with higher lawyer status."

ing her worth as a tenant/client. What changed was her willingness to be explicit about her motivation.

Other writers stress the importance of honest conversation with your client about the racial and cultural differences between you. For many of us conversations about difference will be difficult, but a lot of professional learning will be challenging. If you share that discomfort, your effectiveness may hinge on your developing comfort with this skill. In appropriate circumstances, by acknowledging the effect of racism, sexism, or other injustices on the problems your client has presented to you, or by asking about the ways he sees oppression and the exercise of privilege as having influenced his story, you can begin to reduce the mistrust that a culturally different client may feel in the professional relationship.

In addition, you may look for patterns in your professional relationships to consider how your culture affects the development of empathy for your clients' histories of discrimination and oppression. Are there clients with whom it is easier to empathize? Why? What about clients with whom you have a harder time? What patterns in your culture, your clients' cultures, and the interaction of the two do you discern? By looking for patterns, you can develop a better sense of obstacles and facilitators to your client relationships and make adjustments to minimize the former and maximize the latter.[82]

Conclusion

In this chapter, we have tried to give some concrete guidance to approaching multicultural lawyering situations. This guidance considers both the client

---

82. You might also benefit from learning about cultural identity development theory, as the degree to which a client identifies with his cultural background is important to the development of effective cross-cultural interaction. Cultural identity development theory uses models that identify a progression of consciousness about one's ethnic/racial backgrounds and that anticipate the emotional and psychological implications of each stage of that progression. Each member of an oppressed minority group "will constantly cycle through the five levels again and again as new issues are discovered." Harold Cheatham et al., *Multicultural Counseling and Therapy II: Integrative Practice, in* COUNSELING AND PSYCHOTHERAPY, *supra* note 40, at 162.

Because culture is necessarily "performative[,] improvisational[,] fluid[, and] emergent," Laird, *in* RE-VISIONING FAMILY THERAPY, *supra* note 8, at 24, a member of a cultural community may participate deeply, or very little, in its rituals and practices. The degree of assimilation of ourselves as lawyers and members of our own culture and of a cultural minority client into mainstream American traditions will affect how reliably the heuristics we explored above will fit our own, the client's life experience, and the interaction of the two.

and you the lawyer. Substantively, we suggest the use of heuristics to identify potential areas of cultural difference between you and the client and to anticipate adjustments based on these areas. Attitudinally, we urge that you not employ heuristics heavy-handedly but instead approach each potential area of difference with *informed not-knowing* and *disciplined naïveté;* don't assume that an anticipated difference actually applies to a specific client. For these substantive and attitudinal approaches to work effectively, however, you must apply the same substantive and attitudinal approaches to your own culture. On a substantive level, you would become aware of how your culture affects your values, assumptions, perspectives, and behavior, and, on an attitudinal level, you would beware stereotypes and biases about other cultures that your own culture carries, even if you do not consciously buy into them. By consciously reflecting on your own culture and your client's and by striving to lawyer based on actual values and influences each of you holds, you can begin to lawyer more effectively and accurately in multicultural situations.

CHAPTER 6

Six Practices for Connecting with Clients Across Culture: Habit Four, Working with Interpreters and Other Mindful Approaches

Susan J. Bryant*

Jean Koh Peters**

* Professor of Law and Director of Clinical Programs, CUNY School of Law. I thank my colleagues and students at the CUNY School of Law for their support and insights about the role that culture plays in our legal work on behalf of clients. The rich diversity in the faculty, staff and students of CUNY creates an environment where learning is a daily opportunity. I especially thank Lindsay Parker and Dorothy Mathew for their work on this chapter. Of course, one of the best parts of this ongoing work is the weekly phone calls with Jean where we share ideas about cross-cultural lawyering, writing and so much more. Her model for getting writing done inspires me to do more.

** Clinical Professor of Law, Yale Law School. I thank the Yale Law School for its generous support of this research, year in and year out, since its inception in 1998. David Bartels, Farrin Anello, Elaine Chao and Vanita Shimpi offered wise and generous research assistance on this project. Deborah Tropiano provided unfailingly good-humored and prompt word processing and transcription and Shan Tao labored mightily to try to salvage my dictation from my first forays with voice-recognition software. Mark Weisberg and Marjorie Silver offered warm support and helpful feedback during early drafts of this chapter. I still do not know how I landed the unparalleled pleasure of partnering with Sue Bryant on issues dear to my heart, but I remain grateful for the opportunity to work weekly with one of the finest teachers I know.

We also thank our families, Larry, Alison and Zach and Jim, Liz and Chris for their warm support of our collaboration.

Introduction

Joe, a young white male law student begins his first interview with a Nigerian client in her forties who is seeking asylum in the United States. The interview begins with promise, with the client telling him about her concerns about her family she left behind in her home country. The young lawyer listens attentively and, when the client gets to a natural stopping point, starts in on the questions which he carefully crafted before the meeting. The client lapses into silence, breaks off eye contact, and begins to look very sad. Joe begins to operate on two levels. He continues his questioning, but inside his heart is sinking. What went wrong? How can I get back to that easy conversation we had at the beginning? His mind begins swirling with ideas and his concerns about the interview grow. He feels he cannot sort out his confusion fast enough. He therefore sticks with his agenda and the meeting ends shortly after when his client is offering only monosyllabic answers. He sets up another meeting and goes back to his dorm room. "What do I do next?" he asks himself forlornly.

Harriet, an experienced South Asian-American lawyer, is in the middle of interviewing a Latino teenage boy whom she represents in a neglect case. From the beginning, the interaction is not easy. The client will not make eye contact, will not answer questions, and frankly looks like he doesn't want to be there. Harriet finds herself conscientiously trying different tacks to try to engage her client in conversation relevant to the legal case. After five or six unsuccessful approaches, she finds her client telling her the story that led to his removal from his mother's home. She is conscious to try to maintain the style and form of questioning that led to this change of pace in the interview.

Joe, still thinking about his client, takes out the Habit Four worksheet.[1] He does his best to identify the concrete signs, the specific red flags that led him first to believe that the interview was going wrong and to examine carefully the moments in which the interview changed its timbre. Using the step-by-step process in the worksheet, he develops a number of theories about why the interview went sour, and for each theory, develops a number of changes of pace he could introduce into the interview. He takes a particular look at the part of the interview that went well, trying to understand what the dynamic was there and trying to

---

1. This worksheet can be found in Appendix A.

brainstorm how to return the interview to that spirit. Armed with these thoughts, he enters his second interview. Although the interview has a similar change of mood after a cordial start, Joe tries various different approaches as brainstormed on his worksheet. While none of them is a complete success, he does find that the interview has changed its flavor, and has a more narrative feeling to it. Heartened, he plans to return to the Habit Four worksheet in preparation for the third interview.[2]

Joe and Harriet are engaged in one of the most challenging and rewarding aspects of the affective practice of law—building a genuine, respectful, and fruitful relationship with a client. The law can be a healing profession when we think deeply about the cultural implications of how we communicate with our clients and what we choose to be the subjects of our communication. By considering culture in our client interactions, we shape our definitions of both healing and healing approaches to legal representation. Our previous work, the Five Habits of Cross-cultural Lawyering,[3] gave lawyers approaches for examining the effect of culture and language on their lawyering. This Chapter focuses on six practices for promoting cross-cultural communication, including Habit Four, the habit that identifies moments of faltering communication, which may be based on cultural factors, and suggests ways to think about improving the communication. By using Habit Four and the other Habits, lawyers like Joe and Harriet can become more skilled and reflective practitioners when working with clients who come from cultures different from their own. Habit Four and the other practices discussed here can also address the ways in which shared cultural similarities between lawyer and client can lead to miscommunication.

---

2. The stories and examples in this article are based on real moments in real cases in our practices; we have altered names and details to honor our clients' confidentiality, but we have preserved the details (and the lawyer reactions) that we considered critical to the points illustrated.

3. We have written about the Habits in a number of different forums. Jean published materials about the Habits, set in the context of lawyering for children in child protective proceedings, in her book on the subject. JEAN KOH PETERS, REPRESENTING CHILDREN IN CHILD PROTECTIVE PROCEEDINGS: ETHICAL AND PRACTICAL DIMENSIONS (2d ed. 2001). Sue authored an article for law teachers describing the Habits. Susan J. Bryant, *The Five Habits: Building Cross-Cultural Competence in Lawyers*, 8 CLIN. L. REV. 33 (2001). We have co-authored a chapter, *Five Habits for Cross-Cultural Lawyering*, in RACE, CULTURE, PSYCHOLOGY & LAW (Kimberly Barret & William George eds., 2005). We have collected materials for students and practitioners wishing to learn the Habits on the CUNY Law School website, *available at* http://www.cleaweb.org/documents/multiculture.pdf (under resources for clinical teachers).

Although Habit Four is the focus of this chapter, a brief summary of the other four Habits will help the reader see connections among them. The other Habits involve analytical and reflective thinking about culture, and cultivating the ability to bring culture into the analysis of lawyer-client relationships, the lawyer's role, and its effect on a case. Habit One asks lawyers to identify similarities and differences between the lawyer and the client and to explore how those might affect issues of trust, role of the lawyer, and the content rather than the process of interviews. Habit Two explores how the culture of the courts and other legal players interact with the lawyer's and client's culture, suggesting that lawyers consider culture when designing theories of the case that meet clients' goals. Habit Three—Parallel Universe Thinking—is key to all of the others. Habit Three asks lawyers to imagine other possible explanations or meanings for clients' words and actions. Habit Three recognizes that cultural norms and practices may result in different interpretations of the same actions.[4] Finally, Habit Five recognizes that we approach this work with biases and stereotypes that consciously and unconsciously shape our work. Habit Five asks the lawyer to explore those belief systems without judgment and to take steps to eliminate them if possible and in any event, to minimize their effect.[5] And in those moments where the lawyer has actually, even flamboyantly, erred, Habit Five offers redemption—by looking clear-eyed and non-judgmentally at our mistakes, we can use our mistakes to learn about our hot button issues and the components of our optimal functioning, to aid our work with clients in the future.

Since all of the Habits help the lawyer identify assumptions that may permeate his representation, the reader is entitled to know the assumptions that permeated our reflection on the Habits generally, and Habit Four particularly. We have structured the Habits, taking as given that I) All lawyering is cross-cultural; II) A central goal of lawyering is to remain present with this client, ever respecting her dignity, voice, and story; and III) A cross-culturally competent lawyer must know himself as a cultural being.[6]

Three dynamics drive cross-cultural competence. First, *nonjudgment*—a focus on fact, observation, detail detached from evaluation, criticism, or generalization.[7] Cross-cultural competence requires the lawyer to practice non-

---

4. Parallel universe thinking plays a vital role in cross-cultural communication and Habit Four. *See infra* Section II, Part C.

5. See *supra* ch. 5: Paul R. Tremblay & Carwina Weng, *Multicultural Lawyering: Heuristics and Biases,* at pp. 169–81 (the authors explore the effects that bias and stereotypes can have on lawyers' work and suggest approaches that lawyers can take to minimize these effects).

6. PETERS, *supra* note 3, at 256–259.

7. Tremblay & Weng, *supra* note 5.

judgment with clients, with others in the case, and with herself, observing the actions of all as facts to be reckoned with, but not judged. The risk of negatively judging clients increases when you work cross-culturally due to the confusion inherent in working out of one's own cultural framework, the resultant anxiety, and the attendant loss of control and clarity the lawyer may feel.[8] Second, *isomorphic attribution*—to attribute the same meaning to behavior and words that the person intended to convey. Cross-culturally competent lawyers seek to understand the actions and words that they witness from the perspective of the actor or speaker, rather than from the lawyer's life experience.[9] Third, *daily practice and learnable skill*—through regular practice of simple habits, any lawyer can develop cross-cultural competence; cross-cultural competence is not reserved to the innately skilled, and can be steadily and incrementally learned through daily application.[10]

Habit Four focuses on cross-cultural communication between lawyer and client.[11] This chapter supplements, but does not substitute for, texts on legal interviewing and counseling.[12] As those texts detail, lawyers build or aggravate relationships and gather or miss important information for a number of reasons. Indeed, a lawyer in cross-cultural encounters may be quick to blame

---

8. For more on nonjudgment, in the context of mindful listening, see *infra* Section II, Part B.

9. Cross-cultural theorists have identified the capacity to develop isomorphic attribution as a critical cross-cultural skill. *See* HARRY CHARALAMBOS TRIANDIS, INTERPERSONAL BEHAVIOR (1977). A capacity to make isomorphic attributions requires the lawyer to focus on the differing connotations that a word or act may have in the different worlds inhabited by the client and the lawyer. This capacity is the essence of parallel universe thinking as described below.

10. PETERS, *supra* note 3, at 251–256.

11. In our first description of Habit Four, we offered some tips for improving attorney-client, cross-cultural communication and a way to analyze difficulties. We had not explored the cultural implications for some of the recommended suggestions of interviewing texts. This chapter looks at the interviewing process and points out ways to enhance understanding and connection in cross-cultural exchanges.

12. For students and lawyers wanting to know how to question, actively listen, or plan the structure and content of interviews, there are a wealth of articles and books to read. *See, e.g.,* STEFAN H. KRIEGER & RICHARD K. NEUMANN, JR., ESSENTIAL LAWYERING SKILLS (2d ed. 2003); DAVID A. BINDER, PAUL BERGMAN, SUSAN C. PRICE AND PAUL R. TREMBLAY, LAWYERS AS COUNSELORS: A CLIENT-CENTERED APPROACH (2d ed. 2004); Gay Gellhorn, *Law and Language: An Empirically-Based Model for the Opening Moments of Client Interviews,* 4 CLIN. L. REV. 321 (1998); ROBERT M. BASTRESS & JOSEPH D. HARBAUGH, INTERVIEWING, COUNSELING, & NEGOTIATING SKILLS FOR EFFECTIVE REPRESENTATION 334–38 (1990); Robert D. Dinerstein, *Client-Centered Counseling: Reappraisal and Refinement,* 32 ARIZ. L. REV. 501 (1990).

all interaction difficulties on culture. Habit Four helps the lawyer develop a permeating instinct to consider culture throughout interactions with clients.[13] Culture takes its rightful place as one but not the only explanatory theory for shaping and interpreting interactions with clients.

If the other habits encourage the development of cross-cultural *analytical skills* in a number of concrete settings, Habit Four focuses on the *in-the-moment interaction* between lawyer and client. In this Chapter, we explore how to plan for these moments, to engage mindfully during them, and to reflect and learn from them. We suggest six important practices for improving these moments:

(1) Employ narrative as a way of seeing the client within her own context;

(2) Listen mindfully to promote and understand the client's narrative;

(3) Use parallel universe thinking to explain client behavior and stories;

(4) Speak mindfully, taking into account the client's culture, especially as it relates to how she expects to interact with the lawyer and the legal system;

(5) Work with interpreters in ways that enable the development of genuine communication between lawyers and clients; and

(6) Apply the Habit Four analytical process continuously to identify red flags that the interaction is not working and corrective measures that the lawyer might take.

Habit Four creates this red flag structure for the lawyer to use either BEFORE (preparing for), DURING (in the moment with the client), or AFTER (reflecting upon)[14] the client meeting. In any of these timeframes, the lawyer can identify discrete moments of the client interaction and mine those moments for information about what aids and what hinders constructive lawyer-client communication. Used over time in all three timeframes, Habit Four creates a way for lawyers to improve incrementally their relationships with each client, while continually adding to their repertoire of ideas for future meetings and future clients.

In the examples above, Harriet remembers all too well what it was like to be Joe: conscientiously prepared in an interview that is not flowing smoothly, and feeling helpless to turn the conversation into a fruitful direction. Over

---

13. In our discussion of red flags and correctives, we suggest that lawyers identify a number of explanations for why the interview is failing with culture being one of many explanations. *See infra* Section III.

14. This staging process is referred to as planning, doing, and reflecting—the three stages involved in experiential learning. *See* Stacy Caplow, *A Year in Practice: The Journal of a Reflective Clinician*, 3 CLIN. L. REV. 1, 5 (1996).

many awkward moments with many clients, and many moments of puzzling over them, Harriet developed a repertoire of ideas for rerouting communication from dead ends to a free flow of information both ways. Habit Four, along with the other five practices, we believe, articulates what many thoughtful, experienced lawyers already do to adjust and tailor their communication with each client to that client's needs and culture. Joe was "consciously incompetent" in his communication with his client, and this is a deeply uncomfortable place to be. For the new lawyer, who has difficulty focusing on both the process and content of the interview at the same time, identifying signs of good communication, as well as "red flags" that signal that accurate, genuine communication is probably not occurring, can take the place of more "in the moment" observations. Habit Four offers a way to examine these tough moments of communications and strategize correctives that will improve the communications over time, until, like Harriet, Joe can become "unconsciously competent" at these relationships, due to steady, undiscouraged problem-solving over long experience.[15] We recommend the use of Red Flags as a way to develop a permeating instinct to consider culture throughout interactions with clients.[16]

The six practices—narrative, mindful listening and speaking, parallel universe thinking, effective work with interpreters together with Habit Four red flag analysis—provide an approach that lawyers can use in normal attorney-client tasks that may involve cross-cultural encounters. In a cycle of pro-activity and reactivity, the lawyer plans to use the six practices in upcoming meetings with clients, problem-solves tough interactions in the moment, and then debriefs these tough interactions during a reflective process employing red flag analysis. Based on that reflection, the lawyer can proactively plan for the next encounter and identify concrete strategies to use in the moment. This article discusses the six practices in turn, ending with a concrete description of red flag and corrective analysis.

I. Six Practices of Cross-Cultural Communication

The first practice, seeking narratives from clients, allows the client to shape and sequence the information that he offers to the lawyer. The second practice, listening mindfully, focuses the lawyer's full, nonjudgmental attention on

---

15. See Bryant, *supra* note 3, at 62–63. See also BINDER ET AL., *supra* note 12, at 41–63.
16. Exactly how a lawyer can do this is explored at length in Section III, *infra*.

the client's words and actions during the interaction. The third practice, parallel universe thinking, offers the lawyer alternative explanations for client words or actions which confuse or trouble the lawyer, to prevent the lawyer from filling in the gaps of ambiguity with his own assumptions and values. The fourth practice, speaking mindfully, structures the lawyer's questions and conversation with the client to avoid cultural pitfalls in his own actions and words. The fifth practice, effective work with interpreters, guides the lawyer's partnership with interpreters and translators so that the lawyer can understand the client fully despite a language barrier. And finally, Habit Four, Red Flags & Correctives, outlines a daily habit for client interaction to identify communication problems and fashion correctives for them to improve these interactions over time.

A. Narrative Mode

Ideally, a client is in narrative mode when she is telling a story or describing an experience relevant to the legal questions and case, with little or no prompting from the lawyer, so that the structure of the narrative is very much at the client's discretion. In general, seeking a client's narrative, told in her own voice, in a manner of her own choosing, most strongly vindicates the second principle of the Habits, the goal of being present with this client, ever respecting her dignity, voice, and story. It also promotes the second dynamic of the Habits, achieving isomorphic attribution, because it asks the lawyer to listen to the client's story told from her perspective, crafted and delivered in exactly the way she chooses. Nevertheless, narrative, for a number of reasons, may not always be the proper mode to pursue in an interview; at the end of this section, we suggest some alternate approaches.

1. Why Narrative is the Default Corrective for Habit Four

Habit Four, by default, seeks to elicit a narrative from the client and seeks to keep the client in narrative mode during as much of the client-lawyer interactions as possible. We recommend that lawyers seek to communicate with clients in narrative mode for ten separate reasons:

a. Narrative mode acknowledges the client's authority to tell the story.

In narrative mode, the client starts off with the power to shape her telling of her experience. The client decides what is important to discuss. A client makes decisions about what to tell the lawyer, independent of the questions the lawyer thinks to ask. Because we ask questions based on our cultural frameworks, lawyers may miss important client information if they pursue a strategy of interaction structured by their questions rather than by a client narrative.[17] And finally, the client speaks in narrative without being censored by the lawyer.

b. Narrative mode allows the client to shape, sequence, and pace her disclosure as she will.

The client tells the story as a whole from her point of view. The client chooses the telling detail and lingers on the part of the story that resonates most deeply with her for whatever reasons. The client is also free to hold back what she is not yet comfortable offering. Several cultural factors may cause the client to be reluctant to disclose important facts. For example, the client may violate the high "insider-outsider" norms when she tells narratives that expose the culture or the client's family to legal scrutiny.[18]

c. The client's narrative may also provide the theory of the case.

Because the engine of all litigation and representation is the theory of the case (the story, which, if the fact finder were to believe it, would resolve the case favorably for the client), the client's narrative is an important first step in developing that story in any representation.

d. Many legal representations call for a narrative.

When the lawyer's final end product will need to be a narrative (for example: the affidavit in a asylum interview, the petition in VAWA case, a motion for summary judgment and the affidavits appended to it), starting with the client's narrative is a way to match the client's subjective understanding of her story (and achieving isomorphic attribution) and offers a first draft for how the lawyer will structure the narrative part of the written legal work

e. Narrative combines detail with the client's inner thought processes.

When a client tells a story, we are not only offered any fact and details that the client has chosen to highlight, but we also get insights into the way the

---

17. Habit One explores how a lawyer's culture shapes her questioning of clients. *See* Bryant, *supra* note 3, at 64; PETERS, *supra* note 3, at 262–276.

18. All cultures have people who are considered insider and outsiders. Norms attach to these individuals including who can be told what information and who can be trusted. Some cultures have high inside outside boundaries and newcomers are significantly distrusted. *See* Bryant, *supra* note 3, at 42.

client makes decisions with reasoning and facts on which those decisions were made. Therefore, relevant Storytelling by the client can be critical in helping the lawyer understand why the client acted as she did. Understanding why a client acted the way she did can be critical to drawing the correct inferences. For example, a client whose culture expects an "in your face" response to repression may engage in behavior that denies or defies fear. Both the lawyer and ultimately the fact-finder need to understand the client's actions within her cultural context.[19]

f. Storytelling is a mode that reaches across culture.

There are many ways to tell a story. When lawyers ask clients to tell the story of their experience, clients will resort to the narrative mode which comes most naturally to them, be it linear and chronological, reverse chronological, focused on a group of intertwined characters rather than one central figure, or the like.[20]

g. Storytelling allows the client, not the lawyer to fill in the gaps.

When a client tells her complete narrative, she, not the lawyer, fills in the initial spaces. Filling is a natural part of all communication. Because we fill in based on our experiences, culture shapes what we put in the interstices. When we are working cross-culturally, the odds are greater that we will fill in facts, visual images, and interpretations that are not accurate.

h. Storytelling highlights what important facts and questions need to be followed up on by the lawyer.

An initial narrative will help lay out an agenda for further clarification; once the lawyer has the overview of the narrative, the lawyer can follow up with questions focusing on closing other gaps of information.

---

19. Credibility and relevancy are very culturally driven. When we say a fact is circumstantial evidence proving a particular proposition, we are relying on implicit assumptions. See David A. Binder & Paul Bergman, Fact Investigation: From Hypothesis to Proof 178 (1984). Often these assumptions are embedded with cultural norms, beliefs and values.

20. Western legal culture favors linear and chronological story telling and lawyers will most often question clients in ways that ask the client for this kind of narrative. By encouraging the client to tell the story her way, the lawyer also is able to observe the amount of witness preparation time that may be needed for the client to tell a credible story to the fact finder.

i. Embracing the client's narrative takes the lawyer out of his own.

Immersing himself in the client's narrative helps the lawyer put aside his concerns and remain mindfully connected to the client's described experiences. Once the lawyer intervenes and shapes the information flow, it may be difficult to get the client to return to her narrative.[21]

j. Narrative mode acknowledges the client's power.

It bears repeating: Acknowledging the client's power to tell the story at the pace and in the sequence she chooses can be especially important in cases where the client, for legal purposes, must describe traumatic events. Research on avoiding re-trauma for traumatized clients suggests that service providers reverse the circumstances of the trauma.[22] Therefore, if clients in the traumatic event were helpless and disempowered, concretely acknowledging the client's primacy, power, and control in the lawyer-client relationship can help avoid re-trauma. Narrative mode may be critical to helping the lawyer create a safe environment, putting the client in charge of the flow of information.

* * *

For these reasons, we think that encouraging your client to provide a narrative is the best corrective to use when a red flag occurs. Think of narrative as the default corrective for most red flags.

2. When Narrative Mode is not Appropriate

Nevertheless, narrative may not be appropriate as a mode for conducting certain lawyer-client relationships, for the following reasons:

a. It simply may not be a mode with which this client feels comfortable.

This may be for personal, idiosyncratic, cultural (or a combination of) reasons. The client may prefer not to proceed in narrative mode. For some clients, the open-ended nature of narrative can create anxiety, involving as it does less feedback from the lawyer.

---

21. Especially with a client who may be unfamiliar with legal culture or may come from an authoritarian culture, any hints from the lawyer delivered through questioning that shapes the information flow may in fact limit the information flow. *See* Gellhorn, *supra* note 12, at 346.

22. See Peters, *supra* note 3, at 483–485.

b. Narrative mode may intrude unduly into the client's life.

Where excellent legal representation is possible without narrative (e.g., filling out some immigration applications, completing financial eligibility forms), it may not be necessary to learn the client's entire story. Seeking the narrative from a reluctant client in those instances could be intrusive, voyeuristic, and ultimately disrespectful to the client.

c. Narrative may be culturally uncomfortable for the client.[23]

For some clients, normal cultural exchanges do not properly include stories because a client comes from a culture in which storytelling is not prevalent. Other clients may expect more direction and hierarchy in the lawyer-client relationship, more "leadership" from the lawyer. For still other clients, asking the client to tell certain stories may violate important cultural values. For instance, a woman asked to describe in full detail the abuse by her husband may be restricted by cultural norms from laying bare her husband's violent actions.

d. Narrative may be traumatic for the client.

The costs of such trauma may outweigh the benefits that come from narrative mode. Unless the narrated trauma is central to the legal claim, lawyers should avoid insisting that a client recount difficult experiences.

---

23. *See* Tremblay & Weng, *supra* note 5 (the authors identify many of the cultural beliefs and practices that may make narrative a difficult cross-cultural approach). *See also* Diana Eades, *"I Don't Think the Lawyers Were Communicating With Me": Misunderstanding Cultural Differences in Communicative Style*, 52 EMORY L.J. 1109 (2003). In her article, Eades describes the story of Ms. Kina, an aboriginal woman who stabbed and killed her physically abusive boyfriend after he threatened to rape her fourteen-year-old niece and came after Ms. Kina with a raised chair. Eades discusses the cultural differences in communicative style that led to communication failures between Ms. Kina and her attorneys. For instance, Eades emphasizes that in situations where Aboriginal people want to find out what they consider to be significant or certain personal information, they do not use direct questions as it is important to respect the privacy of others and not to embarrass someone by putting them on the spot. "People volunteer some of their own information, hinting about what they are trying to find out about. Information is sought as part of a two-way exchange. Silence, and waiting till people are ready to give information, are also central to Aboriginal ways of seeking any substantial information." *Id.* at 1117. The lawyers representing Ms. Kina were frustrated because their client would not volunteer information and would only reveal information when questioned in detail. Ms. Kina's lawyers as a result decided that she was passive and uninterested in the entire process of the preparation of her defense while Ms. Kina thought the lawyers were disinterested. *Id.* at 1120.

For these clients, when Habit Four's default to narrative mode will place the client in an awkward situation, the lawyer can try the following alternatives to narrative mode.

3. Alternatives to Seeking Narrative Mode

What should a lawyer do if conversation is faltering but for one of the above reasons or another important reason, the narrative is not of the proper strategy? Here are a few beginning alternative ideas:

a. Ask the client to provide holistic details in a non-storytelling format.

For instance, if it is important to hear about the client's home, but the client does not want to tell you about his family, you can ask for a description of the home and critical locations in the client's story. This provides the lawyer with an integrated sense of the client's views of these important details without asking the client to reveal something he wants to keep private. This approach preserves the client's authority to decide how to describe, as a whole, an important component of his claim, without structure imposed by the lawyer. Other examples of holistic non-narrative-seeking questions include asking the client to describe i) a critical relationship, ii) his education, iii) his experience at his job, in ways that invite but do not require the client to tell stories. All of these alternatives, however, still offer the client an open-ended invitation to describe an important part of the case with little manipulation by the lawyer and with an opportunity for the client to take charge of the description and choose the important details.

b. Ask specific but open-ended questions about relevant issues.

This is actually for many lawyers the first instinct: to come into an interview with a list of questions that track the legal requirement. To avoid the interview devolving into an interrogation, the lawyer should generally prefer open-ended questioning.

c. Ask about the telling detail.

In a previous conversation with the client, the client may have brought up a specific fact, event, person who was particularly important to the client. Asking in further depth about that item of importance to the client will again help the lawyer to get a sense of the client's objective, values, and concerns without requiring her to engage in narrative.

In summary, fruitful narrative drives many cross-cultural interactions with clients. In seeking to improve interviewing and counseling skills, start with widening your repertoire of narrative-seeking approaches. Where narrative is not appropriate, try some of the alternative approaches for starters. Once a client begins richly narrating her experience, the lawyer must next cultivate a second critical cross-cultural communication practice: Listening mindfully.

B. Listening Mindfully

Listening is perhaps the most important and most challenging of cross-cultural skills. Listening is also one of the least studied skills, although it is the most used during any day, the first learned in human development, and the least taught at any time in life.[24]

Mindful listening assists the lawyer in the critical and challenging task of remaining completely open to his client's story while skillfully assembling her legal case. Without mindful listening, lawyers may unconsciously measure their client's stories against story paradigms that the law favors. The lawyer listening to a refugee narrative may be resistant at first to listening carefully and open-mindedly to client explanations for actions that the lawyer believes will be damaging to her legal case. For instance, the lawyer may resist truly listening to a client's explanations for use of false travel papers or for leaving vulnerable children behind in the client's country of origin.

Thus the cross-culturally astute lawyer must figure out how to listen professionally, that is, within the confines of his legal agenda, while remaining extremely open-minded to a client's version of reality and the client's hopes for her legal claim.

With one exception,[25] listening has been largely ignored in lawyering literature. It would appear that the dynamics of listening seemed too obvious to

---

24. Cooper notes that listening, as compared to speaking, reading and writing, is first learned, used 45% of the time, and taught the least. PAMELA COOPER, COMMUNICATION FOR THE CLASSROOM TEACHER 38 (1995) (citing L. STEIL, YOUR PERSONAL LISTENING PROFILE 4 (1980)). For reflections on listening for teachers, see Jean Koh Peters & Mark Weisberg, *Experiments in Listening*, NYLS Clinical Research Institute Paper No. 04/05-5, *available at* http://papers.ssrn.com/sol3/papers.cfm?abstract_id=601182 (last visited May 26, 2006).

25. Legal literature *has* focused on active listening techniques. *See, e.g.*, BINDER ET AL., *supra* note 12, at 41–63. This work has been significant to the training of many generations of new lawyers and takes an important first step in lawyers' thinking about listening. Our only concern about these active listening techniques is that they focus more on techniques that can be used to encourage client conversation by showing external pieces of listening (body language, repeating back client words, showing outwardly that you are listening) without also attending to the essential inner disposition of the lawyer during such

spell out and too basic to be discussed. This non-approach to teaching listening could be justified if we believed that our profession in general provided our clients the listening that they needed. In fact, lawyers as a profession are not reputed to be excellent listeners and many clients might be shocked to know that excellent listening is even a goal for most lawyers. In any case, perhaps it is time for us to break down the concept of listening into daily habits and learnable skills that could improve the quality of our listening throughout our profession.

What are the goals of legal listening? For practitioners seeking cross-cultural competence, the central goal of listening should be isomorphic attribution, understanding events, words, and decisions of the client in the client's own terms—as she experienced them and as she currently interprets them. This is the central agenda for the cross-culturally competent lawyer. Listening with a goal of isomorphic attribution is critical for achieving the second principle of the habits of cross-cultural lawyering: remaining present with this client, ever respecting her dignity, voice, and story.

Two major obstacles can block a lawyer's mindful listening. First, the lawyer's preoccupation with crafting the strongest legal case may skew the way she hears her client's narrative. Until the lawyer is confident that she understands this client's idiosyncratic view of his life, facts of his experience, and goals for the representation, the lawyer should be extremely wary of imposing other agendas even when she is altruistically focused on the client's legal benefit, to avoid distorting the proper hearing of the client's information. Even the most well-meaning lawyer, who "knows" what a successful refugee claim looks like, will be tempted—perhaps unconsciously—to distort her client's claim into a pre-conceived mold without the help of mindful listening discipline.

Second, the lawyer's own cultural makeup may throw up barriers to client-focused listening. Habits One and Two further explore the ways lawyers can identify similarities and differences with clients, and reorient their representations to focus on the interaction between the client and the law, rather than the interaction between the client and the lawyer's own culture, experience, and values. A lawyer focusing on mindful listening must develop strategies to keep her own cultural values from shaping the client interview.

---

listening. Too many lawyers know from good experience that it is possible to employ active listening techniques without a high quality of listening taking place. Tim Floyd, in his chapter below, moves beyond this focus on active listening to discuss "deep attentive listening," as well as the many barriers to such listening by lawyers. *See infra* ch. 16: Timothy Floyd, *Spirituality and Practicing Law as a Healing Profession: The Importance of Listening*, at pp. 486–92.

To overcome these obstacles to excellent listening, lawyers can use mindfulness[26] to refocus continually on the client's meanings and subjective understanding. If lawyers could make only one change in their listening now, a commitment to listen thoroughly and deeply to the client's story as the client understands it, would be one giant step forward in the quality of legal listening across our profession.

The leading American proponent of mindfulness and its practice, Jon Kabat-Zinn, defines mindfulness as "openhearted, moment-to-moment, nonjudgmental awareness."[27] Regular mindfulness practices, such as meditation, yoga, and tai chi, cultivate the mind's ability to maintain an extremely high level of paying attention in the moment. Mindful listening incorporates the four major signature characteristics of mindfulness: 1) awareness that is 2) openhearted, 3) centered in the present moment, and 4) nonjudgmental.

First, mindfulness is awareness, paying attention. Perhaps it should go without saying that we should pay full attention to our clients throughout all our interactions, but many of us ruefully acknowledge how difficult maintaining that attention can be. Who among us has never drifted off to thoughts of our "to do" list during a client meeting? Mindfulness practice focuses on supporting the mind's ability to remain focused, or return to a focus, on the client's expression of her concerns.

Second, mindful listening is openhearted. The mindful lawyer listens, open to the client's full experience, attentive to reason as well as emotion, and ready for the messy as well as the neat, the complex, as well as the straightforward. This lawyer puts aside the two obstacles posed by his preoccupation with crafting the strongest legal case and his own cultural makeup and experiences. These obstacles are fundamentally irrelevant to the client-centered task of thoroughly understanding the client's concerns and experiences in her own

---

26. Len Riskin offers a thoughtful introduction of mindfulness, with exercises, in another chapter of this book. *See generally infra* ch. 15: Leonard L. Riskin, *Awareness in Lawyering: A Primer on Paying Attention.*

27. JON KABAT-ZINN, COMING TO OUR SENSES: HEALING OURSELVES AND THE WORLD THROUGH MINDFULNESS 24 (2005). Legal writers have explored the usefulness of mindfulness in the alternative dispute resolution context. Leonard L. Riskin, *The Contemplative Lawyer: On the Potential Contributions of Mindfulness Meditation to Law Students, Lawyers, and their Clients,* 7 HARV. NEGOT. L. REV. 1 (2002); C. J. Freshman, Adele M. Hayes, & Greg C. Feldman, *Adapting Meditation to Promote Negotiation Success: A Guide to Varieties and Scientific Support,* 7 HARV. NEGOT. L. REV. 67 (2002); Adele M. Hayes & Greg C. Feldman, *Adapting Meditation to Promote Negotiation Success: A Guide to Varieties and Scientific Support,* 7 HARV. NEGOT. L. REV. 67 (2002); William S. Blatt, *What's Special About Meditation? Contemplative Practice for American Lawyers,* 7 HARV. NEGOT. L. REV. 125 (2002).

terms, which forms the essential foundation upon which the legal representation is based.

Third, mindful listening takes place from moment to moment. Throughout the interview, the mindful practitioner remains present with the client in
the now. As simple as this sounds, remaining present is neither easy to achieve
nor maintain. Since our minds inevitably stray as we listen, remaining present requires the practitioner to cultivate ways to return her wayfaring mind
back to total attention to the client.

Fourth, mindful listening is nonjudgmental. Nonjudgment remains one of
the foundational dynamics of the Habits of Cross-Cultural Lawyering, and is
essential to mindful listening because it puts aside evaluation, criticism, and
valuation and adopts the attitude of "witness" rather than judge of the client's
experience. Nonjudgmental listening accepts the client's communications first,
and seeks to explore and understand it fully, before beginning the work of legal
strategy. Kabat-Zinn notes that

> [m]indfulness is cultivated by assuming the stance of an impartial
> witness to your own experience. To do this requires that you become
> aware of the constant stream of judging and reacting to inner and
> outer experiences that we are all normally caught up in, and learn to
> step back from it.[28]

The Sufi mystic poet Rumi[29] offers this image for nonjudgment: "Out beyond ideas of wrongdoing and rightdoing, / there is a field. I'll meet you
there." Mindful listening to the client takes place in that field.

Cultivating mindfulness in listening and, as discussed below, in speaking,
thus dovetails with the three dynamics of the Habits: nonjudgment, isomorphic attribution, and daily habit and learnable skill. Nonjudgment is a central
component of mindful practice. Isomorphic attribution is the goal of mindful listening: client/lawyer communication that achieves a deep understanding of the client on her own terms. And mindfulness is best nurtured in reg-

---

28. Jon Kabat-Zinn, Full Catastrophe Living: Using the Wisdom of Your Body and
Mind to Face Stress, Pain and Illness 33 (1990).

29. COLEMAN BARKS & JOHN MOYNE, THE ESSENTIAL RUMI 36 (Coleman Barks trans.,
Harper Collins 1995). The remainder of the poem reads:
   When the soul lies down in that grass,
   the world is too full to talk about
   Ideas, language, even the phrase *each other*
   doesn't make any sense.

ular practice. Not only will engaging in other mindful practices, such as meditation, yoga, tai chi, and the like, strengthen the lawyer's ability to listen mindfully, but listening mindfully to this client will also strengthen the lawyer's ability to listen mindfully in general.

Here are some concrete ideas for listening mindfully. Consciously choose to be present fully in the client interview. Put aside other distractions; clear your desk, ask your office to hold non-essential calls and interruptions, face your client, and give her your undivided attention. Once the meeting starts, divest yourself of other agendas besides understanding the client's story from her point of view. Pay full attention to the client's words and actions. In times of confusion, focus on observation ("What is the client's body language? What words is she using?") and fact-gathering.[30] Remind yourself that "there is no bad fact," that a deep and rich understanding of your client's point of view will yield the strongest, most authentic theory of the case. Employ strategies that have worked for you before (e.g. note-taking, eye contact, recapping the client's words, and the like) when your mind inevitably wanders, to bring yourself consciously back to listening. One way to do this is to observe yourself during the interview—remain aware of your attitudes, judgments, and inner processes. Use these observations (e.g., "oh no, I hope she's not going to tell me that she left her children behind and fled to the US on her own") to observe your tendency to drift from attending to the client's narrative to your own preoccupations with legal strength and strategy, so that you can bring yourself back to full listening (e.g., *here I go again, jumping ahead to strategy—why don't I save that for later, and focus right now on what she is saying and how she is saying it?*").[31]

While mindful listening is essential to excellent cross-cultural communication, it is not alone sufficient. Mindful listeners will move closer to isomorphic attribution and an in-depth understanding of their client's point of view, but even the perfect listener may not fully understand and ascribe the correct meaning to the language she has heard and the body language she has observed. Where ambiguity remains, the lawyer must employ the remaining four processes of cross-cultural communication: parallel universe thinking, speaking mindfully, proper use of interpreters, and Habit Four analysis.

---

30. This lays the groundwork for Habit Four analysis. *See infra* Section II, Part F.

31. Note that the nonjudgment the lawyer shows here to client is paired with the nonjudgment he shows himself. If the lawyer starts internally chastising himself during the interview, he has left the interview as surely as if he had stood up and walked out the door.

C. Parallel Universe Thinking[32]

Hans, a second-generation German-American clinical professor at a Northeast law school represents Francoise, a West African woman seeking asylum in the United States. His practice is full of African cases, and he "knows what this means": clients who constantly show up late, if they show up at all. He makes an appointment with Francoise to come to his office. Sure enough, she does not appear at the appointed time. Angry and resigned, he calls her again and sets up a second appointment. She does not arrive again. The next day, Francoise arrives without an appointment. Furious, Hans goes to see her in the reception area. Francoise explains that she has just been released from the hospital, and came straight to see him because she was so concerned about her case.

Parallel universe thinking, or Habit Three, asks the lawyer to identify alternatives to assumptions or interpretations he may make about his client's behavior. The Habit itself is simple. When faced with a client behavior, a lawyer should force himself to brainstorm multiple explanations for the actions or words rather than settling on a specific interpretation. To use science fiction terminology, the lawyer should brainstorm the various parallel universes in which the lawyer and client may be interacting, not only to search for open mindedness about the meaning of the client's behavior, but also to avoid rushing to judgment or conclusion about a particular event. Parallel universes also confront a lawyer with the vastness of his ignorance about the client's life and circumstances.

Parallel universe thinking can be done anywhere, anytime, in a matter of seconds. The "no-show" client is a classic example of a situation in which a lawyer has very little information except for his client's actual absence. The lawyer, who immediately jumps to the conclusion that the client doesn't care

---

32. Parallel universe is a concept borrowed from science fiction and quantum mechanics. *See, e.g., Parallel Universe, at* http://en.wikipedia.org/wiki/Parallel_universe (last visited May 26, 2006):

> Parallel universes started as a plot device in science fiction. The idea is that every possible decision in the stream of history actually went every possible way, and that all of those possibilities still exist as part of a multiverse. This is one of the classic versions of alternate history ....

In science, the Many Worlds Interpretation of Quantum Mechanics employs a similar idea. This is often seen as providing a method of reconciling the paradoxical aspects of time travel as predicted by general relativity using the probabilistic nature of quantum mechanics.

about her case, should stop and consider the parallel universe explanation. Maybe the lawyer wrote the time down wrong, perhaps the client got the time of the meeting wrong, perhaps she is delayed and still on her way. Here, Francoise's lawyer jumped to conclusions about his client's failure to come to meetings, assuming, even predicting, that she would be like "all his other African clients." He proceeded with a false certainty about the meaning of her absence as a result. Assuming that the client is indifferent to the case, when many other explanations could be equally true, pushes the lawyer forward to what may well be a false assumption about the client's view about her legal matters. It also prevents him from understanding her behavior on her own terms.

Raymonde Carroll beautifully encapsulates the essential importance of parallel universe thinking.

> Very plainly, I see cultural analysis as a means of perceiving as "normal" things which initially seem "bizarre" or "strange" among people of a culture different from one's own. To manage this, I must imagine a universe in which the "shocking" act can take place and seem "normal," can take on meaning without even being noticed. In other words, I must try to enter, for an instant, the cultural imagination of the other.[33]

Parallel universe thinking is a reactive habit triggered when the lawyer finds herself beginning to make a judgment either negative or positive about the client's behavior. Habit Three asks the lawyer to describe the behavior, but to hold back on interpretations based on an incomplete set of facts. Even a single parallel universe explanation for behavior can jar a lawyer out of a mistaken certainty about his client's motive or intentions. When we are attributing negative meanings to a client's behavior, we should explore other reasons for the behavior. This reminds us that we must explore with the client the actual reason for the behavior rather than operating on our false assumptions.

Another important trigger for parallel universe thinking is certainty. When a lawyer finds herself thinking "I am sure that my client did that because" the lawyer should challenge that assumption with a parallel universe. Note also

---

33. RAYMONDE CARROLL, CULTURAL MISUNDERSTANDINGS: THE FRENCH-AMERICAN EXPERIENCE 2 (1987). As Carroll demonstrates, parallel universe thinking connects directly to the critical dynamics of non-judgment, in its refusal to prejudge confusing behavior, and isomorphic attribution, it its search for the client's understanding of her own behavior. The ease of a parallel universe provides the third dynamic, in that it is easy to learn and integrate into daily life, and thus makes it the ideal habit: essential in its lessons and simple to perform.

that it is not necessary or even expected that the parallel universes generated include the actual explanation for the behavior. While it can be somewhat confusing, in that it offers a multiplicity of explanations for a single event, it is also efficient; it prevents the lawyer from charging forward based on an assumption that is not necessarily true.

Parallel universe thinking opens the lawyer back up to the client, to the vastness of our lack of knowledge about her world, and to a sense of humility in perspective about our relative importance in her life. Its critical quality of nonjudgment is a welcome antidote to the default tendencies of our profession. Our clients may have experienced many events in which they felt wrongly and hastily judged; parallel universe thinking can prevent us joining the ranks of those who have betrayed them in this way. By preventing us from acting mistakenly on false judgment, and lawyering based on a misguided uncertainty about a reality which we do not yet apprehend, parallel universe thinking is a tremendous ally in our ongoing struggle to understand our client in her own terms and not ours.

Habit Three is extremely easy to put into daily practice. When finding that one is making a judgment about a client's behavior, take a moment, and think of a parallel universe, and most of the work is done. Even just the effort of starting to figure out what parallel universes exist will soften a lawyer's dedication to his singular interpretation of a client's behavior. A healthy incorporation of Habit Three into the life of even the busiest lawyer could itself be the singular act that, day to day, increases the cross-cultural awareness that enables the lawyer to practice based on fact and not assumption.

D. Speaking Mindfully—Communicating Within the Client's Context

Lawyers must speak mindfully in beginning interactions with clients in explaining the legal system and the law and in engaging the client to confirm the client's understanding. Lawyering texts alert lawyers to the significance of these tasks in all attorney-client interactions; in cross-cultural interactions, they deserve special attention because they are heavily culturally laden tasks. Below are some concrete suggestions for applying the four components of mindfulness—awareness, openheartedness, a focus on the moment-to-moment, and nonjudgment—to crafting your speaking with your client.

1. Begin your Interactions Thoughtfully

A lawyer working with a client from another culture must pay special attention to the beginnings of communications with the client. Each culture has introductory rituals or scripts that create a sense of welcome and respect as well as trust-building exchanges that promote rapport and conversation. To learn culturally appropriate beginnings, a lawyer can read about the client's culture or, if an interpreter who is familiar with the client's culture will be involved with the interview, the lawyer can consult with the interpreter on appropriate introductory behavior. In addition to learning culture-specific knowledge,[34] a lawyer should pay careful attention to the verbal and nonverbal signals the client is giving to the lawyer from the beginning of the interview.

How will the lawyer greet the client? The lawyer should learn whether any introductory behavior would be viewed as particularly welcoming or as insulting or violating a cultural norm. Take, for example, a strong handshake as a method of greeting and welcoming the client. How will a client interpret it? In some cultures, men and women who are not married to each other do not touch. A handshake offered in that setting might create an awkward beginning. It is also possible that a client from that culture has learned that an "American" greeting involves a strong handshake. Other clients expect more physical exchanges as they come to know a lawyer—a hug, a kiss on each cheek—while others would be horrified by such behavior even by a lawyer that they had known for years. Other cultures expect a bow and a business card exchange as the introductory ritual. Many cultures require different introductory rituals for men and women.

Lawyers should try to identify the range of introductory rituals that might be expected. A lawyer can ask clients if handshakes are appropriate. Clients who come from cultures where touching is not appropriate will usually feel respected by such a question. Lawyers can also let the client take the lead in setting the introductory ritual, waiting to see if the client offers a hand to shake or a cheek to kiss.

What information should be exchanged before the lawyer and client "get down to business?" How do the client and lawyer define "getting down to busi-

---

34. Cross-cultural researchers have identified two different kinds of cultural knowledge: culture general and culture specific. Culture general knowledge is knowledge about concepts and experiences that are likely to occur across cultures. Some culture general concepts include collective and individual culture, time, direct and indirect communication, social role and hierarchy, insider-outsider, categorization, and attribution. *See* Kenneth Cushner & Dan Landis, *The Intercultural Sensitizer, in* HANDBOOK OF INTERCULTURAL TRAINING 189 (Dan Landis & Rabi S. Bhagat eds., 2d ed. 1996); Bryant, *supra* note 3, at 50–51. Culture specific information includes information about the general topics applied to the specific culture as well as history, politics, and geography.

ness?" For one, the exchange of information about self, family, status, or background is an integral part of the business of building a relationship of trust that must precede any genuine discussion of legal issues. For another, it may be introductory chitchat before the real conversation takes place.[35] Of course, these exchanges are especially important for the first meeting with clients when the relationships are first developing. Even if the lawyer and client have a relationship of trust, however, the client may still expect a different kind of interaction at the beginning. These clients expect the lawyer to ask how things are going for them, to inquire about their family and their well being. Again, a mindful lawyer explores culture-specific information, through reading, talking with others who come from the client's culture, and most importantly, taking her cues from the client.

2. Gather Culture Specific Information Before Explaining the Legal Process

An important aspect of attorney-client communication involves providing information to clients about the law and the legal system and the ways the law might be used to solve clients' problems. Before providing this information, a lawyer needs to understand the client's culture and experience to know how to explain the legal system and the lawyer's role. A lawyer needs to know how the client will experience the lawyer's suggestions for handling the problem. Will the concepts and solutions that the lawyer suggests be familiar and comfortable or will they require a stretch for the client to understand and accept within her cultural context?

As described above, narrative provides a good window into exploring the client's values, perspective, and cultural context. When the client is in narrative mode, the lawyer can actively observe the client and her culture and the client's approach to the problem. When the narrative fails to reveal the cultural context or the lawyer wants to confirm his understanding of that context, the lawyer can ask a series of questions that seek to identify the cultural context of the problem and expose differences that will help the lawyer understand the client's worldview.[36] Suggested questions might include the fol-

---

35. See Gellhorn, *supra* note 12, at 325. Gellhorn warns us that even introductory chitchat reveals important clues about client concerns. Often concerns are revealed in response to questions that might be considered "throw away" questions like "how did you get here?"

36. Medical interviewers have described this as developing a medical ethnography of the client. *See* Arthur Kleinman et al., *Culture, Illness and Care: Clinical Lessons from Anthropologic and Cross-Cultural Research*, 88 ANNALS OF INTERNAL MEDICINE 251 (1978).

lowing:[37] Who else has the client talked to and what advice did they give; did they like the advice they were given?[38] Who else besides the client will be affected and consulted?[39] What are the client's ideas about the problem; what would a good solution look like; what are the most important results?[40] Are there other problems caused by the current problem? Does the client know anybody else who had this problem; how did they solve it; does the client consider that effective?[41]

In addition to gathering culture-specific information about the client's problems, lawyers should gather culture-specific information about the client's experiences with legal systems. If the client has come from another country, the lawyer should ask about her experiences of lawyers and judges in her home country, and how problems would be handled in her country of origin.[42] Lawyers need insights about how clients think about conflicts and possible resolution mechanisms.[43] Lawyers should explore what clients understand about the American legal system. Concepts like "prosecutors, jury, or judge" may be strange ones for clients who have not attended high school in the United States

---

37. A similar set of questions are suggested for doctors working in cross-cultural encounters. *See* ANNE FADIMAN, THE SPIRIT CATCHES YOU AND YOU FALL DOWN: A HMONG CHILD, HER AMERICAN DOCTORS, AND THE COLLISION OF TWO CULTURES (2001).

38. This helps the lawyer see whom the client considers involved in the decision and an important decision maker as well as what kinds of solutions to similar problems have been developed within the client's community.

39. These tell you whether the client considers "her" problem actually to belong to a larger collective group. While the American legal system might regard her problem as limited to her rights and responsibilities, a client who comes from a collective culture might see her issue as involving many other people and therefore is not one that she alone can resolve. For example, a client may expect that her mother or father will have a say in what happens to their grandchildren in a custody case or a disabled client may want her adult children to be involved in discussions about her disability case.

40. These are standard client-centered questions that are especially important when the answers are culturally imbedded and inaccessible to the lawyer.

41. These questions allow the lawyer to understand the client's expectations and goals without requiring the client to answer those questions more directly. The solutions might also be new ones for the lawyer to consider.

42. For example, imagine that a client being represented in a divorce action told her lawyers that in her home country she would have to have a trial-reconciliation with her husband before any divorce would be final. This information provides a context for understanding a client's initial reaction to the suggestion that she file for a divorce as a way to deal with spouse abuse.

43. The United States is identified as a very litigious society. The lawyer should explore the client's comfort with pursuing litigation.

or been exposed to the popular culture about lawyers by watching TV shows. These questions also give the lawyer some information about the expectations that the client has for the lawyer. For example, in many legal cultures, the lawyer is the "fixer" or the person-in-charge. In contrast, many law students are taught client-centered lawyering which puts the client in charge and sees the lawyer at most as a partner.

3. Communicate Information Tailored to the Client

Understanding the client's context about what she expects from the lawyer can help shape the information that the lawyer provides to the client. Many lawyers develop scripts for providing this information. Common scripts include ones that lawyers use to open the interview and inform the client about a variety of topics including the purpose of the initial interview, what confidentiality means, the role of various players in the legal system, and other topics common to the lawyer's practice. Lawyers use stock stories or metaphors to explain these concepts to increase a client's understanding of what is going to happen. However, a mindful lawyer uses these scripts cautiously, especially in cross-cultural encounters, and instead, develops a variety of explanations to replace scripts that are tailored to each client's expectations, knowledge of the American legal system, and prior experiences with the law in other countries.[44]

Instead of scripts, a lawyer should have a list of important points they know they want to convey but write them out as concepts to be addressed during the interview, rather than as a script. The lawyer could give the client an opportunity to ask questions about the process of representation before the lawyer launches into his own explanations. The lawyer could fill in any important introductory points not covered by the answers to the client's questions after answering those questions.

4. Confirm Understanding

Both clients and lawyers in cross-cultural exchanges will likely have high degrees of uncertainty and anxiety when they interact with someone they per-

---

44. Perhaps the reader is thinking that the individualized approach takes too much time and thought and those scripts are useful ways for lawyers to communicate efficiently. However, one need only recall all the times lawyers listen to judges' scripts that are used to explain rights to clients to understand that the scripts are often not understood by the clients and that taking the time to give information tailored to the client may reduce client resistance to the lawyer's suggestions and save time in the long run.

ceive to be different.[45] The lack of predictability about how they will be received and their capacity to understand each other often leads to this uncertainty and anxiety. To lessen uncertainty and anxiety, both the lawyer and client will be assisted by using techniques that consciously demonstrate that genuine understanding is occurring and that helpful and expected information is being provided. Active listening techniques, including continuers like, "go on," "Uh-huh," and "yes" communicate that the client is providing useful information.[46] Thanking the client for the information provided is another way to give feedback that the client is giving information that is expected. Feedback that includes rephrasing client information may be used to communicate to the client that the lawyer understands what the client is saying.[47]

In addition to giving the client feedback, the lawyer should look for feedback from the client that the client understands the lawyer or is willing to ask questions if the client does not understand. Until the lawyer knows that the client is very comfortable with a direct style of communication, a lawyer should refrain from asking the client if she understands or agrees. A client who has difficulty telling the lawyer that she does not understand may also have difficulty telling the lawyer she disagrees with the lawyer's suggestions. Instead the lawyer should probe for exactly what the client understands and thinks is a sensible solution.

E. Working with Interpreters

Working with clients who speak a language other than English challenges the lawyer's ability to accomplish the goals of cross-cultural interactions — building relationships and communicating with understanding and accuracy. Relationship building can be difficult when lawyers and clients are "outsiders" to each other. The inability to communicate with a client in her language reinforces to the client that the lawyer is an outsider to her culture. Even when the lawyer speaks the client's language, the difficulties of communicating legal concepts in a language other than English may still make the client feel like

---

45. As described below, this anxiety is heightened even more when communication occurs with an interpreter.

46. Explicit feedback that the client is giving useful information may avoid possible cultural misunderstandings from facial expressions or continuers.

47. *See* Gellhorn, *supra* note 12, at 346. Gellhorn suggests that feedback to clients that rephrases client concerns should not be used too early in an interview as this will limit the client or steer the client in the direction that has been repeated. The client may only be beginning to lay out a host of concerns.

she is an outsider in the legal culture. If clients and lawyers do not share a common language, accurate communication between lawyers and clients depends on the competence of another—the interpreter—and the lawyer's and interpreter's capacities to communicate concepts that may have no easy correlate in the client's language and culture.

To accomplish these goals, a lawyer must focus on developing ways of working with interpreters that enable lawyers to gain a client's trust and that result in good communication between the lawyer and client. To ensure that accurate communication occurs, a lawyer should take these five steps:

1. Assess whether an interpreter is needed;

2. Make sure that the interpreter is competent;

3. Form a professional relationship and prepare the interpreter;

4. Work in ways that lessen the interpretation challenges; and

5. Use Habit Four analysis to plan for, identify, and correct the problems as they occur in the interview.[48]

To take these steps, the lawyer should first develop a basic understanding of languages and the interpretation process.[49] Interpretation is a complex cognitive task requiring the interpreter to capture every element of the message, including the context and integrity, and transfer it wholly and fully to the listener. Lawyers and clients need more than a summary of what each other says; nuance is important and cases are won and deals are made based on those nuances. Credibility determinations may be made based on prior inconsistent statements.[50] Because accuracy and precision are needed, lawyers often tell interpreters that they want "a word for word" interpretation. An accurate, faithful interpretation however is not usually possible by interpreting "word for word." Language is inherently ambiguous and many words are closely related to each other. No two interpreters will interpret the same phrase exactly the same. To convey the meaning of a single word in English, an interpreter may need several words to convey the concept in the client's language. A good interpreter does not summarize and instead focuses on conveying (to the extent

---

48. *See infra* Section III.

49. We are indebted to Angela McCaffrey who first introduced us to the importance of understanding the interpretation process. Her work continues to be mandatory reading for people interested in exploring issues about interpretation. *See* Angela McCaffrey, *Don't Get Lost in Translation: Teaching Law Students to Work with Language Interpreters*, 6 CLIN. L. REV. 347, 375–376 (2000).

50. See Fed. R. Evid. 613.

possible) the whole message and capturing the meaning the client and lawyer intend.

Consecutive interpretation achieves the highest degree of accuracy and faithfulness.[51] The speaker pauses and the interpreter interprets in the other language; the speaker speaks again and the process continues. Because precise wording and accuracy is promoted, most lawyers use consecutive interpretation. Simultaneous interpretation (occurring without pausing) requires greater skill and is used in conferences at the United Nations and in court at counsel table to enable a party to know what is occurring.

Language abilities are domain specific—we learn language related to context. For example, a person who learns and uses English in school and in legal practice and another language in the home will no doubt know the many words for mother, father, refrigerator, or kitchen appliance in the home language and in English. They will know how to describe complex cultural concepts of familial love and family strife in the language used at home and perhaps less well in English. They will experience, however, difficulty explaining legal concepts in the language of the home, lacking the vocabulary and linguistic understanding of how to express those ideas in the home language. Thus, an interpreter often needs to have the particular, context-specific experience to find the words to explain the client's story and the lawyer's conversation.[52]

In addition to having bilingual capacity, interpreters must be effective listeners and predictors, with excellent memory skills. Effective listening requires attention to the meaning of words as well as the meaning derived from their juxtaposition, their context, the intonation and stress of the utterances, and the pace.[53] The same words can have radically different meanings depending on these factors. Consider these examples:

---

51. *See Modes of Interpretation*, Interpreters Office, United States District Court, Southern District of New York, *available at* http://sdnyinterpreters.org/ (last visited May 27, 2006). This site is a wealth of information for working with interpreters in courtroom settings.

52. Consider a client who spoke fluent English when talking about his current living conditions but was much less fluent when speaking about torture that had occurred in his home country. He searched for the words in English to describe what happened. Because these actions and their effect had "occurred" in a different language, his capacity to tell the story in English was severely challenged. Similarly, if an interpreter has never worked with lawyers, she may have difficulty finding the words to explain the concepts in the client's language even where the lawyer is using plain English to explain the concepts.

53. ROSEANN D. GONZALEZ ET AL., FUNDAMENTALS OF COURT INTERPRETATION: THEORY, POLICY AND PRACTICE 380–383 (1991).

- Intonation gives clues to meaning: For example, does the speaker intend a literal interpretation of the spoken word or not? When a client says, "I was surprised to see him," is she surprised? Or is she expressing the opposite emotion by delivering the comment as sarcasm? The stress or intonation will give clues to meaning.

- Context matters—consider legal terminology and ordinary English differences. If I say, "I sent you a pleading in the mail," as a result of your legal training, you might picture a document, relating to a lawsuit, with a stylized beginning and ending, with a back cover. To anyone else, it might mean a request given with an imploring quality.

- Dialects of the same language may cause a similar misunderstanding because the same word may have different meanings in the different dialects. For example, the Spanish language has 19 different dialects. Consider the word, "Ahorita." For Spanish speaking[54] people from the Caribbean, "Ahorita" means "a little later" while for Mexicans it means "right now."

- If the speaker hesitates or emphasizes a point, what is the meaning? In some cultural/lingual traditions, hesitation communicates a lack of commitment whereas in other traditions it communicates respect or normal pacing and nothing more.[55]

What the listener expects to hear based on prior experiences and conversations is also an important part of listening and determining meaning. We fill in stories based on limited information and we fill in even if we do not actually hear the whole conversation. The cell phone user that loses every few words due to connection problems experiences this. We fill in what we do not hear and are not really aware that we did not hear it. We remember and process chunks based on preexisting schemas. So if you hear me say, "hi, I am in the _____, driving to _____ ..." You will hear, "I am in the car, driving

---

54. Sue's colleague Maria Arias, who is originally from the Dominican Republic, offered this example of possible dialect confusion that occurred when she went to work for California Rural Legal Services and encountered a dramatically different meaning to the word "Ahorita."

55. Susan Berk-Seligson, The Bilingual Courtroom: Court Interpreters In The Judicial Process 182–83 (2002). The author compares Latin Americans communication patterns to North Americans and notes that hedging is a manifestation of speaking indirectly and indirection is considered positively by Latin Americans. Latin Americans consider North Americans rude for their desire to get to the point.

to....” We also predict what will follow by listening for conjunctives such as “but” or “however.”

Interpreters in the quest for meaning can predict wrong. Like all of us, they may not be aware that they are filling in based on predictions. When people listen to a language other than their native tongue, it takes longer to process the information. Making predictions in the newer language is harder and causes the interpreter to have to hold the original message in her memory for a longer period, making the task more difficult and slower. This is one of the reasons that mistakes are more likely to be made in the non-native language.

In addition to determining meaning correctly, the interpreter must hold on to the meaning and search for the words to communicate the same meaning in the other language. Actually the interpreter is using her memory in three important ways: (1) to determine the meaning of the speaker’s words, using prior experiences to determine meaning; (2) to remember this meaning; (3) to determine the appropriate terms to express this meaning in the listener’s language, again relying on prior experiences in that language.[56] Experienced interpreters take notes to aid this complicated memory task.[57].

Other factors that influence the interpreter’s capacity to remember include the speed and complexity of the conversation as well as prior experience with the material being discussed. When we are listening to something that is meaningful to us, we are more likely to remember it. For example, if someone rattles off ten single digit numbers, we may not remember them. But what if they are identified as a telephone number that uses an area code that we know—then we really are only remembering seven numbers. And what if we know the exchange numbers—then we only have to remember four.

We hope that understanding some of the complexity of cross-lingual communication convinces you that interpretation is not a job for an amateur. Clients who need interpreters to communicate fully should be offered them and should not be asked to bring relatives or friends to interpret. In addition to recognizing that family members may not have the requisite interpretation skills, the use of relatives or friends creates additional issues. They may be confused about their role in an interview. They may see themselves as protectors, as fact witnesses, as decision makers, as well as interpreters. Clients may also censor themselves in front of family and friends. For these reasons, relatives and friends should only be used in emergency situations. Bar Associations that

---

56. GONZALEZ ET AL., *supra* note 53, at 383.

57. If you want to experience the difficulty of holding on to information and to repeating it, try the shadowing exercises in Appendix B.

have considered the ethical issues posed by lawyers working with interpreters have recognized that both the rules and model codes require use of qualified interpreters to communicate with some clients. Failure to do so may implicate lawyers' obligations to maintain confidences, provide unbiased representation, and perform legal work competently. To meet his ethical obligations, a lawyer should determine if an interpreter is needed and arrange for a competent interpreter.[58]

1. Assess Whether an Interpreter is Needed

A client can appear fluent in English and still not have the fluency to tell a full and coherent story. Many people who came to this country as adults have learned English at a conversational level. They can interact with English speakers and make themselves understood in everyday events like shopping, eating out, and taking the bus. When people with this level of language skills call the office for assistance, staff may not recognize that an interpreter is needed. Conversational English, however, is not proficient enough for clients to engage with legal concepts or conversation in the courtroom.[59]

In evaluating the need for an interpreter, the lawyer should ask the client what language the client would like to use. A lawyer should also make an independent assessment as to whether the client needs an interpreter.[60] Can the client tell the story as richly and fully in English? Can she understand the lawyer's colloquy? To assess English proficiency, a lawyer should look for grammatical structure, vocabulary, and ease of delivery in listening to a client's story. Sometimes the lack of fluency causes clients to become anxious or hostile and creates difficult interactions in the office and in the Court.[61]

---

58. *See* Association of the Bar of the City of New York Comm. on Prof'l and Jud. Ethics, Formal Op. 1995-12 (1995); Pa. Bar Association Comm. on Legal Ethics and Prof'l Responsibility, Informal Op. 93-122 (1993); Utah State Bar Ethics Advisory Op. Comm., Op. 95-06 (1996).

59. McCaffrey, *supra* note 49, at 375.

60. New York City, Pennsylvania, and Utah Ethical Opinions, *supra* note 58.

61. For example, consider a "difficult" Russian client who quickly made enemies of court personnel, social service workers, and her student lawyers. The client had lived in this country for six years and spoke English at a comprehensive level. In a frank conversation with the client about how she came across to others and why she was getting the unfavorable reactions that she was getting, the client explained that this happened because communicating in English made her very anxious; she sounded angry even when she was not, and she found herself talking louder and more emphatically for fear that she was not making herself clear.

Some clients will resist the use of an interpreter. Even if the client would prefer to communicate in English in the office and courtroom, a lawyer who determines that the client lacks sufficient proficiency has an ethical duty to explore the client's reluctance to work with an interpreter. In most situations, a client appreciates having someone who speaks her language as part of the lawyer's team and will view this person as a friend in the interview room. Sometimes the story the client has to tell, however, is shameful to the client or to the client's culture. In these situations, having to tell the story in front of her countryman and requiring an interpreter to repeat it is doubly shameful. Other instances where there may be reluctance include: a client who has been belittled by an abusive spouse for her English skills; a refugee who is worried that people in this country who speak his language will not be sympathetic to his actions; or a client who fears that the interpreter has a view that "all people who come from her province lie." In situations like these, the lawyer will have to assess whether the communication can go forward without an interpreter and whether court appearances and testimony can take place without one. If possible, the lawyer should attempt to answer the client's concerns and if the client insists on not using an interpreter, the lawyer should explain the risks involved.

Similarly, if you speak the client's language, you need to consider whether an interpreter is needed. Depending on your language skills, you may feel comfortable talking with the client about how to get to the office but uncomfortable explaining a legal concept in the client's language. Even if all aspects of the interview can be competently conducted in the client's language—the best alternative for the client—the lawyer should use an interpreter to prepare for court if the client will testify through the use of an interpreter.

2. Work with Competent Interpreters

As we noted above, interpretation is a complex task not suitable for amateurs. How does the lawyer fulfill the ethical duty to work only with a competent interpreter who has the necessary language and listening skills? To determine competence, the lawyer should probe about prior experiences and certifications. Ask how many times and for whom the interpreter has done interpretations. Remember that legal terminology and concepts are domain-specific, thus the subject matter of the interpretations is an important point of inquiry. Is the interpreter certified and by whom?[62] Interpreters should be asked which language is their first language and how they came to know their second language.

Explore the issue of dialects with the interpreter and with the client, making sure to take dialect into account. Clients who come from different countries or different parts of the same country than the interpreter may find the communication incomprehensible or simply more difficult because of a different dialect. To explore bias issues with the interpreter, the lawyer should ask whether there are any historical relationships in the home countries of the client and the interpreter that might influence the interaction.

Community organizations are beginning to form relationships with lawyers to provide competent interpreters with connections to the client's community.[63] Lawyers can increase the competence of these interpreters by participating in interpreter training. In working with the organizations, lawyers should ask what testing is used to ensure that interpreters have the language competence and the needed memory and listening skills.

Working with community-based interpreters can have other advantages: They may connect clients to community support and be a cultural broker for the lawyer, bridging any cultural gaps and misunderstanding between lawyer and client. Lawyers can increase legal knowledge in a community by using

---

62. Certification occurs based on testing of the interpreter's competence in both languages. However, different certifications denote varying degrees of rigor. Sue recalls an interview with a "certified" interpreter with significant interpretation problems. When the interpreter left the room for a break, the client who had established a good relationship with her lawyers using other interpreters said in English, "you speak English up here (gesturing high above her head) and she (the interpreter) speak English down here (gesturing below her knees). Upon investigation, it turned out that the interpreter's "certification" was by the agency employing her.

63. The Asian Pacific American Legal Resource Center (APALRC) in Washington, D.C. has created a multilingual referral hotline and a language interpreter project to facilitate access to legal services within the Asian Pacific American community. The hotline is staffed by law student volunteers who speak up to ten Asian languages. When a client calls the hotline, the staff volunteer conducts a thorough intake of the client's legal problem in his or her native language and then identifies the appropriate legal referral and facilitates the client's placement with one of its legal partners, a legal services organization or a pro bono organization. The Language Interpreter Project supplements this referral process by recruiting and training members of the community in conducting legal interpretation. Once a client is referred to a legal service provider by the hotline then APALRC matches that client with a trained legal interpreter who will then provide interpretation services throughout the legal representation. *See* Asian Pacific American Legal Resource Center (APALRC), *at* http://www.charityadvantage.com/apalrc/home.asp (last visited May 27, 2006).

community members to interpret. Through the training and interpretation process, interpreters learn about the law. By building trust not just with this individual client but also with communities to which the client is connected, the lawyer creates other opportunities for clients and social change lawyering.

3. Prepare Interpreters to Avoid Role Confusion and Increase Accuracy

Another important step to ensuring accurate communications is to make sure that the role of the interpreter is clear. Role confusion can occur for many reasons. Some interpreters work in lawyers' offices and perform multiple functions. They may have independent relationships with the clients—answering the phone, setting up meetings, or assisting clients to fill out basic office forms. In addition to interpreting, this person may be the face of the community in the office, offering a welcoming presence to the client as well as presenting the attorney in the best light.

Sometimes role confusion occurs when both the client and the lawyer try to have side conversations with the interpreter. From the client an interpreter might hear, "Why is the lawyer asking me this? Do I really have to answer?" Or from the lawyer, she might hear, "I am trying to find out why she did that? Can you think of a better way to ask that?" Sometimes the interpreter is embarrassed by what the client has to say or the way the client says it; sometimes the lawyer behaves in culturally inappropriate ways. In these situations, interpreters often are pulled into different roles that are sometimes in conflict with the role of interpreter.[64]

To lessen role confusion, the lawyer should clarify exactly what is expected from the interpreter.[65] If the interpreter has not done legal interpretations, the role should be explained in detail. In addition to explaining the role, the lawyer should take the time to explain why it is important for the interpreter to provide faithful interpretation and the consequences of intentionally or unintentionally altering the client or the lawyer's conversation. For example, where a client will testify in court hearings with a court appointed interpreter, the lawyer wants to know how the client will answer the same question. If the

---

64. In training we have done on these topics, interpreters working in legal offices readily confess that they shorten clients' answers to lawyers' questions because the client gives more information than the lawyer asked for. They also change lawyers' communications when they think the lawyer is committing unintentional cultural faux pas. They "clean" up language for lawyers as well as clients. These interpreters are performing a different role than interpretation.

65. Early in the interview, the client should also be told about the role of the interpreter. McCaffrey, *supra* note 49, at 384.

office interpreter is "helping" the lawyer or client out by speeding up communication by deleting irrelevant information, the lawyer will not have an accurate assessment of how the client will respond to questioning. An interpreter who is not employed as a regular office employee should sign a formal contract with the office that spells out the role expectations and the confidentiality requirements.[66]

In addition to clarifying the role, other important preparatory steps with the interpreter includes explaining the case theory, the information you are seeking from the client, and the information you will be providing to the client. Explain the terms that you will use and put as much as possible in writing so that the interpreter can read it as well as hear it. Remember that if the interpreter has heard the terms and information before, she is more likely to have the right terms ready in the moment. The lawyer can also explore whether the interpreter knows the words in the other language that capture the plain English explanation.

Remind the interpreter that the goal of an interpreted interview is to have a real conversation with someone, not a conversation about them. To accomplish this and promote accuracy, interpreters should be encouraged to use first person pronouns when interpreting. For example, assume that in response to a question, the client says in her language "I do not want to settle this case." By repeating "I do not want" rather than "she does not want," the interpreter remains faithful to the client's voice. The interpreter improves clarity because the pronoun refers to the client. "She" could refer to a number of people. The first person recounting is less likely to be a summary of what has been said. In addition, by using the first person, the repeated conversation is one conversation between the lawyer and client rather than two conversations—the first, between the client and interpreter and the second, between interpreter and the lawyer. Finally, the client who understands some English (and many do) will not hear the repetition as an objectification of her story.

4. Promote Accuracy Through Attention to Process

What can a lawyer do to increase the accuracy of the communication? First, follow the suggestions for communicating with English speaking clients: Use plain English and explain legal terms. The interpreter's job is to interpret the explanation not to explain legal terms. If lawyers avoid speaking too fast and using complex sentence constructions, interpreters will have the time they need to determine meaning. Even excellent interpreters have trouble remembering too much material; thus, a careful communicator pauses to allow interpretation.

---

66. A sample agreement is attached as Appendix C.

The challenge for the lawyer and client is to not pause so often that the flow of an idea is chopped up and, at the same time, pause enough to allow interpretation. A lawyer working with an interpreter for the first time should remember to ask the interpreter if the pace is working to insure accuracy. Lawyers should avoid using words or concepts that are difficult to interpret. For example, idiomatic speech or metaphors are difficult to interpret. Thus, in explaining why a client might not want to take a particular procedural step, a statement like "we might win this battle but lose the war," will make the interpretation difficult.

At the same time that the lawyer uses plain English and pacing that promotes accuracy, a lawyer should be sure that she is not giving the client a "lean" version of the lawyer's normal conversation and that the client is not giving a "lean" version of his story. Interpreted conversations take at least twice as long as other conversations. Cross-cultural and cross-lingual communication requires a lawyer to do more checking to make sure that everyone is understanding each other and all aspects of the communication must be repeated twice. Without careful monitoring by the lawyer, these conversations can become oversimplified, losing the complexity that an English speaking client would get.

In the introductory conversations with the client, the role of the interpreter should be explained. To the extent that the role of the office interpreter will be different than the court interpreter, those differences, too, should be explained at some point, if courtroom appearances are expected. In both the explanation of role and throughout the interview, the lawyer should remember that in most situations the interpreter will be viewed by the client as a natural ally. A lawyer should think about how respect is shown in the client's culture and how to accomplish the interpretation goals showing that respect. Some difficulties may occur if the interpreter is ignored when the lawyer looks at the client rather than the interpreter or the conversation is between two people when three people are in the room. In most offices, interpreters are an important part of the trust building between lawyers and clients, and lawyers should describe the process in detail to avoid misunderstanding and engage in the conversations in ways that promote that trust.

II. Habit Four: Red Flags and Correctives

The final practice is Habit Four, Red flags, and Correctives. How does a lawyer plan for, participate in, and analyze cross-cultural encounters in a way that takes culture into account without attributing all communication difficulties or misunderstandings to cross-cultural differences? An approach which we have used is to pinpoint difficulties—red flags—and identify other possible approaches—correctives—that respond to tentative theories about why the communication difficulty occurred. Some of these difficulties we hypothesize are caused by cross-cultural misunderstandings and other difficulties are rooted in other communication patterns. By using the red flag corrective approach, we hope to be able to communicate better across language and culture.

Habit Four invites the lawyer to bring the wisdom of three interacting time-frames to cross-cultural interactions with clients.

A. Three Time Frames

1. Prepare—Beforehand/Make a Game Plan

In preparing for initial client interactions, lawyers plan their mindful speaking and organize their legal analysis in considering what topics they will encourage their clients to address and how they will open up space for the client's concerns. Preparation also includes consciously thinking about how the lawyer will recognize when the communication is or is not working, identifying red flags, and correctives.

2. Do—in the Moment

During these interactions, the lawyer watches for red flags while listening mindfully to the client. When communication appears to be faltering, the lawyer reaches into her repertoire of ideas for moving back to engaged conversation, beginning with the default of seeking narrative mode.

3. Reflect—After—What Worked, What Didn't

Debriefing the interaction, the lawyer looks at red flag moments, as well as moments of smooth communication, to problem-solve tricky moments of the past interview. Using Habit Four analysis, the lawyer brainstorms some concrete ideas for use in the next interview, should the same red flags arise. This in turns adds to the lawyer's repertoire for in-the-moment problem-solving.

Over the course of a lawyer-client relationship, this third timeframe merges with the first timeframe—debriefing the last interview becomes the concrete fodder for preparing the next interview. During this Habit Four analysis, the lawyer reflects upon what went smoothly and what faltered in the last meeting, and consciously brainstorms new ideas for use in the next interview. In a sense, the lawyer does the in-depth analysis of the client interaction that he was unable to do in the moment. The central time traveling aspect of Habit Four requires you to think about these tough interactive moments and prepare yourself for reentry into the moment. Despite planning, the need for correctives often happens at a time when very little reflection can take place; Habit Four allows the lawyer to reflect after one incident as a way of preparing beforehand for the next incident. Thus, debriefing becomes preplanning for the new event.

B. The Three Steps of Habit Four[67]

1. Describe Red Flag Incidents

Whether you are planning for the interview, in the middle of the interview, or reflecting on the interview, the first step is to identify the concrete signs that communication is faltering. If you are planning for an initial client meeting, you are predicting possible red flag moments. If a meeting has occurred, this step of Habit Four takes place after a critical moment in a relationship. The lawyer identifies a moment in which the client's words or actions troubled or confused them. This first step simply requires the lawyer to describe the actual or predicted moment with some particularity. If you are planning for a follow-up meeting with a client, can you identify a recurrent pattern in those interactions that you've wondered about?

For example, your list might include the following:

- Client appears bored or distracted;
- Client reacts in ways that inhibit development of an important topic by getting testy or withdrawing or changing eye contact;
- Lawyer is doing most of the talking;
- Client is asking no questions;
- The client talks in generalities without providing specific information;
- The lawyer is judging the client negatively;
- The client appears angry; or
- The lawyer is distracted and bored.

2. Brainstorm Possible Reasons for the Red Flag

In our attempt to address the red flags in the interview, we use a corrective based on assumptions about why the communication has reached a red flag moment. In the moment, we do not have time for deep thought about why

---

67. A worksheet that can be used for Habit Four analysis is attached to this chapter as Appendix A.

the communication is faltering and instead jump unconsciously to correctives that we have planned or intuitively use. In reflection, we have the time to think more expansively about why the communication faltered. This step asks the lawyer to do Habit 3 parallel universe thinking about the incident. The goal is to generate as many possible alternate explanations as quickly as possible (to go "for numerosity"), and to write them down as fast as possible.

By brainstorming multiple explanations that include cultural explanations and others, the lawyer does not think about culture in a reductionist fashion. It is not enough to blame the red flags on "culture" generally; instead the lawyer is encouraged to think about cultural explanations that are specific to the client's culture and to culture-general concepts that may be influencing the communication.[68] Similarly, the lawyer must not be too quick to attribute the difficulty to the "cultural" differences and similarities. By identifying the multiple reasons for the failures, we can identify a number of correctives that respond to the causes of the red flags.

For example, what explanations might we come up with for a red flag of "the client talking in generalities without providing specific information" where the client is seeking legal status in this country based on abuse by her citizen husband? A brainstormed list of possibilities might look like this:

- Client is embarrassed by the abuse;
- Client may consider it a violation of her culture to reveal the nature of the abuse to someone outside the culture;
- Something in the way the lawyer asks the questions or looks at the client communicates that the lawyer is not ready to hear about the abuse;
- The client is uncomfortable showing emotion and talking about the details causes emotional reactions;
- Client suffers from post-traumatic stress and telling her story is difficult;
- Client is not talkative; her culture is one where silence and relationship building precede any kind of storytelling;[69]
- She is making up the story and has no specifics; and

---

68. In our five habits materials we identify a number of culture general concepts that might be at play in this example including: insider-outsider status, collective and individual cultures, indirect and direct speech, social role and hierarchy, categorization, attribution, and time. *See supra* note 34. *See also* Tremblay & Weng, *supra* note 5. Tremblay and Weng identify a number of culture specific approaches to clients that may improve or interfere with lawyer and client communication.

69. See Eades, *supra* note 23.

- Client and lawyer share culture and client is embarrassed by the lawyer's success in contrast with her "mistakes."[70]

3. Identify correctives

The third step involves identifying correctives to the red flags. Before interviews, a lawyer identifies potential red flags and correctives based on experience with this particular client or with others based on these explanations. After interviews, the lawyer plans for what he would do if the same or similar incident were to happen again. In a sense the lawyer is thinking on behalf of his future interaction with this client and others.

In creating a corrective, the lawyer should be careful to use a different approach than the one that has led to the red flag. For example, if the client is not responding to a direct approach, try an indirect approach. The corrective should address the most likely explanations for the red flag. For example: We might develop the following correctives to address "the client talks in generalities without providing specific information:"

Parallel Universes	Correctives
Client suffers from post-traumatic stress disorder	Refer client for treatment with someone who can help her remember incidents in a safe environment.
Cultural loyalty	Work with supportive community organization to put client's concerns at ease. Give client the time and space to see lawyer as less of an outsider.
Lawyer's questions or body language communicates that the lawyer is not ready to hear about the abuse	Change the approach. If making eye contact before look away; if asking open-ended before ask closed-ended. Address the issue directly and tell client why you need to hear the information.

---

70. Consider a client one of us represented who was reluctant to reveal spousal abuse that she suffered to a lawyer who came from her country and with whom she had much in common. When asked why she was willing to tell a social worker who did not speak her language or share her cultural heritage, the client explained that she was embarrassed that she had not accomplished all that the lawyer had accomplished and instead had poorly chosen her husband and had not progressed educationally as a result.

Other general suggested correctives that might encourage communication include:

- Turning the conversation back to the client's stated priority;
- Seeking greater detail about the client's priority;
- Giving the client a chance to explain in greater depth her concerns;
- Asking for examples of critical encounters in the client's life that illustrate the problem area;
- Exploring one example in some depth;
- Asking the client to describe in some detail what a solution would look like; and
- Using the client's words.

These are again only a few examples of many correctives that can be fashioned. Encounter by encounter, the lawyer can build a sense of the red flags in this relationship and the correctives that "work" for this client. Client by client, the lawyer can gain self-understanding about her own emblematic red flags and correctives that specifically target those flags. Red flags can remind the lawyer to be aware of the client and focused on the client in the moment. With reflection, the red flags can help the lawyer avoid problems in the future.

4. Use Red Flags and Correctives to Assist in the Communication with Interpreters

Prior to the interview the lawyer should identify red flags that indicate problems with the interpretation. These might include:

- Answers are not responsive to questions;
- Conversations back and forth between client and interpreter or lawyer and interpreter are not being interpreted;
- Long conversations get interpreted with short statements;
- English used by interpreter has grammatical errors or evidences a limited vocabulary;
- Interpreter is not taking notes;
- Client or lawyer is only looking at the interpreter not at each other;
- Inconsistent information is provided by the client; or
- Interpreter starts providing his own facts.

When interpretation difficulties occur, the lawyer should engage in parallel universe thinking about what is causing the difficulty. Sometimes actually taking a break provides the client and the interpreter the opportunity to re-group and gives the lawyer the space to think about what is happening. Is the lawyer or client talking too fast or too much? Are the lawyer and client paus-ing? Does the interpreter have the necessary skills? Is there role confusion? Is the client's dialect interfering with communication? Is the lawyer's use of terms confusing? Has the client's lack of comfort level caused the client to pull back? Has the client or the lawyer formed a relationship with the interpreter rather than with each other?

Correctives:

- Refer back to the preparatory conversation with the client or the inter-preter about role;
- Take a break. Remember that a conversation that occurs through inter-pretation is difficult for everyone. Federal court interpreters change every 30 minutes because they find that accuracy decreases as fatigue sets in;
- Perhaps reschedule and get a different interpreter;
- Constantly confirm your understanding by repeating what you hear and ask the client to do the same;[71]
- Ask the interpreter if they have suggestions;
- Ask the interpreter to clarify differences in what you are hearing the client say—make sure your conversation with the interpreter is inter-preted if it occurs during the attorney-client interview.[72]

Conclusion

Cross-cultural interactions with clients provide endless challenges and endless rewards to the thoughtful lawyer. Building on the thoughtful writing

---

71. Clients need reassurances that we understand their story. Lawyers need reassurance that the clients understands what we are asking or telling. Explain to the client that you are doing this to ensure accurate communication.

72. For example, in one case, the interpreter interpreted the client's statement as "she was burned by a needle on the hand." In prior interpretations of the story, the client story had been that she was burned by a skewer on the arm and her affidavit included these facts. When the interpreter was asked during a break whether it was "on the hand" or "on the arm"—the interpreter explained that in her language the arm below the elbow and the hand were one word. However, given that English had two words to describe this same area, her interpretation was inaccurate.

on legal interviewing, this chapter has identified six essential practices for cross-cultural legal interactions, ending with a permeating strategy of identifying and problem-solving difficult moments in these interactions, before, during, and after they occur, to create a cycle of incremental improvement in these important meetings over time. The practices and the red flag analysis rely, ultimately, on the commitment to nonjudgment that animates all of the Habits. No strategy will protect us from the inevitable mistakes that we will all make, despite our most conscientious planning for narrative interviews, mindful listening and speaking, parallel universe thinking, and work with interpreters. Thankfully, clients are forgiving, as is Habit Four itself, fueled as it is by the redemptive dynamic of examining today's mistakes for ideas about tomorrow's improvements. In the end, Habit Four asks us to work nonjudgmentally with both our clients, and ourselves, to look thoughtfully at the tough moments, and to trust that, over time, we will develop a repertoire of sensitive responses and sophisticated practices in working with our clients from other cultures.

Appendix A

Habit Four Worksheet

Describe Red Flag Incident: Think about a client, or case personage, with whom you have interacted on a number of occasions recently. Can you identify a recurrent pattern in those interactions that you've wondered about? (For instance, the client appears bored or distracted, the client grows testy at certain points in the interview, you find yourself doing all of the talking at certain points, etc.)

I. Brainstorm parallel universes to explain the red flag.

A.	F.
B.	G.
C.	H.
D.	I.
E.	J.

II. Pause to consider culture: Is it accounted for by your parallel universes? Add more parallel universes if necessary.

III. Circle the 2 or 3 parallel universes you consider most likely to account for the red flag (being sure to include at least one which takes culture into account).

IV. Brainstorm Correctives for each universe.

	Parallel Universe 1:	Parallel Universe 2:	Parallel Universe 3:
Possible Correctives			

V. Pause to consider culture; add more correctives if necessary.

VI. Circle the two or three you will try the next time the red flag occurs (being sure to include at least one which takes culture into account).

Appendix B[73]

This appendix contains three short exercises designed to allow the participants the opportunity to play various roles in interpreted conversation. It is called a shadowing exercise and requires that the person in role as interpreter repeat what they have heard from the lawyer to the client. It is designed to give the person playing interpreter the experience of having to remember and repeat what has been said, replicating a small part of the interpreter's task in a real interpretation. There are role plays for three exercises so that each person in a group of three will get to play client, interpreter, and lawyer once.

Person A

Exercise 1—Lawyer

In this exercise, you are a lawyer explaining some rights of workers so you start the exercise. Please read the following all at once without stopping:

All workers have the right to receive pay stubs showing the pay period, the hours worked, the rate you were paid, or if piece rate, the amount of pieces and the rate per piece, any deductions, including those for taxes, FICA, and any other deductions you have authorized. It is very important that you keep your pay receipts. They can assist you in proving that you were employed and what you were paid.

* * *

---

73. Professor Shin Imai from Osgood Hall Law School introduced this exercise to us at an Association of American Law Schools Clinical Teachers Conference. *See also* McCaffrey, *supra* note 49, at 379.

Exercise 2—Interpreter

In this exercise, you play the role of interpreter. You will hear the statement in English (lawyer speak) and your job is to interpret it word for word while retaining meaning for a non-law trained person. You should wait for the lawyer to pause before interpreting.

* * *

Exercise 3—Lawyer

In this exercise, you are listening to a client explain her case.

Person B

Exercise 1—Interpreter

In this exercise, you play the role of interpreter. You will hear the statement in English and your job is to interpret it word for word while retaining meaning for a non-law trained person. You should wait for the lawyer to pause before interpreting.

* * *

Exercise 2—Client

In this exercise, you are a client listening to a lawyer whose statements are being interpreted.

* * *

Exercise 3—Client

Please read the following all at once—you take the lead in this exercise. Do not stop unless stopped:

I worked at the Bloomfield's Department store as a buyer in the men's department. I was being bothered by my store manager, Mr. David Bryant, almost everyday. He was mean and nasty and told me that if I did not sleep with him, he would fire me. I tried to tell my first supervisor, Susan Jones, but she told me I should just keep quiet about it and that my boss was all talk but would not fire me. I put up with his nastiness for 1 year, I developed migraines and felt lousy for almost a year, and then he fired me after all. He called me into his office and told me he had given me plenty of chances and he was giving me no more. Now I have no job. I do not know what to do.

Person C

Exercise 1—Client

In this exercise, you are a client listening to a lawyer explain the law.

Exercise 2—Lawyer

In this exercise, please read the following, pausing for the interpreter to interpret as necessary:

The EPA requires equal pay for equal work on jobs that require equal skill, effort, and responsibility, and which are performed under similar working conditions. The plaintiff must demonstrate the "equal-ness" of the two jobs by showing "substantial equality," not identicalness. Minor differences in the job tasks are viewed as de minimis if the percentage of job time on those tasks is not substantial.

Exercise 3 — Interpreter

You will hear a statement in English and your job is to repeat it word for word while retaining meaning. You may interrupt the speaker if necessary.

Appendix C

INTERPRETER CONFIDENTIALITY AGREEMENT[74]

I, _____

(name of the interpreter), by my initials and signature, agree to the following:

Initials

_____ I respect and understand the importance of the attorney-client re-lationship and agree not to do anything that interferes with that re-lationship.

_____ I agree to protect and hold confidential all privileged and confiden-tial information relating to WCL cases and clients.

_____ I will not discuss the content of the interpreted interview with any-one other than the lawyer.

_____ I will not comment publicly on the case for any reason.

_____ I will not disclose information learned during the interview to others.

I understand that, in addition to breaching the Interpreter Code of Ethics, there may be legal consequences if I break this agreement.

_____

Signature

_____

74. This agreement is reprinted with the permission of Professor Susan Bennett of the American University Law School clinical program. The AU clinical faculty, especially Susan Bennett and Muneer Ahmad, have been leaders in the clinical community on issues in-volved with interpretation.

III

Lawyering and Civil Disputes

CHAPTER 7

Problem-Solving Advocacy in Mediations: A Model of Client Representation*

Harold Abramson**

Introduction

This chapter constructs a self-contained advocacy approach suitable for mediation as a creative problem-solving process. It is an approach based on the model of client representation in my book, *Mediation Representation-Advocating in a Problem-Solving Process.*[1] Although much has been written about how mediators can create a problem-solving process[2] and many mediators have been trained to use a problem-solving approach,[3] surprisingly little has

---

* This chapter is adapted from the author's article, *Problem-Solving Advocacy in Mediations: A Model of Client Representation,* 10 Harv. Negot. L. Rev. 103 (2005). For the original article, I want to thank Lela Love, Ken Rosenblum, and Barbara Swartz for generously finding the time to offer valuable comments, as well as my research assistant, Joseph Wilson, for putting the footnotes in proper form.

** Harold Abramson, Professor of Law, Touro College Jacob D. Fuchsberg Law Center.

1. See Harold I. Abramson, Mediation Representation: Advocating in a Problem-Solving Process (2004) (Recipient of 2004 Book Award of the CPR Institute for Dispute Resolution).

2. See, e.g., Dwight Golann, Mediating Legal Disputes: Effective Strategies for Lawyers and Mediators 14–26 (1996); Christopher W. Moore, The Mediation Process: Practical Strategies for Resolving Conflict 18–19, 55–56 (2d ed. 1996); Jay Folberg & Alison Taylor, Mediation: A comprehensive guide to resolving conflicts without litigation 7–9, 38–72 (1984).

3. Even though I could not find a rigorous study of the approaches taught in mediation training programs, I came across ample anecdotal evidence that suggests that many,

been written on how to represent clients in this burgeoning and increasingly preferred process.[4]

Let me start by defining a problem-solving mediation process. In such a process, the mediator's sole purpose is to assist the clients and their attorneys in resolving the dispute. The mediator knows how to structure a process that can provide both sides an opportunity to fashion enduring, and when at all feasible, inventive solutions that can go beyond what a court might be willing to craft. The mediator serves as a guide by managing a structured discussion that includes gathering specific information; identifying issues, interests, and impediments; and generating, assessing, and selecting options for settlement. The mediator knows how to involve clients constructively and to use various dispute resolution techniques at propitious moments in the mediation session. The mediator poses open-ended and focused questions, reframes issues, conducts brainstorming sessions, and uses recognized strategies for defusing tensions and overcoming impasses. The mediator may use private caucuses to gain confidential information and employ suitable methods for helping participants evaluate the strengths and weaknesses of their legal case, methods that do not involve the mediator rendering his or her assessment. If the dispute does not settle, the mediator may help the participants—the attorneys and the parties—to select a suitable alternative process, including litigation, for ultimately resolving the conflict.

There are, of course, other settlement processes for resolving legal conflicts, a well-recognized reality that has generated much debate over what processes can be rightfully called mediation. After reading and listening to much of the thoughtful debate and observing how loosely the term is used by such diverse sources as judges, the media, and the United Nations, the final clincher in my

---

if not most, training programs teach mediators the interest-based or problem-solving approach. This approach seems to be taught in many court-connected programs, by many private trainers, and at Harvard Law School (where Professors Fisher, Sander, and Mnookin train negotiators and mediators from around the world). Also, although a significant number of mediators are trained in the transformative approach, a number of them also seemed to have been trained in problem-solving.

4. *See* Marc Galanter, *The Vanishing Trial: An Examination of Trials and Related Matters in Federal and State Courts* (Preliminary Version, Oct. 24, 2003) (prepared for the Symposium on The Vanishing Trial sponsored by the Litigation Section of the American Bar Association, December 2003) (In this study, the author has preliminarily documented that while the number of federal lawsuits filed has increased, the number of trials has decreased, from 11.5% in 1962 to 1.8% in 2002, with comparable trends in the state courts. One of the documented replacements for trials is mediation.); *see also* John Lande, *Getting the Faith: Why Business Lawyers and Executives Believe in Mediation*, 5 Harv. Negot. L. Rev. 137 (2000).

intellectual pursuit to define mediation occurred when I encountered an oven advertisement on television. The manufacturer's salesman was presented as a "great mediator" when he offered a range that could "cook two different foods, at two different temperatures."[5] It is just too late to justify a favored, circumscribed definition of mediation. Mediation is simply a negotiation conducted with the assistance of a third party. This generic definition should fit any process that can be legitimately classified as mediation.[6] Instead of debating the definition of mediation, we should focus on defining the adjective in front of the noun. Is the mediation problem-solving, transformative,[7] evaluative,[8]

---

5. Interview with Nicole Kaczmarek, LB Works Operations Manager, Advertising Agency for Maytag Corporation (July 2003) (Maytag Corporation ran a national television advertisement that it called "The Great Mediator (pizza or casserole)." In the advertisement, the "Maytag Man" appears as "a great mediator" who has the answer to the question that has "aroused fierce passions for centuries: What's for dinner?" The mediator presents a new range that can "cook two different foods, at two different temperatures, for one complete meal." The advertisement ran from August 1999 to December 1999. The salesman was mediating using an evaluative approach in which he offered a solution that would meet the needs of both parties to eat different foods.).

6. *See, e.g.*, KIMBERLEE K. KOVACH, MEDIATION: PRINCIPLES AND PRACTICE 23–25 (2d ed. 2000); GOLANN, *supra* note 2, at 14–26; MOORE, *supra* note 2, at ch.2; FOLBERG & TAYLOR, *supra* note 2, at 7–9, 38–72.

7. A transformative mediator engages in a mediation practice based on communication and relational theory. Instead of promoting the goal of settlement for the parties, the transformative mediator allows the parties to determine their own direction and supports the parties' own opportunities for perspective-taking, deliberation, and decision-making. The mediator focuses on the parties' interactions and supports their shifts from destructive and alienating interactions to more constructive and open interactions (referred to as empowerment and recognition shifts). In this model, parties are likely to be able to make positive changes in their interactions with each other and, consequently, find acceptable resolution for themselves, where such terms genuinely exist."
ABRAMSON, *supra* note 1, at 71–2.

8. An evaluative mediator assists the participants in breaking impasses by contributing her views of the merits of the legal case, the consequences of failure to settle, and the benefits of particular settlement proposals. For instance, if each side has strongly conflicting views of the legal merits, the neutral might try to break the impasse by giving an evaluation of the merits of the dispute. By predicting the likely outcome in the adjudicatory forum, the neutral gives the participants a basis against which to assess the attractiveness of emerging options for settlement. If the case is not settling, the neutral might suggest how failure would impact on the interests of each party. If each side has strongly conflicting views of the benefits of a particular settlement proposal, the neutral might give an assessment of how the proposal benefits each side. The neutral might even

or something else? *Mediation Representation* focuses on one particular adjective: problem-solving.

Problem-solving mediations should be distinguished from judicial settlement conferences because some mediations can resemble settlement conferences.[9] These settlement conference-type mediations, like judicial settlement conferences, can consist of the third party hearing each side's arguments, asking questions, challenging partisan points, assessing arguments and legal positions, and hinting at or urging compromised settlement terms. Such mediations, using dispute resolution nomenclature, are often a directive, evaluative process.[10] Attorneys often prefer this sort of mediation process because they know how to represent clients in such a process, using the familiar adversarial strategies of presenting their strongest partisan arguments and attacking the other side's case.

These adversarial strategies may be effective in settlement conference-type processes, as well as in court and arbitrations where each side is trying to convince a third party to make a favorable decision or to steer the negotiations in a favorable direction. However, in problem-solving mediation, there is no third party decision-maker or evaluator, only a third party assistant. The third party assistant is not even the primary audience. The primary audience is the other side, who is surely not neutral and can often be quite hostile. In this different representational setting, the adversarial approach can be less effective, if not self-defeating.

Many sophisticated and experienced litigators realize that mediation calls for a different approach, but they still muddle through the mediation sessions. They are learning on the job. Even though many attorneys prefer a problem-solving-type approach to negotiations,[11] attorneys are still in the early stages

---

present a proposal for adoption by the participants (sometimes known as the "mediator's proposal"). The neutral may present these assessments gently for consideration or may aggressively advocate their adoption."
Id. at 71.

9. *See* Videotape: Comparing Settlement Conferences and Mediations: Instruction Manual and Videotape (Harold Abramson and Catherine Cronin-Harris, NYS Bar Association 1999) (on file with NYS Bar Association); *see also* Carrie Menkel-Meadow, *For and Against Settlement: Uses and Abuses of the Mandatory Settlement Conference*, 33 UCLA L. REV. 485, 507–511 (1985). A significant difference between a directive, evaluative mediation and a judicial settlement conference is the power possessed by the third party. In mediation, the person lacks ultimate decionmaking power while in a judicial settlment conference, the person may be the ultimate decision-maker.

10. A directive evaluative process is when an evaluative mediator presses the parties to move in the direction of the mediator's evaluation.

11. *See* Milton Heumann & Jonathan Hyman, *Negotiation Methods and Litigation Settlement Methods in New Jersey: 'You Can't Always Get What You Want,'* 12 OHIO ST. J. ON

of figuring out how to do it in mediations. Many attorneys went to law school before courses on dispute resolution were offered, and the dispute resolution courses that have emerged in law schools over the last twenty-five years have been largely limited to teaching students to be mediators, not advocates.[12] Continuing legal education programs are only beginning to focus on teaching representation skills, with many programs limited to sharing anecdotal experiences and idiosyncratic advice. *Mediation Representation* provides a comprehensive approach to representing clients in a problem-solving process, an approach that applies from an attorney's first client phone call until the mediation process is concluded.

Developing a model of client representation was an incremental process that drew upon much of the excellent work done in the field of negotiation, mediation, and mediation representation.[13]

I. Three Assumptions When Constructing a Model of Client Representation

Three succinct and widely cited propositions should form the foundation of a model of client representation in problem-solving mediations:

A. Problem-Solving Mediation Can Offer Dispute Resolution Opportunities that are Unavailable in Other Dispute Resolution Forums.

I will not take any space to defend this now widely accepted proposition except to recognize that mediation, when not conducted like a settlement con-

---

DISP. RESOL. 253, 309 (1997) ("While 61% of the lawyers would like to see more problem-solving negotiation methods, about 71% of negotiations are carried out with positional methods instead.").

12. *See* Suzanne Schmitz, *What Should We Teach in ADR Courses: Concepts and Skills for Lawyers Representing Clients in Mediation,* 6 HARV. NEGOT. L. REV. 189, 204 (2001).

13. Much of that work is cited throughout MEDIATION REPRESENTATION but I want to especially acknowledge Eric Galton's pioneering book REPRESENTING CLIENTS IN MEDIATION (1994), Jack Cooley's book MEDIATION ADVOCACY (1996) (2nd ed. 2002), Dwight Golann's book MEDIATING LEGAL DISPUTES (1996), Golann's Videotape & Study Guide: REPRESENTING CLIENTS IN MEDIATION: HOW ADVOCATES CAN SHARE A MEDIATOR'S POWERS (ABA Section of Litigation 2000), and Christopher Moore's book THE MEDIATION PROCESS (2d ed.1996).

ference, has the potential to produce creative and enduring solutions that meet the particular needs of disputing parties.[14]

B. To Realize These Opportunities, Advocates Need an Approach to Client Representation Suitable for Mediation.

As already suggested, the familiar adversarial approach that has proven so effective in judicial trials, as well as in judicial settlement conferences and arbitrations, does not work optimally in a problem-solving mediation. Simply adjusting and refining trial strategies would not be enough to realize the full benefits of mediation. This model had to incorporate a different representation approach, one tailored to realize the full benefits of this forum. Instead of advocating as zealous adversaries, attorneys should advocate as zealous problem-solvers.[15]

C. Mediation is a Continuation of the Negotiation Process.

Any model of client representation had to recognize that parties participating in mediation are simply continuing their negotiation in another forum. Therefore, the model needed to explicitly reveal the relationship between negotiation and mediation.

---

14. *See generally* KOVACH, *supra* note 6; GOLANN, *supra* note 2, at chs. 2, 3; MOORE, *supra* note 2, at 63–68; and FOLBERG & TAYLOR, *supra* note 2, at 7.

15. *See* Andrea K. Schneider, *Shattering Negotiation Myths: Empirical Evidence on the Effectiveness of Negotiation Style*, 7 HARV. NEGOT. L. REV. 143, 196 (2002) (In an extensive study of negotiation styles, 75% of true problem-solving negotiators were considered effective as compared with less than 50% of adversarial bargainers, a percentage that shrunk to 25% when examining adversarial bargainers who were unethical.); ROBERT H. MNOOKIN ET AL., BEYOND WINNING: NEGOTIATING TO CREATE VALUE IN DEALS AND DISPUTES 321–322 (2000); G. RICHARD SHELL, BARGAINING FOR ADVANTAGE: NEGOTIATION STRATEGIES FOR REASONABLE PEOPLE 12–14 (1999). The authors concluded that clients are usually better off when a lawyer adopts a problem-solving approach over an adversarial one. Other studies are cited that suggest that cooperative negotiators are more effective than competitive ones.

II. The Problem: Adversarial Advocacy

The sort of advocacy caricatured in the negotiation session of the movie *Erin Brockovich*[16] has not been uncommon in mediations. Let me describe the sharp exchange of settlement offers in that negotiation. During the rest of this chapter, this dispute[17] will be used as a basis for demonstrating the elements of a formula suitable for representing clients in a problem-solving process. Here is the scene and the transcript.

> The judge just dismissed each of the 84 motions to strike filed by the defendant and upheld the plaintiffs' causes of action in a lawsuit brought by the residents of Hinkley who claimed that the defendant Pacific Gas and Electric had polluted their groundwater. The judge directed the defendants' attorneys to "tell your clients they're going to trial." As a result, the attorneys for both sides agreed to meet at the law office of the plaintiffs' attorney to discuss settling the lawsuit.
> **Scene:** The Waiting Room.
> Ed Masry, the attorney Erin Brockovich works for, glances at the defendants' attorneys who "ooze importance" and whispers to Ms. Brockovich, "The games are about to begin." Mr. Masry recruits and dresses up two of his secretaries to look like attorneys.
>
> **Next Scene:** The Conference Room.
> The four of them, including Ms. Brockovich, walk into the conference room and sit down. Across the table, two attorneys representing the defendant are already seated.
> The lead attorney for Pacific Gas and Electric talks first and presents an opening offer:
> SANCHEZ (PG&E lead attorney): ... Let's be honest here. Twenty million dollars is more money than these people have ever dreamed of.
> ERIN: Oh, see, now that pisses me off. First of all—since the demur, we now have more than four hundred plaintiffs.... and (mocking her) "let's be honest," we all know there's more out there. Now, they may

---

16. Erin Brockovich (Universal Studios 2000).

17. Erin Brockovich was not a lawyer in the movie; she was assisting the attorney as sort of a paralegal. Rather than dealing with the relationship between a paralegal and the attorney who must make all the critical representation decisions, I chose to simplify the discussion here by focusing on Ms. Brockovich's representation choices, as if she were an attorney.

not be the most sophisticated people, but they do know how to divide, and twenty million dollars isn't shit when it's split between them.

And second of all—these people don't dream about being rich. They dream about being able to watch their kids swim in a pool without worrying they'll have to have a hysterectomy at age 20, like Rosa Diaz—a client of ours—or to have their spine deteriorate like Stan Bloom—another client of ours.

So before you come back here with another lame-ass offer, I want you to think real hard about what your spine is worth, Mr. Buda [one of PG&E's attorneys]—or what you'd expect someone to pay you for your uterus, Miss Sanchez [the other PG&E attorney]—then you take out your calculator and multiply that number by a hundred. Anything less than that is a waste of our time.

[Sanchez, throughout her speech, has been reacting in a patronizing manner—as if Erin's words were of no import. As Sanchez picks up a glass of water to sip,]

ERIN: By the way, we had the water brought in special for you folks. It came from one of Hinkley's water wells.

SANCHEZ stares at the water and puts it down and says: I think this meeting is over.

ED responds with: Damn right it is.

[Erin gets up and storms out first.]

This sort of intensive, adversarial posturing can damage, if not derail, a problem-solving process, whether conducted with or without a mediator. Mediation advocates who prefer a problem-solving process need a more suitable approach to client representation.

III. Solution:
The Mediation Representation Formula

In *Mediation Representation*, I present a five component mediation representation formula in which attorneys advocate by using: (1) a creative problem-solving approach to achieve the two goals of (2) satisfying their client's interests and (3) overcoming any impediments to settlement. During the mediation the attorneys (4) enlist the assistance of the mediator while negotiating with the other side at (5) key junctures in the process.

The first three components of the model focus primarily on how to negotiate in the mediation.

A. Negotiation Approach: Creative Problem-Solving

Selecting the negotiation approach was easy. If an advocate views mediation as a problem-solving process, then the attorney should negotiate as a problem-solver.

A problem-solving negotiator who is creative[18] does more than just try to settle the dispute. Such a negotiator creatively searches for solutions that go beyond the traditional ones based on rights, obligations, and precedent. Rather than settling for win-lose outcomes, the negotiator searches for solutions that can benefit both sides.[19] To creatively problem-solve, the negotiator develops a collaborative relationship with the other side and participates throughout the process in a way that is likely to result in solutions that are en-

---

18. *See, e.g.,* Symposium, *Conceiving the Lawyer As Creative Problem Solver*, 34 CAL. W. L. REV. (1998); Thomas Barton, *Creative Problem Solving: Purpose, Meaning, and Values*, 34 CAL. W. L. REV. 273 (1998); Paul Brest & Linda Hamilton Krieger, *New Roles: Problem Solving Lawyers As Problem Solvers*, 72 TEMP. L. REV. 811 (1999); Seamus Dunn, *Case Study: The Northern Ireland Experience: Possibilities For Cross-Fertilization Learning*, 6 ALTERNATIVES 153,153 (CPR Institute, June 2001); Carrie Menkel-Meadow, *Aha? Is Creativity Possible In Legal Problem Solving and Teachable In Legal Education*, 6 HARV. NEGOT. L. REV. 97 (2001); Carrie Menkel-Meadows, *When Winning Isn't Everything: The Lawyer As Problem Solver*, 28 HOFSTRA L. REV. 905 (2000); Carrie Menkel-Meadow, *The Lawyer As Problem Solver and Third Party Neutral: Creativity and Non-Partisanship In Lawyering*, 72 TEMP. L. REV. 785 (1999); Carrie Menkel-Meadows, *Toward Another View Of Legal Negotiation: The Structure Of Problem Solving*, 31 UCLA L. REV. 754 (1984); Linda Morton, *Teaching Creative Problem Solving: A Paradigmatic Approach*, 34 CAL. W. L. REV. 375 (1998); and Janet Reno, *Lawyers As Problem-Solvers: Keynote Address To the AALS*, 49 J. LEGAL EDUC. 5 (1999). *See also,* California Western School of Law, Center for Creative Problem Solving (2004), *at* http://www.cwsl.edu/main/default.asp?nav=creative_problem _solving.asp&body=creative_problem_solving/home.asp (last visited Mar. 12, 2006).

19. Instead of referring to "win-win" solutions, I suggest searching for solutions that can benefit both sides. I avoid using the more familiar, if not overused "win-win" jargon because that jargon carries baggage that can blind people to the underlying valuable point that still retains considerable vitality. The "win-win" attitude can be sharply contrasted with the opposite one of "win-lose." These contrary attitudes neatly capture a fundamental difference between the problem-solving and adversarial approaches.

Many lawyers consider the idea that both sides can secure benefits as naïve, not anchored in reality. However, the notion that both sides might be able to gain something in negotiations reflects an optimistic attitude that can open the mind to creative searches. The likelihood of finding such gains in negotiations is greater than in court. In negotiations, for instance, even the defendant who agrees to pay considerable damages may gain other benefits, such as no publicity, no precedent, and a continuing business relationship, benefits that are usually unavailable in court.

during as well as inventive. Solutions are likely to be enduring because both sides work together to fashion nuanced solutions that each side fully understands, can live with, and knows how to implement. Solutions are likely to be inventive because both sides advocate their client's interests instead of legal positions;[20] use suitable techniques for overcoming impediments; search expansively for multiple options; and evaluate and package options imaginatively to meet the various interests of all parties.

For problem-solving advocacy to be effective, an attorney ought to engage proactively at every stage of representation, from the moment of the first client interview until the negotiation in the mediation is concluded. The attorney should be a constant problem solver. It is relatively easy to engage in simple moves such as responding to a demand with the question "why?" in order to bring the other party's interests to the surface. However, it is much more difficult to stick to this approach throughout the mediation process, especially when faced with an adversarial, positional opponent. Trust the problem-solving approach. When the other side engages in adversarial tactics—a frequent occurrence in practice—the attorney should react with problem-solving responses, responses that might even convert the other side into a problem solver.[21]

In this pitch for a problem-solving approach, I do not blindly claim that it is the only one that results in settlements. Attorneys frequently cite success stories when they use unvarnished adversarial tactics, as occurred in *Erin Brockovich*, or a hybrid of adversarial and problem-solving strategies.[22] The hybrid supporters claim that the best approach is a flexible one, a philosophy that surely is advisable in life generally as well as in legal negotiations. However, flexibility should not be confused with inconsistency. Shifting between adversarial and problem-solving tactics during the course of mediation can undercut creative problem-solving potential. A consistent adherence to problem-solving will more likely produce the best results for clients.

Finally, for the skeptics who think that problem-solving does not work for most legal cases because they are primarily about money, I offer three responses.

---

20. For a full discussion of how to identify client's interests as opposed to positions, see ABRAMSON, *supra* note 1, at ch. 3.2(a) and ROGER FISHER & WILLIAM URY, GETTING TO YES: NEGOTIATING AGREEMENT WITHOUT GIVING IN Ch. 3 (Bruce Patton ed., 2d ed. 1991).

21. *See* ABRAMSON, *supra* note 1, at ch. 1.5.

22. In the hybrid approach, attorneys switch between adversarial and problem-solving tactics, depending on how the mediation is unfolding.

First, whether a legal dispute is mostly about money varies from case to case.[23] An attorney has little chance of discovering whether a dispute is about more than money if the attorney approaches the dispute as if it is only about money.[24] Such a preconceived view backed by a narrowly focused adversarial strategy will likely blind the attorney to the other party's needs and inventive solutions. Both sides are more likely to discover comprehensive and creative solutions if they approach the dispute with open minds and problem-solving orientations.

Second, if the dispute or any remaining issues turn out to be predominantely about money, then at least the attorney followed a representation approach that may have created a hospitable environment for resolving the money issues. A hospitable environment can even be beneficial when there is no expectation of a continuing relationship between the disputing parties.

Third, the problem-solving approach provides a framework for resolving money issues. This type of dispute can sometimes be resolved by resorting to the usual problem-solving initiatives such as the use of objective criteria.[25] If they fail, an attorney might turn to the familiar, adversarial negotiation dance of offers and counter-offers, but a version that has been tempered for a problem-solving process.[26]

---

23. *See* Dwight Golann, *Is Legal Mediation a Process of Repair—or Separation? An Empirical Study and Its Implications,* 7 HARV. NEGOT. L. REV. 301, 334 (2002) (In the only empirical study on the subject, the author found that "almost two-thirds of all [mediated] settlements were integrative in nature.... The results suggest that both mediators and advocates should consider making a search for integrative outcomes an important aspect of their mediation strategy.").

At least one category of disputes is usually primarily about money. The classic personal injury dispute between strangers who will never deal with each other again can be only about money and therefore not open to creative resolutions other than a tailored payment scheme. But, even in these disputes, one side may occasionally want more than money, such as vindication, fair treatment, etc.

24. In a recent case that I mediated, the parties arrived with extreme monetary claims on the table and a long history of failed negotiations. After more than three hours of mediation, the parties and attorneys negotiated a written apology signed by the defendant and a written introduction to future buyers signed by the plaintiff. The monetary issues were then resolved in less than a minute! The parties were apparently already on the same page for settling the money claims but were not ready to settle until some non-monetary needs were met.

25. *See* ABRAMSON, *supra* note 1, at ch. 1.3 (a)(iii) on "Manage Remaining Distributive Conflicts" where the text considers how to use problem-solving moves to resolve easy distributive issues and Subsection E 4(b) of this chapter on "Mediators' Techniques."

26. *See* ABRAMSON, *supra* note 1, at ch. 1.3(a)(iii) on "Manage Remaining Distributive Conflicts" where the text considers how to resolve difficult distributive issues by using tem-

In short, problem-solving provides a comprehensive and coherent structure for representation that can guide an attorney throughout the negotiation in the mediation. By sticking to this approach, the attorney will be prepared to deal with the myriad of unanticipated challenges that inevitably arise as any negotiation unfolds.

Despite these benefits, lawyers gravitate toward an adversarial approach. The reason may seem simplistic, if not superficially glib: lawyers are too preoccupied with litigating. Negotiations are so enmeshed in the litigation process that negotiations and litigation have become an integrated, single process of dispute resolution.[27] Thus, lawyers are likely to approach the negotiated settlement of a court case with a litigator's mindset,[28] one molded by an intensely adversarial legal culture and reinforced by attorney fee arrangements.

As readers of this chapter are likely aware, many lawyers relish and many clients crave a fiercely combative approach to legal representation. Overly optimistic as well as insecure clients want to be protected by aggressive hired guns. They are not very receptive to reality checks and can become perturbed with lawyers who may not appear faithful to the cause when they flag legal risks and inquire about the other side's perspective and needs. Legal training and experience teach lawyers to view legal disputes as zero-sum or distributive conflicts about money in which one party wins and the other one loses. For these and other reasons, it is hardly surprising that when the litigator's mindset is adapted to legal negotiations, the approach is likely to be adversarial.[29] This adversarial approach has been long-standing, despite the finding of at least one prominent study that lawyers would prefer problem-solving strategies.[30]

---

pered adversarial strategies. For example, an attorney can omit the traditional tricks and extreme threats while still engaging in the negotiation dance of offers and counter-offers.

27. *See id.* at 13–14.

28. *See* MNOOKIN ET AL., *supra* note 15, at 108–118, 167–172.

29. One creative solution for changing the litigator's mindset is to change the attorney that tries to settle the case. Instead of the litigator pursuing both the litigation and the negotiations, the litigator only litigates. Any negotiations would be handled by a separate settlement counsel who is committed to a problem-solving approach. For a thoughtful development of this solution, see William Coyne, Jr., *The Case for Settlement Counsel*, 14 OHIO ST. J. ON DISP. RESOL. 367, 367–70 (1999). The author concluded that "… the mindset needed to do effective problem-solving is incompatible with the mind-set needed to pursue litigation whole-heartedly." *Id.* at 393. *See also generally infra* ch. 8: Pauline H. Tesler, *Collaborative Law: Practicing Without Armor, Practicing With Heart,*

30. *See supra* note 11 and accompanying text.

The negotiation in *Erin Brockovich* surely exemplified the classic adversarial approach. It consisted of the exchange of extreme offers and counter-offers backed by muscular language. After the defendant's attorney characterizes her offer as "more money than these people have ever dreamed of," Erin Brockovich responded by scorning the defendant's offer, conveying passionately and vividly her clients' dreams, presenting an extreme and provocative counter-offer, and wrapping up her response with the unsettling water ploy that pointedly raised the health issue. The result of the series of moves was predictable, at least for that negotiation session: an impasse. However, could Ms. Brockovich have been an assertive advocate in a way that would not have sent the other side away? I will suggest how she might have advocated differently, in a way that might have transformed the negotiation into problem solving, as I explore the next four components of the representation model.

B. Goal: Advance Your Client's Interests.

After reflecting on a full range of techniques and moves within the self-contained problem-solving approach, one guiding light stood out because it could instantly shift a negotiator's perspective on a dispute from an adversarial distributive one to a problem-solving mutually beneficial one. This shift can happen when the attorney identifies and advocates her client's interests. More specifically, an attorney should first understand her client's interests, acquire an understanding of the other side's interests, and then advocate to advance her client's interests in a way that sufficiently addresses the other side's interests to move toward an agreement. This focus should be the primary goal in a problem-solving process, a first move that can initiate problem-solving as well as serve as a guiding light throughout the negotiation in the mediation.[31]

In *Erin Brockovich*, Ms. Brockovich might have shifted the negotiation from adversarial to problem-solving by focusing on the parties' interests. Interests reflect parties' needs. The positions that attorneys typically advocate are solutions. The defendant offered twenty million dollars; the plaintiffs counter-offered with a hundred times the value of a spine or uterus. These monetary solutions were offered to meet each side's interests. However, there might have been other solutions. By switching the beginning of the negotiation from ex-

---

31. The attorney should develop a solution that meets her client's interest better than the solution offered by her client's BATNA. For a full discussion of how to identify client's interests as opposed to positions, see ABRAMSON, *supra* note 1, at ch. 3.2(a) and FISHER & URY, *supra* note 20, at ch. 3.

changing initial offers to exchanging information on the needs of each party, an attorney can open the door to a search for creative solutions. It is the first step in a problem-solving negotiation.

In *Erin Brockovich*, consider what might have been the interests of each side and how identifying them would have opened the way to multiple possible solutions. The interests of the ill and scared plaintiffs became clear as the story in the movie unfolded. They wanted recognition that they have been poorly treated and lied to by the defendant; they wanted to be treated with respect and dignity; and they desperately needed health care and a safe place to live for themselves and their families. In view of these interests, solutions other than or including the payment of a lump sum might have included receiving lifetime health insurance, buying out their homes, cleaning up the contaminated groundwater, and/or a public and sincere apology.[32]

For the defendant, PG&E, what were its underlying interests? The company might have wanted to avoid bad publicity and financial distress, if not bankruptcy. In view of these interests, other possible solutions might include burnishing its reputation as a responsible corporate citizen by cleaning up the site, securing government help with the cleanup, or offering health insurance to the residents, which might have been cheaper than paying a single lump sum payment.

There is a second reason for selecting the goal of focusing on a client's interests: to make clear what is *not* the primary goal of problem-solving. Problem-solving is sometimes misconstrued to mean placing a premium on getting along with the other side at the expense of a client's interests.[33] For these reasons, this explicit goal was added to the model: Attorneys should advocate to advance their clients' interests.

---

32. *See generally infra* ch.10: Edward A. Dauer, *Hurting Clients.*

33. Correcting this false perception registered high when drafting the new assessment criteria for the ABA Mediation Representation Competition. We had heard numerous competition judges criticize students' advocacy as too cooperative at the expense of their clients' needs. We resolved to send an unmistakable message to students by adding a separate and specific judging criterion entitled "Advocating Client's Interests." Building a relationship with the other side also is important. A separate criterion focuses on "Problem-Solving Relationship Building." But, the two criteria are not competing with each other.

The Rules Committee of the Mediation Representation Competition of the ABA Section of Dispute Resolution drafted the assessment criteria during 2000–2001 that became effective for the 2001–2002 competition year. The current version of the criteria can be found online, *at* http://www.abanet.org/dispute/rulesandinstructions2004.doc (last visited Dec. 6, 2005). I served as Chair of this committee.

C. Goal: Overcome Impediments

Another primary goal is one that applies to any negotiation regardless of the objective: to overcome any impediments to settlement. This goal entails a return to a basic premise. Parties would not be in mediation unless they were facing an impediment in the negotiation. Otherwise, the parties could probably settle the dispute without the assistance of a mediator. Selecting this goal was obvious. Less obvious, however, was identifying an impasse-breaking strategy that comported with a problem-solving approach.

A number of distinguished authors have devised methodologies that demystify the murky world of impasse-breaking.[34] The methodology developed by Dr. Christopher Moore,[35] for instance, relies on taking three discrete steps that can produce a tailor-made strategy for overcoming impasses. His approach is built around his critical observation that impasses can be divided into five conflict categories that he labels *relationship, data, value, interest, and structural*. Under his approach, you first inquire about the cause of the impasse; then you classify the cause into one of the five impasse categories; and finally, you devise a suitable intervention for overcoming the impasse.

Let me describe Moore's five impasse categories while leaving for the next section how advocates might use his classification system as a basis for enlisting assistance from the mediator.

Relationship Conflicts can arise when participants are deeply upset with each other, cling to destructive misperceptions or stereotypes of each other, or suffer from poor communication. These types of conflicts are common in disputes where parties distrust each other and are occupied with hurling threats. These disabling tensions can arise between clients, between attorneys, and between an attorney and his client. Clearly, a bad relationship between the attorneys in *Erin Brockovich* contributed to that failed negotiation.

---

34. *See* Jean R. Sternlight, *Lawyers' Representation of Clients in Mediation: Using Economics and Psychology to Structure Advocacy in a Nonadversarial Setting*, 14 Ohio St. J. on Disp. Resol. 269, 297–331 (1999) (identifies barriers to negotiations based on economists' insights, psychologists' insights, flaws in rationality assumption, and principal/agent conflicts); Moore, *supra* note 2, at 60–61 (identifies five causes of conflicts—data conflicts, interest conflicts, structural conflicts, relationship conflicts, and value conflicts); Golann, *supra* note 2, at chs. 6–8 (identifies three categories of impasses-process, psychological, and merits); and Frank E.A. Sander & Stephen B. Goldberg, *Fitting the Forum to the Fuss: A User-Friendly Guide to Selecting an ADR Procedure*, 10 Negot. J. 49, 54–59 (1994) (identifies ten impediments to settlement).

35. *See* Moore, *supra* note 2, at 60–61 (author presents a Circle of Conflict in which five sources of conflicts are identified along with possible strategies for intervention).

Data Conflicts can be caused by inadequate, inaccurate, or untrustworthy information. Alternatively, they can be caused by different views of what is relevant information or different interpretations of relevant data. Data conflicts are common in court cases where parties may hold conflicting views of what happened, what might happen in court, or what is an appropriate interpretation of decisive data such as financial statements.

A common data conflict in legal disputes arise from conflicting views of how a court will likely rule. Too many lawyers and clients fail to thoroughly and objectively analyze all the benefits, costs, and risks of pursuing a judicial remedy. This common failure leads to poor legal advice to clients, unrealistically optimistic alternatives to settlement (unrealistic BATNAs), and impasses in negotiations and mediations. Virtually all mediators have seen cases where opposing attorneys were equally optimistic about the judicial outcome. One of the attorneys would, of course, be proven wrong. Inflated assessments can lead clients astray because they will overestimate the benefits of returning to court, and, as a result, they may mistakenly reject what otherwise might have been acceptable settlement proposals.

A data conflict posed one of the impasses blocking settlement in *Erin Brockovich*. The sides could not agree that the town's water was polluted by the defendant, PG&E. The water ploy during the negotiation sharply raised the safety issue in a provocative, confrontational fashion.[36] Ms. Brockovich could have made the same point differently. She could have asked the other side whether they would be willing to drink this glass of water from a Hinkley well. Then she might have stated, while holding the glass of water, that she would not want to drink the water until the people at this table could resolve whether the water was safe (the data conflict). These comments would have directed the discussion to the cause of the impasse and how to garner the information each side would need to assess the safety of the water and, if unsafe, the causation. This plan would have kept both sides engaged specifically in examining ways to overcome the impediment.

Interest Conflicts can arise when parties' substantive, procedural, or psychological/relationship wants conflict with each other.[37] Interest conflicts cover

---

36. Several litigators who have seen the film segment have told me that they would have sipped the water offered by Erin Brockovich. They figured that drinking so little water would have been harmless and yet would have thoroughly defused the tactic.

37. In a problem-solving process in which the concept of "interests" performs such a vital and pervasive role, Moore's narrow and distinctive use of "interest" conflicts can be confusing. I prefer referring to "wants" or "desires" conflicts. Parties may reach an impasse

the classically positional conflict inherent in adversarial negotiations. They can be caused by parties wanting the same thing (such as property), wanting different amounts of the same thing (such as time), wanting different things that the other is not prepared to give (such as one party wanting a precedent that the other party opposes), or even wanting something that another is not even aware of (such as an acknowledgment or an apology). The *Erin Brockovich* negotiation presented the classic distributive conflict over money—the plaintiffs wanted more money than the defendant was willing to pay.

Structural Conflicts can be the murkiest to identify. The two most common as well as easiest structural obstacles to spot are impasses due to unequal bargaining power or impasses due to conflicting goals of attorneys and their clients, which are known as principal-agent conflicts. Other structural conflicts can be more subtle, such as those caused by no deadline, time constraints facing one side, a missing key party, a party without sufficient settlement authority, geographical or technological limitations that impact one side disproportionately, and unequal control of resources for resolving the conflict. Because the causes of structural conflicts also frequently contribute to relationship conflicts, it can be difficult to decipher the nature of the conflict. In *Erin Brockovich,* a structural conflict that contributed to a relationship conflict between the attorneys across the table might have impeded a settlement. A large utility company that thought that it had all the power despite losing a vital motion resented being forced to defend itself against the allegations of uneducated, poor people who were represented by an under-funded and inexperienced attorney.

Value Conflicts can be the most intractable ones because they implicate a party's core personal or moral values. This narrow category can embrace matters of principle, ideology, or religion that can not be compromised. A grassroots environmental group, for instance, may have difficulty settling with a housing developer because to do so might compromise the group's ideology of preserving all large tracts of open space.

Value conflicts can be difficult to recognize in court cases because values can be masked by all too familiar legal categories, arguments, and remedies. When a party wants to win in court, for example, the party may be motivated by the need for a clear victory to preserve a personal value, such as personal integrity.

The last two components of the mediation representation formula focus on the mediation process itself. They address how to enlist assistance from the mediator and how to negotiate at key junctures in the process.

---

because their substantive, procedural, or psychological wants or desires are in conflict with each other.

D. Strategy: Enlist the Assistance of the Mediator

What types of assistance can the third party in the room offer? The mediator can contribute in three general ways: by the way the mediator implements his orientations, uses his techniques, and controls the mediation stages. The particular contributions depend on the type of mediation process envisioned. In a problem-solving process in which the advocate does not scheme to manipulate or "game" the mediator, the third party can be enlisted in the various ways described in this section.

1. Mediators' Orientations

Mediators bring a mix of distinct orientations to the mediation process. These orientations can be grouped into four discrete areas: (1) How will the mediator manage the mediation process? Will she be primarily problem-solving, evaluative, or transformative? (2) Will the mediator approach the problem narrowly as primarily a legal dispute or more broadly? (3) Will the mediator involve clients actively or restrictively? (4) Will the mediator use caucuses extensively, selectively, or not at all? When an advocate knows the mediator's mix, then he knows some of the opportunities for enlisting the mediator for assistance.

Assuming that the dispute in *Erin Brockovich* is now in mediation, Ms. Brockovich might decide that it would be helpful for her clients to personally and passionately convey their fears and suffering to the other side. It became clear after the negotiation session that plaintiffs needed some version of a "day-in-court," and that the defendant did not fully understand the plaintiffs' anguish. Knowing that the mediator conducts most of the mediation in joint sessions, Ms. Brockovich would prepare her client to talk to the other side, reaffirm her preference to minimize the use of caucuses, and be prepared to politely object if the mediator prematurely moves toward a caucus.

The mediator's orientation toward managing the process should be given particular attention because it can singularly shape an attorney's representation strategy. An attorney's entire approach to interacting with and enlisting assistance from the mediator will be influenced by the mediator's process management, that is, how problem-solving, transformative, or evaluative the mediator might be.[38]

For example, realizing that the mediator will stay in a problem-solving mode gives an attorney the freedom and security to share information (including interests), brainstorm options, recognize weaknesses in her client's legal case, and remain open to creative solutions other than the ones in the

---

38. *See* ABRAMSON, *supra* note 1, at chs. 4.2(b)(i) and 5.1(e)(I).

legal papers. The attorney can feel comfortable asking the mediator for help in sorting out interests, facilitating an evaluation of the legal case, or developing multiple options. The attorney also has much freedom and security with a transformative mediator who is trained to support whatever sort of process is structured and implemented by the attorney, client, and the other side. However, the attorney cannot rely on the transformative mediator's expertise or initiatives to create or direct a process, as the transformative mediator is committed to being non-directive.

In contrast, consider the impact of mediator evaluation on advocacy. Whenever an attorney approaches me about this topic, I ask the same simple question: does knowing that the mediator might offer an evaluation influence how you would represent your client in mediation? The answer is "yes" every time.

Mediation evaluations can take a variety of forms. For instance, mediators may assess the reasonableness of settlement options, assess consequences of not settling, or recommend settlement proposals either as the mediation unfolds or as a "mediator's proposal."

Knowing that the mediator may formulate one or more of these types of evaluations can induce the attorney to approach the mediation more like an adjudicatory process than a negotiation. This mediator role can change the nature of the mediation process. Instead of viewing the mediator as a facilitator with whom the attorney can have candid conversations, the attorney is likely to view the mediator as a decision-maker who must be persuaded. Instead of formulating a negotiation strategy based on meeting parties' interests, the attorney is likely to formulate a strategy designed to convince the mediator to recommend a favorable evaluation.

Consider in what specific ways an attorney would circumscribe his representation if the attorney thought the mediator might evaluate. Would the attorney and his client talk less candidly if the attorney were to take into account the possibility of the mediator performing any of these other roles? Would the attorney avoid recognizing any weaknesses in his legal position, other than the safely obvious ones, to the mediator or the other side? Would the attorney eschew compromises, especially ones that deviate from the remedies sought in the legal case? Would the attorney hide and disguise information in order to avoid coloring unfavorably the mediator's view of the dispute? Would the attorney be likely to advance partisan legal arguments at the expense of interest-based creative option building? [39]

---

39. In a passionate article arguing for "flexible mediation that permits judicious use of evaluative techniques," the author still had to recognize that when the advocate knows that the case will be evaluated, the parties are "more likely to present information as advocacy

Affirmative answers to these questions prompt many attorneys to return to the traditional adversarial approach so familiar in the courtroom in which the attorney withholds unfavorable information, hides any flexibility to avoid implying a lack of confidence in the legal case, and presents carefully crafted partisan arguments and positions that are designed to persuade a decision-maker to act favorably.

Alternatively, an attorney might problem-solve but do so in a selective way that reduces the risk of an unfavorable assessment by the mediator. In such a constricted problem-solving approach, an attorney could still share and advocate her client's interests and engage in such problem-solving moves as brainstorming options and designing creative solutions, but only up to a point. The attorney would avoid sharing information or showing flexibility that may risk a less favorable evaluation from the mediator.

Consider what might have been the impact on the parties in *Erin Brockovich* if the case had gone to a mediator who might evaluate and the attorneys had engaged in a constricted problem-solving approach. PG&E would likely be reluctant to disclose its interest in avoiding bad publicity, because this information might be exploited by the mediator. The mediator might attach a financial value to a confidential settlement and then add the value to a recommended payment by PG&E. Disclosing that interest, however, might lead the parties to devise other beneficial solutions.

The utility company would likely be restrained when brainstorming for creative solutions, because it may want to avoid revealing too much flexibility. It may not want to imply that it would be willing to accept something qualitatively or quantitatively less than what it is seeking in court. So, even though the utility company might find it desirable to devise solutions that would avoid negative publicity, for instance, it may not want any appearance of flexibility to influence the mediator when formulating any evaluations or settlement proposals.

In view of this strategic need to hide information and flexibility, the attorneys may have fashioned this constricted form of problem-solving advocacy based on a narrowly focused adversarial plan and presentation. Such an approach requires a sophisticated and nuanced form of advocacy in order to

---

and less as background for negotiation or problem-solving." And, if mediation veers too far from its facilitative assumptions, the author concluded, "it loses some of [its] creative and transformative potential." *See* Jeffrey W. Stempel, *Beyond Formalism and False Dichotomies: The Need for Institutionalizing a Flexible Concept of the Mediator's Role*, 24 FLA. ST. U. L. REV. 949, 950, 983 (1997).

minimize stifling the creative problem-solving potential of the mediation process. The advocacy would consist of a blended problem-solving adversarial strategy that could not be implemented casually because of the need to carefully identify and segregate risky information from safe information and then to artfully and persuasively disclose only the safe information. It is a strategy that would need to be actuated proficiently in the heat of the mediation, realizing that too much candor might result in a less favorable mediator assessment and too little candor might result in a less optimal negotiated result.

An attorney might be more confident pursuing a constricted problem-solving approach if the type of carefully designed safeguard in the Centre for Effective Dispute Resolution (CEDR) Mediation Rules[40] were adopted. The rules ensure that participants approve an evaluation role at the optimum moment in the process as well as limit the type of evaluation. The rules give the mediator *conditional* recommendation authority:

> If the Parties are unable to reach a settlement in the negotiations at the Mediation, and only if all the Parties so request *and the Mediator agrees*, the Mediator will produce for the Parties a *non-binding recommendation on terms of settlement*. This will not attempt to anticipate what a court might order but will set out what the Mediator suggests are appropriate settlement terms in all of the circumstances.[41]

CEDR's Guidance Notes state that

> The intention of paragraph 12 is that the Mediator will cease to play an entirely facilitative role only if the negotiations in the Mediation are deadlocked. Giving a settlement recommendation may be perceived by a Party as undermining the Mediator's neutrality and for this reason the Mediator may not agree to this course of action.[42]

---

40. The Center for Effective Dispute Resolution (CEDR) is a major dispute resolution center based in London. *See* Centre for Effective Dispute Resolution, *at* http://www.cedr.co .uk (last visited Dec. 6, 2005).

41. *See* CEDR Model Mediation Procedure and Agreement para. 12 (8th ed. October 2002), *available at* http://www.cedr.co.uk/library/documents/MMPA_8thEdition.pdf (last visited Mar. 12, 2006) (emphasis added). For a somewhat less strict approach, see The CPR/CCPIT Mediation Procedure for Disputes Submitted to the U.S.-China Business Mediation Center § 7 (2004), *available at* http://www.cpradr.org/pdfs/Intl_China_Procedure04.pdf (last visited June 20, 2006); Daini Tokyo Bar Association's Rules of Procedure for Arbitration and Mediation art. 5, *available at* http://64.233.179.104/translate_c?hl=en&u=http://niben.jp/ english/index.html&prev=/search%3Fq%3DDaini%2BTokyo%2BBar%2BAssociation%26hl %3Den%26lr%3D (last visited June 20, 2006).

42. *See* CEDR, *supra* note 41, Guidance Notes: The Mediation, 9–12 (October 2002).

2. Mediators' Techniques

Basic mediation training emphasizes learning and honing a set of widely used techniques, such as promoting communication through questioning and listening methods, dealing with emotional dimensions of disputes, overcoming impediments including money impasses, helping parties assess their BATNAs, and generating creative options, among other valuable skills. An advocate can solicit the mediator to use any of these techniques at propitious moments in the mediation process.

For example, an advocate might suggest to a mediator that one of the obstacles to settlement is a relationship conflict between the parties. Then the attorney might ask the mediator to assist the parties in implementing a suitable intervention. The mediator might help the parties constructively explain to each other why they are upset, assist them in clarifying their perceptions of each other, focus on other ways to improve their communications, and cultivate their problem-solving attitudes.

For a data impasse, an advocate might ask the mediator to help the parties resolve what data are important, negotiate a process for collecting reliable data, and develop common criteria that can be used to assess the data.

When a data conflict is over the likely judicial outcome, instead of asking the mediator to give a prediction (an evaluation)—a request that would likely compromise the problem-solving process[43]—the attorney can ask the mediator to help each side further analyze the legal case. The attorney might ask the mediator to guide the participants in calculating the value of each client's total BATNA by using a "decision-tree plus" methodology.[44] A client's total BATNA can be divided into two distinct components, public and personal, and a value for each component can be separately calculated.

The *public BATNA* covers the portion that the attorney is qualified to calculate. The attorney has the expertise to predict the likely judicial outcome,

---

43. *See supra* §D.1 p. 241. If an attorney knows that a mediator might offer his or her own evaluation of the legal merits, the attorney will likely shift from a problem-solving to an adversarial mode of advocacy in an effort to induce a favorable assessment.

44. A decision tree is a mathematical technique for estimating the value of an uncertain outcome (e.g. winning in court) by multiplying the probability of an event happening (e.g. winning in court) times the likely outcome if it happens (e.g. what likely to win in court). The plus component involves asking a particular set of questions that will help a client attach a value to a set of personal costs and benefits. *See* ABRAMSON, *supra* note 1, at app. A.

the probability of success, and the likely legal fees and court costs the client will incur. Attorneys frequently make these predictions in their law practices. Based on discovery, legal research, and experience—information that is mostly available to both sides—attorneys routinely estimate these key inputs that are used when employing decision trees for calculating the value of the public BATNA. In *Erin Brockovich,* the judge's ruling denying the defendant's motions surely gave both sides further insight into one key input, the probability of success in court. In addition, as Ms. Brockovich gathered more damaging evidence after the failed negotiations, the plaintiffs' probability of success continued to increase.

The other component, the *personal BATNA*, addresses the portion that the client is uniquely qualified to calculate. It is the component idiosyncratic to the client. For example, the client can best assess the added value of going to court to establish a judicial precedent or to be vindicated. The client can best approximate the added cost of possibly destroying a continuing relationship with the other party by going to court. The client is the expert. Only the client can quantify his or her own subjective views of these additional litigation benefits and costs. This will not be easy for the client to do. Instead of inviting the client to use a formal decision tree, the attorney can take the simpler yet still demanding approach of asking some probing questions. This supplement to decision trees is the plus analysis. For example, the attorney might ask the client—a plaintiff, for instance—to confront and resolve how much less money he would be willing to accept to settle now and not suffer the risks of waiting out the litigation or suffer the risks of destroying a relationship in the litigation. In other words, how much money would the client be willing to sacrifice for settling now?

Factoring in the plaintiffs' personal BATNA weighed heavily in *Erin Brockovich* when the plaintiffs began to abandon their attorneys after the attorneys recommended the use of arbitration. Only after one of their attorneys, Ed Masry, highlighted the personal costs of waiting for any money until trial (the negative personal costs of their BATNA) did the plaintiffs reluctantly accept what they viewed as the faster but less satisfactory forum of arbitration that lacked a jury and right to appeal.

The value of the client's total BATNA is simply the sum of the values of his or her public and personal BATNAs, a critical benchmark when weighing whether to settle or continue litigating.

When encountering an interests conflict, the advocate may ask the mediator to help the parties pinpoint shared or non-conflicting wants, identify objective criteria for overcoming conflicting wants, and search for increased value and productive trades. Court cases typically present conflicting substantive wants because of the nature of the litigation process in which plaintiffs' attorneys draft complaints bursting with demands and defendants' attorneys draft answers rejecting almost everything.

When the interests conflict is the classically distributive one over money, the sort of dispute that may appear unresponsive to the problem-solving methods considered in this chapter, the advocate might consider an approach that avoids the traditional negotiation dance of offers and counter-offers. The advocate might select a method designed to prevent the error of failing to settle due to not revealing the information that would have shown that the parties were within a settlement range. The advocate might ask the mediator to use a scheme that can provide a safe pathway for parties to move toward their bottom lines.[45]

A structural impasse due to an attorney-client conflict can arise due to the inherent structure of the relationship, a bad relationship between the attorney and client, or both. A perceptive advocate might solicit the mediator to help the other side overcome an attorney-client conflict. If it has arisen because the other attorney thinks his client should settle while the client wants to pursue the litigation, for instance, the mediator can facilitate a discussion of the different views and ways to bridge possible differences.

When an advocate recognizes that parties' personal values may be implicated in the impasse, she may enlist the mediator for help by suggesting the nature of the impasse. Then, the mediator might assist the parties in clarifying their core values to find out whether their values are truly at stake or truly in conflict. If in conflict, the mediator may try to help parties work around their personal values because compromise is usually unacceptable. The mediator can help parties search for an overarching shared goal, ways to avoid defining the problem in terms of a particular value, or solutions that do not compromise the value. Or the mediator might assist parties in reaching an agreement to disagree.

Returning to *Erin Brockovich*, Ms. Brockovich, sensing a relationship conflict in that PG&E did not understand her clients' interests and perspective, might ask the mediator to help improve the communications between the parties. In making this request, the parties can benefit from the mediator's training in posing questions, active listening, and reframing what is being said.

---

45. Six such schemes described and analyzed in MEDIATION REPRESENTATION include binding final-offer arbitration, a mediator's proposal, hypothetical testing, confidential disclosure of bottom lines, confidential disclosure of settlement numbers, and a safety deposit box. The book explores the strengths and drawbacks of each of these six methods. *See* ABRAMSON, *supra* note 1, at ch.7.2(d)(iii).

3. Mediators' Control of the Mediation Stages

A problem-solving process follows somewhat predictable stages from beginning to end. The process stages can include the opening statement of the mediator; gathering information (opening statements of parties and attorneys, discussions in joint sessions, and caucuses); identifying issues, interests, and impediments; overcoming impediments; generating options (inventing); assessing and selecting options; and concluding (agreement or impasse).[46] Knowing that a mediator exercises control over the stages gives the advocate other ways to enlist the mediator's assistance. The advocate can request that the mediator use various stages in ways that may advance a client's interests or overcome any impasses.

Frustrated that she could not secure critical data, for instance, Erin Brockovich could plan to raise this data impasse when the mediator reaches the stage of identifying impediments to settlement. Realizing that Pacific Gas and Electric is approaching the dispute as distributive, as if it is only about paying a lump sum of money, Erin Brockovich could plan to invite the mediator to help the parties generate multiple options when the inventing stage is reached.

E. Implement Plan at Key Junctures in the Mediation Process

Finally, these four distinct components of the model must be woven together. I considered how a problem-solving approach that involves the analysis of interests, impediments, and ways to enlist the mediator's assistance, can be implemented by an advocate in the mediation process. The advocate needed a representation plan that could be used throughout the mediation process.[47] However, simply saying "throughout the process" was too vague, leaving the advocate with little practical guidance. So I perused the mediation process to isolate discrete representation junctures where an attorney should consciously implement her focused plan to advance interests and overcome impediments.

I identified six key junctures.[48] Three of the junctures arise before the first mediation session, when (1) selecting a mediator, (2) preparing a pre-medi-

---

46. *See* ABRAMSON, *supra* note 1, at ch. 2.3.

47. *See* ABRAMSON, *supra* note 1, at ch. 5.16 (Checklist for Preparing Case and Mediation Representation Plan).

48. There are other junctures in the mediation process. Attorneys should engage in problem-solving to advance interests and overcome impediments in a way that takes advantage of the availability of a mediator when (1) initially interviewing his client, (2) ap-

ation submission, and (3) participating in a pre-mediation conference. The other three junctures arise in the mediation session when (4) presenting opening statements, (5) participating in joint sessions, and (6) participating in caucuses.

Assuming that Ms. Brockovich thinks her clients should convey personally and vividly that they have multiple interests and that the two sides are likely to reach an impasse over whether the defendant contributed to polluting the town's water (a data conflict), she might prepare a representation plan for four of the junctures as follows. When selecting the mediator (juncture one), she would choose someone who would deeply involve her clients and who would know how to handle complex scientific data. When preparing a pre-mediation submission (juncture two), she would want to explain the substantial data conflict so that the mediator would come prepared to deal with it. During the mediation session, she may want to request a caucus with the mediator (juncture six) to share any information that is especially damaging to the other side, and to discuss with the mediator how to productively present this information to the other side in the joint session (juncture five).

Conclusion

This chapter described the five components of the mediation representation formula, as well as how the formula was derived. This model of client representation that forms the foundation of *Mediation Representation* offers the advocate an approach to representing clients that takes full advantage of the distinctive opportunities in a problem-solving mediation process.

In *Erin Brockovich,* the plaintiffs did not use this approach, however. They used a traditional adversarial approach and achieved a settlement that was impressive, at least based on one criterion. They negotiated the largest payment ever in a direct-action lawsuit, although after a protracted period of angst and uncertainty for the plaintiffs and their attorneys. The plaintiffs were thrilled with the settlement because the payment vindicated them and seemed to offer them ample financial resources to meet their future needs. It was too late, however, for those who died or were destined to die from exposure to the contaminated water. In addition, whether this was the best solution for both sides

---

proaching the other attorney about the use of mediation, (3) preparing the case for mediation, (4) preparing his client, and (5) drafting a settlement agreement or developing an exit plan from an unsuccessful mediation. *See,* ABRAMSON, *supra* note 1, at 8 n.23.

will never be known. Parties are unlikely to know whether they achieved optimum resolutions if they approach disputes as if they are only about money.

Imagine how different the representation and the results might have been, if Ms. Brockovich had identified both sides' interests and the impediments to agreement, and had enlisted help from a mediator at key junctures, searching for solutions that advanced both sides' interests. By fixating less on the size of the check and more on a tailored solution to meet both sides' interests, the result might have materialized sooner; it might have included lifetime health insurance with no deductibles, clean-up of the polluted water, the option of the utility buying residents' homes, individual lump sum payments for pain and suffering, a public and sincere apology by the utility, and more. The plaintiffs would have received what they needed while the utility might have met the plaintiffs' interests at less cost to it while beginning the process of resuscitating its debilitated reputation. This sort of crafted and possibly quicker result exemplifies the potential of mediation when attorneys advocate as problem-solvers.

This model of client representation ought to be applied by an advocate for the duration of the representation, starting as soon as the first client interview. This problem-solving role should be maintained when contacting the other side about the use of mediation, as well as when preparing the case and client for the mediation session. Then, by advocating at every juncture in the ways suggested in this chapter, an attorney should be able to realize the full potential of a problem-solving process.

CHAPTER 8

Collaborative Law: Practicing Without Armor, Practicing With Heart

*Pauline H. Tesler**

Introduction

A profound revolution in the field of family law is transforming how domestic relations lawyers across the English-speaking world think and work. Conceived in 1990 by one disgruntled Minnesota lawyer, collaborative law directly addresses longstanding problems associated with use of the courts as a first resort for resolving domestic relations matters, and consequently the family law bar has embraced it eagerly. The model spread rapidly across the United States and Canada during the 1990's, and is taking root now in Europe, Australia, and New Zealand. As collaborative law enters the conflict resolution mainstream, lawyers have seen significant benefits for clients and their families who elect the collaborative model. More unexpected has been the impact on family law practitioners themselves, who report that engaging in collabo-

* Pauline H. Tesler is a fellow of the American Academy of Matrimonial Lawyers, a certified specialist in family law (State Bar of California Board of Legal Specialization), a founder and first president of the International Academy of Collaborative Professionals, and founding co-editor of the COLLABORATIVE REVIEW. She wrote the first book-length treatise on collaborative law, entitled COLLABORATIVE LAW: ACHIEVING EFFECTIVE RESOLUTION IN DIVORCE WITHOUT LITIGATION (ABA 2001) (hereinafter COLLABORATIVE LAW), and is co-author, with Psychologist Peggy Thompson, of COLLABORATIVE DIVORCE: THE REVOLUTIONARY NEW WAY TO RESTRUCTURE YOUR FAMILY, RESOLVE LEGAL ISSUES, AND MOVE ON WITH YOUR LIFE (2006). In 2002, she received the first "Lawyer as Problem-Solver" award from the American Bar Association. Her website is: www.lawtsf.com.

rative legal practice restores the feelings of pride and satisfaction that accompany performing an important, socially valuable service. Further, many collaborative lawyers look beyond the basics of collaborative legal practice to explore the deeper healing possibilities of this work and, in so doing, find that they too are changed by this work. This mode of practice flourishes best where there is transparent human engagement amongst all participants in the conflict resolution system, including lawyers, clients, and other professionals. In embracing the deep conflict resolution potential of collaborative practice, lawyers often report that—perhaps for the first time in their professional lives—they experience integration of their most significant personal and professional values, in stark contrast with the personal alienation and compartmentalization that so often characterize adversarial litigation practice in the domestic relations courts.[1] Collaborative lawyers are finding that to do this work well requires harmonious engagement of intellect, emotion, values, and even spiritual beliefs in aid of helping the clients find solutions that can last. Pursuing excellence in deep collaborative conflict resolution is leading to abandonment of the armored warrior *persona* so essential for personal survival and professional success as a traditional family law litigator, in favor of integration of personal and professional selves.

The Armored Warrior: Domestic Relations Litigation Practice

There is much truth in the aphorism that criminal lawyers see bad people at their best, while family lawyers see good people at their worst. Divorce is second only to the death of a spouse in terms of the degree of psychological trauma experienced by those going through it. Especially where the divorce is sudden and unexpected, it can precipitate an intense grief and recovery process that may last from eighteen months to several years or more. During that process, moments of hope and optimism are punctuated by periods of overwhelming grief, fear, guilt, and other powerful negative emotions that can

---

1. Empirical research about collaborative law is still in early stages. The observations and conclusions set forth in this chapter are based upon the author's personal experience since the early 1990's as an international trainer of collaborative practitioners and as co-founder and first president of the International Academy of Collaborative Professionals [hereinafter IACP].

sink the client into transient but very real states of diminished capacity.[2] During those periods, clients' ability to process information, prioritize, and make decisions is compromised, at the very same time that the legal divorce process requires them to make major decisions that will shape their own financial and emotional welfare, and that of their children, for the rest of their lives.[3] While most clients will gradually regain the level of functional competency they enjoyed prior to the divorce, the hard work of the divorce must in many cases be accomplished while the client is at lowest ebb, least able to think clearly, most likely to be overwhelmed by states of primitive emotion, and most likely to act and react irrationally.[4]

During this period of emotional challenge, the sole source of professional counsel for most clients is likely to be their divorce lawyer. The grieving client is likely to experience moments during the legal divorce process when it is possible to speak civilly with the soon-to-be ex spouse, moments when the needs of the children are put foremost, moments when simple accommodations and courtesies suddenly seem appropriate, but those are not the moments when the client is likely to call the adversarial family law attorney to set goals and plan strategies. Rather, clients are moved to call their divorce lawyers when relations with their spouses are at their worst, when primitive feelings engender harsh words and vindictive behavior, when fears about financial survival or access to children eclipse perspective, and when anger, disappointment, guilt, and vengefulness are at their peak. Consequently, traditional divorce lawyers tend to devise with their clients mirror-image game plans for trial based upon black and white cartoons, in which each client seeks to be viewed as blameless, and seeks maximum redress from a judge for emotional injuries inflicted by an opposing party characterized at best as impaired and at worst as malevolent.[5]

The divorcing client's emotion-fueled wish to be confirmed as blameless, and for the other to be identified as the villain, cannot readily be satisfied by

---

2. E. M. HEATHERINGTON & J. KELLY, FOR BETTER OR FOR WORSE: DIVORCE RECONSIDERED 9–10, *passim* (2002).

3. *See, e.g.*, Richard A. Gardner, *My Involvement in Child Custody Litigation*, 27 FAM. & CONCILIATION CTS. REV. 1, 3–9 (1989).

4. *Cf.* John H. Wade & Christopher Honeyman, *Negotiating Beyond Agreement to Commitment: Why Contracts are Breached and How to Make Them More Durable*, 20 BOND DISP. RESOL. NEWS 7, 9–10 (2005).

5. *See, e.g.*, Vivienne Roseby, *Uses of Psychological Testing in a Child-Focused Approach to Child Custody Evaluations*, 29 FAM. L.Q. 97, 98 (1999); Andrew Schepard, *War and P.E.A.C.E.: A Preliminary Report and a Model Statute on an Interdisciplinary Educational Program for Divorcing and Separating Parents*, 27 U. MICH. J.L. REFORM 131, 145–47 (1993).

courts operating within the "no-fault" divorce laws of most U.S. jurisdictions which, for the most part, restrict or bar evidence of fault or misbehavior. But an angry or grief-stricken client nonetheless expects the adversarial lawyer to go to battle as a warrior and to win. If evidence of fault is not relevant or admissible, then the client seeks other ways to achieve a victory— any victory— that might satisfy the perceived need to prove who is good and who is not. This is the propelling force behind many costly discovery battles, lengthy searches for hidden assets, allegations and counter-allegations of theft or destruction of property, escalating battles over every detail of daily access to and care of children, and litigation over division of relatively valueless household goods—the kinds of routine pretrial proceedings seen every day in family law court, where—in the words of retired California appellate justice Donald King—"they shoot the survivors."[6]

Thus, clients and lawyers routinely find themselves in high conflict divorce litigation even where the issues are relatively uncomplicated and the clients can ill afford the costs generated by runaway, emotion-fueled court proceedings. It is generally accepted that most family law matters ultimately are settled without full trials, and indeed some data suggests that trials themselves may take place in fewer than 5% of civil cases filed.[7] Nonetheless, trial lawyers are taught that the best way to prepare a case for settlement is to prepare vigorously for trial. Following this common rule of practice, traditional litigators file aggressive pleadings and motions, conduct aggressive discovery, and engage in extreme demands accompanied by the theatrical posturing associated with positional bargaining. In other words, conventional litigation practice —by design— devotes more than 95% of the lawyers' efforts to an event that is expected to occur less than 5% of the time. Finally, literally or figuratively on the courthouse steps, they get to work to resolve the case.

Whether that approach to settlement makes sense in business and commercial disputes is beyond the scope of this chapter, but there can be little doubt that it is destructive and wasteful in domestic relations matters, particularly where there are children involved. To prepare a divorce case aggressively for trial requires that the lawyer relentlessly pare away at the complex and nuanced

---

6. Retired Cal. App. J. Donald King, Address at the *New Ways of Helping Children and Families Through Divorce*, a conference sponsored by the Judith Wallerstein Center for the Family in Transition and University of California, Santa Cruz (November 21, 1998).

7. *See* THE VANISHING TRIAL: THE COLLEGE, THE PROFESSION, THE CIVIL JUSTICE SYSTEM, A REPORT OF THE AMERICAN COLLEGE OF TRIAL LAWYERS 4–10 (American College of Trial Lawyers, October 2004), *at* http://www.actl.com/PDFs/Vanishing_Trial_wAppendices_Final.pdf (last visited Nov. 1, 2006).

circumstances involved in the collapse of a family, simplifying and exaggerating until only those facts remain that might persuade a busy judge to decide a legally cognizable claim in favor of the client. Since domestic relations litigators, like most human beings, like to succeed at what they do, and since family law statutes emphasize justiciable (read "measurable") controversies, it is very common for lawyers to measure their success in family law litigation by the size of the heap of measurable widgets that finally is awarded to the client, whether those widgets are dollars, or teacups, or hours with children. This emphasis on garnering the biggest pile of measurable goodies for the client can encourage lawyers to dispute over matters of relatively little inherent importance, without regard for the consequent irreparable injuries to familial relationships that must—where children are involved— continue long after the judgment has been entered and the lawyer has withdrawn from the case.

Family courts typically have jurisdiction to hear only narrowly defined claims for statutorily constrained kinds of legal or equitable relief, but the matters that keep divorcing clients awake nights frequently lie entirely outside the jurisdiction of the courts to provide meaningful relief. Clients often care far more about matters such as these than about marginal increases in the dollars or hours that can be divided up by a judge:

- Will my children come through this divorce process without harm to their welfare?
- Will they be able to sustain relationships with their cousins, aunts, uncles and grandparents on both sides of the family?
- Will my in-laws be able to remain my friends?
- Will my friends be forced to take sides? Will I have any friends by the time this is over?
- Will my ex-spouse and I be able to cooperate in parenting our children through the difficulties of adolescence?
- Will my ex-spouse and I be able to share the pleasures of milestones like children's high school and college graduations, weddings, the birth of grandchildren?
- Will I be able to look back on this divorce process without shame or remorse about my own behavior?

These highly charged worries concern the health of the invisible or relational estate, the web of human relationships that is so vital to individual and familial health, and which is more often overlooked or damaged than carefully protected during family law litigation. Lawyers as a self-selected group tend to be uncomfortable with emotion, and to be far more at ease with quantifi-able issues and measurable results than with strong feelings, their own or their clients'.[8] And because lawyers are trained in law school to exclude non-justi-ciable matters from consideration, litigators' interviews with clients tend to consist of leading questions designed to spot issues quickly, help the client state a cognizable claim, and facilitate the largest measurable outcome for the client.

Clients, of course, look to their lawyers not only for legal direction, but for guidance about what matters in a divorce and how one should properly con-duct oneself through that life passage. But the temperament of lawyers merges with the limited jurisdiction of the family law courts to send a clear—and highly dysfunctional—message to clients: what matters in divorce is what the law gives judges power to decide and divide. The quality of the ongoing rela-tionship between the divorcing spouses (infamously dismissed in *Cole v. Cole*,[9] as the "foul rag and bone shop of the heart"), so vital to the effective rearing of children during and after divorce, seldom registers as an identified priority in a family lawyer's advice and counsel to a divorcing client. The implicit— and sometimes explicit—message from the legal profession to spouses whose families are unraveling is, "your concerns about the harmful impact of adver-sarial divorce on the human needs of the post-divorce family are not part of my job description; I did not go to law school to hold your hand."[10]

Given the gulf between what traditional lawyers are prepared to focus on in a divorce and the familial, relational, and personal integrity issues that rightly matter greatly to most clients, it should come as no surprise to learn that divorcing clients rarely seem satisfied by the outcome of adversarial di-vorce proceedings, even when their lawyers obtain excellent outcomes for them, measured in dollars and hours. Indeed, family lawyers are more likely than practitioners of other civil specialties to have fee disputes with their clients (because of limited financial resources to meet the high costs of litiga-

---

8. Susan Daicoff, *Lawyer, Know Thyself: A Review of Empirical Research on Attorney Attributes Bearing on Professionalism*, 46 AM. U.L. REV. 1337, 1394 (1997); SUSAN DAICOFF, LAWYER KNOW THYSELF: A PSYCHOLOGICAL ANALYSIS OF PERSONALITY STRENGTHS AND WEAKNESSES *passim* (2004); Stephen Reich, *Psychological Inventory: Profile of a Sample of First-Year Law Students*, 39 PSYCHOL. REP. 871, 871–74 (1976).

9. 633 F.2d 1083, 1088 (1980).

10. Commentators who have emphasized the inherent harms to children from court-based divorce proceedings include JUDITH S.WALLERSTEIN & JOAN BERLIN KELLY, SUR-VIVING THE BREAKUP: HOW CHILDREN AND PARENTS COPE WITH DIVORCE 80 (1980); Schepard, *supra* note 5.

tion) and consequently to be sued for malpractice[11]—not because they are less competent nor their work commonly below the standard of care, but because real human needs are so often ignored, while unrealistic client expectations are routinely encouraged (during the trial preparation phase) and then dashed when resolution is reached, as no amount of money can redress the emotional grievances associated with the end of the marriage, or the emotional injuries inflicted on clients and their children during the adversarial divorce process itself.[12]

While many family lawyers choose this field from a desire to practice law as a helping profession, the harsh reality of domestic relations practice bears little resemblance to anything helpful. The toll upon families experiencing court-based adversarial divorce proceedings can be seen any day of the week in the domestic relations courts of virtually any metropolitan area. What may be less apparent is the toll this mode of practice takes upon practitioners. Conventional adversarial lawyers generally, and family lawyers particularly, show many signs of a profession in trouble. By their middle years—the prime of their professional lives—lawyers are disproportionately likely to experience elevated stress, anxiety, miscarriages, major depression, alcohol and drug abuse, and even suicide, and are far more likely than members of other professions to say that they would not want their children to follow in their chosen career path.[13]

Mediation as a Response to the Deleterious Effects of Domestic Relations Litigation Practice

For all these reasons, many family lawyers greeted the advent of mediation with enthusiasm when it first emerged on the conflict-resolution horizon in

---

11. *See, e.g.,* 10 L. MUTUAL INS. CO. BULL. *passim* (1995).

12. Wade & Honeyman, *supra* note 4, refer to such outcomes, whether negotiated or litigated, as "shallow peace," in contrast to deep resolution.

13. *See, e.g.,* Joseph Bellacosa, *A Nation Under Lost Lawyers,* 100 DICK. L. REV. 505 (1996); Mary Jordan, *More Attorneys Making a Motion for the Pursuit of Happiness,* WASH. POST, Sept. 4, 1993; Connie J. A. Beck et al., *Lawyer Distress: Alcohol-Related Problems and Other Psychological Concerns Among a Sample of Practicing Lawyers,* 10 J.L. & HEALTH 1, 45–58 (1995–96); William W. Eaton et al., *Occupations and the Prevalence of Major Depressive Disorders,* 32 J. OCCUPATIONAL MED. 1079 (1990); Patrick Schiltz, *On Being a Happy, Healthy, and Ethical Member of an Unhappy, Unhealthy and Unethical Profession,* 52 VAND. L. REV. 871, 883–884 (1999); Andrew H. Benjamin, Bruce Sales & Elaine Darling, *Comprehensive Lawyer Assistance Programs: Justification and Model,* 16 L. & PSYCHOL. REV. 113 (1992); NANCY J. CAMERON, COLLABORATIVE PRACTICE: DEEPENING THE DIALOGUE ch. 3, *passim* (2004).

the 1970's, hoping that many divorcing couples might thereby avoid the downward slide toward costly, damaging, high conflict proceedings and have a better prospect of co-parenting their children effectively after the divorce. But while mediation[14] remains a useful conflict-resolution option for some divorcing couples, the initial high hopes have not borne fruit. For many divorcing couples, mediation simply is not sufficiently protective or powerful to be the best dispute resolution choice.[15]

Divorcing couples frequently display significant imbalances in terms of acceptance of the divorce itself, relative progress through the stages of grief and recovery, sophistication about money and negotiations in circumstances where resources may be scarce, emotional maturity, commitment to civil behavior, power imbalances, and intention to reach reasonable, equitable outcomes. For such couples, a single neutral mediator will be hard-pressed to facilitate efficient, reasonable negotiations and equitable outcomes. The very steps that might be taken to ameliorate such imbalances can easily offend one or both of the participants, causing resistance or even termination of the mediation. On the other hand, a mediator who pushes the parties toward agreement without regard for the negative impact of such imbalances is likely to facilitate unbalanced agreements that do not sufficiently resolve deep grievances or protect the interests of disadvantaged parties.

The challenges of addressing such imbalances in power, commitment, and understanding are inherent in the very structure of mediation. A neutral, by definition, must not only remain detached and unaligned, but must be perceived as such by both parties if the mediation is not to terminate. If one or both parties misuse the mediation process—whether by overbearing or disrespectful behavior, lack of full candor, explicit or implicit threats, delays, lack of follow-through, and the like, no professional in the picture is mandated to work privately with the difficult client outside the negotiations room to "recalibrate" the bad faith behavior, returning only when the client is ready to participate in good faith bargaining.[16] Hence, mediation can readily be expe-

---

14. It is difficult to make useful generalizations about mediation, because the term encompasses such a broad spectrum of different models that no statement is likely to be true for all or even most forms of mediation that are being practiced with divorcing couples. Joan B. Kelly, *A Decade of Divorce Mediation Research*, 34 FAM. & CONCILIATION CT. REV. 373–85 (1996). *See also supra* ch. 7: Harold Abramson, *Problem-Solving Advocacy in Mediations: A Model of Client Representation.*

15. JANET R. JOHNSTON & VIVIENNE ROSEBY, IN THE NAME OF THE CHILD 230–31 (1998).

16. In most (though not all) family mediation models, the clients are urged to retain independent counsel to advise and represent them. But those lawyers can be highly adver-

rienced by both clients as unsafe and insufficiently protective. For these reasons, family lawyers often regard mediation[17] as suitable primarily for higher-functioning clients who are able to behave civilly under pressure and who can sustain a commitment to consensual conflict resolution without the built-in support of legal counsel in the mediation room, at the heart of the negotiation process.[18]

The Advent of Collaborative Law: What it is and How it Came into Being

By the late 1980s, the inherent limitations of mediation as a way for lawyers and clients to avoid the stresses and strains of adversarial family law practice had become apparent. Stuart Webb, a Minneapolis family lawyer, was, like many family lawyers, frustrated with his inability—despite the best of intentions—to provide his clients either a consistently healthy negotiations process or a reasonably high likelihood of satisfactory outcomes in most divorce cases. And, like many family lawyers, he found the toll upon himself in terms of stress and professional dissatisfaction increasingly intolerable. He did something about it. As he contemplated abandoning the practice of law entirely, it suddenly occurred to him that he had nothing to lose by trying to practice family law in an unprecedented way that *would* be more positive for himself and his clients. The worst that could happen would be failure in the endeavor, which would result in giving up the practice of law. On January 1, 1990, he announced that he was now the world's first "collaborative lawyer" and he invited his colleagues to consider practicing family law in this new way with him.

Fifteen years later, collaborative law—also referred to as "collaborative practice," "collaborative family law practice," and "collaborative divorce"—is well-established in forty states and nearly every major metropolitan area in the United States, as well as across Canada the UK, Ireland, Austria, Switzer-

---

sarial and positional in their advice and counsel. The lawyers' job description remains unchanged structurally, and the threat of litigation, implicitly or explicitly, always remains. *See* Abramson, *supra* note 14, at pp. 226–27, 229–30.

17. These comments pertain to voluntary private-sector mediation, not compulsory court-annexed mediation. Wade & Honeyman, *supra* note 4.

18. For a more extended discussion of the differences between mediation and collaborative law, see Pauline H. Tesler, *Collaborative Law: A New Paradigm for Divorce Lawyers*, 5 PSYCHOL. PUB. POL'Y & L. 967, 973–74 (1999).

land, Australia, and New Zealand.[19] Recognizing a better way when they see it, family lawyers have embraced this new model with alacrity wherever it has been introduced, and have created a broad array of international, statewide, and local organizational structures[20] to support delivery of consistent, high quality collaborative legal services to family law clients.[21]

Collaborative lawyers are not neutrals. They remain advocates for their respective clients, providing built-in advice and counsel at the heart of the conflict resolution process. In collaborative law, structural and contractual "carrots and sticks" encourage a respectful, careful, consensual conflict resolution process that takes place entirely outside and without reference to the court system, aimed solely at reaching creative, acceptable, interest-based[22] resolutions that are likely to last because they begin and end with the actual concerns of clients rather than the jurisdictional mandate of the court.

The core element and *sine qua non* of collaborative law is a formal written agreement signed by both clients and both lawyers that limits the work of the lawyers to facilitating settlement of all issues,[23] and that disqualifies the lawyers from ever representing these clients in adversarial proceedings against one an-

---

19. *See* the website of the International Academy of Collaborative Professionals, http://www.collaborativepractice.com [hereinafter IACP website].

20. *See, e.g., id*; Collaborative Practice California, http://www.cpcal.com; the Collaborative Law Institute of Texas, http://www.collablawtexas.org; the Massachusetts Collaborative Law Council, http://www.massclc.org; the Collaborative Family Law Council of Wisconsin, http://www.collabdivorce.com; The Collaborative Law Institute of Minnesota, http://www.collaborativelaw.org; Resolution-First For Family Law, http://www.sfla.org.uk; San Francisco Bay Area Collaborative Law Group, http://www.collaborativepracticesfbay.com; Collaborative Lawyers of Southwest Florida, http://www.collaborativelaw-swfla.com; Collaborative Divorce Vancouver, http://www.collaborativedivorcebc.org; The New York Collaborative Law Group, http://www.collaborativelawny.com; and many more.

21. Collaborative law has also begun to take its place in the spectrum of conflict resolution modes available to civil and commercial practitioners and clients, but at a less rapid speed than in the family law bar.

22. Interest-based bargaining was first described by Roger Fisher & William Ury, *in* GETTING TO YES: NEGOTIATING AGREEMENT WITHOUT GIVING IN (1991). *See generally* Abramson, *supra* note 14.

23. This is a form of "limited purpose retention," which comports with professional ethical mandates provided the lawyers ensure fully informed consent on the part of the clients. While collaborative family lawyers are responsible for assisting clients to resolve all issues in the divorce, they generally do not conduct extensive formal discovery, nor do they use adversarial court procedures to resolve issues. See, by way of analogy, CAL. R. CT. 5.70, 5.71, concerning "unbundled" practice of law. Collaborative law has been expressly recognized in at least two state family codes, Texas (TEX. FAM. CODE § 6.603) and North Carolina (N.C. Gen. Stat. §§ 50-70 to 50-79).

other.[24] Beyond that core element, a growing body of practical techniques and tools has emerged over time that helps practitioners to facilitate authentic, interest-based solutions meeting the reasonable needs of both parties to a divorce. The first practical development was recognition of the critical importance of collegial trust relationships for high quality collaborative conflict resolution.[25] Collaborative lawyers need colleagues whom they can trust to adhere to a high standard of honesty and collegiality if clients are to be guided effectively through difficult stages of the divorce process. Building and sustaining trust requires ongoing, transparent relationships with colleagues. Toward that end, the early and mid 1990s saw the emergence of "practice groups," small voluntary local associations of practitioners who are likely to have cases in common. Because no formal credentialing is required to become a collaborative lawyer, there is no ready way to track exactly how many collaborative lawyers there are. However, a reasonable estimate[26] is that as of mid-

---

24. New practitioners at first may struggle with the unfamiliar idea of a disqualification requirement; it has been attacked by litigators worried about losing market share and its necessity questioned by at least one academic conflict resolution theorist, John Lande, *Possibilities for Collaborative Law: Ethics and Practice of Lawyer Disqualification in a New Model of Lawyering* , 64 OHIO ST. L.J. 1315 (2003). But all collaborative law trainers and experienced practitioners agree that this element is central to the power of collaborative law and that without it, collaborative law would be structurally indistinguishable from conventional settlement negotiations. The reasons are twofold. First, it keeps the clients and lawyers at the table in the face of apparent impasse longer because of reluctance on the part of all participants to terminate the collaborative representation. Disqualification thus provides considerable motivation for all participants to push through impasse to resolution, a structural incentive/disincentive that does not exist in other alternate dispute resolution models. Second, its existence pushes lawyers to change their unexamined and sometimes unconscious adversarial habits of practice in order to enhance their success at helping angry, fearful, or grieving clients to reach resolution. While nothing prevents traditional lawyers from staying at the table and changing their stripes, nothing in traditional practice encourages them to do so. The disqualification provision, on the other hand, distributes the risk of failure not only to the clients, but also to the lawyers. The clients must retain new counsel if they decide to abandon collaboration and take their disputes to court, just as the lawyers must bow out of the case and hand it over to litigation counsel if they cannot succeed in facilitating consensual resolution. In the words of one delighted client, "This is great! If you guys can't deliver on what you promise, you are out of a job!"

25. *See* Ronald J. Gilson & Robert H. Mnookin, *Disputing Through Agents: Cooperation and Conflict Between Lawyers in Litigation*, 94 COLUM. L. REV. 509 (1994). *See also* ROBERT H. MNOOKIN, SCOTT R. PEPPET, & ANDREW S. TULOMELLO, BEYOND WINNING (2000).

26. Based upon anecdotal reports from trainers, mailing lists maintained by IACP, and informed estimates, we approximate that 1 out of 7 trained lawyers elect to join IACP.

2005, approximately 7,000–8,000 practitioners in forty states, six Canadian provinces, six European countries, and two Pacific Rim countries, have participated in formal collaborative law trainings. Most of these lawyers join or start local practice groups after being trained.[27]

These practice groups have become not only trust-building vehicles, but also venues for skill development, training, case conferencing, mentoring, public education, and marketing. Everywhere that collaborative lawyers are found, they belong to practice groups, and the practice groups have been a vital force in the movement of the collaborative law model into the mainstream of divorce conflict resolution. Some groups affiliate with local bar associations, while others remain informal voluntary associations. Some are open to all, while others choose to remain small. Membership in practice groups is seen as an essential starting point for building trust, fostering consistency and congruence, and maintaining high standards of practice.[28]

In the early 1990's, a second important resource evolved. Practitioners in California, Minnesota, and Ohio drafted and shared carefully wrought participation documents: retainer agreements, formal stipulations for collaborative representation, and plain-English contracts that set out the key elements of the process, important informed-consent information and disclaimers, and good faith undertakings.[29] By sharing these forms and engaging in multi-state efforts aimed at improving them, collaborative lawyers learned the importance of collegiality for sending a consistent, congruent message to the bar, the bench, referral sources, and clients about this new mode, collaborative law. This early collegiality supported creation of the International Academy of Collaborative Professionals (IACP), which has helped practitioners to build a strong, unified collaborative movement. After fifteen years, the collaborative law movement remains remarkably coherent, and remarkably free of factions

---

27. As of mid-2005, IACP was aware of 170 local and state practice groups. *See* IACP website, *supra* note 19.

28. *See, e.g.,* Chip Rose, *Essential Elements ... For the Successful Collaborative Law Practice Group,* 2 THE COLLABORATIVE REVIEW 5 (2000); TESLER, COLLABORATIVE LAW, *supra* note *, ch. 9, 171–178, *passim* (2001); Cynthia Brewster et al., *Collaborative Law Affiliations: Trainings, Practice Groups, and Marketing, in* COLLABORATIVE LAW: A NEW MODEL FOR DISPUTE RESOLUTION pt. 4, chs. 22–26 (Sheila Gutterman ed., 2004).

29. Sample forms can be found in TESLER, COLLABORATIVE LAW, *supra* note *, app., the first book-length treatment of this dispute-resolution model. These forms are constantly evolving as collaborative practitioners suggest improvements. An important vehicle for sharing such "upgrades" is the collaborative law listserv, collablaw@yahoogroups.com, a lively discussion and networking forum for new and experienced practitioners.

and schisms. Practitioners have modeled for themselves what they recommend to clients: transparency, cooperation, and keeping the focus on broad shared principles rather than minor differences.

As standard documents were being developed and shared, local practice groups recognized the need for congruence and predictability in how a case would be handled, so that lawyers and clients electing collaborative law in that community could rely on agreed protocols for what would and would not take place at each stage in a collaborative case. Many local groups have adopted written practice protocols, and while minor differences can be found from one community to another, with some brief and general while others are quite detailed, the broad steps and stages of a collaborative representation and the broad guiding principles set forth in these protocols are remarkably consistent from community to community, state to state, and even nation to nation. Typically they provide that negotiations will proceed in well-defined phases, utilizing agreed agendas and interest-based rather than positional bargaining; that all discovery will be early, complete, and voluntary; that all experts and consultants participating in the process will be retained jointly as neutrals and will be barred from participation in litigation; and, that all negotiations will be conducted in face to face "four-way meetings" involving both clients and lawyers rather than through lawyers bargaining as agents. A case begins with Opening Moves (explaining the process, setting up a "container" of agreed modes of behavior and good faith bargaining, signing the formal participation agreements); proceeds to Midgame (sharing and developing information, identifying goals and priorities, brainstorming solutions, arriving at agreement); and reaches final resolution at Endgame (preparing and signing the settlement agreement; signing and processing necessary court forms and documents leading to entry of judgment, and gathering for a more or less ceremonial signing and completion of the case).[30]

The Evolution of Interdisciplinary Collaborative Practice in the Family Law Field

In the early 1990's, as collaborative law was emerging as a new force in the family law field, a parallel model arose in the San Francisco Bay Area among

---

30. The chess metaphor employed here is one of many used to help clients understand that a collaborative divorce has an identifiable beginning, middle, and end—a useful orientation in time and space for clients who may be experiencing the confusion associated with high stress levels.

mental health professionals who were discouraged about the negative impact upon families of their court-based work in contested custody trials. Peggy Thompson, Ph.D., and her colleague Nancy Ross, L.C.S.W, synthesized understandings from the realms of high conflict divorce counseling, communications theory, grief counseling, child development, and family systems theory in a new, client-centered divorce coaching model that they named Collaborative Divorce. Collaborative Divorce rapidly matured into an interdisciplinary approach in which specially trained collaborative lawyers, financial neutrals, child development specialists, and licensed mental health divorce coaches work in a coordinated team model to help a divorcing couple communicate better, develop well-informed parenting plans, participate more effectively in collaborative legal negotiations, and develop resolutions that incorporate sophisticated financial planning.[31]

Some communities in the U.S. and Canada (notably New Orleans, Vancouver, Milwaukee, and Phoenix) embraced the interdisciplinary team approach from the start, training lawyers, financial neutrals, and mental health professionals together in how to become effective collaborative practitioners. Elsewhere, lawyers have been the leading edge, and collaborative law has been the first to take root, for instance, in Dallas, Boston, and Los Angeles.

However collaborative practice begins in a community, lawyers who become deeply involved in collaborative representation eventually see that their work will be more effective, and difficult clients will have a better chance of reaching resolution, with the help of an interdisciplinary team of collaborative professionals than with collaborative lawyers alone. In the words of psychologist Abraham Maslow, "He that is good with a hammer tends to think everything is a nail."[32] Working with interdisciplinary teams, clients learn with their coaches to manage strong emotions and to communicate more reasonably and effectively at legal four-way meetings, and their lawyers are given information and tools to help them better manage conflict. The neutral financial consultants help clients gather data and understand the economic realities of their divorce efficiently and effectively, and the child specialist facilitates the development of parenting plans based on sound information about the preferences and needs of children rather than on "he said/she said" advocacy.

---

31. Pauline Tesler, *It Takes a System ... to Change a System: An Interview With Peggy Thompson*, 4 COLLABORATIVE REVIEW (Issue 2, 2002); A. RODNEY NURSE & PEGGY THOMPSON, COLLABORATIVE DIVORCE: A FAMILY CENTERED APPROACH (forthcoming 2006).

32. *See, e.g.,* Abraham Maslow, Father of Modern Management, *Maslow's Hammer: When all you have is a hammer...,* at http://www.abraham-maslow.com/m_motivation/Maslows_Hammer.asp (last visited Feb. 21, 2006).

Best of all, lawyers learn to share the load. Few lawyers are trained to deal effectively with the strong feelings that commonly surface during the intensely stressful process of divorce. When coaches, child specialists, and financial neutrals are involved, clients can meet with the professional best able to guide them through emotional meltdowns, returning to legal negotiations better able to work. In the interdisciplinary team model, collaborative lawyers learn to share responsibility appropriately, to communicate transparently and clearly, and to listen deeply to the other professionals working with the clients. These relational skills also enhance authentic communications between lawyer and client, and between lawyer and lawyer. Clients' actual concerns can be heard and addressed more clearly in a process that is explicitly aimed at identifying and attending to the human as well as legal and financial needs of both clients and those whom they love. When lawyers learn to work this way with their clients, it is not only the clients whose stress levels fall and whose satisfaction levels rise. For lawyers, to embrace this mode of practice is to embark on law as a healing profession.[33]

The Future of Collaborative Practice: Where it is Going and What Impact it is Having on Practitioners and Clients

New collaborative practitioners sometimes bring from conventional family law practice a picture of divorce as beginning with the filing of a petition or complaint and ending with entry of a judgment—in other words, bounded by pieces of legal paper in a court file. From this perspective, the point is to get to the agreement and judgment as efficiently and cost-effectively as possible. Such a view of collaborative law is "lawyer-centric," focusing entirely on events that happen in the lawyer's office and in court, according to a timetable

---

33. In 2004, the IACP adopted a comprehensive set of *Ethical Guidelines and Standards for Collaborative Practitioners, Trainers, and Trainings* that set forth current understandings about best practices for lawyers, mental health coaches, child specialists, and financial neutrals. These are voluntary aspirational standards rather than gatekeeper credentialing tools. They reflect a remarkable degree of consensus internationally about what it means to be a capable collaborative practitioner. These documents can be viewed *at* http://www.collaborativepractice.com.

dictated by local procedure, within a framework of rights and entitlements prescribed by statute. While the final agreement may be arrived at consensually by the clients, it emerges from a process that is constrained by the habits and norms of third party decision-making.[34]

As collaborative lawyers learn to listen to clients' actual concerns rather than determining *a priori* what is relevant and extracting information via leading questions, the focus can change from deductive to inductive, from identifying rights and predicting ranges of probable trial outcomes to facilitating conversations about shared principles and possible solutions, outside the constraints under which trial judges are permitted to decide issues.[35] In this collaborative conflict-resolution mode, solutions emerge from clear communication about facts, priorities, and options rather than from predictions about the behavior of local judges. In this inductive, client-centered, interest-based mode of collaborative practice, deep conflict resolution becomes possible, because where the clients have a will to do so and the lawyers help them, negotiations can address any concern that matters to a client, and solutions can go far beyond what a judge is permitted to do. This process recognizes that clients' experience of divorce begins long before the filing of a legal paper, and will continue long

---

34. The result is almost always "shallow peace" rather than deep resolution. *See, e.g.,* Marygold Melli, *The Process of Negotiations: An Exploratory Investigation in the Context of No Fault Divorce*, 40 RUTGERS L. REV. 1333, 1143–44 (1996).

35. For example, in a long term marriage, California judges abuse their discretion if they make orders that terminate spousal support (alimony) unless the supported spouse is found to be fully self-supporting at the marital standard of living. The amount of support that California judges order is based on current needs, capped by the marital standard of living. But in collaborative divorces, couples often prefer to work out support arrangements that provide the supported spouse with greater financial resources immediately after separation in order to go back to school and build a new career, in return for an agreement that support will at some specified point terminate. Or, some spouses prefer to trade their entitlement to spousal support entirely, for a larger share of the marital property. None of these creative options can be ordered at trial by judges. Similarly, in California and many other jurisdictions, step-parents have no custodial rights or support duties, no matter how long their familial relationship with step-children may have lasted. While such courts are powerless to hear claims relating to step-parent rights or duties, in a collaborative representation such concerns might be very significant in the negotiations. Many other common concerns of divorcing spouses lie beyond the effective power of courts to issue orders. Depending on the jurisdiction, such issues might include: linking custody or visitation rights to participation in substance abuse, anger-management, or mental health treatment; providing for support of handicapped adult children; providing for college education; creation of trusts for children; negotiating deferred sale of family residence; planning structured sale of assets for maximum tax advantage; etc.

after the judgment is filed and the professionals have moved on to other cases.[36] It also recognizes that for clients, the bounds of family court jurisdiction do not necessarily match the bounds of what matters most for the long term health of a family that is breaking down and restructuring.

It is not that collaborative lawyers ignore legal rights and entitlements or that the allegiance of the collaborative lawyer is to anyone other than his or her client. Rather, experienced and capable collaborative practitioners advise about the law but also remind their clients that legal rights and entitlements may be only a small part of what matters most to them, and counsel clients that they need not be limited by the bounds of the family code unless they so wish. Good collaborative lawyers not only explain legal rights, but also deconstruct the law, explaining its origin, function, and limitations, and addressing what matters to the client whether a court could or not.

A wise collaborative lawyer provides even *more* law than a conventional lawyer, not less:

> The diversity of legal treatment of the common issues arising out of a divorce in jurisdictions whose populations are virtually indistinguishable from our own is substantial, and instructive not because of the many and varied conclusions that have been reached by legislatures and courts in those other states, but rather because those conclusions, like our own, have been reached by reasoned and principled people seeking to carefully craft solutions to the same questions our clients face today.[37]

When shown that the results for similarly situated couples litigating the same issues in San Francisco, Boston, Chicago, Dallas, or Miami would diverge significantly (as, for instance, with respect to alimony/spousal support rights), our clients can readily see that there is nothing inherently superior about a specific state's laws, and that the spectrum of potentially useful solutions available to them is far wider than what may be available at the local courthouse.

When lawyers listen to what their clients really care about, and help them to articulate those concerns as interests that any reasonable person can be ex-

---

36. Mental health professionals know that from the perspective of clients, the divorce may have begun when the couple met, or even earlier, and when there are children, it will never end.

37. Don Royall, *Complex Financial Issues in Collaborative Cases: Is Less Emphasis on the Law a Good Idea?*, 6 THE COLLABORATIVE REVIEW 22, 27 (Winter 2004). *See also*, Pauline H. Tesler, *Law and Collaboration* 6 THE COLLABORATIVE REVIEW 9–13 (Winter 2004).

pected to respect, a human interaction takes place quite different in kind from lawyer-directed issue-spotting—a more leisurely dialogue in which the outcome is discovered gradually rather than predicated from the start. The collaborative lawyers bring to that discussion understanding, wise counsel, and expressive help instead of directive focus on getting the biggest pile of goodies. In such conversations, open dialogue can occur and genuine human contact is possible. In such conversations, the lawyer who brings his or her full self, including values, life experience, and empathy as well as legal knowledge and negotiating skills, will be more effective in facilitating genuine communication and deep resolution between clients than the lawyer who comes wearing the personal armor of a litigator, because that armor blocks important information about who these human beings are, what each wants and needs and cares about, and what beliefs or feelings might be standing in the way of effectively communicating and reaching an agreement. The eminent twentieth-century philosopher Martin Buber called such genuine interactions "I-Thou" experiences as distinct from "I-It" experiences.[38] It is not only the clients who benefit from the human interactions at the core of effective collaborative practice. When the professional life of a lawyer is characterized by trust, transparency, collegial collaboration, and "I-thou" interactions, professional satisfaction grows as the boundary between personal and professional selves becomes less rigid, more permeable.

Conclusion

Collaboration is a form of practice that flourishes at its highest potential when the armor is laid down. The "I-Thou" quality of good collaborative negotiations enters the room only when the litigator's weapons have been put

---

38. These ideas are discussed at length in BUBER, I AND THOU (Touchstone 1996), first published in 1923 in German. According to Buber, human beings may adopt two attitudes toward the world: *I-Thou* or *I-It*. "*I-Thou* is a relation of subject-to-subject, while *I-It* is a relation of subject-to-object. In the *I-Thou* relationship, human beings are aware of each other as having a unity of being. In the *I-Thou* relationship, human beings do not perceive each other as consisting of specific, isolated qualities, but engage in a dialogue involving each other's whole being. In the *I-It* relationship, on the other hand, human beings perceive each other as consisting of specific, isolated qualities, and view themselves as part of a world which consists of things. *I-Thou* is a relationship of mutuality and reciprocity, while *I-It* is a relationship of separateness and detachment." Alex Scott, *Martin Buber's I and Thou*, *at* http://www.angelfire.com/md2/timewarp/buber.html (2002) (last visited Feb. 21, 2006).

aside. In the authentic human interactions that can then take place during honest, well-managed, respectful, interest-based collaborative negotiations, the benefits flow to all participants. For example, collaborative lawyers report that at the final four-way meetings, after the settlement agreement has been reviewed and signed, after moments of generosity have been recalled and the clients have been congratulated for moving through a difficult life passage with grace and consideration, after the lawyers have thanked one another for a job well done, it is not uncommon for both clients to embrace one another and the lawyers before leaving. This kind of ending marks a process that acknowledges the human complexity of the divorce passage; that models and holds out high expectations for how participants will comport themselves during that difficult transition; that helps them to rise to those expectations; and that attends to the human needs of all the participants, lawyers, and clients alike.

When collaborative trainers relate such anecdotes to aspiring new practitioners, it is not unusual for a participant to come up after the training to say (often tearfully) that he or she was ready to leave the practice of law, but that collaborative law has provided new hope of integrating personal values and professional life. The promise is real. Collaborative practice is a direct pathway to practicing law as a healing profession. And the first persons healed are often the lawyers.

CHAPTER 9

THE CULTURE OF LEGAL
DENIAL*

*Jonathan R. Cohen***

*[The] question of guilty clients ... is the oldest of the old, old questions
for lawyers.*[1]

I. Introduction

Basic morality teaches that if a person injures another, he should take responsibility for what he has done. Lawyers, by contrast, typically assist injurers in the reverse—denial. Legal culture masks the immoral as the normal.
"You prove it," says the defendant's lawyer, "and if you cannot, then my client
will not pay." How did lawyers grow so comfortable in assisting injurers in a
basic act of moral regression? Can this be changed?

* This chapter is reprinted by permission of the Nebraska Law Review. It appears in
substantially similar form as a section of a longer article of the same title in 84 NEB. L. REV.
247 (2005). That longer article also addresses ways in which economic incentives within
litigation, the choice of dispute resolution mechanism, legal education, and broader aspects of our cultural composition facilitate denial within ordinary civil disputes.
** Professor of Law, University of Florida, Fredric G. Levin College of Law. I thank
Thomas Cotter, Susan Daicoff, Steven Hartwell, Rebecca Hiers, Richard Hiers, Michelle
Jacobs, B.J. Krintzman, Samuel Levine, Lyrissa Lidsky, William Page, Juan Perea, Marty
Peters, Carrie Petrucci, Sharon Rush, Andrea Kupfer Schneider, Thomas L. Shaffer, Marjorie Silver, David Wexler, and Walter Weyrauch for their comments and suggestions. All
errors are mine alone.
1. Thomas L. Shaffer, *Should a Christian Lawyer Serve the Guilty?*, 23 GA. L. REV. 1021,
1023 (1989).

In a prior essay, I addressed denial from the perspective of the client.[2] There I argued that, possible economic benefits notwithstanding, failing to take responsibility poses serious spiritual and psychological risks to injurers. Here I focus on the role of the lawyer. This chapter examines the practice of lawyers assisting clients in denying harms they commit and suggests some ways of changing that practice.[3] Lawyers commonly presume that their clients' interests are best served by denial. Yet such a presumption is not warranted. Given the moral, psychological, relational, and sometimes even economic risks of denial to the injurer, lawyers should consider discussing responsibility taking more often with clients. Even if a lawyer anticipates that denial will benefit a client financially, a lawyer should not assume that such expected economic benefit outweighs possible moral, psychological, and relational costs to the client. Hence, under the existing professional ethics norms (commonly called the "zealous advocacy" framework[4]), lawyers should consider counseling clients about responsibility taking far more often than they do. As we shall see, the failure of lawyers to offer such counseling does not rest upon the strictures of legal ethics codes. Indeed, properly understood, existing legal ethics standards often require such consideration.

For the lawyer who decides to discuss responsibility taking with a client, the question of how to do so requires careful consideration. Obstacles to such

---

2. Jonathan R. Cohen, *The Immorality of Denial*, 79 TUL. L. REV. 903 (2005) [hereinafter *Immorality*].

3. Though I will not address it here, the obverse problem of lawyers assisting clients in bringing unwarranted accusations also merits serious consideration.

4. In recent years, attempts have been made to "soften" the level of zeal with which lawyers are to pursue their work. For example, whereas ABA Model Code of Professional Responsibility Canon 7 (1983) stated that, "A lawyer should represent a client zealously within the bounds of the law," ABA Model Rules of Professional Conduct Rule 1.3 (2003) now states only that, "A lawyer shall act with reasonable diligence ... in representing a client." (However, the Comment to Rule 1.3 does provide, "A lawyer must ... act with commitment and dedication to the interests of the client and with zeal in advocacy upon the client's behalf.") Such change notwithstanding, the grip of the "zealous advocacy" paradigm on the minds of lawyers is quite strong. *See, e.g.,* Monroe H. Freedman & Abbe Smith, *Zealous Representation: The Pervasive Ethic, in* UNDERSTANDING LAWYERS' ETHICS 71 (2004) ("This ethic of zeal ... established in Abraham Lincoln's day ... continues today to be '*the* fundamental principle of the law of lawyering' and 'the dominant standard for lawyerly excellence.'") (citations omitted). *See also* Leonard L. Riskin, *Mediation and Lawyers*, 43 OHIO ST. L.J. 29, 43–48 (1982) (describing the adversarial paradigm as lawyers' "standard philosophical map"). On the historical development of the zealous advocacy framework, see Geoffrey C. Hazard, Jr., *The Future of Legal Ethics*, 100 YALE L.J. 1239 (1991); Freedman & Smith, *supra*.

counseling include client reticence to disclose mistakes, the lawyer's fear of appearing judgmental or disloyal, and expectations by both lawyers and clients that the lawyer's essential role is to minimize the client's financial liability. ("Your job is to get me off. If I wanted someone to tell me to take responsibility for what I have done, I would have gone to a minister or psychologist.") Such obstacles, however, are not insurmountable, and can often be met with good client counseling. Critical to such counseling is a strong lawyer-client relationship based upon trust. Further, great rewards may await clients and lawyers who discuss responsibility taking. Responsibility taking after injuries can help clients maintain morally-grounded lives, and the lawyer who discusses that path with clients may discover a deepened sense of purpose in her work.[5]

Within our culture, people, especially lawyers, commonly focus on individuals' rights and overlook individuals' responsibilities. Denial is almost always within an injurer's legal rights, yet often deeply at odds with his responsibilities. The argument presented here is at its root a simple one flowing from the premise that it is immoral to deny responsibility for an injury one has committed. Some readers may find the picture painted too simple or "reductionist" and feel that the critique of denial has been pushed too far. My goal here is to identify and explore what I consider a largely unrecognized aspect of legal practice—a missing "piece of the puzzle." I do not mean to suggest that this missing piece forms the whole puzzle. Yet before a synthesis can be achieved between what is recognized and what is largely unrecognized, the unrecognized must first be recognized.

The eighteenth century founder of Hasidic Judaism, known as the Baal Shem Tov, once claimed that,

> The chief joy of the Satan ... is when he succeeds in persuading a man
> that an evil deed is a *mitzvah* [a deed commanded by God]. For when

---

5. For reasons I describe in greater detail elsewhere, my focus here is upon civil rather than criminal cases. *See Immorality, supra* note 2, at 905–06. For fine presentations in criminal law raising related concerns, see Robert F. Cochran, Jr., *Crime, Confession, and the Counselor-at-Law: Lessons from Dostoyevsky,* 35 Hous. L. Rev. 327 (1998) (speaking on the risk of psychological guilt to the guilty-in-fact criminal defendant who denies his guilt at law); Stephen P. Garvey, *Punishment as Atonement,* 46 UCLA L. Rev. 1801 (1999) (commenting on the possibility of atonement through criminal punishment). *See also* John Braithwaite, Crime, Shame and Reintegration (1989) (remarking on the role of shame in reintegrating criminals into society). The criminal setting raises enough distinct issues (e.g., the Fifth Amendment right against self-incrimination, power disparities between the state and the accused, etc.) so as to merit separate treatment. Note too that I will not address the influence of liability insurance on the injurer's denial, as an in-depth treatment of this significant subject is also beyond the scope of this chapter.

a man is weak and commits an offense, knowing it to be a sin, he is likely to repent of it. But when he believes it to be a good deed, does it stand to reason that he will repent of performing a *mitzvah?*[6]

Our legal system masks the vice of denial after injury as a virtue. We have developed a culture of legal denial. To fix this problem, we must first understand it.

II. Clients and Lawyers

A. Client Ethics

Before addressing the topic of denial, it is helpful to take a step back to understand the broader ethical domain within which that topic resides. When discussing ethics, lawyers almost always focus on *professional* ethics. As the name suggests, professional ethics concern the professional. Professional ethics address, for example, what ethical obligations a lawyer has to the client, to the court, and to third parties. Codes of professional ethics, such as the *ABA Model Rules of Professional Conduct* ("*Model Rules*") and the *ABA Model Code of Professional Responsibility* ("*Model Code*"), are paradigmatic of this focus. In the language of philosophers, these codes address role ethics, that is, the ethical obligations entailed when acting in a certain professional role.

In contrast, the root ethical issue raised by denial falls into a different, and sadly often overlooked, domain. One might call this the domain of *disputant* ethics, *client* ethics or, perhaps most basically, *interpersonal* ethics.[7] Consider questions like, "Are there times when taking revenge is morally acceptable?" or, "If a person apologizes for injuring me, must I forgive him?" These questions had ethical relevance long before mechanisms such as courts or professional lawyers existed. In legal conflict, lawyers are ultimately the secondary figures. They are the agents of the parties. The domain of disputant ethics addresses the ethics of the parties themselves. It explores how people should treat one another after injury or when in conflict. Within it we find matters such as apology and forgiveness, respect and revenge, and responsibility and rela-

---

6. Louis I. Newman, *The Baal Shem Tov, in* CREATORS OF THE JEWISH EXPERIENCE IN ANCIENT AND MEDIEVAL TIMES 287, 302 (Simon Noveck ed., 1985).

7. For further discussion, *see* Jonathan R. Cohen, *A Taxonomy of Dispute Resolution Ethics, in* HANDBOOK OF DISPUTE RESOLUTION 244 (Robert Bordone & Michael Moffitt eds., 2005).

tionships. The focus is on the ethics of the parties, not the ethics of the lawyers.

B. Responsibility Taking as the Moral Response to Injury

A foundational question within the realm of disputant ethics is, "What should a person do who injures another?" The answer is so simple that even children know it. The ethical response to injuring another is to take responsibility for what one has done. Usually one should begin by apologizing. Next one should try to make amends, for example, by offering fair compensation to the injured party. Ideally the injurer and the injured will have a direct dialogue through which a remedial plan acceptable to both is established.[8] In short, the injurer should *actively* take responsibility for what he has done. Conflict is not the inevitable result of injury. Where an injurer fails to take responsibility after an injury, conflict is quite likely. Conversely, the ethical path of active responsibility taking by the injurer usually results in relational repair and speedy private settlement. The injurer's choice of whether to take responsibility voluntarily is often simultaneously a choice of whether cooperation or conflict will ensue.

The response where the injurer denies responsibility is, by contrast, an act of moral regression. It compounds the primary injury with a secondary one. Even if the injured party can prevail at trial—and often the injured party cannot, either from lack of evidence or from the skill of the injurer's lawyers— such compensation will be delayed and usually reduced by the cost of the injured's legal fees, commonly one third for a contingency case. Further, in terms of the *injurer's* morality, passive accountability enforced by a court is not an ethical substitute for voluntary, internally-chosen responsibility taking.[9] The former, though certainly necessary where an injurer fails to take responsibility, can hardly be called ethical behavior by the injurer at all, while the latter reflects the true internalization of ethical norms. Note too that the injurer who fails to take responsibility puts himself at serious psychological risk.[10] The guilt of not making amends, even if not consciously recognized,

---

8. There are, of course, circumstances where direct dialogue may be inappropriate, even with a mediator present. *See, e.g.,* Lisa G. Lerman, *Mediation of Wife Abuse Cases: The Adverse Impact of Informal Dispute Resolution on Women,* 7 Harv. Women's L.J. 57 (1983) (arguing mediation is inappropriate where domestic violence exists).

9. *See Immorality, supra* note 2, at 920–23.

10. *See id.* at 933–37.

can be haunting. Also of note is what one might call relational risk.[11] Many injuries occur in the context of prior relationships (e.g., family, business, neighbor, etc.) and until the injurer makes amends it can be impossible for those relationships to go forward. Finally, many also see failing to take responsibility as placing the injurer at spiritual risk. For example, both Christian and Jewish scriptures advise injurers to first make amends with injured parties before seeking Divine forgiveness.[12]

If the ethical response of taking responsibility for injury is so clear, and if failing to follow that response poses significant moral, psychological, relational, and perhaps even spiritual risks to injurers, then why do so many injurers fail to take responsibility? Elsewhere I explore the contribution of our legal system and legal culture to that practice,[13] but let us recognize two factors internal to the injurers themselves: greed and shame.[14] Despite knowing that responsibility taking is the ethical response to injury, many injurers place money before morality. They fear, sometimes rightly and sometimes wrongly, that responsibility taking will be more costly economically than denial, and, consciously or not, overlook their moral obligation for financial reasons. For example, an injurer with solely pecuniary motivations may see denial largely as a no-lose gamble. "If the denial succeeds, I will pay nothing, but if the denial fails I will just have to pay what I would if I took responsibility directly. So why shouldn't I deny?"[15] Yet greed is not the only motivation for denial. Indeed, it may not even be the primary one. Sociopaths aside, most people who commit injuries experience guilt for what they have done, whether consciously or subconsciously. That guilt can readily translate itself into a feeling of internal shame.[16] To take responsibility is to face one's shame squarely—to bring it out in the open. Yet, like the child who lies when caught with his hand

---

11. See id. at 922.

12. In Judaism, see, e.g., MISHNAH YOMA 8: 9 ("For transgressions against God, the Day of Atonement atones, but for transgressions against another human being, the Day of Atonement does not atone until one has made peace with that person."). In Christianity, see, e.g., Matthew 5: 23–24 ("Therefore if thou bring thy gift to the altar, and there rememberest that thy brother hath ought against thee; Leave there thy gift before the altar, and go thy way; first be reconciled to thy brother, and then come and offer thy gift."). For further discussion, see Immorality, supra note 2, at 929–32.

13. Jonathan R. Cohen, The Culture of Legal Denial, 84 NEB. L. REV. 247, at section III (2005) [hereinafter Legal Denial].

14. See Immorality, supra note 2, at 938 (discussing greed), 940 (discussing shame avoidance).

15. For further discussion, see Legal Denial, supra note 13 at section III.A.

16. See Immorality, supra note 2, at 935.

in the cookie jar, many injurers unreflectingly choose to deny. Though such does not provide a basis for moral excuse, their denials and other avoidances reflect a shame-avoidant myopia, the belief that they can avoid facing the shame of their error altogether if only they can avoid facing it now.[17] As Mark Twain's Huckleberry Finn put it, "That's just the way: a person does a low-down thing, and then he don't want to take no consequences of it. Thinks as long as he can hide it, it ain't no disgrace."[18] Sadly such responses usually escalate the conflict and ultimately compound the injurer's sense of shame.

Though it is possible to raise some (largely unsatisfactory, in my view) moral defenses to the approach of denial after injury (e.g., based upon the possibility of generating fairer ultimate settlement outcomes), I will not explore these here.[19] Let me mention, however, two serious and related issues: ambiguity and prematurity. Some may assert that questions of fault, both moral and legal, are typically complex and ambiguous. They may argue that for a person unilaterally to take responsibility prior to full legal proceedings is premature. "Fault is only known after a court has passed its judgment, not before." Elsewhere, I respond to this argument at greater length, but let me make a few basic points here.[20] First, in many instances of injury, fault, in both moral and legal senses, is quite clear to one such as an injurer who knows the facts.[21] We should not let the complexity of some cases lead us into believing that fault is always ambiguous. To assert that a person who injures another should never take responsibility absent full legal proceedings is simply untenable. Many injurers quite rightly assume responsibility of their own initiative day in and day out. Second, where fault is ambiguous, say because of factual or legal ambiguity, possible "injurers" should *not* take responsibility on their own, but, generally speaking, should await a court's determination. Third, where parties know they are at fault in one area but unsure of the extent of their fault in another area,

---

17. *See id.* at 940.

18. *See* 8 THE WORKS OF MARK TWAIN: ADVENTURES OF HUCKLEBERRY FINN 268 (Victor Fischer et al. eds., 2003). Though *Huckleberry Finn* is an American classic, it is also a very problematic work. *See* SHARON RUSH, HUCK FINN'S HIDDEN LESSONS: TEACHING AND LEARNING ACROSS THE COLOR LINE (2006) (arguing teaching *Huckleberry Finn* creates emotional segregation among Black and non-Black children).

19. *See Immorality, supra* note 2, at Part IV.B.

20. *See id.* at Part IV.B.3.

21. Legal and moral fault can of course differ. For example, in American legal ethics discourse, there is a debate dating back to David Hoffman's 19th-century remarks on whether a lawyer should assert a statute of limitations defense to an otherwise just debt. *See* DAVID HOFFMAN, A COURSE OF LEGAL STUDY 754 (2d ed. 1972) (1836).

they should at least take responsibility for the former area. Finally, though a party may not initially be sufficiently aware of facts to properly accept responsibility, when an injury or claim of injury occurs, the putative injurer has some duty of investigation to determine what occurred and should take responsibility, if appropriate, after such ambiguities are resolved.

C. The Typical Pattern of Denial

In contrast to the moral path of active responsibility taking, lawyers commonly lead injurers in the opposite direction: responsibility avoidance. Key to this path are both silence and denial.[22]

Suppose a client who has injured another enters a lawyer's office. What is likely to happen? Soon into the conversation, the client will share his story with the lawyer. The client's account may (less likely) or may not (more likely) include an admission of fault, but it probably will indicate that the injured party has filed or is likely to file a claim. If she has not done so already, usually the lawyer will instruct the client to cease communicating with the other party. "It is best to let me do the talking. Anything you say to the other side can be used against you in court. You can talk with me, and you can talk with your spouse if you want, for those conversations are protected by legal privileges. By the way, be careful even when speaking with friends. They can be subpoenaed and made to testify to your conversations."

The message that injurers should refrain from communicating about the case and only speak, if at all, after the lawyer grants permission is so well known that many clients internalize it before they see their lawyer. As a sheriff who was removed from office for public drunkenness said to the press in explaining his refusal to comment on his case, "I'm seeing an attorney (today), and as soon as he tells me [what] I need to say, then I can talk to you."[23] A similar theme is found in instructions sent by some insurance companies to their insured motorists instructing them not to apologize if they are in an ac-

---

22. Twenty five years ago, William Felstiner et al. famously described the injured party's steps toward litigation as "naming, blaming, and claiming." *See* William Felstiner et al., *The Emergence and Transformation of Disputes: Naming, Blaming, Claiming…*, 15 LAW & SOC'Y REV. 631 (1980–81). By way of parallel, the injurer's steps toward litigation might be described as "injuring, avoiding, and denying." Perhaps empirical research will someday be conducted on this latter topic assessing the frequency at which each stage is reached akin to Felstiner et al.'s earlier research.

23. Karen Voyles, *Lafayette Sheriff Is Relieved from Duty*, GAINESVILLE SUN, Aug. 22, 2002, at A1.

cident.[24] Perhaps most basically the public learns this lesson through the celebrated *Miranda* warnings in the criminal context. "You have the right to remain silent. Anything you say can and will be used against you in a court of law. You have the right to speak to an attorney, and to have an attorney present during any questioning."[25] The lesson is simple: statements made to the other side could be used against you in court, so remain silent and let your lawyer do the talking.

If the lawyer does start speaking for the client, that pattern of silence is likely to continue, if not grow into outright denial. Should the lawyer speak with the other party, it is extremely unlikely that she will admit her client's fault.[26] An exception helps prove the rule here. In 1987, the Veterans Affair Medical Center in Lexington, Kentucky ("Lexington VA") switched from the widespread "deny and defend" approach of responding to medical errors[27] to an approach of responsibility taking.[28] This involved admitting fault, apologizing, and offering fair compensation.[29] Although the responsibility-taking approach to medical error has since grown markedly[30]—in part because this moral response has proved financially viable[31]—when the Lexington VA implemented that approach, most lawyers who learned of it were highly skeptical. As hospital attorney Ginny Hamm stated, "The attorneys around here in

---

24. *See* Jonathan R. Cohen, *Advising Clients to Apologize*, 72 S. CAL. L. REV. 1009, 1012–13 n.9 (1999) [hereinafter *Advising Clients*].

25. There is no single form to the *Miranda* warnings mandated by constitutional law. The quotation above is among the most common and simple language.

26. Throughout this chapter, for literary convenience, I use masculine terms to describe the client and feminine terms to describe the lawyer. No gender implications are intended.

27. *See* Rachel Zimmerman, *Doctors' New Tool to Fight Lawsuits: Saying 'I'm Sorry'*, WALL ST. J., May 18, 2004, at A1 (describing "deny and defend" as the traditional approach to responding to medical errors). *See also* Marianne D. Mattera, *Memo From the Editor: Better to Beg Forgiveness?*, MED. ECON., June 4, 2004, at 5 ("[I]t's long been a tenet of liability insurers that you never admit a mistake or apologize for a mishap, lest it come back to bite you in court.").

28. Jonathan R. Cohen, *Apology and Organizations: Exploring an Example from Medical Practice*, 27 FORDHAM URB. L.J. 1447, 1451 (2000) [hereinafter *Apology and Organizations*].

29. *Id.* at 1452–53.

30. *See* Zimmerman, *supra* note 27 (discussing the growth of apology in medical practice); Jonathan R. Cohen, *Toward Candor after Medical Error: The First Apology Law*, 5 HARV. HEALTH POL. REV. 21 (2004) (discussing the rise of new laws to exclude medical apologies from admissibility into evidence) [hereinafter *Toward Candor*].

31. *See Apology and Organizations*, *supra* note 28, at 1453–54; Zimmerman, *supra* note 27.

Lexington [thought] we were *crazy*."[32] The moral response to injury is commonly viewed by the legal community as bizarre.

And how will the lawyer respond if the other side files a complaint? Typically the response will be denial, or at least the denial of everything that arguably can be denied.[33] The lawyer will admit to facts both inconsequential and indisputable. Matters of consequence, however, are likely to be disputed. Notwithstanding that (a) modern federal civil pleading practice takes a liberal attitude toward discovery[34] and permits a general denial only where the defendant "intends in good faith to controvert all the averments" of the plaintiff's complaint;[35] (b) Rule 36 provides that a party's denial in response to a request for admission must "fairly meet the substance of the requested admission;"[36] and (c) the unwarranted denial of a factual contention is an explicitly enumerated basis for Rule 11 sanctions,[37] the reality in practice still has a strong residue of general denials and demands of strict proof. As attorney Dmitry Feofanov writes:

> Every lawyer (including myself) has been told by his or her mentors that the "right way" to respond to certain allegations in a complaint is as follows: if the complaint alleges that a document says so-and-so, respond, "the document speaks for itself." If the complaint alleges that venue is proper, respond, "calls for legal conclusion." Add, "to the extent there remain any factual allegations, they are denied." If an allegation cannot be denied, ask for "strict proof."[38]

---

32. *Apology and Organizations*, *supra* note 28, at 1449 (emphasis added) (quoting Lexington VA attorney Ginny Hamm, who served both as the hospital's counsel and as a member of its risk management committee).

33. A similar approach holds in depositions, where witnesses are coached to say no more than they must.

34. *See* Fed. R. Civ. P. 26(b)(1) ("Parties may obtain discovery regarding any matter, not privileged, that is relevant to the claim or defense of any party....").

35. Fed. R. Civ. P. 8(b).

36. Fed. R. Civ. P. 36(a).

37. Fed. R. Civ. P. 11(b)(4).

38. Dmitry N. Feofanov, *Of Speaking Documents and Talking Clams: A Proper Answer Under Federal and State Rules*, DCBA Brief Online (Journal of the DuPage County Bar Ass'n) (Nov. 2002), *at* http://www.dcba.org/brief/novissue/2002/art21102.htm (last visited Aug. 5, 2005). *See also* David J. Luban, *The Ethics of Wrongful Obedience, in* Ethics in Practice: Lawyers' Roles, Responsibilities, and Regulation 94 (Deborah L. Rhode ed., 2000).

> Every litigation associate goes through a rite of passage: she finds a document that seemingly lies squarely within the scope of a legitimate discovery request, but her supervisor tells her to devise an argument for excluding it. As long as the argument isn't frivolous there is nothing improper about this, but it marks the

Why do lawyers do this? The strategic rationale may be summarized in one word—caution.[39] "We can always admit something later, but if we admit it now, there is no going back. Let's take some time to see what develops and be sure we are on top of the facts." The defense lawyer might add a further point. "If we don't deny, the rules state that we will be taken as having admitted everything the plaintiff asserts.[40] Once a complaint has been filed (and it's almost always written in plaintiff-biased language), we cannot be neutral. Silence is not really an option, for if we simply say nothing, that has the effect of an admission. Despite initial appearances, the rules are actually cast in favor of our denying."

So normalized is the denial modality that, should a settlement be reached, even in cases where, realistically speaking, all the parties recognize the fact of the injurer's wrongdoing, a usual term in the settlement will be a disclaimer of any wrongdoing by the injurer. Coca-Cola's recent settlement of racial discrimination claims is illustrative. Under the settlement, the largest such settlement in U.S. history, Coca-Cola agreed to pay $156 million, but admitted no fault.[41] Assuming, *arguendo*, Coca-Cola actually was at least in part at fault, what would have been so wrong if, when reaching the settlement, Coca-Cola had admitted its fault?[42] Some may contend that Coca Cola is unusual, that it had concerns about negative publicity and suits by parties who did not join the settlement. But in essence it is not. The usual civil settlement is of a no-fault form: the injurer pays money, the injured releases the injurer from all present and future claims, and the injurer admits no fault. But why should not the injurer (verbally) acknowledge fault along with the payment? Some claim that, "The payment is the acknowledgment of fault." Such a statement simply re-

---

first step onto the slippery slope. For better or for worse, a certain kind of innocence is lost. It is the moment when withholding information despite an adversary's legitimate request starts to feel like zealous advocacy rather than deception. *Id.* at 106.

39. Observe, however, that risks attach to *both* admitting responsibility (e.g., one's admission being used against one in court) and denying responsibility (e.g., relational damage from denial may lead to an escalation of hostilities).

40. *See* Fed. R. Civ. P. 8(d) ("Effect of Failure to Deny. Averments in a pleading to which a responsive pleading is required ... are admitted when not denied in the responsive pleading.").

41. *See* Greg Winter, *Coca-Cola Settles Racial Bias Case*, N.Y. Times, Nov. 17, 2000, at A1.

42. For further discussion and examples, *see* Jonathan R. Cohen, *Legislating Apology: The Pros and Cons*, 70 U. Cin. L. Rev. 819, 854–55 (2002).

flects how socially-entrenched the pattern of denial is. How strange it is that the verbal admission of fault is often harder to extract than a payment.

Query too whether the courts should rubber-stamp such settlements that are predicated on fault avoidance. On the one hand, such settlements may foster private dispute resolution and docket clearing, and may also avoid the efforts that might need to be expended to determine and describe the extent of fault. On the other hand, such settlements may have an anti-therapeutic, "band-aid" effect, helping the injurer to patch over but never fully address the roots of the injury, thereby increasing the likelihood of re-injury.[43] Further, and perhaps most fundamentally, is the issue of the linkage between our courts and truth. Unlike purely private settlements, many settlements to court cases become court orders. The imprimatur of the courts is upon them. Our courts articulate the pursuit of truth and justice as central ideals. It seems plausible that our courts may have an interest in not lending their name and power to settlements with significant components of nondisclosure if not falsity.

1. Denial Reinforcement, Fault Projection, and Conflict Escalation

The lawyer's denials are likely to produce several negative consequences. Three of the most salient are reinforcing the injurer's denial, projecting fault on the injured party, and overall conflict escalation.

The external story of denial the lawyer pens will likely serve to reinforce any internal sense of denial the injurer may have. Parties in conflict commonly have fairly strong, self-serving cognitive biases.[44] Further, whether or not the story is true, by writing the story one is led to believe it.[45] Thus, the external act of legal denial may promote an internal psychological denial by the client. The story advanced in the written legal denial may become a piece of the mask the client uses to prevent himself from squarely facing his acts.[46] Further, in

---

43. For an argument against allowing criminal *nolo contendere* and *Alford* pleas in which fault is also not admitted based on such anti-therapeutic effects, see Stephanos Bibas, *Harmonizing Substantive-Criminal-Law Values and Criminal Procedure: The Case of Alford and Nolo Contendere Pleas*, 88 CORNELL L. REV. 1361 (2003).

44. For references, see Chris Guthrie, *Framing Frivolous Litigation: A Psychological Theory*, 67 U. CHI. L. REV. 163, 206 n.199 (2000).

45. *See, e.g.*, E. Tory Higgins & William S. Rholes, *"Saying Is Believing": Effects of Message Modification on Memory and Liking for the Person Described*, 14 J. EXPERIMENTAL SOC. PSYCHOL. 363 (1978).

46. On such legal masking of persons, see generally JOHN T. NOONAN, PERSONS AND MASKS OF THE LAW: CARDOZO, HOLMES, JEFFERSON, AND WHYTHE AS MAKERS OF THE MASKS (1976); Walter O. Weyrauch, *Law as Mask: Legal Ritual and Relevance*, 66 CAL. L. REV. 699 (1978).

many cases, a denial-based collusion of sorts may arise between the client and the lawyer. "I the client want to believe a narrative proclaiming my innocence that you the lawyer will help write. Moreover, I am concerned that if I tell you the truth—that I was at fault—you will not fight for me as vigorously." "I the lawyer do not want to know everything that you have done, for I want to write a narrative proclaiming your innocence, and not only may my ignorance be of strategic benefit at trial,[47] but it is easier for me (e.g., there is less cognitive dissonance and value conflict for me) if I think you are innocent, or at least do not know you are guilty."

Psychologists often speak of the linkage between denial and projection. Projection is a process of unconsciously attributing to the other person characteristics of oneself that one denies to oneself. Like slave-owners who saw slaves rather than themselves as "lazy," or invading "settlers" displacing natives they saw as "nomadic," the very faults one refuses to recognize in oneself one may project onto others.[48] A somewhat analogous process takes place in many legal disputes, though now the denial and projection are conscious processes.

Suppose an accident has occurred through the injurer's negligence. How is the accident to be explained? If the injurer denies that he was at fault for the accident, then he must assert that someone or something else caused the accident.[49] And who is to become the most likely target of such projection? None other than the injured party. "If I did not cause the accident, you must have,"

---

47. The allusion here is that the lawyer's willful or contrived ignorance might benefit the client by in essence helping the client or his witnesses commit perjury at trial. *See, e.g.,* MODEL RULES OF PROF'L CONDUCT R. 3.3(a)(3) (2003):

> A lawyer shall not knowingly offer evidence ... that the lawyer knows to be false. If a lawyer, the lawyer's client, or a witness called by the lawyer, has offered material evidence and the lawyer comes to know its falsity, the lawyer shall take reasonable remedial measures, including, if necessary, disclosure to the tribunal.

On such contrived ignorance, see David Luban, *The Social Responsibilities of Lawyers: A Green Perspective,* 63 GEO. WASH. L. REV. 955, 980–81 (1995).

48. *See* Albert Memmi, *Mythical Portrait of the Colonized, in* THE COLONIZER AND THE COLONIZED 79, 79–89 (1991).

49. Implicit here is the binary conception of fault common within much legal thinking, critiqued long ago by John Coons in his call for the apportionment of responsibility. *See* John E. Coons, *Approaches to Court-Imposed Compromise—The Uses of Doubt and Reason,* 58 Nw. U. L. REV. 750 (1964). For further discussion and references, see Carrie Menkel-Meadow, *From Legal Disputes to Conflict Resolution and Human Problem Solving: Legal Dispute Resolution in a Multidisciplinary Context,* 54 J. LEGAL EDUC. 7, 20–21 (2004). Though I will not explore it here, I would note as well the possibility that responsibility need not be divided solely among the parties (so their shares of responsibility sum to one), but that richer understandings of causality that recognize the role of circumstance (e.g., "It was just

the injurer decides.[50] Perhaps the injurer will go so far as to file a counterclaim. From the injured party's perspective, the situation is quite remarkable: "You injure me, and not only don't you compensate me, but you have the gall to claim that I have injured you!"

As should be clear, the injurer's choice of whether to take or deny responsibility strongly influences the course the dispute will take. The injurer's response is often a crossroads or tipping point for the subsequent encounter.[51] Accepting responsibility usually yields swift settlement, while denying or failing to take responsibility usually produces conflict escalation. Recall that many injuries occur by accident. The injurer had no intention of committing harm. The decision not to take responsibility, by contrast, is usually far from accidental. Had the injurer accepted responsibility, including offering compensation, the injured party may have forgiven, at least in the sense of reducing anger. But where the injurer denies or fails to take responsibility, hostilities usually grow.

2. Lawyers Benefit from Conflict Escalation

Are the economics of lawyering an important driver of the practice of denial? Unlike the plaintiff lawyer who works on a contingency fee, most defense lawyers earn their livelihood from the process of litigation. As a litigation partner who represented corporate defendants at a law firm where I once worked joked (I paraphrase), "Our good clients come to us ahead of time seeking advice about how to avoid a lawsuit. But our best clients come to us after the fact."

I am not asserting that most defense lawyers consciously decide against counseling responsibility taking at the outset of the case based on economic self-interest. Most are aware of the professional requirement to put their clients' interests before their own and would not, I suspect, consciously do otherwise. Yet the obliviousness of many defense lawyers to the possibility of discussing responsibility taking with their clients does work to the lawyer's economic benefit. Not only might the defense lawyer's legal fees for the instant case be reduced if it settles rapidly, but her reputation as a "tough litigator," critical for attracting future clients, may be damaged. If one-third of

---

an accident. No one was a fault.") may also be possible. For a brief discussion, see *Apology and Organizations, supra* note 28, at 1462.

50. *See* ROBERT M. BASTRESS & JOSEPH D. HARBAUGH, INTERVIEWING, COUNSELING, AND NEGOTIATING: SKILLS FOR EFFECTIVE REPRESENTATION 280 (1990) ("A typical problem arises from the client's inclination to blame other for the consequences of his or her own conduct.").

51. *See* THOMAS C. SCHELLING, MICROMOTIVES AND MACROBEHAVIOR 99–110 (1978).

an apology had monetary value, I suspect many more plaintiffs' lawyers would seek apologies.[52] If advising responsibility taking increased a defense lawyer's billable hours, I suspect many more would talk about that path with clients.[53]

3. Some Objections

Can the typical practice of failing to consider talking with injurers about responsibility taking be defended? Usually that practice is done automatically, so possible justifications are never offered. In a previous work, I suggested and largely rejected one possible justification—that ultimately fairer results could occur when the injurer denies responsibility.[54] Here I consider, and largely reject, several other possible responses. These are: (1) that denial is permitted if not required by the ethics of zealous advocacy; (2) that lawyers already do discuss responsibility taking with clients; (3) that the lawyer cannot simply know whether the client is guilty-in-fact or innocent-in-fact, and given that ambiguity, the safe route is to assume the latter; and (4) that if the lawyer raises the possibility of responsibility taking with the client, the lawyer risks alienating the client. While I largely reject these possible responses, I believe much can be learned from their consideration.

a. The Defense of Zealous Advocacy

A first response for many lawyers is to seek refuge in the ethics of zealous advocacy. "Who are you to suggest that I defend clients out of personal greed, putting my interest before theirs? Did you learn nothing of legal ethics? I am duty bound to be a zealous advocate for my client. To do anything less than

---

52. *See Advising Clients, supra* note 24, at 1045.

53. Though I suspect counseling responsibility taking will generally work against a defense lawyer's economic interests, countervailing factors may exist. First, the lawyer may offset some of the billable hours she loses litigating with increased billable hours spent in client counseling, for, as discussed below, effectively counseling responsibility taking often takes some time. Second is the possibility that the lawyer, like some collaborative lawyers, may increase her client base by developing a reputation as a wise counselor. Though fees per client may decrease, the overall number of clients may rise.

54. *See Immorality, supra* note 2, at Part IV.B.2. The claim against responsibility taking runs roughly as follows. If split-the-difference forces drive settlement outcomes, then an initial denial of fault by the injurer could ultimately lead to a fairer result than an initial acceptance of fault. Note, however, FED. R. CIV. P. 68: If an offer of settlement is made and rejected and if "the judgment finally obtained by the offeree is not more favorable than the offer, the offeree must pay the costs incurred after the making of the offer." This provides a strong incentive for a plaintiff who receives a fair offer to accept it, and for the defendant who makes a fair offer to stick to it.

fighting with all my efforts on behalf of my client would be shirking my professional duty." They might invoke Lord Brougham's famous call toward thick-skinned battle,[55] or may turn to the words of the adversary system's greatest modern defender, Monroe Freedman:

> In the adversary system, it is not the role or function of the advocate to act upon conclusions of ultimate facts such as guilt or innocence. That function is assigned to the judge or jury, which bases its decision on the adversaries' presentation of their clients' cases. Thus, the fact of guilt or innocence is irrelevant to the role that has been assigned to the advocate.[56]

The vision of the lawyer as a zealous advocate, fighting relentlessly on behalf of her client, is a powerful one.[57] The problem, however, is in what one might call the *advocacy bias* in legal representation, that is, in reducing the lawyer's entire role to that of a partisan combatant in litigation.[58] Observe that my goal in this chapter is not to enter the longstanding debate about whether

---

55. Lord Brougham stated,

An advocate, in the discharge of his duty, knows but one person in all the world, and that person is his client. To save that client by all means and expedients, and at all hazards and costs to other persons, and, among them, to himself, is his first and only duty; and in performing this duty he must not regard the alarm, the torments, the destruction which he may bring upon others.

2 Trial of Queen Caroline 3 (James Cockroft & Co. 1874).

56. Monroe Freedman, Lawyers' Ethics in an Adversary System 57 (1975).

57. *See, e.g.,* Model Code of Prof'l Responsibility Canon 7 (1983) ("A Lawyer Should Represent a Client Zealously Within the Bounds of the Law"); EC 7-1 ("The duty of a lawyer, both to his client and to the legal system, is to represent his client zealously within the bounds of the law...").

58. *See generally* Murray L. Schwartz, *The Professionalism and Accountability of Lawyers*, 66 Cal. L. Rev. 669 (1978) (arguing for differentiated legal ethics standards for different tasks); Carrie Menkel-Meadow, *Ethics in Alternative Dispute Resolution: New Issues, No Answers from the Adversary Conception of Lawyers' Responsibilities*, 38 S. Tex. L. Rev. 407 (1997) (similar). Observe too that Lord Brougham began his statement with the important qualification, "[a]n advocate," not "a lawyer" or "an attorney." *See supra* note 55. It may be helpful to recall here the British division between solicitors, who focus significantly on legal counseling, and barristers who argue in court. The American approach of merging these two functions into a single professional, the lawyer, yields problems (though of course some benefits too), for ethical norms (e.g., of partisanship and zeal) perhaps appropriate for debate in court carry poorly to other areas. Roughly put, this chapter concerns the mistake of unreflectingly carrying the lawyer-as-barrister's approach of denial to the role of the lawyer-as-solicitor.

and how a lawyer should *advocate* for guilty clients,[59] but, roughly put, to explore how lawyers should *counsel* guilty clients.[60] Lawyers serve their clients not only as advocates, but also as counselors. The Comment to Model Rule 1.3 articulates this often overlooked distinction well: "A lawyer must also act with commitment and dedication to the interests of the client and with zeal in advocacy on the client's behalf." The lawyer's ethical duty, in other words, is not zealous advocacy *per se* but acting "in a manner consistent with the best interests of his client."[61] Zealous advocacy is a means or technique, but not an end. As a first approximation (for lawyers of course have other duties as well), the client's best interests are the general end of legal representation.

Recognizing that the lawyer should act in the best interests of the client implicates two fundamental questions: (1) what are the client's best interests, and (2) what technique or approach will best serve those interests? In response to the first question, most civil defense lawyers presume that the client's "best interests" means the client's best *financial* or *pecuniary* interests.[62] But why should that presumption be made? Do not clients have moral, psychological, relational, and spiritual interests as well? Failing to pay compensation for an injury one has caused can be financially beneficial, but it can be harmful to the injurer in these other ways. How can the lawyer know *a priori* which outweighs which? She cannot. The common practice of automatically reducing the client's "best interests" to "best financial interests" is error.

A second common error is assuming that, even if a client's ends are purely financial, the most effective strategy for pursuing them is a combative one. Even from the pecuniary viewpoint, compromise can sometimes be more effective than combat. The experience of the Toro Corporation ("Toro"), a manufacturer of lawn care products, is telling. For years, Toro responded with an aggressive "litigate everything" strategy to the roughly 125 annual personal in-

---

59. In American discourse, that debate begins with 19th-century Hoffman-Sharwood dialogues. For a description and references, see Thomas L. Shaffer, *The Problem of Representing the Guilty, in* ON BEING A CHRISTIAN AND LAWYER 57, 57–69 (1981). It has continued with the many modern discussions of the ethics of zealous advocacy. For references, see *Immorality, supra* note 2, at 907 n.11.

60. For two fine works in this vein, see Thomas L. Shaffer, *The Problem of Ministry to the Guilty, in* ON BEING A CHRISTIAN AND LAWYER, *supra* note 59, at 71, 71–79 (1981); Cochran, *supra* note 5.

61. MODEL CODE OF PROF'L RESPONSIBILITY EC 7–9 (1983).

62. For a critique, see Carrie Menkel-Meadow, *Portia in a Different Voice: Speculations on a Women's Lawyering Process*, 1 BERKELEY WOMEN'S L.J. 39, 57 (1985). Similarly, most criminal defense lawyers presume "best interests" means minimum time in jail.

jury claims arising from the use of its products.[63] In 1991, amidst (like the Lexington VA) much skepticism from the Bar, Toro switched to a conciliatory mode of response, seeking to mediate cases and making what it saw as fair offers of compensation in mediation. Following this change, Toro's average total cost per claim fell from $115,620 to $30,617. By 1999, Toro had saved over $75 million by switching from a combative to a conciliatory approach.

b. Counseling Clients About Such Matters Already Occurs

Another response is not to fight the criticism that lawyers should think about discussing responsibility taking with clients, but to suggest that they already do. This argument may branch in one of three directions.

A first branch stresses the strategic benefits of conceding adverse facts at trial. Some attorneys may reason, "Surely a good lawyer needs to know the weaknesses of her client's case. It is better to present damaging facts to the jury on direct examination than to have them brought out on cross examination. Even if her concern is only strategy, the lawyer who ignores the weaknesses of her client's case is foolhardy." Though I accept the innoculatory efficacy of disclosing weaknesses at trial, a trial strategy of conceding weaknesses is very different from a philosophy of actively accepting responsibility. As discussed, the passive accountability a trial can produce by no means fully substitutes for active responsibility taking. For example, if the injured party lacks sufficient evidence to prove its burden, morality still calls for the injurer to actively take responsibility. A rationale of strategic concession, by contrast, would suggest the injurer remain silent at trial for disclosure would be strategically disadvantageous.

A second branch of justification points to the general importance of moral counseling in legal representation. This idea is reflected, for example, in calls within both the *Model Rules* and *Model Code* for lawyers to discuss moral dimensions of cases with clients.[64] In so far as it goes, such a view is accurate — discussing moral matters with clients is undoubtedly a proper part of legal representation. The problem with this justification is that, with rare exception, this particular moral matter, which is among the most significant moral

---

63. For more details about Toro, see *Apology and Organizations, supra* note 28, at 1460–61.

64. *See* MODEL RULES OF PROF'L CONDUCT R. 2.1 (2003) ("In representing a client, a lawyer shall exercise independent professional judgment and render candid advice. In rendering advice, a lawyer may refer not only to law but to other considerations such as moral, economic, social and political factors, that may be relevant to the client's situation."); MODEL CODE OF PROF'L RESPONSIBILITY EC 7–8 (1983) (similar).

matters in legal representation, is usually not discussed explicitly. Further, discussing responsibility taking with clients can be quite different from discussing many other moral considerations. Consider, by contrast, a fine example offered by Shaffer and Cochran. They ask how a lawyer should counsel a residential property owner who is considering raising legal objections to a proposed zoning change that would permit a nearby residence to be turned into a group home for developmentally challenged men, thus possibly harming property values in the neighborhood.[65] There are, no doubt, important ethical considerations at stake, considerations the lawyer might properly raise with the client. Yet such a client is likely to be relatively comfortable talking about such ethical matters, for any mistakes he might make are prospective in nature. The person who has injured another, by contrast, is likely to feel ashamed about what he has already done, making a moral dialogue with the client far more challenging.[66]

A third branch of justification suggests that lawyers already do talk with clients about responsibility taking. Some may argue, "One should not be overly cynical or simplistic. Lawyers are not mindless hired guns. They are counselors too. As counselors, they often help clients face issues that are difficult for those clients to face. While lawyers may not often use the term 'responsibility taking,' it is wrong to suggest that lawyers never talk with clients about having to face matters clients would rather avoid."

If it is true that lawyers commonly discuss or even think about discussing responsibility taking with clients, then I will happily pack up my bags and go home. At this point in time, however, I do not think this is the case. Like the criminal law presumption of "innocent until proven guilty," the normal mode of civil defense is to deny.[67] (The very word "defendant" is suggestive of this: the defendant *defends* against the charge.) Lawyers who impress upon clients adverse facts commonly do so late in the dispute, often with the goal of "soften-

---

65. Thomas L. Shaffer & Robert F. Cochran, Jr., Lawyers, Clients, and Moral Responsibility 116–34 (1994).

66. See David A. Binder & Susan C. Price, Legal Interviewing and Counseling: A Client-Centered Approach 10–11 (1977) (identifying the client's shame about mistake, which they label the "ego threat," as a primary barrier to full disclosure by the client to the lawyer).

67. Some may ask whether empirical data exists showing the frequency with which lawyers discuss responsibility taking with clients. To my knowledge, such data does not exist. (Such counseling occurs, of course, in private lawyer-client interactions.) However, from both conversations with numerous lawyers and many anecdotal accounts (e.g., the Bar's reaction to the Lexington VA's approach), I think it fair to say that the normal approach to civil defense is denial.

ing" their own client about the possibility of settlement.[68] Further, the perspective underlying such conversations tends to remain that of liability minimization.

c. The Lawyer's Epistemological Demurrer

A third line of response focuses on the lawyer's lack of knowledge. "When a client enters my office, he does not come with a label of 'innocent' or 'guilty' attached. One only knows these things after trial, not before. Further, even if the client does remember the facts accurately—and often they do not—many, especially the 'guilty' ones, are less than candid with me about what happened. The terminology of 'injurer' you use simply is not helpful. What I have are clients, and I cannot know which are 'injurers' and which are not.[69] How then can I speak with them of responsibility taking?"

Such reasoning, called by Deborah Rhode the lawyer's "epistemological demurrer," is often offered to justify the lawyer's partisanship.[70] Though this excuse *qua* justification may be critiqued in a variety of ways, it contains an important element of truth. In many cases, the proposition is true that the lawyer does not know whether her client is innocent-in-fact or guilty-in-fact.

The flaw in the argument, however, is in moving from this proposition to the conclusion that the lawyer should not discuss responsibility taking with clients. First, often lawyers do know or can determine with confidence the merits of their client's claims.[71] Second, and more fundamentally, a lawyer need not know with certainty whether the client is innocent-in-fact or guilty-in-fact to consider discussing responsibility taking with the client. When it comes to responsibility taking, the critical issue is not what the lawyer knows to be true

---

68. *See also infra* Part D.2.b. (discussing lawyers use of mediation to indirectly break bad news to clients).

69. As Paul Tremblay states, "[I]n law offices, clients and client agents do not present unambiguous stories of injustice, corruption, or unconscionability. Well, maybe they do, but it is always *the other side* who fits that description." Robert F. Cochran, Jr., et al., *Symposium: Client Counseling and Moral Responsibility*, 30 PEPP. L. REV. 591, 621 (2003).

70. *See* Deborah L. Rhode, *Ethical Perspectives on Legal Practice*, 37 STAN. L. REV. 589, 618–20 (1985).

71. Such views are common. *See, e.g.,* FREEDMAN, *supra* note 56, at 53; Marvin E. Frankel, *The Search for Truth: An Umpireal View*, 123 U. PA. L. REV. 1031, 1039 (1975); Rhode, *supra* note 70, at 619. One of the leading models of ethical lawyering even rests in part on this view. *See* William H. Simon, *Ethical Discretion in Lawyering*, 101 HARV. L. REV. 1083, 1089–90 (1988) ("[T]he central thrust of the approach defended in this essay is to insist that the [lawyer's] decision[s] should often turn on 'the underlying merits.'"); WILLIAM H. SIMON, THE PRACTICE OF JUSTICE: A THEORY OF LAWYERS' ETHICS 9 (1978).

but rather what the client knows to be true. To use an analogy, many great sports coaches are not themselves great athletes. Rather, what great coaches know best is how to *assist* athletes. So too legal counselors do not usually know all that their clients know. Indeed, many clients, especially those who have committed injuries, are reticent. Yet the challenge of providing legal counseling that assists the client in making the best choices for himself still remains. Even if she does not know with certainty that the reticent client is guilty-in-fact, a good lawyer might help the client who does know with certainty that he is guilty-in-fact think about the possibility of responsibility taking.

d. Client Alienation

Though in its specifics it may take numerous forms, a fourth justification of the defense lawyer's usual approach focuses on the risk of client alienation. "Many clients come to me precisely with the expectation that I will help them deny. If they wanted someone to tell them to take responsibility, they would have gone to a minister or psychologist. If I raise responsibility taking with them, I will alienate them, and if I alienate them, I can no longer serve them. If I raise responsibility taking with them, they will see me as judgmental, paternalistic and maybe even disloyal. Further, who am I to substitute my morality for theirs? While it may be true that there are examples like Toro where responsibility taking saves the client money, surely that is not the norm. If it were the norm, many more clients would take responsibility out of self-interest. The fact that clients so often choose to deny indicates that many expect that more is to be gained than lost financially by denying.[72] And if this is what the client wants—if what the client cares about is money—who am I to second guess him? It is not my job to be holier-than-thou and substitute my morals for the client's. I am there to serve the client, not to judge him. That is for the judge and jury."

In the ensuing section, I address the question of how to lessen the risk of client alienation when discussing responsibility taking, for, particularly if done poorly, the risk of client alienation is substantial. Let me first respond briefly to the charge that to discuss responsibility taking with clients is to impose the lawyer's morality upon the client. I do not suggest that a lawyer should substitute her moral values for her client's. The rules of legal ethics are clear, and in my view right, that it is for the client to determine the ultimate ends of legal representation, and that the lawyer who feels unable to abide by her client's

---

72. See *Legal Denial, supra* note 13, at section III.A.

ends should seek to resign.[73] Observe too that I have *not* argued here (though probably such arguments can be made) from what one might label the public or social perspective that the lawyer should discuss responsibility taking with the client so as to produce more just outcomes.[74] Nor do I dispute the claim that under our current legal system denial is often best for the injurer economically. Rather my argument is that lawyers should not *assume* that clients have solely economic interests. A default presumption should not be set focusing solely on the client's economic interests and ignoring the client's possible moral, psychological, relational, and spiritual interests. Indeed, no default presumption should be set at all. If it is for the client and not the lawyer to determine the ultimate ends of legal representation, then the lawyer must speak with the client and explore what those ends are. The lawyer must learn, rather than presume, the client's interests.

---

73. *See, e.g.,* MODEL RULES OF PROF'L CONDUCT R. 1.2(a) (2003) ("A lawyer shall abide by a client's decisions concerning the objectives of representation....); R. 1.16(b)(4) (2003) ("[A] lawyer may withdraw from representing a client if ... the client insists upon taking action ... with which the lawyer has a fundamental disagreement...."). Some may ask whether the lawyer's decision to seek to resign (I write "seek" as in adjudicatory matters withdrawal can require the leave of the court) should be more than a matter of personal preference but rather one of professional obligation. Suppose, for example, that after discussing responsibility taking with a client who the lawyer is convinced is at fault (e.g., because the client has admitted his fault to the lawyer), the civil client nevertheless insists on denial. Can the argument be made that the lawyer should be under a professional duty to withdraw (e.g., that the legal profession should not be complicit in wrongful denial) or otherwise modify her approach to legal representation? Such an argument would be antithetical, of course, to the traditional understanding of zealous advocacy, and such a rule, if adopted, could significantly impede lawyer-client communication. Yet perhaps the case can be made. For related discussions, see SIMON, *supra* note 71; LUBAN, *supra* note 47.

Observe too that for the lawyer who believes her client is at fault, how she assists that client in denial in litigation while simultaneously complying with the rules of procedure is far from apparent. *See* Fed. R. Civ. P. 11(b):

> By presenting to the court (whether by signing, filing, submitting, or later advocating) a pleading, written motion, or other paper, an attorney ... is certifying that to the best of the [attorney's] knowledge, information, and belief, formed after an inquiry reasonable under the circumstances ... (2) the claims, defenses, and other legal contentions therein are warranted by existing law or by a nonfrivolous argument for the extension, modification, or reversal of existing law or the establishment of new law; ... (4) the denials of factual contentions are warranted on the evidence or, if specifically so identified, are reasonably based on a lack of information or belief.

74. For such approaches to legal ethics, see, *e.g.,* Robert W. Gordon, *The Independence of Lawyers,* 68 B.U. L. REV. 1 (1988); ANTHONY T. KRONMAN, THE LOST LAWYER: FAILING IDEALS OF THE LEGAL PROFESSION (1993).

The description of legal counseling within Ethical Consideration 7-8 of the *Model Code* captures well the approach envisioned here:

> A lawyer should exert his best efforts to insure that decisions of his client are made only after the client has been informed of relevant considerations. A lawyer ought to initiate this decision-making process if the client does not do so. Advice of a lawyer to a client need not be confined to purely legal considerations. A lawyer should advise his client of the possible effect of each legal alternative. A lawyer should bring to bear upon this decision-making process the fullness of his experience as well as his objective viewpoint. In assisting his client to reach a proper decision, it is often desirable for a lawyer to point out those factors which may lead to a decision that is morally just as well as legally permissible. He may emphasize the possibility of harsh consequences that might result from assertion of legally permissible positions. In the final analysis, however, the lawyer should always remember that the decision whether to forego legally available objectives or methods because of non-legal factors is ultimately for the client and not for himself. In the event that the client in a non-adjudicatory matter insists upon a course of conduct that is contrary to the judgment and advice of the lawyer but not prohibited by Disciplinary Rules, the lawyer may withdraw from the employment.[75]

When it comes to responsibility taking, the first two sentences of the paragraph above are particularly telling. A lawyer should exert his best efforts to insure that decisions of his client are made only after the client has been informed of relevant considerations. A lawyer ought to initiate this decision-making process. For most injurers, the decision of whether to take or deny responsibility is the most fundamental ethical choice they will make, or will have made for them, during litigation. It is laced with moral, psychological, relational, and economic considerations—considerations which can often point in different directions. If there are to be any areas where the lawyer helps the client think seriously about the implications of his decisions, surely this should be one of them.

D. Counseling Responsibility Taking

Often the lawyer either knows or suspects that her client is at fault for what occurred. In some cases, this occurs during the initial client interview. In other

---

75. MODEL CODE OF PROF'L RESPONSIBILITY EC 7–8 (1983).

cases, the lawyer develops this sense over time based on what the client has said, what the client has not said, or information garnered from sources other than the client. Whatever the source, how is the lawyer to raise the question of responsibility taking without alienating the client?

Before answering the question, two preliminary comments to frame the discussion may be of help. First, I mentioned earlier by way of a hypothesized defense of denial the idea that some clients seek lawyers precisely because they want to deny harms they commit, and that both the lawyer and the client have the expectation that it is the lawyer's job to help the client deny. The more this is true, then of course the more difficult raising the question of responsibility taking with clients will become. In my opinion, however, this characterization is often inaccurate. Many clients come to lawyers because they have a problem, if not a crisis, with legal dimensions, and what they seek from their lawyers is help in handling the problem.[76] Many clients do not arrive with a rigidly predetermined approach to their problem in mind. Rather they seek professional help to handle something they cannot adequately handle on their own. Sometimes such help is purely "technical," as when a lawyer knows the correct terminology to use when drafting a will. Yet often the help is of a broader nature, including not only legal advocacy but counseling and advice.

Second, in my view, the willingness of many clients to think seriously about responsibility taking and discuss it with their lawyers depends significantly on the *lawyer's* willingness to "go there." The lawyer is the professional experienced in handling such matters, and most clients take cues from lawyers about what to discuss and what not to discuss. Consider by analogy what is for many among the hardest matters to discuss—death. In her pioneering work on caring for the terminally ill, Elisabeth Kübler-Ross found that whether patients would in fact talk with their medical professionals about death—a subject many patients wanted to discuss—depended significantly on the willingness of the medical professionals to talk with them about death. Where the professionals were comfortable talking about death, patients would discuss death with them. However, where the professionals were uncomfortable talking about death, patients would not.[77] A similar lesson applies to responsibility

---

76. Such a conception underlies, for example, Brandeis' "lawyer for the situation" (*see* Geoffrey C. Hazard, Ethics in the Practice of Law (1978)) and subsequent views of lawyers as problem solvers. *See* Carrie Menkel-Meadow, *Toward Another View of Legal Negotiation: The Structure of Problem Solving*, 31 UCLA L. Rev. 754 (1984); Robert H. Mnookin et al., Beyond Winning: Negotiating to Create Value in Deals and Disputes (2000).

77. *See* Elisabeth Kübler-Ross, On Death and Dying 244–68 (1969).

taking. The willingness of clients to talk about responsibility taking with their lawyers may depend significantly on the willingness of the lawyers to talk with them about it.

1. Trust & Relationship, Not Magic Bullets

For many lawyers, raising the subject of responsibility taking with clients is a "difficult" or intimidating conversation to initiate.[78] Few enjoy being the bearer of bad news.[79] The lawyer may fear that if she raises responsibility taking, the client will grow angry with her and view her as judgmental, paternalistic, and perhaps even disloyal. Is there an approach to such conversations that fully avoids such risks? No, there is no "magic bullet" for making the process of discussing responsibility taking with clients risk-less and effortless.[80] Yet not discussing the issue with the client is often inadequate too. The basic choice of whether to take or deny responsibility should be the client's. To know, rather than presume, what the client wants, the lawyer must discuss it with the client. Further, the potential moral, psychological, and relational costs of failing to take responsibility are precisely the type of important considerations that a client might overlook on his own, making the potential service to the client of raising the issue particularly valuable. Thus, from the viewpoint of client service, there are risks both to raising and to not raising responsibility taking with clients. Though not easy to have, if the lawyer wishes to best serve the client, such conversations are frequently necessary.

How then should the lawyer do this? Below I offer some general thoughts. Much, however, depends on the particular client, the particular lawyer, their particular relationship, and the particular case. There is no simple recipe for effective communication. Effective communication is highly context- and people-dependent. The general thoughts below are no substitute for the lawyer giving careful attention to the particularities of each case.

If there is one word that captures what is needed to make such conversations effective, it is *trust*. Raising the subject of responsibility taking involves drawing attention to a mistake or mistakes the injurer has made, which in turn may press upon the injurer's sense of shame. How will the injurer react to hav-

---

78. On approaching such conversations, see generally Douglas Stone et al., Diffi-cult Conversations: How to Discuss What Matters Most (1999).

79. Yet often lawyers must bear "bad news" and should learn to do so skillfully. For advice, see Linda F. Smith, *Medical Paradigms for Counseling: Giving Clients Bad News*, 4 Clin. L. Rev. 391 (1998).

80. *Id.* at xvii.

ing his attention so focused? If the injurer distrusts the lawyer, he will proba-bly react negatively. Likely he will hear the conversation as words of accusa-tion and rebuke, and will grow angry at the messenger rather than facing the message. On the other hand, if the injurer trusts the lawyer, the chances are far greater that he will hear the words as ones of care and face the difficult matters implicated. At first, the lawyer's role may seem oppositional; however, at a deeper level the injurer may experience it as supportive. To use a rough parallel, it is easier to heed constructive criticism from a trusted friend than from a stranger.

The first questions the lawyer should thus pose are ones to herself. "Am I trustworthy? Have I acted toward this client in a manner such that he trusts me?" If the answers to such questions are "no," constructively discussing re-sponsibility taking will be difficult. This challenge of being trustworthy is nontrivial for many lawyers. An important part of many lawyers' jobs is *not* telling the whole truth. In litigation, for example, to best serve their clients, lawyers commonly present half the truth.[81] Though they may not actively lie, they often must selectively omit and slant, with the hope of persuading the judge or jury to accept the version of the facts most favorable to their client. The adversarial trial system is designed this way. While being trust-worthy in the jury's eyes is important to trial advocacy, being less than fully candid is also an important legal skill. In certain respects, lawyers are called upon to be fully trustworthy in some areas but not others. This is no sim-ple task.

Related to trust is the quality of the lawyer-client relationship generally. As mentioned, the more the client feels his lawyer cares about him, the more re-ceptive he is likely to be to conversations of responsibility taking. As typified by the growth of the mega law firm, we live in an age when legal services have in significant ways become commodified. Lawyers jump from firm to firm and city to city. Relationships with clients are often short-lived. Constrained by the billable hour, conversations with clients are often brief. When stacks of documents are being sifted through in discovery, it may not matter exactly which lawyer does the sifting. But when it comes to raising the subject of re-sponsibility taking, it does. The lawyer-client anonymity common in law prac-tice today is antithetical to such conversations. Though I will not argue here the position that "once there was a time" when lawyers did speak with clients

---

81. Deception is common in legal negotiations as well. For a critique, see Gerald B. Wetlaufer, *The Ethics of Lying in Negotiations*, 75 Iowa L. Rev. 1219 (1990).

about responsibility taking—both for fear of romanticizing the legal past[82] and, more fundamentally, because I do not believe that sufficient data about past and current legal counseling exist to make such a comparison—I note the possibility that such counseling may have once occurred more than it now does.[83]

Before raising the subject of responsibility taking, it is important that the lawyer listen carefully to the client's story and demonstrate to the client that she understands his account. Not only will this help the client to feel that the lawyer is on his side, but it also helps encourage the client to listen to the lawyer. There has been much discussion in negotiation theory about the importance of demonstrating empathy (*i.e.* demonstrating to the other side that one understands what they are saying) so that they will, in turn, listen to what one has to say.[84] A similar dynamic occurs here. A client who feels heard will be more willing to listen.

2. A Spectrum of Discourse: Confrontation, Indirection, and Engagement

How then is the lawyer to raise the issue of responsibility taking with the client? As mentioned, I do not believe there is a single optimal approach. Rather, it is helpful to think of a range of approaches. One way to characterize that range is in terms of a "confrontation" spectrum. Below I discuss three points on this spectrum. I will call these confrontation (most confrontational), engagement (moderately confrontational), and indirection (least confrontational). Visually, one might image these as:

	Confrontation	Engagement	Indirection	
More Confrontational	←	———————→		Less Confrontational

Two further notes. First, the word "confrontational" has different possible meanings. One can "confront an issue," "confront a person," or "confront a person about an issue." The sense of "confrontational" intended here is the third—the lawyer confronting the client about responsibility taking. (It is hard to imagine many circumstances where the second sense confrontationalism—

---

82. For references, see Rhode, *supra* note 70, at 592–93 ("Bar literature has long hosted laments for some happier era when law was a profession, not a business, and lawyers were stewards of societal values, not servants of private profit.").

83. For one such view, see Paul J. Zwier & Ann B. Hamric, *The Ethics of Care and ReImagining the Lawyer/Client Relationship*, 22 J. Contemp. L. 383, 387 (1996).

84. *See* Mnookin et al., *supra* note 76, at 49.

purely toward the person—is appropriate in the lawyer-client relationship.) Second, for expository purposes, I will discuss these three approaches in the following order: confrontation, indirection, and engagement. In so doing, I do not mean to imply the third approach of engagement is a golden mean between the other two. While I am fondest of that approach, I stress that I believe there is no single optimal approach appropriate in all circumstances. The need for context-sensitivity in making such determinations is paramount.

a. Confrontation

The clearest way to raise an issue with a client is to do so directly. "Let me be straight. From everything you've told me, it sounds like you were at fault here. In my judgment, you've got a basic choice to make. You can deny what you did or you can take responsibility for it. In my view, there are pros and cons to each which we can discuss if you like, but that, as I see it, is the basic issue you face."[85]

To some lawyers such directness may seem the stuff of science fiction. To others it may not. Thomas Shaffer recalls an experience as a young lawyer in the early 1960s sitting in a partner's office listening to the telephone conversation between the partner and a corporate client about whether the client was under a legal obligation to desegregate its factories. The laws were in the process of revision, and the partner walked the client through complex details of why, despite the revision, the client was not legally obligated to desegregate.

> The [corporate secretary] said, at the end of all this, 'Well, what do you think we ought to do?' My senior in the practice of law said, 'Oh, I don't think there's much doubt about what you ought to do: you ought to integrate those factories.' The secretary said, 'All right,' and hung up his telephone [and the corporation proceeded to desegregate its factories.][86]

The approach of Dallas attorney John McShane is also very interesting. David Wexler writes that McShane,

> has a substantial criminal law practice that 'focuses solely on rehabilitation and mitigation of punishment.' McShane is in private practice, and he can pick and choose his clients. He chooses only those who

---

85. Should the client insist on denial, the lawyer must then consider her response carefully. *See supra* note 73.

86. SHAFFER & COCHRAN, *supra* note 65, at 31.

agree to use the crisis occasioned by the criminal case as an opportunity to turn their lives around.[87]

This might involve the client entering a drug treatment program, so that later evidence of "the client's well-documented recovery, rehabilitation and relapse prevention plan [can be] presented to the judge in mitigation of punishment."[88]

Neither the Shaffer nor McShane examples are ones of pure confrontation. They are not "on all fours" with the hypothesized lawyer who bluntly confronts the client about responsibility taking. In the Shaffer case, the corporate secretary invites the lawyer's opinion. Further, the matters of legal and moral responsibility clearly differ. In McShane's practice, the responsibility-taking focus is not simply toward the crime, but also toward underlying substance abuse problems. Moreover, McShane describes his communication style as compassionate rather than brusk and judgmental.[89] Nevertheless, these examples are suggestive of some important lessons.

A first lesson is what one might call being "tough on the problem, but supportive of the person."[90] Squarely confronting a client about a difficult issue does not mean being disrespectful. Indeed, the more respectfully confrontation is handled, the more likely it is to be effective. Similar to a patient who wants his doctor to "tell it to me straight," many clients value blunt communication from their lawyers.[91] For some, the more direct the communication, the more respectful it is ultimately taken to be. The speaker's candor conveys that the speaker sees the listener as an adult who can hear "the truth" and make his own decision about it. In a way this is the opposite of the paternalist who couches what she says for fear of the listener's negative reaction.

A second lesson is not to be overly fearful of alienating the client. This is true not simply because the lawyer (like McShane) has the right to determine the style of her practice and whom to represent but, more deeply, because the essential goal of legal representation is serving the client's best interests rather

---

87. David B. Wexler, *Robes and Rehabilitation: How Judges Can Help Offenders "Make Good,"* 38 CT. REV. 18, 19 (2001).

88. John V. McShane, *The Need for Healing: Addressing the Causes of Wrongdoing Helps the Client and Society,* 89 A.B.A. J. 59 (May 2003).

89. *Id.*

90. *See, e.g.,* SHAFFER & COCHRAN, *supra* note 65, at 99; ROGER FISHER ET AL., GETTING TO YES: NEGOTIATING AGREEMENT WITHOUT GIVING IN 17–39 (2d ed. 1991).

91. As Thomas Morgan writes, "The thought that a lawyer should give a client the kind of candid, tough advice which the lawyer would give a good friend may seem radical or unnatural. Any other approach, however, may be less natural." Thomas D. Morgan, *Thinking About Lawyers as Counselors,* 42 FLA. L. REV. 439, 459 (1990).

than avoiding client alienation. Akin to calls for "radical honesty" in psychotherapeutic counseling, there is a serious argument to be made that by
telling the client the truth the lawyer best serves the client, even if that means
at times alienating the client.[92] What is essential is that the lawyer help the
client, not that the lawyer be liked by the client. The lawyer who fears alienating the client should ask herself whether she does so with the client's best
interests at heart (e.g., "The client needs legal help, and if I alienate him, he
won't get that help.") or her own best interests at heart (e.g., "If I alienate the
client, he'll drop me and I'll lose income.").

A third lesson is that the justification for the confrontational approach gains
particular force when one thinks, as with the addiction issues McShane addresses, of the possibility of future repetition of wrongful conduct by the
client. This applies not only to individuals but in the organizational context
as well, where unaddressed problems can recur for decades (e.g., the American Catholic Church and pedophilia).

Finally, a confrontational approach need not be dramatic. One method, for
example, is to raise the possibility of responsibility taking as one option in a
manner-of-fact discussion of the menu of options the client faces. Rather than
singling out responsibility taking for special treatment, approaching responsibility taking as a normal, possible option may help avoid anxiety in discussing that issue.

b. Indirection

At the opposite end of the spectrum from confrontation lies indirection.
Here the lawyer's goal is not to raise the issue of responsibility taking herself
but to send the client down a path along which the issue *might* get raised. Unlike direct confrontation, there is no guarantee the issue will get raised along
such a path. Simultaneously, there is far less risk of client alienation.

Perhaps the most common indirect path is to bring the client to mediation.
As part of working toward settlement, mediators, particularly evaluative
ones,[93] often engage in "reality checking," that is, asking questions and presenting facts that are difficult for a party to face. Many lawyers bring their

---

92. *See, e.g.,* Brad Blanton, Radical Honesty: How to Transform Your Life by
Telling the Truth (1996).

93. For discussions of different styles of mediation, see Leonard L. Riskin, *Under-
standing Mediators' Orientations, Strategies, and Techniques: A Grid for the Perplexed*, 1
Harv. Negot. L. Rev. 7 (1996); Leonard L. Riskin, *Decisionmaking in Mediation: The New
Old Grid and the New New Grid System*, 79 Notre Dame L. Rev. 1 (2003).

clients to mediation for precisely this reason.[94] They want the mediator to be the "bad guy" rather than having to be the "bad guy" themselves. Though reality checking is not identical to raising responsibility taking, the two have much overlap. Note too that a central feature of mediation is to bring the parties face-to-face.[95] The typical pattern of denial in litigation is characterized by compartmentalization—the communication between the parties is highly restricted and stylized, the handling of the disputed is delegated, history is reduced to facts relevant to proving legal fault at trial, and so on.[96] When an injurer comes face-to-face with the person he injured, the injurer can no longer hide not only from the injured party, but also from aspects of himself, such as a sense of guilt or shame, that he might rather ignore. (This helps explain why emotional outbursts are not uncommon in mediation.) Further, as evidenced by the prevalence of apology within mediation, mediation often does lead to responsibility taking.

Sometimes even more oblique means can be helpful. "Perhaps you might want to take a few weeks to think things over?" "What does your spouse think about this?" "When you look back at this years from now, what do you want say about it all?" "Have you prayed about this?" Such questions too may help move the client from narrow compartmentalization and short-run, shame-avoidant myopia to a place where the client can be in touch with a fuller range of long-run interests, including moral, psychological, and relational interests. (We sometimes use the word "wise" to describe the lawyer who can help clients shift from a narrow focus to a broader one.) Perhaps the lawyer can suggest others persons (with their permission, of course) who have been in similar situations in the past with whom the client might talk. Perhaps something as minor as the lawyer having photos of her family in her law office can impart

---

94. *See, e.g.,* Bobbi McAdoo, *A Report to the Minnesota Supreme Court: The Impact of Rule 114 on Civil Litigation Practice in Minnesota,* 25 HAMLINE L. REV. 401, 429 (2002) (reflecting a sample in which a significant (forty-seven percent) of cases the desire to provide a "needed reality check" for their own clients was a factor prompting lawyers to choose mediation).

95. Though sometimes face-to-face contact between the parties is broken during mediation (e.g., as when a mediator caucuses privately with one side), and while not all mediations do involve face-to-face contact of the parties (e.g., as in "online" mediations of e-commerce disputes or with mediations conducted with only the parties' lawyers attending), face-to-face contact between the parties remains a defining feature of most mediation. Additionally, the non-verbal communication present in face-to-face meetings generally helps promote trust among the parties. *See* Janice Nadler, *Rapport in Legal Negotiation: How Small Talk Can Facilitate E-mail Dealmaking,* 9 HARV. NEGOT. L. REV. 223, 228–29 (2004).

96. *See Legal Denial, supra* note 13, at section III.B.

to the client the idea that what takes place within law is not ultimately separate from what takes place in life. Of course, there is no guarantee that such indirection will lead the client to address the question of responsibility taking, but sometimes it may.

c. Engagement

Somewhere between direct confrontation and oblique indirection lies engagement. The idea here is to try to raise the issue of responsibility taking by, to the degree necessary for the client to make his legal choices, "going through" the client's experience.

The first, indispensable step is listening. As mentioned, in part this is a matter of trust. To be willing to listen to their lawyers, most clients must first feel heard. But there is more than just trust at stake. Powerful emotions like guilt, shame, and anger often attach to injuring others. Until those emotions are at some level recognized and processed, the ability of the client to think clearly about denial and responsibility taking may be greatly impaired.

To provide effective legal counsel, often the lawyer must listen for not just the "facts" alone, but the client's *experience* of those facts. "Tell me about it from the start." "How did you feel when that happened?" "How are you feeling about it today?" Though some may find the overall approach advanced in this chapter quite judgmental,[97] the nonjudgmental, Rogerian roots of client-centered counseling are very much what I have in mind.[98] First, the lawyer listens nonjudgmentally to the client's experience. Occasionally, this may happen during the first meeting, but typically it will take longer for a sufficient level of trust to be established for the client to feel comfortable sharing such feelings. As Bastress and Harbaugh write, "[C]onfrontation—unless it relates to clarification of factual inconsistencies—should not ordinarily be used in the early stages of the lawyer-client relationship. The typically threatening nature of confrontation can damage and stunt an undeveloped relationship."[99]

After the client has discussed his experience, the client's choice of whether to take or deny responsibility can then be broached. "I'd like to talk with you next week[100] about some different possible paths we might take, and hear

---

97. While the approach advocated here does call for moral judgment of the client's acts, the need for that judgment is rooted ultimately in client service.

98. *See* BINDER & PRICE, *supra* note 66, at 14–15; BASTRESS & HARBAUGH, *supra* note 50, at 32.

99. BASTRESS & HARBAUGH, *supra* note 50, at 281.

100. I write "next week," as time can be essential in helping clients address such matters.

where you want to go with this. Is there any part of what occurred for which you feel responsible, and if so, would you be willing to pay something for that? Would you rather we litigate this? Maybe we can talk about some of the different options."

Some may ask whether such an approach invites the lawyer to "practice psychology without a license." In my view, the answer is no. The goal here is for the lawyer to provide the client with a full range of legal services. For legal counseling on such matters to be effective, addressing the client's emotions to a certain degree is often important, if not essential. I would caution, however, that it is critical for a lawyer to know the limits of her professional role and skills, and to refer clients to other professionals, like psychologists, when appropriate.[101] Injurers, especially those who do so intentionally, often also need psychological counseling. The lawyer should not seek to provide such counseling. However, the lawyer must be sensitive to the role psychological and emotional issues can play in the client's legal choice-making.[102] A similar point would apply, for example, to religious counseling. The lawyer need not work through with the client the ramifications of taking or denying responsibility in terms of the client's religious belief system. The client should go to his clergy for that. That, however, does not mean the lawyer should simply ignore the possibility that the case has religious dimensions for the client.

Let me make three further comments about these different approaches. First, these approaches, especially engagement and confrontation, require a moderate degree of emotional competency by the lawyer.[103] The lawyer needs to be comfortable with the client discussing or otherwise expressing feelings like shame, guilt, and anger. Not all lawyers possess such counseling skills, and even those who do must be sensitive to cultural barriers.[104] Second, clients will differ in their capacities and desires to discuss such emotions. For some, state-

---

101. Recall that the implicit classification of the client's problems as legal rather than, say, psychological, is done by the client when he seeks legal counsel. The client may of course be in error. *See* Walter O. Weyrauch, *Foreword: Legal Counseling as an Intellectual Discipline*, 42 FLA. L. REV. 429, 432 (1990).

102. *See generally* PRACTICING THERAPEUTIC JURISPRUDENCE: LAW AS A HELPING PROFESSION (Dennis P. Stolle et al. eds., 2000).

103. *See* DANIEL GOLEMAN, EMOTIONAL INTELLIGENCE: WHY IT CAN MATTER MORE THAN IQ (1997); Marjorie A. Silver, *Emotional Intelligence and Legal Education*, 5 PSYCH. PUB. POL'Y & L. 1173 (1999).

104. As Michelle Jacobs writes, "Though, legal educators appear to assume counseling skills are innate, clinicians would agree that in fact they are difficult to learn and effectively employ." Michelle S. Jacobs, *People from the Footnotes: The Missing Element in Client-Centered Counseling*, 27 GOLDEN GATE U. L. REV. 345, 412 (1997). *See also* Carolyn C. Hartley

ments such as, "I felt horrible when I realized I had ..." come easily. For others, they come not at all. Lawyers should be sensitive to such variety. Third, under any of these approaches, the lawyer's goal should not be "salvational"—to turn the client into a moral being and persuade the client to make the moral choice.[105] But neither should the lawyer assume the worst about the client's morals. The goal rather is similar to that of much moral counseling: to have a conversation that assists the client by helping him understand the possible ramifications, including moral ramifications, of his choices.[106] The choices are fundamentally the client's. The lawyer's essential role remains that of service.

3. A Skeptical View and an Optimistic Response

Upon hearing my central claims—that, morally speaking, injurers ought to take responsibility of their own initiative and that, from the viewpoint of client service, their lawyers ought to consider discussing this possibility with them—some will react with skepticism. "If men were angels," a skeptic might say, "there would be no need for law. Many clients and many lawyers are greedy. Whether consciously or not, they will place their own financial interests before some claim of what is right for them to do. Further, people who injure others are likely to be low on the 'responsibility taking' scale to begin with. If they were sensitive toward others, they would have been less likely to have committed the injury in the first place.[107] Your vision is idealistic, but not realistic."

There is much force to the skeptic's view, and I suspect that in many cases the skeptic will be descriptively right. Yet the possibility for change should not be disregarded either. As discussed above, injurers have moral, psychological, and relational interests as well as economic interests. Such noneconomic interests give even self-interested injurers reasons to think seriously about re-

---

& Carrie J. Petrucci, *Practicing Culturally Competent Therapeutic Jurisprudence: A Collaboration Between Social Work and Law*, 14 WASH. U. J.L. & POL'Y 133, 162 (2004).

105. *See* Serena Stier, *Legal Ethics: The Integrity Thesis*, 52 OHIO ST. L.J. 551, 566 (1991).

106. On the merits of such moral counseling, see generally Robert M. Bastress, *Client Centered Counseling and Moral Accountability for Lawyers*, 10 J. Legal Prof. 97 (1985); SHAFFER & COCHRAN, *supra* note 65. *Cf.* HAZARD, *supra* note 76, at 147 ("A legal adviser should be reticent about incorporating morals or policy into his advice...."). For a history of scholarship concerning the related topic of "moral activism" by lawyers, see Paul R. Tremblay, *Moral Activism Manque*, 44 S. TEX. L. REV. 127, 137–47 (2002).

107. Though obviously true in cases of intentional injuries, even in negligence cases, a greater sensitivity toward others may lead to increased caution, which may decrease the chances of injury.

sponsibility taking. The possibility that responsibility taking will turn out to be economically beneficial should also not be discounted. Indeed, even if their lawyers fail to raise responsibility taking with them, such reasons may lead some injurers to consider the topic seriously.

Injury often offers the injurer a character-building opportunity. For the injurer who would deny out of greed, it may be the chance to place morality before money. For the injurer who would deny out of shame, it may be the chance to accept one's human imperfection. So too lawyers who discuss responsibility taking with clients may find a deepened sense of meaning in law practice, a meaning derived from providing a fuller range of service to the client, and, simultaneously, from being a member of a profession that fosters moral behavior, social healing, and just outcomes.[108] The public perception of lawyers may also improve, for little causes greater loss of public respect for the legal profession than the view that lawyers help the guilty-in-fact go free. For those lawyers who would fear losing business, recall the advice of attorney Abraham Lincoln: "Discourage litigation. Persuade your neighbors to compromise whenever you can. Point out to them how the nominal winner is often a real loser.... As a peacemaker the lawyer has a superior opportunity of being a good man. There will still be business enough."[109] Even if denial is the norm, the hope exists that individual clients and individual lawyers will choose another path.[110]

Finally, and it is here that I place my greatest hope, is the chance that, as individual clients and individual lawyers choose a different path, the norms within our legal culture will shift. I suspect that many injurers deny and many lawyers fail to discuss with them the possibility of responsibility taking because "that is the way it is done." Without reflection, they simply slip into the common mode of response.[111] Yet as discussions of responsibility taking be-

---

108. *See generally* STEVEN KEEVA, TRANSFORMING PRACTICES: FINDING JOY AND SATISFACTION IN THE LEGAL LIFE (1999) (discussing lawyers who found satisfaction through transforming their legal practices); HOWARD GARDNER ET AL., GOOD WORK: WHEN EXCELLENCE AND ETHICS MEET (2001) (emphasizing the importance of ethical pursuits to job satisfaction generally).

109. Abraham Lincoln, *Lecture Notes*, *in* 2 COLLECTED WORKS OF ABRAHAM LINCOLN 81, 81 (Roy P. Basler ed., 1953).

110. *See* REINHOLD NIEBUHR, MORAL MAN AND IMMORAL SOCIETY: A STUDY IN ETHICS AND POLITICS (1932).

111. *See* Gerald J. Postema, *Moral Responsibility in Professional Ethics*, 55 N.Y.U. L. REV. 63, 69 n.22 (1980) (quoting G.K. Chesterton, *The Twelve Men*, *in* TREMENDOUS TRIFLES 57–58 (1955)) ("[T]he horrible thing about all legal officials, even the best, about all judges, magistrates, barristers, detectives, and policemen, is not that they are wicked (some of

come more widespread, the modality that once seemed inevitable may no longer seem inevitable. The experience over the past two decades with medical error may be instructive. In 1987, when the Lexington VA switched from the denial approach to the responsibility approach after medical error, it was viewed as bizarre. Roughly two decades later numerous medical providers have adopted this approach,[112] and discussions of apology in the medical context are becoming increasing common.[113] Innovative laws are being passed both requiring the disclosure of serious medical errors and even excluding apologies made after medical errors from admissibility into evidence.[114] Minor fissures can sometimes tumble a wall that once appeared rock solid.

III Conclusion

Denying, rather than taking, responsibility after one injures another is a basic act of moral regression. Our legal system, however, helps mask that immoral act as normal. This is no small feat, and the ramifications of what one might call the "pattern defect" of legal denial are multifaceted. In terms of legal practice, I invite you to think seriously about discussing responsibility taking with clients. Though a client may benefit from denial economically, denial may harm the client's moral, psychological, and relational interests. We should not presume which factors the client values most, but rather learn the skills of legal counseling needed to explore such matters with clients. In addition, as a society, we should consider addressing structural factors that may buttress the practice of denial we see in ordinary civil legal disputes. Factors to consider include economic incentives within litigation, the nature of different dispute resolution mechanisms, the methodology of legal education, and even broader aspects of our cultural composition, such as rights-based ideology and social denials of structural injustices.[115]

Some of you practicing lawyers and law students patient enough to have read this chapter may respond with a variant of the following: "This idea of counseling responsibility taking is a little 'out there.' It's not what is commonly

---

them are good), not that they are stupid (several of them are quite intelligent), it is simply that they have got used to it.").

112. *See* Zimmerman, *supra* note 27.

113. *See, e.g.,* Mattera, *supra* note 27; Douglas N. Frenkel & Carol B. Liebman, *Editorial: Words that Heal*, 140 ANNALS OF INTERNAL MED. 482 (2004).

114. *See Toward Candor, supra* note 30.

115. *See Legal Denial, supra* note 13, at Part III.

practiced. But perhaps you are right. Maybe we lawyers should sometimes talk with clients about taking responsibility? I don't really know." To you I would make a two-fold recommendation. First, when the time is right for you, give it a try. On the day when you have a client who you think might benefit from such a conversation and with whom you feel you could have such a conversation, take the risk. Second, at some later point, reflect on the experience.

CHAPTER 10

HURTING CLIENTS

Edward A. Dauer*

One of the most valuable lessons I learned in law school wasn't on the bar exam, and probably never will be. Nonetheless—even if I did not realize it at the time—its significance to the art of legal counseling outweighs everything the bar exam has ever asked about the Rule against Perpetuities, and about Evidence, and Secured Transactions, and nearly everything else. The lesson happened in Victor Brudney's Corporations class, on a Spring day about 40 years ago.

The case *du jour* involved a particularly truculent course of litigation between two shareholders unhappily trapped together in a closely-held corporation, one of whom was suing the other for some cause of action like self-dealing or misappropriation of corporate assets. After extracting the obligatory briefing of the case, Professor Brudney asked the class, "What is this lawsuit about?" A few students raised their hands. "The fiduciary obligation of directors is blah blah blah …" "The plaintiff is representing the corporation in a derivative capacity, according to the rule in etc. etc. etc.…" One particularly perspicacious soul suggested that "The shareholders' agreement failed to specify any restrictions on the freedom of the shareholders to compete with the corporation, so that and so on and so on …" None of this impressed Professor Brudney. He scowled, shook his head, and thundered at us, "What this case is about—is that *these two people hate each other.*"

I think about Victor Brudney every time I drive through Teller County, Colorado. Route 24 goes all the way across Teller County. It's a two-lane road for most of its length, winding through mountains and sparsely settled terrain on the edge of the Pike National Forest. But because it connects Colorado Springs with the ski areas in Summit County, for most of the year it carries a heavy

---

* Dean Emeritus and Professor of Law, University of Denver Sturm College of Law.

flow of traffic. On property owned by Jineen McWherter, abutting Route 24 about 40 miles from the city and in plain view of all that traffic, there is a large billboard. It is twenty-two feet wide and sixteen feet high. It is mounted on three telephone poles sunk into deep concrete footings. The metal sign is bright crimson enamel with large, bright white letters. At night it is illuminated by a bank of flood lamps fed with a power line strung hundreds of feet from the Rural Electric Cooperative Association poles for only this purpose. For more than three years the sign said,

We regret

doing business with

Hotchkiss Realty

Apparently that had some effect on Hotchkiss Realty, because the sign later sprouted what I can describe only as the billboard equivalent of pocket parts. The bottom of the sign was extended a couple of feet on each side and the third line of lettering was covered over with amended text, so that the sign read,

We regret

doing business with

A.J. and Lenore *Hotchkiss* Who Now Own Prudential *Realty*

Two years later, in July of 2005, almost overnight all of that disappeared. Sixteen feet wide, ten feet high, mounted on telephone pole pylons and illuminated with flood lamps, there is now Teller County's largest happy-face, and the legend,

We won the appeal.

Hotchkiss was 100% wrong!

I have long wondered what the real facts of that dispute were,[1] but one doesn't just wander unarmed up to the door of someone who would deal with their enemies in that way. An outline, however, was available from the Internet: Apparently, the McWherters felt the Hotchkisses had done them harm as brokers in a deal between them and the Fletchers, in which McWherter lost

---

1. The unpublished opinion of the Colorado Court of Appeals reads, in its entirety, "Judgment reversed and case remanded with directions." McWherter v. Fletcher, 2005 Colo. App. Lexis 873 (June 9, 2005).

some money and was out to recover it from the hides of Hotchkiss. For the Hotchkisses' part, A.J. still thinks the McWherters are "whacked out."[2]

To some extent this kind of behavior is "irrational:" the financial, not to mention the emotional, costs of erecting and maintaining the sign must have been considerable. Its impact on the litigation could not have been helpful for Jineen McWherter. As economic behavior, this was preposterous. But, just as for the protagonists in Victor Brudney's corporations case, the emotional component was no less real and certainly no less motivating.

The lesson itself is a generalization from these kinds of examples. Most lawsuits seem to be about money. The plaintiff demands the defendant's money, and the defendant does whatever can be done to keep the plaintiff from having it. Money is not, however, what some clients who sue for money actually want. Lawsuits are about money only because, most of the time, money is the only thing a client can get from bringing a lawsuit. Anything else—like satisfaction and consolation and vindication (or their baser forms in revenge and retribution, *a/k/a* "justice")—is derivative, and money is only the surrogate. It is hard to measure exactly how often this is so; but for reasons to be offered anon, it is so often enough to be worth our careful attention: this client whom we represent in this matter on this day may well be motivated to bring an action for money not by the need for money, but by the need to accomplish something else. Without knowing about and knowing how to respond to whatever the something else is, we lawyers risk missing the opportunity to help that client find more satisfaction and wellbeing than a money lawsuit might bring. And at lower cost.

Lawyers don't always think about this deeply enough. Sometimes we commit clients to the path of litigation without questioning critically whether conventional litigation is what this client really wants or needs. Some clients, to be sure, come to us saying they want to sue for money; some lawyers don't know how to do anything else; and sometimes for whatever reason the lawyer-client counseling never gets to what else might matter more. Even when the suit is successful, the money judgment may be a poor substitute for the balm the hurting client might otherwise have had. And given the financial and emotional costs of bringing a lawsuit—even a successful one—the process and its outcome may in retrospect feel something like having burned the forest to catch the stag.

Law students don't always think about this enough either; and for that they cannot really be blamed. Bar exams ask about the Fertile Octogenarian vari-

---

2. The story up to the time of the appeal is chronicled in Terje Langeland, *Sign of the Times: Teller County Feud Advertised on Billboard* (Dec. 18–24, 2003), *at* http://www.csindy .com/csindy/2003-12-18/news2.html (last visited Nov. 14, 2005).

ation on contingent remainders under the Rule Against Perpetuities; law school exams ask for instant recall of the eighth exception to the hearsay rule; all of most law students' casebooks are *case*books; and cases are for good reasons (but not for *really* good reasons) limited to the facts that the law makes germane—regardless of the facts that may be germane to the client. Some students, like those whose early instruction includes live-client clinics, gain a broader appreciation early on. The rest of us need to be reminded that sometimes clients hurt, that sometimes hurt matters, and that sometimes suing for money may not be the best way to help the client fix the hurt.

Clients Hurt and Hurt Matters

The field of medical malpractice has been a fertile one in which to study these phenomena. Perhaps because the data are better there (there is a patient record and an insurance file for every claim, and the judgments and settlements are all reported to a federal data bank), or maybe just because there has been intense public interest in the "malpractice liability crisis" which, some say, threatens to do in modern medicine, more data have been collected about patients and patient claims in medical malpractice than in any other part of civil litigation. What we see in all that data is that, at least among malpractice plaintiffs, Jineen McWherters abound.

Three significant investigations have been conducted into the needs and drives of people who feel themselves hurt by bad medicine and who bring legal claims against the doctors who, they believe, have hurt them. Although the studies were done at different times, in different countries, and with different methodologies, their results are remarkably consistent. People who allege injury from medical malpractice and who bring lawsuits demanding money *most of the time* are not suing because of money.

One of the three studies was done by Dr. Charles Vincent and his colleagues among patients and their families who brought malpractice claims in England.[3] Vincent asked these people why they had brought their claims and what they hoped to achieve. In one part of the survey the respondents were asked to indicate which of a list of goals best described their motives to sue. Here are the results, edited from Vincent's Table 4:

---

3. Charles Vincent et al., *Why do People Sue Doctors? A Study of Patients and Relatives Taking Legal Action*, 343 Lancet 1609 (1994).

	Agree %
So that it would not happen to anyone else	91.4
I wanted an explanation	90.7
I wanted the doctors to realise what they had done	90.4
To get an admission of negligence	86.7
So that the doctor would know how I felt	68.4
My feelings were ignored	66.8
I wanted financial compensation	65.6
Because I was angry	65.4
So that the doctor did not get away with it	54.7
So that the doctor would be disciplined	47.6
Because it was the only way I could cope with my feelings	45.8
Because of the attitude of the staff afterword	42.5
To get back at the doctor involved	23.2

Notice that while the desire for money did have significant salience, it mattered less frequently to these respondents than did explanation, prevention of further harm, and a host of other nonmonetary concerns. "So that the doctor would be disciplined" was not far behind, and "So that it would not happen to anyone else" was way ahead.

In another part of the study Vincent asked the question, "What could have been done that would have led you not to bring this claim?" These results were even more interesting. From Vincent's Table 5:

Explanation and apology	37
Correction of mistake	25
Pay compensation	17
Correct treatment at the time	15
Admission of negligence	14
Investigation by drug company/hospital	3
Disciplinary action	4
If listened to and not treated as neurotic	5
Honesty	4

Here we see "pay compensation" as one of the least significant factors. If the respondents were paying attention to the questions and answering accurately, the difference between the 65% compensation result for suits once begun and the 17% score for claims before they were filed suggests that, whatever the initial motivations may have been, they became transmogrified once the litigation began. People *brought* claims mostly to effect correction or recognition; they *pursued* claims once begun, they more frequently said, for money. It can't be proven just from these data, but it is certainly a tempting hypothesis that the litigation process itself changed the more authentic emotional motives into the more readily counted financial motives.

The second of the three studies was done in the United States by Dr. Gerald Hickson and his colleagues at Vanderbilt University, among families who had sued for neonatal birth injuries.[4] These kinds of injuries—including what are sometimes called "bad babies"—are seldom if ever trivial. Yet Hickson, using a methodology different from Dr. Vincent's, found motivations strikingly consistent.

Hickson's group was interested in the factors that "prompted" claims-making, and so included within the response codes both motivations and influences, or precipitating events:

What motivated you to bring this lawsuit?	
Advice of a third person:	~33%
Physician not completely honest:	~25%
Needed compensation:	~24%
Only way to find out what happened:	~20%
Punish doctor / assure it won't happen again:	~20%

Once again the need for compensation played a relatively minor role, even among families who had suffered very significant traumas and injuries, and even though the data set included only closed money claims. Moreover, the response rate for "punish doctor / assure it won't happen again" was 46% among families whose baby had *died*.[5]

The methodologies and therefore the implications of both of these studies can, of course, be criticized. They were both surveys, and there is reason to believe that people responding to surveys will give responses that make them seem like good people—"I am doing this for the good of humanity, not to line my own pocket." No amount of methodological elegance can completely remove that concern. The third study, however, does very largely put that concern to rest. It is a remarkable piece of data collection just completed by Dr. Marie Bismark in New Zealand.[6]

---

4. Gerald Hickson et al., *Factors That Prompted Families to File Medical Malpractice Claims Following Perinatal Injuries*, 267 JAMA 1359 (1992); *further analyzed in* FRANK A. SLOAN ET AL., SUING FOR MEDICAL MALPRACTICE 65, 68 (1993).

5. SLOAN, *supra* note 4, at 66.

6. A summary of the data and analysis can be found in Marie Bismark & Edward Dauer, *Motivations for Medico-Legal Action: Lessons from New Zealand*, 27 J. LEGAL MED. 55 (2006).

New Zealand differs from both the U.S. (Hickson's venue) and the U.K. (Vincent's) in that there is no civil liability for medical malpractice. A patient (or patient's family) who believes they were injured by medical care may bring a claim to the Accident Compensation Corporation (ACC) and will be compensated within that agency's scheme on a no-fault basis. It is not necessary to prove negligence, and the scheme has been described as the world's easiest compensation system for ordinary people to navigate. At the same time, the same people may if they wish bring a "complaint" to a wholly separate tribunal, the Health and Disability Commission (the HDC). Unlike the ACC, which can only award money damages, the HDC cannot award money damages at all. It can intervene in the doctor's practice; it can order corrective action; it can in a proper case suspend a physician's license. But it cannot order the doctor to pay the patient any money.

Bismark analyzed the self-reported reasons why people brought complaints to the HDC. In some senses these reports are purer than those of either Vincent's or Hickson's respondents. Because the HDC-complaint patients *cannot* be paid in money, and because the HDC process *cannot* have any impact on the ACC claim, these reports of motivation-to-complain are almost perfectly uncorrupted by the wish for money, however sublimated that wish may be. Here, then, is what Bismark's respondents report:

Desired outcome	Complainants (n=154[7])
Lessons learned/system change	70 (45%)
Explanation	52 (34%)
Compensation for economic losses	28 (18%)
Discipline/punishment	18 (12%)
Apology/expression of responsibility	16 (10%)
Review of provider's competence	11 (7%)
Intervention with care or waiting lists	6 (4%)

Again we can see strong feelings toward punishing the wrongdoer, toward preventing whatever happened to the patient from ever happening to anyone else, toward having recognition of the hurt the patient endured. These feelings are *real*; and these feelings cause people to bring complaints and legal claims. But not for money, or at least not usually.

---

7. Twenty-eight respondents also expressed a need for economic compensation. It has not yet been determined whether these were people whose HDC complaint preceded their ACC claim. The data analysis is continuing.

"Accountability"

The practical question is how we turn these sorts of empirical findings into useful observations about lawyering. But before we get there we can do some filtering and deepening of the meaning of the data, for it appears that there is a more organized way to understand what's going on. In a number of focus groups that Leonard Marcus and I conducted a few years ago,[8] in which we had all of the interests involved in malpractice litigation assembled to talk about what they needed and wanted out of the process, the most frequently-voiced need of the patients and their representatives was the word "accountability." When doctors make errors and hurt other people, the injured people insist that the doctors must be "held accountable." Accountability is called for not only by the victims of medical malpractice, but by the families who lost loved ones in 9-11, by people "taken" by corporate accounting scandals, even by people who had donated their loved ones' cadavers to the UCLA Medical School only to discover that someone at UCLA was making money selling the corpses on the used body parts market.[9] Its occurrence is so common, and seemingly so diverse, that it is tempting to consider the word "accountability" as having no distinctive meaning simply because it may have so many.

A closer examination of the med-mal data we just looked at, however, suggests a four-fold set of meanings that are broad enough to capture all the uses yet clear enough to be helpful. In particular, when people say they demand accountability, their demand may be for one (or more) of the following four kinds of things: *Sanction, Correction, Restoration, and Communication.* Here's what these four mean:

Sanction. People who do bad things should be punished. Punishment serves as vengeance; as expression of outrage, personal or social; as moral desert; as restoration of the equilibrium of good and evil that was upset by the wrongdoer's doing of the wrong. The effect of all of these is the same: Punishment means inflicting harm on a wrongdoer even when its infliction does not in any objective way necessarily benefit the victim. Like what Jineen McWherter was doing to A.J. and Lenore Hotchkiss, and what Victor Brudney thought the litigants were up to in his corporations case.

---

8. A report of the focus groups can be found in Edward A. Dauer et al., *Prometheus and the Litigators: A Mediation Odyssey*, 21 J. LEGAL MED. 159 (2000).

9. These and other cases, and the derivation of the "accountability" concept, are discussed in a paper I will be presenting at University College (London) in February 2006, Edward A. Dauer, *Accountability and Legal Responses to Medical Error* (on file with the author).

Restoration. In contrast to Sanction, which imposes a loss on the wrong-doer without necessarily achieving a gain for the victim, Restoration focuses on compensation for the victim first, and only secondarily on its impact on the wrongdoer. "He messed up and now I have to pay all these bills, and I've lost income, and so he has to *pay me back.*" People who sue for money and re-ally want the money are suing for Restoration. (Actually, there are two kinds of restoration—one is "fix what you broke." The other is "pay me money." The latter is usually called compensation.)

Correction. Someone who did the bad deed once just might do it again, unless something's done to prevent it. (Legal theorists call this "deterrence," and weave elaborate economic theories about it.) Punishment swift and sure should do the trick. Indeed, it would even be good if the punishment were public—behead one traitor in the public square and everyone might act bet-ter in the future. Accountability of this sort changes (if it doesn't kill) the wrongdoer; the threat of it guides the behavior of everyone else; and holding accountable today's wrongdoer (even if it does kill him) seems like a morally defensible way to make real the threat of doing the same to others. Recall here the commonly heard plaint in the malpractice complaints data, "I want to be sure what happened to me never happens to anyone else; that's why I'm suing *this* bastard."

Communication. This fourth aspect of accountability is the most difficult to define, but the most interesting in practice. It includes such familiar phrases as *"You owe me an explanation."* and *"Come clean."* and *"You let me down; come forward and 'fess up."* and *"Take responsibility."* Common to all of those is the idea of disclosure and communication. It seems to be heard most often when one person (the victim) trusted or depended on another (the wrongdoer) who failed to live up to the expectations of that trust. Politicians are often "held ac-countable" in this way, as are employees and, notably, professionals who hold themselves out as caring as much for their clients as for themselves. The de-sire for accountability in the classic hit-and-run, or in a fraud committed by a total stranger, is seldom of this fourth type. But it is frequently this type of accountability that attends a breach of faith or an injury caused by the lack of care from someone in whom someone else placed their trust. Trustees are not allowed simply to offer restoration or to suffer a flogging stoically. They de-serve more: they have to face the one they hurt and *explain* themselves. Later on we'll talk about apology and voluntary disclosure—two of the ways Com-munication gets expressed.

So, in short, out of any statistically sufficient group of people who were hurt through someone else's fault and who were moved to make a "legal claim" about it (for money, of course), we would find that some of them (probably a minority, though that can change from one setting to the next) demand the money because they want the money (Restoration); another group demand the money because they want to hurt the hurter back (Sanction); some demand the money because they care about the deterrent effect of bringing the claim (Correction); and a fourth group demand the money because the *process* of suing for the money requires the miscreant to recognize the hurt they caused, and to confront it if not confess it (Communication).

There are a couple of advantages to thinking about all of this in the way we just did—having four descriptions of what injured people want and one concept that embraces them all. For one, a lawyer consulting an injured client doesn't need an extensive knowledge of human psychology to be sensitive to what the client may really be saying they want. There is no question but that this four-fold way is simplistic, and would probably not earn a passing grade in an upper-level Psych course. But extensive taxonomies of mental states are more than what most lawyers ordinarily need. What we do need, however, is something that reminds us to think about the alternatives when a hurting client arrives demanding a lawsuit for money. Simple though it may be, the four-fold might be helpful in preventing us from clumsily hurting the client even more.

The second advantage is that having a unifying concept—Accountability—moves us closer to actually using these ideas in practice. Here's why: In what is probably a substantial number of all the cases, the four kinds of accountability people demand may just be four *seemingly* different facets of the same thing. To put that another way, injured people may have a real need for achieving accountability, and the four variations are just different ways by which they can do that. Now that's a hypothesis a Psych post-doc could get their teeth into, because saying that the four are really all the same means that if we satisfy one of them, we may well have slaked the thirst for any of the others.

That is not just a theoretical possibility. We know both anecdotally and systematically that among two groups of equally injured people, prompt full disclosure and recognition of the hurt offered to one group will result in that group producing fewer demands for any other kind of accountability. Medical patients to whom prompt disclosure of an error was made (Communication) are both less likely to sue for money (Restoration)[10] *and* less likely to "report" the doctor to the licensing authorities (Sanction, Correction).[11] We know from

---

10. Examples abound. For one, see Kathleen M. Mazor et al., *Health Plan Members' Views About Disclosure of Medical Errors*, 140 ANN. INT. MED. 409 (2004).

11. Amy B. Witman et al., *How do Patients Want Physicians to Handle Mistakes*, 156 ARCHIVES INT. MED. 2565 (1996).

both ordinary experience and through methodologically rigorous experiments that offering apologies reduces not just the cash settlement value of a post-injury claim, but also causes the apologee to regard their injury as less serious than they would have without that balm. Something cognitively significant is going on[12]—something important for lawyers who counsel hurting clients (and, as we'll see, for lawyers who counsel hurters as well as hurtees).

But one final digression. Although most of the studies that lead us to these ideas have been done in the setting of medical injuries, there is very good reason to believe that the same would be true almost everywhere when people injure other people. This drive toward effecting accountability, and each of the four guises that make it up, is a deeply rooted piece of human nature. It is, indeed, so basic to our make-up that we should expect to see it operating no matter the way or the setting or the device by which the hurt hurt. Victor Brudney's corporate antagonists, Jineen McWherter with her billboard, and all of the people in the U.S., the U.K., and New Zealand who suffered from medical error, may all have been acting from the same deeply basic motive.

Why People Act That Way

"Motive" isn't the right word now, because we are about to switch from Psych 101, where "motives" are valid concepts, to Evolutionary Biology, where the only things we are allowed to talk about are behavioral tendencies and traits. (Bear with me here. This is actually kind of fun.) So we'll call acting-to-effect-accountability a behavioral tendency, and its four guises a suite of behavioral traits.

You may have heard of the Darwin Awards. "The Darwin Awards salute the improvement of the human genome by honoring those who remove themselves from it in really stupid ways."[13] Evolutionary theory holds that the genetic predispositions toward behaviors are selected for over time in the same way that physical traits are. If some behavioral tendency (such as eating) helps

---

12. Jennifer K. Robbennolt, *Apologies and Legal Settlement: An Empirical Examination*, 102 MICH. L. REV. 460 (2003); Ronald S. McCord et al., *Responding Effectively to Patient Anger Directed at the Physician*, 34 FAM. MED. 331 (2002).

13. Winners (and losers) are chronicled on the Darwin Awards website, *at* http://www.darwinawards.com (last visited Nov. 14, 2005). One "Honorable Mention" was Genadi Lambas, 48, who, on November 15, 2004 tried to cross the Mediterranean to visit his family in landlocked Moldova on a raft made of a mattress tied to 448 empty mineral water bottles. *Id.*

the individual survive long enough to breed, that gene has a higher chance of being passed to the next generation than does a gene that causes someone to act in a way that reduces their chances of breeding (such as having no fear of sabretooth tigers). "Useful" genes are accordingly selected for; self-destructive genes are accordingly selected against. So how did Jineen McWherter get hers?

We need to explain why people sometimes act in ways that seem to be contrary to their individual best interests. Why would anyone devote their time and resources to pursuing Correction, or any other aspect of Accountability other than individual Restoration? Why do the New Zealanders bring complaints to the HDC? An economist would find Jineen's actions "irrational"—she must have spent a great deal on a project that could not possibly have returned her anything. Yet many of us have experienced anger and the urge to get back at someone who cut us off on the highway, or who cheated us on the used car lot, even if following that urge might risk much and net nothing.

The answer, evolutionary theorists tell us, stems from the fact that humans, for good and sufficient physiological reasons, cannot survive as solitary animals. We evolved living in smallish groups; and we are dependent for our individual survival on the survival of the group—without it, we die. Without us, it dies. Cooperation is the key to group survival. The saga of the stag hunt tells it well.[14] Hunting stag is a group activity; hunting hare can be done alone. Bagging a stag is better all around than catching a hare is. Is it better to hunt hare, or to contribute to hunting stag? If everyone cooperates in hunting stag, everyone—and the group—is better off. But if anyone "cheats" and goes off to hunt hare for themselves, the success of the stag hunt is endangered. So, will Tumak[15] hunt hare, or help hunt stag? This is what game theorists call a prisoner's dilemma—if everyone cooperates, Tumak and everyone else win big; if Tumak "cheats" and hunts hare, Tumak wins a little; if Tumak cooperates in the stag hunt while others cheat, Tumak loses big. The "equilibrium solution" is for everyone to cheat. In a world of rational maximizers, where everyone does what maximizes their individual advantage, the equilibrium outcome is less positive for the group than it would be in a world where everyone cooperates.

---

14. *See generally* B. Skyrms, The Stag Hunt and the Evolution of Social Structure (2004).

15. Tumak, for those not among the Paleolithic cognoscenti, was the name of the male lead opposite Raquel Welch in the 1969 remake of "One Million Years BC," a film in which the 60 million years that elapsed after the dinosaurs died and before humans lived were ignored in the name of, well, art. *See, e.g.,* http://www.filmbug.com/asin/B00018D3ZA (last visited Nov. 9, 2005).

But individual competition in a world of scarcity matters too (why else do law students care so much about graduating in the top 10% of the class?) In the whole of the environment, then, the behavior patterns that get selected for are some optimal blend of self-interest and group-interest, and thus (ethnologists believe) we see the evolution of altruism and reciprocity. Cheating, however, is still pretty tempting, and so backup systems also have survival value. One of those is called "strong reciprocity."[16] Strong reciprocity is a behavioral tendency we have inherited, courtesy of both individual and group natural selection, to reward cooperators and punish cheaters even when doing that might cost the individual who does the punishing more than they could gain for themselves alone by doing it. It greatly improves the prospects for cooperation, and so contributes to the survival prospects for the group and, accordingly, for its members.

There is still, however, a "free rider" problem to get over. Why should anyone do such things? Why should *I* punish the miscreant who went off and hunted hare? Why should *I* run down and cut off the aggressive driver who cut me off? Punishing them is likely to be personally risky if not just costly. If someone else did it, I would be better off without risking anything of my own. Hence again the solution would be, that none of us would ever do anything to punish cheaters. But we do. Jineen McWherter sure did.

The mechanism for making "strong reciprocity" work is anger. Watching a cheater cheat makes Tumak angry. Anger, as the people back in Psych 101 tell us, results in cognitive distortions—angry people tend to *underestimate* the cost to themselves of the actions they are thinking of taking to get back at the object of their wrath; and they tend to *overestimate* the magnitude of the actual threat.[17] Detecting a cheater produces anger, which in turn supports strong reciprocity and a system for enforcing group norms that overcomes the free rider problem. Tumak picks up his club, and the group is better off.

I am not suggesting that Jineen McWherter was driven inexorably by her DNA to risk her individual reproductive fitness by erecting an enormous billboard just to punish A. J. Hotchkiss for having cheated on the norms of Jineen's tribe. I am suggesting that the underlying behavioral trait that Jineen

---

16. *See, e.g.,* Lee Dugatkin, Cheating Monkeys and Citizen Bees 13–20 (1999); J. Maynard-Smith, *The Evolution of Behavior*, 239 Sci. Am. 176 (1978); Robert L. Trivers, Social Evolution 388 (1985).

17. Richard McElreath et al., *The Role of Cognition and Emotion in Cooperation, in* Genetic and Cultural Evolution of Cooperation 144–149 (Peter Hammerstein ed., 2003).

and most of the medical malpractice victims exhibit is an expression of a deeply rooted and very basic suite of behavioral propensities—to achieve accountability (now read, social cooperation) even when there is nothing in it for them alone. That makes what we see in the medical malpractice data far more likely to be a generalized phenomenon, happening across differences in time and setting and place. This is deep stuff.

Counseling

Suppose all of this is true. (It is.) The practical question is whether it matters. Does knowing about the origin and distribution of feelings a person experiences after an injury help at all, really? (It does.)

Let's take an anonymous version of a real case—one of many cases like it in which I have personally seen the value of knowing about these things. The year was 1985. Three years earlier a young mother of three children was injured in an accident, received three units of whole blood in the ER, and six months later was diagnosed with HIV. The virus moved rapidly to AIDS and the patient's condition deteriorated tragically. She and her husband sued the blood bank that collected the blood, the hospital where she received it, and the physicians who gave the orders to infuse it. The defendants mounted a staunch defense: until 1985, three years after this transfusion, there was no test for HIV, and no way for anyone to screen blood other than by screening donors for "life-style" risks. Blood, as every first-year Torts student should know, is not a product under Restatement Torts 402A, but a service. There is no strict liability for blood products. The plaintiff would have to prove that the blood center was negligent—that it failed to live up to the appropriate standard of care.

The lawsuit went to trial against the blood bank, and the blood bank won. The plaintiffs appealed, and the judgment was affirmed. The plaintiffs appealed to the state's supreme court where, on a narrow evidentiary point, the judgment was reversed and the case was remanded. The second trial began. We are now four years into the litigation. The plaintiff died while her attorney was making closing arguments to the jury.[18] The second jury returned a verdict for the plaintiffs and this time the defendant appealed. While on appeal for the second time the case was settled. I do not know the amount of the

---

18. The sequence of the proceedings is in fact true and is based on an actual case. The balance of the description is generic.

settlement. My guess, knowing something about these cases in general, is that it cost the blood bank about as much to settle the case as it spent to that point defending it. The injured patient, meanwhile, died after spending her final years in litigation and in poverty. This was a legal tragedy that followed a medical tragedy. Should something else have been done?

The answer is obviously yes. But how could the case have gotten there?

I recognize that it is hard for contingency fee lawyers to live on 30% of an apology, but I think in most instances we guide our clients into litigation for better but still not very good reasons. That more likely cause of what I think of as counseling errors came to me some years later, in the form of a preposterous statement made by an otherwise decent member of the bar. I was arguing on that occasion for a greater use of ADR techniques such as mediation in civil claims, on the ground that mediation's flexibility of remedy could be more satisfying to at least some clients than a money judgment would be. The lawyer in question said, with a straight face, "My clients all want money. That's all the legal system can give them, and they know that. So when they come to see a lawyer, they have already decided that money is what they want."

"Baloney,"[19] I carefully explained.

These days I begin my own law school course in the subject of ADR by challenging my students with what I call Maslow's Dictum, after Abraham Maslow who is reported to have first uttered it:

> *If all you have is a hammer,*
> *everything looks like a nail.*

If all we lawyers know is litigation and its appurtenant histrionics, bargaining, threats, and bluster, then of course that's what we'll offer our clients. And the clients will respond with reinforcement of the choice. As Robert Redmount taught us many years ago,[20] an injured client is often putty in the lawyers' hands. By selective questioning, by indicating what parts of the story are "relevant" and what parts aren't when we do our interviewing and counseling, by offering limited options for remedy, and in all by imposing on the client's facts what Leonard Riskin termed the "lawyer's standard philosophi-

---

19. The actual word was "bullshit," but one can't put that in the text of learned scholarship.

20. Robert Redmount, *Humanistic Law Through Legal Counseling*, 2 CONN. L. REV. 98, 98–99 (1969); Robert Redmount, *Attorney Personalities and Some Psychological Aspects of Legal Consultation*, 109 U. PA. L. REV. 972, 982–990 (1961).

cal map,"[21] lawyers tell clients what the lawyer expects the client to say. They dutifully respond and we call it authentic.

The patient, and her family, were really, really angry in this case. The infected blood carried a death sentence whether the blood center meant it to or not, and the whole medical apparatus was trusted to save her life, not to take it. Some lawyers consider their clients' emotions as problems to be managed as well as can be in the course of getting at the legal facts that really matter. In doing that they miss the point that feelings are facts just as much as physical wounds are, and in the process miss the chance to help their clients more effectively. In some cases, underestimating the affect of a matter can lead to results that make things worse, like this case.

The same thing is true for transactional lawyers. A colleague of mine was consulted once by a client for whom he had done some legal work in the past. He knew that this client owned a small corporation that was moderately successful, since he had formed the company and counseled with its owner on other things a few years before. On this day the client presented this question: "Is it possible for a corporation like mine to have two kinds of stock—one that has the right to vote on things and one that doesn't?"

The answer to that question is easy enough—classes of stock in closely-held corporations can be created with or without almost any voting rights one might want; and it is not a difficult matter to amend the By-laws to allow the issuance of new classes of stock even after the corporation has been formed. My friend the lawyer, however, wanted to know why the client wanted to know about this, and so he asked him, "Yes, we can do that; but tell me why you would want to?"

The client's answer was not unexpected: "Because I want to give someone who is going to work for the company an economic stake in the business but not the right to mess around with it." Ah, well, that's different. Now the possibilities widen. What seemed like the client's question was actually the client's answer to a question one layer down. Having discovered that, there became available to the lawyer a much wider array of possible answers—employee benefit plans funded with company stock but managed by a Trustee, incentive salaries tied to performance, and numerous other ways to link an employee's fortune to a company's without dealing in stock at all.

This lawyer was still curious. "Any particular employee?" The next answer *was* unexpected. After some hesitation the client revealed that his plan was to bring his son into the business—a son who, the father thought, had been mis-

---

21. Leonard L. Riskin, *Mediation and Lawyers*, 43 OHIO ST. L.J. 29, 43–48 (1982).

led in life by the blandishments of Boulder or Madison or Berkeley or wherever. That was the father's plan for repairing a badly frayed filial fabric. The
young man's goals should be made consistent with those of the family business, which was how the father was going to relate to the wayward son; but
he wasn't yet to be trusted with the right to vote.

Redrafting the corporation charter and issuing a new class of stock would
have been a perfectly valid legal answer to a seemingly legal question, just as
the plaintiffs' counsel in the blood case would not be faulted—under traditional standards—for having brought a well-framed and well-tried liability
suit. But just creating the new class of stock would have been a very bad answer to the client's real question. Indeed, it is far from clear that the client's
real question, of how to bond with the son he wished he had, is something a
lawyer should have responded to at all. It is fair to suggest, however, that any
such two-classes-of-stock plan would have been useless at best and, more
likely, disastrous at worst.

Another example[22] makes the same point in a more common setting. A
commercial artist drew a new logo for a minor league baseball team and came,
somehow, to an intellectual property lawyer to draft the contract, between
him and the team, by which he would be compensated for giving the team the
logo. The lawyer gave all the right advice about securing copyright protection,
and laid out the pros and cons of the two major avenues for selling such
things, *viz.* an outright sale of the artwork for some number of dollars, or a
license agreement under which the artist would receive a royalty for every tee-
shirt or baseball cap sold that bore the logo. What the lawyer ignored throughout the interviewing and counseling of this client, however, was the half dozen
times the client said, mostly in asides, how his love of baseball and of this team
in particular came from his own childhood dream of playing on a professional
baseball team some day, and how he might prefer the license deal because it
would better make him feel that he was "part of the team," and how an outright sale would be just a commercial deal and that would be the end of it.

On the one hand, those feelings might indicate a preference for a license
agreement over an outright sale. But the possibilities could go even deeper
than that. How about his becoming the Art Director for the team; or (in this
very different case) taking a small share of the ownership? What did this client
really want? Money? I don't think so. Feelings matter.

---

22. This one is taken from videotapes that accompany R. HAYDOCK ET AL., LAWYERING:
PRACTICE AND PLANNING (1996).

Here's the point: To do the best for the HIV patient, and the artist, and the erring Dad, the lawyer has to have two things. One is the ability to hear what clients are saying, and to appreciate what they are saying might mean. The other is the willingness to believe that, even if all that emotional stuff doesn't fall neatly into the lawyer's standard philosophical map, it is the stuff of which good counseling is made—not stuff to be worked around while some satisfactory "legal" solution is conjured up.

With that, let's go back to the hard case—the infected blood—and see how that might have worked out. We can do it from two sides—the patient and the blood center. Blood center first.

One alternative approach, pretty familiar these days to any lawyer who has learned anything at all about "ADR" techniques such as mediation, would be to catalogue the blood center's interest, find out or guess what they could about the plaintiff's interests, and engage in either direct or mediated interest-based negotiation. That would have been an improvement over what actually happened; but the blood center could have done even more, and particularly so if they had gotten to it sooner than they did.

By the time the blood center responded to the problem, the plaintiff had already been through a longish process with her own lawyers, who very likely steered her toward voicing threats of a lawsuit if not the lawsuit itself. The blood center isn't necessarily to be blamed for that. It may well have been the long-standing advice of its counsel, or of its liability insurer, not to go looking for trouble. One liability insurer I know of, for example, has two general rules for its insured docs. Rule No. 1: If the doctor knows of an adverse event and hears a patient making rumbling noises, the doctor is not to speak with that patient until the insurance company appoints defense counsel. Rule No. 2: Defense counsel won't be appointed until the patient has actually filed a claim. So there we have a patient, disappointed or worse by the course of their care, maybe wanting the Communication part of accountability, but unable even to *talk* with the doc until they file a formal claim. And of course once they file a formal claim the expectations everyone brings to the rest of the opera pretty much preclude any effective conversations from ever occurring thereafter.

Suppose, however, that the blood center had taken a different approach. Their counsel knows, let's say, all the stuff we've talked about in the first half of this essay, and particularly these facts: This patient is angry; people who entrusted their wellbeing to others and who feel abandoned get *really* angry; anger enhances the perceived gravity of the harm, it reduces the perception of the costs of responding to it, it drives people to put up big billboards along Route 24 (or the equivalent, to file very expensive and nasty lawsuits); and the patient's drive for, say, Sanction or Correction is one of the maybe-exchange-able guises of the more general motive to achieve Accountability. Suppose, then, the blood bank stepped up to the plate before the patient determined to file a claim; suppose it opened the books, so to speak, about what had happened, and how, and opened a conversation about what might be done about it; took care of the patient's immediate needs, expressed recognition of the patient's hurt and (gasp now, all ye traditional defense counsel) *apologized.*

As it happens, we *do* know what would probably have happened had they done all of that, because there are liability-management programs now going on across the country that tell us what happens.[23] The data are there, and they are robust. The blood bank's liability costs would have gone down, the total number of claims for all transfusion-associated injuries would have gone way down, and the destruction of the blood center's public image attributable to avoidable litigation would have all but disappeared. Yes, it might have cost some money as well, but the evidence strongly suggests it would have cost much less than it actually did.

There you are, then, counsel to a blood center, or a hospital, or a doctor, or a retail store that sells things that can injure people if they're defective.

---

23. One private insurance company (COPIC) has found a very favorable effect from its program of "3Rs"—Recognize, Respond and Resolve—in which physicians are encouraged to initiate communication with patients immediately after an unexpected result rather than waiting for the patient to discover and press a claim. Modest compensation is offered for actual monetary needs and the physician, where appropriate, apologizes and offers to continue to work with the patient. In over 930 instances of matters handled through the 3Rs program, there have been two formal claims (both now settled) and no lawsuits. The mean claim payment was an extremely modest $5,326 (compared to over $300,000 for the average paid claim outside the program). Data provided to the author by COPIC and cited with COPIC's permission. The equally well-known Lexington, VA program had similar results: a policy of voluntary disclosure accompanied with an offer of restoration had economic results favorable to the hospital, as well as some suggestion of therapeutic advantage. Steve S. Kraman & Ginny Hamm, *Risk management: Extreme Honesty May be the Best Policy*, 131 ANN. INT. MED. 963 (1999).The disclosure studies are several, varying in their approach, and consistent in their results: Mazor, for example, found that nondisclosure of an error would increase the patient's propensity to sue by a minimum of 17% (for a monitoring error with a non-serious outcome) to nearly 650% (for a missed allergy diagnosis). Kathleen M. Mazor et al., *Health plan Members' Views About Disclosure of Medical Errors*, 140 ANN. INT. MED. 409 (2004). Whitman reported a near doubling of the probability of suit and more than a doubling of the probability of reporting the physician to a medical licensure board, if an error were made but not voluntarily disclosed, suggesting that punishment (reporting) and communication (disclosure) are exchangeable in at least that direction. Amy B. Whitman et al., *How do Patients Want Physicians to Handle Mistakes?*, 156 ARCHIVES INT. MED. 2565 (1996).

Knowing all of this, how do you counsel the client? I'd tell them they should develop an early-intervention risk management system before the next injury happens. Runs counter to the scorch-the-earth approach of yesteryear? Right; but ya gotta believe it. Knowing why people sue rather than assuming you know why this person wants to sue, should at the very least open options to consider, for responding to other peoples' hurt.

To illustrate this practical point, I offer one more "war story." A few years ago the FDA ordered blood centers and hospitals to conduct "look-back" programs for Hepatitis C ("HCV"). Until 1990 or so there was no blood test for HCV, yet it was blood-transmissible. The disease itself could lurk undetected for many years, until it erupted in serious and even life-threatening liver disease. Some people who received transfused blood prior to 1990 might have HCV without knowing it. Most blood donors, however, are repeat players—if they donated today, they probably did years before as well. So, in 1993, when a blood donor shows up and—now that there is a good test—shows markers for HCV, it is possible to "look back" at all of that donor's pre-1990 donations, and to trace them to their recipients. The FDA ordered exactly that, and required that the hospitals contact those identified recipients and call them in for testing. Some would undoubtedly test positive for the disease.

How should a hospital blood bank deal with the legal risk of such a program? Conventional counsel gave the conventional defense advice: gird your loins, admit nothing, and fight the first few claims to victory at almost any cost. What we have just been discussing, however, counsels otherwise. What is likely to cause lawsuits is anger, and anger will come when the people called back feel not just injured, but abandoned—when they feel the blood center needs to be held accountable. Full disclosure, stepping up to the plate with explanation and care, should slake that demand for accountability (Sanction, Correction) by responding to other of its facets (Communication, Restoration.) That, fortunately, is what some blood centers decided to do; and, so far as I know, those centers have not had a single lawsuit filed.

Let's look at the harder side—the young mother with then-unmanageable AIDS. How might her lawyer have done better? Which brings up a question that should have been raised earlier: If it matters to know how a client feels, in addition to knowing "the facts" of how the matter happened, how does a lawyer do that? We needn't get deeply into the nuances of client counseling to see two very effective techniques. One is, just ask. In the case of the family corporation and the question about the shares of stock, the lawyer took the client's question as an answer to a question one layer down, and peeled that layer away: "Why do you want to do that?" Maybe something as straightforward as, "How do you feel about all of this?" And if that doesn't get anything, then it's still possible to pick up clues from the rest of the counseling dialogue—like the artist who let drop more than once that a licensing deal would help him feel like part of a baseball team—his childhood ambition. The critical *sine qua non* of hearing is listening, and that means believing that such things really can matter.

That may not always be as easy as it sounds. Asking Mrs. HIV how she feels is likely to open the sluice-gates to a torrent of emotions ... emotions that many lawyers find uncomfortable, if not discomfiting. But those feelings are the facts, just as much as the facts are the facts, and knowing about them opens options on this side of the aisle as well.

The transfusion injury victim and her husband present themselves to the lawyer. Early on, the husband says something like, "They poisoned my wife and she's going to die and I want to see them bleed now." Knowing that a money judgment alone may not be as satisfying as something more sensitively tuned could be, and knowing that the anger is an appropriate and a deeply-rooted response, the lawyer decides to explore the emotional affect more. What is it that these people really want / need / might get from the object of their wrath? Surely money would be helpful, particularly for excess medical costs and lost wages, the lost value of household production, and whatever other economic consequences the family has suffered. There is neither need nor reason to avoid that part of it. But there could be more, and it may be that if the money claim is used only for what money can easily do, then the rest of the motivations might be addressed by something more efficient and less destructive to pursue. It would certainly make no sense to commit these people to a lawsuit as the dominant feature of their final months together, if their underlying needs can be met more effectively. Even the money items might not need money. Health care costs, for example, don't require money. What the plaintiff really needs is health care, and it may be that the blood center, if it is part of an integrated health care system, can provide that care more efficiently by providing it in kind.

Beyond that, and calling on what we know from the medical malpractice studies and from our recently-gained insights into anger and accountability, there may be a drive to have Communication, Sanction, or Prevention as well as Restoration. It is very likely that the family does want to prevent such a tragedy from happening again; that they do want recognition of the terrible harm they have suffered; that they do want the blood center to feel their pain if not its own. They might even want Restoration beyond compensation—lifestyle counseling, for example, for this extraordinary disease, or some public vindication that this case of HIV was the result of an innocent transfusion, not the lifestyle assignations that attended AIDS in its early days (the implication of illicit drug use or sexual promiscuity still).

Now the creative part: What could a blood center be asked to do to meet these kinds of needs? Name a fellowship residency after these victims and devote the residency to research in transfusion safety. Publicly appear hand in hand with the family, expressing sincere remorse. Communicate openly about the blood transfusion process rather than, as too many defense lawyers recommend, forcing the patient-now-plaintiff to go the wrong way through a funnel sieve to get basic information about what happened. And more, maybe much more.

But again, how does the lawyer know the client's authentic needs and wishes? Even assuming they are already formed (which Redmount tells us they usually are not[24]), direct questions may be helpful but could be premature. One technique that can be used to good advantage is—again, listen first—to feed back to the client what you hear them say, and not just the facts. "What I hear in your voice is a real anger that you are innocent of everything yet your life has been so grossly affected." Or, "What I hear you saying is that you are terribly afraid of having your family impoverished by these enormous medical expenses." Let it come out. Then, when the time seems right, offer the client lots of options—including a full-bore lawsuit—while explaining the pros and cons of each. Pros and cons means suitability as measured not by each option's legal sufficiency, but by its resonance with what you have heard the clients say. Some ideas will be rejected, and in the explanation of *why* they are rejected there will often be a clearer description of the underlying *what*. "I don't want to do that, because what I really want to do is ..."

* * *

This essay was not intended to be a how-to textbook for client counseling, though client interviewing and counseling is where the affective assistance of counsel, or its opposite, is most effectively given. Interviewing and counseling, of course, are subjects with deep and useful literatures: what causes clients to withhold saying what they mean or feel? What blocks lawyers from hearing the cues that reluctant clients are sending? How can these causes of interference be overcome? These are skills that require clinical experience to learn well. One essay won't do.

The point of this essay, however, is more foundational, or at least more straightforward—and, I hope, at least a little convincing in light of the discussion we have just explored. Remember Victor Brudney. When listening to what one of those mutually-hated victims of the other is saying, think of the

---

24. *See* Redmount, *Attorney Personalities, supra* note 20.

legal or litigation categories into which those facts might be framed *if they need to go there.* But at the same time, listen to the affect of what the client is saying, with the possibility in mind that maybe those facts shouldn't go there.

I cannot resist one final personal tale. This year my niece entered medical school. My wife, a nurse with a lifetime of experience in medicine and in patients, bought her a stethoscope to celebrate the beginning of our niece's career. She wrote a card to go in the gift box: "When you use this stethoscope with your patients, listen not just with your ears, but with your heart."

The title of this essay was a double entendre, in case you hadn't noticed. If we lawyers are sensitive to the affect of injury as well as we are to its effect, we have the opportunity to be of immense assistance to our hurting clients. If we are not, then hurting clients is a greater risk in doing what we do.

CHAPTER 11

Overcoming Psychological Barriers to Settlement: Challenges for the TJ Lawyer

Bruce J. Winick*

Introduction

An important direction in therapeutic jurisprudence ("TJ") scholarship has been its concern with how law is applied. Not only can the rule of law itself be regarded as a therapeutic agent, but even when legal rules remain static, the way they are applied can have important therapeutic consequences for those affected. Judges,[1] lawyers,[2] police officers,[3] expert witnesses testifying in

* Copyright 2005 by Bruce J. Winick. Professor of Law and Professor of Psychiatry and Behavioral Sciences, University of Miami, Coral Gables, FL. Comments to the author should be addressed to bwinick@law.miami.edu.

1. *See, e.g.,* Judging in a Therapeutic Key: Therapeutic Jurisprudence and the Courts (Bruce J. Winick & David B. Wexler eds., 2003); Bruce J. Winick, *Therapeutic Jurisprudence and Problem Solving Courts*, 30 Fordham Urb. L.J. 1055 (2003); William Schma, *Judging for the New Millennium*, 37 Ct. Rev. 4 (2000).

2. *See, e.g.,* Susan S. Daicoff, Lawyer, Know Thyself: A Psychological Analysis of Personality Strengths and Weaknesses (2004); Practicing Therapeutic Jurisprudence: Law as a Helping Profession (Dennis P. Stolle, David B. Wexler & Bruce J. Winick eds., 2000) [hereinafter Practicing Therapeutic Jurisprudence]; Symposium, *Therapeutic Jurisprudence and Preventive Law: Transforming Legal Practice and Education*, 5 Psychol. Pub. Pol'y & L. 793-1210 (Bruce J. Winick, David B. Wexler & Edward A. Dauer, eds. 1999) [hereinafter Symposium].

3. *See, e.g.,* Ulf. Holmberg & Sven-Ake Christianshon, *Murderers' and Sexual Offenders' Experiences of Police Interviews and Their Inclination to Admit or Deny Crimes*, 20 Behav.

court,[4] and governmental officials at every level have a wide range of discretion in how they apply the law and how they function can impact the psychological wellbeing of the individuals whose lives they touch. It therefore is important that these legal actors understand that, among their other roles, they function as therapeutic agents. It is hoped that this understanding will be transformative. If they know that their actions either can impose psychological harm or facilitate emotional wellbeing, they should strive to minimize the anti-therapeutic consequences of their conduct and maximize its therapeutic potential.

This book focuses on the role of the lawyer as a therapeutic agent. Therapeutic jurisprudence has spawned a reconceptualization of the role of the lawyer. It envisions lawyers who practice their profession with an ethic of care, enhanced interpersonal skills, a sensitivity to their clients' emotional wellbeing as well as their legal rights and interests, and a preventive law orientation that seeks to avoid legal problems. This has been described as the therapeutic jurisprudence/preventive law model of lawyering.[5]

This chapter explores the role of the lawyer representing a client in a potential or actual civil dispute. The client is involved in a controversy, and this has brought her to the law office. Will a lawsuit be necessary, or can it be avoided? The client is likely to be in a state of emotional turmoil, and the TJ lawyer will be highly sensitive to the emotional dimensions of the lawyer/client relationship as well as the protection and promotion of the client's legal rights. How can the lawyer reduce the client's emotional stress and facilitate her ability to resolve the conflict and experience psychological healing? This is the challenge facing the TJ lawyer, and it often raises difficult problems that call for highly sensitive interviewing and counseling.

If litigation can be avoided, the client most often will be much better off. Yet, the client will often bring to the law office a variety of emotional responses to the controversy that can make settlement quite difficult. The client may in-

---

SCI. & L. 31 (2002); Bruce J. Winick, *The Jurisprudence of Therapeutic Jurisprudence*, 3 PSY-CHOL. PUB. POL'Y & L. 184, 203–04 (1997).

4. *See, e.g.,* Bruce J. Winick, *Therapeutic Jurisprudence and the Civil Commitment Hearing,* 10 J. CONTEMP. LEGAL ISSUES 37 (1999).

5. *See generally* PRACTICING THERAPEUTIC JURISPRUDENCE, *supra* note 2; Symposium, *supra* note 2; Dennis P. Stolle, David B. Wexler, Bruce J. Winick & Edward A. Dauer, *Integrating Preventive Law and Therapeutic Jurisprudence: A Law and Psychology Based Approach to Lawyering,* 34 CAL. W. L. REV. 15 (1997); David B. Wexler & Bruce J. Winick, *Putting Therapeutic Jurisprudence to Work,* 89 A.B.A. J. 54 (2003); Bruce J. Winick, *The Expanding Scope of Preventive Law,* 3 FLA. COASTAL L.J. 189 (2002).

sist that the lawyer bring a lawsuit. In her mind, nothing else will do. The client may be angry with her adversary. Not only has the client suffered physical injury, economic loss, or frustrated expectations, but the client's feelings are hurt and the client wants revenge. Sometimes the client is in denial about what has happened or the extent to which she is at fault. These clients present difficult challenges for the lawyer. This chapter discusses how the lawyer can deal with these psychological barriers to settlement.

I. Counseling the Client About Litigation and How to Avoid It

Sometimes litigation may be unavoidable. However, it always imposes significant costs, is fraught with delay, and poses risks that are difficult to calculate.[6] It often hardens feelings and produces nastiness, concealment, and outright dishonesty. Moreover, a lawsuit predictably will impose serious emotional costs on the parties.[7] It ranks among the most stressful experiences the individual will endure in life, comparable to the stress caused by the death of a loved one, the breakup of a relationship, or the loss of a job.[8] Controversies often involve parties who have had an existing relationship—spouses heading for divorce, business partners, employers and employees, manufacturers and their suppliers or customers, and neighbors. Litigation may provoke such strong anger and resentment that wounds will never heal and the relationship may be permanently severed. A lawsuit typically will provoke fear and anxiety that may be debilitating, and sometimes a form of depression.

The TJ lawyer should counsel the client about these negative effects of litigation, and explore all possible alternatives that might avoid them. Sometimes

---

6. *See, e.g.,* David M. Trubek et al., *The Costs of Ordinary Litigation*, 31 UCLA L. Rev. 72 (1983); Bruce J. Winick, *Therapeutic Jurisprudence and the Role of Counsel in Litigation*, 37 Cal. W. L. Rev. 105, 108 (2000).

7. Marc Galanter, *The Day After the Litigation Explosion*, 46 Md. L. Rev. 3, 8–11 (1986). As the following discussion shows, litigation ordinarily is antitherapeutic for both parties. There are, of course, exceptions. Sometimes a lawsuit can be cathartic. In some instances, for example involving a victim of domestic violence, it can be empowering in ways that can be psychologically beneficial. *See* Trina Grillo, *The Mediation Alternative: Process Dangers For Women*, 100 Yale L.J. 1545, 1573 (1991). Although sometimes these psychological benefits may outweigh the antitherapeutic effects of litigation described herein, other ways of achieving them—in counseling, for example—frequently will exist.

8. Barbara S. Dohrenwend et al., *Exemplification of a Method for Scaling Life Events: The PERI Life Events Scale*, 19 J. Health & Soc. Behav. 205 (1978).

the claim or defense is considerably weaker than the client may think, and the attorney may have to advise the client to let the matter go and move on with the rest of his life. In any event, the lawyer should explore with the client the various alternative dispute resolution mechanisms that exist, each of which is likely to be superior to litigation as a mechanism for resolving the controversy. These include negotiation and settlement, mediation, arbitration, and collaborative law.[9] Direct negotiation between the parties, perhaps including their lawyers, may be the best alternative. Settling the matter for themselves will generally feel better to the parties than having a solution imposed by the court or an arbitrator.[10] Negotiation can itself be a healing process, bringing together disputants to discuss and resolve their differences and to achieve reconciliation.[11] However, anger and other strong emotions that the controversy may have provoked may make it impossible for such direct settlement discussions to occur.

In such cases, mediation should be considered. The attorney should counsel the client about the differing kinds of mediation—facilitative, evaluative, and transformative—and their advantages and disadvantages.[12] If the conflict

---

9. *See generally* ROBERT A. BARUCH BUSH & JOSPEH P. FOLGER, THE PROMISE OF MEDIATION: THE TRANSFORMATIVE APPROACH TO CONFLICT (2005); STEVEN GOLDBERG ET AL., DISPUTE RESOLUTION (3d ed. 2000); KIMBERLEE K. KOVACH, MEDIATION: PRINCIPLES AND PRACTICE (1994); LEONARD L. RISKIN & JAMES E. WESTBROOK, DISPUTE RESOLUTION AND LAWYERS (2d ed. 1997); JOHN WINSLADE & GERALD MONK, NARRATIVE MEDIATION: A NEW APPROACH TO CONFLICT RESOLUTION (2000); Carrie Menkel-Meadow, *Pursuing Settlement in an Adversary Culture: A Tale of Innovation Co-Opted or "The Law of ADR"*, 19 FLA. ST. U. L. REV. 1 (1991); Judith Resnik, *Many Doors? Closing Doors? Alternative Dispute Resolution and Adjudication*, 10 OHIO ST. J. ON DISP. RESOL. 211 (1995); Leonard Riskin, *Understanding Mediators' Orientations, Strategies, and Techniques: A Grid for the Perplexed*, 1 HARV. NEGOT. L. REV. 7 (1996). For discussion of the relatively new dispute resolution model known as collaborative law, see *infra* note 13 and accompanying text.

10. A body of literature on the psychology of choice suggests that, in general, people feel better about choices that they make for themselves and perform more effectively in such circumstances, compared to when they experience their choices as having been coerced or pressured. *See* BRUCE J. WINICK, CIVIL COMMITMENT: A THERAPEUTIC JURISPRUDENCE MODEL ch. 2 (2005); BRUCE J. WINICK, THE RIGHT TO REFUSE MENTAL HEALTH TREATMENT ch. 17 (1997); Bruce J. Winick, *On Autonomy: Legal and Psychological Perspectives*, 37 VILL. L. REV. 1705, 1755–68 (1992).

11. *See* Gerald R Williams, *Negotiation as a Healing Process*, 1996 J. DISP. RESOL. 1 (1996); Winick, *supra* note 6, at 113.

12. For analysis of facilitative and evaluative mediation, see *supra* ch. 7: Harold Abramson, *Problem-Solving Advocacy in Mediations: A Model of Client Representation*, at pp. []; Kimberlee K. Kovach & Lela P. Love, *Evaluative Mediation is an Oxymoron*, 14 ALTERNATIVES TO HIGH COST LITIG. 31 (1996); Michael L. Moffitt, *Schmediation and the Dimensions Of Definition*, 10 HARV. NEGOT. L. REV. 69, 83–84 (2005); Ellen Waldman, *The Eval-*

arises out of a relationship that the client has had with his present adversary, the attorney may wish to suggest the use of transformative mediation or another approach that focuses on relationship issues and not merely the conflict at hand. Resolving the instant dispute without addressing the relationship issues that might have caused it may miss the opportunity that the conflict presents for healing the relationship itself.

In this connection, the lawyer also should consider the emerging dispute resolution mechanism of collaborative law.[13] Because it focuses on resolving the dispute in ways that do not irreparably damage the relationship, collaborative law is particularly well suited for conflicts between individuals who wish to preserve their business or personal relationship beyond the dispute that has placed it at risk. A collaborative approach, of course, requires a willingness to attempt it on both sides, and this may not be possible.

If none of these approaches are appropriate in the circumstances, the attorney may consider the possibility of arbitration. Particularly when both parties can agree upon a trusted friend, family member, or member of the clergy to hear both sides and render either a decision or a recommendation, this mode of dispute resolution can be far superior to litigation. Arbitration can impose its own costs and delays, but these typically are far less than litigation. There may be reasons to prefer litigation to arbitration, particularly given the tendency of arbitrators sometimes to impose a compromise resolution, and the pros and cons of this technique should be fully explored with the client. If any of these alternative dispute resolution mechanisms can be used, they generally will be much better for the client than litigation. This is, of course,

---

uative-Facilitative Debate in Mediation: Applying the Lens of Therapeutic Jurisprudence, 82 MARQ. L. REV. 155 (1998) (comparing evaluative and facilitative mediation and discussing the therapeutic effects of facilitative mediation); For discussion of transformative mediation, see BUSH & FOLGER, *supra* note 9; JOSEPH P. FOLGER & ROBERT A. BARUCH BUSH, DESIGNING MEDIATION: APPROACHES TO TRAINING AND PRACTICE WITHIN A TRANSFORMATIVE FRAMEWORK (2001).

13. For discussion of the collaborative law model in the divorce context, see PAULINE H. TESLER, COLLABORATIVE LAW: ACHIEVING EFFECTIVE RESOLUTION IN DIVORCE WITHOUT LITIGATION (2001); Pauline H. Tesler, *Collaborative Law: A New Paradigm for Divorce Lawyers*, 5 PSYCHOL. PUB. POL'Y & L. 967 (1999); Pauline H. Tesler, *The Believing Game, The Doubting Game, and Collaborative Law: A Reply to Penelope Bryan*, 5 PSYCHOL. PUB. POL'Y & L. 1018 (1999); Pauline H. Tesler, *Collaborative Law: What it is and Why Lawyers Need to Know About It*, 13 AM. J. FAM. L. 215 (1999), *reprinted in* PRACTICING THERAPEUTIC JURISPRUDENCE, *supra* note 2, at 187; *supra* ch. 8: Pauline H. Tesler, *Collaborative Law: Practicing Without Armor, Practicing With Heart.*

a decision for the client.[14] But the attorney should discuss with the client the negative consequences of using litigation to resolve the dispute, and the advantages of considering these various alternatives. Litigation generally should be considered only as a last resort, not as a preferred mode of resolving the dispute. Yet, the client, as a result of the strong emotions that the controversy has provoked, may be unable to hear the attorney's advice. Moreover, the client consulting an attorney as a result of the conflict may see the task at hand as bringing a successful lawsuit. Discussing these alternative modes of dispute resolution with the client, therefore, may present difficult interviewing and counseling challenges.

II. Psychological Barriers to Settlement and How to Overcome Them

Sometimes the client's emotional reactions to the conflict will make these discussions about alternatives to litigation quite difficult. Indeed, these emotional reactions may constitute psychological barriers to the client's considering alternative possibilities and participating appropriately in settlement discussions or other modes of dispute resolution. These present special challenges for the TJ lawyer. The remainder of this chapter discusses these psychological barriers and suggests ways in which the lawyer can seek to overcome them.

A. The Client Who Wants to "Sue the Bastards"

Clients may come to the law office demanding that their attorneys "sue the bastards." They are there to interview the attorney for the role of trial lawyer. Litigation is the goal, and they are ready for war. In interviewing the lawyer, they are not looking for a peacemaker, but for a pit bull. Such clients might have unrealistic expectations about litigation success and the amount of re-

---

14. The prevailing model of the lawyer/client relationship is client centered counseling, in which the client makes the ultimate decision. *See generally* ROBERT M. BASTRESS & JOSEPH D. HARBAUGH, INTERVIEWING, COUNSELING & NEGOTIATING: SKILLS FOR EFFECTIVE REPRESENTATION 334–38 (1990); DAVID A. BINDER ET AL., LAWYERS AS COUNSELORS: A CLIENT CENTERED APPROACH 2–13 (2d ed. 2004); Robert D. Dinerstein, *Client-Centered Counseling: Reappraisal and Refinement*, 32 ARIZ. L. REV. 501 (1990); Bruce J. Winick, *Redefining the Role of the Criminal Defense Lawyer at Plea Bargaining and Sentencing: A Therapeutic Jurisprudence/Preventive Law Model*, 5 PSYCHOL. PUB. POL'Y & L. 1034, 1067 (1999).

covery they will receive. They may overlook problems of collection. They may underestimate the likelihood that their adversary will be open to a negotiated compromise. As a result, litigation seems to them to be the only possibility.

To the extent that the client's desire to pursue a lawsuit is based on misconceptions about any of these matters, the lawyer must attempt to dispel them and provide the client with a new sense of reality. How can the lawyer do this? This can be seen as a task not unlike cognitive restructuring, a therapeutic approach used by clinicians in dealing with a variety of problems that bring their patients to the office.[15] Therapists specializing in cognitive behavioral therapy often seek to break down the patient's cognitive distortions, and to help the patient to replace them with new and more adaptive cognitive strategies.[16] To the extent that the client's announced decision to pursue litigation is based upon misconceptions or cognitive distortions, the lawyer should attempt to demonstrate to the client the erroneous nature of her assumptions. This requires careful and sensitive interviewing to uncover the client's misconceptions or distortions, and skilled counseling to persuade the client to discard them.

The attorney's role in correcting the client's false assumptions can also be seen as an exercise in reframing.[17] Just as changing the picture frame on a work of art sometimes allows us to see the art differently, helping the client to interpret the situation differently than he initially may have seen it can constitute a creative way of helping the client to better understand the situation. Even if the reality of the situation is the same, framing it differently can permit the client to deal with it more effectively. The client laboring under false assumptions about how a lawsuit might turn out may see litigation as the only possible way of redressing the wrongs that she has suffered. Such a client may

---

15. *See* Bruce J. Winick, *Applying the Law Therapeutically in Domestic Violence Cases,* 69 U. Mo. Kan. City L. Rev. 33, 77 (2000) ("Cognitive restructuring seeks to break down the [individual's] cognitive distortions and to replace them with more accurate, functional, adaptive, and effective thought patterns."); *see also* Jacqueline B. Persons, Cognitive Therapy in Practice: A Case Formulation Approach (1989); Dennis P. Saccuzzo, *How Should the Police Respond to Domestic Violence: A Therapeutic Jurisprudence Analysis of Mandatory Arrest,* 39 Santa Clara L. Rev. 765, 781 (1999).

16. *See, e.g.,* Albert Bandura, Social Foundations of Thought and Action: A Social Cognitive Theory 338 *passim* (1986); Aaron T. Beck, Cognitive Treatment of Depression (1992); Aaron T. Beck et al., Cognitive Therapy of Personality Disorders (2003); Donald. Meichenbaum, Cognitive Behavior Modification: An Integrative Approach (1977).

17. *See, e.g.,* Richard Bandler & John Grinder, Reframing: Neuro-Linguistic Programming and the Transformation of Meaning (1981).

be psychologically unable to consider the possibility of settling the dispute. The purpose of hiring a lawyer, in her view, is to bring a lawsuit. However, the TJ lawyer, understanding that litigation often is the worst means of resolving a dispute, faces the challenge of helping the client to reframe the purpose of hiring the lawyer; it is not to litigate the controversy, but to resolve the conflict. Once the client can see it in this way, the purpose of the attorney/client relationship will be redefined. If the problem is defined as how to win a lawsuit, then a lawsuit will surely occur. If the problem can instead be defined as how to resolve the dispute, then many creative possibilities will emerge.

As a creative problem solver, the TJ lawyer must strive to see the problem in different ways, rather than merely accepting the way the client defines the problem.[18] And the lawyer must attempt to allow the client to see the problem in different ways, rather than in the way he initially defines it. How the problem is defined will dictate the solutions that are attempted. Once the client can redefine the problem as resolving a dispute, rather than as winning a lawsuit, an entirely new range of options become possible. Litigation is only one way of resolving the dispute, and once the client redefines the goal, the lawyer can counsel the client about the various alternative dispute resolution modes that are available, and which ones would be most advisable in the circumstances.

B. The Angry Client

Some clients will be so angry with their adversary that they will not be able to consider the possibility of settlement. Some will want to punish their adversaries by bringing litigation. They are self-righteous, and seek revenge and retribution.

When anger seems to be the principal motive for litigation, the lawyer needs to acknowledge the client's strong feelings, but seek to determine whether they drive the client's decision to bring litigation. If so, the lawyer should raise the question of whether these strong feelings should justify the high costs and other negative effects of bringing a lawsuit. Pursuing a lawsuit out of anger and the desire for revenge may be unhealthy, and the attorney needs to develop creative ways of conveying this to the client without appearing to be paternalistic. The lawyer's task is to get the client to question his as-

---

18. For a useful analysis of creative problem solving, see Edward A. Dauer, *Reflections on Therapeutic Jurisprudence, Creative Problem Solving, and Clinical Education in the Transactional Curriculum*, 17 St. Thomas L. Rev. 483 (2005).

sumptions by introducing information that the client may not have considered or fully considered. In doing this, of course, the lawyer must remember that the ultimate decision is up to the client. It may be useful to invoke the adage, attributed to Confucius, that "if you devote your life to seeking revenge, first dig two graves."[19] The client may not agree with Confucius, but at least should consider the point before launching into litigation. Most anyone who feels he has been wronged will feel angry and desire retribution. These are appropriate human feelings, but may not justify a lawsuit. The attorney should seek to ascertain whether other reasons justifying litigation might exist—obtaining compensation for an injury suffered, preventing a future injury, or vindicating the client's reputation, for example. If so, litigation might be legitimate, but if not, pursuing a lawsuit is unlikely to be an appropriate outlet for anger or the desire for retribution.

The attorney should suggest to the client that there are other, more healthy outlets for anger. Pursuing a lawsuit will prevent the client from letting go of his anger for the several years that it will last. Not only will it produce psychological difficulties that will prevent the client from enjoying life, but it can produce physical illness as well—high blood pressure,[20] headache,[21] back or neck pain,[22] and heart attack or stroke.[23] The TJ lawyer will be aware that it

---

19. Jordana Lewis & Jerry Adler, *Forgive and Let Live*, NEWSWEEK, Sept. 27, 2004, at 52.

20. *See, e.g.,* Stephan Bongard & Mustafa al'Absi, *Domain-Specific Anger Expression and Blood Pressure in an Occupational Setting*, 58 J. PSYCHOSOMATIC RES. 43 (2005) (Anger linked to elevated blood pressure and heart rate); Jennifer L. Schum et al., *Trait Anger, Anger Expression, and Ambulatory Blood Pressure: A Meta-Analytic Review*, 26 J. BEHAV. MED. 395 (2003) (Anger related to elevated blood pressure).

21. *See, e.g.,* Ephrem Fernandez, *The Relationship Between Anger and Pain*, 9 CURRENT PAIN & HEADACHE REP. 101 (2005) (Exploring the interrelationship between anger and chronic pain including headache); Felicity Materazzo et al., *Anger, Depression, and Coping Interactions in Headache Activity and Adjustment: A Controlled Study*, 49 J. PSYCHOSOMATIC RES. 69 (2000) (Anger related to headache activity).

22. *See, e.g.,* John W. Burns et al., *Anger Management Style, Blood Pressure Reactivity, and Acute Pain Sensitivity: Evidence for "Trait X Situation" Models*, 27 ANNALS BEHAV. MED. 195 (2004) (Anger management style is related to acute and chronic pain); John W. Carson et al., *Forgiveness and Chronic Low Back Pain: A Preliminary Study Examining the Relationship of Forgiveness to Pain, Anger, and Psychological Distress*, 6 J. PAIN 84 (2005) (Chronic lower back pain linked to anger).

23. *See, e.g.,* Matthew M. Burg & Brian C. Sirois, *Negative Emotion and Coronary Heart Disease*, 27 BEHAV. MODIFICATION 83 (2003) (Negative emotions, including anger, hostility and anxiety are related to coronary heart disease); Susan A. Everson et al., *Anger Expression and Incident Hypertension*, 60 PSYCHOSOMATIC MED. 730 (1998) (Extreme anger and expression of anger linked to cardiovascular disease); Janice E. Williams et al., *The As-*

will likely be more therapeutic for the client to let go of the anger and get past the controversy. The lawsuit will absorb the client's energies and upset his equilibrium, causing him to put good energy after bad. The lawyer should advise the client to reflect upon the lessons that the dispute may offer, and move on, rather than maintaining the bad feelings it has engendered.

This is an extraordinarily sensitive conversation to have with a client who is angry. The attorney should display empathy, showing the client that he understands the client's strong feelings and perhaps even shares them. Empathy can be a critical tool in cutting through a strong emotional reaction on the part of the client that might prevent the client from seeing the situation clearly and following counsel's advice. Conveying empathy involves the ability to enter the client's feelings and to see the world through her eyes. It is the ability of the lawyer to perceive the client's meanings and to communicate that feeling back to the client. Empathy involves both a cognitive and an affective component—both an intellectual response to the client, conveying the sense that the attorney thinks the same way as the client, and an emotional response, conveying the sense that the attorney feels the way the client does.[24] Conveying empathy is not the same as conveying pity, which can be offensive, and is more than conveying sympathy. It involves having an emotional response to the client's story in which the attorney experiences the client's pain or grief as her own, and, in the process, forges an emotional bond with the client. Al-

---

sociation Between Trait Anger and Incident Stroke Risk: The Atherosclerosis Risk in Communities (ARIC) Study, 33 STROKE 13 (2002) (Anger found to be related to risk of stroke).

24. Gerald A. Gladstein, *Understanding Empathy: Integrating Counseling, Developmental, and Social Psychology Influences*, 30 J. COUNSELING PSYCHOL. 467 (1983); Daniel R. Shuman, *The Use of Empathy in Forensic Examinations*, 3 ETHICS & BEHAV. 289 (1993); Bruce J. Winick, *Client Denial and Resistance in the Advance Directive Context: Reflections On How Attorneys Can Identify And Deal With A Psycholegal Soft Spot*, 4 PSYCHOL. PUB. POL'Y & L. 901, 910 (1998); "The word empathy is derived from the Greek *empatheia*, which implies an act of appreciation of another person's feeling experience." *Id.* Empathy involves the capacity to perceive the client as having goals, interests, and emotions similar to those of the attorney; to imagine the situation of the client; and to respond in ways calculated to ease the client's pain. It involves "exuding a feeling of caring and sincerely trying to understand the other in a nonjudgmental and helping way." Winick, *supra* at 910, *citing* ARNOLD P. GOLDSTEIN & GERALD Y. MICHAELS, EMPATHY: DEVELOPMENT, TRAINING AND CONSEQUENCES (1985); Carl R. Rogers, *Empathic: An Unappreciated Way of Being*, 2 COUNSELING PSYCHOLOGIST 2 (1975). To be effective at expressing empathy, attorneys must learn to project themselves into the feelings and situations of their clients, expressing the warmth and understanding that create a comfortable space within which clients can express their own emotions.

though the attorney must be careful not to over-identify with the client and to preserve her professional objectivity, the ability of the lawyer to convey empathy when appropriate can be an essential mechanism for piercing the emotional barriers that might stand in the way of settlement.

The lawyer should listen to the client, not only hearing his words, but also being sensitive to his non-verbal forms of communication.[25] The lawyer should avoid paternalism and confrontation. Paternalism is offensive, sometimes making it difficult for the client to hear the attorney and follow her advice. Confrontation, although sometimes appropriate, similarly can be counter productive, especially if the attorney has not yet earned the client's trust, sometimes leading the client to question whether the attorney is an opponent rather than an ally.

"Where would the client like to be in a couple of years?" the lawyer might ask. What are his post-dispute goals, and will holding on to the controversy further or frustrate these goals? The lawyer must be careful to allow the client to answer these questions for himself, rather than telling him what he should do.[26]

When the client's anger is so strong that it seems to prevent rational consideration of the options, the lawyer might suggest the advisability of obtaining counseling. This, too, is a highly sensitive conversation, and the lawyer should raise the question in ways that the client does not perceive as insulting or demeaning. The lawyer should have a familiarity with mental health or counseling services and providers in the community, and, if asked, should be prepared to recommend referrals to those who are well regarded. In having

---

25. Steven Keeva, *Beyond the Words: Understanding What Your Client is Really Saying Makes for Successful Lawyering*, 85 A.B.A. J. 60 (1999).

26. Allowing the client to reach her own conclusions can be seen as an application of principles drawn from the social psychology of persuasion. The elaboration likelihood model of persuasion is particularly useful in this context. *See* RICHARD E. PETTY & JOHN T. CACIOPPO, COMMUNICATION AND PERSUASION: CENTRAL AND PERIPHERAL ROUTES TO ATTITUDE CHANGE (1986). This model posits that the impact of certain persuasive elements will be influenced by the extent to which the individual listening to the message is herself actively involved in the processing of the presented information. Central route persuasion focuses on the content of the message itself and posits that persuasion is maximized when the individual has a high likelihood of elaboration, *i.e.*, of engaging in issue-relevant thinking about the message itself. The likelihood of persuasion is maximized to the extent that the message has personal relevance to the individual and the individual has prior knowledge concerning the issue in question. *See* Wendy Wood, *Retrieval of Attitude-Relevant Information from Memory: Effects on Susceptibility to Persuasion and on Intrinsic Motivation*, 42 J. PERSONALITY & SOC. PSYCHOL. 798 (1982); Wendy Wood & Carl. A. Kallgren, *Communicator Attributes and Persuasion: Recipients' Access to Attitude-Relevant Information in Memory*, 14 PERSONALITY & SOC. PSYCHOL. BULL. 172 (1988).

these conversations, the lawyer should be attentive to the client's non-verbal forms of communication. Some clients will deeply resent the suggestion that they need therapy or mental health counseling. In such circumstances, the lawyer should avoid incurring such resentment, which has a high potential for destroying the client's trust and confidence in the attorney. Instead, the attorney might provide anecdotal accounts of friends or family members who have confronted similar difficulties, and for whom unresolved anger produced serious additional problems. These accounts can involve individuals in these situations who have benefited from professional counseling about their problems. The lawyer, however, should avoid drawing inferences from these accounts for the client. It would be better to allow the client to draw such inferences for himself.

Allowing the client to ventilate his anger and other strong feelings will often be a prerequisite for the client to consider alternatives other than litigation. This can be an occasion for active and reflective listening, in which the lawyer restates the client's feelings. The client's anger and related strong feelings may well be fully legitimate, and if so, the attorney can say so. But whether they justify litigation is an altogether different question.

"If we can resolve the dispute through a settlement that brings adequate compensation, thereby avoiding the time and expense of litigation, would this satisfy you?" the lawyer might ask. "Would an apology suffice, if coupled with reasonable compensation?" Does the client think that it might be possible to reconcile with his adversary? Is this a personal or business relationship that the client would wish to continue should they be able to resolve the dispute in a satisfactory way? The client may think that none of this is possible, but if he can acknowledge that reconciliation would be beneficial, the lawyer may be able to persuade him that an attempt at settlement through the use of a dispute resolution mechanism other than litigation should be given a try. Creative questions of this kind might allow the client to get past his anger, which otherwise may prevent clear thinking about his options.

When these strategies fail to succeed, and the attorney is left with the feeling that litigation is being sought by the client as a result of anger and a desire for revenge, the attorney may face a significant ethical dilemma. If a lawsuit seems to lack merit or to be unjustified other than as an expression of anger, the lawyer may be unwilling to take the case. Indeed, it may be unethical for the lawyer to do so.[27] Functioning as an instrument of the client's anger

---

27. *See* Model Rules of Prof'l Conduct R. 3.1 (2003) ("A lawyer shall not bring or defend a proceeding, or assert or controvert an issue therein, unless there is a basis in law

will seem inappropriate to many lawyers, particularly if other justifications for litigation do not exist. In such circumstances, the attorney can tell the client that in his professional opinion, litigation is not warranted in the circumstances, and that settlement should be sought, or the matter dropped if unmeritorious. If the client is unwilling to follow the attorney's advice in this regard, the attorney can suggest that, although other attorneys might agree to pursue litigation on the client's behalf, he is unwilling to do so. Sometimes the attorney has a professional responsibility to say no to a client and this may often arise when dealing with the angry client. Sometimes the lawyer must refuse to respond to the client's lower self. "Take some time and think it over," the lawyer can tell the client, encouraging him to get in touch with his higher self and to let it be his guide.

C. The Client in Denial

Some clients will grossly misperceive the realities of the situation. Some will be plagued with denial, rationalization, or minimization, psychological defense mechanisms that will prevent them from considering settlement or even participating appropriately in the attorney/client relationship. Some will experience similar psychological defense mechanisms that will make it difficult for them to accurately understand the conduct and purpose of their adversaries. A spouse in a divorce proceeding, for example, may refuse to acknowledge that the marriage is over, and as a result, to even consider settlement possibilities. Similarly, a business partner or affiliate may be unable to accept the reality that the business relationship will no longer exist. Another example is the defendant in a personal injury action who has harmed someone, but seems psychologically unable to accept responsibility for his wrongdoing.

How can the TJ lawyer deal with these psychological defense mechanisms that may interfere with the client's ability effectively to deal with the problem and to participate in settlement? Once again, sensitive interviewing and counseling strategies are called for.[28] It is essential that the attorney establish a relationship of trust and confidence with the client. This is an important mission of the first client interview.

---

and fact for doing so that is not frivolous ..."); FED. R. CIV. P. 11 (Good faith pleading requirement).

28. *See* Winick, *supra* note 24, at 908–17 (discussing how lawyers can deal with resistance and denial in the context of advising clients concerning advance directive instruments for health and mental health care).

At the outset, it is important for the attorney to understand the psychological dimensions of the client's response. Denial and similar psychological defense mechanisms are responses to the strong feelings of anxiety that this situation provokes in the client. The concept of denial is derived from the early work of Sigmund Freud, who viewed denial as a protective personality mechanism that, by reducing anxiety, allows the individual to continue to function.[29] Under the classic psychoanalytic paradigm, denial is an unconscious process designed to protect the individual and to preserve his functioning.[30] With this understanding of the nature of denial, the TJ lawyer will be highly sensitive to the client's psychological state. The attorney should be supportive and non-judgmental, and should convey empathy where appropriate.[31] The attorney must strive to create a climate in which the client can feel comfortable in discussing highly personal and sensitive matters that produce intense anxiety. It is useful, in this connection, to discuss with the client the attorney/client privilege and the confidentiality that covers conversations occurring within the professional relationship. The attorney should tell the client that, for the lawyer to represent him effectively, the client must open up to the lawyer and be fully forthcoming. This includes expressing his feelings about the conflict and about his adversary. Unless the client feels that the attorney is an ally and confident, he will not feel free to share thoughts and feelings with counsel.

Success in having such sensitive conversations with the client requires that the attorney possess heightened interpersonal skills.[32] TJ lawyers need to possess good listening skills and to pay attention not only to what the client says, but to non-verbal forms of communication.[33] They need to develop their emo-

---

29. *Id.* at 904.

30. *Id.*

31. *Id.* at 906–17.

32. *See* Jonathan R. Cohen, *The Culture of Legal Denial*, 84 Neb. L. Rev. 247, 271–82 (2005) (making suggestions concerning how the lawyer can discuss responsibility-taking with the client, including techniques of building trust and confidence, listening, conveying empathy, and the differing styles of confrontation that the lawyer can use in raising the subject with the client—confrontation, indirection, and engagement), *reprinted in* (in part) *supra* ch. 9, at pp. 305–12; Winick, *supra* note 24, at 906–17 (discussing techniques for attorneys to use in holding sensitive conversations with their clients about the advisability of executing advance directive instruments for health and mental health care); Winick, *supra* note 14, at 1065–78 (discussing techniques for criminal defense attorneys to use in having sensitive conversations with their clients about rehabilitation).

33. Keeva, *supra* note 25; Winick, *supra* note 24, at 912–13.

tional intelligence[34] and be affective lawyers.[35] It is essential that the lawyer convey to the client that unless she is willing to consider and discuss with her attorney issues relating to the conflict even though they may provoke intense anxiety, embarrassment, or internal conflict, the lawyer will be compromised in her ability to achieve the client's best interests.

In having these conversations, lawyers should be careful to avoid acting paternalistically. Rather, they should respect their client's autonomy, persuading them of the merits of their advice, instead of coercing them. In having these conversations, the TJ lawyer will benefit from an understanding of the technique of motivational interviewing, originally developed in the context of substance abuse counseling.[36] Because individuals suffering from alcoholism or other forms of substance abuse frequently are in denial about their problem or minimize its significance, an important challenge for the substance abuse counselor is to help the individual to recognize the existence of the problem and motivate her to deal with it. This technique has been suggested for use by criminal defense attorneys, representing clients in plea bargaining, diversion, or sentencing.[37] In this context, motivational interviewing can be a technique for helping their clients to accept responsibility for their wrongdoing and understand that they have a problem with which they need to deal. This approach may similarly be useful in the context of counseling clients about the settlement of civil disputes, particularly when denial, minimization, rationalization, or some other psychological defense mechanism appears to be present.

How does this approach work? Several basic principles underlie motivational interviewing. First, the interviewer needs to express empathy by trying to understand the individual's feelings and perspectives (through careful and

---

34. *See* DANIEL GOLEMAN, EMOTIONAL INTELLIGENCE (1997); DANIEL GOLEMAN, WORKING WITH EMOTIONAL INTELLIGENCE (1998); Marjorie A. Silver, *Emotional Intelligence and Legal Education*, 5 PSYCHOL. PUB. POL'Y & L. 1173 (1999).

35. *See* Peter Margulies, *Representation of Domestic Violence Survivors as a New Paradigm of Poverty Law in Search of Access, Connection and Voice*, 63 GEO. WASH. L. REV. 1071 (1995); Carrie J. Menkel-Meadow, *Narrowing the Gap by Narrowing the Field: What's Missing from the MacGrate Report—Of Skill, Human Science, and Being a Human Being*, 69 WASH. L. REV. 593 (1994); Linda G. Mills, *On the Other Side of Silence: Affective Lawyering for Intimate Abuse*, 81 CORNELL L. REV. 1225 (1996); Linda G. Mills, *Affective Lawyering: The Emotional Dimensions of the Lawyer-Client Relation*, *in* PRACTICING THERAPEUTIC JURISPRUDENCE, *supra* note 2, at 419.

36. *See generally* WILLIAM R. MILLER & STEPHEN ROLLNICK, MOTIVATIONAL INTERVIEWING: PREPARING PEOPLE TO CHANGE ADDICTIVE BEHAVIOR 33–51 (2d ed. 2002).

37. *See* Astrid Birgden, *Dealing with the Resistant Criminal Client: A Psychologically-minded Strategy for More Effective Legal Counseling*, 38 CRIM. L. BULL. 225 (2002).

respectful listening) without judging, criticizing, or blaming. Reflective listening and acceptance are essential to this process. It is often the case that the individual is reluctant and ambivalent in the beginning. Those traits should not be seen as pathological, but rather considered an ordinary aspect of human behavior.[38]

Second, the interviewer, in a non-confrontational way, should seek to identify discrepancies between the individual's present attitudes or behavior and important personal goals. The interviewer thus must elicit the individual's underlying goals and objectives, and through interviewing techniques, including open-ended questioning, reflective listening, the provision of frequent statements of affirmation and support, and the elicitation of self-motivational statements, should attempt to enable the individual to recognize the existence of a problem that denial or a similar psychological defense mechanism makes it difficult for him to manage. It is important that the interviewer point the individual in the right direction, but it must be left to the individual to express the intention to change or to come to terms with the problem.[39] Only when people perceive the discrepancy between how they are thinking or behaving and the achievement of their personal goals will motivation for change be created.[40] Third, when resistance is encountered, the interviewer must attempt to roll with the resistance rather than become confrontational. This requires listening with empathy and providing feedback to what the individual is saying by introducing new information, thereby allowing the individual to remain in control, to make his own decisions, and to create solutions to his problems. The interviewer should avoid arguing with the individual, which can be counterproductive and create defensiveness.[41]

Faced with the client whose denial or other defense mechanism prevents effective representation concerning possible settlement, the TJ lawyer can adapt the technique of motivational interviewing to attempt to counsel the client about the realities of the situation and the advantages of pursuing settlement strategies. Treating the client with dignity and respect, conveying empathy, respecting the client's autonomy, and using a form of motivational in-

---

38. MILLER & ROLLNICK, *supra* note 36, at 37.

39. *Id.* at 38–39.

40. In a useful discussion, Astrid Birgden ties motivational interviewing to the literature on readiness for change. Birgden, *supra* note 37. Sometimes legal involvement may provide a catalyst for change, increasing the likelihood that motivational interviewing will succeed. *See supra* ch. 2: Susan Brooks, *Using Social Work Constructs in the Practice of Law*, at pp. 63–66.

41. MILLER & ROLLNICK, *supra* note 36, at 39–40.

terviewing can help to break through the psychological denial and resistance that may pose an insurmountable barrier to fully exploring with the client settlement options and alternative dispute resolution mechanisms. Motivational interviewing can allow the client to understand that her denial, minimization, or rationalization is inconsistent with achievement of her long-range objectives, and that their continuation is not in her best interests. Such conversations can be expected to touch pent-up fear and anxiety that the client has been holding. In an empathic way, the attorney can assure the client that confronting rather than denying these strong emotions will have long-term therapeutic benefits for the client and will enable the lawyer to help her deal more effectively with the controversy. In appropriate circumstances, the attorney can suggest referring the client for mental health counseling concerning the feelings that now are coming to the surface.

D. The Client Who Cannot Admit That She Was Wrong

Some clients will find it difficult to admit that they made a mistake or committed negligence or some other legal wrong. In general, people are reticent to disclose their mistakes, and sometimes seem psychologically unable even to admit them to themselves. Many clients accused of wrongdoing come to the lawyer's office with the expectation that they should deny wrongdoing. They assume that such a defensive posture will limit the amount of any recovery against them, and that admitting responsibility will result in a higher award of damages. Indeed, there seems to be a general culture of denial that pervades legal practices relating to the resolution of civil disputes.[42] Client expectations that they should deny wrongdoing are fostered by the general practice of many lawyers in civil cases in assisting their clients in denying the wrongs they have done.

TJ lawyers face a special challenge when the client is unable or unwilling to accept responsibility for her wrongdoing. The client generally has the right to deny wrongdoing. Only if there is no genuine basis in law or fact for such a denial will the attorney encounter an ethical restriction on permitting such a denial.[43] But there often are harmful psychological and spiritual consequences for the client who falsely denies her wrongdoing.[44]

---

42. Cohen, *supra* note 32.

43. *See supra* note 21 and accompanying text.

44. Cohen, *supra* note 32; Jonathan R. Cohen, *The Immorality of Denial*, 79 TUL. L. REV. 903 (2005).

In Chapter 9 of this book, Professor Jonathan Cohen offers a powerful critique of this general practice.[45] He documents the harmful consequences of this practice on clients. His thesis is not that lawyers should talk their clients into acknowledging their guilt, but that they should consider discussing the subject of taking responsibility for their actions with them, something they rarely do. Lawyers frequently tell their clients to deny responsibility for the harms they have done, and advise them not to apologize to their victims. This posture makes settlement much more difficult, escalates the conflict, and is more likely to result in litigation that not only is expensive, but that brings forth dishonesty and concealment on the part of the client. Professor Cohen makes a compelling case that this practice presents serious moral, psychological, relational, and even economic risks to the client, and as a result, challenges the general assumption made by many lawyers that denial of wrongdoing is in the client's best interests.

Critics of this proposal may question whether it is the lawyer's role to save her client from immorality. But, Professor Cohen does not argue that the lawyer should impose her morality on the client. It is for the client to determine the ultimate ends of legal representation in the client-centered model of the lawyer/client relationship that our system embraces.[46] The lawyer's conduct in this regard typically is based on the assumption that it is in the client's best interests to deny wrongdoing. Professor Cohen shows that this assumption frequently is erroneous, and that also erroneous is the assumption that clients have only economic interests. Lawyers should not ignore their clients' other interests—moral, psychological, relational, and spiritual interests—and unless these other interests are explored in candid conversations with the client, the assumption that denial of wrongdoing is best for the client may be false. An important goal of TJ lawyering is to understand the client holistically. In addition to focusing on the client's legal/economic rights and interests, the TJ lawyer is concerned with these related interests, particularly those that can significantly impact the client's emotional wellbeing. Sometimes a practice of denying wrongdoing will succeed in avoiding liability or limiting recovery, particularly when the plaintiff will face difficulty in proving his case or substantiating the full amount of damages suffered. Perhaps this is the client's most important objective. But in deciding whether to deny or accept responsibility for his actions, the client should at least consider what the likely impact may be on his sense of integrity and emotional state and whether he

---

45. Cohen, *supra* note 32.
46. *See* sources cited *supra* note 14 and accompanying text.

values having a continued personal or business relationship with the party he has injured. Professor Cohen's conclusion therefore is correct that the lawyer should openly discuss with the client whether to admit or deny wrongdoing and the consequences of both. If the client, following this discussion, expresses the willingness to accept responsibility for his wrongdoing, the next question is whether he should offer an apology to the injured party.

Raising the question with the client of whether he should accept responsibility for wrongdoing and offer an apology, may be delicate and somewhat awkward. After all, the client has come to the lawyer's office presumably to seek advice about avoiding or limiting responsibility. The lawyer may be concerned that the client will perceive his raising the questions of taking responsibility and apologizing as judgmental or even disloyal, perceptions that might destroy the client's trust in the attorney.

How can the lawyer have these difficult and sensitive conversations with the client? The techniques described above for dealing with the client in denial are applicable here. The lawyer should treat the client with dignity and respect, be a good listener, convey empathy, and avoid acting paternalistically. The lawyer should point out the likely negative effects of denying wrongdoing and the positive consequences for facilitating settlement and for the client's psychological wellbeing of accepting responsibility.

E. Counseling the Client About Offering (or Accepting) an Apology

Moreover, these techniques can facilitate the client's willingness to offer an apology for his wrongdoing. An apology can do much to create the opportunity for successful settlement of the dispute, and if the apology is accepted, this can do much to repair the relationship between the parties and diminish the chances that conflict between them will again arise. The injured party may desire an apology as much as or even more than compensation. An apology, especially if made publicly, can bring a much-needed feeling of vindication. The making of an apology and its acceptance by the injured party, often will dissipate the anger and bad feelings that existed between the parties, restore the injured party's sense of equilibrium, and permit a healing of the relationship. By contrast, when an individual who has wronged another refuses to take responsibility for his actions and to apologize for them, the anger and bad feelings that are likely to exist between the parties can prevent clear thinking about settlement possibilities, can distort the ability of the parties to be realistic in negotiations and to understand the value of settlement, and can prevent them from accurately comprehending and evaluating settlement offers and making effective counter-offers. Compromise may be impossible in this climate, and the dispute is much more likely to end up in litigation.

The attorney for the party against whom a claim of wrongdoing is made, however, may be concerned that allowing the client to apologize may present risks should negotiations fail and the dispute become a lawsuit. In such an event, it is possible that the apology would be admissible in evidence, seriously undermining the defendant's ability subsequently to contest liability.[47] While the legal culture of today still discourages apology,[48] this is beginning to change as commentators extol the virtues of apology in facilitating settlement.[49] A number of jurisdictions recently have enacted legislation preventing an apology from being used against its maker at trial.[50] Some jurisdictions, however, only prevent the admissibility of apologies that are expressions of sympathy, providing no protection for those that acknowledge fault.[51] While such partial apologies may be effective in limited circumstances, they often may backfire, increasing feelings of resentment on the part of the injured party.

To be effective, an apology typically must acknowledge wrongdoing, offer an explanation for it, express shame and remorse, and include a willingness to make reparations.[52] Furthermore, the injured party must feel that the maker of the apology is sincere in his expression of remorse.[53] Successful apologies

---

47. *See* Fed. R. Evid. 801(d)(2) (party admissions exception to the hearsay rule).

48. Jennifer K. Robbennolt, *Apologies and Legal Settlement: An Empirical Examination*, 102 Mich. L. Rev. 460, 461 (2003); *see also* Hiroshi Wagatsuma & Arthur Rosett, *The Implications of Apology: Law and Culture in Japan and the United States*, 20 Law & Soc'y Rev. 461 (1986) (comparing practices in Japan and the U.S.).

49. *See, e.g.,* Jonathan R. Cohen, *Advising Clients to Apologize*, 71 S. Cal. L. Rev. 1009 (1999); Steven Keeva, *Does Law Mean Never Having to Say You're Sorry?* 89 A.B.A. J. 64 (1999); Aviva Orenstein, *Incorporating a Feminist Analysis into Evidence Policy Where You Would Least Expect It*, 28 Sw. U. L. Rev. 221 (1999); Robbennolt, *supra* note 48, at 461; Daniel R. Shuman, *The Role of Apology in Tort Law*, 83 Judicature 180 (2000).

50. *See* Robbennolt, *supra* note 48, at 470–71; *id.* at 470 n.44 (listing statutes); *see also* Jonathan R. Cohen, *Legislating Apology: The Pros and Cons*, 70 U. Cin. L. Rev. 819 (2002); Edward A. Dauer, *Apology in the Aftermath of Injury: Colorado's "I'm Sorry" Law*, 34 Colo. Law. 47, 51 n.2 (2005).

51. Robbennolt, *supra* note 48, at 471.

52. *See* Erving Goffman, Relations in Public: Microstudies of the Public Order 113 (1971); Aaron Lazare, On Apology 39 (2004); Robbennolt, *supra* note 48, at 477–80; Steven J. Scher & John M. Darley, *How Effective Are the Things People Say to Apologize? Effects of the Realization of the Apology Speech Act*, 26 J. Psycholinguistic Res. 127, 134–36 (1997); Wagatsuma & Rosett, *supra* note 48.

53. Lazare, *supra* note 52, at 39.

satisfy a number of psychological needs on the part of the injured party—the restoration of his self-respect and dignity, the assurance that both parties have shared values and that there is safety in their relationship, the desire for meaningful dialogue with the person who wronged him, the recognition that the offense was not his fault, and the feeling that the wrongdoer should suffer reparation for the harm done.[54] An apology that meets these needs, or at least many of them, facilitates the process of forgiveness.[55]

On the other hand, partial apologies—those that merely express sympathy, but do not acknowledge fault or express remorse and the desire to make reparations—are likely to be unsuccessful. An apology that seems insincere or is devoid of sympathy, sorrow, remorse, or admission of wrongdoing will not prompt forgiveness and may even fuel animosity if the injured party perceives the apology as a thinly veiled attempt to escape liability. This conclusion is supported by recent empirical research showing that not only is the likelihood of settlement substantially increased when there is a full apology, but that a partial apology reduces the likelihood of settlement to less than that existing when there was no apology at all, particularly when the injury is severe.[56] A partial apology therefore may backfire.

As a result, the attorney should counsel the client about the value of a sincere apology accompanied by an admission of wrongdoing, the expression of remorse, and an offer to make reparations for the wrong. Such an apology will significantly increase the likelihood that the apology will be accepted, that forgiveness will be granted, and that a settlement of the dispute will be reached. In addition, such a full apology may be necessary for healing, both of the injured party and of the client. Accepting responsibility and making amends to the injured party can be vital to the emotional wellbeing of the client when he knows he was at fault. Acceptance of the apology can provide needed closure for both parties, allowing them to move forward with their lives and, when desired, to heal their relationship. It can diffuse the stress, anger, hostility, hatred, resentment, and fear that is associated with holding a grudge. Moreover, experiencing forgiveness, which will come with the genuine acceptance of an apology, can produce health benefits for the individual.[57] Attorneys representing both alleged wrongdoers and parties injured as

---

54. *Id.* at 44; Robbennolt, *supra* note 48, at 477–80.

55. LAZARE, *supra* note 52, at 228–50.

56. Robbennolt, *supra* note 48, at 471, 515–16.

57. Patients who report an inability to forgive others may experience higher pain and psychological distress that are mediated by relatively higher levels of anger. Carson et al.,

a result therefore should discuss with their respective clients the value of a full apology and its acceptance in producing forgiveness, reconciliation, settlement, and healing.

In discussing apology or its acceptance with the client, the lawyer will need to display the enhanced interpersonal skills discussed above, avoid paternalism, convey empathy, and use a form of motivational interviewing. Sometimes these techniques will allow the client to concede to himself and his lawyer that he was wrong, or at least partially at fault. This doesn't necessarily mean that the client will be willing to acknowledge his wrongdoing to the injured party and apologize to her. The client may still wish to deny wrongdoing and attempt to avoid liability. This is his right, but the attorney should tell him that this course will likely provoke litigation, that the client's wrongdoing may be exposed in discovery or trial, and that this exposure following denial will likely make the injured party less willing to compromise the claim or lead the jury to impose a higher award. If he accepts wrongdoing and tenders an appropriate apology, on the other hand, the client can avoid the dishonesty in which his denial will likely lead him to engage, and the feelings of guilt and inner conflict that this can provoke. It also can produce a more advantageous settlement.

Conclusion

The TJ lawyer representing a client involved in a civil dispute can perform an enormous service to the client by exploring the possibilities for avoiding litigation. The attorney needs to become an expert in the various modes of alternative dispute resolution and in how to counsel the client about them and about the disadvantages of litigation.[58] Settlement will almost always be better than litigation. However, a number of psychological barriers to settlement may exist. This chapter has described several of these psychological obstacles and offered suggestions concerning how the attorney can attempt to overcome them.

---

supra note 22 (suggesting a relationship between forgiveness and pain, anger, and psychological distress in patients with chronic low back pain).

58. For a discussion of alternative modes of dispute resolution that contains several helpful comparative tables, see Frank E. A. Sander & Stephen B. Goldberg, *Fitting the Forum to the Fuss: A User-Friendly Guide to Selecting an ADR Procedure*, 10 Negot. J. 49 (1994).

Therapeutic jurisprudence calls for an increased psychological sensitivity in the attorney/client relationship and an awareness of some basic techniques of psychology—enhanced interpersonal skills, well developed interviewing and counseling skills, and approaches for identifying and dealing with a variety of emotional responses that the dispute is likely to produce. Practicing therapeutic jurisprudence in the civil settlement context can provide the opportunity to help the client through one of life's most difficult challenges. Moreover, practicing in this way can bring much personal and professional satisfaction.

IV

LAWYERING AND THE
CRIMINAL JUSTICE SYSTEM

CHAPTER 12

THE TJ CRIMINAL LAWYER: THERAPEUTIC JURISPRUDENCE AND CRIMINAL LAW PRACTICE

*David B. Wexler**

This chapter offers a simple yet, I hope, useful model of the components or ingredients of a therapeutic jurisprudence[1] criminal law practice. These components can perhaps best be illustrated by a concrete case. The case I have selected, *United States v. Riggs*[2] is, in its facts and legal import, an "ordinary" one, not unlike the steady diet of cases handled by most criminal defense lawyers.

I. United States v. Riggs

Riggs suffers from paranoid schizophrenia and, without medication, experiences auditory hallucinations and paranoia.[3] These symptoms began to assert themselves approximately two years before his first arrest—on Maryland state charges of drug distribution and possession of a shotgun (found during

---

* John D. Lyons Professor of Law and Professor of Psychology, University of Arizona, and Professor of Law and Director, International Network on Therapeutic Jurisprudence, University of Puerto Rico. The author may be contacted at davidbwexler@yahoo.com. This chapter draws upon David B. Wexler, *A Tripartite Framework for Incorporating Therapeutic Jurisprudence in Criminal Law Education, Research, and Practice*, 7 FL. COASTAL L. J. 95 (2005), and David B. Wexler, *Therapeutic Jurisprudence and the Rehabilitative Role of the Criminal Defense Lawyer*, 17 ST. THOMAS L. REV. 742 (2005).

1. *See* the bibliography on the website of the International Network on Therapeutic Jurisprudence, *at* http://www.therapeuticjurisprudence.org (last visited Nov. 23, 2005).

2. 370 F.3d 382 (4th Cir. 2004), *vacated and remanded*, 125 S. Ct. 1015 (Jan. 24, 2005).

3. *Id.* at 383.

a subsequent search of his home).[4] But Riggs did not receive any psychiatric treatment until *after* his arrest.[5] Riggs began taking oral medication to control the schizophrenia, and was sentenced on the state charges to three years probation, which he successfully completed.[6] At some point, Riggs failed to take his medication for two or three days,[7] began hallucinating, and believed people were trying to hurt him.[8] Riggs' failure to take his medication was, the parties agreed,[9] the cause of Riggs' later legal trouble.

A few days after discontinuing his medication, Riggs was stopped for driving a vehicle with expired plates.[10] Riggs was clutching his jacket and refused to show his hands.[11] A pat-down frisk revealed a .22 revolver in Riggs' jacket, leading to the federal firearm violation.[12]

Riggs pled guilty to the federal offense and resumed taking his oral medication.[13] Moreover, after the federal arrest, Riggs' mother began reminding Riggs daily to take his oral medication, and his treating physician started Riggs on long-acting intramuscular injections of antipsychotic drugs—drugs that remain in the bloodstream for a month, assuring adequate medication even if Riggs were to fail to take the oral medication religiously.[14]

Riggs was on pre-sentence release for almost two years.[15] That period was marked by its uneventful nature, during which Riggs took his medication without incident.

At the federal sentencing hearing, evidence was presented regarding the intramuscular injections, Riggs' oral medication compliance, and his mother's role in providing reminders.[16] Moreover, "Riggs emphasized to the court that he wanted to continue taking his medication, an intent that his consulting clinical psychologist believed."[17]

---

4. *Id.* at 390 (Duncan, J., dissenting).
5. *Id.*
6. *Id.* at 383.
7. *Id.* at 390 (Duncan, J., dissenting).
8. *Id.* at 383.
9. *Id.* at 390 (Duncan, J., dissenting).
10. *Id.* at 383.
11. *Id.*
12. *Id.*
13. *Id.*
14. *Id.*
15. *Id.*
16. *Id.* at 390 (Duncan, J., dissenting).
17. *Id.*

Under the then-existing sentencing guidelines, the district court granted a diminished capacity downward departure, and sentenced Riggs to three years probation, of which 12 months was to be served under home confinement with an electric home monitoring system. The court did not believe the non-incarcerative downward departure to be barred by a need to protect the public:

> I really do think that to the extent one can tell, based upon the facts as they now exist, things are under control, that you have been taking your medication, your mother is making sure, and … [your] treating physician is making sure you take your medication, and as long as you do that I think you are going to be law abiding.[18]

The preceding facts are more or less sufficient for our purposes. In terms of the human drama and legal niceties, however, there is more to the story: the government appealed—on public protection grounds—the district court's grant of the downward departure, and a divided panel of the Fourth Circuit agreed with the government, vacated the sentence, and remanded for re-sentencing. The majority noted that "although Riggs has been complying with his treatment program, we see no adequate assurance in the record that he will continue to do so."[19] The dissent strongly disagreed with the position that, despite the apparent success of Riggs' treatment plan, "the possibility that the defendant *might*, at some future time, decide not to take his medications requires the defendant's incarceration to protect the public."[20] But significantly, *Riggs* was decided before—and was ultimately vacated and remanded in light of—the U.S. Supreme Court's landmark decision in *U.S. v. Booker*,[21] which in essence converts the federal sentencing guidelines from mandatory to advisory only, and subjects imposed sentences to a "reasonableness" review.

Before proceeding to piece together the components of TJ lawyering, two observations are in order: First, the thrust of *Booker* is likely to lead federal courts to pay greater attention to general factors in sentencing, including treatment and rehabilitative goals.[22] In any case, after *Booker*, the sort of proba-

---

18. *Id.* at 384.
19. *Id.* at 386.
20. *Id.* at 387 (Duncan, J., dissenting).
21. United States v. Booker, 543 U.S. 220 (2005).
22. *See, e.g.*, the treatment-oriented provision in 18 U.S.C. §3553(a)(2)(D) (2003), which is receiving much post-*Booker* attention. U.S. v. Ranum, #04-CR-31, E.D. Wis., 2005; U.S. v. Jones, 352 F.Supp.2d 22 (D.Me., Jan. 21, 2005). Even before *Booker*, a federal judge wrote an op-ed piece in the New York Times urging a more flexible and therapeutic approach for the federal justice system. Donald P. Lay, *Rehab Justice*, N.Y. TIMES, Nov. 18, 2004, at A31.

tionary sentence imposed by the district court in *Riggs* should be less likely to be reversed on appeal.[23] *Booker*, if it is not undone by Congress, surely ushers in the distinct possibility of a true therapeutic jurisprudence perspective in federal criminal court.

Next, recall Riggs' symptoms surfaced two years before his initial arrest, but that Riggs did not receive mental health treatment until after he was arrested. And it was not until his second arrest that his medication regimen was augmented by a monthly intramuscular injection.

This noteworthy, but not at all uncommon, sequence of events underscores the difficulty of the position of those who "prefer that the judicial system was out of the business of organizing and providing social services to individuals and families,"[24] or who oppose "making the judiciary more like the public health arena."[25] Of course, the more "macro" issues of prevention, treatment, and services need to be seriously and vigorously attended to,[26] and the legal profession needs to be an important participant and advocate in that venture.[27] But, as the facts of *Riggs* suggest, no matter what the available resources, the criminal justice system will often function as a legal emergency room.[28] It is thus crucial for lawyers to concern themselves with treatment issues at the "micro" level[29] of the individual case and client. I now turn to the nature of TJ criminal lawyering.

---

23. In fact, when the Fourth Circuit considered its earlier *Riggs* opinion in light of *Booker*, it reinstated its prior opinion reversing the district court's grant of a downward departure and remanding for re-sentencing. But the now unanimous panel recognized the greater flexibility wrought by *Booker*, as well as the appropriateness of a "reasonableness" review. United States v. Riggs, *supra* note 2.

24. Jennie J. Long, *Book Review of 'Winick and Wexler (eds.) Judging in a Therapeutic Key'*, 40 CRIM. L. BULL. 541, 542 (2004) (reviewing JUDGING IN A THERAPEUTIC KEY (Bruce J. Winick & David B. Wexler eds., 2003)).

25. Jessica Pearson, *Special Issue: Models of Collaboration in Family Law: The Bookshelf: Bruce J. Winick and David B. Wexler (Eds.), Judging in a Therapeutic Key: Therapeutic Jurisprudence and the Courts*, 42 FAM. CT. REV. 384, 385 (2004).

26. *See* Long, *supra* note 24; Pearson, *supra* note 25.

27. Cait Clarke & James Neuhard, *Making the Case: Therapeutic Jurisprudence and Problem Solving Practices Positively Impact Clients, Justice Systems and the Communities they Serve*, 17 ST. THOMAS L. REV. 779 (2005).

28. Of course, as a matter of policy, we would surely want to avoid a situation where treatment and services are provided and are available *primarily* through the courts, thereby in essence rewarding criminal behavior. Pearson, *supra* note 25, at 386 ("Will we reward criminal behavior with jobs, housing, and education?").

29. Long, *supra* note 24, at 542.

II. The Components of TJ Criminal Lawyering

Several factors facilitated the district court's decision to grant Riggs a probationary sentence: Riggs' mental condition seemed very much "under control," according to the court, thanks to the medication; Riggs was receptive to taking the medication, was reminded daily by his mother, and was, in any case, administered a monthly long-acting intramuscular injection. Moreover, the adequacy of the treatment plan was evidenced by an almost two year period of successful pre-sentence release.

The above factors can be grouped into three categories: (1) *treatment and social service resources* (here, the availability and suitability of both the oral and intramuscular medication); (2) *the legal landscape* (the ability under the law to defer sentence and permit a period of pre-sentence release); and the less obvious and more nuanced category that we might call (3) *theory-inspired practices* (reflected here by the involvement of defendant's mother and, arguably, by the positive and reinforcing judicial remark that matters were "under control"). We will now explore further this tripartite classification or, in keeping with the standard vocabulary of the therapeutic jurisprudence "lens,"[30] will look at the criminal lawyer's potential role through a TJ trifocal.

A. Treatment and Social Service Resources

The availability of treatment is of course an essential ingredient in TJ criminal lawyering—and, ideally, in preventing many of the incidents that trigger the involvement of the criminal justice system. Services are necessary for mental health problems, such as encountered in *Riggs*, as well as for substance abuse, domestic violence, child abuse, and the like.

Lawyers need to have a basic understanding of these problem areas and of the programs designed to deal with them. Through judicial colleges and associations, judges are beginning to receive basic instruction in these areas,[31] and lawyers and law students likewise need an exposure to this material. An introductory course in social work and social welfare, especially if brought to life by a series of guest speakers from local programs and agencies, would be

---

30. *E.g.,* Law in a Therapeutic Key: Therapeutic Jurisprudence and the Courts xix (David B. Wexler & Bruce J. Winick eds., 1996).

31. *See* the website of The National Judicial College, *at* www.judges.org (last visited Nov. 23, 2005).

a wonderful addition to the law school curriculum and to continuing legal education programs.[32]

Mostly, of course, this overall category is the proper province of the mental health, social work, and criminal justice fields, but lawyers need to grasp the essentials and need to know how to relate to, ask questions of, and coordinate with those allied professions: "Is this a condition that can be improved by medication? Is there any kind of appropriate long-acting medication available for patients who are forgetful about daily medication-taking?"

The need for basic knowledge and inter-professional cooperation, moreover, extends as well to "jobs, housing, food, education, and health care."[33] For we cannot "address the causes of recidivism without creating jobs for offenders or places where they can live,"[34] and cannot adequately tackle problems of domestic violence and child abuse and neglect when breadwinners cannot find jobs.[35]

Lawyers are not equipped to be social science researchers delving into the efficacy of treatment programs. But lawyers should be competent consumers and conveyors of that research. They can synthesize and draw bottom-line conclusions about the research.[36] They can, moreover, serve as compilers of (and, when appropriate, complainers about) their clients' experiences in given programs.[37] Working in partnership with social workers, the legal profession—especially in law school clinics and Public Defender offices—can incorporate this material in useful up-to-date manuals of services and resources.[38] And lawyers acutely aware of service shortcomings can, especially if they are institutional defenders,[39] advocate freely for needed programs and resources.

---

32. *See, e.g.*, Rosalie Ambrosino et al., Social Work and Social Welfare: An Introduction (5th ed 2005). Such a course is now available at The University of Arizona James E. Rogers College of Law.

33. *See* Pearson, *supra* note 25, at 386.

34. *Id*

35. *Id. See also* Long, *supra* note 24. This task shows the blurring of law and social work as well as the blurring of functions between criminal defense lawyers and civil legal aid lawyers.

36. *E.g.*, David R. Katner, *A Defense Perspective of Treatment Programs for Juvenile Sex Offenders*, 37 Crim. L. Bull. 371 (2001).

37. A book by a physician could serve as a model for attorneys. Lonny Shavelson, Hooked: Five Addicts Challenge Our Misguided Drug Rehab System (2001).

38. An excellent judicial manual, Judging In the 21st Century: A Problem-Solving Approach (2005) [hereinafter Judging in the 21st Century], was produced by Canada's National Judicial Institute, *available at* http://www.nji.ca (last visited Nov. 23, 2005), under "education" and "publications."

39. Clarke & Neuhard, *supra* note 27.

B. The Legal Landscape

I noted above that although the category of treatment and social services resources is primarily within the province of social work, it is, nevertheless, influenced by the needs of clients of the legal profession. Similarly, the present category, focusing on the legal landscape, while quite clearly in the lawyer's domain, ideally should be shaped by therapeutic considerations. What are at issue here are the various legal provisions (usually statutory) that facilitate or impede the practice of therapeutic jurisprudence in a given jurisdiction.

As I suggested earlier in the discussion of the *Riggs* case, a rigid, inflexible sentencing scheme, especially one characterized by mandatory incarcerative penalties, is surely a major impediment. By contrast, the ability to defer the imposition of sentence, also involved in *Riggs*, is surely a major facilitator; the deferral can allow rehabilitative efforts to get meaningfully underway, and can, as in *Riggs*, allow for gauging their likely success.[40]

Jurisdictions may differ markedly in the TJ "friendly features" of their legal landscapes, or at least in the extent to which certain facilitative features are present, absent, or ambiguous. For instance, in some jurisdictions sentence may be deferred (either indefinitely or for a time-limited period) in the sole discretion of the court,[41] but in others the situation is less clear. At the other end of the criminal process, some jurisdictions allow for motivating and rewarding an offender by the possibility of early termination of probation[42] or parole,[43] whereas others do not permit or are silent on the possibility.[44]

With regard to probationary sentences in general, the therapeutic jurisprudence literature recommends, in addition to the possibility of early ter-

---

40. Bruce J. Winick, *Redefining the Role of the Criminal Defense Lawyer at Plea Bargaining and Sentencing: A Therapeutic Jurisprudence/Preventive Law Model*, in Practicing Therapeutic Jurisprudence: Law as a Helping Profession 245 (Dennis P. Stolle et al. eds., 2000) [hereinafter Practicing TJ]; United States v. Flowers, 983 F. Supp. 159 (EDNY 1997). In traditional TJ terminology, deferral of sentence could be regarded as an "opportunity spot." *See* David B. Wexler, *Psycholegal Soft Spots and Strategies*, in Practicing TJ, *supra*, at 61.

41. *Flowers*, *supra* note 40. In Western Australia, the court may defer sentence, but for only a period of six months. W. Austl. Consolidated Acts, *Sentencing Act of 1995*, Section 16(1) and (2).

42. Ariz. Rev. Stat. § 13-901(E) (2003).

43. Joan Petersilia, When Prisoners Come Home: Parole and Prisoner Reentry (Studies in Crime and Public Policy) 211 (2003) ("goal parole").

44. *Id. See also* David B. Wexler, *Spain's JVP (Juez de Vigilancia Penitenciaria) Legal Structure as a Potential Model for a Re-Entry Court*, 7 Contemp. Issues L. 1, 7 (2003–2004) [hereinafter *Spain's JVP Law*].

mination, a process of ongoing judicial supervision by means of periodic review hearings.[45] The review process is meant to monitor compliance—of both the offender and the social service agencies—and, in cases of successful offender compliance, to provide an opportunity for the court to reinforce and praise the offender's efforts.[46]

A careful, systematic examination of the criminal code in a given jurisdiction will reveal a great many instances of provisions friendly or hostile to a therapeutic jurisprudence approach; it would likely also call attention to provisions which, if used creatively, could pave the way for an increased therapeutic jurisprudence practice. For instance, the therapeutic jurisprudence literature suggests the value of "behavioral contracting" to set appropriate conditions of probation.[47] For example the simple "allocution" provision requiring judges to ask offenders whether they have anything to say before sentence is imposed[48] could, combined with the pre-sentence guidance and preparation provided clients by defense counsel, constitute a convenient context for discussing and setting the terms of a behavioral contract. The careful and creative examination of criminal codes for their therapeutic jurisprudence potential is a crucial enterprise and a very fertile field for the TJ criminal law practitioner.

C. Theory-Inspired Practice

It is not at all uncommon, of course, for a lawyer to try to postpone a pending case and attempt to connect a client with an appropriate treatment or service. Increasingly, in fact, some lawyers are envisioning such activities as the core of their professional role.[49] They intend, in essence, to specialize in knowing appropriate treatments and programs, in accessing those services for their clients, and in navigating the legal landscape so as to achieve a rehabilitative

---

45. David B. Wexler, *Robes and Rehabilitation: How Judges Can Help Offenders Make Good*, 38 Ct. Rev. 18 (Spring 2001) [hereinafter *Robes and Rehabilitation*]. For a general resource on the use of therapeutic jurisprudence in judicial settings, most of which are pertinent in the criminal context, see Judging in a Therapeutic Key: Therapeutic Jurisprudence and the Courts (Bruce J. Winick & David B. Wexler eds., 2003) [hereinafter TJ Judging].

46. *Robes and Rehabilitation, supra* note 45.

47. *E.g.*, TJ Judging, *supra* note 45, at 213, 227.

48. *E.g.*, Allocution under §726 of the Canadian Criminal Code.

49. *E.g.*, Cait Clarke & James Neuhard, *From Day One: Who's in Control as Problem Solving and Client-Centered Sentencing Take Center Stage*, 29 N.Y.U. Rev. L. & Soc. Change 11 (2004).

result. These lawyers, then, will seek to develop expertise in the first two categories—the treatments and the relevant law—already discussed in the present chapter.

But in order to most effectively engage criminal clients in rehabilitative enterprises, there is an important third dimension to the role, the somewhat fancy-sounding category of Theory-Inspired Practices, a name I have chosen principally for its appropriate acronym, TIPs.[50] If the first examined category—treatment and services—is primarily in the mental health/social work realm, and if the second category—the legal landscape—is primarily in the legal realm, the final category—theory-inspired practices—is overwhelmingly and vigorously interdisciplinary.

The theory-inspired practices category is robustly interdisciplinary because its thrust is to search for promising developments and insights in the relevant mental health/social work/criminal justice disciplines (psychology, social work, and criminology have thus far been most heavily involved) and to explore creatively how, without running afoul of important justice goals (due process and the like), those insights might best be brought into law reform, into the legal process, or into the realm of judging and lawyering.[51]

The third category is somewhat more nuanced and subtle than the other two categories. Nonetheless, intuitive and psychologically-sensitive lawyers and judges likely already employ a number of devices that are completely consistent with the TIPs literature.

For example, in the *Riggs* case, Riggs' mother was enlisted to provide reminders regarding Riggs' taking his daily medication. Many have noted that involving a family member for such purposes is a worthwhile component of facilitating treatment adherence.[52] Likewise, the district court's statement that

---

50. The term, however, is also accurate insofar as the suggestions are actually more "inspired" by theory than they are "based" on such theory.

51. Behavioral science titles that have inspired my own efforts in therapeutic jurisprudence/criminal law scholarship include Donald Meichenbaum & Dennis C. Turk, Facilitating Treatment Adherence: A Practitioner's Guidebook (1987) (This work prompted David B. Wexler, *Health Care Compliance Principles and the Insanity Acquittee Conditional Release Process*, 27 Crim. L. Bull. 18 (1991)); What Works: Reducing Reoffending (James McGuire ed., 1999) (This work inspired, for example, David B. Wexler, *Relapse Prevention Planning Principles for Criminal Law Practice, in* Practicing TJ, *supra* note 40); and Shadd Maruna, Making Good: How Ex-Inmates Reform and Rebuild Their Lives (2001). (Maruna's work inspired *Robes and Rehabilitation, supra* note 45; David B. Wexler, *Some Reflections on Therapeutic Jurisprudence and the Practice of Criminal Law*, 38 Crim. L. Bull. 205 (2002) [hereinafter *Reflections*]).

52. *See supra* sources cited in note 51.

Riggs seemed to have matters "under control" serves not only as a statement of factual/legal relevance, but, according to the literature, likely serves as well to reinforce and maintain the offender's successful reform efforts.[53]

While it is likely that sensitive lawyers and judges will intuit and use several techniques that happen to be supported by the therapeutic jurisprudence literature, it is also likely—extremely likely—that, without periodic exposure to the pertinent TJ literature—the actual use of recommended TIPs will be hit-and-miss and far and few between. For instance, the therapeutic jurisprudence literature, in addition to promoting the involvement of family (like Riggs' mother) in the treatment process, suggests a great many additional techniques—behavioral contracting is one of many important ones[54]—to enhance client adherence to treatment plans. The practice TIPs are meaningful for they suggest not merely the importance of lawyers contemplating rehabilitative efforts "from day one," but suggest also *how* lawyers might guide clients along a promising rehabilitative path.

The TIPs category, therefore, gives lawyers practice tips on the "how" of effective TJ criminal lawyering, sometimes called TJ's "principles"[55] or "instrumental prescriptions:"[56] *how* lawyers can put clients at ease by according them "voice" and "validation;" *how* lawyers can develop a respectful—and influential—relationship with their clients; *how* lawyers can reduce perceptions of coercion and give clients a meaningful choice to opt in or out of particular programs; *how* lawyers can work with clients to increase empathy to victims and increase also the genuineness of any acceptance of responsibility or tendered apology; *how* lawyers can help clients develop relapse prevention strategies, engage in efforts of behavioral contracting, and propose a plan for conditional release on probation or parole; *how* lawyers can work with clients to increase offender compliance with release conditions; and *how* lawyers can recognize client strengths and reinforce client efforts at desistance from crime.[57]

---

53. *See supra* sources cited in note 51. Many problem-solving courts, such as drug treatment courts and mental health courts, use periodic review hearings and graduation ceremonies to explicitly reinforce successful reform efforts. *See infra* text accompanying note 128.

54. *See supra* sources cited in note 51.

55. TJ JUDGING, *supra* note 45, at 105.

56. Robert F. Schopp, *Therapeutic Jurisprudence: Integrated Inquiry and Instrumental Prescriptions*, 17 BEHAV. SCI. & L. 589 (1999).

57. All of these, and more, are discussed from a judicial perspective in TJ JUDGING, *supra* note 45. In my Therapeutic Jurisprudence courses at the University of Arizona and the University of Puerto Rico, I ask the law students to explore how those principles can

III. Getting Down to Details

The nature of criminal law practice is changing, at least for some, and the indications are that the change will continue to gain strength and numbers. With the above organizational framework in mind, I would like, in the remainder of this chapter, to sketch the changing role of the criminal law practitioner, and to provide some detail and some concrete examples of how therapeutic jurisprudence can recognize and contribute to the rehabilitative role of the criminal defense lawyer.

Some lawyers have already begun to practice criminal law in a specifically therapeutic key.[58] Mostly, interested lawyers will likely augment a traditional criminal law practice with the more holistic approach suggested by therapeutic jurisprudence, and the present chapter seeks to point interested practitioners in that direction.

Some lawyers may even decide to go "all the way," and to limit their criminal law practice to a concentration in therapeutic jurisprudence. For instance, in *The How and Why of Therapeutic Jurisprudence in Criminal Defense Work,*[59] Dallas, Texas attorney John McShane provides a brief overview of his perspective and his practice.

> Application of therapeutic jurisprudence in criminal defense work involves a threshold recognition that most criminal defense attorneys and the criminal justice system generally address the symptoms of the client's legal problem rather than the cause. For example, in the classic case of the habitual driving under the influence (DUI) offender, the symptom is the repeated arrests and the cause is usually alcoholism. It is the long-standing policy of the firm of McShane, Davis and Nance to decline representation of this type of defendant unless he or she contractually agrees to the therapeutic jurisprudence approach. If this approach is declined by the potential client, referral is

---

best be employed by practicing lawyers. As the present chapter illustrates, specific therapeutic jurisprudence scholarship on criminal lawyering is, however, now fortunately emerging. *See also* Gregory Baker & Jennifer Zawid, *The Birth of a Therapeutic Externship Program: Hard labor but Worth the Effort,* 17 St. Thomas L. Rev. 709 (2005); Clarke & Neuhard, *supra* note 49.

58. *Reflections, supra* note 51.

59. John V. McShane, The How and Why of Therapeutic Jurisprudence in Criminal Defense Work (2000) (unpublished manuscript, on file with author).

made to a competent colleague who will then represent the client in the traditional model.[60]

Referral to outside counsel is also made if the defendant has a viable defense. In the criminal arena, therefore, the firm "focuses solely on rehabilitation and mitigation of punishment."[61] Representation is agreed to if the client is in turn willing "to accept responsibility for his actions, submit to an evaluation, treatment, and relapse prevention program, and to use this approach in mitigation of the offense in plea bargaining or the sentencing hearing."[62] McShane seeks to defer disposition of the case so as "to allow the client the maximum opportunity to recover."[63] A packet of mitigating information is assembled and eventually submitted to the prosecutor in an effort at plea bargaining, or, failing that, to the court at sentencing. The packet consists of items such as "AA Meeting Attendance Logs, urinalysis lab reports, reports of evaluating and treating mental health professionals, and letters of support from various people in the community such as AA sponsor, employer, coworkers, clergyman, family, and friends."[64]

There is much more to this, of course, and there are indeed a variety of models that criminal defense attorneys might use in practicing therapeutic jurisprudence. Although McShane and his firm have chosen to refer a client to outside counsel unless the client chooses, from the beginning, to accept responsibility, that course of action is in no sense required. As noted earlier, a lawyer might well choose to practice "traditional" criminal law, but infuse the practice with therapeutic jurisprudence concerns throughout the process. Indeed, as we will see, a TJ criminal lawyer can play an essential role even after conviction in the appeal process, in release planning, in prisoner reentry, and beyond.

In the remainder of this chapter, I will identify the potential rehabilitative role of the attorney from the beginning stages—possible diversion, for example—through sentencing and even beyond—through conditional or unconditional release, and possible efforts to expunge the criminal record. I will try to sketch more clearly the role and practice setting of the TJ criminal lawyer, taking into account certain important skills, legally-relevant doctrines, and the kind, content, and timing of certain important conversations with clients.[65]

---

60. *Reflections, supra* note 51, at 206–07.

61. *Id.*

62. *Id.*

63. *Id.*

64. *Id.*

65. Recently, Broward County Public Defender Howard Finkelstein—who, incidentally, was (with Judge Ginger Lerner-Wren) instrumental in creating the nation's first men-

A. The Criminal Lawyer as Change Agent

Before proceeding to particular stages in the criminal process, and looking at the criminal defense lawyer's potential rehabilitative role in each, we need to address a more general and basic set of issues. A typical initial response to a proposed broadening of the traditional role of defense counsel is, "Hey, I'm not a therapist." True, a lawyer is not a therapist or social worker, and is not expected to be. But, as social worker and drug court consultant Michael Clark makes clear,[66] lawyers (and others in the legal/judicial system) can nonetheless be quite effective as "change agents."

Clark notes that, if change is forthcoming, the lion's share of change will come from the client, together with whatever internal or social strengths and supports can be mustered. Client "hope and expectancy" accounts for another chunk of the change. And a whopping amount of positive change is attributable to "relationship" factors—the connection between client and change agent (e.g., relations characterized by empathy, acceptance, encouragement). Much rehabilitative work lies in encouraging active and meaningful client participation, in developing a strong relationship between client and change agent, and in fostering client hope and expectancy. Writing in the context of drug courts, Clark underscores that "all professionals working with drug court participants, especially judges, lawyers, and probation officers, may adopt and utilize techniques that most effectively induce positive behavior change."[67]

Clark and others have written about how a professional can strive to develop a relationship of respect[68] and trust,[69] and about the importance of giving a client "voice"—of clients being able to "tell their story,"[70] unconstrained

---

tal health court—has forbidden his attorneys from advising indigent criminal defendants to plead guilty at arraignment unless they have had meaningful contact with their clients in advance. *See* CrimProf Blog, *at* http://lawprofessors.typepad.com/crimprof_blog/ (last visited June 8, 2005).

66. Michael D. Clark, *A Change-Focused Approach for Judges, in* TJ JUDGING, *supra* note 45, at 137.

67. *Id.* at 147.

68. *Id.* at 148 (*e.g.*, respectful communications, eye-contact, attentive listening).

69. Marcus T. Boccaccini et al., *Development and Effects of Client Trust in Criminal Defense Attorneys: Preliminary Examination of the Congruence Model of Trust Development*, 22 BEHAV. SCI. & L. 197 (2004) (stating that lawyers should invite client participation, take client phone calls, ask for suggestions, and listen to suggestions).

70. Clark, *supra* note 66, at 142.

by rigid notions of legal relevance.[71] Important, too, are matters of emotional intelligence and cultural competence.[72]

These skills—on building a strong interpersonal relationship, on attentive listening, and on becoming an "effective helper"[73]—can be acquired and improved by lawyers, and are increasingly important components of law school courses on interviewing and counseling, and in legal clinics. Proposals are now emerging, too, to introduce lawyers and law students to techniques of "motivational interviewing."[74] Keeping the importance of these skills always in mind, we may now turn our attention to the lawyer's role in various stages of the criminal process.

B. Diversion and Problem-Solving Courts[75]

Lawyers need to be versed in the various treatment programs available in their jurisdictions,[76] and in informal and formal schemes for diversion. Diversion is sometimes spelled out by statute, and may operate either pretrial or

---

71. *Cf.* Jack Susman, *Resolving Hospital Conflicts: A Study on Therapeutic Jurisprudence,* in LAW IN A THERAPEUTIC KEY, *supra* note 30, at 907, 909–10 (stating that patients prefer informal dispute resolution proceedings, for such proceedings allow for greater dialogue); Thomas D. Barton, *Therapeutic Jurisprudence, Preventive Law, and Creative Problem Solving: An Essay on Harnessing Emotion and Human Connection,* 5 PSYCHOL. PUB. POL'Y & L. 921, 921 (1999).

72. Marjorie A. Silver, *Emotional Competence, Multicultural Lawyering and Race,* 3 FLA. COASTAL L.J. 219, 220–21 (2002); Carolyn Copps Hartley & Carrie J. Petrucci, *Practicing Culturally Competent Therapeutic Jurisprudence: A Collaboration Between Social Work and Law,* 14 WASH. U. J.L. & POL'Y 133 (2004); Marjorie A. Silver, *Emotional Intelligence and Legal Education,* 5 PSYCHOL. PUB. POL'Y & L. 1173, 1173 (1999).

73. Richard Sheehy, *Do You Have the Skills to be an Effective Helper,* 29 FLA. B. NEWS 14 (2002), *available at* http://www.flabar.org/DIVCOM/JN/JNNews01.nsf/cb53c80c8fab d49d85256b5900678f6c/b82d3f3cd077d99c85256bb200527098?OpenDocument (last visited Mar. 16, 2005).

74. Astrid Birgden, *Dealing with the Resistant Criminal Client: A Psychologically-Minded Strategy for More Effective Legal Counseling,* 38 CRIM. L. BULL. 225 (2002) (stating that motivational interviewing, or MI, finds a line between a "heavy handed" approach and "hands off" approach). For a bibliography on motivational interviewing, including discussion of the impact a helping professional can have on a client's stages of change, go to http://www .motivationalinterview.org/library/index.html (last visited Mar. 13, 2005).

75. *See generally* TJ JUDGING, *supra* note 45; NORA V. DEMLEITNER ET AL., SENTENC-ING LAW AND POLICY 546 (2004).

76. This is true, of course, whether we are talking diversion, sentencing, or parole. For a good example of scholarship in this area, see Katner, *supra* note 36.

post-adjudication (deferral of judgment). In diversion, issues often arise regarding the appropriateness of conditions, such as those relating to drug testing or to search and seizure.[77]

Problem-solving courts, such as drug treatment courts ("DTCs"), may also operate pre- or post-adjudication; increasingly, they operate post-guilty plea. Lawyers need to know about these courts, their programs, their eligibility requirements,[78] and about the actual functioning of the courts and programs,[79] including rates of successful graduation versus the 'flunk out' rate, and the amount of time an average client might expect to spend in jail (for being sanctioned) under a DTC program as compared to expected jail time in the conventional system.[80]

There is an emerging literature on the role of counsel in this area,[81] given the non-traditional aspects and atmosphere of DTCs and other problem-solv-

---

77. Terry v. Superior Court, 73 Cal.App.4th 661, 86 Cal.Rptr.2d 653, 666 (1999). Conditions may also be imposed when one is released pretrial on bail or on one's own recognizance. In *In re* York, 9 Cal.4th 1133, 1151 (1995), the California Supreme Court upheld conditions, such as random drug testing and unannounced searches, beyond those relating to assuring the defendant's presence in court. For a discussion of conditions of release, *see infra* Part 5, "Probation." In Alabama v. Shelton, 535 U.S. 654, 656 (2002), the Supreme Court discussed the availability of 'pretrial probation' (adjournment in contemplation of dismissal), and noted that the conditions imposed under that arrangement are basically the same as those available under 'regular' probation.

78. In New South Wales, Australia, where the drug court is statutorily based, the drug court, in written opinions, decides eligibility requirements and other interpretative matters. *See* Lawlink New South Wales, *Caselaw New South Wales, at* http://www.lawlink .nsw.gov.au/lawlink/caselaw/llcaselaw.nsf/pages/cl_index (last visited June 4, 2005) [hereinafter New South Wales]. A body of case law is developing. For some TJ implications of this development for the lawyer's role, see *infra* Part 6, "Appeal."

79. For example, one of my students at the University of Puerto Rico reported that clients in one area of the island were expected to enroll in a treatment program that involved little more than hour upon hour of daily prayer.

80. *See* Mark A.R. Kleiman, *Drug Court Can Work: Would Something Else Work Better?*, 2 Criminology & Pub. Pol'y 167 (2003) (stating that recent research suggests a client, although successful in the program, may spend about as much time in jail under DTC as under the traditional criminal justice option). In terms of their actual functioning, the operation of DTCs has been affected in several jurisdictions by the passage of drug treatment initiatives. These initiatives generally mandate treatment and probation, and forbid incarceration, for qualifying defendants. The initiatives have been worrisome to some DTC judges, for the laws may remove the motivational "stick" of possible incarceration. *See* Michael M. O'Hear, *Statutory Interpretation and Direct Democracy: Lessons from the Drug Treatment Initiatives*, 40 Harv. J. on Legis. 281, 289–90 (2003).

81. For the most recent contributions, see generally Clarke & Neuhard, *supra* note 49; William H. Simon, *Criminal Defenders and Community Justice: The Drug Court Example,*

ing courts ("PSCs"). One of the most important issues relates to the client's consent to opt out of the 'ordinary' criminal justice system and into a PSC program. In an important article, former drug court defense attorney Martin Reisig underscores the necessity of obtaining true client consent to enter the program.[82] According to Reisig, obtaining adequate client consent is always important, but it is clearly crucial in post-adjudication jurisdictions, given the fact that fully one-third of those who enter a DTC program may flunk out of it and be returned to the criminal court not to stand trial but as convicted defendants. Real consent is crucial, says Reisig, for purposes of due process. Moreover, consent is important therapeutically as well: imagine how 'sold out' a client may feel being rushed into a DTC program from which he/she later flunks out, only then to face the court as an already convicted defendant.

Reisig notes that, even in a therapeutically-oriented law practice, the criminal defense lawyer needs to convince the client that the strengths and weaknesses of the case can and will be evaluated more or less along traditional lines.[83] A study of clients in mental health court revealed that those who believe they have a real choice regarding participation also perceived less coercion than do others.[84] Yet, a number of clients reported that they were unaware they had a choice.[85]

---

40 Am. Crim. L. Rev. 1595 (2003); Jane M. Spinak, *Why Defenders Feel Defensive: The Defender's Role in Problem Solving Courts*, 40 Am. Crim. L. Rev. 1617 (2003). For a recent defense of the traditional model, see Abbe Smith, *The Difference in Criminal Defense and the Difference it Makes*, 11 Wash. U. J.L. & Pol'y 83 (2003). Melding therapeutic elements and traditional ones will lead to interesting discussions about accommodating conciliatory and adversarial postures. This is a crucial—perhaps *the* crucial—future issue, but, at this early stage, is beyond the scope of the present chapter. As evidenced by Clarke & Neuhard, *supra* note 49, at 36–47, this is a case where the general will flow from the specific; where concrete examples will be necessary to confront ethical issues. In the present chapter, I try to present important but relatively non-controversial aspects of the lawyer's role—aspects easy to accommodate in a traditional practice.

82. Martin Reisig, *The Difficult Role of the Defense Lawyer in a Post-Adjudication Drug Treatment Court: Accommodating Therapeutic Jurisprudence and Due Process*, 38 Crim. L. Bull. 216 (2002).

83. The conventional wisdom has it that the quicker the entry into a treatment program, the better. Judge Peggy F. Hora, Judge William G. Schma & John Rosenthal, *The Importance of Timing*, in TJ Judging, *supra* note 45, at 178. Be that as it may, the supposed advantage of early enrollment can be dwarfed by the due process considerations and by the anti-therapeutic aspects of having been rushed into a treatment track.

84. Norman J. Poythress et al., *Perceived Coercion and Procedural Justice in the Broward Mental Health Court*, 25 Int'l J.L. & Psychiatry 517, 526 (2002).

85. *Id.* at 530.

Apparently, some clients do not understand a general statement, made by the judge to the courtroom audience as a whole, regarding voluntary participation. This suggests the need for a change in the judicial role and, in any case, suggests a highly significant role for counsel. Although observations of mental health court reveal that "there is little that reflects traditional 'lawyering' as the attorneys are relegated to relatively minor roles in the hearings,"[86] pre-selection legal advice and counseling is essential.

The therapeutically-inclined criminal defense attorney must consider what kind of dialogue to have with the client. What should the lawyer tell the client about the pros and cons of opting into DTC or mental health court? What information should be provided to the client regarding the program, the nature of the treatment, the consequences of success or failure, the alternatives, and the amount of incarceration one might expect under either option?[87]

What outcomes other than incarceration time might be important? Might success be measured not only by "graduation" rates but also by small successful steps in peoples' lives? What if drug court participation gives many clients a new outlook on life, or a glimpse of a way to live life without drugs, or a family who now backs his or her efforts to get clean?[88]

Should the client, if free on bail (as many are), visit any of the treatment programs before making a decision? Should the client be invited or encouraged by counsel to sit in on a drug court session (typically open to the public) before making up his or her mind? Note that in many drug treatment courts, case calendaring is used to promote vicarious learning by clients—cases are ordered so as to give new clients a glimpse of the hard work, but also of the opportu-

---

86. Roger A. Boothroyd et al., *The Broward Mental Health Court: Process, Outcomes, and Service Utilization*, 26 INT'L J.L. & PSYCHIATRY 55, 67 (2003).

87. Thus, consider the question asked critically by attorney Mae Quinn, "is it not a defense attorney's 'therapeutic jurisprudential' obligation to inquire whether certain drug court practices are perceived by client as confusing or too invasive ... ?" *See* Mae C. Quinn, *Whose Team am I on Anyway? Musings of a Public Defender about Drug Treatment Court Practice*, 26 N.Y.U. REV. L. & SOC. CHANGE 37, 53 n.100 (2000–2001). This question should be answered, assuming a correct understanding of therapeutic jurisprudence, with a resounding "yes."

88. These are all examples given by New South Wales Magistrate Neil Milson, as reported by Michael Pelly, *When Treatment is Scarier than Jail*, SYDNEY MORNING HERALD, Feb. 26, 2004, at 15. Magistrate Milson's insights tie in nicely with the program development and evaluation research literature, where "outcomes" are defined as "measurable changes in the client's life situation or circumstances." PETER M. KETTNER ET AL., DESIGNING AND MANAGING PROGRAMS: AN EFFECTIVENESS BASED APPROACH 113 (2d ed. 1999).

nity and hope for real recovery that lies ahead.[89] A lawyer, or paralegal, might play an important role in maximizing the vicarious learning by sitting through the session and explaining to the prospective DTC client exactly what is happening and why different clients are receiving different dispositions.

Lawyers exploring the consent question should also consider how a client's active addiction impedes attentive listening and interacts with nuanced notions of consent. They should also ask how much effort is and should be expended in "regular" court to advise clients about the collateral consequences of a proposed plea—and should consider whether enrollment in a treatment option should call for the same or a higher standard.

The drug court community sometimes speaks of the four "Ls" that drive people to treatment: lovers, livers, law, and labor. Clients typically opt for drug court and like programs when faced with loss of family, or health, or liberty, or employment. Some practitioners and judges in the field thus feel that an overly complex consent procedure is not workable with many clients. Those experts believe a preferable approach would be to keep things simple and allow for an easy exit if the client wants out of the program. Such an easy exit should, of course, be especially consistent with a "pre-plea" kind of program.

---

89. *See* Judge Peggy F. Hora et al., *Promoting Vicarious Learning Through Case Calendaring, in* TJ JUDGING, *supra* note 45, at 300–01:

> DTCs (Drug Treatment Courts) design the courtroom process itself to reinforce the defendant's treatment. The court may set up its daily calendar so that "first-time participants appearing in Drug Court … are the last items on the session calendar. This gives them an opportunity to see the entire program in action, and know exactly what awaits them if they become a participant." The DTC may handle program graduates first in order to impart a sense of hope to the new and continuing program participants who may experience hopelessness at the beginning of the process. The court may then devote the next portion of the calendar to defendants who enter the court in custody. This procedure is designed to convey to all DTC participants the serious nature of the court and the gravity of the defendant's situation. This demonstrates that a violation of DTC rules may not get a defendant ejected from the program, but the court may use jail time as a form of "smart punishment" to get the defendant to conform to treatment protocol. Those DTCs that do not have treatment facilities in their jails recognize that incarceration represents a break in treatment for the individual. However, the shock of incarceration may serve to break down the person's denial of her addiction. Finally, the court handles the cases involving new defendants who wish to enter the DTC program. All of these procedures are founded on the therapeutic ideal that every aspect of a DTC can and does have a powerful impact on the success of the defendant in treatment.

Id.

C. Pleas and Sentencing Considerations[90]

It is always important to remember that the overwhelming majority of cases are resolved by plea,[91] and typically through a process of plea negotiation.[92] Accordingly, a TJ criminal lawyer will, in appropriate cases, try to assemble a rehabilitation-oriented packet to present to the prosecutor in hopes of securing a favorable plea arrangement. Failing that, the packet may be presented to a court at sentencing.

The area of plea negotiation is immense, and beyond the scope of this chapter. What are within the chapter's scope are some factors that may enter into a client's decision regarding a plea.

One factor that should enter into the determination of whether a client will go to trial or enter a plea is the likely loss, for one insisting on going to trial, of what in practice typically amounts to a 'plea discount'[93] for a defendant's saving the government the trouble of going to trial, and saving the victim and the government witnesses the trouble and often the trauma of a trial. Closely related to this is sentence leniency, often given for a defendant's 'acceptance of responsibility,' which will kick in more clearly if it occurs early in the process, and is perceived as genuine rather than as purely strategic.[94]

A genuine acceptance of responsibility—especially if coupled with an apology[95]—is generally regarded as therapeutically welcome by the victim[96] and

---

90. *See generally* DEMLEITNER ET AL., *supra* note 75, at 405–32; TJ JUDGING, *supra* note 45, at 165–76.

91. DEMLEITNER ET AL., *supra* note 75, at 405.

92. Plea negotiations may involve bargaining over the sentence or over the charge itself (an indirect way, of course, of affecting sentence). DEMLEITNER ET AL., *supra* note 75, at 413–25. The TJ literature has raised the question whether charge bargaining might feed into offender cognitive distortion and denial more so than sentence bargaining. *See* David B. Wexler, *Therapeutic Jurisprudence and the Criminal Courts, in* LAW IN A THERAPEUTIC KEY, *supra* note 30, at 157, 162 n.37. Therapeutic jurisprudence thinking has also questioned whether "no contest" pleas feed into offender denial and minimization. *Id.* at 165–76.

93. DEMLEITNER ET AL., *supra* note 75, at 305.

94. United States v. Jeter, 236 F.3d 1032 (9th Cir. 2001).

95. Carrie J. Petrucci, *Apology in the Criminal Justice Setting: Evidence for Including Apology as an Additional Component in the Legal System,* 20 BEHAV. SCI. & L. 337, 340, 359 (2002).

96. *Cf.* Judge William G. Schma, *Judging for the New Millennium, in* TJ JUDGING, *supra* note 45, at 87, 89 (victims prefer defendants to enter guilty pleas, rather than no contest pleas); *see also* Edna Erez, *Victim Voice, Impact Statements and Sentencing: Integrating Restorative Justice and Therapeutic Jurisprudence Principles in Adversary Proceedings,* 40

as a good first rehabilitative step for the defendant.[97] Other cooperative efforts, such as rendering substantial assistance[98] and pre-sentencing proactive repayment of victims[99] (which often, but not always, accompany a guilty plea), are also typically considered by the sentencing judge.[100]

The rub in all this, of course, especially as it relates to the role of the criminal lawyer, is that if courts regard these behaviors and gestures as being engaged in merely in the hopes of receiving a lesser punishment, the courts may find the acts to be without merit.[101] But there is also the other side to this coin: if a defendant does not plead guilty and goes to trial, he or she can, if convicted, expect to lose the typical 'plea discount.'[102] Moreover, if the defendant goes to trial, testifies, loses, and is regarded by the judge as having committed perjury at the trial, the court may well enhance the sentence further for this supposed obstruction of justice.[103]

In light of all the above, how should a defense lawyer go about advising a client, discussing these issues and potential consequences with a client, and trying to work with the client to create a genuineness even within a strategic legal context? Are there psychological approaches that may be useful? For example, one psychological approach to 'empathy training' is a 'perspective-taking' approach, where a psychologist working with an offender might ask the offender to re-enact the crime, playing the role of the victim:

> The offenders read heart-wrenching accounts of crimes like their own, told from the victim's perspective. They also watch videotapes of victims tearfully telling what it was like to be molested. The offenders then write about their own offense from the victim's point of view, imagining what the victim felt. They read this account to a therapy group and try to answer questions about the assault from the vic-

---

Crim. L. Bull. 483 (2004); Stephanos Bibas & Richard A. Bierschbach, *Integrating Remorse and Apology into Criminal Procedure*, 114 Yale L.J. 85 (2004).

97. *See generally supra* ch. 9: Jonathan R. Cohen, *The Culture of Legal Denial*.

98. Demleitner et al., *supra* note 75, at 318.

99. *Id.* at 341; United States v. Kim, 364 F.3d 1235 (11th Cir. 2004).

100. Michael O'Hear, *Remorse, Cooperation, and "Acceptance of Responsibility": The Structure, Implementation and Reform of Section 3E1.1 of the Federal Sentencing Guidelines*, 91 Nw. U. L. Rev. 1507, 1510 (1997).

101. United States v. Martin, 363 F.3d 25 (1st Cir. 2004).

102. Demleitner et al., *supra* note 75, at 314.

103. United States v. Dunnigan, 507 U.S. 87, 90–94 (1993); United States v. Grayson, 438 U.S. 41, 44–54 (1978).

tim's perspective. Finally, the offender goes through a simulated reenactment of the crime, this time playing the role of the victim.[104]

It is interesting to consider how the 'perspective-taking' approach could be imported into the law office. Perhaps lawyers, preferably in combination with social workers or like professionals, could create a "bank" of videotapes of victim statements, and ultimately suggest that a client, in preparing a written apology letter (or videotape), include a section where the client imagines the many ways in which the crime likely affected the victim's life.[105]

D. Deferred Sentence and Post-Offense Rehabilitation

Recall that, in his practice, John McShane tries to delay the imposition of sentence for as long as possible,[106] and urges the client to begin to pick up the pieces and to engage in available rehabilitative efforts, whether they be attendance at Alcoholics Anonymous or a more elaborate treatment program. McShane emphasizes to the client that, up to this point, the existing evidence already, by definition, "exists;" it perhaps can be given a "spin," but it cannot be changed. On the other hand, suggests McShane, from here on out the client can build his or her own case, can help create evidence that is favorable and that can work to the client's advantage.

In order to accomplish some meaningful rehabilitation—rather than a mere gesture, however genuine—it is of course important to have some time on your side. For this reason, deferring the imposition of sentence can be highly important.[107] Federal case law allows for post-offense rehabilitation ef-

---

104. Allison R. Shiff & David B. Wexler, *Teen Court: A Therapeutic Jurisprudence Perspective, in* LAW IN A THERAPEUTIC KEY, *supra* note 30, at 287, 297.

105. Note that such a procedure would work even if we are dealing with an early stage in the proceedings, where a victim impact statement, ARIZ. REV. STAT. § 13-4424 (2004), would not yet have been prepared. To establish the genuineness of an offender's apology, an expert witness—a professional who is not part of the offender's treatment team—might be called to counter any claim of malingering. *See* Bruce J. Winick, *Redefining the Role of the Criminal Defense Lawyer at Plea Bargaining and Sentencing: A Therapeutic Jurisprudence/Preventive Law Model, in* PRACTICING TJ, *supra* note 40, at 245, 265–66.

106. See *supra* text accompanying note 63.

107. *See, e.g.,* United States v. Flowers, 983 F. Supp. 159, 163–65 (E.D.N.Y. 1997). Winick's writing on the topic applauds Federal District Judge Jack B. Weinstein's on-point scholarly opinion in *Flowers* permitting deferred sentencing. Winick, *supra* note 104, at 245, 267–71. This is a "legal landscape" topic, see *supra* text accompanying note 40, that clearly warrants attention on the state law level as well.

forts to be taken into account when sentence is eventually imposed.[108] This is a highly important area that also needs to be researched on a state-by-state basis. Some state courts may be explicit on the matter.[109] In others, post-offense rehabilitation may not be the subject of case law, but may be the sort of factor that can be brought to bear where courts have considerable discretion in sentencing, perhaps under a statutory "catch-all" provision that allows for mitigation for "any other factor that the court deems appropriate to the ends of justice."[110]

E. Probation[111]

A client who successfully establishes a course of post-offense rehabilitation will typically hope for a probationary sentence in order to remain (relatively speaking) at liberty and to pursue a satisfying life path. The sanction of probation, when legally available for a given offense, is chock full of therapeutic jurisprudence considerations,[112] which can inform and enrich the role of defense counsel. Some of the relevant psychological and criminological work relates to bringing into the probation area notions of psychological compliance principles,[113] relapse prevention principles,[114] and reinforcement of desistance from crime.[115] Let us consider some of these propositions and, following that, consider how they might be employed in the lawyer/client interaction. I make the assumption in these examples that probation is legally available and that it is also a plausible disposition.

Regarding compliance, adherence to probation conditions might be enhanced if probation is conceptualized more as a behavioral contract than as a judicial fiat. If certain family members are aware of the client's agreement to

---

108. Winick, *supra* note 104, at 258–63; DEMLEITNER ET AL., *supra* note 75, at 342. United States v. Atlas, 94 F.3d 447 (8th Cir. 1996). For a recent case, see United States v. Smith, 311 F. Supp. 2d 801, 804–06 (E.D. Wis. 2004).

109. DEMLEITNER ET AL., *supra* note 75, at 343.

110. ARIZ. REV. STAT. § 13-702(D)(5) (2003).

111. *See generally* DEMLEITNER ET AL., *supra* note 75, at 519–34.

112. Faye S. Taxman & Meredith H. Thanner, *Probation from a Therapeutic Perspective: Results from the Field*, 7 CONTEMP. ISSUES L. 39 (2004).

113. David B. Wexler, *Health Care Compliance Principles and the Judiciary*, in TJ JUDGING, *supra* note 45, at 213–26.

114. David B. Wexler, *Problem Solving and Relapse Prevention in Juvenile Court*, in TJ JUDGING, *supra* note 45, at 189 [hereinafter *Problem Solving*].

115. *Robes and Rehabilitation*, *supra* note 45, at 249.

abide by certain conditions, that too is thought to increase the likelihood of compliance. Also, if a person is presented with some "mild counterarguments" regarding his or her likely compliance, the person may be encouraged to explain why "this time is different," and may thereby anchor himself/herself to the view that compliance is desirable and is now attainable.[116] Regarding relapse prevention, some promising rehabilitative techniques urge offenders to think through the chain of events that leads them to criminality so that they may be aware of patterns and of high risk situations (e.g., going to a disco on weekend nights). The offenders are then encouraged to think of ways of avoiding or coping with the high risk situation (e.g., not going to that disco on weekends, and going to a movie instead), and of ultimately embodying their thinking in a "relapse prevention plan" that they may employ in the future to reduce the risk of re-offending.[117] Regarding the reinforcement of desistance from crime, the literature suggests that desistance is more a process than a specific event. Moreover, desistance can best be maintained if, especially in the early stages, it is reinforced through the recognition of respected members of the community.[118]

How might these 'principles' be translated into law practice? Here are some ideas, which I present as food for thought.[119]

The defense lawyer could be one of those "respected members of the community," proud of the client's efforts and positive about the client's prospects. The lawyer and client might talk about others who know the client and his (or her) genuine steps toward reform: an AA sponsor, the receptionist at the drug treatment clinic, a mental health professional, an employer, teacher, coworker, member of the clergy, family member, and/or friend. The lawyer and

---

116. David B. Wexler, *Health Care Compliance Principles and the Judiciary, in* TJ JUDGING, *supra* note 45, at 213–26.

117. *Problem Solving, supra* note 114. This is, of course, a highly skimpy and oversimplified summary of a meaty process. Moreover, the relapse prevention approach needs to be fused with an approach that looks at how offenders can lead "good lives," not simply at how they can avoid re-offending. Tony Ward & Claire Stewart, *Criminogenic Needs and Human Needs: A Theoretical Model,* 9 PSYCHOL. CRIME & L. 234 (2003). For a discussion of merging risk management and good lives considerations in the area of sex offenders, see Astrid Birgden, *Therapeutic Jurisprudence and Sex Offenders: A Psycholegal Approach to Protection,* 16 SEXUAL ABUSE: J. RES. & TREATMENT 351 (2004).

118. *Robes and Rehabilitation, supra* note 45, at 249–54.

119. "At this exciting—but early—stage of development, these 'principles' must, of course, be taken more as suggestions for ongoing discussion, dialogue, and investigation than as hard and fast rules to be set in stone." TJ JUDGING, *supra* note 45, at 105–06.

client might decide which of them might approach which person regarding the willingness to provide a letter of support or testimony.[120]

The lawyer might be guided by the relapse prevention principles to work with the client to come up with and present to the court a proposed probationary plan.[121] The lawyer, perhaps working with a social worker or like professional, might engage the client in a discussion of the chain of events that has led to criminality or drug abuse and might encourage the client to recognize situations which, for the client, seem to be high risk. The lawyer can also prompt the client to consider ways in which the high risk situations can be best avoided.

In terms of the division of labor between lawyer and client, it is important to recognize that it is the *client* who should develop an appreciation of the high risk situations and their alternatives. The goal is for the client to recognize this and to buy into a change of behavior that should reduce the risk of criminality. It is thus important for the client to be fully involved in the thinking process, and lawyers should resist the temptation of thinking for the client and of proposing a plan for the client's acquiescence.

Perhaps the best role for the lawyer here is to prompt and prod the client by asking a series of questions. For instance, UK psychologist James McGuire has developed a course to teach problem-solving skills to offenders, and some of the questions he employs are: "Does most of your offending behavior occur in the same place? At similar times of the day or week? In the presence of the same person or persons?"[122]

This is an area where psychologists and other professionals accustomed to the problem-solving and relapse prevention approach might be very useful. They might be able to suggest some interviewing techniques—or specific questions—to elicit from the client the high risk situations and ways of avoiding them. They may also be able to alert lawyers to the types of patterns and offense pathways often associated with particular offenses or offenders.

---

120. *See Reflections, supra* note 51, at 214.

121. The proposed probationary plan would be derived from some of the relapse prevention principles, and may serve in a very rough way to start a client on the road to relapse prevention, but it is of course no substitute for a full-fledged relapse prevention program led by mental health professionals and trained probation officers. The lawyer's effort might more properly be viewed as resulting in a "safety" plan rather than in a true "relapse prevention" plan. Indeed, one of the proposed conditions of the probationary plan might be a client's full participation in a relapse prevention program, ultimately resulting in the preparation of a true relapse prevention plan. *Problem Solving, supra* note 114, at 198 n.2.

122. *Problem Solving, supra* note 114, at 196.

For example, youths usually get into car accidents not when driving alone but rather when other kids are in the car.[123] Criminologists and insurance companies—and now lawyers—may know this, but it is important for a youthful offender to personally realize it, and this may be accomplished by the lawyer engaging the client in a type of Socratic dialogue: "Well, when do you seem to get picked up for driving violations? Day or night? When you are alone or when you are with others? Which others? Your parents? Your friends?" And then, if the client recognizes that he or she gets into trouble when driving with certain peers, the lawyer might ask the client to propose a plan to reduce the likelihood of future violations or accidents, hopefully producing a response such as: "Well, I will make sure to drive alone, or with other kids only if an adult is present, or with Jane, who always wants me to drive carefully."

This questioning process could result in a preliminary probationary plan to be presented to the court. Note that the proposed conditions are now in essence coming from the client, not from the lawyer or the court, and thus should be understandable to the client and perceived as reasonable, enhancing the chance for compliance if probation is granted.[124] Probation under this scheme will look more like a behavioral contract than like judicial fiat.

---

123. *Passengers Hazardous to Teen Drivers*, Ariz. Daily Star, Mar. 22, 2000, at A6. *See generally* L. H. Chen et al., *Carrying Passengers as a Risk Factor for Crashes Fatal to 16- and 17-Year-Old Drivers*, 283 JAMA 1578 (2000); R. Foss, *Reducing Fatal Crash Risk Among Teenaged Drivers: Structuring an Effective Graduated Licensing System*, 283 JAMA 1617 (2000). For a recent discussion of offense pathways, or offense process approaches, see Devon L. L. Polaschek, *Relapse Prevention, Offense Process Models, and the Treatment of Sexual Offenders*, 34 Prof. Psych.: Res. & Prac. 361 (2003).

124. A related dialogue springs from some of the research on risk management and the difference between "static" (unchanging) and "dynamic" (changeable) risk factors. Gender and race would be static risk factors, whereas drug use and employment status would be dynamic ones. One approach to risk management is the changing or elimination of dynamic risk factors, factors theoretically within the control of the individual under assessment. Emerging therapeutic jurisprudence literature suggests a motivational role for lawyers in prompting clients to change some dynamic risk factors so as to maximize liberty and, at the same time, to take a substantial step in the rehabilitative direction. *See* Bruce J. Winick, *Domestic Violence Court Judges as Risk Managers, in* TJ Judging, *supra* note 45, at 201. An interesting exercise in the risk management area is to ask what the lawyer-client conversation might look like. Keeping with the legal education analogy, might the lawyer in this context sometimes need to do a bit of "lecturing" rather than relying principally on the "Socratic method"? For example: "It is known that factor X makes people more at risk for engaging in violent behavior. If you can change factor X, we can present that to the judge, and hopefully the judge will be impressed. Would you like to give that a shot? How?" Note that the proposed sharing of decision-making between lawyer and client taps into

Ideally, the client should play some role in presenting the proposal to the court, and a give and take might follow, leading to acceptance, modification, or, in disappointing cases, to rejection of the plan.[125] If the client is likely to speak to some of this in court, either proactively or at least in responding to the court's questions and concerns, then the lawyer will need to prepare the client for the sentencing hearing.

As part of the preparation, the lawyer could present the type of 'mild counterarguments' that research suggests can be useful in grounding a client in the propriety of the present plan. For instance: "OK, now I want to ask you some questions that the judge or prosecutor might ask at the hearing, like: Why should I feel comfortable granting probation? Judge X granted you probation last time around, and probation was revoked very soon thereafter."

One would hope the client would personally come up with a suitable answer: "This time is different. I have been going to AA meetings for almost a year, and I have good attendance records. I have a job now, and I want to keep it. I don't go to that bar where I used to get into trouble. And I'm going to enroll in an anger management class that my lawyer and I visited a couple of weeks ago."

Knowing something about the compliance principles, including the fact that compliance is increased if some family or friends are aware of a client's proposed course of action, also suggests a role for the lawyer. The lawyer might discuss this with the client and suggest to the client the usefulness of having some agreed-upon family members or friends familiarize themselves with the proposed conditions and attend the hearing. For therapeutic—as well as ethical—reasons, the lawyer should be clear that the client truly agrees

---

standard social work notions of client empowerment and self-determination. *See* Hartley & Petrucci, *supra* note 72, at 177.

125. Even if the plan is rejected, the effort was not necessarily wasted: the process may have started the client on a course of cognitive restructuring and relapse prevention, and these cognitive/behavioral changes can benefit the client even during incarceration and can surely be beneficial when planning for prison release and reentry. At some point, the lawyer should discuss with the client the usefulness of even the rejected plan, but of course should wait until the timing is right—until the dust settles and the client is able to think beyond having to face an incarcerative penalty. When a disappointing disposition occurs, this "long range" view of rehabilitation is also important in terms of defense counsel "believing in" the client and some of the client's strengths and achievements: "the defendant's forceful efforts and the intervention of a respected legal professional who 'believed in' the defendant may still, despite the setback, sow the seeds for eventual desistance on the part of the defendant." *See Reflections, supra* note 51 (referring to criminological work on offender desistance and the role of narrative development).

with the idea of involvement of family and friends. Ordinarily, if probation is granted, the court will have no further contact with the defendant unless revocation is sought for an alleged violation of the terms of probation. Taking a page from the apparently successful ongoing judicial supervision practices of drug treatment court, I have elsewhere urged ordinary criminal courts to schedule periodic review hearings in probation cases.[126] Review hearings can monitor not only the defendant's compliance, but can also assess whether various agencies have been providing the offender with appropriate services.[127] If such hearings are held, defense counsel should recognize that there is a meaningful role to play even if all is going well. Defense attorneys easily understand their role when violations are alleged and when revocation or other adverse sanctions will possibly result. But attorneys can play an important role in routine review hearings by marshalling, with the client, impressive evidence of success, and presenting it to the court, thereby helping to reinforce desistance from criminal activity.[128]

Drug treatment (and other problem-solving) courts also hold "graduation ceremonies" for clients who successfully complete the program. Graduates and their families attend, and applause is common. Again, receiving praise in this sort of official setting seems to be very meaningful. Accordingly, these ceremonies are not merely "ceremonial," but appear to have real rehabilitative value, and suggest an important, albeit unconventional, role for counsel.[129] Given the drug court graduation experience, courts and counsel should consider some sort of in-court acknowledgement when probation is terminated. Indeed, when the probationary period has been going well, counsel should, when available under the local legal landscape, move for the early termination

---

126. *Robes and Rehabilitation*, *supra* note 45, at 251.

127. This ties in with the "good lives" perspective mentioned earlier. *See* Ward & Stewart, *supra* note 116 and accompanying text.

128. *Robes and Rehabilitation*, *supra* note 45, at 251–52; *see also* Quinn, *supra* note 87, at 39 (counsel important at drug treatment court post-adjudication status hearings even when all is going well and when sanctions are not at issue). Caroline S. Cooper & Shanie R. Bartlett, *SJI National Symposium on the Implementation and Operation of Drug Courts*, *available at* http://spa.american.edu/justice/publications/juvrptt.htm. (last visited Jan. 27, 2005) (surveying drug court participants themselves report value in regular judicial contact). One DTC judge told me that, with retained counsel, to cut down on expenses, the judge only asks counsel to come to a review hearing if the judge expects "to be mean." This raises an interesting question regarding costs, therapeutic aims, and retained versus publicly-provided legal services.

129. *Robes and Rehabilitation*, *supra* note 45, at 251.

of probation, hopefully accompanied by an in-court acknowledgement of the probationer's successful conduct.[130]

F. Appeal

Following conviction, and especially after the imposition of an incarcerative sentence, the issue of an appeal will arise. With retained counsel, counsel and client will engage in a cost/benefit analysis of sorts. In most cases, however, the client will be indigent, and, given the right to appointed counsel in the first appeal,[131] there are no real disincentives to filing an appeal. Not surprisingly, therefore, the great bulk of appeals result in affirmances.

Therapeutic jurisprudence considerations abound in the kind of conversations lawyers should have with clients both before an appellate brief is filed and in the aftermath of an appellate determination.[132] One crucial therapeu-

---

130. Ariz. Rev. Stat. § 13-901(E) (2002).

> The court, on its own initiative or upon application of the probationer, after notice and an opportunity to be heard for the prosecuting attorney, and on request, the victim, may terminate the period of probation or intensive probation and discharge the defendant at a time earlier than that originally imposed if in the court's opinion the ends of justice will be served and if the conduct of the defendant on probation warrants it.

Id. Under certain drug treatment initiatives, a similar court hearing can be held to underscore the "successful completion of treatment." Cal. Penal Code § 1210(c) (2004).

131. Douglas v. California, 372 U.S. 252 (1963).

132. In the event of an appellate reversal, counsel will need to explain what has happened and what comes next, especially in terms of possible new trials and the like. It is crucial, in such cases, that a client not think incorrectly that complete freedom has been won. Of course, all of this should ideally have been first explained to the client earlier, at the time counsel explained the arguments to be made and the relief sought. A valuable educational exercise would be for lawyers and law students to contemplate the kind of conversation to have with a client before a brief is filed and after an appellate ruling. Also to be considered is whether the conversation should be face-to-face or through correspondence. Of course, the post-ruling conversation will differ markedly if the appellate court reverses or affirms the court below. Mainly, the lawyer will be dealing with appellate affirmances. The present chapter discusses possible lawyer-client dialogue and conversations not only in the context of appeals, but also in the context of diversion decisions and in the context of formulating proposed conditions of probation and parole. Important as they are, these are only illustrative of the TJ-tinged conversations that can be had throughout the criminal process. For example, the nature—or at least the tone—of a conversation regarding a motion to suppress evidence may be a bit different from the conventional one when it is inspired by a TJ perspective. Legal clinics can discuss what these conversations might look like.

tic consideration is whether the appellate court accorded appellant and counsel "voice"—whether it truly attended to the client's case.

The "real" way an appellant can be shown to have had "voice" is through a conversation with counsel, and, for that to happen, in a meaningful way, an appellate court opinion, as opposed to a per curium summary affirmance is essential.[133] Since criminal appeals are typically taken because there is nothing to lose, success on appeal is generally quite an uphill battle.

The appellate lawyer's task in discussing an appellate affirmance is a highly sensitive one. On the one hand, it is important for counsel to convey the message of voice and validation. On the other hand, it is crucial that counsel not simply serve as an apologist for an appellate affirmance; that appellant know that counsel is truly on the appellant's side, giving the case the best possible shot. The following remarks are intended to open a discussion about how to strike an appropriate balance.

If the appellate affirmance is much in line with what counsel anticipated (or feared), it is probably helpful for counsel to express that view to the client. "Yeah, as I feared, the court reaffirmed what it had said five years ago in *State v. Wilkins*. We tried to get the court to overrule *Wilkins* or at least to limit it, and the court seemed to understand what we were arguing, but they didn't buy it." Unless counsel truly believes the appellate court was muddled, inattentive, or outright stupid, it would seem to be without much purpose so to characterize the ruling. Such a characterization suggests that the client was not accorded "voice" and "validation," even with a professional advocate speaking for the client, which would be likely to affect the client's acceptance of the ruling and adjustment to the situation. In the great majority of cases, one would hope the appellate opinion would reflect the fact that the appellant—and thus the attorney as well—was accorded voice and validation.[134]

The conversation a lawyer might have with a client following an appellate ruling relates also to the conversation the lawyer should have had with the client earlier—when the appeal was filed or during the preparation of the appellate brief. Except when the attorney regards a case to be wholly without merit, a brief on the merits is likely to be filed. At this stage, it is important

---

133. *See* Amy D. Ronner & Bruce J. Winick, *The Antitherapeutic Per Curiam Affirmance,* in TJ JUDGING, *supra* note 45, at 316; *see also* Amy D. Ronner & Bruce J. Winick, *Silencing the Appellant's Voice: The Antitherapeutic Per Curiam Affirmance,* 24 SEATTLE U. L. REV. 499, 500–07 (2000).

134. These issues, and conversations, can be applied as well to the trial level when trial courts prepare written opinions, as does the drug treatment court of New South Wales. *See* New South Wales, *supra* note 78 and accompanying text.

for the lawyer to explain the points and arguments to be made, but also to indicate the state of the prevailing law and the lawyer's general assessment of what the appellate court will do and why. This is to give the client a realistic view of what to expect, and it also sets the stage for the later conversation—the one following the appellate court's ruling.

And what if the lawyer finds the case completely without merit? *Anders v. California*[135] allows the lawyer to move to withdraw, accompanied by a "minor brief" referring to anything in the record that may arguably support an appeal. The more recent case of *Smith v. Robbins*[136] although it does not contemplate attorney withdrawal, and does not require the lawyer to characterize the case as frivolous, in some ways permits a lawyer to do even less than in *Anders*: to merely summarize the case, with references to the record, and to offer to brief any points suggested by the appellate court.

A useful exercise would be to consider, keeping in mind the therapeutic jurisprudence considerations, what a lawyer faced with such a case should do, and what the lawyer/client conversation might look like. Might it be preferable for the lawyer to explain why the case, given the state of the law, seems without merit, but, in lieu of withdrawing, to offer to "dress up" the *Anders* brief as a short brief on the merits? Are there any ethical restrictions on such a strategy, such as an ethical obligation not to file a frivolous appeal?[137] If so, how might ethical considerations form part of the lawyer's conversation with the client on why another course of action seems in order?

G. Corrections, Reentry, and Beyond

If a client is confronting an incarcerative sentence, the TJ Criminal lawyer should, at some point, engage the client in a dialogue regarding the sentence and the future. Some of this discussion can occur in the legal context of an expected or hoped-for release or conditional release date. Relevant legal considerations will be earning and forfeiting good time credits, [138] including sentence reductions for engaging in certain treatment programs.[139] Crucially im-

---

135. Anders v. California, 386 U.S. 738 (1967).

136. Smith v. Robbins, 528 U.S. 259 (2000).

137. *Id.* at 278.

138. James B. Jacobs, *Sentencing by Prison Personnel: Good Time*, 30 UCLA L. Rev. 217 (1982).

139. Lopez v. Davis, 531 U.S. 230 (2001) (discussing operation and limitation of Federal Bureau of Prisons regulation according early release for completion of a substance abuse program). The U.S. Sentencing Commission's Ad Hoc Advisory Group on Native

portant, too, is whether the jurisdiction authorizes discretionary parole release and, if so, when the client will be eligible for parole consideration.[140]

Over the last couple of decades, as part of the development to reduce sentencing disparity, many jurisdictions have abolished discretionary parole eligibility, perhaps throwing the baby out with the bathwater by sapping the system of a tool to motivate prisoners and to orient them toward release. Recently, however, the crucial question of prisoner reentry has surfaced as a major concern of public policy.[141] Proposals have emerged to reform and reinvigorate the parole process,[142] as well as to borrow from the drug court model and to create reentry courts.[143] A reentry court could have conditional release authority[144] or could operate post-unconditional release to work with ex-offenders who volunteer to participate in a program geared toward smoother reentry.[145]

This new urgency should carry with it a major role for lawyers—and a very major need for the creation of new structures for providing legal services in this arena. In therapeutic jurisprudence terms, there is much meaningful work for an attorney at the parole grant hearing stage. The prior detailed discussion of relapse prevention planning and probation is fully applicable.[146] The discussion proposes a very substantial role for the lawyer in working with the client and others to establish a plan—and proposed conditions—for conditional release.

Once the client has been released from confinement, conditionally or unconditionally, counsel can also help in the tremendously difficult task of reen-

---

American Sentencing Issues recently proposed the adoption of a similar program for sex offender treatment. Report of the Native American Advisory Group, 26–30, Nov. 4, 2003, *available at* http://www.ussc.gov/NAAG/NativeAmer.pdf (last visited April 23, 2005).

140. Petersilia, *supra* note 43.

141. *See id.*; *see also* Fox Butterfield, *Repaving the Long Road Out of Prison*, N.Y. Times, May 4, 2004, at 25A (discussing strong interest in reentry, and innovative programs to provide released inmates immediately with clothing, housing, mental health and drug treatment, and employment opportunities); Terry Carter, *End Mandatory Minimums, ABA Commission Urges*, 3 A.B.A. J. E-Report 1, June 25, 2004. (In lieu of mandatory minimums, the report proposes the use of "guided discretion").

142. Petersilia, *supra* note 43.

143. *Spain's JVP Law, supra* note 44.

144. *Id.*

145. Shadd Maruna & Thomas P. LeBel, *Welcome Home? Examining the "Reentry Court" Concept from a Strengths-Based Perspective, in* TJ Judging, *supra* note 45, at 255, 257.

146. *See supra* text accompanying notes 110–129.

try and readjustment.[147] On the strictly legal side, the client should be clearly informed of any imposed parole conditions. The possibility of parole revocation as well as the applicability of recidivist statutes[148] will underscore the high stakes involved in a return to criminality.

Unfortunately, the collateral consequences of a criminal conviction[149] are a further impediment to successful reentry, but they are crucial components of an important lawyer/client conversation.[150] Because the restoration of some rights is possible,[151] the lawyer can play an important role in restoration and expungement efforts.[152]

Conclusion

This chapter has merely scratched the surface of the ways in which lawyers interested in therapeutic jurisprudence might invigorate and enlarge their traditional roles, but I hope it will motivate the development of a true TJ crim-

---

147. Alan Feuer, *Out of Jail, Into Temptation: A Day in a Life, in* TJ JUDGING, *supra* note 45, at 13–19. *See also* Butterfield, *supra* note 140; Anthony C. Thompson, *Navigating the Hidden Obstacles to Ex-Offender Reentry*, 45 B.C. L. REV. 255 (2004) (an excellent piece on the role of the lawyer in re-entry, and on the workings of the Offender Reentry Clinic at NYU law school).

148. Julian V. Roberts, *The Role of Criminal Record in the Sentencing Process*, 22 CRIME & JUST. 303 (1997).

149. Sabra Micah Barnett, *Collateral Sanctions and Civil Disabilities: The Secret Barrier to True Sentencing Reform for Legislatures and Sentencing Commissions*, 55 ALA. L. REV. 375 (2004).

150. These collateral consequences accompany the conviction, and thus attach to probationers as well. Joshua R. DeGonia, *Defining a Successful Completion of Probation Under California's Expungement Statute*, 24 WHITTIER L. REV. 1077 (2003).

151. *E.g.*, ARIZ. REV. STAT. §§13-904–912 (2004).

152. Margaret Colgate Love, *Starting Over With a Clean Slate: In Praise of a Forgotten Section of the Model Penal Code*, 30 FORDHAM URB. L.J. 1705 (2003). These too could serve as reintegration ceremonies, or redemption rituals, praising and reinforcing the offender's desistance. *Robes and Rehabilitation, supra* note 45, at 250–51. Of course, some "collateral" consequences are purely informal rather than imposed by law: apartment complexes that may refuse to rent to those with a record, or employers who refuse to hire. Here is an area where the new reentry court concept may help, for landlords and employers may be more willing to consider one with a criminal record if the person is part of—or a graduate of—an official program. TJ criminal lawyers will need to play a role in the creation of these programs, and in informing clients of their existence, eligibility requirements, benefits, and potential costs.

inal defense bar[153] among private lawyers, public defenders, law school clinics, and privately-supported defense organizations. I hope it will foster further exploration, both within and outside of the legal academy,[154] of how TJ principles can inform the effective *and* affective assistance of counsel in criminal defense representation.

---

153. The present chapter focuses on the role of the criminal defense attorney. A virtually untouched but crucial area of inquiry relates to the use of the therapeutic jurisprudence perspective in the role of the prosecutor in their dealings with defendants as well as with victims.

154. I hope the chapter will be useful in legal education, both in general courses in criminal law and procedure, to explicate and legitimate a non-traditional role, and in sentencing and correction courses. I especially hope it will find its way into clinical legal education. There, the topics explored here can be further developed in teaching, in practice, and in student research projects. After all, the legal clinics are where the initial training of many of tomorrow's criminal lawyers is likely to begin.

CHAPTER 13

A PUBLIC DEFENDER IN A
PROBLEM-SOLVING COURT

*Lisa Schreibersdorf**

Not long ago, while helping a client draft an answer to a guardianship petition, I found myself in a lengthy discussion with her about the details of her life. We talked about her relationship with her family, her income, and expenses, her children, her dog, and the jewelry she had been forced to pawn. I listened to her feelings about losing the things that connected her to her past and her despair at how the guardianship had caused her to lose control over her finances.

Strangely, guardianship work is not the legal work for which I signed on. I am a public defender—a criminal defense trial attorney—by training. But now, in order to help clients who have been admitted to the mental health court, I find myself in areas of the court building I never expected to go, having discussions I never expected to have.

As I walked back to my office, I thought about this client and wondered whether I could have said something more inspiring, or listened better. I reminded myself that I had no law school class or CLE training about giving life advice to clients. There is no body of case law, no precedent and no legal authority for such discussions. The only source of knowledge in such a situation is an attorney's own life experience, and her willingness to share that wisdom with people who happen to be her clients.

When I started working as a public defender, I did not expect that I would be sharing my own personal truths with my clients. Certainly, I expected that

* Executive Director, Brooklyn Defender Services, New York. After all these years of legal writing, I found it extremely difficult to articulate these non-legal ideas. I would like to acknowledge the assistance of Laura Saft, Sharon Creal and Carol Fisler for their part in helping me get these thoughts down on paper. Thanks also to Marjorie Silver for her patience and understanding.

I would become an expert in constitutional law and suppression of unlawful evidence, that I would spend my time litigating and negotiating, and that I would gauge my success by wins and losses. While much of that has come to pass, I am continually surprised that, as I represent clients in treatment court, I am compelled to listen well, impart wisdom, and have expertise as to the issues of addiction and mental illness. And although I would not have been able to predict it, my concern for the wellbeing of my clients in the treatment courts has brought with it a healing process for me as a person, and an emotional recovery from the draining work of being a public defender.

Twenty-one years ago, I took a job with the Legal Aid Society in New York City, and there began representing clients accused of crimes in one of the poorest urban areas in the country. My experience as a public defender began as a trial attorney and eventually led to my current role as Executive Director of Brooklyn Defender Services, a medium-sized public defender office. To date, I have represented thousands of people accused of a wide variety of criminal acts, from trespassing and shoplifting to robbery and murder.

From the beginning, I loved being a public defender. I liked going to court every day and I thrived on the companionship of my colleagues. I was excited by the cases and the challenge of developing my litigation skills. As a new public defender in a large office, I was inspired by the idea of a shared mission—that there were other attorneys learning and growing as lawyers and also working hard to see that clients got a fair shake in court. And then there's the thing that drives many public defenders—the desire to fight for the underdog.

It did not take very long for me to realize, though, that the skills I was learning were not enough. Many of my clients needed more from me than successful legal arguments, good plea negotiations or a winning trial strategy. A lot of my clients, particularly those involved in drug and property crimes, were struggling with substance abuse, mental illness, homelessness, health issues, and other overwhelming circumstances. Many of the families with whom I was in touch had multi-generational problems, including alcoholism, child abuse, and domestic violence.

Having seen that so many of my clients were coming into the criminal justice system because of underlying problems in their lives, I started to feel dissatisfied that the notions of compassion, understanding, redemption, and rehabilitation were rarely part of the discussion in court. It was mostly an uphill battle to convince prosecutors and judges that a criminal act might be an aberration for a particular individual or that poverty or other circumstances made that act understandable or even laudable.

One troubling case during the crack epidemic of the 1980s stands out in my memory. My client, Ronald F., was a teenager who lived in one of the poorest and most dangerous housing projects in Brooklyn. Ronald had agreed to sell drugs for a well-known drug dealer in his neighborhood. When I asked Ronald why he sold drugs, he explained that the drug dealer was one of the only people in his neighborhood who had money to give to his mother and children and that he was always kind and protective towards Ronald. He saw the drug dealer as a role model. Ronald knew selling drugs was illegal, but he did it out of loyalty and respect for the dealer he had come to know. What was compelling about Ronald was that he respected the drug dealer for the same reasons I would respect someone, for the manner in which he cared for his loved ones.

Ronald was arrested when he sold drugs to an undercover officer. Normally, it would have been possible to get a probationary sentence in such a case, but this particular client was unlucky. In the criminal justice lottery system, he had drawn a particularly harsh judge and an unsympathetic prosecutor. They were not willing to plea bargain. Despite my best efforts, I could not convince the judge or the prosecutor to give Ronald a non-jail disposition. It was very upsetting to me when Ronald had to accept a one-to-three year jail sentence. At the time, I felt this was a professional failure on my part.

Now I see Ronald's case as a failure of our criminal justice system. When we expose an essentially innocent child to the violence and culture of prison, we get back a damaged individual, someone whose formative years have warped him in ways that are unimaginable to those of us who have not endured a prison sentence. The person who comes out of prison is exponentially more troubled than when he went in, and often becomes a burden on his family and community—both financially and emotionally. In addition, the felony conviction on his record makes it difficult for him to reintegrate into society. A person who has been in prison is disenfranchised in many ways, most particularly by the extreme likelihood that he will become unemployed or underemployed after his release.

It is upsetting to realize that because people from certain neighborhoods and certain racial or ethnic groups are more likely to be arrested, poor communities of color bear the brunt of the problems associated with stiff prison sentences.[1] The difficulties families face when their loved one is in prison and the obstacles the community faces when prisoners are released has always been difficult for me to witness, as an attorney and as a person. It is also hard to accept that from the eyes of my clients' families and community, the judicial

---

1. Some examples include deportation, eviction, caring for the children of the inmate, and even bearing the costs of exorbitant collect calls from prison.

system is a punishing, harsh, unpredictable institution. The sense of fairness, justice, and mercy that I believe in does not exist for many of the citizens the court is supposed to serve.

At some point in my career as a public defender, I started to feel an almost unbearable sense of loss. Large numbers of incarcerated people and long prison sentences were creating devastating problems for the community. Meanwhile, families were begging me to get help for their drug addicted or mentally ill loved ones.

As a trial attorney, there was a limit to the impact I could have on such a problem. I could, on a case-by-case basis, refer clients for drug or mental health treatment. And if I was able to convince a prosecutor and judge that such a disposition was appropriate, I might be able to divert a client from jail. Even if I were successful, though, there were major obstacles the client faced in such a situation. For example, many judges had a particularly harsh view of anyone who was given the "gift" of treatment. Many times, a client who had been doing well in a program for months was returned to jail because of one positive drug test or a relatively minor infraction. Often, such a jail sentence was harsher than the sentence I could have plea bargained in the first place.

In the mid 1990s, in what can only be described as a sea change, the court system began to adopt the medical community's view that addiction was a disease that could be treated. The notion that a substance abuser was suffering from a treatable disease went together with the understanding that relapses and backsliding were normal parts of recovery from that illness. The acceptance of those notions was instrumental in humanizing the court's response to drug addicts in the criminal justice system.

In 1996, Brooklyn became one of the first locations in the country to start a drug court.[2] Drug court is premised on the notion that addiction should be treated rather than punished. In drug court, case managers work for the judge

---

2. Brooklyn was selected, in part, because of the progressive attitude of the District Attorney, Charles J. Hynes, towards treatment programs. *See* Carol Fisler, *Building Trust and Managing Risk: A Look at a Felony Mental Health Court*, 11 PSYCHOL. PUB. POL'Y & L. 587, 589 (2005) ("Brooklyn had been the focal point for many of New York's important problem-solving initiatives, largely because of the vision of its district attorney, Charles J. Hynes, who is committed to crime reduction strategies ..."). His office had already initiated the DTAP program, which gave drug addicted felons a chance to obtain drug treatment. *See* The National Center on Addiction and Substance Abuse at Columbia University, *Innovative Drug Treatment Alternative to Prison Program Reduces Crime, Prison Costs* (2003), *available at* http://www.casacolumbia.org/absolutenm/templates/PressReleases.aspx?articleid =261&zoneid=46 (last visited June 25, 2006).

by evaluating clients for treatment and referring them for appropriate serv-ices. The premise in drug court is that the arrest of the drug addict can act as a catalyst for change in his or her life. The judge is an active participant in the process of recovery, filling a variety of non-traditional judicial roles, such as motivating people to enter treatment, monitoring their progress, and sup-porting their efforts. When drug court clients come to court, the judge re-wards their progress or penalizes them according to a predetermined set of graduated sanctions that mete out punishments for missed appointments, positive drug tests or other lapses in treatment progress. After such punish-ments, clients are returned to the program to continue with treatment. Drug court introduced the concept of audience participation— when a client reaches a milestone, the entire courtroom applauds.

Although my fellow public defenders and I were skeptical that the court system could change its view of drug addiction so completely and so suddenly, we decided to take a leap of faith in favor of this new court. When the court lived up to its promises, we were genuinely pleased to see our clients getting what they deserved—treatment rather than prison.

For those of us who had spent years advising clients to take substantial jail sentences on drug-related cases, the formation of drug court was a relief. We were happy for anything that would stop the madness of having to pressure our clients, many who were actually going through withdrawal, to accept harsh jail sentences in order to avoid even harsher sentences later.

Over time, our collective sense of relief changed to one of support as drug court has become a resounding success. Many clients not only succeed in hav-ing their case dismissed, but they also turn their lives around. At any gradu-ation ceremony, the audience is silent as the clients tell the riveting stories of their lives lost to drugs and restored to them because of drug court. As a de-fense attorney, the unfolding of this human drama is made more powerful by the memory of the hundreds of clients who never got this opportunity, but who went to prison instead.

The use of special treatment courts creates its own set of issues for a pub-lic defender, and particularly for me as a chief defender. For example, what does a defense attorney do if a client is innocent? One of my office's first cases in drug court was an older man, in his 50's. He was homeless and dirty when he was arrested. He told his lawyer that he did not sell drugs. He said to his lawyer, "Look at me, who would trust me with drugs, who would buy drugs from me?" His attorney, a veteran trial attorney, believed that the client was innocent. But the client had already been offered a chance to be treated for his drug addiction in treatment court. The client was tired of living in the street and he wanted to accept the treatment offer.

The attorney who represented this client was troubled, but eventually decided that he would not try to persuade the client to go to trial. He allowed the client to plead guilty, despite the attorney's belief that the client was innocent of the crime. Fortunately, this client succeeded in drug court, became clean and sober and, two years later, had his case dismissed.

The real problem would have been if the client did not make it through the treatment program. Then, he would be serving a substantial jail sentence for a crime he did not commit. Such a potential is troubling in our system of justice, which is built on the notion that conviction and incarceration of an innocent person is an unacceptable outcome.

Another problem in drug court is that improper police behavior cannot be litigated. Because clients plead guilty when they go to drug court, they waive objections to constitutional violations that have occurred. As defense attorneys, we must advise individuals regarding their own personal situation and cannot let our broader concerns jeopardize the best interest of an individual client. Thus, most of the clients who are offered treatment accept it, even if there is a problem with what the police did during the arrest.

The concern, for those of us who hear from our clients and the community about problematic police activity, is that drug court eliminates an avenue of challenge to such behavior. Since the majority of the complaints we hear about occur in drug arrests, it is troubling that suppression issues are not litigated in drug court.

I was pleased that I was asked to participate in planning our second and third drug courts and, later, our mental health court[3] in Brooklyn. There was little in my training as a trial attorney that prepared me for the task of sitting on a planning committee. Even so, I agreed to participate, because of the extreme importance of having defense attorneys play a role in planning these programs. As the only person in court who is permitted to speak with the defendant once charges are filed, defense attorneys have the most significant interactions with accused people in the criminal justice system. Public defenders, in particular, have a lot to contribute when planning a treatment court because we represent the vast majority of drug-addicted and mentally ill

---

3. Mental Health Court is similar to drug court but it treats people who have serious mental illnesses. Many of these clients also suffer with drug or alcohol problems. Maia Szalavitz, *The Brooklyn Mental Health Court*, GOTHAM GAZETTE: N.Y.C. NEWS & POL'Y, Nov. 2002, *available at* http://www.gothamgazette.com/article//20021101/9/100 (last visited June 25, 2006) ("Since about 50 percent of the severely mentally ill have drug problems and about 50 percent of addicts have additional mental illnesses of varying severity, this is a large group of people who often have contact with the criminal justice system.").

clients. We know what clients' concerns are when they are offered treatment and what might work to address those problems. We also understand that our fellow defense attorneys are worried about the erosion of procedural and substantive safeguards guaranteed to our clients by the Constitution.

When I work on planning and implementing a new court, I view my role as the spokesperson for the client who will not or cannot meet the requirements of the court. I know there is a lot of optimism about drug and mental health court because, at least in Brooklyn, we have seen so many successful outcomes. But as a public defender I want to be sure that everyone is treated fairly, and in this case the person who received an opportunity in drug court and could not comply with its mandate is the person who most needs my advocacy on his or her behalf.

As a defense attorney on the planning team, I focus on the fact that constitutional rights and due process need to be part of the plan for a specialty court—giving life to principles such as the right to counsel, the right to be heard, and the prohibition against cruel and unusual punishment strengthens a treatment court, since applying such principles makes our system resilient and just.

One very important notion that our treatment courts have adopted is that clients who attempt treatment should not be given a longer sentence if they fail than if they had not tried treatment at all. The reason this is important is because clients should still be punished for their original crime, not for their treatment failure.

After the experience of helping plan a treatment court and then spending time appearing in that court, I have learned that what I really care about in a drug or mental health court is certainty. It is important that the court's procedures allow an attorney to negotiate a pre-determined time that the client will stay in the program as well as a defined outcome upon ultimate success or failure. By determining each of these issues at the outset of treatment, our courts avoid the temptation to punish someone for their failure in recovery rather than for the crime that brought them into the criminal justice system. Equally as important is a pre-agreed positive outcome and defined treatment period—a client working hard to succeed in treatment day by day needs to know what he is working towards and for how long.

Planning a new court and then standing next to a client who graduates from that court is a uniquely satisfying experience. During the week I was writing this chapter, my client Moises graduated from drug court. The courtroom erupted with applause while he radiated with pride and satisfaction. I remembered that just months ago, I spent the better part of a day with Moises, discussing whether he should agree to go to an in-patient rehab at his case manager's suggestion. He did not want his wife to know he had a drug problem. I told him she probably knew about his problem despite his attempts to hide it and perhaps this was a chance at a real new beginning in their relationship. I was glad that I was part of a process that worked for him. I was also gratified when I remembered the many hours I spent with a group of dedicated professionals sitting at a table planning a court that would someday help people like Moises.

As for my own personal experience, nothing compares with representing clients in mental health court. The possibility of diverting a mentally ill person from prison is profoundly important because prison is an atrocious place for inmates with mental illness. Prisoners who suffer with mental illness tend to be harassed and abused by other inmates. Also, because they are not always able to comply with directions given to them by corrections officials, prisoners with mental illness are placed into solitary confinement more often than inmates without mental illness. Solitary confinement can take a huge toll on anyone, but for someone with a mental illness it can mean severe and permanent damage and extreme mental anguish.[4] There are many suicide attempts and other self-destructive behaviors associated with mentally ill prisoners.

One reason I enjoy appearing in mental health court is that there is a real sense of gratification when I can help someone so vulnerable avoid a harrowing and dehumanizing experience. But truth be told, I have learned a lot from my clients in mental health court. I have learned about struggling with aspects of oneself that are distasteful or difficult to accept. I have watched people work very hard just to get through one day and then wake up the next day and struggle just as hard to get through another. And most compelling, I have seen that there is redemption for people who used to be thought of as hopeless.

It is not always easy to represent clients with mental illness. Such clients and their cases present a unique set of challenges for a public defender. Most difficult among those challenges is deciding when to substitute your own judgment about what is best for the client for a client's stated desire. When a client is mentally ill, it is irresponsible to allow him to make all the decisions. On the other hand, for defense attorneys, it is anathema to our role to make decisions for clients or substitute our judgment for theirs. Balancing these two important

---

4. For more information about the effects of incarceration upon the mentally ill, see the various news articles provided on the Urban Justice Center website at www.urbanjustice.org/ujc/press/mental.html (last visited June 25, 2006). For example, see Cara Matthews, *Mentally Ill Inmates' Treatment Decried*, ROCHESTER DEMOCRAT AND CHRONICLE, June 8, 2006, *available at* http://www.urbanjustice.org/pdf/press/democrat_chronicle_08jun06.pdf (last visited June 25, 2006).

principles is difficult, but because the implications are so serious for the clients, the lawyer must wrestle with these issues on a case-by-case basis.

It is rewarding to participate in a program that has addressed a myriad of thorny issues responsibly and conscientiously.[5] In fact, the mental health court in Brooklyn is a wonderfully humane and supportive environment for my clients with mental illness. Recently, the judge, the social worker, the assistant district attorney, and I discussed with each other and with the client her need for hospitalization. She was so depressed that she did not have the strength to take her medication as the judge had ordered. The kindness and compassion that were expressed towards this woman stood in stark contrast to what would be more likely to occur in another courtroom—the shackling of a client and removal of that person to jail for failing to comply with the judge's directive.

In my opinion, one of the most important factors in the success of our mental health court is the judge.[6] He and his staff are able to maintain a high level of control in the courtroom despite the erratic nature of the people who appear there. The judge treats the clients with a level of firm compassion that has caused attorneys, clients, and family members to respect him and the court. And he has stood solidly on his commitment not to punish a mentally ill defendant who could not benefit from the treatment plan more harshly than a similarly situated non-mentally ill defendant.

Every time I witness the interplay of the judge, the treatment staff, the prosecutor, the defense attorneys, the clients, and the court personnel, I am gratified that I had even a small part to play in the formation of the mental health court. And as I stand next to a graduate, I know that in another time or place, instead of applause, that person could have been experiencing the deadly silence of a few years in solitary confinement. It is impossible to stand next to a graduating client in such a situation and not be profoundly moved and forever changed.

I find that the positive feelings I get from representing clients in treatment court are an important counterbalancing force to the stress and difficulties associated with traditional public defense work.[7] The recognition of the hu-

---

5. Some of the issues include: When can the court force the client to take medication? What can the court do if the client's illness does not respond to treatment? How will the court react to illegal drug or alcohol use?

6. Brooklyn's Mental Health Court is presided over by The Honorable Matthew D'Emic. http://www.courtinnovation.org/index.cfm?fuseaction=Document.viewDocument&documentID=554&documentTopicID=25&documentTypeID=8 (last visited June 26, 2006).

7. See supra ch. 1: Marjorie A. Silver, Emotional Competence and the Lawyer's Journey, at pp. [] (discussing challenges and stresses of criminal defense work).

manity of my clients and their families by a treatment court and the joy it brings is an antidote to the sadness and misery witnessed each day by public defenders in other courtrooms. For this reason, it is my office policy that all attorneys represent clients in drug or mental health court. Unlike many other defender offices, Brooklyn Defender Services does not limit treatment court appearances to one or two attorneys. We feel it is important for every attorney to see the most positive aspects of the criminal justice system so that they, too, can have a balanced view of the justice their clients deserve.

The hopefulness and humanity of the treatment courts have altered the way our clients are viewed when they are in the criminal justice system. For myself, being part of the journey taken by those clients as they progress through the drug or mental health court has balanced the frustration, bitterness, and despair that drags many public defenders into their own depression, alcoholism, and divorce.

Public defenders are not the only professionals who benefit from the humane treatment of drug addicted or mentally ill defendants. I have seen judges, prosecutors, private defense attorneys, court personnel, law clerks, and treatment professionals change the way they view criminal defendants when they spend time in a treatment court. When compassion, understanding, and humanity are valued in a court, it changes everyone.

CHAPTER 14

Defining the Lawyer-Self: Using Therapeutic Jurisprudence to Define the Lawyer's Role and Build Alliances that Aid the Child Client

*Kristin Henning**

Introduction

The application of therapeutic jurisprudence to juvenile court is not new. In fact, juvenile courts were designed to meet an explicit rehabilitative agenda and have historically relied on paternalistic judges to dole out an array of therapeutic services to youth charged with crime.[1] Today, therapeutic outcomes are not limited to judicial paternalism and rehabilitative programming, but may also be achieved or hindered through the child's daily interaction with lawyers, probation officers, the police, and even his own family. The child's interactions

---

* Copyright © 2005 by Kristin Henning. Associate Professor of Law, Georgetown University Law Center. J.D., Yale Law School, L.L.M., Georgetown Law Center; A.B., Duke University. The author has represented juveniles in the District of Columbia for the last ten years. She previously served as lead attorney for the juvenile unit of the D.C. Public Defender Service and is currently the Deputy Director of the Juvenile Justice Clinic at Georgetown.
    1. Josine Junger-Tas, *The Juvenile Justice System: Past and Present Trends in Western Society, in* Punishing Juveniles: Principle and Critique 30 (Ido Weijers & Antony Duff eds., 2002) [hereinafter *Juvenile Justice System*].

with key players in the juvenile justice system will inevitably shape the child's perceptions of justice, authority, and morality and may alter or reinforce the path the child has set for his own future. Because the attorney-client relationship may be the sole means by which the child may participate in the process of justice and earn credibility and respect with others in the system, the attorney-client relationship warrants special care and attention in the juvenile court.

This chapter considers ways in which therapeutic jurisprudence may inform and improve attorney-child relationships in the juvenile justice system. Therapeutic jurisprudence recognizes that there is considerable therapeutic value to attorney-client relationships that educate, empower, and validate the client. Attorneys who validate clients are neither patronizing nor paternalistic, but instead seek and respect the client's perspective, identify and affirm the client's strengths, and convey empathy for the client's plight. Attorneys who empower clients give voice to the client's views and attempt to understand the client from the client's own cultural, ethnic, gendered, and socioeconomic perspective. Therapeutically inspired attorney-client relationships not only yield immediate benefits of client-satisfaction and positive self-esteem, but may also promote effective long-term rehabilitation for children accused of crime.

The attorney-child relationship is also influenced by a myriad of external factors that may impede or enhance the attorney-client dynamic. Notwithstanding the child's independent legal interests, the child always exists within the context of family and community and is generally dependent on parents, teachers, and other significant adults for basic necessities and guidance. Thus, successful lawyering on behalf of children may require the lawyer to build alliances and forge partnerships that will inform and improve attorney-child interactions and aid the lawyer in representing the whole child. In a delinquency case, alliances with family members, teachers, social workers, psychologists, public benefits attorneys, and special education advocates may facilitate a more informed choice among case-related alternatives, empower the child to participate more effectively in the juvenile justice system, and increase the child's opportunity for favorable outcomes. The second half of this chapter explores the value of interdisciplinary partnerships.

I. Defining the Lawyer-Self

A. Selecting the Appropriate Attorney-Client Paradigm

The selection of an appropriate attorney-child paradigm cannot be taken lightly in the juvenile justice system. The attorney-client relationship is the primary means by which an accused child may exercise or waive important constitutional rights; it is the lens through which the child views, understands, and evaluates the juvenile court system; and it is the relationship through which the child comes to understand broader notions of law, liberty, justice, and fairness. The attorney-client relationship is also the means by which the child will develop positive or negative responses to the rehabilitative goals of the court.

Lawyers interested in the study of effective attorney-client relations will find a wealth of literature on the theories and practice of client counseling, client interviewing, "affective" advocacy, and moral responsibility. [2] In the literature, the lawyer is left to choose from among a variety of attorney-client paradigms creatively named: the hired gun, the guru, the godfather, the authoritarian, the friend, the best interest or guardian advocate, and the client-centered or collaborative lawyer among others.[3] The lawyer's choice of paradigms often depends more on the lawyer's values, experience, and ego than on the client's expressed or negotiated preference in the attorney-client relationship. The selection of an appropriate attorney-client framework is especially complicated when the client is a child or an adolescent who has limited life experience, incomplete cognitive and psychosocial development, and limited ability to effectively negotiate roles and responsibilities within the attorney-client dyad.[4] The traditional paternalistic and rehabilitative mission of the juvenile court further complicates the role of the child's lawyer.

Principles of law and ethics are obvious and important means by which the lawyer may select among the various advocacy models. Today, emerging principles of therapeutic jurisprudence provide an additional consideration in the evaluation of lawyering paradigms. This section looks at the therapeutic values and skills that lie at the heart of a successful and satisfactory attorney-

---

2. For a representative sampling, see DAVID A. BINDER ET AL., LAWYERS AS COUNSELORS: A CLIENT-CENTERED APPROACH (2d ed. 2004); Robert F. Cochran et al., *Client Counseling and Moral Responsibility*, 30 PEPP. L. REV. 591 (2003) [hereinafter *Client Counseling*]; Linda G. Mills, *Affective Lawyering: The Emotional Dimensions of the Lawyer-Client Relation, in* PRACTICING THERAPEUTIC JURISPRUDENCE: LAW AS A HELPING PROFESSION 419 (Dennis P. Stolle et al. eds., 2000); ROBERT F. COCHRAN ET AL., THE COUNSELOR-AT-LAW: A COLLABORATIVE APPROACH TO CLIENT INTERVIEWING AND COUNSELING (1999) [hereinafter COUNSELOR-AT-LAW]; THOMAS L. SHAFFER & ROBERT F. COCHRAN, LAWYERS, CLIENTS AND MORAL RESPONSIBILITY (1994).

3. COCHRAN ET AL., COUNSELOR-AT-LAW, *supra* note 2, at 165–82 (discussion array of client-counseling models).

4. Melinda G. Schmidt et al., *Effectiveness of Participation as a Defendant: The Attorney-Juvenile Client Relationship*, 21 BEHAV. SCI. & L. 175, 176–78 (2003).

client dyad and considers whether therapeutic preferences conflict or converge with other more important values and norms.

1. Values

Therapeutic jurisprudence is a study of the ways in which legal rules, legal procedures, and the roles of legal actors—such as lawyers, judges, and probation officers—produce intended or unintended therapeutic or anti-therapeutic consequences for parties in the relevant system of justice.[5] Therapeutic jurisprudence seeks to promote policies, systems, and relationships, consistent with principles of justice and constitutional law, that will secure positive therapeutic outcomes and minimize negative or anti-therapeutic consequences.[6] Modern applications of therapeutic jurisprudence in the juvenile justice system suggest that when children perceive legal rules, procedures, and actors as unfair, they have less respect for the law and legal authorities and are less likely to accept judicial interventions.[7] By contrast, when children believe the legal system has treated them with fairness, respect, and dignity, they are more inclined to accept responsibility for their conduct and engage in the process of reform.[8] Long before the evolution of therapeutic jurisprudence as an organized school of thought, the Supreme Court in *In re Gault*[9] recognized that the appearance and actuality of fairness, impartiality, and orderliness in the juvenile court may be just as, if not more, therapeutic for the child than programming.[10] That is, the child's perception about whether she is being treated fairly in the system is "integral to the child's behavioral and psychological development."[11]

Research suggests that litigants evaluate fairness and impartiality by opportunity for voice, validation, participation, autonomy, choice, accuracy of outcomes, and access to information.[12] In a juvenile case, the child has voice when he is given an opportunity to tell his story and express his own views

---

5. Bruce J. Winick, *The Jurisprudence of Therapeutic Jurisprudence*, 3 PSYCHOL. PUB. POL'Y & L. 184, 185 (1997) [hereinafter *Jurisprudence of TJ*].

6. *Id.* at 188.

7. Amy D. Ronner, *Songs of Validation, Voice and Voluntary Participation: Therapeutic Jurisprudence, Miranda and Juveniles*, 71 U. CIN. L. REV. 89, 93 (2002).

8. *Id.* at 94.

9. 387 U.S. 1 (1967).

10. *Id.* at 26.

11. Ronner, *supra* note 7, at 114 (quoting *In re Amendment to Rules of Juvenile Procedure*, 804 So.2d 1206, 1211 (Fla. 2001)).

12. Stephen J. Anderer & David J. Glass, *A Therapeutic Jurisprudence and Preventive Law Approach to Family Law*, in PRACTICING THERAPEUTIC JURISPRUDENCE, *supra* note 2, at 231.

and opinions before important decisions are made.[13] Validation goes further by ensuring not only that the child's story is heard, but also that the fact-finder has really listened to and considered his views.[14] Voice and validation have both symbolic and utilitarian value for the accused. Meaningful participation in the process not only allows the respondent to feel like a valued member of society whose opinion is worthy of consideration, but it also gives the respondent confidence in the accuracy of results and allows him to feel more in control of the outcome even if he is not the ultimate fact-finder. [15] In effect, voice and validation provide the accused with a real opportunity to influence the judge's final decision and increase the probability of either a favorable or a more equitable outcome.[16] In the disposition stage of a juvenile case, for example, participation enhances the child's perception that his interests are being considered in determining whether he needs treatment at all and, if so, whether that treatment may be accomplished in the least restrictive placement.

Individual autonomy, self-determination, and choice are other important components of therapeutic jurisprudence that promote the psychological well-being of those who are involved in legal proceedings.[17] Studies in the psychology of choice indicate that people who make choices for themselves function more effectively and have greater satisfaction. [18] Paternalism, by contrast, is anti-therapeutic because it breeds apathy, hinders motivation, and limits the potential for rehabilitation.[19] By facilitating the child's choice and self-determination in the disposition phase of a juvenile case, the system can enhance the child's motivation and increase the efficacy of treatment in which the child

---

13. Allen E. Lind et al., *Voice, Control, and Procedural Justice: Instrumental and Noninstrumental Concerns in Fairness Judgments*, 59 J. PERSONALITY & SOC. PSYCHOL. 952, 952 (1990).

14. Juan Ramirez, Jr. & Amy D. Ronner, *Voiceless Billy Budd: Melville's Tribute to the Sixth Amendment*, 41 CAL. W. L. REV. 103, 121 (2004).

15. Lind et al., *supra* note 13, at 952.

16. *Id.* at 952–53 (but also acknowledges potential for "frustration effect" caused by repeated unfavorable outcomes or biased communications of others that may subvert the impact of voice).

17. Winick, *Jurisprudence of TJ, supra* note 5, at 192; Bruce J. Winick, *Client Denial and Resistance in the Advance Directive Context: Reflections on How Attorneys Can Identify and Deal with A Psycholegal Soft Spot*, 4 PSYCHOL. PUB. POL'Y & L. 901, 916 (1998) [hereinafter *Client Denial*].

18. Winick, *Client Denial, supra* note 17, at 916.

19. Winick, *Jurisprudence of TJ, supra* note 5, at 192; Ramirez & Ronner, *supra* note 14, at 120–21; Bruce J. Winick, *Therapeutic Jurisprudence and the Civil Commitment Hearing*, 10 J. CONTEMP. LEGAL ISSUES 37, 45 (1999) [hereinafter *Civil Commitment*].

chooses or agrees to participate.[20] Children who design or actively participate in the development of their own treatment plans are more likely to follow through and succeed.[21]

Because meaningful choice is virtually impossible without information, children in court are also likely to measure fairness and impartiality by access to information.[22] Information relieves stress, increases the respondent's understanding and acceptance of procedures, and may increase the respondent's expectations for a positive result.[23] Individuals who obtain information about the law and the legal process also perceive that they have greater control within the system.[24] In a juvenile case, the accused child is powerless to make critical decisions without information about basic statutory and constitutional rights. The child may also feel alienated, anxious, and vulnerable when he does not understand what is happening to him or why he is being evaluated, referred for treatment, or removed from his home.

2. Attorney-Client Paradigms and Values

Proponents of procedural justice and therapeutic jurisprudence recognize the central importance of attorneys in securing therapeutic objectives.[25] In the criminal and juvenile justice systems, the attorney gives voice to the client's story and advances the client's participatory and dignitary interests in the system.[26] The attorney also arms the client with information and makes the proceedings seem less coercive. The selection of an appropriate attorney-client paradigm thus clearly lies at the heart of positive therapeutic outcomes. While some attorney-client paradigms, such as collaborative or client-centered models of advocacy will produce positive therapeutic outcomes for the child, other paradigms, such as authoritarian, best-interest, and parent-directed models of advocacy, will be anti-therapeutic and produce psychologically dysfunctional responses from the child.

---

20. Winick, *Jurisprudence of TJ, supra* note 5, at 197.

21. David Wexler, *Problem Solving and Relapse Prevention in Juvenile Court, in* JUDGING IN A THERAPEUTIC KEY: THERAPEUTIC JURISPRUDENCE AND THE COURTS 189, 193 (Bruce J. Winick & David B. Wexler eds., 2003) (excerpted from David B. Wexler, *Just Some Juvenile Thinking About Delinquent Behavior: A Therapeutic Jurisprudence Approach to Relapse Prevention Planning and Youth Advisory Juries,* 69 UMKC L. REV. 93 (2000)).

22. *See* Winick, *Civil Commitment, supra* note 19, at 46–47.

23. *Id.* at 46–47.

24. *Id.* at 46–57.

25. Ramirez & Rommer, *supra* note 14, at 108.

26. *Id.* at 121.

a. Authoritarian and Best Interest Models of Advocacy

In authoritarian models of advocacy, the advocates presume that their clients lack the competence or wisdom to make the right legal decisions.[27] In response, the authoritarian lawyer adopts a directive, and sometimes coercive, role in the attorney-client dyad,[28] and expects that his client will passively follow his direction, either by choice or default.[29] Authoritarian lawyers deprive the client of control by manipulating information or controlling the content and sequence of meetings with the client.[30] Attorneys control content by interrupting the client, limiting topics of conversation, withholding information, or narrowing the alternatives from which the client may choose.[31] Attorneys may also influence client decisions by speaking in legalese, framing issues in a narrow and limiting fashion, or strategically arranging the list of options to exaggerate or emphasize negative or positive outcomes.[32]

The opportunity for coercion is particularly great when the client is a child. Differences in age and experience combined with the child's natural inclinations to defer to adults create inherent power imbalances between the child and the attorney.[33] When the lawyer is concerned about the child's need for psychiatric or psychological treatment, for example, the lawyer may manipulate the options available in order to earn the child's consent to a residential treatment program despite the child's desire to remain at home. The client who feels stifled by the control of an authoritarian lawyer will often be dissatisfied with the legal process and unwilling to follow through with recom-

---

27. Rodney J. Uphoff, *Relations Between Lawyer and Client in Damages: Model, Typical, or Dysfunctional?*, 2004 J. Disp. Resol. 145, 152; Robert F. Cochran, *The Rule of Law(yers): The Practice of Justice: A Theory of Lawyers' Ethics by William H. Simon*, 65 Mo. L. Rev. 571, 589 (2000) (book review).

28. Cochran et al., Counselor-at-Law, *supra* note 2, at 2 (stating that the authoritarian lawyer exercises "predominant control over and responsibility for the problem-solving").

29. Joseph Allegretti, *The Role of a Lawyer's Morals and Religion when Counseling Clients in Bioethics*, 30 Fordham Urb. L.J. 9, 12 (2002).

30. Cochran et al., Counselor-At-Law, *supra* note 2, at 11, 14–16.

31. *Id.* at 137.

32. *Id.* at 137; Lynn Mather, *What do Clients Want? What do Lawyers Do?*, 52 Emory L.J. 1065, 1070 (2003) (discussing malleability of legal language).

33. Ellen Marrus, *Best Interests Equals Zealous Advocacy: A Not So Radical View of Holistic Representation for Children Accused of Crime*, 62 Md. L. Rev 288, 342 (2003) (stating that "children naturally look to adult authority figures to make decisions for them").

mendations and court orders made by those who have never heard or considered his views.[34]

Like the authoritarian lawyer, the best-interest or paternalistic advocate believes that his clients, particularly his child clients, are not able to identify and act in accord with their own best interests. As a result, some more experienced, rational adult must be given authority to make decisions on the child's behalf. [35] By advocating for what they believe to be best for the child, the paternalistic advocate—like others in the juvenile justice system—hopes to divert the child from a life of crime and protect the child from the consequences of his risky behavior. Evidence suggests that paternalistic, best interest advocacy is pervasive on behalf of children in contemporary juvenile courts.[36] Because juvenile court is traditionally committed to rehabilitation in lieu of punishment, many advocates believe that children do not need the vigorous assistance of counsel and view best interest advocacy as an essential tool in the rehabilitative process.[37] In some jurisdictions, lawyers will assume the role of guardian advocate and lobby the court to provide services and treatment that are purportedly best for the child. In other jurisdictions, lawyers will defer to the direction and control of a parent who presumptively knows and desires what is best for the child.

The paternalistic advocate, who is frequently more concerned about the rehabilitative needs of the child and less about the child's guilt or innocence in the delinquency case, will often conduct little or no investigation and decline to challenge facts alleged in the petition. These lawyers may also routinely waive Fourth and Fifth Amendment rights, fail to explore creative alternatives to incarceration, and generally look to probation officers to secure treatment

---

34. Allegretti, *supra* note 29, at 13 (stating that an authoritarian model produces less satisfaction for clients); Cochran et al., Counselor-At-Law, *supra* note 2, at 115 (positing that clients who lose trust in their lawyers are less likely to fully disclose important information, less likely to follow through on necessary steps and less likely to comply with any agreement reached by the parties); *cf.* Ronner, *supra* note 7, at 93–96 (arguing that attorneys who give voice to child can increase likelihood that juvenile will have positive response to judicial decisions and rehabilitative objectives).

35. Emily Buss, *"You're My What?" The Problem of Children's Misperceptions of Their Lawyers' Roles*, 64 Fordham L. Rev. 1699, 1701–02 (1996) (best interest model involves substitution of the lawyer's judgment for the child client's judgment).

36. Kristin N. Henning, *Loyalty, Paternalism and Rights: Client Counseling Theory and the Role of Child's Counsel in Delinquency Cases*, 81 Notre Dame L. Rev. 101 (2005) (documents history and persistence of paternalistic advocacy in juvenile justice system).

37. *In re* Gault, 387 U.S. 1, 16–17 (1967); Mary Berkheiser, *The Fiction of Juvenile Right to Counsel: Waiver in the Juvenile Courts*, 54 Fla. L. Rev. 577, 586 (2002).

for the child.[38] Because these advocates often have little confidence in the child's views and opinions, they may neglect to meet with their clients before court and instead draw from their own wisdom and experience to evaluate the advantages and disadvantages of the child's case-related options. In some cases, the advocate may coerce the child to plead guilty to expedite the rehabilitative process. In other cases, the paternalistic advocate may defer to the judge or probation officer for a determination of what is best for the child at disposition, or in some instances, actually request more restrictive or longer periods of confinement when the advocate believes such penalties are appropriate.[39] Even if the attorney questions his own ability to decide what is best for the child, the paternalistic advocate may look to the child's parent for guidance and direction. Like the advocate who usurps decision-making authority for himself, the parent-directed advocate presumes that the child lacks the judgment, wisdom, and experience to make good decisions on his own behalf, but views the parent as an experienced and responsible adult who has special insights into the needs of the child and the family.

Although the best interest advocate believes that he is advancing the rehabilitative interests of the child, evidence suggests that by usurping voice and autonomy from a child in the juvenile justice system, the paternalistic advocate may actually impede rehabilitation by stifling the child's commitment to and cooperation with the disposition plan.[40] A child who is deprived of a meaningful opportunity to participate in his juvenile case is likely to perceive the system as unfair and likely to resent and resist any efforts to engage him in the rehabilitative process.

b. Client-Centered and Collaborative Models of Advocacy

In stark contrast to best interest and authoritarian models of advocacy, client-centered and collaborative models advance therapeutic goals and produce positive therapeutic outcomes. Client-centered advocacy rejects lawyer paternalism and manipulation and recognizes individual autonomy and self-

---

38. Henning, *supra* note 36, at 142–43; *cf.* Winick, *Civil Commitment, supra* note 19, at 41–43 (describing the conduct of best interests lawyers in the civil commitment process to include deference to expert witnesses, little cross examination, failure to meet with clients, little or no investigation, failure to challenge allegations, failure to explore alternatives to hospitalization and waiver of patient's right to testify).

39. Janet E. Ainsworth, *Re-imagining Childhood and Reconstructuring the Legal Order: The Case for Abolishing the Juvenile Court*, 69 N.C. L. Rev. 1083, 1127 (1991).

40. *See supra* notes 8–24 and accompanying text.

determination as a foundation of the American legal system.[41] Client-centered advocates recognize that client participation in the attorney-client relationship may reduce the anxiety that often accompanies the client's passive or blind role in the legal process.[42] They also believe that clients are more likely to accept and comply with decisions they make for themselves.[43] The client-centered lawyer ultimately respects and validates the client's interests and gives the client voice in the proceedings. When the client seeks advice from the lawyer, the lawyer may provide information about several possible courses of action, but will urge the client to make decisions for himself.

Collaborative models of advocacy seek to refine client-centered paradigms. Critics of client-centered advocacy worry that excessive deference to clients will deprive the client of important insight from the lawyer and produce unnecessarily poor decisions.[44] Critics also believe that clients rarely come to the attorney-client relationship with a preconceived set of goals and interests, but instead shape and construct those goals through interaction with the lawyer.[45] Although collaborative lawyers, like client-centered advocates, value attorney loyalty and client autonomy, the collaborative lawyer will engage the client in a realistic and objective appraisal of all of the legal and non-legal advantages and disadvantages of a contemplated course of action.[46] The collaborative lawyer will also provide clients with relevant information about available options, help clients clarify personal goals and objectives, and give clients emotional and social support for their decisions.[47] Both the collaborative and client-centered lawyer will provide the client with an opportunity for meaningful participation and secure positive therapeutic outcomes by educating, informing, empowering, and validating the client within the system.

3. Conflicting Norms

Notwithstanding its benefit to the mental health of juveniles, therapeutic jurisprudence is not both a means and an end unto itself. The goals and val-

---

41. Robert D. Dinerstein, *Client-Centered Counseling: Reappraisal and Refinement*, 32 ARIZ. L. REV. 501, 510–13 (1990); Mather, *supra* note 32, at 1068; Cochran, *supra* note 27, at 590–91.

42. Dinerstein, *supra* note 41, at 548–49; Ronner, *supra* note 7, at 93.

43. Jason J. Kilborn, *Who's in Charge Here? Putting Clients in Their Place*, 37 GA. L. REV. 1, 36 (2002); Dinerstein, *supra* note 41, at 547–48.

44. Dinerstein, *supra* note 41, at 505–06.

45. *Id.* at 517.

46. COCHRAN ET AL., COUNSELOR-AT-LAW, *supra* note 2, at 135; Allegretti, *supra* note 29, at 18–19.

47. COCHRAN ET AL., COUNSELOR-AT-LAW, *supra* note 2, at 113.

ues of therapeutic jurisprudence must be evaluated in light of other potentially competing legal and social norms, values, and principles.[48] In juvenile court, lawyers must weigh the therapeutic benefits of voice and autonomy with normative objections to ceding autonomy to children, societal commitment to producing healthy well-adjusted children, the need for public safety, and the constitutional rights of parents to raise children as they deem appropriate. Reliance on therapeutic principles to promote the child's psychological health is appropriate only if those principles do not abrogate important constitutional mandates or conflict with other more highly valued norms.

In the search for an appropriate attorney-child paradigm, a careful evaluation of competing values suggests that client-centered and collaborative models of advocacy are consistent not only with therapeutic objectives, but also with fundamental principles of constitutional law and justice, public safety, and societal efforts to develop productive, law-abiding children. Even though client-centered models may be inconsistent with the rights of parents to rear children without the interference of others, the child's constitutional right to counsel and rules of professional ethics support client autonomy and may outweigh the parents' rights in the juvenile justice context.

a. Normative Objections to Ceding Authority to Youth

Opponents of client-directed advocacy in juvenile court argue that children should not be allowed to direct lawyers because they lack the experience, judgment, and cognitive capacity to act in their own best interests.[49] Normative opposition to the allocation of decision-making authority to children is well documented in laws that use age to grant or deny certain rights or privileges to children and adolescents. State statutes that require children to attend school or that deny children the right to contract, marry, vote, drive, or purchase alcohol, tobacco, or pornographic material all seem to reflect a societal presumption that children lack the wisdom, judgment, and cognitive capacity to make good decisions in these areas.[50] Societal norms that guide the legislative allocation of decision-making authority between children and adults are necessarily concerned with balancing competing interests such as respect for parental authority, the need to protect society from the consequences of

---

48. Winick, *Jurisprudence of TJ, supra* note 5, at 197–98.

49. Marrus, *supra* note 33, at 343.

50. Elizabeth S. Scott, *The Legal Construction of Adolescence*, 29 Hofstra L. Rev. 547, 547, 557–58 (2000).

immature and unwise decisions of children, and the state's obligation to protect certain constitutional rights of the child.[51]

The paternalistic ideology of the traditional juvenile justice system promotes and supports best-interest advocacy on behalf of children charged with delinquency. Since the inception of the first juvenile court, the legacy of paternalism has shaped and continues to shape the attitudes of many juvenile defenders who have a sincere desire to aid in the rehabilitation of children.[52] Even when the child's attorney wishes to advocate for the child's expressed interests, the attorney will often face tremendous systemic opposition from judges, prosecutors, and probation officers who expect defense counsel to participate as a part of the juvenile justice team.[53] Prosecutors may resent defenders who seek to vindicate their client's legal rights and interfere with the child's potential for rehabilitation, while judges may chastise attorneys for seeking to litigate legal issues or challenging factual allegations on the merits.

Therapeutic jurisprudence, on the other hand, offers a useful shift from traditional responses to presumed youth and adolescent irresponsibility and dependence. Therapeutic jurisprudence suggests that we may actually enhance the quality of adolescent decision-making and ensure that children become responsible members of society precisely by giving them voice and respect in the juvenile justice system. Attorney-client paradigms that allocate decision-making and choice to the child improve the child's psychological well-being by facilitating self-regulation and responsibility, encouraging positive self-determination, and enhancing the child's appreciation for law and authority.[54] By contrast, authoritarian and paternalistic models of advocacy which deprive the child of a meaningful voice in the attorney-client relationship, and thus in the juvenile justice system as a whole, hinder the public safety and rehabilitative objectives of the court.[55] Likewise, authoritarian and paternalistic mod-

---

51. *Id.* at 557–58 (discussing allocation of children's rights based on a myriad of sociopolitical factors).

52. Janet E. Ainsworth, *Youth Justice in a Unified Court: Response to Critics of Juvenile Court Abolition,* 36 B.C. L. Rev. 927, 1129–30 (1995).

53. *See* Henning, *supra* note 36, at 116–18.

54. Carolyn Copps Hartley & Carrie J. Petrucci, *Practicing Culturally Competent Therapeutic Jurisprudence: A Collaboration Between Social Work and Law,* 14 Wash. U. J.L. & Pol'y 133, 153 (2004); Wexler, *supra* note 21, at 191–93; Ronner, *supra* note 7, at 111–12.

55. *See supra* notes 5–20 and accompanying text; *see also* Rhonda Gay Hartman, *Adolescent Autonomy: Clarifying an Ageless Conundrum,* 51 Hastings L.J. 1265, 1330–31 (2000) (stating that in the civil commitment context, evidence suggests that allowing adolescent to direct his own care enhances the effect of therapy).

els of advocacy that deprive the child of his own rights and due process ultimately undermine the child's respect for the rights of others and eventually erode society as a whole.[56]

Authoritarian and paternalistic lawyering also frequently produces poor and unsatisfactory legal outcomes by inhibiting a full exchange of information between the lawyer and the child.[57] When the lawyer controls the client interview, limits free input from the child, and excludes the child's voice from the system, the lawyer deprives both himself and the court of important information and insight. Without critical input from the child, the diagnostic team assigned to develop the child's treatment plan will likely have an inaccurate or incomplete picture of the child's needs.

Moreover, even accepting that many youth and adolescents will have cognitive and psychosocial limitations that affect judgment, lawyering models that give the child voice and validation in the juvenile justice system present minimal risk of harm to the child or the community. Because delinquency cases are adversarial hearings in which the judge makes the final decision about questions of guilt, innocence, detention, and disposition, the child's voice is but one of many that will influence judicial outcomes. Thus, even where the child wisely or unwisely instructs counsel to advocate for his release back into the community, it is the judge, after hearing arguments from prosecutors, parents, probation officers, and victims, who will decide whether release is consistent with the rehabilitative needs of the child and the safety of the public. Even where there is an adverse ruling, the child who has been given an opportunity to participate in the hearing will, hopefully, still perceive that the process has been fair and learn to respect law and authority.[58]

b. Rights of the Child's Parent

In selecting an appropriate attorney-client paradigm for the representation of children, principles of therapeutic jurisprudence must also be weighed against the rights and interests of parents. Given the long legal and social history of paternal control over almost every facet of a child's life, the law is generally reluctant to interfere with the rights of parents to raise and direct their

---

56. Ramirez & Ronner, *supra* note 14, at 121.

57. COCHRAN ET AL., COUNSELOR-AT-LAW, *supra* note 2, at 115 (stating that clients who lose trust in their lawyers are less likely to disclose important information); Allegretti, *supra* note 29, at 13–14.

58. Ramirez & Ronner, *supra* note 14, at 120 ("[W]hat influences [individuals] most is not the result, but their own assessment of the fairness of the process itself."); *see also supra* notes 16–17 and accompanying text.

children as they deem appropriate.[59] In some areas of the law, parents may even have a constitutional right to make decisions for the child.[60] In addition, from a therapeutic perspective, the participatory and dignitary interests of an accused child may conflict with the participatory interests of the parent. While parents who feel engaged in the child's decision-making process will be more likely to support the child in juvenile court proceedings, parents who feel excluded from the attorney-client relationship altogether may refuse to help the attorney, the child, or the court in the rehabilitative plan.[61] Attorneys who respect the rights and interests of parents may reject client-centered models of advocacy that challenge the authority of parents within the home and instead look to the parents to determine and articulate the goals and objectives in the juvenile case.

When the rights and norms of different groups conflict, lawyers, judges, and legislators must look to overarching principles of law and ethics as a means by which to weigh and prioritize competing interests.[62] In weighing the therapeutic interests of parents and children in juvenile court, lawyers should recognize that the denial of parental control in the attorney-child relationship does not preclude parental involvement and influence in the juvenile justice system as a whole. In most juvenile courts today, parents generally have an opportunity to communicate directly or indirectly with the judge through probation officers, prosecutors, or other court officials.[63] When the child, however, is denied meaningful participation in the attorney-client relationship, the child generally has no other means by which to be heard in the system.

The balancing of therapeutic interests, alone, cannot determine the allocation of decision-making authority among parents and their children. The

---

59. Martin Guggenheim, *Minor Rights: The Adolescent Abortion Cases*, 30 HOFSTRA L. REV. 589, 593–94 (2002); Scott, *supra* note 50, at 551.

60. *See, e.g.*, Pierce v. Society of Sisters, 268 U.S. 510, 518 (1925) (finding that compulsory public school attendance unreasonably interferes with parental right to direct the upbringing and education of children).

61. Bruce C. Hafen & Jonathan O. Hafen, *Abandoning Children to Their Autonomy: The United Nations Convention on the Rights of the Child*, 37 HARV. INT'L L.J. 449, 483–84 (1996) (discussing fear that denial of parental rights may have long term effect of reducing parental commitment to childrearing); Scott, *supra* note 50, at 551 (recognizing that parental rights and authority might be viewed as legal compensation for the burden of responsibility to provide food, shelter, health care, affection and education).

62. Winick, *Jurisprudence of TJ, supra* note 5, at 197–98.

63. In many jurisdictions, the parent will be a formal party to the proceedings. *See, e.g.*, ALA. CODE § 12-15-31(5) (1995) (giving court jurisdiction to make parents parties to all juvenile court actions).

parties must also consider the competing legal interests. Although the constitutional rights of parents are significant, they are not without limits. [64] Recognizing the diversity of circumstances in which children and parents are involved, courts and legislatures have chosen to allocate the rights of children and parents on an issue-by-issue basis, and in each instance have considered a wide range of sociopolitical variables including the age of the child, the liberty and due process rights of the child, the rights of the parents, and the needs of society.[65] Likewise, in selecting an appropriate attorney-client paradigm in the juvenile justice context, lawyers, too, must weigh the constitutional rights of parents against the liberty and due process interests of the accused child.

c. Constitutional Rights in the Juvenile Justice System

Notwithstanding the history of paternalism in the juvenile justice system, due process is now guaranteed as a fundamental right in the juvenile court.[66] After years of procedural irregularity, unfettered discretion, and the appearance of judicial partiality, the Supreme Court, in *In re Gault* and a series of cases that followed, held that due process and fundamental fairness would no longer be sacrificed in favor of some nominal commitment to rehabilitation.[67] To ensure due process, the Court determined that an accused child would be entitled to adequate notice of the charges, the right to counsel, the right to be free from self-incrimination, the right to confront and cross examine witnesses, and the right to require the government to prove guilt beyond a reasonable doubt.[68] The right to counsel—or more importantly, the right to direct and control counsel—clearly falls at the center of all other rights. [69] As

---

64. Bellotti v. Baird, 443 U.S. 622 (1979) (striking down requirement of parental consent for abortion).

65. Scott, *supra* note 50, at 557–58.

66. *In re* Gault, 387 U.S. 1 (1967) (defining basic procedural due process requirements owed to an accused juvenile).

67. *Id.* at 33–56; *In re* Winship, 397 U.S. 358, 368 (1970); Breed v. Jones, 421 U.S. 519, 541 (1975).

68. *Gault,* 387 U.S. at 33–56 (requiring adequate notice of charges, right to counsel, privilege against self-incrimination, and rights of confrontation and cross-examination); *Winship,* 397 U.S. at 368 (finding that guilt must be proved beyond a reasonable doubt in delinquency proceedings).

69. Susan D. Hawkins, Note, *Protecting the Rights and Interests of Competent Minors in Litigated Medical Treatment Disputes,* 64 FORDHAM L. REV. 2075, 2076 (1996) (arguing that control over the decision-making process lies at the heart of the American legal system when personal legal rights are at stake); Shannan L. Wilber, *Independent Counsel for Children,* 27 FAM. L.Q. 349, 353 (1993) (arguing that our emphasis on individual rights and

an advocate for the interests of the child, the child's lawyer is the primary means by which the child may effectively assert or waive all other individual legal rights in the system.

The Court's commitment to fundamental fairness also suggests that an accused child has the same interest in fair and accurate fact-finding as an accused adult in a criminal case.[70] Adversarial, client-directed models of advocacy have been identified as essential to fair and accurate fact-finding.[71] As the Supreme Court has recognized, society is better served when the lawyer is advancing the interests of the client rather than joining together and acting in concert with the government.[72] Considering the indispensable role of the attorney in ensuring due process and protecting the constitutional rights of children, client-centered and collaborative paradigms of lawyering are not only therapeutically preferred, but also constitutionally required. By contrast, paternalistic models of advocacy in the juvenile justice system may deprive the child of fundamental rights.

d. Principles of Professional Ethics

Principles of professional ethics further promote client-centered and collaborative models of advocacy over paternalistic or parent-directed alternatives. The *Model Rules of Professional Conduct* remind lawyers that clients must be treated with respect, clients' interests are foremost, and attorneys should intrude on clients' decision-making authority to the least extent possible.[73] Even when the parent hires an attorney for the child, the *Rules* prohibit interference from a third-party payer and prohibit the attorney from communicating about the case with the parent, absent consent of the

---

personal autonomy are furthered by role of attorney which enables litigants to pursue and protect their legal rights); Martin Guggenheim, *The Right to Be Represented But Not Heard: Reflections on Legal Representation for Children*, 59 N.Y.U. L. REV. 76, 81, 86–87 (1984) (arguing that child's constitutional rights would be meaningless if the attorney were allowed to assert and waive those rights in his own discretion).

70. *Gault*, 387 U.S. at 30 (finding no material different between criminal and juvenile delinquency proceedings when considering the child's need for counsel); *Bellotti*, 443 U.S. at 634 (recognizing the child's right against the deprivation of liberty without due process of law as virtually coextensive with that of an adult).

71. Strickland v. Washington, 466 U.S. 668 (1984); Polk County v. Dodson, 454 U.S. 312 (1981).

72. *Polk County*, 454 U.S. 312; U.S. v. Cronic, 466 U.S. 648, 655–57 (1984).

73. MODEL RULES OF PROF'L CONDUCT R. 1.2, 1.14 cmt 1 & cmt 3 (2002) [hereinafter MODEL RULES].

child.[74] The *Rules* also entitle the child to conflict-free representation by the lawyer.[75] Recent developments in juvenile justice policy challenge the traditional assumption that parents are the best decision-makers for an accused child. Today, parents may be held civilly or criminally liable for the misconduct of their children, forced to pay the cost of treatment and services for a delinquent child, or held in contempt for failing to ensure their child's compliance with the conditions of probation.[76] Considering the ever-expanding risk of parental liability, allocating decision-making authority to parents may compromise the child's right to conflict-free advocacy.[77]

The *Model Rules* also require the lawyer to maintain, as far as reasonably possible, a "normal" attorney-client relationship with clients of potentially diminished capacity, including minors.[78] Therapeutic jurisprudence implicitly assumes that affected parties will have the cognitive capacity to appreciate and value concepts such as voice, participation, and fairness.[79] Even if the youth's cognitive and psychosocial capacities are not fully developed, most adolescents in the juvenile justice system will be able to communicate basic goals and concerns to their lawyers and intuitively grasp notions of fairness.[80] Commentary to the *Model Rules of Professional Conduct* recognizes that "children as young as five or six, and certainly those of ten or twelve" have the ability to "understand, deliberate upon and reach conclusions about matters affecting [their]

---

74. *Id.* at R. 1.8(f).

75. *Id.* at R. 1.7.

76. For a representative sampling, see S.D. CODIFIED LAWS § 26-7A-51 (1999) (parent may be held in contempt for failing to bring child to court when promised); ALA. CODE § 12-15-11 (1995) (court may order parent to reimburse state for expense of evaluations, commitment, special schools, detention, counseling or other treatment ordered for juveniles); ALASKA STAT. § 47.12.155(b)(3) (2004) (parent may be held jointly or independently responsible for restitution to victims); N.Y. PENAL LAW § 260.10 (McKinney 2000) (parent guilty of misdemeanor when parent "refuses to exercise reasonable diligence in the control of the child to prevent his from becoming a juvenile delinquent"); CAL. CIV. CODE § 1714.1 (Deering 2005) (parent or guardian may be civilly liability for the willful misconduct of minors).

77. *See* MODEL RULES R. 1.7 (noting that absent the consent of both parties, the lawyer generally cannot advise two parties who have conflicting interests in the same proceedings).

78. *Id.* at R. 1.14.

79. *Cf.* Winick, *Civil Commitment, supra* note 19, at 49 (applying therapeutic jurisprudence to civil commitment context and recognizing that some clients may be so impaired that they will not realize procedural justice of a fair, participatory hearing).

80. Scott, *supra* note 50, at 555 n.35 (noting that adolescents are close to adulthood and by the age of 14 and 15 generally have cognitive capacity for reasoning and understanding process).

own well-being."[81] Collaborative models of advocacy, which recognize cognitive reasoning and moral judgment as evolving skills that improve with experience, provide the child with an opportunity to try on and enhance newly acquired cognitive abilities.[82] The therapeutic value of voice, the guarantee of due process, and ethical considerations that require lawyers to maintain a "normal" relationship with minors all suggest that client-directed and collaborative models of advocacy provide an appropriate framework in which to advance the interests of youth in the juvenile justice system.

e. Attorney Satisfaction

Finally, client-centered relationships have benefits for the health and satisfaction of the lawyer.[83] Attorneys often experience high burnout in juvenile court as they attempt to reconcile the internal tension between their legal obligation to advocate for the expressed interests of the child and their own well-meaning, paternalistic desires to advocate in the best interests of the child.[84] The attorney should find solace in therapeutically-inspired relationships that motivate compliance and yield greater rehabilitative outcomes for the child.[85] The lawyer who understands and applies principles of therapeutic jurisprudence need not choose between due process and rehabilitation. Therapeutic, client-centered models of advocacy advance rehabilitative objectives without excluding the child's voice.

---

81. MODEL RULES R. 1.14 cmt. 1.

82. COCHRAN ET AL., COUNSELOR-AT-LAW, *supra* note 2, at 170 (stating that individuals develop their own code of personal morality and adopt virtues such as courage, truthfulness, faithfulness and mercy through the trial and error of exercising moral judgment); William A. Kell, *Ties That Bind?: Children's Attorneys, Children's Agency, and the Dilemma of Parental Affiliation*, 29 LOY. U. CHI. L.J. 353, 375 (1998) (discussing the benefits of encouraging children to exercise their own developing decision-making skills with the aid of a "teacher). If the child, however, is so cognitively limited that he cannot articulate and act in his own interests, the Rules permit the attorney to employ alternative, protective measures on the client's behalf and principles of therapeutic jurisprudence may not apply. MODEL RULES R. 1.14 cmt 5 & cmt 7.

83. Hartley & Petrucci, *supra* note 54, at 153.

84. Thomas F. Geraghty, *Justice for Children: How Do We Get There?*, 88 J. CRIM. L. & CRIMINOLOGY 190, 236 (1997); Ainsworth, *supra* note 39, at 1129–30; David A. Harris, *The Criminal Defense Lawyer in the Juvenile Justice System*, 26 U. TOL. L. REV. 751 (1995); *cf.* Winick, *Civil Commitment*, *supra* note 19, at 57 (discussing advocate's internal tension in civil commitment context).

85. Winick, *Civil Commitment*, *supra* note 19, at 57.

4. Skills: The Lawyer as an Agent for Change

Once the lawyer accepts the client-centered or collaborative paradigm as the appropriate model of advocacy, the lawyer must learn and apply relevant skills for effective and affective lawyering.[86] Lawyers who are committed to advancing the participatory interests of their clients and promoting other components of therapeutic jurisprudence will again find guidance in the wealth of literature on collaborative lawyering, client interviewing, and affective counseling.[87]

As a starting point, therapeutic jurisprudence requires the lawyer to relinquish his own ego needs and focus on the client. Client-centered and collaborative lawyers do not assume they know what is best for the client, but instead help the client explore and clarify his own goals and objectives.[88] Lawyers who are committed to voice and validation will give the client a safe space to speak and express emotions, elicit the client's views through open-ended questions, and offer verbal and nonverbal responses that express interest and sympathy and confirm that the lawyer is listening.[89] The lawyer also understands that good decision-making is predicated on the lawyer's ability to create an appropriate environment for counseling.[90] For children, who generally demonstrate better cognitive capacity in contexts that are familiar to them and devoid of stress,[91] the collaborative counselor will provide a comfortable physical and emotional environment and allocate sufficient time for questions.[92]

Effective therapeutic counseling also requires the lawyer to become culturally competent in dealing with clients of different socioeconomic, ethnic, and racial backgrounds. To achieve cultural competence, the lawyer must first be cognizant of and examine his own attitudes and beliefs about other groups.[93] The lawyer must also increase his knowledge about diverse popu-

---

86. Mills, *supra* note 2, at 421–22 (recognizing affective lawyering as a psychology-based approach to lawyering that offers emotional ways for lawyers to connect with clients).

87. *See Juvenile Justice System, supra* note 1.

88. Kilborn, *supra* note 43, at 36; Dinerstein, *supra* note 41, at 508, 516; COCHRAN ET AL., COUNSELOR-AT-LAW, *supra* note 2, at 113.

89. Winick, *Client Denial, supra* note 17, at 912; COCHRAN ET AL., COUNSELOR-AT-LAW, *supra* note 2, at 33–37, 40–48 (discussing array of passive and active listening skills).

90. Uphoff, *supra* note 27, at 155–57; COCHRAN ET AL., COUNSELOR-AT-LAW, *supra* note 2, at 113.

91. *See* Emily Buss, *Confronting Developmental Barriers to the Empowerment of Child Clients*, 84 CORNELL L. REV. 895, 918–19 (1999); Thomas Grisso, *The Competence of Adolescents as Trial Defendants*, 3 PSYCHOL. PUB. POL'Y & L. 3, 16–18 (1997).

92. COCHRAN ET AL., COUNSELOR-AT-LAW, *supra* note 2, at 152–53.

93. Hartley & Petrucci, *supra* note 54, at 170.

lations and acquire skills that facilitate healthy cross-cultural communications.[94] Specifically, the lawyer must recognize and acknowledge differences in the communication styles among different racial and ethnic groups, including differences in nonverbal communication such as the use of personal space, body movements, and gestures.[95] Culturally competent lawyers communicate respect to clients by acknowledging the range and validity of diverse perspectives and by providing them with an opportunity to share their views.[96]

While attorneys should not try to be therapists or social workers, therapeutically-inclined lawyers should understand the basic principles of psychology and develop skills necessary to accommodate the psychological dimensions of the attorney-client relationship.[97] Lawyers will need appropriate interpersonal skills to deal with the client's psychological and emotional issues such as denial, anger, frustration, despair, resentment, indifference, and helplessness which are common among those who enter the legal system.[98] Empathy is thus an essential skill in effective therapeutic lawyering.[99] Empathy involves both an "intellectual response" that suggests that the listener thinks the same way as the speaker and an "emotional response" that suggests that the listener feels the same way as the speaker.[100] As the lawyer evolves as an empathetic counselor, the lawyer should learn to read nonverbal cues, project himself into the feelings of his clients, and express warmth and understanding.[101]

In juvenile cases, the lawyer should engage the child in one-on-one, age-appropriate dialogue and repeat information as many times as the child needs to hear it.[102] Age-appropriate consultation is essential to empower children

---

94. *Id.*

95. *Id.* at 179.

96. *Id.* at 179–80. *See generally supra* ch. 5: Paul R. Tremblay & Carwina Weng, *Multicultural Lawyering: Heuristics and Biases; supra* ch. 6: Susan J. Bryant & Jean Koh Peters, *Six Practices for Connecting with Clients across Culture: Habit Four, Working with Interpreters, and Other Mindful Approaches.*

97. Winick, *Client Denial, supra* note 17, at 903–04 (exploring ways in which principles of psychology enhance the effectiveness of lawyers in advance directive and preventive lawyering context); Hartley & Petrucci, *supra* note 54, at 140–41.

98. Winick, *Client Denial, supra* note 17, at 903–04, 909.

99. *Id.* at 909–10.

100. *Id.* at 910.

101. *Id.* at 909.

102. Wallace J. Mlyniec, *A Judge's Ethical Dilemma: Assessing a Child's Capacity to Choose,* 64 FORDHAM L. REV. 1873, 1898 (1996); Dinerstein, *supra* note 41, at 556.

who are unsophisticated and lack knowledge about legal matters.[103] Research suggests that psychosocial impediments to effective adolescent decision-making, such as lack of trust for adults, limited risk perception, and poor risk preference, are likely to improve as the attorney-client relationship improves.[104] Because youth tend to have higher levels of trust and satisfaction with attorneys who spend more time working with them,[105] the child's lawyer must set aside adequate time for meetings with young clients. The lawyer may ultimately improve the quality of adolescent decisions by encouraging the child to slowly identify and consider all of the long-term implications of any decision.[106] When the lawyer equips the child with all of the relevant information and provides the appropriate environmental and emotional supports, the child may make well-reasoned decisions and appropriately direct counsel in the legal representation.

Therapeutic jurisprudence also recognizes the child's entry into the juvenile justice system as a "teachable moment" that presents the child with an opportunity for change and rehabilitation.[107] It is at this moment that lawyers have a unique role in promoting the child's psychological well-being and assisting in the child's positive development.[108] Therapeutic jurisprudence draws from a variety of psychological tools that increase positive self-motivation and improve psychological functioning.[109] Studies in the social psychology of adolescent delinquent behavior suggest that undesired behavior may be corrected when the child begins to identify personal ambitions and gain confidence in his ability to achieve personal goals.[110] Legal actors, such as lawyers in the ju-

---

103. *See* Cochran, *supra* note 27, at 592 (stating that effective legal counseling may empower politically disadvantaged clients); Uphoff, *supra* note 27, at 768 (same); Dinerstein, *supra* note 41, at 519 (same).

104. Schmidt, *supra* note 4, at 193–94.

105. *Id.* at 180 (discussing study conducted in 2000 finding that youth were more likely to be satisfied with their lawyers, regardless of the ultimate outcome of the case, when the lawyer spent time with them); *see also* Hartley & Petrucci, *supra* note 54, at 159 (reporting that time defendants spent with lawyer had a significant impact on perceived justice in the system).

106. *See* COCHRAN ET AL., COUNSELOR-AT-LAW, *supra* note 2, at 172.

107. Astrid Birgden, *Dealing with the Resistant Criminal Client: A Psychologically-Minded Strategy for More Effective Legal Counseling*, 38 CRIM. L. BULL. 225, 237 (2002).

108. *See* Winick, *Jurisprudence of TJ*, *supra* note 5, at 202.

109. *Id.* at 194.

110. Georgia Zara, *Therapeutic Jurisprudence as an Integrative Approach to Understanding the Socio-Psychological Reality of Young Offenders*, 71 U. CIN. L. REV. 127, 140–41 (2002).

venile justice system, may motivate the child by challenging negative internal and external messages and helping the child identify a greater range of positive alternatives and positive self-images.[111]

Rather than coercing the child into change through paternalistic advocacy, the therapeutic lawyer must learn to actively engage the child in the design of his own treatment plan.[112] Through a series of probing and directed questions at the disposition phase, the lawyer may help the child identify an array of realistic disposition alternatives, lead the child through a reflection on his own strengths and needs, and encourage the child to consider the likely response of the court, victims, and others impacted by the child's conduct.[113] When the lawyer engages the child in this way, the lawyer becomes an agent in the child's rehabilitation and motivates the child to take responsibility for change.[114]

Collaborative models of advocacy provide a useful framework through which the lawyer can guide the process of self-actualization and change. In the collaborative paradigm, the client controls the decisions, but the lawyer offers advice and structures the counseling process in a way that is likely to foster good decision-making by the client.[115] Collaborative lawyers are "nondirective" as to the client's ultimate decision, but "directive" as to the process to be followed in reaching that decision.[116] The lawyer's responsibility is not just to passively or neutrally list alternatives, but also to ensure that the client will consider and evaluate all of the available options and choose the best alternative. The collaborative lawyer will empower the child to identify the widest range of alternatives through techniques such as brainstorming that encourage the client to think broadly, be creative, and withhold judgment until all options have been discussed.[117] The lawyer will also help the child evaluate alternatives by encouraging the child to identify all consequences that might flow from an identified alternative. With the lawyer's help, the child will decide whether each consequence is positive or negative, con-

---

111. *Id.* at 135–43.

112. Wexler, *supra* note 21, at 192; Ronner, *supra* note 7, at 112.

113. *See* Wexler, *supra* note 21, at 192–93 (in the relapse prevention context, the lawyer will help the child identify specific methods for avoiding and coping with high risk situations and prepare the child to address likely concerns of the court in the disposition hearing).

114. *Id.* at 192–93.

115. COCHRAN ET AL., COUNSELOR–AT–LAW, *supra* note 2, at 6; Cochran et al., *Client Counseling, supra* note 2, at 598 ("The client makes the ultimate decision, but the lawyer is actively involved in the process.").

116. COCHRAN ET AL., COUNSELOR–AT–LAW, *supra* note 2, at 131; Allegretti, *supra* note 29, at 16.

117. COCHRAN ET AL., COUNSELOR–AT–LAW, *supra* note 2, at 139–40.

sider the relative importance of each consequence, and assess the likelihood that each consequence will occur.[118] In identifying potential consequences, the lawyer will encourage the client to consider not only the impact his choices will have on himself, but also to consider the impact his choices will have on others.[119]

Moreover, because the collaborative lawyer wants his client to avoid mistakes, the lawyer may appropriately advise and persuade the client in the decision-making process.[120] When trust and rapport are well-established in the attorney-client relationship, the lawyer may even tell the client that he is choosing a patently bad alternative and explain why.[121] When the lawyer is not overbearing and delays advice until he has an appropriate rapport with the child, the child retains individual autonomy and is free to reject the lawyer's opinion.[122]

Paternalistic advocacy persists in juvenile courts today not only because the experienced, well-educated lawyer thinks he knows better than his immature client, but also because the paternalistic model is often less time-consuming for the lawyer. Unlike best-interest models of advocacy, collaborative and client-centered lawyering requires the lawyer to devote an indeterminable amount of time to explaining relevant legal rights and procedures and to engage the client in a process that facilitates good decision-making. Because the collaborative model requires considerable time and training, it may be resisted by those lawyers who have high caseloads or work in resource poor defender offices. Although systemic reform is beyond the scope of this chapter, child advocates committed to a therapeutic agenda need to encourage policymakers to allocate adequate resources to therapeutic processes and procedures that will improve rehabilitative outcomes and enhance public safety.

II. Building the Child's Legal Team

By definition, therapeutic jurisprudence is an interdisciplinary enterprise that looks to psychology, mental health, and other related disciplines to in-

---

118. *Id.* at 146.

119. COCHRAN ET AL., COUNSELOR-AT-LAW, *supra* note 2, at 147.

120. Dinerstein, *supra* note 41, at 517 (drawing from medical doctrine of informed consent in which persuasion is not only acceptable is necessary).

121. Allegretti, *supra* note 29, at 18–19 (noting that in the collaborative model, as between friends, the lawyer should advise the client when the lawyer believes the client is making a bad decision); COCHRAN ET AL., COUNSELOR-AT-LAW, *supra* note 2, at 132.

122. COCHRAN ET AL., COUNSELOR-AT-LAW, *supra* note 2, at 175.

form and shape the development of law.[123] Collaborations between lawyers, social workers, and mental health experts provide opportunities for training, consultation, and dialogue in legal offices, law school classrooms, and continuing legal education programs. Specifically, mental health professionals bring expertise and skill in the application of psychological tools that may improve the attorney-client relationship. In addition, because therapeutic jurisprudence recognizes that all clients exist in a larger network of familial and communal relations,[124] therapeutic lawyers who represent children will learn to engage the child at multiple levels and may partner with parents, teachers, mentors, and other relevant adults in the child's life.

A. Interdisciplinary Collaboration: Expanding the Lawyer's Skill Set

Probably the greatest benefit the lawyer will gain in collaboration with mental health professionals is training. Consistent with the lawyer's potential as a therapeutic agent, lawyers would benefit from training in relapse prevention, adolescent development, theories of cognitive change, and the social psychology of persuasion among others.[125] As but one of many examples, forensic psychologist Astrid Birgden has developed a framework for training criminal defense lawyers in motivational interviewing. In Dr. Birgden's framework, the lawyer will use directive, but client-centered counseling to help clients recognize problem behavior or thinking, articulate concerns about their behavior, and become optimistic about the prospect for change.[126] At varying stages of the relationship, the lawyer will motivate change by inviting the client to consider a new perspective, such as that of the judge or victim, asking the

---

123. Winick, *Jurisprudence of TJ, supra* note 5, at 185; Hartley & Petrucci, *supra* note 54, at 151.

124. Hartley & Petrucci, *supra* note 54, at 140–43 (urging lawyers to adopt generalist approach to social work which includes recognition of organizational context of client interaction).

125. *See* Wexler, *supra* note 21, at 190–93 (encouraging juvenile courts and its lawyers to learn rudimentary principles of relapse prevention and self change); Birgden, *supra* note 107, at 229 (proposing that sophisticated research-based clinical therapy of motivational interviewing can be applied by lawyers); Hartley & Petrucci, *supra* note 54, at 133 (encouraging application of generalist theories of social work); Winick, *Client Denial, supra* note 17, at 914 (arguing that attorneys should acquire basic understanding of the social psychology of persuasion).

126. Birgden, *supra* note 107, at 234.

client to elaborate when the client displays some recognition of the problem or desire to change, and shifting focus away from negative aspects of the problem and redirecting attention to the possibility of a positive outcome. Neither the tone nor the content of motivational counseling should be coercive, paternalistic, or judgmental. Consistent with the child's constitutional rights, motivational interviewing may only be appropriate when the child has made a decision to plead or the evidence of guilt is overwhelming.[127] Although motivational interviewing is a sophisticated, research-based clinical therapy designed for mental health professionals, Dr. Birgden argues that lawyering skills such as open-ended questioning, reflective listening, and empathy equip lawyers with the rudimentary foundation they need to apply motivational methods in legal counseling sessions.[128]

When psychological techniques are beyond the ability of lawyers, the lawyer may consult with an expert or refer the client for counseling.[129] External referrals may be appropriate when sophisticated methodologies are necessary to deal with a particularly resistant client or a client with a significant mental health history.[130] In the juvenile justice context, crisis intervention, counseling, or individual therapy may be required to stabilize the youth, diffuse immediate crises within the family, or to decrease anxiety, hostility, or depression among family members.[131] Such referrals should be handled with sensitivity as the client may be offended at the suggestion that he needs counseling and may perceive the lawyer's suggestion as paternalistic.[132]

Therapeutic jurisprudence is concerned not only with individual relations between legal actors and consumers: it is also concerned with broader procedural and organizational features within the relevant system of justice.[133] Thus, in the juvenile justice system, therapeutic jurisprudence recognizes that the very structure of the juvenile court process may produce therapeutic or antitherapeutic outcomes. One of the most pervasive changes in juvenile justice policy in recent years has involved the implementation of multi-systemic or family-focused therapeutic responses to juvenile crime. Juvenile justice strate-

---

127. *Id.* at 239 (finding that motivational interviewing by lawyer does not presume that client is guilty).

128. *Id.* at 237.

129. Winick, *Client Denial, supra* note 17, at 907–09.

130. Birgden, *supra* note 107.

131. Janet Gilbert et al., *Applying Therapeutic Principles to a Family-Focused Juvenile Justice Model (Delinquency)*, 52 ALA. L. REV. 1153, 1180 (2001).

132. Winick, *Client Denial, supra* note 17, at 908.

133. Gilbert, *supra* note 131, at 1201.

gies no longer focus on the child alone as the cause of his delinquent behavior, but now reflect a growing recognition of the multidimensional causes of delinquency to include family, peers, schools, neighborhoods, and communities.[134] Juvenile drug courts, truancy courts, Unified Family Courts, and family-focused juvenile justice systems that employ Multisystemic Therapy (MST), Multidimensional Treatment Foster Care (MDTFC), and Functional Family Therapy (FFT), all recognize the need for multidimensional responses to the risk factors associated with delinquency.[135]

The influx of multi-systemic responses to juvenile crime has radically altered the way attorneys interact with and advocate on behalf of children in juvenile court. Because multi-systemic models require extensive collaboration between treatment providers, the state juvenile justice agency, the school system, the court, and various social services agencies,[136] therapeutic lawyers in modern juvenile justice systems must advance the participatory interests of children not only in the juvenile court itself, but also in the public school system, the public housing authority, and the public benefits office among others. The lawyer must arm the child with information, give the child voice, and validate the child's concerns in all of the interrelated systems. Lawyers who are interested in motivating change and facilitating positive self-actualization will necessarily be concerned with reducing negative messages from other systems, generating positive educational, housing, and community-based alternatives, and building positive and supportive relationships within the child's family, peer group, school, and community.[137] Not surprisingly, the shift to multi-

---

134. Scott W. Henggeler & Ashli J. Sheidow, *Conduct Disorder and Delinquency*, 29 J. MARITAL & FAM. THERAPY 505 (2003); Gilbert, *supra* note 131, at 1169.

135. Family-focused strategies such as MST, FFT, and MDTFC recognize the role of family, schools, and community in the onset, prevention, and resolution of adolescent delinquent behavior. Family-focused and multi-systemic interventions thus seek to build supportive intra-family relationships, improve supervision and disciplinary practices among caregivers, monitor school attendance, increase positive collaboration between the family and the school, develop supportive mentoring relationships with adults, and reduce the child's exposure to delinquent peers. For an overview of clinical procedures, policies, and rationale for MST, FFT, and MDTFC, see Henggeler & Sheidow, *supra* note 134; Cindy M. Schaeffer & Charles M. Borduin, *Long-Term Follow-up to a Randomized Clinical Trial of Multisystemic Therapy With Serious and Violent Juvenile Offenders*, 73 J. CONSULTING & CLINICAL PSYCHOL. 445 (2005); Barbara J. Burns et al., *Comprehensive Community-Based Interventions for Youth with Severe Emotional Disorders: Multisystemic Therapy and the Wraparound Process*, 9 J. CHILD & FAM. STUD. 283 (2000); Gilbert, *supra* note 131, at 1156.

136. Gilbert, *supra* note 131, at 1176.

137. *Id.* at 1172 (discussing the need to foster pro-social relationships for the child).

systemic models of rehabilitation has led to greater collaboration among attorneys, children, teachers, counselors, social workers, and other relevant adults in the child's life. Interdisciplinary partnerships are also consistent with principles of collaborative and client-centered advocacy, which encourage the child to make use of all available resources and consult with other professionals when necessary.[138]

The collaboration of social workers and attorneys is increasingly common in the domestic relations, family law, and juvenile justice contexts.[139] Social workers have collaborated with lawyers as consultants, resource developers, agents, independent service providers, and co-advocates on behalf of the child.[140] Because the social worker is trained to work with the client at micro (individual), mezzo (familial), and macro (communal) levels,[141] the social worker is well suited to collaborate with lawyers in the contemporary multisystemic juvenile justice system. In some cases, the social worker may provide direct services to a child with extreme and immediate emotional needs.[142] In other cases, social workers may enhance attorney-client relations by training or modeling effective interviewing and counseling skills.[143] The social worker may also broaden the lawyer's perspective and help advance the child's participatory interests in the many systems the child will encounter.[144] In the juvenile case, for example, the social worker may educate the attorney and the child on creative alternatives to incarceration, make appropriate referrals, provide the client and the lawyer with information to challenge court-ordered diagnostic assessments, and help engage the child's family, school, or neighborhood in the treatment plan. Together, the lawyer, the child, and the social worker may develop a more comprehensive treatment plan, win the support of judges and prosecutors, and influence the disposition of the child's case.

Child advocates also have many opportunities to collaborate with special education and public benefits attorneys. Because effective treatment in the ju-

---

138. COCHRAN ET AL., COUNSELOR-AT-LAW, *supra* note 2, at 140, 155.

139. Hartley & Petrucci, *supra* note 54, at 133; Jacqueline St. Joan, *Building Bridges, Building Walls: Collaboration Between Lawyers and Social Workers in a Domestic Violence Clinic and Issues of Client Confidentiality,* 7 CLIN. L. REV. 403 (2001); Louise G. Trubek, *Context and Collaboration: Family Law Innovation and Professional Autonomy,* 67 FORDHAM L. REV. 2533 (1999).

140. St. Joan, *supra* note 139, at 431 (describing various models of social work-attorney collaboration).

141. Hartley & Petrucci, *supra* note 54, at 140.

142. St. Joan, *supra* note 139, at 419 (describing example).

143. *Id.* at 405.

144. *Id.* at 415.

venile justice system often requires comprehensive intervention to improve educational opportunities for the child and to improve housing conditions and
economic sufficiency within the family, [145] the juvenile lawyer must be familiar with an ever-expanding range of legal matters and interdisciplinary resources. Like the juvenile justice system, both the school system and the public benefits office have daunting administrative procedures that leave the child
and his family feeling vulnerable, anxious, and alienated. Like social workers,
education advocates and public benefits attorneys provide information, make
collateral systems more accessible, and increase the child's opportunity to influence outcomes in both the juvenile case and related fora. The civil legal
services lawyer may help the child obtain subsidies for food, clothing, housing, utilities, medical assistance, and childcare. The education advocate may
help the child navigate school disciplinary hearings, explore public, private,
and charter school options, and obtain auxiliary education equipment and
services such as hearing aids, tutors, and transportation. The simultaneous
resolution of multiple legal and social issues is therapeutically advantageous
as it may provide the child and his family with a sense of completeness and
increase the child's hope for an overall positive change.[146]

Notwithstanding the benefits discussed herein, interdisciplinary collaborations among lawyers, social workers, and other professionals must be approached with forethought and care as they may jeopardize both the legal
rights and the participatory interests of the child. Therapeutic juvenile justice
models such as juvenile drug courts and all-inclusive Unified Family Courts
may compromise due process and feel very paternalistic for the accused
child.[147] In these models, defense attorneys must be ever vigilant in protecting the child's constitutional rights and be careful not to be co-opted by the
best-interest standard of other members of the juvenile justice "team." The
lawyer should carefully explain both the advantages and disadvantages of collaboration and clearly secure the child's consent before developing partnerships and sharing confidential information with other professionals.[148] In contemplating collaboration with a social worker, for example, the lawyer should

---

145. Gilbert, *supra* note 131, at 1169.

146. Barbara A. Babb, *Fashioning an Interdisciplinary Framework for Court Reform in
Family Law: A Blueprint to Construct a Unified Family Court*, 71 S. CAL. L. REV. 469 (1998).

147. *See* Mae C. Quinn, *Whose Team Am I On Anyway? Musings of a Public Defender
about Drug Treatment Court Practice*, 26 N.Y.U. REV. L. & SOC. CHANGE 37, 54–55 (2000);
Anne H. Geraghty & Wallace J. Mlyniec, *Unified Family Courts: Tempering Enthusiasm with
Caution*, 40 FAM. CT. REV. 435, 439 (2002).

148. St. Joan, *supra* note 139, at 415.

explain that the social worker generally has a different ethical and professional obligation than the lawyer. When the client withholds consent, or when systemic and ethical barriers prohibit full interdisciplinary collaboration, the lawyer may often seek the social worker's advice without disclosing confidential or identifying information about the child.[149]

B. Ecology of the Family

The unique interaction between children and their parents merits special attention for lawyers representing youth in the juvenile justice system. Although therapeutic jurisprudence argues against delegation of the child's participatory rights and interests to the parent, therapeutic jurisprudence would not exclude parents from the attorney-client relationship entirely.[150] In fact, principles of therapeutic jurisprudence recognize that familial support may play an important role in ameliorating the coercive nature of the juvenile court process and may compliment the child's voice in the juvenile hearing. Although I have found no empirical studies on the therapeutic value of parental support, it is widely assumed among judges, legislators, law enforcement officers, and attorneys that moral support from parents may make juvenile defendants more confident in their rights and counterbalance coercive law enforcement practices.[151] In the interrogation context, for example, state legislatures may deem juvenile confessions *per se* involuntary unless a parent or guardian is present at the time of questioning.[152]

---

149. *Id.* at 432 (describing consultant model in which lawyer and social work never share identifying information).

150. *See supra* ch. 2: Susan Brooks, *Using Social Work Constructs in the Practice of Law* at pp. [].

151. *See* Ronner, *supra* note 7, at 102–03 (discussing police tactics that deprive suspects of psychological confidence and advantage by secluding them from family and friends who may offer moral support); *but see* Hillary B. Farber, *The Role of the Parent/Guardian in Juvenile Custodial Interrogations: Friend or Foe?*, 41 Am. Crim. L. Rev. 1277 (2004) (arguing that parents may intentionally or unwittingly join in coercive police tactics).

152. *See, e.g.*, Colo. Rev. Stat. § 19-2-511 (2003); Conn. Gen. Stat. § 46b-137 (2003). In jurisdictions where voluntariness is determined by a judicial evaluation of the totality of the circumstances, judges generally view the parent's presence as a positive factor ameliorating the threat of coercion. *See, e.g.*, A.M. v. Butler, 360 F.3d 787 (7th Cir. 2004) (court considering failure to contact child's mother as one of factors important to finding that confession was involuntary); State v. Presha, 748 A.2d 1108, 1110 (N.J. 2000) (court should consider absence of parents as highly significant factor in evaluating whether child's waiver was knowing, voluntary and intelligent).

In some cases, parents may also help the child exercise his constitutional right to counsel. In introductory attorney-client interactions, the parent may explain the lawyer's obligations to the child, help bridge trust between the child and the lawyer, and help the child articulate questions and concerns. When the parent is familiar with how the child receives and processes information, the parent may help the lawyer explain legal concepts in terms the child will understand. The parent may also help the lawyer and the child plan meaningful case strategies and choose between various options in the case.[153] Even as adolescents begin to assert their independence from parents, adolescents generally remain emotionally attached and regularly seek guidance, acceptance, and approval from parents and other significant adults.[154] Thus, in the decision-making process, the lawyer may encourage the child to talk to family members who may provide additional information and offer an alternative perspective.[155] Parental support may even enhance the lawyer's own cultural competence and make the lawyer a better advisor, counselor, and advocate for the child.

Collaboration between the lawyer and the child's parent may also improve the child's self-image, enhance the child's opportunity to influence the factfinder, and increase the likelihood of favorable outcomes. In fact, family-focused responses to juvenile crime are designed to keep families together and avoid the unnecessary placement of youth in out-of-home residential facilities.[156] A prosecutor who is pleased with pretrial interventions in the child's home, school, or community may be inclined to dismiss charges or divert the child from formal court proceedings.[157] A judge who is satisfied that negative community factors have been corrected may also be more inclined to allow the child to remain in or return to his home at the time of disposition.

Consistent with principles of client autonomy and self-determination, the lawyer should provide the child with information about his right to engage parents in the decision-making process, but should give the child an oppor-

---

153. Catherine Ross, *Implementing Constitutional Rights for Juveniles: The Parent-Child Privilege in Context*, 14 STAN. L. & POL'Y REV. 85, 107 (2003).

154. Laurence Steinberg, *Autonomy, Conflict and Harmony in the Family Relationship*, *in* AT THE THRESHOLD: THE DEVELOPING ADOLESCENT 257–58 (Shirley Feldman & Glen R. Elliott eds., 1993); RALPH J. GEMELLI, NORMAL CHILD AND ADOLESCENT DEVELOPMENT 467 (1996).

155. COCHRAN ET AL., COUNSELOR-AT-LAW, *supra* note 2, at 155 (suggesting that an attorney might direct the client by asking "Is there anyone else that you would like to talk to about this choice?").

156. Gilbert, *supra* note 131, at 1172.

157. *Id.* at 1194.

tunity to specify the nature, extent, and content of the consultation with parents. Initial attorney-client meetings conducted without parents provide the child a safe space in which to consider his right to confidentiality and understand the limits of parental control over case-related decisions. In jurisdictions where communications between the child and the parent are privileged or where the attorney-client privilege extends to parents of a minor child,[158] the lawyer should inform the child that he may invite his parent to participate in attorney-client interviews and consultations. In jurisdictions where there is uncertainty about the parameters of the attorney-client and parent-child privileges, the lawyer should advise the child not to discuss the details of his factual involvement in the alleged offense, but may offer to speak to the parents on the child's behalf or encourage the child to talk generally with parents about legal options, disposition alternatives, and general fears and concerns.

In negotiating an appropriate framework for the interaction among attorneys, children, and their parents, the child and the lawyer should carefully identify and evaluate all of the benefits and risks of collaborating with parents. The lawyer and the child might consider the child's ability to communicate with counsel and understand important legal issues without the parents' assistance, the potential that parents will provide information or insight not otherwise available to the child or his lawyer, and the existence of unique cultural, ethnic, religious, or moral norms that are shared between the parent and the child but not with the lawyer. The lawyer might also help the child consider strategic advantages that might be gained by including the parents in attorney-client discussions and earning the parents' support for the child's stated objectives such as in-home or other community-based alternatives to detention.[159]

---

158. Only three states have enacted statutory parent-child privileges, and only one state has clearly recognized such a privilege at common law. CONN. GEN. STAT. §46b-138a (2003); IDAHO CODE ANN. §9-203(7) (2004); MINN. STAT. §595.02(j) (2002); In re Mark G., 410 N.Y.S.2d 464, 464–65 (N.Y. App. Div. 1978). Only one state has explicitly extended the attorney-client privilege to parents by statute, but a few courts have found that the parents' present will not waive the attorney-client privilege when the child looks to the parent as an advisor and clearly intends that the communications remain confidential. WASH. REV. CODE §5.60.060 (2004 & Supp. 2005); State v. Sucharew, 66 P.3d 59 (Ariz. Ct. App. 2003) (noting privilege is generally waived when a third party is present, but finding that parents presence did not waive privilege in that case); Kevlik v. Goldstein, 724 F.2d 844 (1st Cir. 1984) (same); United States v. Bigos, 459 F.2d 639 (1st Cir. 1972) (same). Lawyers will need to thoroughly research the nature and extent of local parent-child and attorney-child privileges to preserve the child's right to be free from self-incrimination.

159. See Gilbert, supra note 131, at 1189–90 (noting that when child and family participate in services, they may prevent the child's removal from the home).

If the child decides to include the parents in an attorney-client consultation, the lawyer is provided with an opportunity to employ motivational strategies that will promote the psychological well-being of the entire family.[160] Like strategies for individual relapse prevention, family-focused interventions encourage legal actors to avoid "doing for" the family and stress enabling the family to do for itself.[161] Family-focused juvenile justice models are designed to develop feelings of self-worth and teach families that they are primarily responsible for, and capable of, achieving treatment goals.[162] Together, the family intervention specialist and the family will agree on appropriate goals and methods to achieve those goals.[163] The interventions will identify and draw on strengths within the family and maximize the capacity of family members to effect change in their own lives.[164] Family intervention specialists also teach families to advocate on behalf of children in other systems.[165] In meetings with the attorney, the client, and the client's parents, the lawyer may advance the rehabilitative process by helping to mend relationships within the family and secure the parents' support for the child's stated objectives. When parents are angry, for example, about court fines and missed hours at work, the lawyer may help the child develop a plan to pay parents back, increase household chores, or take greater responsibility for the care and supervision of younger siblings.

Although a lawyer who collaborates in family-focused advocacy may advance significant therapeutic interests, the lawyer must never lose sight of his role as counselor or advisor for the child and may not allow parents to usurp control over the child's legal representation. In the initial interaction with parents, the lawyer must clearly identify the child as his client and advise the parent that the child will be the ultimate arbiter of all key decisions, including those about whether to plead or go to trial.[166] Collaboration with parents also does not relieve the attorney of his duty to educate the child about his constitutional and statutory rights within the juvenile justice system or to provide the child with candid advice about how the child should proceed in the case.

---

160. *See* Winick, *Jurisprudence of TJ, supra* note 5, at 202.

161. Gilbert, *supra* note 131, at 1206.

162. *Id.* at 1178, 1180.

163. *Id.* at 1178.

164. *Id.* at 1176, 1178, 1186.

165. *Id.* at 1174.

166. Nancy J. Moore, *Conflicts of Interests in the Representation of Children*, 64 FORD-HAM L. REV. 1819, 1824–25, 1830 (1996).

Conclusion

Application of therapeutic jurisprudence to juvenile court has evolved considerably since the inception of the juvenile court movement. While judges in early juvenile courts offered kindly, paternalistic guidance and treatment to children in lieu of punishment, due process has changed the landscape of the modern juvenile court. Today, therapeutic outcomes are not only achieved through rehabilitative programming, but are also deeply intertwined in both the process of justice itself and the legal relationships in which the child will engage. Lawyers, judges, probation officers, parents, and teachers all have a role to play in the therapeutic success of the juvenile justice system. As the primary ally and voice for the child, the child's attorney plays a significant role in advancing therapeutic objectives for the child. By applying basic principles of psychology and selecting the appropriate attorney-client paradigm, the attorney may become a positive therapeutic agent and empower the child to comply with the court's rehabilitative efforts without violating overarching principles of law and justice. By building alliances within the child's family, school, and community, the lawyer may improve the child's self-image and help the child conceive of and pursue a greater range of positive alternatives.

V

LAWYERING WITH MINDFULNESS, SPIRITUALITY & RELIGION

CHAPTER 15

Awareness in Lawyering: A Primer on Paying Attention

*Leonard L. Riskin**

Introduction

Many lawyers who wish "to practice law as a healthy, healing profession, one that the lawyer finds fulfilling and rewarding and that is beneficial and therapeutic for the client"[1] could face at least two problems. The first is the dominance of the narrow mindset—which I have elsewhere called the "Lawyer's Standard Philosophical Map"—that governs much of legal education and many aspects of law practice.[2] The second is the natural tendency of the human mind—exacerbated by the conditions of contemporary law practice—to get distracted and to focus excessively on the self. These problems combine to make it difficult for many lawyers to be sufficiently "present"—mentally and emotionally—with their clients, their counterparts, and themselves, to practice law in the ways envisioned in this book. In meeting the challenges of being present, two states of mind are particularly useful: a mindful, non-judgmental awareness and an attitude of loving-kindness. All people experience such states of mind at some times. But for most of us, most of the time, it is impossible to sustain such states of mind in the face of difficult circumstances.

* Copyright © 2006 Leonard L. Riskin. Chesterfield Smith Professor of Law, Frederic C. Levin College of Law, University of Florida. Thanks to Melissa Blacker, Lynn Rossy, Ferris Buck Urbanowski, and Rachel Wohl for their comments on a draft of this chapter.

1. *Preface, supra* at p. xv.

2. *See* Leonard L. Riskin, *Mediation and Lawyers*, 43 Ohio St. L.J. 29, 44–45 (1982) [hereinafter Riskin, *Mediation and Lawyers*].

Fortunately, however, we can deliberately cultivate such states of mind through specific meditative practices and can integrate these practices, and the perspectives they produce, into our professional lives. Beginning about 1998, some law firms, law schools and professional organizations of lawyers and mediators have been offering instruction and support for such meditative practices—and many lawyers are participating.[3]

This chapter explains the nature of the states of mind characterized by mindfulness and loving-kindness and gives practical suggestions on how to develop these states of mind and deploy them in relation to law practice situations in order to provide better service to your clients and gain more satisfaction from your work. Because of space limitations, and the "practical" orientation of this book, this chapter is necessarily brief. It deals with just a few meditative practices and describes only their principal features and potential benefits—omitting many of their philosophical and psychological underpinnings. I hope that interested readers will follow the trails marked in the footnotes and in the Appendix.

I. Mindfulness and Loving-Kindness

A. Mindfulness

Mindfulness, as I use the term, means being aware, moment-to-moment, without judgment and without commentary, of whatever passes through the sense organs and the mind—sounds, sights, bodily sensations, odors, thoughts, judgments, images, emotions.[4] One develops the ability to be mind-

---

3. *See* Leonard L. Riskin, *The Contemplative Lawyer: On the Potential Benefits of Mindfulness Meditation to Law Students, Lawyers, and their Clients,* 7 Harv. Negot. L. Rev. 1, 33-35 (2002) [hereinafter Riskin, *Contemplative Lawyer*]; Leonard L. Riskin, *Mindfulness: Foundational Training for Dispute Resolution,* 54 J. Legal Educ. 79, 85–88 (2004) [hereinafter Riskin, *Foundational Training*]; Initiative on Mindfulness in Law and Dispute Resolution, *at* http://www.law.missouri.edu/csdr/programs/mindfulness (last modified Sept. 23, 2005).

4. *See* Bhante Henepola Gunaratana, Mindfulness in Plain English (1992). It is important to distinguish mindfulness from the other major form of meditation, known as "concentration." In concentration meditation, the mediator focuses attention exclusively on one object, such as a mantra or an image or a mental state. *See* Daniel Goleman, The Varieties of The Meditative Experience 7–20 (1977) [hereinafter Goleman, Varieties of Meditative Experience]; Gunaratana, *supra,* at 3; Kathleen Riordan Speeth, *On Psychotherapeutic Attention,* 14 J. Transpers. Psychol. 141, 146–48 (1982). In the West, perhaps the most popularly-known examples of concentration meditation are Transcendental Meditation (*see* Charles N. Alexander et al., *Transcendental Meditation, Self-Actualization,*

ful through "formal" practices, such as meditation and mindful yoga, then deploys mindfulness in everyday life. The purpose of the practice, as Jon Kabat-Zinn tells us, is not to become a good meditator, but to live with more freedom from habitual ways of perceiving and acting, and thus to be more present in your life and your work, to enjoy life more, and to help others more readily and fully.[5]

During the last twenty years, this ancient practice has found many uses in modern Western society—in health care, athletics, management, and more recently, in programs for lawyers, law students, and mediators.[6] Mindfulness meditation and the mindful awareness that it fosters can help people deal better with stress, listen better to themselves and others, perform better, and achieve more satisfaction from their work. For these reasons and others, they can help lawyers who wish to serve their clients more comprehensively and gain more satisfaction from their work.

Mindfulness can help in several ways.

1. Dealing with Stress, Creating Calm, and Enhancing Presence

First, mindfulness can enable the lawyer to deal better with stress and to develop a calm state of mind that will foster the ability to think clearly. Second, it can permit the lawyer to deal more effectively with distractions so that he can listen carefully and otherwise pay attention to—that is, be "present" with—his work and his client. Such presence not only allows the lawyer to learn more about the client; this form of non-judgmental attention often can help "heal" the client—perhaps in the same way that the close presence of a human caretaker can enhance the health of a houseplant. And the emotional calm has a contagious effect, spreading from lawyer to client and to those the client touches.[7] As the poet William Butler Yeats put it: "We can make our

and Psychological Health: A Conceptual Overview and Statistical Meta-Analysis, 6 J. Soc. Behav. & Personality 189 (1991)), and the method known as the "Relaxation Response," which was developed by Herbert Benson of Harvard Medical School. Herbert Benson, The Relaxation Response (1975).

5. See generally Jon Kabat-Zinn, Coming to Our Senses: Healing Ourselves and the World Through Mindfulness (2005).

6. See Riskin, Contemplative Lawyer, supra note 3; Riskin, Foundational Training, supra note 3; Initiative on Mindfulness in Law and Dispute Resolution, supra note 3; The Harvard Negotiation Insight Initiative, at www.pon.harvard.edu/hnii (last visited Apr. 30, 2006).

7. See Joseph P. Forgas, On Feeling Good and Getting Your Way: Mood Effects on Negotiator Cognition and Bargaining Strategies, 74 J. Personality & Soc. Psychol. 565 (1998) (documenting the phenomenon of "emotional contagion").

minds so like still water that beings gather about us, that they may see their own images, and so live for a moment with a clearer, perhaps even with a fiercer, life because of our quiet."[8]

Mindfulness also can enhance "emotional intelligence"[9] and so enable the lawyer to deal more appropriately with her own emotions and those of her client and others involved in a dispute or transaction.

2. Transcending Habitual Ways of Perceiving and Behaving

The biggest challenge to providing "affective assistance" is the dominance of an adversarial perspective in legal education and law practice. I have elsewhere called this the "Lawyer's Standard Philosophical Map":

> On the lawyer's standard philosophical map … the client's situation is seen atomistically; many links are not printed. The duty to represent the client zealously within the bounds of the law discourages concern with both the opponent's situation and the overall social effect of a given result.

---

8. William Butler Yeats, *quoted in* SHARON SALZBERG, LOVINGKINDNESS: THE REVOLUTIONARY ART OF HAPPINESS 189 (1997).

9. To over-simplify, and put it into the contemporary idiom, mindfulness practice tends to produce what Daniel Goleman has called "emotional intelligence," which entails five "basic emotional and social competencies": self-awareness, self-regulation, motivation, empathy, and social skills. DANIEL GOLEMAN, EMOTIONAL INTELLIGENCE: WHY IT CAN MATTER MORE THAN IQ (1995) [hereinafter GOLEMAN, EMOTIONAL INTELLIGENCE]; DANIEL GOLEMAN, WORKING WITH EMOTIONAL INTELLIGENCE (1998) [hereinafter GOLEMAN, WORKING WITH]. Goleman argues, marshaling a great deal of empirical evidence, that emotional intelligence is much more important than academic intelligence in predicting success at virtually any occupation or profession—assuming, of course, an adequate level of academic intelligence. Mindfulness meditation can help develop the first four of these emotional intelligence competencies—self-awareness, self-regulation, motivation, and empathy; these, in turn, are likely to help produce the fifth emotional intelligence competency—social skills.

These emotional intelligence elements provide the foundation for, but do not guarantee, the development of certain practical skills, or emotional *competencies*. GOLEMAN, WORKING WITH, *supra*, at 25. As Goleman explains, "[B]eing good at serving customers is an emotional competence based on empathy. Likewise, trustworthiness is a competence based on self-regulation, or handling impulses and emotions well." *Id.*

For an excellent discussion of how the "emotional sense" can help a lawyer perform better in all manner of activity, see Erin Ryan, *The Discourse Beneath: Emotional Epistemology in Legal Deliberation and Negotiation*, 10 HARV. NEGOT. L. REV. 231 (2005).

See generally supra ch. 1: Marjorie A. Silver, *Emotional Competence and the Lawyer's Journey.*

Moreover, on the lawyer's standard philosophical map, quantities are bright and large while qualities appear dimly or not at all. When one party wins, in this vision, usually the other party loses, and, most often, the victory is reduced to a money judgment. This "reduction" of nonmaterial values—such as honor, respect, dignity, security and love—to amounts of money, can have one of two effects. In some cases, these values are excluded from the decision makers' considerations, and thus from the consciousness of the lawyers, as irrelevant. In others, they are present but transmuted into something else—a justification for money damages ... The lawyer's standard world view is based upon a cognitive and rational outlook. Lawyers are trained to put people and events into categories that are legally meaningful, to think in terms of rights and duties established by rules, to focus on acts more than persons. This view requires a strong development of cognitive capabilities, which is often attended by the under-cultivation of emotional faculties.[10]

This perspective has its virtues, of course,[11] but it also carries problems. It severely limits a lawyer's ability to see things broadly or deeply, to develop curiosity, to listen fully to clients and others, to learn about people's underlying interests, and to think creatively. And it seems to render irrelevant attempts at self-understanding or at seeking out, or even noticing, what connects people (in addition to what separates them). Thus, it may contribute to many problems in law practice and in the legal system—such as excessive adversarialism, inadequate solutions, high costs, delays, and dissatisfaction among both lawyers and clients—all of which produce suffering.[12] To help clients more fully, lawyers must transcend the dominating influence of the standard philosophical map and recognize it as simply one perspective. To do that the

---

10. Leonard L. Riskin, *Mediation and Lawyers*, 43 OHIO ST. L.J. 29, 44–45 (1982) [hereinafter Riskin, *Mediation and Lawyers*]. Of course this map is overdrawn; it exaggerates a common tendency. Many lawyers practice in more balanced ways. And transactional lawyers tend more often to draw on wider perspectives. But as I said twenty years ago, it describes the way most lawyers think most of the time. *Id.* at 46. Other limiting mind-sets also contribute to the problems I describe. *See, e.g.,* ROBERT H. MNOOKIN ET AL., BEYOND WINNING: NEGOTIATING TO CREATE VALUE IN DEALS AND DISPUTES 9–91 (2000) (describing limiting mind-sets associated with client counseling and negotiation) [hereinafter BEYOND WINNING].

11. *See* Riskin, *Mediation and Lawyers*, *supra* note 10, at 47.

12. *See supra* ch. 7: Harold Abramson, *Problem-Solving Advocacy in Mediations: A Model of Client Representation.*

lawyer must be aware of the psychological contours of that map. And mind-fulness is a premier method for developing such awareness.

Mindfulness can help lawyers achieve a distance from the adversarial per-spective in another way—by nurturing positive emotions, as well as feelings of kindness and compassion toward self and others. There is a strong interdepend-ency among attitude, mood (or state of mind or emotional tone), and behavior. The better mood a person is in, the more likely he or she will spot opportunities for collaboration, i.e., for getting beyond adversarial relations.[13] A bad mood tends to narrow one's focus, a good mood to expand it.[14] And the more one col-laborates successfully, the more likely one is to be in a good mood. In other words, a positive mood and collaborative behavior are mutually reinforcing.

Mindfulness can contribute to reducing the pull of negative emotions and to strengthening positive emotions in several ways. First, mindfulness can help diminish pessimism[15] by helping lawyers become aware of the extent to which their thoughts contribute to pessimism and the extent to which their thoughts—as well as the circumstances to which they relate—are always tran-sient and often in error.[16] In addition, it generally improves one's mood by

---

13. *See* Max H. Bazerman & Margaret A. Neale, Negotiating Rationally 121–22 (1992); Ryan, *supra* note 9, at 269. *See generally* Clark Freshman et al., *The Lawyer-Nego-tiator as Mood Scientist: What We Know and Don't Know About How Mood Relates to Suc-cessful Negotiation*, 2002 J. Disp. Resol. 1.

14. Martin E. P. Seligman, Authentic Happiness: Using the New Positive Psy-chology to Realize Your Potential for Lasting Fulfillment 39 (2002).

15. Pessimism, as Seligman uses the term, does not mean seeing the glass as half-empty. "[P]essimists tend to attribute the causes of negative events to stable and global factors ("it's going to last forever, and it's going to undermine everything"). The pessimist views bad events as pervasive, permanent, and uncontrollable, while the optimist sees them as local, temporary, and changeable." Seligman, *supra* note 14, at 177–78. "[P]ositive emotions are the fuel of win-win (positive sum) games, while negative emotions like anger, anxiety, and sadness have evolved to switch on during win-loss games." *Id.* at 180. Seligman maintains that all emotions have feeling, sensory and thinking components, and that "[t]he feeling component of all negative emotions is aversion—disgust, fear, repulsion, hatred, and the like.... The type of thinking such emotions ineluctably engender is focused and intolerant, narrowing our attention to the weapon and not the hairstyle of our assailant. All of this culminates in quick and decisive actions: fight, flight, or conserve." *Id.* at 31. Reducing pes-simism in lawyers may not be entirely beneficent. In one study, law students who were more pessimistic, as measured by a questionnaire, did better on law school examinations. Selig-man speculates that they were more able to identify problems, an essential skill on most law school examinations. *See id.* at 178.

16. *See* Zindel V. Segal et al., Mindfulness-Based Cognitive Therapy for De-pression: A New Approach to Preventing Relapse 134–36 (2002).

helping reduce and better address the experience of stress. Recently, scientists have found evidence that mindfulness meditation can increase the type of brainwave activity associated with happiness—actually shifting a person's disposition, not just her mood.[17]

Psychologist Martin Seligman, a leading exponent and proponent of "Positive Psychology," which emphasizes the study and promotion of positive emotions, argues that the despair that is so prevalent among lawyers—especially young associates in large law firms—is due to three factors: pessimism; "low decision-latitude in high stress situations"; and being part of a win-lose profession."[18] By increasing a lawyer's positive emotions toward his client, his counterpart, and himself, mindfulness meditation can enhance the likelihood that the lawyer will be able to address underlying interests of his client and the other party and to collaborate more effectively. In Seligman's words, "A positive mood ... buoys people into a way of thinking that is creative, tolerant, constructive, generous, undefensive and lateral."[19] This should enable the lawyer to create better processes and outcomes and more satisfaction, by giving him more "decision latitude" and allowing him, when appropriate, to convert "win-lose" situations to "win-win" situations.[20]

B. Loving-Kindness

Mindfulness practices *tend* to promote positive mind states, but not consistently and sometimes only over a period of time. However, other medita-

---

17. Richard J. Davidson et al., *Alterations in Brain and Immune Function Produced by Mindfulness Meditation*, 65 Psychosomatic Med. 564 (2003). Davidson and his colleagues found that mediators had increased levels of brainwave activity in the left prefrontal cortex (which is known to correlate with the experience of happiness) and decreased activity in the right prefrontal cortex. High activity in the right prefrontal cortex is associated with the experiences of stress and anger. *See also* Daniel Goleman, *Finding Happiness: Cajole Your Brain to Lean to the Left*, N.Y. Times, Feb. 4, 2003, at F5.

18. Seligman, *supra* note 14, at 177–81.

19. *Id.* at 39.

20. Of course, I am presenting a simplified, but I hope not too simplistic, explanation of the relationship between mindfulness and collaborative behavior. For a more critical—and pessimistic—discussion, see Scott Peppet, *Can A Saint Negotiate?*, 7 Harv. Negot. L. Rev. 83 (2002). *See also* Van M. Pounds, *Promoting Truthfulness in Negotiations: A Mindful Approach*, 40 Willamette L. Rev. 181 (2004); Bazerman & Neale, *supra* note 13, at 122 (asserting that negotiators in a good mood may be more vulnerable to certain psychological traps, which are known as the framing, escalation of commitment, and availability effects).

tive practices are specifically designed to deliberately and directly cultivate such positive states of mind.[21] The most fundamental of such meditations are those that develop loving-kindness toward self and other. These practices are grounded upon the notion that one cannot truly send positive wishes to another unless he has positive feelings toward himself. Thus, the practices begin with developing a positive state of mind as to oneself, which is followed by sending good wishes to others.

II. Developing Mindfulness and Loving-Kindness

This Part offers practical suggestions on developing and reinforcing the foundation for mindfulness and loving-kindness. After that, Part III offers ideas about how to integrate them into daily life and law practice.

A. Building the Foundation: Meditation Practices

1. Mindfulness

Mindfulness means being aware, moment to moment and without judgment of whatever passes through the senses and the mind—sounds, sights, smells, other bodily sensations, emotions, and thoughts and images. We aspire to be *aware* that we are hearing while we are hearing; to be aware that we are thinking while we are thinking; and so forth. With such non-judgmental awareness, we gain a kind of freedom. For instance, if, while we are interviewing a client, we become aware that our mind has wandered off to thoughts about next week's football game, we can swiftly bring our attention back to the client. If we become aware of an impulse to get away from our client— manifested, perhaps, by feelings of aversion or anxiety or fear and accompanying bodily sensations—we can make a discerning judgment about whether to follow that impulse in light of the circumstances and our obligations as a lawyer.

We cultivate mindfulness through a progression of meditative practices. The most basic of these is concentration on the breath. From there we move to bodily sensations, thoughts, emotions, and finally, to choiceless awareness

---

21. *See* SHARON SALZBURG, LOVING-KINDNESS: THE REVOLUTIONARY ART OF HAPPINESS (1997).

or bare attention, a non-judgmental awareness of whatever arises through any of the sense organs or the mind.[22]

As indicated in Section B, *infra*, it is helpful to have support for your meditation practice, including individual and group educational activities. However, to give you a sense of meditative practices and an opportunity to practice on your own, I set forth below a series of instructions for the following meditations:

   a. Awareness of Breath

   b. Awareness of Bodily Sensations

   c. Awareness of Thoughts

   d. Awareness of Emotions

   e. (Almost) Choiceless Awareness

a. Awareness of Breath

1) Basic Meditation on the Breath

Sit comfortably with your back and neck erect—either on a chair with your feet flat on the floor, or on a meditation cushion on the floor with your legs crossed—and your hands on your knees or your thighs.[23] Begin to settle yourself by bringing attention to sound. As best you can, observe sounds as they arise, stay present, and fall away, and do this without worrying about the cause of each sound and without judging the sounds. However, if thoughts about the source of sounds and judgments arise, simply be aware of them, and return the attention to sound.

After a few minutes, bring your attention to the sensation of your breath at the place where it is easiest for you to notice. This might be at the nostrils,

---

22. Different teachers present these practices in different ways and in different orders and combinations. The meditation instructions that follow are based on my own experience as a student and teacher of meditation. They draw on numerous sources, many of which I can no longer identify. For other instructions and a sense of the variety of practices, see generally: JOSEPH GOLDSTEIN, THE EXPERIENCE OF INSIGHT (1987); GUNARATANA, *supra* note 4; JON KABAT-ZINN, FULL CATASTROPHE LIVING (1990); JON KABAT-ZINN, WHEREVER YOU GO, THERE YOU ARE (1994); JACK KORNFIELD, A PATH WITH HEART: A GUIDE TO THE PROMISES AND PERILS OF SPIRITUAL LIFE (1993); BREATH SWEEPS MIND: A FIRST GUIDE TO MEDITATION PRACTICE (Jean Smith ed., 1998).

23. Meditation traditionally has been done sitting, standing or lying down. In addition there are various forms of walking meditation, which are particularly useful in bringing mindfulness into daily life. For further information on walking meditation, which means being present while walking, see JOSEPH GOLDSTEIN, INSIGHT MEDIATION: THE PRACTICE OF FREEDOM 136–37 (1993) and MATTHEW FLICKSTEIN, SWALLOWING THE RIVER GANGES: A PRACTICE GUIDE TO THE PATH OF PURIFICATION 78–82 (2001).

as the air enters and leaves, or in the chest or abdomen, as they rise and fall with inhalations and exhalations. Focus on the sensations of one inhalation at a time, one exhalation at a time. When you notice that your mind has wandered, this is a moment of mindfulness! Gently escort your attention back to the breath. If you have a lot of trouble concentrating on the breath, you might try one of the following: 1. Silently note "rising" and "falling," or "in" and "out," or "up" and "down" with each breath. 2. Silently count each exhalation until you reach ten; when you reach ten, or go past ten or lose count, begin again at one. During such activities, the words should be in the background, the sensations in the foreground.

The first time you do this meditation, try it for five minutes. As you become comfortable with it, extend the practice to fifteen minutes or more, ideally twice a day. Notice, without judgment, how the mind wanders, and its propensity to latch on to—get carried away with—thoughts, feelings, and sensations.

2.) Extended Meditation on the Breath

When you become comfortable with the Basic Meditation on the breath—which could be a matter of days, weeks, or months—you may want to move to a more extended version of the breath meditation.

Begin with the Basic Meditation on the Breath, as described in the preceding instructions. This time, when you become aware that the mind has wandered, notice where it has gone. Become aware of whether it is in the past or future, and its focus, e.g., on thoughts, bodily sensations, emotions; notice its impermanence, and then gently return the attention to the breath.

* * *

Comment on Breath Meditation

These meditations on the breath tend to create a calm state of mind that enables one to perceive and think more clearly. The difference between the Basic and the Extended Awareness of Breath Meditations is this: In the Basic method, when you notice that the mind has wandered from the breath, you simply bring the attention back to the breath; in other words, you are trying to ignore any distractions so that you can be "absorbed" in the breath. In the Extended form, when you observe that the attention has wandered from the breath, you notice where it has gone—momentarily concentrating on that—and then bring the attention back to the breath. This subtle distinction will be clearer after you practice a bit.

How long should you practice? As a general matter, you will get more benefit from more practice. I suggest quickly working up to fifteen minutes twice each day, and gradually increasing the time up to thirty and then forty-five minutes. It is especially important to practice every day, even if it is for a very short time.

b. Awareness of the Body—The Body Scan

It is best to do this for thirty to forty-five minutes, but shorter times can work as well. Get into a comfortable position. The ideal position for the body scan is lying on your back on a yoga mat or blanket or soft carpeting, with your feet hanging loosely to the side, arms by your side, and hands palm-up. Sitting in a chair also works, and lessens the chance of falling asleep.

Begin meditating on the breath, as described above. After about three minutes, on an out breath, move the awareness from the breath down the left side of the body to the toes on the left foot. Notice any sensations in the toes—on the skin, in the muscles. If you observe no sensations at all in the toes, that is o.k. After a few moments, on an out breath, move your attention to the bottom of the foot. Gradually, in this manner, move your attention systematically throughout the body, moving, more or less, as follows, noticing, as best you can, any sensations on the skin, in the muscles, in the joints:

- the left ankle, calf, knee, thigh, buttock;
- the right toes, foot, ankle, calf, knee, thigh, buttock;
- the genital area;
- the abdominal area, chest, upper back;
- shoulders, lower back;
- the left upper arm, elbow, lower arm, hand, fingers and thumb (as best you can, moving the attention from one digit to another);
- the right upper arm, elbow, lower arm, hand, fingers and thumb (one digit at a time);
- the neck, front, sides and back;
- the cheeks, chin, lips, mouth (roof, floor, sides, tongue, teeth), eyes, eye lids, ears;
- the head—sides, back, top;
- the entire body, noticing any sensations on the skin, in the tissue, in the bones and joints, as they arise in any part of the body.

As you are moving the attention through the body, here are a few suggestions:

- The attitude here is non-judgmental curiosity. You are trying to observe what's going on in the body, not to judge it. If, however, it turns out that the mind is judging—*e.g.* if the thought arises, "I wish my hair were thicker"—simply observe that judging, and don't judge yourself harshly for having such a judgment.

You may find it helpful to imagine that you are breathing into and out of the part of the body on which you are focusing.

- When you notice that the mind has wandered away from the part of the body on which you are focusing, that is a moment of mindfulness; simply return the attention to that part of the body.[24]

- If, however, the attention is distracted by a very strong unpleasant sensation, such as a pain or an itch, instead of drawing the attention back to the part of the body on which you are focusing, simply focus on the unpleasant sensation. As best you can, observe it without judgment. But as judgment arises, notice that, too. Observe the changing nature of the physical sensation, and notice the thoughts associated with it. Usually such thoughts relate to wishing the sensation would go away. In this sense, there is a distinction between pain—the physical sensation—and suffering—wishing things were other than the way they are.

- Use the breath as a source of stability. In the same way that a swimmer may occasionally return for temporary support to the side of the pool or a pier in a lake, when you lose track or get stuck in any sounds, bodily sensations or feelings, bring the attention momentarily to the breath, until the attention feels stable enough to return the part of the body on which you are focusing.

c. Awareness of Thoughts

To prepare for Awareness of Thoughts Meditation, begin with a brief Extended Awareness of the Breath Meditation, as described above. Once the mind is relatively settled, bring the attention to thoughts and thinking. The idea is to become aware, without judgment, of thoughts as they arise, stay present, and drop out of awareness. For most people, this is more challenging than being aware of the breath and bodily sensations. For that reason, you may find it helpful to silently "label" thoughts as they arise. For instance, you might say "thinking" when you notice a thought arise.

---

24. After you become familiar with the body scan (*e.g.*, after you have done it several times), you might address distractions by using the "triangle of awareness"—thoughts, bodily sensations, and emotions (an idea developed at the Stress Reduction Clinic at the University of Massachusetts Medical School and used in its teaching programs). For example, when you notice that the mind is distracted by thinking, try also to observe any bodily sensations and emotions that accompany the thoughts.

The main idea here is to be *aware* that you are thinking *while* you are thinking, and to have enough distance from the thinking that you can decide whether that's what you want your mind to be doing.

*   *   *

Comment

This meditation is particularly useful in helping us learn to deal with distracting thoughts. In addition, it gives us the opportunity to notice that we have almost no control over what thoughts arise, though we do have choices over how we respond to them. If we have enough presence of mind to be aware of thoughts as they arise, we also have a chance to assess their validity[25] and appreciate the saying, "Don't believe everything you think."

d. Awareness of Emotions

Prepare for this by meditating on the breath and then doing a brief (say, two-minute) body scan. Once the mind is settled, open the awareness to emotions. Try to notice—again, without judgment—feelings such as fear, sadness, joy, revulsion, anxiety. Once again the appropriate attitude is curiosity, mingled with a compassion for self. If you observe carefully, you will see that what we think of as an emotion is closely connected to thoughts and bodily sensations. You may find it helpful to silently label the emotions that you recognize. As in all the meditations in this sequence, you may find it useful to use the breath as a source of stability, returning to it whenever you lose track of where your attention is or should be or when you need a "rest."

e. (Almost) Choiceless Awareness

Prepare for this by meditating on the breath and then doing a brief body scan. Once the mind is settled, open the awareness to all of the objects that we addressed in the previously described meditations—sounds, the breath, bodily sensations (this includes sounds and the breath as well as smells), and emotions.[26] Once again, use the breath as a source of stability. It may be helpful for you to keep in mind categories of experiences and to label experiences accordingly. For instance, you might employ the "triangle of awareness"[27]—

---

25. For an example of this ability in the negotiation context, see Andrea K. Schneider, *Effective Responses to Offensive Comments*, 10 NEGOT. J. 107 (1994).

26. I call this "(Almost)" Choiceless Awareness, because in Choiceless Awareness (a.k.a. Bare Attention) one does not choose to focus on the breath, or anything else.

27. This notion was developed at the Stress Reduction Clinic at the University of Massachusetts Medical School and is used in its teaching programs.

thoughts, bodily sensations, and emotions; try labeling your experiences in terms of these three categories and noticing any relationships among them.[28]

2. Loving-kindness

The central idea in loving-kindness meditation is to send certain kinds of good wishes to others. In order to do that, however, you must have similar good feelings about yourself. And in the West, many people have lots of negative feelings about themselves. So in doing the loving-kindness meditation, we typically begin by sending these good wishes—in the form of a series of phrases—to ourselves. We do this mindfully, noticing any resistance to sending or receiving such wishes. Then we bring to mind a series of others—one person or one group at a time—and send these wishes to them, also mindfully, again noticing any resistance or opening to sending such wishes. We start by sending these good wishes to people we care about very much, and move on to others we know less well or may even dislike.[29]

The following instructions include phrases that many people find helpful. They are

> May I/you be safe.
> May I/you be happy.
> May I/you be healthy and strong.
> May I/you care for myself/yourself with joy and ease
> If these do not resonate with you, make up your own, similar phrases.

* * *

After seating yourself comfortably, begin to calm the mind and body through observation of the breath. Find the place where it is easiest to notice the sensation of the breath—which could be at the nostrils, in the chest, or in the belly. After a few minutes, get a sense of your body, noticing any sensations.

---

28. As you may notice, the three factors often are deeply interrelated. Each affects the others.

29. As is the case with all the meditations described in this chapter, loving-kindness meditations come in a wide variety of formulations. The language set forth below draws heavily on meditation instructions recorded by Melissa Blacker of the Stress Reduction Clinic at the University of Massachusetts Medical School and available for purchase at http://www.umassmed.edu/cfm. She, in turn, drew on loving-kindness materials prepared by Michelle McDonald-Smith and Sharon Salzburg, "almost like a folksong." Email from Melissa Blacker, University of Massachusetts Medical School, to Leonard Riskin (Aug. 30, 2005) (on file with author). For more on loving-kindness, see SHARON SALZBURG, LOVING-KINDNESS (1995); KABAT-ZINN, *supra* note 5.

a. Cultivating Loving-Kindness Toward Yourself

This is very good.

Safety

Open to the possibility that you could feel safe.

- Notice any thoughts, emotions, or sensations that arise.
- Notice any resistance, fear, or sadness that arises.
- Notice any softening to that idea, any feeling of safety.

Silently repeat, several times: "May I be safe from all inner and outer harm."

- Notice any thoughts, emotions, or sensations that arise.

Happiness

perhaps change to

Open to the possibility that you could be happy, in the very life you are leading—not in a different life in which circumstances are different or you are different.

I AM... rather than may I

- Notice any thoughts, emotions, or sensations that arise.
- Notice any resistance, fear, or sadness that arises.
- Notice any softening to that idea, any feeling of happiness.

Silently repeat, several times, "May I be happy, peaceful, and calm."

- Notice, with curiosity, any thoughts, emotions, and bodily sensations that arise.

Health

Open to the possibility that you could be healthy and strong.

- Notice any thoughts, emotions, or sensations that arise.
- Notice any resistance, fear, or sadness that arises.
- Notice any softening to that idea, any feeling of strength and health.

Silently repeat, several times, "May I be as healthy and strong as it is possible for me to be."

- Notice, with curiosity, any thoughts, emotions, and bodily sensations that arise.

Caring for yourself

Open to the possibility that you could care for yourself with a sense of joy and ease.

- Notice any resistance, fear, or sadness that arises.
- Notice any softening to that idea, a sense of what it would be like to care for yourself with joy and ease.

Silently repeat, several times: "May I care for myself with joy and ease."

- Notice, with curiosity, any thoughts, emotions, and bodily sensations that arise.

Repeating all the phrases

Silently repeat all the phrases:

"May I be safe from all inner and outer harm."
"May I be happy, peaceful, and calm."
"May I be as healthy and strong as it is possible for me to be."
"May I care for myself with joy and ease."

- Notice, with curiosity, any thoughts, emotions, and bodily sensations that arise.

b. Sending Loving-Kindness to Others

Now call to mind the image of a person you love. It could be a friend, a relative, a mentor. Don't try to make a rational choice, just accept whatever image arises first. Silently repeat the phrases, but directed at that person:

"May you be safe from all inner and outer harm."
"May you be happy, peaceful, and calm."
"May you be as healthy and strong as it is possible for you to be."
"May you care for yourself with joy and ease."

- Notice, with curiosity, any thoughts, emotions, and bodily sensations that arise.

Next call to mind, one at a time, images of individuals and groups such as the following, and send to each the wishes embodied in these phrases, observing, with curiosity, any thoughts, emotions, and bodily sensations that arise.
A friend or family member.
Someone you don't know well, an acquaintance.
Someone you don't know at all but see occasionally—perhaps someone who walks on your block or works in a business you frequent.
Someone whom you dislike or whom you consider an enemy. (You may find it difficult to send good wishes to such a person. If this is the case, try

imagining that person as an infant or a young child—or on her or his deathbed.)

All people in your town, nation, or continent, and in other parts of the world.[30]

B. Reinforcing the Foundation

Meditation is the key to building the foundation for states of concentration, mindfulness, and loving-kindness, as I am using those concepts. You can dramatically increase the impact of meditation through regular practice and a variety of supporting activities:

- **Meditate regularly on your own.** Establish a routine of meditating once or twice each day, preferably at regular times. Most people find it best to meditate first thing in the morning and again in the evening. Begin with fifteen minutes and gradually increase up to 50 minutes.
- **Sit regularly with a group.** In most mid-size or large communities in the U.S., groups (organized in varying degrees), meet weekly to meditate. Often the sittings include talks on philosophical and practice issues.[31]
- **Attend meditation retreats.** Day-long and multi-day retreats permit the mind to become still so that you can get a deeper level of calm and greater insight into how the mind works. Some such retreats are designed especially for lawyers.[32]
- **Attend lectures and workshops on meditation.** Numerous programs are available in most large U.S. cities. In addition, special workshops on meditation for lawyers and mediators are now common features of dispute resolution conferences and the subject of multi-day workshops and retreats. Other workshops are based principally on particular skills, such as negotiation, and include a large mindfulness component.

---

30. Some people will extend these wishes to animals, plants, and "all beings."

31. In some contexts, "mindfulness meditation" is also known as "vipassana" or "insight meditation." For a listing of insight meditation resources, see http://www.geocities .com/~madg/links.html#us_practice, as well as other resources listed in the Appendix to this chapter. You will also find mindfulness meditation used by some practitioners of Zen and other schools of meditation.

32. For information about retreats and other mindfulness meditation programs for lawyers, see the following websites, which are listed in the Appendix at the end of this chapter: The Center for Contemplative Mind in Society Law Program; The Initiative on Mindfulness in Law and Dispute Resolution; The Harvard Negotiation Insight Initiative.

- **Read about meditation practices.** There is a vast literature on meditation, with many orientations, including religious, spiritual, philosophical, practical, and scientific. And there is a growing literature on mindfulness as it relates to law and dispute resolution.
- **Keep a journal of your meditation insights and experiences.** This can help you keep track of what you are learning. During meditation retreats it usually is unwise to write in a journal, and it is almost always a bad idea to stop a meditation, when you get a "great idea," in order to write it down. Such activities could interfere with developing the states of mind you are seeking to cultivate, which are about observing, not about thinking. However, after retreats and after meditating in other settings, you may find it useful to make notes or comments as a way of preserving your insights.
- **Engage in other mindfulness-generating activities.** Some forms of yoga take a very mindful focus, as do T'ai Chi, Qi Gong, and other processes, such as the Feldenkrais method.[33] Many mindfulness programs offer instruction in walking meditation.

III. Bringing Mindfulness and Loving-Kindness into Daily Life and Law Practice

Mindfulness and Loving-Kindness can help you prepare for, conduct, and reflect on many lawyering activities.

A. Preparing for Activities

I find it very useful to use meditative practices to prepare for various challenging activities, and for transitions between ordinary activities.

In preparing for activities you expect to be challenging, the most appropriate meditative practice to use might depend on your current state of mind and the nature of the prospective activity. Your level of experience with various meditative practices also might have an impact.

Here are a few suggestive examples:

- **Before a difficult trial, negotiation, mediation, or meeting**
  - **If you are feeling very anxious or agitated:**

---

33. *See* Feldenkrais Educational Foundation of North America, *at* http://www.feldenkrais .com/ (last visited Dec. 28, 2005).

A meditation on the breath or on bodily sensations could help calm the mind and body.

As you feel more calm, and depending upon your level of experience and comfort with the other meditations, you may wish to extend your focus to thoughts and emotions, and even practice (almost) bare attention. Such awareness could give you insight into particular issues or concerns that might be bothering you. In negotiations, for example, as Roger Fisher and Daniel Shapiro put it, most people have the same "core concerns": appreciation, affiliation, autonomy, status, and role.[34] Any of these could manifest itself in thoughts, emotions, and bodily sensations. And, of course, any of these could get in the way of your mindful attention to the task at hand. However, if you can muster moment-to-moment awareness and equanimity about concerns you are experiencing—say a sense of threat to your status—that, in itself, could diminish the power of such concern, and allow you to maintain the appropriate focus. Similarly, such non-judgmental awareness may give you reason to suspect that your negotiation counterpart has similar concerns, and give you the presence of mind to address such concerns.[35]

Such meditations also will heighten your general level of awareness, enhancing the likelihood that you will be able to maintain a mindful awareness in the midst of the negotiation.

- **If you are feeling antipathy toward any of the parties or lawyers or insecure about their attitudes toward you or about your own competence or ability to perform (any of which could be a cause of the anxiety or agitation above):**

You might do a loving-kindness meditation, in which you include, in addition to yourself, the parties and lawyers on both sides, and other affected persons. This can help you keep focused on the task at hand and the interests of others, and less focused on your own ego-centric needs, which otherwise could cause a good deal of distraction. In addition, such meditation usually generates energy and positive states of mind that will improve your chances of making good judgments and collaborating, as appropriate.

You might also meditate on your intentions. You may notice, for example, that negative thoughts arise about your negotiation counterpart—or about yourself. You also may notice thoughts or impulses about how to negotiate— *e.g.,* to follow adversarial strategies or problem-solving strategies. The mind-

---

34. Roger Fisher & Daniel Shapiro, Beyond Reason: Using Emotions as You Negotiate 15–21 (2005).

35. *See id.* at 115–82 (for ways to do this).

ful, non-judgmental awareness of such thoughts and impulses can allow you to examine them and make a discerning choice about whether and how to follow them.[36] In other words, the non-judgmental awareness provides a degree of freedom from impulsive and habitual patterns of behavior.

B. Carrying Out Activities

Building the foundation (through a regular meditation practice and related supporting activities) and meditating before particularly challenging events will enhance the likelihood that you will be able to be mindful in everyday life. Such a foundation improves your alertness and skill at noticing when you are *not* mindful—*e.g.,* when you are distracted by strong emotions, self-centered thoughts or other cognitive processes, or strong sensations in the body—and in being able to return your attention to the task at hand. The real challenge to being mindful is remembering to be mindful. Here are a few suggestions for injecting mindful awareness into routine activities of everyday life and particularly challenging professional situations.

- **Find a few routine activities to do mindfully.**

Such activities as walking, waiting for an elevator or a stoplight, doing the dishes, answering the phone, as well as transitions between activities can provide good reminders. You could even choose something that you find irritating, say a truck horn or alarm.

- **Drop your attention to your breath and to bodily sensations.**

When you are feeling agitated, say, during a negotiation, such a shift in focus can have a calming effect that can enable you to think more clearly. Even when you are not feeling agitated, periodically shifting to such a focus can calm the mind and free you from the constraining effects of strong emotions that might otherwise impair your judgment.

- **Try the "STOP" technique**

The instructions for this simple method, developed and taught by the Stress Reduction Clinic at the University of Massachusetts Medical School, are to:

---

36. I saw Professor Clark Freshman demonstrate this exercise at a conference sponsored by the Center for Contemplative Mind in Society at the Fetzer Institute in Kalamazoo, MI in 2003. *See generally* Clark Freshman et al., *Adapting Meditation to Promote Negotiation Success: A Guide to Varieties and Scientific Support,* 7 Harv. Negot. L. Rev. 67 (2002).

- Stop whatever you are doing or thinking.
- Take a breath.
- Observe and "open" to the breath, bodily sensations, emotions. Also observe and open to all the senses and the external environment.
- Proceed. That is, continue with whatever you were doing. [37]
- **Notice distractions to listening, and keep listening.**

While you are listening to someone speak—in a negotiation, an interview, a conversation—try to really pay attention. To do that you may have to notice when you are not listening—*e.g,* when the mind is distracted by emotions, discursive thought, thinking about what *you* will say next, worries, bodily sensations, desires—and to bring your attention back to the speaker. Also notice any impulses to interrupt the speaker—because of impatience, because you think you know what the speaker will say next, because you have a need to say something—and allowing the temptation to be present without following it. Use silence, and notice your and the other person's reactions to silence.[38]

- **Mentally send loving-kindness to others:**

Try sending good wishes to others, mentally. They can include people you pass on the street, friends, enemies, and the lawyers and clients on the other side of your cases. Observe any resistance you feel to doing this as well as your reactions.

C. Reflecting Upon or Reviewing Activities

It is especially useful to practice mindfulness meditation during a break or shortly after completing a significant activity, such as a negotiation, for two reasons: First, it can help you in the transition, to decompress or detach, so that you can be present with whatever happens next. Second, sometimes while practicing mindfulness meditation—even if you try to focus on the present moment—your mind will automatically generate insights about what happened or about why you or others did what they did. Even without looking for them, you may get ideas about what to do next or how to undo mistakes.

In addition to mindfulness practice at such points, some people find it helpful to deliberately reflect on the dispute resolution activity, calling to mind

---

37. For a more extended version of this technique, see "The Three-Minute Breathing Space," *in* SEGAL, *supra* note 16, at 173–75.

38. For further reading on mindful listening, see REBECCA Z. SHAFIR, THE ZEN OF LISTENING: MINDFUL COMMUNICATION IN THE AGE OF DISTRACTION (2000).

any discomfort, unease, or difficulty that might have kept them from being more present. [39] This can produce much insight.

Conclusion

I hope this has whetted your appetite to know more about how awareness skills can help you feel and perform better as a lawyer. In one sense, being mindful is the easiest task in the world. All you need to do is pay attention, and you can do that right now. In another sense, it is the hardest job you will ever undertake. You could view the simplest meditations, such as awareness of the breath, as a series of constant failures. This is because the essence of being mindful is to notice when we are mindless, when in the words of Ellen Langer, "The light's on, but nobody's home,"[40] or when we are controlled by habitual thought patterns or impulses. But your diligence will be amply repaid. Mindful awareness gives you and your clients the greatest gift of all, your presence.

Appendix: Resources on Mindfulness for Lawyers Organizations and Websites

Initiative on Mindfulness, Law and Dispute Resolution, University of Missouri-Columbia School of Law, http://www.law.missouri.edu/csdr/mindful ness.htm. This will be moved in 2007 to the University of Florida Levin College of Law.

Harvard Negotiation Insight Initiative, Program on Negotiation at Harvard Law School. Contact Erica Fox, at Efox@law.harvard.edu; http://www .pon.harvard.edu/hnii.

Center for Contemplative Mind in Society, 199 Main St., 3rd Floor, Northampton, MA 01060. The Center's law program has sponsored a series of insight meditation retreats for lawyers and law students. For information, contact Mirabai Bush, executive director, 413/268-9275; or Doug Chermak, law program director, 510-597-1650, d_chermak@yahoo.com; http://contem plativemind.org.

---

39. *See* Daniel Bowling, *Who am I as Mediator? Mindfulness, Reflection and Presence*, ACRESOLUTION, Fall 2005, at 12–15.

40. ELLEN J. LANGER, MINDFULNESS 9 (1983).

The **Center for Mindfulness in Medicine, Health Care, and Society** at the University of Massachusetts Medical School provides training in mindfulness for a wide range of organizations, operates a stress and pain reduction clinic, and conducts research on the effects of mindfulness practices. Saki Santorelli, Director, Center for Mindfulness in Medicine, Health Care, and Society, Department of Medicine, University of Massachusetts Medical School, 55 Lake Avenue North, Worcester, MA 01655; Tel: 508/856-5493; Fax: 508/856-1977; http://www.umassmed.edu/cfm.

Forest Way Insight Meditation Center, P.O. Box 491, Ruckersville, VA 22968. Offers insight meditation retreats. Tel: 804/990-9300; Fax: 804/990-9301; Email: forestway@cstone.net.; Web site: www.forestway.org.

Insight Meditation Society, 1230 Pleasant Street, Barre, MA 01005; Tel: 978/355-4378; http://www.dharma.org.

Mid-America Dharma Group. Includes information or links to information about retreats and sitting groups across the U.S. and Canada, http://www.midamericadharma.org.

Spirit Rock Meditation Center, 5000 Sir Francis Drake Blvd, P.O. Box 169 Woodacre, CA 94973; Tel: 415/488-0164; Fax: 415/488-017.

Website maintained by Steven Keeva, author of the book **Transforming Practices: Finding Joy and Satisfaction in the Legal Life**, http://www.transformingpractices.com.

Vipassana Meditation Centers operated by S.N. Goenka and his assistants around the world, http://www.dhamma.org.

Shinzen Young (insight meditation teacher), www.shinzen.org.

Inquiring Mind, the Quarterly Journal of the Vipassana Community. Excellent listing of insight meditation retreats and sitting groups, www.inquiringmind.org.

Books and Articles

Bringing Peace into the Room: How the Personal Qualities of the Mediator Impact the Process of Conflict Resolution (Daniel Bowling & David Hoffman eds., Jossey-Bass 2003).

Mark Epstein, Thoughts Without a Thinker: Psychotherapy from a Buddhist Perspective (Basic Books 1995).

Mark Epstein, Going to Pieces Without Falling Apart: A Buddhist Perspective on Wholeness (Broadway 1998).

Daniel Goleman, Emotional Intelligence: Why it Can Matter More than IQ (Bantam 1995).

Daniel Goleman, Working with Emotional Intelligence (Bantam 1998).

Joseph Goldstein, Insight Meditation: The Practice of Freedom (Shambhala 1994) *(Highly recommended for basic introduction to mindfulness.)*

Henepola Gunaratana, Mindfulness in Plain English (Wisdom 1992) *(Highly recommended for basic introduction to mindfulness.)*

Thich Nhat Hanh, The Miracle of Mindfulness (1999).

Phil Jackson & Hugh Delehanty, Sacred Hoops: Spiritual Lessons of a Hardwood Warrior (Hyperion 1995).

Phil Jackson & Charley Rosen, More than a Game (2001).

Jon Kabat-Zinn, Full Catastrophe Living: Using the Wisdom of Your Mind to Face Stress, Pain & Illness (Delta 1990).

Jon Kabat-Zinn, Wherever You Go, There You Are: Mindfulness in Everyday Life (Hyperion 1994). *(Highly recommended for basic introduction to mindfulness.)*

Jon Kabat-Zinn, Coming to Our Senses: Healing Ourselves and the World Through Mindfulness (Hyperion 2005).

Steven Keeva, Transforming Practices: Bringing Joy and Satisfaction to the Legal Life (Transaction Books, 1999).

Leonard L. Riskin, *The Contemplative Lawyer: On the Potential Contributions of Mindfulness Meditation to Law Students and Lawyers and their Clients,* 7 Harv. Neg. L. Rev. 1–66 (June 2002) (the centerpiece of a Symposium on Mindfulness in Law and ADR). A webcast of the live symposium held at Harvard Law School in March 2002 is available at http://www.pon .harvard.edu/news/2002/riskin_mindfulness.php3.

Leonard L. Riskin, *Mindfulness: Foundational Training for Dispute Resolution,* 54 J. Legal Educ. 79–91 (2004).

Leonard L. Riskin, *Knowing Yourself: Mindfulness, in* The Negotiator's Fieldbook (Christopher Honeyman & Andrea K. Schneider, eds., 2006).

Zindel V. Segal, J. Mark G. Williams & John D. Teasdale, Mindfulness-Based Cognitive Therapy for Depression: A New Approach to Preventing Relapse (Guilford 2002).

Saki Santorelli, Heal Thy Self: Lessons on Mindfulness in Medicine (Bell Tower, 1999).

Breath Sweeps Mind: A First Guide to Meditation Practice (Jean Smith ed., Tricycle 1999).

Eckhart Tolle, The Power of Now (New World Library 1999).

Audiotapes and Videotapes

The DHARMA SEED TAPE LIBRARY, http://www.dharmaseed.org/, offers a variety of audiotapes and videotapes, including some intended for beginners.

MINDFULNESS MEDITATION PRACTICE TAPES with Jon Kabat-Zinn, Saki Santorelli, Melissa Blacker, Florence Meyer, and others are available through http://www.umassmed.edu/cfm.

CHAPTER 16

Spirituality and Practicing Law as a Healing Profession: The Importance of Listening

*Timothy W. Floyd**

Lawyers and Brokenness

Lawyers are in the midst of the world's brokenness in unique ways. The very nature of legal problems implies broken relationships. If lawyers are involved in a situation, it's usually because people are in conflict with each other, or at least feel a need to protect themselves in anticipation of conflict in a relationship. Marriages and families fall apart; someone has been injured on the job or on the highway; employees believe that they are not treated fairly by their employer; crimes of violence are committed that shock and divide a community; long-standing business and commercial relationships come to an end; surviving family members battle over the property left by a loved one. People turn to lawyers to manage and resolve these conflicts that derive from broken relationships. Moreover, lawyers often deal with the individual manifestations of that brokenness: people who seek legal counsel are often wounded—sometimes physically, often psychologically and emotionally—by the events that gave rise to the legal problem.

---

* Professor of Law and Director, Law and Public Service Program, Mercer University Walter F. George School of Law.

At their best, lawyers can be agents of healing and reconciliation. It is possible to practice law in ways that heal our brokenness—but it is rare. Too often lawyers and the legal system aggravate the brokenness in the situation. Practicing law in healing ways is a daunting task because it goes against the grain of prevailing modes and conceptions of practice. Indeed, to practice law in healing ways raises spiritual issues and requires spiritual practices.

Healing of our brokenness is a deep spiritual need, and whether and how we can practice law as a healing profession is a deeply spiritual issue. The word healing resonates with the deepest longings of our souls, because healing is a deep spiritual need—on a personal level and collectively in our relationships with each other. Healing appeals to us because we know that we are broken and in need of healing.

When we look around us, we cannot escape the realization that we live in a broken world. Global conflicts rage, and the atrocities that people inflict on one another are staggering. Closer to home, our communities are marked by pain and injustice. Even (perhaps especially) in our families, we hurt each other physically and emotionally. Many people around the world suffer from scarcity and deprivation, while other people waste food and other resources. Our relationship with the environment is broken: fragile ecosystems are ravaged by short sighted exploitation and finite resources are consumed at alarming rates.

The brokenness also manifests in our individual lives. We are alienated from our true selves; we look for meaning and validation in consumerism and materialism; we numb ourselves with substances; we rarely experience deep joy, and when we do the experience is all too fleeting; in our fear and pain, we feel the pull of violence and hatred.[1]

Religious faith and spirituality embody the belief that this brokenness is not the way the world is meant to be. Thomas Merton claimed that "there is in all things ... a hidden wholeness." [2] Spirituality recognizes our connections to each other and to all of creation. People are meant to live together in peace

---

1. Obviously most of us don't kill or engage in acts of violence directly. But we subscribe to the myth that violence is redemptive, turning to military might and capital punishment to make us secure and save us from harm. *See* WALTER WINK, ENGAGING THE POWERS: DISCERNMENT AND RESISTANCE IN A WORLD OF DOMINATION 13–30 (1992) (Volume Three of the Powers Trilogy), in which he explores—and debunks— the "myth of redemptive violence."

2. PARKER PALMER, A HIDDEN WHOLENESS: THE JOURNEY TOWARD AN UNDIVIDED LIFE 4 (2004) [hereinafter HIDDEN WHOLENESS].

and justice. And we are also created to have wholeness within ourselves: we are meant to experience fulfillment in this world and to realize our deepest hopes and dreams.

A central part of the religious impulse among human beings is the drive to find wholeness in the midst of the world's brokenness. The word "religion" is derived from the Latin *religare*, "to bind together." Our spirituality is based upon trust that the brokenness in the world is not the way things are meant to be; it is trust that, despite the outward evidence, at its deepest level our existence has a hidden wholeness. Religious faith insists that the brokenness we experience in our lives is not indicative of ultimate reality.

Flowing from the spiritual insight that brokenness is not what should be, our faith traditions call us to bind together that which has been estranged and alienated. In my own Christian tradition, we are called to heal the brokenness through concrete acts of feeding the hungry, clothing the naked, comforting the sick, and visiting the prisoner.[3] Judaism calls upon people to engage in Tikkun Olam—to engage in acts of social justice to repair the world's brokenness.[4] Likewise, it is a fundamental tenet of Islam that Muslims are to restore right relationships, with God and with other human beings.[5]

In this chapter, I use the framework of *listening* to explore spirituality and the practice of law as a healing profession. In this regard, listening is a spiritual practice; it includes the ideas of paying attention, of seeing clearly, of understanding deeply, and of reaching out in empathy and understanding.[6]

I'll discuss listening in two senses: of "listening to our lives" and of listening to others. It is crucial for lawyers to "listen to their lives"—to listen for the inner voice of vocation that calls us to bring our souls and our roles as lawyers into harmony, and to pay attention to what is going on around us to discover possibilities of healing and reconciliation in our work as lawyers. Moreover, it is essential to engage in deep attentive listening to clients and other persons involved in legal problems. Deep listening and understanding is a profoundly spiritual act and perhaps the most healing act we can do in our work as lawyers.

---

3. *Matthew* 25: 31–46.

4. Wayne D. Dosick, Living Judaism: The Complete Guide to Jewish Belief, Tradition, and Practice 37–50 (1998).

5. Feisal Abdul Rauf, What's Right with Islam 11–40 (2004).

6. Accordingly, "listening" as I use the term has much in common with Buddhist practice. *See, e.g.,* His Holiness The Dalai Lama, An Open Heart: Practicing Compassion in Everyday Life (2001).

Listening to our Lives

Listening for the Voice of Vocation

Many enter the legal profession with the hope of making a difference for the better in the world. Many students enter law because they want to contribute to peace, justice, and reconciliation. All too often, those hopes and dreams are dashed in the first year of law school. In law school students soon learn that caring about the people involved in legal problems is "naïve" and that social justice and social change are not highlighted in the standard curriculum of law schools. Students are taught that hard headed realism and cold analytical reasoning are the lawyer's stock in trade. Of course dispassionate reasoning and analysis is a strength of the legal profession—the problem comes when law students and lawyers believe that people and their relationships, their pain and their joy, are not important.

There is a tremendous amount of distress in lawyers and law students. Rates of clinical depression and other psychological disorders and of alcohol and other substance abuse are markedly higher among law students and lawyers than among the general population.[7] Many express dissatisfaction with their career choice and large numbers are leaving the profession. I'm convinced that for many this distress is the result of disillusionment, of believing that we cannot practice law consistently with who we really are at our deepest levels. Some law students and lawyers are concerned that doing what the legal profession requires will cause them to compromise or betray fundamental values. They worry that they might gain the world but lose their souls.[8]

In order to practice law as a healing profession, we must have hope that our efforts as lawyers can make a difference. We should see our work as a calling, a vocation. To believe that our work is a vocation is to insist that our work has meaning beyond acquiring money, status, prestige, and power.

The work of the novelist, essayist, and minister Frederick Buechner and of educator and writer Parker Palmer is helpful on issues of vocation. Both insist that we can find work that makes a contribution to the world's need and also brings deep personal fulfillment, or, as Palmer puts it, that we can "join soul and role."[9] Buechner defines vocation as "the place where your deep glad-

---

7. See Larry Krieger, *Institutional Denial About the Dark Side of Law School, and Fresh Empirical Guidance for Breaking the Silence*, 52 J. LEGAL EDUC. 112 (2002).

8. *See Mark* 8:36.

9. *See* PALMER, HIDDEN WHOLENESS, *supra* note 2, at 13–29.

ness meets the world's deep need."[10] Unlike many discussions of vocation, which are oriented toward doing what we ought to do to serve the world, Buechner's definition starts with the self and focuses on our own fulfillment, while also emphasizing service to the world's needs. As Palmer states approvingly, this definition of vocation "begins, wisely, where vocation begins—not in what the world needs (which is everything), but in the nature of the human self, in what brings the self joy, the deep joy of knowing that we are here on earth to be the gifts that God created."[11]

The conventional concept of vocation insists that our lives must be driven by "oughts." The vocation that I'm advocating, by contrast, insists that we do not find our callings by conforming ourselves to some abstract moral code nor to what others tell us we should do. We find our callings by claiming authentic selfhood, by being who we are, by dwelling in the world as ourselves rather than as we think we ought to be. As Palmer puts it: "The deepest vocational question is not 'What ought I to do with my life?' It is the more elemental and demanding 'Who am I? What is my nature?'"[12]

Those questions of core personal identity require us to listen to our inner voice. Instead of the "oughts" and commands of external voices, we must hear the voice of the soul. Too many lawyers sacrifice the person they truly are at the deepest levels to do what they believe lawyers must do. Ignoring the inner voice, or living a divided life, is ultimately destructive. Vocation as listening to the inner voice, however, offers the possibility of "living divided no more" in the hope of uniting the deepest aspirations with the reality of work.[13]

For those who are concerned that this call to listen to your inner voice is self-indulgent, let me add that the authentic voice of vocation is anything but

---

10. FREDERICK BUECHNER, WISHFUL THINKING: A SEEKER'S ABC 119 (1993).

11. PARKER PALMER, LET YOUR LIFE SPEAK: LISTENING FOR THE VOICE OF VOCATION 16–17 (2000) [hereinafter LET YOUR LIFE SPEAK].

12. *Id.* at 15.

13. Palmer describes the journey toward the wholeness at the core of authentic vocation:

> What a long time it can take to become the person one has always been! How often in the process we mask ourselves in faces that are not our own. How much dissolving and shaking of ego we must endure before we discover our deep identity—the true self within every human being that is the seed of authentic vocation.... From the beginning, our lives lay down clues to selfhood and vocation, though the clues may be hard to decode. But trying to interpret them is profoundly worthwhile—especially when we are in our twenties or thirties or forties, feeling profoundly lost, having wandered, or been dragged, far away from our birthright gifts.

LET YOUR LIFE SPEAK, *supra* note 11, at 9, 15.

selfish or hedonistic; I'm not saying "if it feels good, do it." But I am saying, if after giving certain work in the world a fair shot, and engaging in honest and searching introspection, it does **not** feel good, don't do it.

As Palmer puts it: "Our deepest calling is to grow into our own authentic selfhood, whether or not it conforms to some image of who we *ought* to be. As we do so, we will not only find the joy that every human being seeks—we will also find our path of authentic service in the world. True vocation joins self and service."[14]

More concretely, there are certain practices that can help us listen for that inner voice of vocation:

- **Developing habits of reflection and contemplation.** The demands of preparing for class, of billing hours, of going to court, make practices such as meditating, praying, reading, and reflecting seem like luxuries. But making time to cultivate the inner life and to better understand ourselves is a necessity. Practices that lead to self-awareness and understanding should become habits.

- **Learning to distinguish the inner voice of vocation, purpose, and meaning from those external voices that tell us what we should do.** The external world tells us that rewards such as higher grades, more money, winning cases, or making partner bring fulfillment. If we really pay attention to our inner voice, we may just find that the satisfaction and fulfillment of service to others is deeper and more long-lasting than the satisfaction that we get from coming out ahead in the external measures of success. The joys that come from making a difference in someone's life are more satisfying than the temporary thrill of winning a competition.[15]

- **Taking time to remember to focus on purpose.** It is helpful to take time to reflect on why you decided to enter law school or the legal profession. An example: re-reading the law school application personal essay once a year can be a helpful reminder of purpose in the middle of the stresses and pressures of law school or law practice. Or writing down in a sentence or two why you came to law school and keeping those words in a conspicuous place.

---

14. *Id.* at 16.

15. *See generally* Lawrence S. Krieger, *What We're Not Telling Law Students—and Lawyers—That They Really Need to Know: Some Thoughts-In-Action Toward Revitalizing the Profession From Its Roots*, 13 J.L. & HEALTH 1 (1998–99).

Listening for Opportunities for Healing and Reconciliation

In order to practice law as a healing profession, we must not only learn to listen to our inner lives. We must also learn to pay attention to what is going on around us. It is necessary to "listen to your life as a lawyer." I take the concept of "listening to your life" from the novelist, essayist, and minister Frederick Buechner. A consistent theme of his writings for years has been listening to our lives. "If I were called upon to state in a few words the essence of everything I'd been trying to say both as a novelist and as a preacher, it would be something like this: *Listen to your life.* See it for the fathomless mystery that it is. In the boredom and pain of it no less than in the excitement and gladness: touch, taste, smell your way to the holy and hidden heart of it, because in the last analysis, all moments are key moments, and life itself is grace."[16]

We lawyers need to "listen to our lives as lawyers" in order to see the hidden meanings and grace notes. My faith tradition tells me that when we listen to our lives, we are listening for the voice of God. How does God speak in our lives? God is not a puppeteer pulling the strings or a chess player moving the pieces. Rather, God is present in all our moments as one who always offers the possibility—even in the hardest and most hair-raising events—of new life, healing, and reconciliation.[17] "There is no event so commonplace but that God is present within it, always hiddenly, always leaving you room to recognize [God] or not...."[18] To use Buechner's analogy, God is the director who conveys to us from the wings how to play the roles given us in a way "to enrich and ennoble and hallow the vast drama of things including our own small but crucial parts in it."[19]

If lawyers listen to their practice in this way, they may perceive tremendous possibilities for healing, peace, and reconciliation. Because lawyers work in the midst of conflict, they have the potential to bring about those goals as much or more than any group. To realize that potential, lawyers must be open to possibilities of healing and reconciliation in legal conflicts; they must pay

---

16. FREDERICK BUECHNER, LISTENING TO YOUR LIFE 2 (1992) (emphasis added).

17. God's offering of new possibilities is at the core of prophetic faith: "Do not remember the former things, or consider the things of old. I am about to do a new thing; now it springs forth, do you not perceive it? I will make a way in the wilderness and rivers in the desert." *Isaiah* 43:18–19.

18. FREDERICK BUECHNER, NOW AND THEN: A MEMOIR OF VOCATION 3 (1983).

19. BUECHNER, LISTENING TO YOUR LIFE, *supra* note 16, at 323.

attention to what is going on, and perceive how to play their roles in ways that lead to healing and to peace.[20]

But remaining open to those possibilities is especially difficult in our current legal culture. The modern American legal system is characterized by unproductive conflict that creates a spiral of alienation and distrust. Fear and hostility dominate the litigation process. The costs in hours, dollars, aggravation, and humiliation are great. The prevailing paradigm is competitive and adversarial and assumes a zero-sum game in which one party can achieve its interests only at the expense of another party. Seeking cooperative and collaborative resolutions in this prevailing culture is swimming upstream against a hard current. Lawyers and their clients are often perceived as lying and engaging in other repugnant behavior.[21]

But there are alternative visions of new ways to practice that bring about healing rather than further division. This book itself, and the skills and competencies described in the book, is powerful evidence of that movement and those possibilities. Many examples of this new vision exist. To list a few:

- Therapeutic jurisprudence, which is the "study of the role of the law as a therapeutic agent." It focuses on the law's impact on emotional life and on psychological well-being. Therapeutic jurisprudence focuses on this previously underappreciated aspect, humanizing the law and concerning itself with the human, emotional, and psychological side of law and the legal process.[22]
- Collaborative law, in which both parties agree to forego litigation as a vehicle for resolving the conflict, and also utilize multi-disciplinary teams of professionals to take a holistic view of the conflict and possible resolutions.[23]

---

20. Paying attention is also a central ethical issue. The great Protestant moral theologian H. Richard Niebuhr insisted that the primary moral question is not "what is good or right?" or even "what should I do?" Rather, the first question in ethics should be "What is going on?" Paying close attention, truly understanding what is going on and understanding the people involved, is essential to acting morally.

21. In WHY LAWYERS (AND THE REST OF US) LIE AND ENGAGE IN OTHER REPUGNANT BEHAVIOR (1998), Mark Perlmutter has eloquently described the pathologies that are generated by the unproductive conflict of our litigation system. His book also offers much hope: he describes possibilities of engaging in cooperation and healing in litigation.

22. See, e.g., supra Introduction at pp. xxiv–xxvi; ch. 11: Bruce J. Winick, Overcoming Psychological Barriers to Settlement: Challenges for the TJ Lawyer at pp. 341–42.

23. See infra ch. 8: Pauline H. Tesler, Collaborative Law: Practicing Without Armor, Practicing With Heart.

- Transformative or understanding-based mediation, (as described by Bush and Folger in *The Promise of Mediation*,[24] and as practiced by Gary Friedman and Jack Himmelstein, at the Center for Mediation in Law[25]) in which the primary goal is not to reach a settlement of the parties' differences, but to help the parties better understand each other and reach their own resolution of the conflict.

Perhaps most impressive are examples from the criminal context, the arena in which I work and am most familiar. One might expect that criminal law is the most difficult area of law in which to find possibilities of reconciliation and healing, but even here the new field of restorative justice has changed the way many think about criminal law and has gained a foothold in the administration of criminal justice in many places. Restorative justice is a framework that views criminal law through a new lens: rather than focusing on punishing offenders who violate the state's rules (and a corresponding focus on the rights of the accused), restorative justice emphasizes the harm done to persons and the community and seeks ways to restore relationships that have been broken by criminal acts.[26]

Concrete examples of new visions of healing in the criminal justice system include:

Victim Offender Conferencing. Many prosecutors' offices include a victim/witness unit to keep victims informed, and to assist with victims' needs. Some prosecutors, including those in Minneapolis, Des Moines, and Milwaukee, are also moving toward a restorative justice practice called Victim-Offender Conferencing (VOC), which allows a victim and offender to meet in a safe setting to actively explore the impact and effect of the crime on their lives.[27] Although the VOC is run by a trained facilitator, it is not a mediation;

---

24. ROBERT BARUCH BUSH & JOSEPH FOLGER, THE PROMISE OF MEDIATION: RESPONDING TO CONFLICT THROUGH EMPOWERMENT AND RECOGNITION (1994).

25. *See* The Center for Mediation in Law, *at* www.mediationinlaw.org (last visited Mar. 12, 2006) (in which the directors of the center describe their "understanding-based" model of mediation).

26. *See* HOWARD ZEHR, CHANGING LENSES: A NEW FOCUS FOR CRIME AND JUSTICE (1990) and HOWARD ZEHR, THE LITTLE BOOK OF RESTORATIVE JUSTICE (2002). Zehr is often called the father of the restorative justice movement. *See also* Ellen Waldman, *Healing Hearts or Righting Wrongs?: A Meditation on the Goals of "Restorative Justice,"* 25 HAMLINE J. PUB. L. & POL'Y 355 (2004).

27. David Lerman, an Assistant District Attorney and the coordinator of the Milwaukee County Community Conferencing Program, is one such prosecutor. His article, *Restoring Dignity, Effecting Justice*, describing VOC can be found in 26 HUM. RTS. Q. 20–21, *passim* (Fall 1999) or online, *at* http://www.abanet.org/irr/hr/fall99humanrights/lerman.html

there is not a presumption that the parties have equal rights and responsibilities. Rather, there is an understanding that one party has been wronged, and that the other is there to accept responsibility. The VOC allows the victims to ask questions such as "Why me?" and "How did you get in?" Offenders in turn, learn the real human consequences of their actions. In addition, the VOC enables community members to convey the moral outrage of the community.

During a VOC, it is common for the offender to apologize directly to the victim. Sometimes a victim will forgive the offender for committing the act, although this is never a requirement. Generally, an agreement is reached as to how the offender can repair the harm done, which often includes a plan for the offender to gain skills that will reduce the likelihood of recidivism. VOC can occur at any point in the criminal justice process: a conference can be held after a plea, but before sentencing; before a plea, with contemplation of a dismissal or reduced charges on successful completion of the agreed-upon plan; or several years after a criminal act, while the offender is imprisoned.

Storytelling is a powerful theme in VOC, allowing victims and offenders to tell the stories of what happened and the impact of criminal wrongdoing on them and others in the community. By focusing on harm, harm reduction, and accountability, as opposed to simply finding guilt and meting out punishment, restorative justice practices such as VOC foster understanding of the human consequences of crime and builds human relationships. As David Lerman describes the consequences: "This is naturally empowering. Victims are empowered because they feel less fear, which transforms the cycle of fear into an opportunity for hope. The community is empowered because it does not lose an individual to isolation and alienation. Offenders too are empowered by the realization that they are not being treated as throw-away people."[28]

The Georgia Justice Project describes itself as "an unlikely mix of lawyers, social workers, and a landscaping company."[29] GJP defends people accused of crimes and, win or lose, stands with its clients while they rebuild their lives, in the belief that this is the only way to break the cycle of crime and poverty.

(last visited Mar. 12, 2006). My description of VOC is taken largely from Mr. Lerman's article.

28. *Id.*

29. *See* Brenda Sims Blackwell & Clark D. Cunningham, *Taking the Punishment out of the Process: From Substantive Criminal Justice Through Procedural Justice to Restorative Justice*, 67 LAW & CONTEMP. PROBS. 59 (2004) (describing the history and mission of the Georgia Justice Project); *see also* the website of GJP: www.gjp.org (last visited Mar. 12, 2006) (containing a comprehensive description of the mission and structure of the Georgia Justice Project).

GJP ensures justice for the indigent criminally accused by providing them with the same quality of legal representation usually only afforded those who can hire their own lawyers, but it also provides much more. GJP carefully selects which clients and cases it takes on, and agrees to represent indigent individuals accused of crimes only if those individuals are willing to work, accept counseling or treatment, and pursue job training or educational opportunities so that they will be better equipped to live more productive lives once their legal problems are behind them.

The staff of GJP includes social workers and drug treatment counselors who work with the clients of the office. In addition, GJP operates New Horizon Landscaping, which is a vital component of GJP's mission. The landscaping company provides an employment opportunity for many GJP clients. NHL enables GJP clients to learn valuable skills that they can take into the market place as well as providing them with a means to establish a credible employment history. Without the landscaping company, the prospects for gainful employment for many GJP clients after their legal troubles are behind them would be bleak. The recidivism rate for GJP clients is less than one-third the national average (18.8% compared to the national average of over 60%).[30]

Victim-Based Defense Outreach: Defense attorneys who represent the accused in criminal cases increasingly are recognizing the potential of the adversarial process to re-traumatize victims. To assist defense teams in capital cases in reaching out to survivors, capital defense lawyer Richard Burr and Tammy Krause and Howard Zehr of Eastern Mennonite University have developed a process of defense-based survivor outreach founded on the principles of restorative justice. This process asks the following questions: (1) Who was hurt? (2) What are their specific needs? and (3) Who is obligated to meet their needs? Rather than simply trying, convicting, and punishing the defendant, this framework expands the focus of the criminal prosecution to address the judicial needs of survivors, to allow for cooperation between the defense and the prosecution that may benefit survivors, and to include expressions of offender accountability.[31]

---

30. *See* http://www.gjp.org/about (last visited Mar. 12, 2006).

31. For descriptions of defense-based victim outreach and of the program at Eastern Mennonite University, see Richard Burr, *Litigating with Victim Impact Testimony: The Serendipity that has Come from Payne v. Tennessee*, 88 CORNELL L. REV. 517 (2003), and Kristen F. Grunewald & Priya Nath, *Defense-Based Victim Outreach: Restorative Justice in Capital Cases*, 15 CAP. DEF. J. 315 (2003). *See also* the website of the program at EMU, called JustBridges: http://www.emu.edu/ctp/justbridges.html (last visited Mar. 12, 2006).

The defense-based outreach to survivors that comes from this framework asks two basic questions of survivors: (1) What is most important to you? and (2) What are your needs within the judicial process? As Burr states,

> From these modest inquiries can arise a range of potential benefits for survivors. For example, survivors may:. gain formal introduction to defense team members, thereby overcoming the first and in many ways most formidable barrier produced by the adversarial process;. receive timely information about upcoming hearings and dates;. learn about the judicial process and the possible roles survivors can play;. get answers to at least some of their questions about the case and the crime;. gain opportunities to talk with others about the victim in a variety of settings;. identify and articulate their judicial needs;. decide which track—trial or guilty plea—best serves their interests;. meet with defense attorneys and, in appropriate situations, the offender;. encourage plea agreements that take their interests and needs into account.[32]

In a recent plea agreement in a highly publicized federal death penalty case, the family of the murder victim wanted to avoid trial, believing that it would be too traumatic, and they wanted to avoid the years of appeal and post-conviction review that would follow if the offender were sentenced to death. The defendant was willing to plead guilty in exchange for a sentence of life without the possibility of release. The survivors had other needs, including a desire that the defendant stop making public statements or giving interviews about the case, that the defendant be cut off from the possibility of any personal financial gain from selling the film or literary rights to the story of his case, and that, should they choose, they would have the opportunity to meet the defendant with a third-party facilitator present. In large part through the efforts of defense-based victim outreach, the plea agreement incorporated all these elements.[33]

The possibilities of healing alternatives in law practice are already taking shape in various ways, but they cut against the grain of prevailing cultures of hostility and distrust. Taking a holistic approach to criminal representation or reaching out to the victims in murder cases, for example, both run very much counter to the prevailing mindset of criminal litigation. Alternative ways of

---

32. Burr, *supra* note 31, at 51–52.
33. *Id.* at 52.

practice depend upon our faith in the possibility of new ways, and upon our courage in acting upon that faith. Although he is discussing nonviolence in a violent world, Parker Palmer's insights apply as well to practicing law in healing ways in an adversarial and destructive legal system:

> The bad news is that violence is found at every level of our lives. The good news is that we can choose nonviolence at every level as well. But what does it mean, in specifics, to act nonviolently? ... In particular, we must learn to hold the tension between the reality of the moment and the possibility that something better might emerge.... The insight at the heart of nonviolence is that we live in a tragic gap—a gap between the way things are and the way we know they might be. It is a gap that never has been and never will be closed. If we want to live nonviolent lives, we must learn to stand in the tragic gap, faithfully holding the tension between reality and possibility.[34]

Practicing law in healing ways requires us to stand faithfully in that tragic gap between reality and possibility. We can stand there, but only if we have vision that there is a reality of peace, justice, and reconciliation that is deeper and more real than the conflicts in which we are immersed. [35] Faith is not the same thing as certainty; indeed, certainty can be the enemy of faith. And it doesn't mean we won't have moments of doubt.[36] Faith does require a vision of things not readily apparent, it requires risk in the midst of uncertainty, and it requires courage to act on that vision. It takes vision like that of Martin

---

34. Parker Palmer, A Hidden Wholeness, *supra* note 2, at 175.

35. The prophet and poet known as Second Isaiah (who wrote from the darkness of exile) expressed this hope:
> Why do you say, O Jacob, and speak, O Israel, "My way is hidden from the LORD, and my right is disregarded by my God"? Have you not known? Have you not heard? The LORD is the everlasting God, the Creator of the ends of the earth. He does not faint or grow weary; his understanding is unsearchable. He gives power to the faint, and strengthens the powerless. Even youths will faint and be weary, and the young will fall exhausted; but those who wait for the LORD shall renew their strength, they shall mount up with wings like eagles, they shall run and not be weary, they shall walk and not faint."

Isaiah 40:27–31.

36. Doubt can, and usually does, coexist with faith; as the father of an ill son said to Jesus: "Lord, I believe; help my unbelief." *Mark* 9:24.

Luther King, Jr., who in the teeth of brutal injustice and oppression insisted that "the moral arc of the universe is long but it bends toward justice."[37]

Listening to Clients and Others in Legal Conflict

Listening for the inner voice of vocation and listening for possibilities of healing and reconciliation in our work are essential to practicing law in healing ways. But if we are to practice law as a healing profession, it's not just a matter of our inner lives. Even more important are our relationships with people, in reaching out in compassion and understanding. The law always concerns relationships among people, and at its best attempts to help them live together harmoniously and helps to heal conflicts when they arise.

Once again, the idea of listening provides my framework. But this time I mean listening in a more traditional sense. Lawyers must listen—pay close attention—to the people involved in legal problems. That includes first and foremost the persons to whom lawyers are closest, their clients. It also requires paying attention to the other people involved in clients' disputes, including those the legal system views as adversaries. Reaching out in understanding and empathy is the essential in healing our brokenness. And, deep attentive listening is the key to such understanding.

William Stringfellow, lawyer, theologian, and activist, insists that: "Listening is a primitive act of love in which a person gives himself to another's word, making himself accessible and vulnerable to that word."[38] Reaching out to another in compassion and empathy is at the heart of the spiritual life. It is a form of love, but using the word "love" gives me pause. This kind of love is not emotional attachment or feelings of intimacy, and it's not a general yearning that we should all get along. Indeed, the love to which I refer is not a *feeling* at all. Love is action: paying close attention to a person, trying our best to understand that person, and taking action to respond to that person's needs. It's what the New Testament always refers to as *agape*, as opposed to *eros* (erotic love) or *philia* (brotherly love).

---

37. The phrase "arc of the moral universe" or variants on it occur throughout King's writing and speeches. *See, e.g.*, Taylor Branch, At Canaan's Edge: America in the King Years 1965–68, at 170 (1988).

38. *See* The Internet's Largest Collection of Quotations About Listening, *at* http://www.listen.org/quotations/morequotes.html (last visited Mar. 26, 2006) (This website attributes the quote to William Stringfellow's work titled *Friend's Journal.*).

Stringfellow's point is that if we truly listen to someone, if we listen with complete intensity, in a manner sensitive to her hopes and enthusiasms and which delights in her delights, and most importantly, that suffers when she suffers, we have loved that person.[39] Approaching clients in this spirit is a service to God through attentive, loving listening.

But this kind of listening doesn't come naturally or easily, at least not most of the time. Listening is not the passive response of not talking while another is talking. Genuine listening means suspending judgment and refraining from disagreeing or giving advice or talking about your own experience; it often takes a deliberate effort to suspend our own needs and reactions. "Temporarily, at least, listening is a one-sided relationship.... You need to be silent; you need to be selfless." [40]

Empathetic listening is the selfless setting aside of ourselves in order to understand another. According to Scott Peck: "An essential part of true listening is the discipline of bracketing, the temporary giving up or setting aside of one's own prejudices, frames of reference and desires so as to experience as far as possible the speaker's world from the inside, stepping inside his or her shoes."[41] Or, as the great fictional lawyer Atticus Finch put it, "You don't really know someone until you put on his shoes and walk around in them for a while."[42]

Deep attentive listening is difficult for all of us; it doesn't come naturally. It requires great effort, concentration, and discipline. Again, from Stringfellow:

> Listening is a rare happening among human beings. You cannot listen to the word another is speaking if you are preoccupied with your appearance, or with impressing the other, or are trying to decide what you are going to say when the other stops talking, or are debating about whether what is being said is true or relevant or agreeable. Such matters have their place, but only after listening to the word as the word is being uttered.[43].

---

39. For a beautiful meditation on Stringfellow and listening, see the sermon "Spiritual Poverty," at http://uumiddleboro.org/Previous%20Sermons/Sermons-2001/sermon%2005-06-01.htm (last modified Feb. 8, 2006).

40. MICHAEL P. NICHOLS, THE LOST ART OF LISTENING 64 (1995).

41. M. SCOTT PECK, THE ROAD LESS TRAVELED 127–28 (1978). Peck's chapter on "The Work of Attention" id. at 120–131, describes very well what I am trying to say here in the text.

42. HARPER LEE, TO KILL A MOCKINGBIRD (1960).

43. See The Internet's Largest Collection of Quotations About Listening, supra note 38.

Unfortunately, this kind of attentive listening is particularly difficult for lawyers. There are many barriers to effective listening in the practice of law:

- Lawyers' education and training condition them to evaluate, to judge, to make counter-arguments; what lawyers may think of as "listening" is often simply preparing their response.
- Lawyers are trained in law school to separate the relevant from the irrelevant, to spot the issues and ignore everything else. Much of what the client says would be irrelevant if the problem was a law school examination — and yet much of this legally "irrelevant" information is crucial to providing effective representation. We are taught in law school that feelings are irrelevant to legal analysis. But in the law office, feelings are facts. The client's feelings, motivations, relationships, and priorities can be even more important than the historical events that constitute the legally relevant facts.
- Lawyers tend to be competitive; as a result, many may have the urge to argue with a client, or to "one-up" the client's knowledge or experiences. This may happen without any awareness on the lawyer's part — but the client may feel it acutely.
- Lawyers, especially newer lawyers, are sometimes anxious about their own competence or ability to represent the client adequately. In their anxiety, they tend to talk in order to show off their own knowledge and expertise. Truly paying attention to the client then gets lost in the lawyer's talking.
- More experienced lawyers may believe that they have seen it all, that they don't have anything to learn from a particular client, or that all clients in particular kinds of cases are alike (e.g., "you've seen one child custody dispute you've seen them all"; or, "I know what an injured client needs without asking"). It is obvious that these assumptions prevent truly listening to the client.
- Legal problems almost always cause stress and anxiety for the client. This makes clients less likeable and harder to be with. In addition, clients in the midst of this stress and anxiety may look to the lawyer as their "savior" from all the problems that brought them to the lawyer in the first place. Lawyers are particularly ill-equipped to deal with such situations; they typically have little or no training in setting appropriate boundaries, in understanding transference and counter-transference, and even in knowing when and how to refer a client for professional counseling or therapy.[44]

---

44. *See generally* Marjorie A. Silver, *Love, Hate and Other Emotional Interference in the Lawyer/Client Relationship*, 6 CLIN. L. REV. 259 (1999); *supra* ch. 1: Marjorie A. Silver, *Emotional Competence and the Lawyer's Journey*.

Clinical law teachers have emphasized for years that effective lawyers must be good listeners. Truly listening to clients is essential to quality representation, and fortunately there are now many good resources available on skills and techniques of effective listening.[45] Listening is a skill that can be practiced and improved. Asking open ended questions, thoughtfully formulating active listening responses, giving appropriate nonverbal cues—all are essential skills that can and should be practiced.

But improved listening skills alone will not necessarily result in improved listening. Effective listening is much more than technique—it is an attitude, a motivation, a disposition. To listen to someone, we must suspend the interests of the self. We must suppress our own urge to disagree, exercise judgment, give advice, or talk about our own experience. As I've emphasized, it requires effort and concentration.

To put in that effort, lawyers must understand the importance of listening. Fortunately, there are payoffs. Lawyers are more effective lawyers when they listen, and listening enables lawyers and clients to find healing resolutions to conflicts. To be more concrete about the benefits of listening:

- Being listened to is itself therapeutic for the client. The great psychotherapist Carl Rogers insisted that there is great healing power for the client simply in being heard.[46] Although lawyers are not therapists, it is undeniable that the very act of listening, of paying close attention to the client, can be very beneficial for the client, especially in overcoming the isolation and anxiety that often accompany a legal problem.
- Having a lawyer who listens is empowering for the client. For many clients, not being heard is part of what brought them to a lawyer. When the lawyer doesn't listen, that aggravates the injury. But being heard, maybe for the first time, enables clients to take responsibility for their conflict and work out resolutions.
- Lawyers can better serve clients when they really understand the client. Simply learning all the facts can make a big difference. At least as important as the facts is understanding the client's goals and motivations. Listening is also more likely to make the representation helpful to the client. Instead of imputing ends to the client—assuming we know what the

---

45. *See, e.g.,* ROBERT F. COCHRAN ET AL., THE COUNSELOR AT LAW: A COLLABORATIVE APPROACH TO CLIENT INTERVIEWING AND COUNSELING (1999); DAVID BINDER ET AL., LAWYERS AS COUNSELORS: A CLIENT CENTERED APPROACH (2004).

46. CARL ROGERS, ON BECOMING A PERSON: A THERAPIST'S VIEW OF PSYCHOTHERAPY (1961).

client's needs and goals are—listening forces us to learn who the client is and what she wants and needs, including her deep hopes and fears that often get overlooked in standard conceptions of the lawyer's role.

- When the lawyer listens to the client, the client is more apt to listen to and trust the lawyer. Listening breeds listening. If the lawyer truly listens to the client and to the context, both the lawyer and client will probably be changed by the relationship. [47] Lawyers and clients who truly listen will grow in spirit; they will in turn be more open to possibilities of healing in practice. Together they are more likely to desire a healing resolution—and to be able to find one.

The listening I describe is also necessary in understanding the other parties in the conflict. Understanding the fears and anxieties, as well as the hopes and aspirations, of all parties to conflict is essential to working out healing resolutions. The empathy and care for the client I advocate is certainly client-centered, but that client-centeredness does not imply blind loyalty and zealous advocacy at the expense of third parties and the public. Most clients do not want to destroy their adversary. And understanding the other parties to the dispute—their motivations, their hopes, their fears and anxieties—is crucial to reaching a healing resolution.

The healing power of listening to a client was brought home to me in my recent representation of a person who was convicted of murder, sentenced to death, and ultimately executed in 2003. Although I've been a full-time law teacher for most of my legal career (over 25 years), I've also represented several persons who were defendants in capital cases. I have done this work in part because it resonates with the deepest longings of my own soul; I feel called to this work. There are stresses, trials, and tribulations involved in the work, to be sure, but I have found deep satisfaction in representing people who are facing the ultimate punishment. It would not be enough to sustain me in this work if I only did it because of my commitment that capital punishment is morally wrong or bad public policy; I'm convinced that one cannot do this

---

47. As Scott Peck puts it:

> Moreover, since true listening involves bracketing, a setting aside of the self, it also temporarily involves a total acceptance of the other. Sensing this acceptance, the speaker will fell less and less vulnerable and more and more inclined to open up the inner recesses of his or her mind to the listener. As this happens, speaker and listener begin to appreciate each other more and more, and the duet dance of love is begun again.

PECK, *supra* note 41, at 128.

work without the conviction that one is called to do it. And from that calling comes deep satisfaction from doing the work that one is meant to do.

But it was in my representation of this most recent client that I have best discovered the possibilities of practicing law as a healing profession. At some point in the representation, I forced myself to do the hard work of truly listening to this man. It was not easy to hear him express the anguish of his deep guilt and profound remorse for the brutal crime that he had committed. In fact, a part of him believed that execution was the appropriate punishment for him, but he was torn about that: he also had deep concerns about what would happen to his daughter if he was executed. For my part, I could not help but think about the young woman that he had killed—and the fact that I had a daughter about the same age. Since he spent eight years on death row and learned the stories of many other people facing execution—and several who were executed—we also had many conversations about the arbitrariness and unfairness of the criminal justice system.

Now, none of these feelings (his or mine) were legally relevant to the issues I was litigating on his behalf in direct appeal and post-conviction proceedings. Nonetheless, in the eight years that I represented him, I spent many hours just being with him and listening to the concerns of his heart.[48] We most often discussed matters that had nothing to do with the legal issues in his case; and we frequently explored issues of our shared religious faith. Some criminal defense lawyers I know have expressed concern to me that I let myself get "too close" to this client—that I should have stuck to the legal issues and not developed a personal relationship with him. Especially since we "lost" his case and as a consequence he faced the ultimate punishment, they believe that it is dangerous for the lawyer to care too much and to lose emotional distance. But I am convinced that the relationship we developed over those several years helped us both—lawyer and client—face the end of the case and the end of his life with courage and strength that we otherwise may not have had.

Despite the circumstances of his looming execution and the fact that he committed a brutal crime, I gained a lot from him: I drew from his spiritual wisdom and my own spirit grew over time. The case also caused me to step back and listen to my life, to see the notes of grace in unexpected and unlikely places, and to see possibilities of new life, healing, and reconciliation. He faced his execution with dignity, courage, and grace. And I was able to deal with the

---

48. Having said that, I would also insist that my listening to him, my getting to know him very well, did in fact make me a better advocate. Particularly in clemency proceedings, I was a more effective advocate because I knew so much about my client.

execution (which I attended and witnessed) with more strength and peace than I would have if we had not built a relationship through many hours of attentive listening.

And I gained much from the relationships that I developed with those in his life who loved him and stood by him until the end. Despite his execution, new possibilities of healing and reconciliation sprang forth for those who knew and loved him. I could not have been a part of that or contributed to it without deep attentive listening to him over the years.

Conclusion

I've emphasized two kinds of listening: of listening as self-reflection, as "listening to your life," and of listening as paying deep attention to another. But these are really two sides to the same coin. Listening to one's life, that is, engaging in self-reflection and awareness, is essential to truly listening to others, that is, to understanding and reaching out in empathy and compassion. For helping professionals such as therapists, counselors, clergy, and social workers, listening to others is central to the work. The education of the other helping professionals, however, focuses much more on self-awareness and understanding than does the education and training of lawyers. Those professions understand that truly listening to others requires a high degree of self-awareness. It is also the case that truly listening to another person helps us understand ourselves better.

Moreover, when we reach out to another in understanding and empathy, we satisfy the deepest needs of our own souls. Lawyers who listen grow spiritually, and lawyers who grow spiritually are better able to practice law as a healing profession.

CHAPTER 17

SOJOURNER TO SOJOURNER

Calvin G.C. Pang[*]

I write as a sojourner[1] and a struggler.[2] With respect to spirituality, it is the way I interact. I claim neither learned expertise nor enlightenment, but offer what I have, and receive what others offer. For me, much remains ineffable and mysterious about spirituality, and the limits in my maturity and understanding make it impossible to write with authority. Even on matters about which I am reasonably sure, my stabs at certitude leave me feeling glib.

To complete this chapter, I must write in part for myself. As such, it serves as an extended journal entry, a piece of reflection and self-processing. This

---

[*] Associate Professor of Law, William S. Richardson School of Law, University of Hawaii.

1. I think of "sojourner" as used by Professor Milner Ball in his work, *Called by Stories: Biblical Sagas and Their Challenge for Law.* In describing the primary guiding image in this book, Professor Ball mentioned Abraham, Moses, and John the Baptist as three who were chosen *to receive and go forth* with directives from God. MILNER S. BALL, CALLED BY STORIES: BIBLICAL SAGAS AND THEIR CHALLENGE FOR LAW 2 (2000). These "going forths" were coupled with God's promise of a productive return. All three men were, in Professor Ball's words, "messenger(s), representative(s), ambassador(s)," as well as "outlaw(s)," outsiders who were "passing through." *Id.* These men were "caught up in the going forth and returning of the word," and as such, were "sojourners." *Id.* Although sent forth and therefore "alien" to where they were sent, they were also embraced in their journey as they moved from one wilderness to another. These sojourners, according to Professor Ball, were "passing through," not "passing by;" because they remained "deeply engaged in the life that lies close at hand." *Id.* Like these sojourners, I see myself and others with our individual callings and directives, being sent forth with a promise of productive return. Our journeys challenge us to remain engaged with the people and experiences we encounter as we live out our calling and its purposes.

2. Alan Perry, a founding partner for a growing law firm in Mississippi, wrote a compelling essay to describe how he reconciled his "faith life" with his "professional life as a lawyer." Alan W. Perry, *Javert or Bebb,* 27 TEX. TECH L. REV. 1271, 1271 (1996). Mr. Perry began his essay by noting how words from "fellow strugglers" have had the most impact on his life. I found Mr. Perry's essay helpful because of the honesty and humility with which he wrote. As a fellow struggler, I found his words resonant.

will at least get the words out. I realize that I must also write for a reader, perhaps a fellow sojourner. I will share some of the things I understand, experience, have come to believe, and still question. Hopefully, some of this will engage, if not match a part of the reader's sojourn and reality.

What is spirituality? One mainstream dictionary defines it as "the quality or fact of being spiritual."[3] Fair enough—it would explain the slew of titles and phrases that begin with "the spirituality of" referencing the spiritual quality of a particular thing, whether it be an aspect of nature, a religious belief system, or Harry Potter.[4] Although I believe that all spiritual matters are ultimately linked, I will focus here on a personal spirituality, a person's "quality or fact of being spiritual." It is the way I think of and experience spirituality daily.

Harder still is defining "spiritual." In an earlier piece, I described the spiritual as a personal dimension that is in us whether or not we consciously give it attention, nourishment, or value.[5] It is as much a part of us as our more obvious physical, mental, and emotional aspects. As a wise colleague from my university's religion department told me, it is the "animating" dimension of our being, the dimension that enhances everything and makes our other qualities more vibrant.[6] Even when we let it lie quiet, it nudges, even gnaws, moving us to ponder our purpose and meaning and, ultimately, to locate and fit ourselves within a larger truth.[7] I do not mean to reduce spirituality to a concrete quality or a physical situs,[8] yet I know it by its tangible force and effect. While

---

3. THE RANDOM HOUSE DICTIONARY OF THE ENGLISH LANGUAGE 1840 (2d ed. 1987).

4. The Harry Potter series spawned at least two works dealing with spirituality. These include FRANCIS BRIDGER, A CHARMED LIFE: THE SPIRITUALITY OF POTTERWORLD (2002), and CONNIE NEAL, THE GOSPEL ACCORDING TO HARRY POTTER: SPIRITUALITY IN THE STORIES OF THE WORLD'S MOST FAMOUS SEEKER (2002).

5. See Calvin Pang, Eyeing the Circle: Finding a Place for Spirituality in a Law School Clinic, 35 WILLAMETTE L. REV. 241, 252–53 (1999).

6. Id. at 260 n.58. Indeed, the word "spirit" comes from the Latin spirare meaning "to breathe," the function fundamental and essential to life. JONATHAN KRAMER & DIANE DUNAWAY KRAMER, LOSING THE WEIGHT OF THE WORLD 40 (1997). The nexus between breath and life, and a view of breath as more than a physical life force is captured in spiritual traditions. Jews use the term ruah, to refer to "the breath" meaning the spirit of God that infuses creation. Id. Similarly, Taoists use the term chi which also means "breath," and is used to refer to a vital spiritual life energy. Id. at 41.

7. See Pang, supra note 5, at 257 (noting that spirituality is "the part of us that (1) sets us searching for meaning and purpose in life; (2) strives for transcending values, meaning and experiences; and (3) motivates the pursuit of virtues such as love, truth, and wisdom").

8. Others, however, have tried. See, e.g., Sharon Begley, Religion and the Brain, NEWSWEEK, May 7, 2001, at 50 (describing the field of "neurotheology" which posits a neurobiological basis of spirituality).

evanescent and hard to pin down,[9] it's there.[10] I once heard it described as the core in us that never gets damaged, providing an eternal font of confidence and hope.[11] Indeed, my religion department colleague recalled that in his volunteer work with the dying, he could always reach and administer to a spiritual core, even while the person's physical and mental faculties ebbed toward shutdown.[12]

I could spend much time and effort refining a definition for spirituality[13] but as writers Ernest Kurtz and Katherine Ketcham noted, it's spirituality that defines *us*.[14] In trying to encapsulate it, we discover our limitations; in seek-

---

9. As Ernest Kurtz and Katherine Ketcham put it, "spirituality slips under and soars over efforts to capture it, to fence it in with words." ERNEST KURTZ & KATHERINE KETCHAM, THE SPIRITUALITY OF IMPERFECTION 16 (paperback ed. 2002). They noted that in discovering "a helplessness before the very word," we experience "the powerlessness that is the necessary beginning of spirituality itself." *Id.* at 22.

10. Kurtz and Ketcham recounted a story in which students contemplating Lao-Tzu's dictum, "Those who know do not say; those who say do not know," asked their teacher for help in discerning its meaning. The teacher said "Which of you knows the fragrance of a rose?" Each student indicated his knowledge. But when the teacher asked, "Put it into words," all fell silent. *Id.* at 15 (endnote omitted).

11. Audio tape: Interview with John O'Donohue on "Embracing Beauty," by New Dimensions Radio Program #3084 (Mar. 23, 2005), *available at* http://www.newdimensions .org/NEW/audio-books/3084.shtml (last visited Feb. 11, 2006).

12. *See* Pang, *supra* note 5, at 260 n.58.

13. I find Professor Lucia Ann Silecchia's thoughts about defining spirituality to be most sensible. Professor Silecchia wrote:

Defining spirituality is a task far better suited to philosophers and theologians than lawyers ... [n]evertheless, a basic vocabulary for discussing spirituality is needed, and this may be the first challenge to those who would tackle spiritual matters in law practice, law schools or elsewhere. Arriving at a helpful vocabulary to describe the life of the spirit raises many questions including:

- What is spirituality as popularly understood and as defined in traditional thought?
- How, if at all, is spirituality different from religion, and what are the distinctions between these two interrelated but distinct concepts?
- How, if at all, is spirituality different from related but more tangible and familiar notions of ethics, service, or compassion—issues generally discussed in professional settings with much more freedom and unreserved approval than spirituality itself?
- What are the basic contours of different spiritual traditions and do these differences have an impact on the ways in which spirituality can best be integrated with professional life?

Lucia Ann Silecchia, *Integrating Spiritual Perspectives with the Law School Experience: An Essay and an Invitation*, 37 SAN DIEGO L. REV. 167, 175–76 (2000) (footnotes omitted).

14. KURTZ & KETCHAM, *supra* note 9, at 16.

ing to prove it, we learn that it is truer to say that it proves *us* in that our spirituality provides experiences against which we measure our humanness, or as Kurtz and Ketcham put it, "our human be-ing."[15]

Giving attention to the spiritual can be a challenge for lawyers. Our professional culture gives it little room to flourish. It begins in law school where intellectual rigor and rational thought dominate and are rewarded. Spirituality rarely if ever appears in classroom discourse and, while tacitly encouraged as a pursuit in one's personal life, spiritual development is purely "extracurricular," outside institutional requirements and deemed unimportant in the making of lawyers. Life and livelihood[16] curl away from each other like drying cardboard layers. In law school, if not before, a further separation occurs as we adopt a schedule of work frenzy that only gets worse for many who proceed to traditional lawyering jobs. The pace and quantity of work leaves little space for anything but work and consigns other dimensions of our lives to wherever we can find room for them. In the process, our spiritual side often becomes a casualty of inattention, gross neglect, or worse, conscious rejection. Lacking spiritual anchorage, we are without the means to respond to the despair—the despiriting—that overwhelming and unforgiving workloads and other professional demands visit upon us. The visible rewards of our profession—money, power, and prestige—provide some justification for the torrid pace, but they ultimately prove insufficient, and only distract us from receiving and responding to an internal knocking at the door.[17] A developing

---

15. *Id.*

16. The distinction of life and livelihood comes from Matthew Fox's work, *The Reinvention of Work*. In it, he argued that "life and livelihood ought not to be separated but to flow from the same source, which is Spirit, for both life and livelihood are about Spirit. Spirit means life, and life and livelihood are about living in depth, living with meaning, purpose, joy, and a sense of contributing to the greater community." MATTHEW FOX, THE REINVENTION OF WORK 1–2 (1994).

17. Believing that they were giving me the best education in Honolulu where I grew up, my parents sent me to two Roman Catholic schools. For years, I daily encountered various symbols of Catholic doctrine and belief—crucifixes, statuettes of Mary and a variety of saints, and pictures depicting the life of Christ. The one picture that stays with me is that of Jesus Christ knocking on a door. True to the way such pictures were drawn, Jesus was a handsome bearded man with fair skin, kind eyes, and flowing brown hair. To me, the picture had no meaning other than what it depicted: Christ knocking on a door. Only after many years had passed did I realize the picture's significance: that my God is always there ready to meet me if only I would open the door and let Him work in me. This doesn't keep me from ignoring the knocking even though I understand the importance of the one calling to me. Ignoring the knocking occurs for all the reasons I do not respond to any caller: I want to be left alone; I don't hear the knocking; I'm too busy or enamored with

work addiction and how it keeps us too busy and even too numb, further the estrangement between life and livelihood.[18]

Law is full of cleavings and classifications that create "others" from which we separate and grow distant. Even with best intentions, our work of ordering, reducing, discerning, clarifying, and focusing has the effect of slicing off, squeezing out, covering, and discarding. What drops off the edge of the table may well be a piece of our living truth, something that completes us even though we deem it inconvenient, undesirable, or impractical.[19] Not to say that what we do is inherently bad, only that the habits of our work keep us in the pattern of parsing and compartmentalizing even when integration and connectivity are more useful and deeply satisfying. Thus, the linking and blending of our spirituality into our work, a trying human task under normal circumstances, can even be harder for lawyers.

But try we must. Our challenge is, as Professor Joseph Allegretti wrote, "to link what [we] do on the job with [our] deepest values and commitments. [We] need to reconnect what [we] do on Monday with what [we] pray and profess on Sunday."[20] But how? As Professor Allegretti noted, "Too often spirituality ... has been seen as something you can do only if you *escape* your or-

---

what's before me; and I know who's at the door but for a variety of reasons — fear, dislike, shame, anxiety, irritation, lack of regard — don't want any part of Him.

The picture of Christ knocking was probably intended to illustrate the words of *Matthew* 7:7–8: "Ask, and it shall be given you; seek, and ye shall find; knock, and it shall be opened unto you: For everyone that asketh receiveth; and he that seeketh findeth; and to him that knocketh it shall be opened."

18. Fox, *supra* note 16, at 35. Fox suggests that the seductiveness and acceptability of work addiction allow it to flourish: "Everywhere I go it seems people are killing themselves with work, busyness, rushing, caring and rescuing. Work addiction is a modern epidemic and it is sweeping our land.... I call it the cleanest of all the addictions. It is socially promoted because it is seemingly socially productive." *Id.*

19. Professor Milner Ball alludes to this in his work, *The Promise of American Law.* Starting with Thomas Reed Powell's "notorious dictum" alleging that when "you can think about something which is attached to something else without thinking about what it is attached to, then you have what is called a legal mind," Professor Ball points to the "reductionist conversion" lawyers undergo starting in law school. MILNER S. BALL, THE PROMISE OF AMERICAN LAW 128–29 (1981). Professor Ball is not a pessimist, however, and drawing on the writings of Professor James White, he calls not only for the animation of our imagination, but the inspiriting of the heart. *Id.* at 137–38. In another work, MILNER S. BALL, THE WORD AND THE LAW (1993), Professor Ball devotes the initial chapter to describing the law-related practices of several individuals who work in an expansive, risky, lyrical, ultimately spiritual, and thus, spirited way.

20. JOSEPH ALLEGRETTI, THE LAWYER'S CALLING 4 (1996).

dinary life."[21] Popular author Robert Fulghum, on looking over his busy life, which included 35,000 hours for eating, 2,508 hours brushing his teeth, 30,000 hours waiting in traffic, 217,000 hours at work, and 870,000 hours coping with odds and ends, figured that, "There's not a whole lot [of time] left over.... The good stuff has to be fitted in somewhere or *else the good stuff has to come at the very same time we do all the rest of the stuff.*"[22]

Fulghum's point is well taken. Our spiritual lives need not be like a clay pot of summer flowers set on the back porch to be tended a few minutes a day. We can live them at the very same time we do all the rest of the stuff. I don't mean to suggest a facile remedy like diets that promise weight loss without altering lifestyle, activity level, or food choices. Nor am I devaluing periods of Sabbath when we are especially focused on the things to which our spiritual dimension turns us.[23]

I am suggesting, as others have, that in the course of living and working, we strive to become perceptive to the spiritual. In his book, *Work as Spiritual Practice*, Lewis Richmond noted that, "[t]he world is full of spiritual opportunity [and the] trick is to be alert enough to notice it."[24] Professor Allegretti referred to spirituality as an "attentiveness to the sacred in our life."[25] Frederic and Mary Ann Brussat premised their book, *Spiritual Literacy*, on the idea that we cultivate "the ability to read the signs written in the text of our experience" and in doing so, "discern and decipher a world full of meaning."[26] They described spiritually literate people as those able "to locate within their daily life points of connection with the sacred."[27]

---

21. Joseph Allegretti, *Neither Curse Nor Idol: Towards a Spirituality of Work for Lawyers,* 27 Tex. Tech L. Rev. 963, 964 (1996).

22. *Quoted in* Kramer & Kramer, *supra* note 6, at 33–34 (emphasis added).

23. Professor Allegretti characterizes spirituality as "*a person's orientation toward the divine.*" Allegretti, *supra* note 21, at 964 n.1. Keeping with my thought that spirituality is a dimension that does and affects things, I think Professor Allegretti's characterization to be apt to the extent that it refers to one of the most important, and for many, the most important function of our spirituality. It turns us toward the recognition of something bigger and better than our ordinary existence and uncovers the possibility of reliance, release, and redemption. This directive, orienting nature of our spiritual dimension is also noted by Kurtz and Ketcham who wrote that "[s]pirituality points, always, beyond: *beyond* the ordinary, *beyond* possession, *beyond* the narrow confines of the self, and—above all—*beyond* expectation." Kurtz & Ketcham, *supra* note 9, at 31.

24. Lewis Richmond, Work as Spiritual Practice 9 (1999).

25. Allegretti, *supra* note 20, at 5.

26. Frederic Brussat & Mary Ann Brussat, Spiritual Literacy: Reading the Sacred in Everyday Life 15 (1996).

27. *Id.*

Spiritual literacy doesn't just come, and even when we develop it, "we [can] lose track of it and [not] know how to find it, rekindle it, [or] nurture it."[28] It takes a certain discipline and willingness to discern. I lose my way daily, and recognizing my disability, find myself relying on my God to help me see His face and be mindful of Him. Yet I persist because an awareness of the spiritual helps me to see and filter things differently. At one level, things do not change. The phones still ring, deadlines loom, human misery remains the norm, adversaries threaten, and the day's busyness presses on.[29] However, at another level, everything changes. As Professor Allegretti noted, "the lawyer now *sees* herself in a different light[;] [h]er work has a different wider frame of meaning. It has a different orientation."[30] The scene changes not, but our lenses do, and this is what spiritual awareness provides.

As lawyers who place a premium on foresight as well as insight, our habits can make it hard to see the sacred in our ordinary lives. We race because our schedules demand it, and wear blinders to keep us aligned with and focused on specific destinations. This affects what we can see and easily averts our minds and hearts from the here and now. Joan Chittister makes the point with this exchange:

"Where shall I look for Enlightenment?" the disciple asked.

"Here," the elder said. "When will it happen?" the disciple asked.

"It is happening right now," the elder answered.

"Then why don't I experience it?" the disciple persisted.

"Because you do not look," the elder said.

"But what should I look for?" the disciple continued.

"Nothing. Just look," the elder said.

"But at what?" the disciple asked again.

"At anything your eyes alight upon," the elder answered.

"But must I look in a special way?" the disciple went on.

"No. The ordinary way will do," the elder said.

"But don't I always look the ordinary way?" the disciple said.

"No, you don't," the elder said.

"But why ever not?" the disciple asked.

---

28. RICHMOND, *supra* note 24, at 20.

29. *See* ALLEGRETTI, *supra* note 20, at 32 (In describing what happens to a person who finds his work embedded in a calling, Professor Allegretti wrote "At first glance, nothing changes. The lawyer ... still spends her time meeting with clients, doing research, drafting documents, and resolving disputes.").

30. *Id.* (emphasis added).

"Because to look, you must be here. You're mostly somewhere else," the elder said.[31]

Many engage in practices that keep them "here," and I consider these to be spiritual practices. Quiet prayer and journaling[32] are my vehicles. They pull me into the present, and in the case of prayer, into a Presence. I find myself having to be attentive and bearing an "interior disposition"[33] that releases me from the noise of pending projects and plans. It readies me to process and receive from a larger reality that's always in front of me if only I would "look."[34] Others use yoga, meditation, and mindfulness practice.[35] Steven Keeva, an *American Bar Association Journal* editor who regularly writes a section on life and law practice, described these as "paying attention in a particular way: on purpose, in the present moment and without judgment."[36] While these practices are technically things to do, they actually embody and connect with a *way of being.*

It's more than just "stopping to smell the roses," which reminds busy, driven people that simple natural beauty could touch us if we would slow down enough to perceive and partake in it. This message made popular in song and greeting cards, is not a bad one,[37] but there's a larger, more enduring piece. Be-

---

31. JOAN CHITTISTER, THERE IS A SEASON (1995), *quoted in* BRUSSAT & BRUSSAT, *supra* note 26, at 34–35.

32. Although I use journaling to reflect on things that already happened, it has a way of keeping me in the present. For me, what is "present" about journal writing is the *processing* I do. *That* act is in the present. It requires concentration and a willingness to stay with and examine not only what is before me, but also the larger deeper themes of my life.

33. *See* MARY ROSE O'REILLEY, RADICAL PRESENCE: TEACHING AS CONTEMPLATIVE PRESENCE 13 (1998).

34. Spiritual "viewing" is distinct from physical seeing. It is "an inner vision that looks at the world in a way that sees 'self' *in context.*" KURTZ & KETCHAM, *supra* note 9, at 69.

35. *See generally* Leonard Riskin, *Mindfulness in the Law and ADR,* 7 HARV. NEGOT. L. REV. 1 (2002); *supra* ch. 15: Leonard L. Riskin, *Awareness in Lawyering: A Primer on Paying Attention.*

36. Steven Keeva, *A Mindful Law Practice,* 90 A.B.A. J. 78, 78 (Mar. 2004).

37. I would even give it a spiritual quality. In developing their notion of spiritual literacy, the ability to see the sacred in everyday life, the Brussats created an "Alphabet of Spiritual Literacy" which consists of words beginning with each letter of the alphabet. Each word, such as "Attention," "Beauty," "Compassion," etc., encapsulates a spiritual practice which can give meaning to one's life. In the case of "Beauty," the Brussats counsel the reader to "[w]alk the path of beauty. Relish and encourage its inward and outward expressions. Acknowledge the radiance of the creation." BRUSSAT & BRUSSAT, *supra* note 26, at 19. I particular like the last sentence which not only recognizes the inherent good of beauty but pays attention to the fact of its creation. This acknowledges a source, a creator, and even a divine source, a "Creator."

yond being sufficiently present to receive gifts and the joy they bear, we need something that imbues these gifts with meaning. Spirituality and finding pieces of it in our daily life hoist us towards a glimpse of the possibility, and even better, the reality of something beyond the material and the obvious. In my case, it keeps me connected with my God and allows me to let His purposes unfold, though sometimes in unbecoming spurts. Having a sense of purpose in my work, of a specific calling,[38] and pausing often to let it reorient me through the day, I not only enjoy the metaphorical rose, but understand where it comes from, marvel at its creation and design, and receive it for the gift it is.[39]

Staying in the present and the ordinary to touch the transcendent also helps me to stay with myself and not escape my inadequacies. In our professional culture, we radiate an aura of competence and power which we learn to wear as naturally as a coat and tie.[40] The aura, however, can be as illusory

---

38. Others have written about their lawyer's work as a "calling," a sense, even a certainty of being called for a purpose determined by a higher being. Earlier, I mentioned Professor Joseph Allegretti's book *The Lawyer's Calling,* ALLEGRETTI, *supra* note 20, which is premised on attorneys being oriented and acting according to a calling to a higher purpose. Two other works I've found helpful include Professor Timothy Floyd's *The Practice of Law as a Vocation or Calling,* 66 FORDHAM L. REV. 1405 (1998) and John Cromartie's *Reflections on Vocation, Calling, Spirituality and Justice,* 27 TEX. TECH L. REV. 1061 (1996). *See also supra* ch. 16: Timothy Floyd, *Spirituality and Practicing Law as a Healing Profession: The Importance of Listening.*

39. My fundamental beliefs and understanding of the world makes apt the call for being present and attentive. I do believe what lawyer-lay theologian William Stringfellow once wrote: "Biblically, the Holy Spirit means that militant presence of the Word of God *inhering in the whole of creation.*" William Stringfellow, *The Secret of the Holy Spirit,* 58 WITNESS 4 (1974), *quoted in* Mary Lou Suhor, *Bill—Recollections of an Editor, in* RADICAL CHRISTIAN AND EXEMPLARY LAWYER 73 (Andrew W. McThenia, Jr. ed., 1995) (emphasis added).

My ability to see what inheres to the creation before me is a matter of tuning in. To illustrate, let me share a personal story. I pray while jogging. Often while praying, I begin to notice a breeze that sometimes blows so strongly that it roars in my ears and slows my already middle-aged pace to a standing dance. So frequently does this occur that I began thinking of the breeze as God's response to me. Maybe it is. However, it also got me thinking that these cool trade breezes, common in Hawaii, are already enveloping me well before I notice them. They remain off my radar until I center myself in the present which always occurs when I pray.

40. Working in Hawaii where temperatures infrequently dip below 70 degrees, complying with court rules by wearing a coat and tie is something I had to grow into. Early in my career, a federal magistrate threatened me with contempt of court when I failed to wear a tie to what I incorrectly thought would be an informal scheduling conference in his chambers. Now I always have the required "uniform" but leave my collar unbuttoned, tie down, and jacket slung on my arm until I'm close to the courthouse door. Even with these adjustments, I'm still warm but not enough to drip perspiration or appear red-faced. Thus, the

and transient as any external projection and when it goes away, imperfections remain, sore and exposed. An attention to spiritual opportunities helps me to accept my weaknesses and even construe them as gifts.[41] As Ernest Kurtz and Diane Ketcham wrote, "Spirituality which is rooted in and revealed by uncertainties, inadequacies, helplessness, the lack and failure of control, supplies a context and suggests a way of living in which our inadequacies can be endured."[42] "[F]ounded in the recognition of one's creatureliness and finitude,"[43] this spirituality of "imperfection"[44] provides release from the need for absolute control and unattainable perfection. Kurtz and Ketcham noted that in this release, we discover "the fruit of grace;"[45] in learning to receive from and rely on something beyond us, we cultivate an attitude of humility[46]

---

dignity and respect communicated by my coat and tie remain un-betrayed. An expectation of competence and confidence from clients as well as from ourselves is also *di rigeur* in our profession, and I venture to think we bring into any professional situation a mix of real and projected competence. At least on the "projected" end, the tricks are many: color and quality of clothes, framed diplomas and awards, a certain voice and texture of speech, and an emotional steadiness, to name some. But projections only go so far and so, on the hottest of days, when sweat and a red face are simply unavoidable, the coat and tie get exposed for what they are: keepers of body heat that wilt their wearers—all in the name of dignity.

41. As an example, I often compare myself to colleagues I consider brilliant and academically accomplished, and find myself wishing I could be like them. When I settle into a moment of honesty, I know that their "natural" gifts are not mine but that I have what I need to accomplish that to which I am called. Beside the fact that weaknesses can either cultivate or reveal strengths, or become strengths depending on how and when they are used, they bear messages on who we are, why we're here, and what we should be doing.

42. Kurtz & Ketcham, *supra* note 9, at 43.

43. *Id.* at 47.

44. *Id.* at 2. In introducing the spirituality of imperfection, Kurtz and Ketcham wrote:
[T]hrough the centuries, a recurring spiritual theme has emerged, one that is more sensitive to earthly concerns than heavenly hopes. This spirituality—the spirituality of imperfection—is thousands of years old. [I]t is the timeless, eternal and ongoing, for it is concerned with what in human beings is irrevocable and immutable: the essential imperfection, the basic and inherent flaws of being human.
Id.

45. *Id.* at 40 (quoting Caussade, 1 Lettres Spirituelles 96, 117 (1962)).

46. *See id.* at 185–96. Kurtz and Ketcham point out that humility does not demand responding to "Me First" by saying "Me Last," but instead, avoids comparisons. *Id.* at 188. They quoted Dag Hammarskjöld from his work, *Markings*: "Humility is just as much the opposite of self-abasement as it is of self-exultation. To be humble *is not to make comparisons*. Secure in its reality, the self is neither better nor worse, bigger nor smaller, than anything else in the universe. *It is*—is nothing, yet at the same time one with everything." *Id.* at 187 (endnote omitted). Humility advances self-acceptance by tempering our response to life's highs and lows: "when we are down, we need to get up; and when we are up, we

and gratitude.[47] This helps me to see and behave differently, and thus engage life, and by extension, the practice of law in a different way.

I am not alone in trying to locate my work within a larger journey, the specifics of which aren't always clear or readily discoverable. I find support and affirmation in hearing and reading the words of other sojourners, particularly those who are lawyers. Sometimes I am even lucky enough to meet one of them. I am grateful for two symposia in the 1990s, one at Fordham University School of Law,[48] the other at Texas Tech University School of Law,[49] that assembled attorneys, academics, theologians, and religious leaders to seriously consider the intersections, as well as the raw sometimes unforgiving tensions between faith, faith traditions, and the work of lawyers. While framed in the terms of faith and religion, these symposia delved into spirituality, both generally and in the individual lives of their participants. The Texas Tech symposium, in particular, gathered lawyers with visions, shaped by personal spirituality, that challenge, dictate, and ultimately alter their work to make it meaningful although not always easier.

---

need to remember that we have been, and certainly will be again, 'down.'" *Id.* at 193.

I very much like the story the authors recount about Lucifer, the great angel turned into Satan. Thinking himself above God's command for all angels to serve humans and worship Christ, Lucifer was cast out from Heaven and became a devil. Kurtz and Ketcham shared St. Augustine's observation that "It was pride that changed angels into devils; it is humility that makes men as angels." *Id.* at 188.

47. *See id.* at 175–84. I also like what Kurtz and Ketcham say about gratitude which they describe as "the vision that 'sees' gift and recognizes how *gift-ed* we are." *Id.* at 177. Conjoined with this sense of giftedness is a sense of release or surrender—surrender of claims and demand to control. *See id.* at 181.

48. Fordham University School of Law hosted "The Relevance of Religion to a Lawyer's Work: An Interfaith Conference," which sought to do two things: "develop ... a range of scholarly literature which would address systematically the range of theoretical issues raised by the existing religious lawyering literature[,]" and "bring together lawyers, judges, law professors, religious leaders, and theologians ... to develop agendas for further scholarship, teaching, bar programs, and congregational activities." Russell G. Pearce, *Foreword: The Religious Lawyering Movement: An Emerging Force in Legal Ethics and Professionalism,* 66 FORDHAM L. REV. 1075, 1077 (1998). An intriguing and enlightening array of voices follow the aforementioned cite.

49. Texas Tech University School of Law hosted the "Faith and the Law Symposium" which assembled "prominent persons from all sorts of legal specializations, professional roles, and career experiences ... [and] from many different religious traditions" to "reflect on how they have reconciled their professional life with their faith life." Thomas Baker & Timothy Floyd, *A Symposium Precis,* 27 TEX. TECH L. REV. 911, 911 (1996). As requested by faculty editors Thomas Baker and Timothy Floyd, the authors for this symposium submitted personal narratives, often using story-telling to convey the power and nuances of their messages.

One participant of the Texas Tech symposium was Dan Edwards,[50] an attorney and Episcopalian priest. His essay provides an example of how one's spirituality, often given form and traction by one's religion or faith tradition,[51] compels one to proceed with a vision, and thus, a path that may otherwise be hidden. His essay contains three short stories. Binding the stories is what Professor Howard Lesnick called "constituent qualities of a religious[52] outlook": obligation, integration, and transcendence.[53] By "obligation," Professor Lesnick meant a binding,[54] a sense of being impelled or led to act.[55] Of "integration," he described the "'connection between faith and work,'" where work becomes an expression, even an embodiment of faith.[56] About "transcendence," the most defining of the three, Professor Lesnick referred to "the more," a sacredness or holiness that is, at one level, apart from the mundane, and at another, so a part of it.[57]

---

50. Dan Edwards, *Reflections on Three Stories: "Practicing" Law and Christianity at the Same Time*, 27 Tex. Tech L. Rev. 1105 (1996).

51. *See* Pang, *supra* note 5, at 245–46, 254–55 (distinguishing spirituality from religion which I believe is a "framework or system of values and beliefs, often organized and institutionalized, that serves as a vehicle for spiritual expression and development"). *See also* Silecchia, *supra* note 13, at 176–77 (while eschewing a definition of spirituality, Professor Silecchia stated that spirituality is not religion, explaining that "[r]eligion, as commonly defined, entails a belief system with doctrines, explanations of the divine, and an established set of practices followed by its adherents to assist them in drawing closer to the divine.").

52. I construe these as "constituent" qualities of a *spiritual* outlook and use them thusly here. I don't think this strays too far from what Professor Lesnick contemplated. In developing and articulating these constituent qualities, he sought to encompass "qualities that ... virtually *all* religious perspectives share, across as well as within sectarian boundaries." Howard Lesnick, *The Religious Lawyer in a Pluralistic Society*, 66 Fordham L. Rev. 1469, 1472 (1998) (emphasis added). That he attempted to find universal qualities rather than ones more specific to particular faith traditions, suggests an attention to something bigger, more eternal than man-hewn institutions.

53. *Id.* at 1500.

54. *Id.* at 1473 (noting that "the words, religion and obligation, have a common Latin root, *ligare*, to bind").

55. *Id.* at 1475.

56. *Id.* at 1486 (quoting Thomas L. Shaffer & Mary M. Shaffer, American Lawyers and their Communities: Ethics in the Legal Profession 199 (1991)). Drawing on Professor Thomas Shaffer's work, Professor Lesnick alluded to another kind of "integration"—a community of people—which cultivates an understanding of the immersion, the integration of faith and work.

57. *See id.* at 1487–89. Quoting Mircea Eliade, a historian of religion, Professor Lesnick wrote, "the sacred manifests itself as reality, a reality 'of a wholly different order from "natural" realities.'" *Id.* at 1487 (footnote omitted).

In Father Edwards' stories, all three constituent qualities appear, in various forms and degree. These stories recount how Father Edwards felt bound to and moved by the sacred, or a sense of it, and how his response transformed him and thus his views and methods of work. They reveal what one sees and how one becomes "more" when attentive to the spiritual.

In his first story, entitled "The Jesus Prayer and the United States v. Alejandro,"[58] Father Edwards described his early spiritual journey which was characterized by struggle and search. In the midst of this journey, he was appointed to represent a person who had illegally re-entered the United States and owned a rap sheet over three pages long. The charges on the sheet were not minor and included child molestation and murder. Father Edwards recounted how he met the client in a sparse jailhouse cubicle lit only by a single naked bulb. A barred window separated them. The attorney-later turned-priest struggled to see "something of Christ" in the man before him, hoping to squeeze his still-forming faith into his encounter with this far too imperfect client.[59] At first, he hoped to see Christ in his client "but didn't truly believe" he would.[60] Then while observing his client's face and struggling through an interview made choppy by a language barrier, a short prayer came to him. It was "the Jesus Prayer"[61] which, during this period of his life, he had been saying "methodically, by rote, but not really getting anywhere with it." But at this instant, the prayer intruded "spontaneously and uninvited." It humbled him, and he found himself asking for forgiveness from the Christ he suddenly saw *in* the unfortunate Juan Alejandro.   Striking yet common is how spiritual attentiveness supports a vision of "the nobility of every human soul."[62] Clients are often the focus of this attentiveness, as they probably should be, in light of their normative role in our professional life. As those we serve, clients, more than any other group, should enjoy the most sympathetic turn of our lenses. Yet, they don't always get it because the demands on our attention, energy, and time either harden what we can see, or worse, move our eyes off the target. Thus, clients can become objectified, commodified, and otherwise processed for easier management. What I suggest is that spiritual at-

---

58. Father Edwards changed the names of all clients mentioned in his essay.

59. Edwards, *supra* note 50, at 1107.

60. *Id.*

61. Father Edwards describe the short prayer as an "ancient prayer practice of the Eastern Orthodox Church" which practitioners recite like a mantra: "Lord, Jesus Christ, Son of the Living God, have mercy on me, a sinner." *Id.* at 1106.

62. James F. Nelson, *The Spiritual Dimension of Justice*, 27 Tex. Tech L. Rev. 1237, 1246 (1996).

tentiveness brakes this tendency and restores at crucial moments the inherent worthiness and deservedness of the client. At best, it can "[get you] so deep into someone's life that you reach the place from which whatever the person had done, you could defend from your heart."[63]

Father Edwards did not tell us how Juan Alejandro's story ended or how his "vision" altered his approach to his client and the legal case. Since his point was to describe how this encounter radically kindled his spiritual search, he did not have to. The story, however, illustrates a lawyer finding the sacred amid fallenness, and how this discovery transformed him. Although his story did not detail the remainder of his journey with this client, his moment of revelation changed him and, in the process, likely changed how he lawyered. It would be akin to how Professor William Stuntz supposed Jesus Christ, worked as a carpenter. Professor Stuntz posited that Christ's tables were probably not different but were "*made*" differently.[64] He felt certain that Christ, whether one views him as deity or spiritual exemplar, made tables with motivations and attitudes that were different, treated his customers and coworkers differently, and simply practiced differently from carpenters who lived without spiritual awareness or behavioral standards expressive of one's spirituality.[65]

Indeed, Father Edwards wrote that his "living faith" necessarily entails a life of service, and that its key element is "that it is personal ... grounded in genuine care for the person served."[66] This was the point of his second story, "The Foot of the Cross: In the Matter of _____." This story concerned a client, Giles Woods,[67] who was charged with killing his ex-wife. Father Edwards represented him not in the criminal case but in a guardianship proceeding to determine who would legally assume the supervision and care of Woods' children. Woods' ex-in-laws sought this role, much to Woods' consternation about the care they could provide, and the likelihood they would alienate his children from him. However, because Woods was in jail and unable to effectively

---

63. Emily Fowler Hartigan, *Advocacy and Innocence, in* RADICAL CHRISTIAN AND EXEMPLARY LAWYER 125 (Andrew W. McThenia, Jr. ed., 1995). This may well be an extreme place to be yet there is something to this acceptance and thus vulnerability that a lawyer extends to a client. Quoting the writings of William Stringfellow, Professor Hartigan referred to advocacy's "most profound invitation and ... most forbidding requirement" to be "making oneself vulnerable in behalf of another, even upon death." *Id.* at 123–24.

64. William J. Stuntz, *Christian Legal Theory,* 116 HARV. L. REV. 1707, 1722 (2003) (reviewing CHRISTIAN PERSPECTIVES ON LEGAL THOUGHT (Michael W. McConnell et al. eds., 2001)).

65. *Id.*

66. Edwards, *supra* note 50, at 1112.

67. Another pseudonym.

offer an alternative to his ex-in-laws, his case proved challenging from the out-set. The result was predictably unfavorable, with the judge instructing the in-laws, who were appointed the guardians, to discourage contact between Woods and his children. The judge also advised Woods to "cease to exist in [his children's] lives."[68]

Father Edwards understood the significance of the case to his client, a worthy and sympathetic man despite his heinous mistake. Father Edwards understood that Woods loved his children despite killing their mother, and that the hope of reuniting and reconciling with his children would facilitate Woods' spiritual sur-vival. So, the judge's decision and stance were devastating. As Father Edwards wrote, "each of [the judge's] words was a nail in my client's hands and feet."[69]

At one level, Father Edwards felt the sting of failure, stating, "[i]f no lawyer had taken his case, the result could not have been worse."[70] However, with a spiritual lens,[71] he saw and understood something else. If all he could do was sit with Woods and "be his advocate and in some sense his friend," he would do it because compassionate ministry required it. He wrote: "I was not able to win Giles Woods' case; but I was able to care for him when so many peo-ple hated him, and I was at his side when he lost."[72] Maintaining a vision of his client's inherent worthiness, and advocating with a "genuine care for the person served," Father Edwards not only took Woods' case, but stood with him at the nadir, sharing what felt like a kind of death. Another priest once told him, "The foot of the cross is the hardest place to be."[73] Father Edwards stayed, and in so doing, not only saw and honored the wholeness of his client, but nurtured his own.

Of course, perceiving and responding to the wholeness of others extend beyond clients: judges, witnesses,[74] opposing parties and their attorneys,[75]

---

68. Edwards, *supra* note 50, at 1110.

69. *Id.*

70. *Id.*

71. Father Edwards wrote that "the narrative of my faith made sense of that experience for me; and, in fact, enabled me to play my part in Mr. Woods' story." *Id.* at 1112.

72. *Id.*

73. *Id.* at 1110.

74. *See* Samuel J. Levine, *The Broad Life of the Jewish Lawyer: Integrating Spirituality, Scholarship and Profession*, 27 Tex. Tech L. Rev. 1199, 1207 (1996) (describing a prosecu-tor's need to be concerned with the well-being of those who witness crimes and not to treat them as simply another piece of evidence).

75. I recall a state attorney general who was particularly stubborn about sticking to his position on evicting a client of ours. It was only after my student and I decided to remold our approach around our belief that the state attorney was a decent vibrant human being,

staff,[76] clerks, and everyone in between, even the difficult ones, can be viewed "from that place of inner innocence."[77] It was about a "difficult" one that Father Edwards wrote his third short story, "Evil as Springboard: State v. Selby." He characterized this case as one filled with "moral malignancy" and touched with a "sinister spirit." The "moral morass" left him gasping and moved him to search for a "world view which made sense of the senselessness."[78] Rather than sink him, the baseness of the *Selby* case launched him into a quest for "a story big enough to include such a cruel and cynical chapter without col-

---

did we make significant headway toward keeping our client housed. It was as if the attorney elevated himself to the level at which we placed him—and should have placed him at the outset. As my student pointed out, we did not get the better of him, but the better in him. For a more detailed description of this case, see Pang, *supra* note 5, at 262–64. *See also* Tom Matheny, *My Faith and My Law,* 27 Tex. Tech L. Rev. 1211, 1215–16 (1996) (recounting an encounter early in his career with a well-known experienced opponent in whom the author had enough faith and belief to reveal his inexperience and vulnerability—the opponent's response to the author was predictably noble).

76. In a story he entitled "The Case of the Coughing Stenographer," Michael Woodruff described how as a young attorney, he overcame an initial hesitation and interrupted a court proceeding to fetch a cup of water for a stenographer who was caught in the throes of a prolonged coughing spell. Although a simple gesture, it showed a refusal to let the coughing stenographer and her obvious human need disappear amid the strictures of court protocol, the solemnity of the ongoing proceedings, or the gross inaction of others in the courtroom. Michael Joseph Woodruff, *Lawyers and Sacred Gold,* 27 Tex. Tech L. Rev. 1411, 1412–13 (1996).

77. *See* Hartigan, *supra* note 63, at 125 (while grappling with advocacy for a difficult client, Professor Hartigan recounted a conversation with a senior litigation partner who responded by telling "stories of the damndest unlikeliest people whom he had come to see from that place of inner innocence"). Another view was provided by William Stringfellow who wrote:

> There is a boy in the neighborhood ... whom I have defended in some of his troubles with the law.... He is dirty, ignorant, arrogant, dishonest, unemployable, broken, unreliable, ugly, rejected, alone. And he knows it.... There is nothing about him that permits the love of another person for him. He is unlovable. Yet it is his own confession that he does not deserve the love of another that he represents all the rest of us in this regard. We are *all* unlovable. More than that, the action of this boy's life points beyond itself,..., it points to God who loves us though we hate Him, who loves us though we do not please Him, who loves us not for our sake but for his own sake, who loves us freely, who accepts us though we have nothing acceptable to offer him.

William Stringfellow, My People is the Enemy 97–98 (1964), *quoted in* Andrew W. McThenia, Jr., *An Uneasy Relationship with the Law, in* Radical Christian and Exemplary Lawyer 178 (Andrew W. McThenia, Jr. ed., 1995).

78. Edwards, *supra* note 50, at 1108.

lapsing into chaos and despair."[79] He ultimately found it. For Father Edwards, the "Christian narrative" which climaxes in the "grim victory of evil on the cross juxtaposed with the joyful mystery of Resurrection" became the story that made sense of the senselessness.[80]

In the "Selby" story, Father Edwards dwelled on the part of him that cried out for meaning amid the squalor of the case. This is the dimension of which I spoke earlier in this chapter. Even before we have a name, a conceptualization, or a vocabulary for our spiritual selves, it is already there, working, nudging, demanding, and even convicting. It sets us off to search as Father Edwards did, a search that yields discovery but not all the answers at once. For Father Edwards, his search kindled a Christian faith that eventually led to his ordination. For others, a different path may be cut.

Obligation, integration, transcendence. Receiving the unmistakable nudge—obligation, seeing and responding to work with new purpose and eyes—integration, and being transformed into "more" simply by being who we were meant to be—transcendence, are parts of the spiritual journey. As Father Edwards found, it is a walk, arduous and puzzling at times, that brushes us against "the moment-to-moment hurly burly of everyday life."[81] As sojourners we are "passing through," not merely "passing by,"[82] and the friction from ordinary human encounters, engagements, and exchanges often forms the context for, as well as the content of, our pilgrimage. Juan Alejandro, Giles Woods, and even the sinister Selby were part of the "common lot of humanity" within which Father Edwards searched for and ultimately found the sacred.[83] This is context. They were also his clients for whom he provided succor in a manner informed by a living faith. For them and with them, his "inner work"— working on that "large world within [his] soul"—shaped and gave meaning to his "outer work."[84] This is content.

Each was a "hard" client, troubled and disturbing, and yet it was just their fallenness that elevated Father Edward's consciousness of the spiritual and allowed "the more" to kick in. It helped that he was, as Professor Lesnick wrote, "[open] to awe, triggered perhaps by the apprehension of awesome power but

---

79. *Id.*

80. *Id.*

81. Lesnick, *supra* note 52, at 1489.

82. *See supra* note 1 and accompanying text.

83. Edwards, *supra* note 50, at 1112.

84. *See* Fox, *supra* note 16, at 20–21 (introducing the concepts of "inner" and "outer" work).

also by an 'appreciation of the possibility of meaning and moral order.' "[85] It also helped that he was a sojourner and a struggler, "straining forward toward mystery, toward a luminous darkness, toward an insatiated desire for a meaning beyond meaning."[86] It left him open to utter transformation.

Transformation is what I see daily in my work as a law school teacher. In three years, I watch students evolve into novice lawyers, in some cases, very good ones. That most succeed with this transformation is a tribute to their perseverance, intelligence, toughness, and I hope, heart. Yet there is another transformation that's troubling. As Professor Lawrence Krieger has pointed out, empirical studies consistently reveal how law students with initially normal psychological markers shift to major psychological distress by the first year.[87] This sets a pattern that persists through graduation and into post-graduation careers.[88] Professor Krieger described a "dark side" of law school culture that overly relies on objective analytical thought, and overly values external measures of success, such as high grades, academic honors, "prestige" jobs, and financial affluence.[89] Unwittingly or not, this undermines a "sense of self-worth, security, authenticity and competence,"[90] and what inheres to at least some of our graduates is a woundedness that erodes their choices, visions, and values.

In modest ways, I let students know that it is not only legitimate but necessary to give attention to their spiritual selves and be available to experience the spiritual in their day-to-day lives. For example, in my elder law clinic, I encourage my students to mine their work not only for facts and insights essential to developing their legal cases, but also for understanding how an elderly client's inclinations, motivations, and emotions arise from a weave of personal meaning and purpose. Thus, a simple advance health care directive will entail not just a mechanical recordation of competently rendered health care instruc-

---

85. Lesnick, *supra* note 52, at 1488–89 (quoting Daniel C. Maguire, The Moral Code of Judaism and Christianity: Reclaiming the Revolution 33 (1993)).

86. Laura Jones, *What Does Spirituality in Education Mean? Stumbling Toward Wholeness*, 6 J.C. & Character 1, 3–4 (2005) (quoting R.J. Nash, Spirituality, Ethics, Religions, and Teaching: A Professor's Journey 18 (2002)).

87. Lawrence S. Krieger, *Institutional Denial about the Dark Side of Law School, and Fresh Empirical Guidance for Constructively Breaking the Silence*, 52 J. Legal Educ. 112, 114 (2002).

88. *See id.* at 114–15 (noting that lawyers ranked highest in major depressive disorder among 104 occupational groups and show five to fifteen times the normal incidence of clinical psychological distress as well as high levels of substance abuse).

89. *Id.* at 114, 116–17.

90. *Id.* at 125.

tions, but also a quiet invitation to the client to discuss her instructions and choices in ways that reveal a larger search for significance and human worth. Thankfully, many clients oblige us with stories I suspect they have retold and refined to make sense of and find meaning in their long lives. In listening to these stories, my clinic students are disarmed.[91] In that moment of vulnerability they receive experiences and visions they would not otherwise have. If they can remember the word "spiritual," a term that is missing from law school vernacular, they will know what touched them and what is being touched. I hope that like Father Edwards, whose spiritual transformation often occurred in moments of vulnerability and even helplessness, my students will place their metamorphosis into lawyers within a larger spiritual transformation that comes when inner callings are identified and nurtured, when connections are forged between one's deep human core and one's work, and when sacredness is celebrated.

Our profession is not an easy one.[92] Its challenges and demands can overwhelm, demean, and destroy.[93] One response is to harden our hearts and ride on the material spoils available to many practitioners. But this is hardly living. Another response is to consciously allow the animating, integrating, and grandly sustaining part of ourselves—our spirituality—to work. It is there in each of us, ready to help us discern meaning in our work, indeed, in all of our

---

91. Authors Ernest Kurtz and Katherine Ketcham describe the storytelling tradition of Alcoholics Anonymous as forming a language of recovery that opens both the teller and the listener to "the experiencing of those [spiritual] realities we seek." KURTZ & KETCHAM, *supra* note 9, at 160. The use and receipt of language in storytelling shapes what is experienced, "mak[ing] it possible to *see*—and thus to *understand*—reality differently." *Id.*

92. *See* Ann Juergens, *Essay on Professionalism and Personal Satisfaction: Practicing What We Teach: The Importance of Emotion and Community Connection in Law Work and Law Teaching,* 11 CLIN. L. REV. 413 (2005). Professor Juergens began her essay thusly:

> Lawyers' work at its best is arduous. Its intellectual content is challenging, for lawyers contend with the rule structures that regulate the affairs of our civilization, its citizens and the market. Though less recognized, the emotional content of law work is at least as taxing as the cerebral, because lawyers deal with the effects of law on peoples' lives. At times the effect of law is to bring joy—as with the completion of a transaction, a vindication of rights or giving voice to the muted. Yet law is commonly engaged not with beauty, rather with problems caused by misunderstanding, greed and fear. Time and again, the effects of the law on peoples' lives are troubling, grief-filled or violent.

Id. at 413–14 (footnotes omitted).

93. *See* Krieger, *supra* note 87, at 114–15 (citing several studies ranking lawyers at or near the top of the list of professionals with major depressive disorder, suicide, clinical psychological distress, and substance abuse).

life activities. It helps us to locate our ordinary lives within, as Father Edwards found, an extraordinary transcending story.

Engaging our spiritual dimension does not make our lives perfect. It is not an anodyne. And while spiritual inquiry[94] produces forward movement and some answers, it is just as likely to raise more questions and deepen the mystery. Yet, the ensuing journey of discovery enriches and transforms us by returning us to a core primal reality that somehow links us. From this inner work comes external vision and hope; and from inner reflection comes, as Professor Lucia Silecchia wrote, "outward manifestation of the spiritual life in outreach to others."[95] Ours is a profession of service, and spirituality reminds us of where our service ethic comes from—not from an institutionally prescribed formula, but from a deep human, and perhaps, divine calling. Virtue moves from inside out.

Professor Silecchia used the word "invite" to move legal educators and lawyers to explore the integration of spirituality into their endeavors.[96] It is a gentle and respectful term, and I adopt it here. However, let it be understood that "invitation" exists on at least two levels: first, the one extended by Professor Silecchia, and second, in which the spirit inside us beckons and *invites*, and it is we who must receive and accept.

---

94. In an earlier work, I raised some of these questions: Why am I here? Why am I putting up with this, for what larger purpose? Where am I going and how did I get here? What is this all doing to me? Do I have it in me to get through this? Is there enough good in this to make it worthwhile? With whom must I connect to get through this? Pang, *supra* note 5, at 278–79.

95. Silecchia, *supra* note 13, at 186.

96. Professor Silecchia characterized her piece on integrating spiritual perspectives as "an essay and an invitation." Silecchia, *supra* note 13, at 167.

CHAPTER 18

THE GOOD LAWYER: CHOOSING TO BELIEVE IN THE PROMISE OF OUR CRAFT

*Paula A. Franzese**

I have come to the frightening conclusion that I am the decisive element. It is my personal approach that creates the climate. It is my daily mood that makes the weather. I possess tremendous power to make life miserable or joyous. I can be a tool of torture or an instrument of inspiration, I can humiliate or humor, hurt or heal. In all situations, it is my response that decides whether a crisis is escalated or de-escalated, and a person humanized or de-humanized. If we treat people as they are, we make them worse. If we treat people as they ought to be, we help them become what they are capable of becoming.

— Goethe[1]

The ability to derive meaning from one's experiences as a lawyer depends in significant measure on the strength of one's capacity to believe in the nobility and the promise of our craft. It is not so much the ability to feel optimistic at the start of one's professional path, when spirits tend to be high and expectations great, but rather it is the capacity *to persist* in this hopefulness, over time and against all odds, that is the stuff of miracles.

---

* Peter W. Rodino Professor of Law, Seton Hall University School of Law.

1. Johann Wolfgang van Goethe. This quote is also attributed to Dr. Haim Ginott. For a source attributing the quote to Goethe, see Wynn Wolfe, *Begin the Soliloquy*, SUNRISE MAGAZINE, April/May 2002, *available at* http://www.theosociety.org/pasadena/sunrise/51 -01-2/oc-wynn2.htm (last visited Dec. 6, 2005).

Entire books have been devoted to the shortcomings and failings of the legal profession.[2] Lawyers are vilified in countless realms.[3] Many in our ranks have opted out.[4] Others share feelings of significant discontent.[5] Against this backdrop, it takes courage to choose to believe that the law can and does afford profound opportunities to do well and, more essentially, to do good. Often, it takes a great leap of faith to "love the law, and treat it as an honorable profession."[6] But that choice, consciously rendered, becomes its own reward.

---

2. *See, e.g.*, SOL M. LINOWITZ & MARTIN MAYER, THE BETRAYED PROFESSION: LAWYERING AT THE END OF THE TWENTIETH CENTURY (1994) (recounting inadequacies and shortcomings of contemporary law practice); ANTHONY T. KRONMAN, THE LOST LAWYER (1993) (deploring near-disappearance of the "lawyer-statesman ideal"). These themes are explored in some of my earlier writings. *See* Paula A. Franzese, *To Be the Change: Finding Higher Ground in the Law*, 50 ME. L. REV. 11 (1998); Paula A. Franzese, *Back to the Future: Reclaiming Our Noble Profession*, 25 SETON HALL L. REV. 488 (1994) (reviewing SOL M. LINOWITZ & MARTIN MAYER, THE BETRAYED PROFESSION: LAWYERING AT THE END OF THE TWENTIETH CENTURY (1994)).

3. Lawyers provide fodder for commentators, comedians and pundits alike. A new book by Marc Galanter, LOWERING THE BAR: LAWYER JOKES AND LEGAL CULTURE (2005), puts lawyer jokes into an historical perspective and concludes that they have gotten increasingly nastier and more hostile over time. A reviewer observed: "Historically, lawyer jokes poked fun at lawyers, but did so with some sense of appreciation for their ability to be persuasive and eloquent at a moment's notice. Over the past few decades, however, they have become downright cruel." Kate Coscarelli, *A Man Walks Into a Bar Association...*, THE STAR-LEDGER (New Jersey), Oct. 11, 2005, at 25 (book review).

4. Examples of attrition in the legal profession abound. *See generally* Martin E. P. Seligman et al., *Why Lawyers Are Unhappy*, 23 CARDOZO L. REV. 33, 37 (2001) (noting that many practitioners are either "retiring early or leaving the profession altogether"); *see also* Wolfson Andrew, *Life Changes Everything; Professionals Leave Lucrative Jobs For Work They Find More Satisfying*, THE COURIER-JOURNAL (Louisville, Kentucky), Jan. 16, 2005, at 1E ("Disillusioned by increasing competition, the unrelenting demands for more billable hours and the contentiousness of clients and fellow lawyers, many attorneys are leaving the profession for careers that often pay less but promise to be more satisfying, lawyers and bar officials say."); Tom McCann, *Chef, Author, Teacher: Ex-Lawyers Pursue Their Dreams*, CHI. LAW., Sept. 2004, at 14; Maura Dolan, *Miserable With the Legal Life More and More Lawyers Hate Their Jobs, Surveys Find*, L.A. TIMES, June 27, 1995, at A1.

5. Benjamin Sells has written poignantly about the feelings of depression, alienation, and loss of meaning experienced by many lawyers. BENJAMIN SELLS, THE SOUL OF THE LAW (1994).

6. This was Justice Cardozo's advice to the first graduating class of New York University Law School. The difficulty of a disenchanted lawyer's ability to appreciate that advice is embodied in the main character of John Grisham's *The Rainmaker*. *See* JOHN GRISHAM, THE RAINMAKER 111 (2005).

There is a force that meets good with good, as it greets the generous impulse with a sigh of relief and a compassionate embrace.

What we think about most expands. What we think about most, we move towards. With our thoughts and core belief systems, we create a whole range of experiences. In the world of those experiences, we do not get what we want. We get what we *are*. And we are who and what we choose to love, not who or what loves us. True love looks for ways to make other people's lives better.

A few years ago my daughter Nina, then seven, discovered *The Wizard of Oz* for the first time. Thereafter, whenever meeting someone new, she would whisper to me, "Mommy, is that person a good witch or a bad witch?" It occurred to me that this is actually a good lens through which to view our craft. As lawyers, we have the choice, always, to be good witches or bad, to use the power that comes with our skill and expertise as a tool to heal or to humiliate, to transcend or to add injury. The challenge is to be a good witch in what can sometimes feel like a wicked world.

It takes fortitude to choose to believe that, as the wielders of the law, we are capable of accomplishing great good. But it is cowardly to summarily negate this premise. We all know our share of cynics, described by one writer as "those people who tell you they see things as they *really* are, and that things are really rotten. They believe that no one is sincere, and that everyone has secret, selfish reasons for the things they do. They'll tell you that everything is rigged against you, and no one means what they say. The world, according to the cynic, is a cold and cruel place."[7]

Cynicism has been described as a belief in nothing.[8] "People who are cynical, or jaded, *make* their own lives cold because they lack courage. It takes courage to believe in things; sometimes things *will* disappoint you, sometimes people will let you down. To have faith is to risk having your heart broken, and the cynic isn't willing to take that risk."[9]

As lawyers, we have to be willing to take that risk. People can be cruel, but it is up to us to help them anyway. "If we treat people as they are, we make them worse. If we treat people as they ought to be, we help them become what they are capable of becoming."[10] To choose to see the potential that resides not

---

7. Phillip van Munching, Boys Will Put You on a Pedestal (So They Can Look Up Your Skirt): A Dad's Advice For Daughters 132 (2005).

8. *Id.*

9. *Id.*

10. This saying is adapted from the writings of Johann Wolfgang von Goethe. *See* Wolfe, *supra* note 1.

just in some of us, but in all of us, and to act on that promise, is to risk a broken heart. But a broken heart has more room.

As a young attorney and new law professor, I remember phoning home and speaking with my dad. I had been working on a housing court reform project and felt agitated and disappointed at how local politics, greed, and petty squabbles were getting in the way of real reform. I was complaining when my father interrupted me and said, "Could it be that you're thinking too much about what you're not getting, when you should be thinking about what you're not giving? We get what we give. Is there something that you are withholding from this enterprise?" At the close of the conversation, sensing my weariness, my dad reminded me that no act of generosity, no matter how it is received or perceived, is ever wasted. He continued, "Our lives are shaped most not by what we take with us, but by what we leave behind."

Those words became a prophecy of sorts. My dad died, unexpectedly, only days later. Carlos Castaneda wrote, in one of the Don Juan allegories, "There is one simple thing wrong with you—you think you have plenty of time."[11] That is the trouble with all of us. The time is now for us to remember who we are and what we stand for.

There has never been a more important time for us, the lawyers, to show up forcefully and powerfully. We are the crusaders for justice and the reminders of hope, even in, *especially in*, cultures fraught with hostility, anger, and despair. Abuses are perpetrated in the name of the law. Too many are denied, by poverty or circumstance, access to the law. We live in a world divided by fear. That fear can make us doubt ourselves, believing that we are somehow ill-suited or ill-equipped to meet the challenges at hand. At those times, especially, we must define our mission mightily. Could it be that "[o]ur deepest fear is not that we are inadequate?" Could it be that "[o]ur deepest fear is that we are powerful beyond measure?"[12]

We are here to close the gap between what is and what ought to be. We are here to be the voices of compassionate honesty in a world that is filled with too much brutality. We are here to make the difference, with one kind impulse and one generous response, rendered one person, one cause, and one day at a time. We are here to use our unique expertise to give people hope. And this is what we as lawyers do, first and foremost. We give people hope.

---

11. Carlos Castaneda, Journey to Ixtlan 81 (1972).
12. Marianne Williamson, A Return To Love: Reflections on the Principles of a Course in Miracles 190 (1992).

When all is said and done, our clients may not remember what we did or what we said. But they will remember how we made them feel.[13] Everyone has something to teach us, and everyone is entitled to dignity. The antidote to hate is not more hate. The antidote to fear is not more fear. It is our capacity to love that softens the hard edges and lightens the dark places.

When we anchor ourselves in love in all situations, we find ourselves becoming midwives to the birth of a new way. We usher in a chain reaction of the human spirit when we choose to see what needs to be seen, and decide to respond with compassion and respect. We become the change that we are hoping for when we finally acknowledge that every small deed matters, that every word has power and that each of us, in our responses to everyone and everything, is the decisive element.

There will always be the naysayers, the cynics and the critics; those who would confuse gentleness for weakness and the impulse to do good with false piety. But we know better. And by our example, we demonstrate. Gentleness comes from strength. Cruelty comes from weakness.

When I was in the fifth grade, our teacher challenged us to raise dollars for afflicted families. I took this imperative very seriously. I worked hard, going from door to door to raise funds. Finally, I had collected twenty-seven dollars. I proudly presented the donation, only to overhear a group of my classmates making fun of me. (I will not mention names, but I could.) They passed notes around to each other. One said, "Who does she think she is?" I felt ashamed. Shortly thereafter, I came to learn the story of the starfish. A young boy is enjoying the seashore, as are thousands of beautiful, living starfish. Suddenly, the tide begins to pull out, leaving the starfish stranded. The boy begins picking them up, one at a time, and casting them back out to sea. Soon, a man happens by, observes the scene and says, "Hey, kid, give it up. Can't you see that with the tide pulling out as quickly as it is, what you're doing doesn't matter?" The boy looks down at the starfish in his hand, the one whose life is about to be spared. With tremendous sincerity and strength of purpose, the boy replies, "But it does matter to *this* starfish."[14]

---

13. There is a quote attributed to Maya Angelou that says, "I've learned that people will forget what you said, people will forget what you did, but people will never forget how you made them feel." *See* Maya Angelou on Wikiquote.org, *at* http://en.wikiquote.org/wiki/Maya_Angelou (last visited Feb. 4, 2006).

14. *See The Starfish Story, at* http://muttcats.com/starfish.htm (last visited Dec. 6, 2005), *adapted from* Loren Eiseley's *The Star Thrower, available at* http://www.lunar archives.com/deepin/eiseley.htm (last visited Dec. 6, 2005). The website notes that the story

As I write this, as you read this, there is a starfish in each of our hands. Let us seek the wisdom to see that it is there, and find the courage to respond with compassion. We heal this world not with the grand or sweeping gesture, but with the earnest effort, rendered one person at a time. The Talmud says, "Whoever saves one life, it is as if he has saved the whole world."[15]

My fifth grade experience taught me to always have an answer, in my heart, to the question, "Who does she think she is?" Who do any of us think we are? Marianne Williamson, founder of the international network of peace activists known as The Peace Alliance, ventured a response. She said:

> We ask ourselves, Who am I to be brilliant, gorgeous, talented, and fabulous? Actually, who are you *not* to be? You are a child of God. Your playing small doesn't serve the world. There's nothing enlightened about shrinking so that other people won't feel insecure around you. We were born to manifest the glory of God that is within us. It's not just in some of us; it's in everyone. And as we let our own light shine, we unconsciously give other people permission to do the same. As we are liberated from our own fear, our presence automatically liberates others.[16]

As attorneys, who do we think we are? We are the champions of the underdog, the agents for change, the vessels for justice to work miracles in a world desperately in need of our light. We must decline the opportunity to believe less than this. We cannot allow anyone else's limiting thoughts or harsh judgments to infect our own.

There is the parable of the sage, an elder in her community, well known for her capacity to respond to struggle and conflict with grace. A more cynical member of the community attempted repeatedly to diminish her achievements and to mock her message. He doubted her sincerity and challenged her commitment to social change, often hurling criticisms that included, "You think that you are better than us. You are a phony. Your agenda is no more than pie-in-the-sky. You refuse to fight back because you are weak," and so on.

---

has "appeared all over the web in various forms, usually with no credit given to Mr. Eiseley." *Id.*

15. The above is a paraphrase of a Talmudic passage that reads as follows: "Whosoever destroys a single soul of Israel, scripture imputes [guilt] to him as though he had destroyed a complete world; and whosoever preserves a single soul of Israel, scripture ascribes [merit] to him as though he had preserved a complete world." SEDER NEZIKIN, *Tractate Sanhedrin 37a* (this quote comes from a Hebrew-English edition of The Babylonian Talmud).

16. WILLIAMSON, *supra* note 12, at 191.

Throughout, the elder declined the opportunity to respond or to defend herself until, one day, the critic came knocking on her front door. She opened the door and, again, out came his litany of verbal assaults. Finally, the sage answered with a question. She asked, "Sir, if someone offers you a gift, but you decline to accept it, to whom does the gift then belong?" The disgruntled young man paused, and then replied, "It belongs to the person who offered it." "Yes," said the elder. She continued, "Similarly, if I decline to accept your criticisms and harsh judgments, to whom do they then belong?" The man was left speechless, never to return again.[17]

It is important that we take good care in determining which of the criticisms to come our way belong more to the giver than to us. Similarly, we must be careful of our judgments of others. We cannot admire or detest something about a colleague, an adversary, a client, or any other unless it reflects something that we love or hate about ourselves. When tempted to criticize someone, it is essential that we first ask, why are we feeling so strongly?

Words have power. Particularly as attorneys, we must accept responsibility for our words, rendered both on and off the record. Eastern traditions encourage the practice of right speech.[18] The principle of right speech refers to

---

17. This parable is adapted from *The Saturday Zen Story (To Whom Does a Gift Belong?)*, a variation of this story is available online, *at* http://ginasmith.typepad.com/gina _on_gina/2005/01/the_saturday_ze.html (last visited Dec. 6, 2005). In that variation, the story features an undefeated old warrior, who is challenged by a young warrior. *Id.* The young warrior began the fight by hurling insults at the old master, waiting for the old master to take the first step and show his weakness. For hours, the young warrior continued to throw insults at the old master, but the old master remained motionless and unaffected. The young warrior finally left the field, feeling shamed. When the old master's students asked him how he was able to endure the insults with such dignity, the old master responded, "If someone comes to give you a gift and you do not receive it ... to whom does the gift belong?" *Id.*

18. A central tenet in the Buddhist religion, the Right Speech is part of the Noble Eightfold Path, which describes the way to the end of suffering. The Right Speech is the third step to the end of suffering, and the first principle of morality (there being three principles within the eightfold path: the Threefold Practice) and refers to the great power of words to influence ethics. "Buddha explained right speech as follows: 1. to abstain from false speech, especially not to tell deliberate lies and not to speak deceitfully, 2. to abstain from slanderous speech and not to use words maliciously against others, 3. to abstain from harsh words that offend or hurt others, and 4. to abstain from idle chatter that lacks purpose or depth." *The Eightfold Path*, The Big View, *at* http://www.thebigview.com/buddhism/index.html (last visited Dec. 6, 2005). *See also* KEVIN GRIFFIN, ONE BREATH AT A TIME: BUDDHISM & THE TWELVE STEPS 119 (2004); HUSTON SMITH & PHILIP NOVAK, BUDDHISM: A CONCISE INTRODUCTION 43 (2004); PETER HARVEY, AN INTRODUCTION TO BUDDHISM: TEACHINGS, HISTORY & PRACTICES 69 (1990).

the speaker's personal and professional imperative to speak wisely and honestly. To practice right speech also means that one must avoid wrong speech such as gossip, petty judgments, and abusive or hurtful language.

As lawyers, we tend to talk too much. We need to be in the practice of routinely checking our egos at the door, so that we can better discern when it is appropriate to speak and when it is best to be silent. For that matter, too many of us seem to think that brutal honesty is a virtue. It is not. Compassionate honesty should be the norm. What we say should facilitate tolerance and understanding.

As attorneys, we are uniquely situated to practice this art. We possess a baseline expertise and set of skills that render us at least nominally conversant with the predicates to successful negotiation. Our abilities as facilitators, mediators, and peacemakers can be honed if we want them to be. Growing bodies of literature on therapeutic jurisprudence and the humanistic practice of law are readily available.[19] Courses in the law school curriculum are beginning to reflect those precepts,[20] while more traditional offerings on alternative dispute resolution, mediation, and clinical work remain readily available. Thereafter, continuing legal education training, mediation certification processes, access to meaningful role models (through the organized bar as well as more informal mechanisms), and a multi-disciplinary world of offerings[21] provide

---

19. Bruce J. Winick and David B. Wexler have written extensively on the application of Therapeutic Jurisprudence in various areas of law. *See generally* BRUCE J. WINICK, CIVIL COMMITMENT: A THERAPEUTIC JURISPRUDENCE MODEL (2005); BRUCE J. WINICK & DAVID B. WEXLER, JUDGING IN A THERAPEUTIC KEY: THERAPEUTIC JURISPRUDENCE AND THE COURTS (2003); BRUCE J. WINICK, THERAPEUTIC JURISPRUDENCE APPLIED: ESSAYS ON MENTAL HEALTH LAW (1997); LAW IN A THERAPEUTIC KEY: DEVELOPMENTS IN THERAPEUTIC JURISPRUDENCE (Bruce J. Winick & David B. Wexler eds., 1996); DAVID B. WEXLER, THERAPEUTIC JURISPRUDENCE (1989); *see also* INVOLUNTARY DETENTION & THERAPEUTIC JURISPRUDENCE: INTERNATIONAL PERSPECTIVES ON CIVIL COMMITMENT (Kate Diesfeld & Ian R. Freckelton eds., 2003).

20. For example, the following law schools have offered courses on Therapeutic Jurisprudence or other courses incorporating social science in the practice of law: Florida Coastal School of Law, Hamline University School of Law, New York Law School, Seattle University Law School, South Texas College of Law, University of Baltimore School of Law, University of Miami School of Law, and William & Mary Law School. A list of these courses, along with links to their course descriptions and syllabi, are available online, *at* http://www.law.arizona.edu/depts/upr-intj/intj-c.html (last visited Dec. 6, 2005).

21. For example, the American Bar Association offers a complimentary online CLE program entitled "Practicing Preventative Law." According to its description, the CLE course is intended to "explain the concepts behind therapeutic jurisprudence and show how it can be applied in a number of practice settings, including domestic relations, criminal law, and

opportunities to hone the craft of effective and compassionate communication. Wisdom and compassion are indivisible. As Karl Llewellyn observed, "Compassion without technique is a mess; and technique without compassion is a menace."[22]

When the student is ready, the teacher appears. As we declare our intention to get better at being voices of reason, no matter the adversity, and at maintaining our heads and hearts, no matter that others are losing theirs, paths are cleared and a way appears. There is a force that meets good with good.

Throughout, it is essential to persist in the capacity to remain humble, respectful, and confident. These virtues can co-exist only in the presence of great gratitude. A heart that is grateful has room for little else. A holy man was asked, "What is the most powerful prayer that we can say?" His response: "Thank you." Get in the habit of saying thank you, and really meaning it, many times a day. Rather than focus on scarcity, lack, and all that is missing from life, dwell with gratitude on the good already there. This is, by the way, the surest way to attract even more good. What we think about most expands.

Confidence is sometimes confused with cockiness or arrogance. This misunderstands the virtue and source of authentic confidence. Confidence is born of a wholesome discipline and a gentle trust. It is the trust that all is unfolding as it should, that there is a time to every purpose, that our contributions matter, and that there are countless clients and causes out there, some of them as yet nameless and unknown, waiting for us to make the difference that only we can make.

To make that contribution, we must free ourselves from the fear of rejection. We cannot fail. We can only produce results. And we are the ones in charge of our reactions to those results. It has been said that experience is not

---

litigation, and how it can be used to bolster the attorney-client relationship." American Bar Association, *CLE Now! Online, Complimentary ABA-CLE Programs, at* http://www.abanet.org/cle/clenow/preventivereg.html (last visited Dec. 6, 2005). Other classes offered by different organizations include: "Therapeutic Jurisprudence: Using the Law to Improve the Public's Health," offered by Georgia State University's College of Law and Center for Law, Health & Society (held June 13–15, 2005, in Atlanta, Georgia); "Finding Your Center in the Midst of Stress," offered by the Martin County Bar Association Committee on Continuing Legal Education and the Spirit Rock Mediation Center (held in May of 2001 in Woodacre, California); "Self-Awareness for Mediators and Lawyers: A Workshop on Mindfulness Mediation," offered by the Iowa Peace Institute (offered in May 2001 in Grinnell, Iowa), *available at* http://www.transformingpractices.com/er/rs8.html (last visited Dec. 8, 2005).

22. *See* Roger C. Cramton, *Beyond the Ordinary Religion,* 37 J. LEGAL EDUC. 509, 510 (1987) (quoting Karl N. Llewellyn, Cramton's mentor).

what happens to us. Experience is what we do with what happens to us. On my son Michael's recent class trip to the Thomas Edison Museum, I was touched by a story told to us by the tour guide. Apparently, the great Thomas Edison encountered significant difficulties and obstacles on the road to inventing the light bulb. During this protracted process of trial and error, several of his colleagues and competitors mocked him, asking, "So, Tom, how does it feel to have failed to come up with a light bulb, after 2,000 tries?" Edison is said to have responded, "What failure? I now know 2,000 ways how not to make a light bulb." He persisted, and he succeeded.

There is something to be said about the power of optimism in the face of all disappointment. I am reminded here of the story of the parent who has two children, one an avowed optimist and the other an avowed pessimist. The parent, trying to bring both children back to center, fills the pessimist's room with a host of toys and gadgets, designed to entice and enthrall even the most recalcitrant of youngsters. Into the optimist's room, the parent places fifty pounds of horse manure. The child needed to learn, thought the parent, that sometimes life stinks.

The parent waits a while, and then ventures into the pessimist's room. There she finds the child scowling as he asks angrily, "How dare you patronize me with these mundane offerings?" The parent shrugs, and proceeds to the optimist's room. There, he is astonished to find the child gleefully whistling while at work, busily spraying air freshener and shoveling the manure into a corner. The parent asks, "Son, in the midst of all of this, how can you maintain so hopeful and cheerful a countenance?" The little boy replies with great sincerity, "Mommy, don't you get it? With all this horse manure, there has to be a pony!"[23]

It may sometimes feel that no matter how earnestly you shovel, you just cannot keep up. Amidst it all, trust that there are ponies. The rewards will come. No matter how disheartened or fatigued you become, do not let anyone or anything shake you from this resolve. Give no one permission to diminish your capacity to feel hopeful about the promise of your life's work.

There will always be colleagues, clients, outcomes, and people who disappoint you. Forgive them, if not for their sakes, then for yours. The goal is to be governed by what you admire, and not by what you detest. Again, this requires that you exercise care in your thought patterns. All action begins with

---

23. Lou Cannon, Governor Reagan: His Rise to Power 13 (2003) (President Reagan, "in the bleak days" following the Watergate Scandal, would often begin his addresses with this story.).

a thought. We tend to attract what we think about most. To frequently dwell on the negative—that guy is a bad faith player, this case is hopeless, that judge is a jerk—helps to guarantee that the disdainful will keep showing up. An angry person lives in an angry world. By contrast, the good begins to appear as we consciously rein in our thoughts (and that is not easy; as our minds are active (often overactive), and programmed from a very early age to fixate on the negative), and decide to focus with gratitude on the acts of virtue and generosity demonstrated by others.

To change our professional (and personal) lives for the better, we must change our thoughts for the better. We can choose to think the best, work for the best, and expect the best, all the while celebrating the success and achievements of others. To herald and be glad for others' accomplishments is the surest way to assure our own success. What we think about most expands.

Ultimately, true meaning is derived when we remember that our life's work is all about service. Toward the end of his life, Albert Schweitzer said to a group of young professionals, "I do not know what your destinies will be, but one thing I do know: the only ones among you who will be really happy are those who have sought and found how to serve."[24] As lawyers, we are not automatons, technicians or hired guns. We are fiduciaries of the public trust. We cannot serve only for ourselves. The very premise is a contradiction in terms. "A thousand fibers connect us with all of humanity. And among those fibers, our actions run as causes, and they come back to us as effects."[25]

When all is said and done, let it be said that we learned to use our power and expertise to be a source of comfort to those in despair. Let it be said that we invoked the form, but, most essentially, the spirit of the law, to give people hope. Let it be said that we were intelligent, but, most of all, that we were kind.

---

24. This quote is attributed to Albert Schweitzer (1875–1965), winner of the 1952 Nobel Peace Prize. *See* Albert Schweitzer on Wikiquote.org, *at* http://en.wikiquote.org/wiki/Albert_Schweitzer (last visited Feb. 4, 2006).

25. This quote is attributed to Herman Melville (1819–1891). *See* Herman Melville on Wikiquote.org, *at* http://en.wikiquote.org/wiki/Herman_Melville (last visited Feb. 4, 2006).